Kentucky Women

Kentucky Women

THEIR LIVES AND TIMES

EDITED BY

Melissa A. McEuen and Thomas H. Appleton Jr.

The University of Georgia Press *Athens and London*

Athens, Georgia 30602
www.ugapress.org

Set in Minion Pro by Graphic Composition, Inc.
Printed and bound by Thomson-Shore, Inc.
The paper in this book meets the guidelines for
permanence and durability of the Committee on
Production Guidelines for Book Longevity of the
Council on Library Resources.

Most University of Georgia Press titles are
available from popular e-book vendors.

Printed in the United States of America
15 16 17 18 19 P 5 4 3 2 1

Library of Congress Cataloging-in-Publication Data

Kentucky women : their lives and times /
edited by Melissa A. McEuen and Thomas H. Appleton Jr.
pages cm. — (Southern women: their lives and times)
Includes bibliographical references and index.
ISBN 978-0-8203-4752-3 (ebook) —
ISBN 978-0-8203-4452-2 (hardcover : alk. paper) —
ISBN 978-0-8203-4453-9 (pbk. : alk. paper)
1. Women—Kentucky—Biography. 2. Women—Kentucky—History.
3. Kentucky—Biography. I. McEuen, Melissa A., 1961– editor.
II. Appleton, Thomas H., 1950– editor.
HQ1438.K4K43 2015
920.73—dc23
[B]
2014023187

British Library Cataloging-in-Publication Data available

In Memory of Our Mothers

Margaret Glennan Appleton
(1919–1995)

Peggy Brown McEuen
(1933–2013)

Contents

Acknowledgments

As editors, we wish to thank the sixteen talented scholars who enthusiastically joined us in our exploration of women in Kentucky history. Most have full-time teaching responsibilities and other research projects in progress, so we appreciate their meeting our deadlines and responding to suggestions promptly. They have been a pleasure to work with. We also are grateful for the support we have received from our institutions, Transylvania University and Eastern Kentucky University. At Transylvania, William Pollard, vice president and dean of the college, and Kathleen Jagger, who succeeded him in that position, supported the project at every stage; the Dr. Byron and Judy Young Faculty Development Fund underwrote the precious resource that historians need and treasure: time. At Eastern Kentucky University, John Wade, dean of the College of Arts and Sciences, and Christiane Diehl Taylor, chair of the history department, have been unfailingly generous and supportive, while F. Tyler Huffman of the department of geography and geology kindly shared his expertise in producing the map of the commonwealth that appears in this volume.

Directors and staff members at the following institutions have assisted us and the contributors and have kindly granted permission to publish from their collections and publications: *Appalachian Journal*; Ashland, the Henry Clay Estate; Berea College; Cincinnati Historical Society; Columbia University; Filson Historical Society; Hindman Settlement School; Indiana State Museum and Historic Sites; Kentucky Department for Libraries and Archives; Kentucky Historical Society; Kentucky State University; Library of Congress; Southern Foodways Alliance, Center for the Study of Southern Culture, University of Mississippi; the *Times Leader* (Princeton, Kentucky); University of Chicago; University of Kentucky Special Collections and Archives; University of Nebraska–Lincoln Libraries; University of North Carolina, Southern Historical Collection; University of Wisconsin, Madison; and the Wisconsin Historical Society.

When the project was in its infancy, James C. Klotter, state historian of Kentucky, gave willingly of his time and deep knowledge of the commonwealth's history, to help nurture it. We appreciate his helpful advice as well as that provided by editors of other volumes in the *Southern Women: Their Lives and Times* series, in particular Janet Allured, Beverly Greene Bond, and Joan Marie Johnson.

Finally, this book exists because Nancy Grayson, former executive editor at the University of Georgia Press and the founding editor of its *Southern Women* series, wanted a volume on Kentucky. We salute her passion for the project and the series as well as her unyielding advocacy for women's history and southern history in general. These fields have been greatly enriched by her guidance and commitment to them. We appreciate those at the press who have maintained that commitment and all there who have assisted us, especially Beth Snead.

Melissa A. McEuen and Thomas H. Appleton Jr.

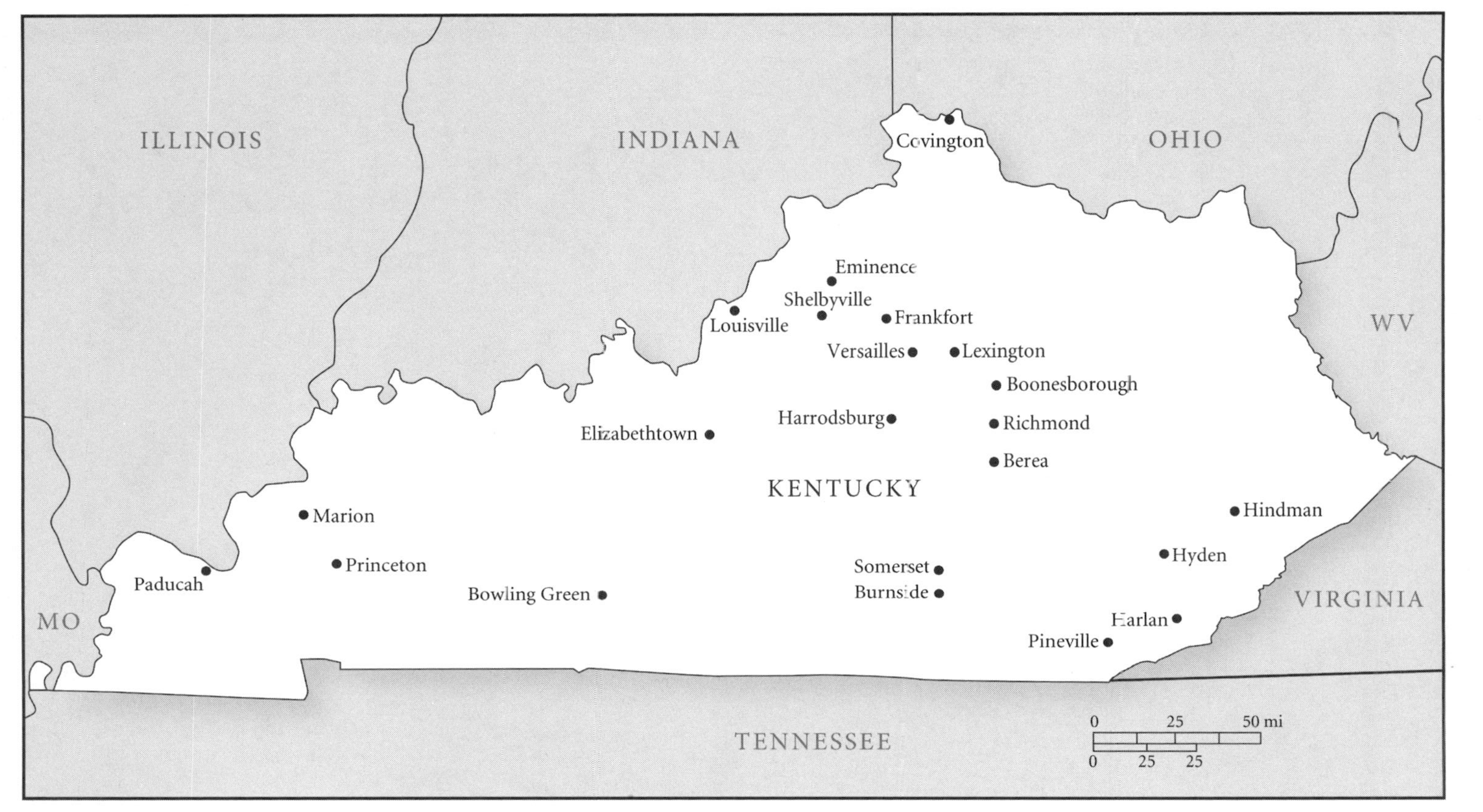
ILLINOIS
INDIANA
OHIO
WV
VIRGINIA
TENNESSEE
MO
KENTUCKY
Covington
Eminence
Shelbyville
Louisville
Frankfort
Versailles
Lexington
Boonesborough
Harrodsburg
Richmond
Berea
Elizabethtown
Marion
Princeton
Paducah
Bowling Green
Somerset
Burnside
Hindman
Hyden
Harlan
Pineville
0
25
50 mi
0
25
25

Kentucky Women

Introduction

THOMAS H. APPLETON JR. AND MELISSA A. MCEUEN

In an essay published in 1992 to commemorate the bicentennial of Kentucky statehood, the historian Margaret Ripley Wolfe demonstrated how, for too long, women constituted the "fallen leaves and missing pages" from published histories of Kentucky. "Their stories need telling," she insisted, "for their legacy matters to present and future generations."[1] Happily, during the last two decades, scholars in diverse disciplines have heeded Wolfe's clarion call. Significant, pathbreaking monographs and articles have enriched our understanding of women's experience in the Bluegrass State. We hope this volume will hasten the day when a comprehensive history of women in the commonwealth will be written.

In the meantime, students of Kentucky women can be grateful for the recent work of such excellent biographers as Melba Porter Hay, Yvonne Honeycutt Baldwin, Melanie Beals Goan, Catherine Fosl, Catherine Clinton, and Lindsey Apple, writing on Madeline McDowell Breckinridge, Cora Wilson Stewart, Mary Breckinridge, Anne Braden, Mary Todd Lincoln, and Susan Clay Sawitzky, respectively. Valuable scholarly articles have appeared from Nancy Disher Baird and Carol Crowe-Carraco on motherhood in late antebellum Kentucky, Deborah L. Blackwell on Eleanor Marsh Frost and Appalachian reform, and Randolph Hollingsworth on the idea of womanhood in pioneer Kentucky. One is grateful, too, for the insightful memoirs of Linda Scott DeRosier and Bobbie Ann Mason in which they reflect on their childhoods in rural Kentucky.[2]

As we imagined this volume of essays, our goal was to fashion a history as varied and diverse as Kentucky itself. The table of contents reveals coverage from frontier days to the twenty-first century, from the Appalachian region in the east to the Pennyroyal in the west. It features women with well-known names as well as those whose lives and work deserve greater attention. Arranged chronologically based on the subject's date of birth, the volume highlights politics, family connections, medical advances, racial challenges and triumphs, widowhood, gender inequality in divorce, agrarian life, urban experiences, activism, entrepreneurship, and visual art and literature. The list of contributors is also marked by diversity, with established scholars alongside those currently securing their places in academe with exciting, new interpretations of Kentucky's past, the southern experience, and women's history. In debating which women should be profiled and who should be invited to contribute an entry, we considered "the art of the possible." Some women merited an essay but could not be included because there were no accessible primary sources on which to rely or there was no expert available to undertake the assignment. In our judgment the essays that follow are both grounded and groundbreaking.

Craig Thompson Friend leads off the volume with an intriguing essay exploring the "female frontiers" of three persons: Nonhelema Hokolesqua, a female Shawnee chief who experienced the frontier of the 1760s; Jemima Boone Callaway, a daughter of Rebecca and Daniel Boone who lived on the frontier in the late 1770s and 1780s; and Matilda Lewis Threlkeld, a young slave brought to western Kentucky in the early 1800s. Each vignette examines the evolving nature of womanhood within larger gendered constructs. Together, their lives and experiences demonstrate that in the violent, male-oriented culture of early Kentucky, the female frontier was defined not by women's shared responsibilities but by women's shared vulnerability.

History-minded Kentuckians familiar with the heroic work of Anne McCarty Braden in the modern civil rights movement might initially question the early placement of Catherine Fosl's essay. But as she forcefully argues, it is impossible to make sense of Braden's odyssey away from her segregationist upbringing to become a lifelong "race radical" without first understanding the depth of her roots in Kentucky and the origins of her steadfast claim to a white southern identity. Part of that journey involved coming to terms with the vivid stories she heard as a child in a family whose ancestors had come into Kentucky with Boone in the eighteenth century. A portion of Fosl's essay examines the sources of Braden's antiracist passions through the meanings she attached to the tales of frontier Kentucky that peppered her childhood, particularly the stories of her five times great-grandmother Anne Pogue McGinty, one of the first white settlers of Harrodsburg and a rebel in her own right.

Mary Jane Warfield became known primarily for her 1833 marriage to and 1878 divorce from the outspoken antislavery crusader Cassius M. Clay. As William Kuby's essay poignantly reveals, when the couple's tumultuous marriage ended, Mary Jane was left with no financial resources, despite her success in maintaining the Clay property and increasing the family fortune during the many years her husband served as minister to Russia. Ultimately, her post-marital plight inspired her daughter Mary Barr Clay to join the women's rights movement and to fight against the gender inequalities that her mother had faced in divorce.

Angela Esco Elder focuses on two of the most prominent women widowed by the Civil War, the sisters Emilie Todd Helm and Mary Todd Lincoln. After her husband was killed in battle in 1863, Emilie Helm embarked on a "career" as a Confederate widow. Elder asserts that it was a part she was born to play. The younger Todd sister achieved a kind of professional fame as a widow. Through her we can see more clearly the society that created her role, built her stage, and applauded her performances. Helm's experience with grief contrasts sharply with that of her more famous sister Mary, who, by her own society's standards, did everything exactly wrong as a widow.

Andrea S. Watkins has mined the revealing, introspective diaries of two Union women to illuminate the course of the Civil War for Kentucky women. From their vantage points in Bowling Green and Lexington, respectively, Josie Underwood and Frances Dallam Peter described how women experienced the physical and emotional hardships of war. In a state torn by the issues of slavery, secession, and war, women faced the division of friends and family as the conflict began. Longtime friendships were strained, and families sometimes refused even to mention relatives who aligned with the "wrong" side. Women later saw their homes destroyed, fields emptied, and personal fortunes disappear.

Laura Clay, the best-known southern suffragist of her day, has long fascinated students of women's struggle to secure the franchise. Despite her decades-long activism in Kentucky and beyond—she was on the executive board of the National American Woman Suffrage Association (NAWSA) for fifteen years—Clay ultimately opposed the ratification of the Nineteenth Amendment and vigorously worked against it. As Mary Jane Smith makes clear, Clay's reform agenda was overshadowed by her concern about the power of the federal government to interfere in southern political affairs, especially race relations, which could potentially upset the order of southern white supremacy to which the Kentuckian was committed.

Another "homegrown" activist, Sophonisba Preston Breckinridge, spent her adult life at the University of Chicago, where she helped personalize social work and establish high standards of academic rigor for the discipline in the United States and overseas. She was active in virtually every reform—including legal aid for immigrants, civil rights for blacks, labor legislation for workers, equal rights for women, and juvenile courts for youth—of the Progressive and New Deal eras. Throughout her long life, Anya Jabour emphasizes, Breckinridge maintained a connection to her native commonwealth, both by fostering relationships with her socially prominent Kentucky kin and by writing editorials for her hometown newspaper on issues ranging from woman suffrage to lynching.

Two reform-minded women inspired by the work of Sophonisba Breckinridge and other Progressives were Katherine Pettit and May Stone, who in the initial years of the twentieth century founded the Hindman and Pine Mountain settlement schools in the mountainous eastern region of Kentucky. In a wide-ranging essay Sarah Case explores Pettit and Stone's competing desires: to bring Progressive values of efficiency, faith in science, temperance, and greater gender equality to mountain people while at the same time preserving their "old-timey" handicrafts and music and celebrating them as pure Anglo-Saxon folk. The work and agenda of these two schools, she maintains, point to the ambivalence with which mountain reformers, and Americans generally, regarded modernity and progress.

Juilee Decker brings expertise as an art historian to her profile of Enid Yandell, a sculptor whose life and art are at the nexus of public art, occupational identity, and philanthropy. The Louisville native, who worked with such noted sculptors as Lorado Taft and Auguste Rodin, cultivated her status as a "pioneer" woman in art with commissions at the Columbian Exposition (1893) and the Centennial Exposition in Nashville (1897). Her early large-scale work of Daniel Boone served to reinforce her identity as both a pathbreaker and a Kentuckian. The first woman inducted into the National Sculpture Society, Yandell promoted art education through her founding of the Branstock School of Art in Massachusetts. Though Yandell was awarded public recognition during her lifetime, Decker asserts, the scholarship and exhibition records to date fail to reflect fully her significance as an artist, educator, and philanthropist.

Like Yandell, Madeline McDowell Breckinridge was the descendant of a distinguished Kentucky family. Despite—and likely because of—personal unhappiness and disability, she became the commonwealth's foremost reformer of the Progressive Era. Long recognized for her efforts on behalf of woman suffrage, Breckinridge also advocated a host of other reforms, from vocational education to juvenile courts to kindergartens. With charisma approaching that of her great-grandfather Henry Clay, she led Lexington's gentry women, her friends from school days at Miss Porter's, and her editor husband into the reform movement on the state and national levels. As Lindsey Apple reminds us, nineteenth-century male historians and moralists lamented that none of the Great Compromiser's descendants attained his prominence. In doing so they betrayed their own bias. In truth, Breckinridge came closest to filling the shoes of the great family's patriarch.

While Madeline Breckinridge campaigned for tuberculosis sanitaria, her fellow Lexingtonian Linda Neville targeted the eye disease trachoma. Shocked by what she witnessed on a visit to remote eastern Kentucky in 1908—scores of children and adults permanently blind from a totally preventable disease—Neville committed her life to ending the scourge. For more than forty years she brought patients to Lexington for treatment or persuaded specialists to accompany her to the mountains to operate clinics. By 1952 her activism had virtually eradicated the disease in Kentucky, and the last of her clinics closed, no longer needed. James Duane Bolin chronicles here the inspiring story of Linda Neville, thanks to whom untold thousands of Kentuckians, young and old, were spared a life without sight.

Spirited activism also characterized the life and work of Elizabeth "Lizzie" Fouse, an African American woman born in the last years of Reconstruction. According to Karen Cotton McDaniel, Fouse serves as the quintessential exemplar of black women's leadership in community building in a border state during the first half of the twentieth century. McDaniel's essay investigates the circumstances surrounding the 1925 death of a black woman whom police incarcerated for perceived drunkenness. In fact, the woman was seriously ill with a gastrointestinal ailment and died in her jail cell. Fouse organized a petition drive among local women in an effort to prevent future outrages. In so doing, she raised the consciousness of black citizenry and helped bring about changes in the Lexington police department's treatment of prisoners.

The year 1925 also saw the founding of the Frontier Nursing Service (FNS) in the Knott County community of Hindman. Melanie Beals Goan considers the motives that drove Mary Breckinridge to launch a health service for expectant mothers in such a remote mountain area. She contends that the highly intelligent and talented Breckinridge spent much of her life seeking an outlet that was within the bounds of women's accepted spheres. Establishing the FNS afforded her a position of power, yet the service's focus on mothers and babies protected her from appearing self-serving. As head of the FNS, she wielded a great deal of influence for more than forty years. Regrettably, in her attempt to maintain her authority and to build a legacy for herself as she aged, she ultimately undercut her goal of making health care universally affordable and accessible.

The southeastern region of the state also figures prominently in the novels and short stories of Harriette Simpson Arnow, who, in the judgment of Martha Billips, "arguably stands as Kentucky's most accomplished woman writer." In such works as *Hunter's Horn* (1949) and *The Dollmaker* (1954), Arnow describes the hardships, particularly for women, of living in an isolated mountain culture dependent on subsistence farming. Her most famous character, Gertie Nevels, and her husband typify the men and women of the Appalachian diaspora who abandoned the land in search of better opportunities in the urban, industrial Midwest. While her formative years in and around Burnside in Pulaski County "contributed indelibly" to Arnow's development as a writer, she had to leave that world in order to write about it, Billips argues.

Georgia Montgomery Davis Powers's life sits at the intersection of two historical subfields: the civil rights movement in Kentucky and women in the civil rights movement nationally. Because neither has received adequate attention from historians, it is little wonder that the colorful and active Montgomery, who was the first woman and the first person of color in the Kentucky state senate, rarely appears in larger civil rights narratives. She is best recognized outside Kentucky, if at all, as the lover of Martin Luther King Jr., an affair she revealed in her 1995 autobiography, *I Shared the Dream*. Yet, as Carolyn R. Dupont shows us, Montgomery went to Frankfort when the capital was still segregated, held her seat for twenty-one years, and left a lasting legacy as an advocate for women and children and in issues of fair housing and employment.

The first—and, to date, the only—woman governor of the commonwealth, Martha Layne Collins, came of age when social and religious forces often still dictated that men alone should hold political power. Yet the Shelby County native rose through the ranks of the Democratic Party and won statewide races to become clerk of the Kentucky Court of Appeals and lieutenant governor. In 1983 she defied the odds to win the governorship. While her administration was not without its missteps, as John Paul Hill demonstrates, Collins established herself as a skilled executive attuned to the needs of her constituents. Understanding her political ascendancy illuminates the difficulties that women in general, and women in the conservative South in particular, faced in their attempts to gain personal freedom and political power in the 1970s, 1980s, and onward.

The concluding essay in the volume, by Melissa McEuen, introduces the "ham lady" of western Kentucky, Nancy Newsom Mahaffey. The Princeton native and resident is an internationally recognized expert on the production of dry-cured ham, or, as it is known in the American South, "country" ham. In producing her award-winning hams, Mahaffey follows a recipe that the Newsom family brought with them to Kentucky in the early 1800s. She has also been one of the commonwealth's most notable voices in the "heritage foods" revival of the last twenty years. Praised for her leadership in small-town economic development and revitalization, Mahaffey has emphasized the efficacy of linking southern foodways and historic preservation with tourism—a recipe for rural areas seeking to meet the challenges of a new century.

These, then, are the essays that await. While we recognize that students of

Kentucky history, women and gender studies, and southern history, as well as scholars in those disciplines, will likely be our primary audience, we are confident that the profiles in this volume will inform and delight nonspecialists as well. Above all, we hope that our collection inspires continuing and sustained research in the fascinating story of Kentucky women.

NOTES

1. Margaret Ripley Wolfe, "Fallen Leaves and Missing Pages: Women in Kentucky History," *Register of the Kentucky Historical Society* 90 (1992): 65, 89.

2. Melba Porter Hay, *Madeline McDowell Breckinridge and the Battle for a New South* (Lexington: University Press of Kentucky, 2009); Yvonne Honeycutt Baldwin, *Cora Wilson Stewart and Kentucky's Moonlight Schools* (Lexington: University Press of Kentucky, 2006); Melanie Beals Goan, *Mary Breckinridge: The Frontier Nursing Service and Rural Health in Appalachia* (Chapel Hill: University of North Carolina Press, 2008); Catherine Fosl, *Subversive Southerner: Anne Braden and the Struggle for Racial Justice in the Cold War South* (Lexington: University Press of Kentucky, 2006); Catherine Clinton, *Mrs. Lincoln: A Life* (New York: HarperCollins, 2009); Lindsey Apple, *Cautious Rebel: A Biography of Susan Clay Sawitzky* (Kent, Ohio: Kent State University Press, 1997); Nancy D. Baird and Carol Crowe-Carraco, "A 'True Woman's Sphere': Motherhood in Late Antebellum Kentucky," *Filson Club History Quarterly* 66 (1992): 369–94; Deborah L. Blackwell, "Eleanor Marsh Frost and the Gender Dimensions of Appalachian Reform Efforts," *Register of the Kentucky Historical Society* 94 (1996): 225–46; Randolph Hollingsworth, "'Mrs. Boone, I presume?': In Search of the Idea of Womanhood in Kentucky's Early Years," in *Bluegrass Renaissance: The History and Culture of Central Kentucky, 1792–1852*, ed. James C. Klotter and Daniel Rowland (Lexington: University Press of Kentucky, 2012), 93–130; Linda Scott DeRosier, *Creeker: A Woman's Journey* (Lexington: University Press of Kentucky, 1999); Bobbie Ann Mason, *Clear Springs: A Memoir* (New York: Random House, 1999). Since 1982 Kentucky's state historian, James C. Klotter, has published three valuable critiques of recent scholarship on the commonwealth. See in particular "Moving Kentucky History into the Twenty-first Century: Where Should We Go from Here?" *Register of the Kentucky Historical Society* 97 (1999): 83–112; and "Charting the Path of Twentieth-Century Kentucky: Current Courses and Future Directions," *Register of the Kentucky Historical Society* (forthcoming).

Nonhelema Hokolesqua, Jemima Boone Callaway, and Matilda Lewis Threlkeld

(1718–1786; 1762–1829; 1799–c. 1885)

Searching for Kentucky's Female Frontier

CRAIG THOMPSON FRIEND

In 1892 Frederick Jackson Turner figuratively stood at Cumberland Gap and watched "the procession of civilization, marching single file—the buffalo following the trail to the salt springs, the Indian, the fur-trader and hunter, the cattle-raiser, the pioneer farmer—and the frontier has passed by."[1] But Turner did not look closely enough, for there were women within that procession. For Turner, successive waves of *men* interacted with the western wilderness, and in return the wilderness imbued *men* with "American character," all done apparently without the assistance or even the presence of women.

Turner's exclusion of women reflected the nineteenth-century literature on which he grounded his scholarship. In the 1820s and 1830s Kentucky's first historians—Humphrey Marshall, John Bradford, Timothy Flint, and John McClung—minimized women's roles in frontier history. Plenty of examples lingered in public memory to demonstrate female ancestors' roles on the frontier, but they were not to be celebrated in the narratives of antebellum Kentucky's increasingly patriarchal culture, which demanded the myth of docile, domestic, and dependent women to justify men's dominance as protectors and providers. Women's diminished roles in these histories tainted the narrative of the frontier and poisoned Turner's thesis.[2]

Well into the twentieth century, women remained peripheral and passive participants in frontier histories. Some scholars such as Thomas Perkins Abernethy omitted women completely. Exceptional women such as Mary Draper Ingles and Rebecca Bryan Boone received sporadic treatment, although always as they related to the male sphere of discovery, conquest, and civilization at the heart of Turner's thesis. In Etta DeGering's 1966 study of Rebecca Boone, undertaken because "it is high time the woman who stood so loyally by his side receive the honors due her," the author insipidly concluded that Boone was a "modern Ruth—'Wither thou goest, I will go'—she followed her Daniel." The historical imagination seemed intent on portraying women as compliant partners in the male arena of the frontier. In those few cases where women had pushed the traditional wifely roles that historians ascribed to them, scholars such as Thomas D. Clark dismissed them as "women unworthy of the name of woman" or as "women of easy virtue."[3]

New social historians of the 1960s and 1970s rejected this phallocentric orientation of frontier studies, purposefully seeking out women subjects. Yet, like their predecessors, they found it very difficult to cast off the Turnerian context that framed frontier historiography. Even with the rise of women's history and its early paradigms of "separate spheres" and "the cult of domesticity," historians continued to understand frontier women as submissive and reluctant participants in frontier conquest. Men were brave and adventurous; women were dragged along, forced to abandon kin in the East as they articulated what Joan Cashin described as "bewilderment, anger, and despair about the dramatic changes in their lives." Still, social historians did interpret something new: by exerting moral authority, frontier women acted as "gentle tamers" of the frontier and of their men. In her survey of Kentucky women's history, Margaret Ripley Wolfe encapsulated this type of thinking, portraying Rebecca Boone's arrival at Boonesborough thusly: "Even under primitive conditions, a feminine presence at this wilderness outpost reportedly brought civilizing influences."[4]

Recognition that women might have experienced the frontier differently from men opened up analytical possibilities. As early as 1979, Helen Deiss Irvin declared that "to learn of a woman migrant on horseback fording a swift river, one child in her arms and one hanging on behind her, to find other women improvising a substitute for flax, defending a fort under siege, or fighting off Indian attackers, is to see women as active participants in the rough, precarious life of the settlements." Ten years later, western historian Glenda Riley challenged scholars to consider further how "women's shared responsibilities, life styles, and sensibilities constituted a female frontier, that is, a comparable set of orientations and responses that in most ways transcended the region of the frontier in which they settled, the occupations of the men of their families, and the historical period in which they lived." Whether farming or hunting, trading or herding, men's activities were determined by economic variables. Women's activities, in contrast, were defined by gender and manifested in spheres of home, family, community, education, and religion. Riley insisted that being a woman, more than anything else, defined the female frontier. In the 1990s and early 2000s a new wave of historians began to look for women's shared responsibilities, lifestyles, and sensibilities on Kentucky's frontier, particularly as they manifested in familial, communal, educational, and religious experiences. Religion, in particular, proved a fertile field because the Great Revival of 1801 seemed to mark the culmination of women's frontier experience. Stephen Aron found women frustrated by the creation of a best poor man's country and turning to "otherworldly aspirations." Ellen Eslinger concluded that by empowering women, "camp meeting communitas temporarily narrowed gender differences." Both historians identified shared experiences that indicated a female frontier in Kentucky.[5]

Still, there was something unsatisfying about the female frontier paradigm and its seemingly negligible manifestation on the Kentucky frontiers as a reaction to men's activities. If activities in home and family, community, education, and religion defined frontier womanhood, how were frontier women any different from those who lived in the East and acted in the same spheres? What Riley seemed to overlook was the frontier context itself. The West was not just another region: it was an arena in which white men and women sought to supplant Indians, violently if necessary. The female frontier had to evidence more than just civilizing influences; it had to verify women's shared stake in survival and success. Elizabeth Perkins first broached this part of Kentucky's female frontier by concluding that by "using the sanctions of moral coercion and public shaming," women "staked their claim in the common defense by attempting to curb the rashness of men and, alternately, by ridiculing their overt cowardice." Perkins's not-so-gentle tamers essentially turned upside down the traditional narrative of adventurous and brave men versus submissive and dependent women. Similarly, I discovered a frontier in which conventional gender roles failed: faced with an unrelenting threat of Indian attack, death, and capture, women became more violent and aggressive, forcing men to appropriate hypermasculine ways to demonstrate their manliness. Still, despite the new attention given women, none of us produced a comprehensive female frontier in Kentucky. That undertaking is awaiting its author.[6]

Additionally, we all assumed that the story of Kentucky's frontier women is about *white* women. While there have been some efforts in recent years to complicate Kentucky's frontier story by including Native American and African American women, for the most part we have simply added multicultural examples, leaving those women on the margins of a narrative that relates the triumph of white men *and* white women over the Others. Contributing to the problem, historians have tended to gloss over white women's roles in that colonization process by suggesting a common experience among white women, blacks, and Indians in reaction to white men's consolidation of power. For example, I recently concluded that "white men came to champion patriarchy and in turn codified 'gendered and racial inequality'"; and Joan Cashin described southern frontiers as regions where white women "tended to perceive slaves as individual human beings . . . [and] a few planter women even sympathized with and identified with slaves as individual human beings." Such statements may be substantiated, but they simultaneously excuse us from truly discovering the ways in which white frontier women benefited from displacement and eradication of Native Americans and enslavement of African Americans. In her critique of the current state of frontier women's history, Antonia Casteñeda complained that "theoretical approaches that incorporate the historical realities of people of color, and their own interpretation of their realities, are still wanting." Specifically, she decried interpretations in which gender trumped race on the frontier and in which women of all colors formed "harmonious, co-operative, mutually supportive relations," the consequence of which is a perpetuation of white women as "gentle tamers" rather than invasive colonizers and oppressive slaveholders.[7] The remainder of this essay takes up Casteñeda's appeal and seeks out Kentucky's female frontiers. To do so we must abandon Turner's Cumberland Gap for more revealing panoramas.

Stand on the southern bank of the Ohio River at its confluence with the Scioto River in 1758 and watch the Shawnee women pulling weeds and tending crops for the last time. This is the northeasternmost corner of Kentucky. Among the farmers strides a tall, powerful woman, giving instructions about the migration that will soon be undertaken. Across the river is a significant village: lower Shawnee Town, one of many multinational villages that arose in the 1730s and 1740s as the Shawnees returned to the Ohio River valley.

A century earlier, the Shawnees had lived in summer villages located along waterways north of the Ohio River and in winter hunting camps constantly relocating throughout the hunting grounds to the south, the most notable of which was Eskippakithiki in north central Kentucky. But their successful buffalo- and deerskin trade with the French drew the attention and ire of the powerful Iroquois who forced the Shawnees from the region in an effort to lay claim to Kentucky and its wealth. Not until Iroquois hegemony weakened in the early eighteenth century did the Shawnees move back and reclaim their traditional Ohio valley homeland and the Kentucky hunting grounds. Their villages filled with other refugees of the Iroquois empire: Lenni Lenapes, Mingos, and Wyandots who built new economic relationships with the French and shared in Kentucky's bounty. By the mid-1740s lower Shawnee Town had grown so large that it spilled over onto the southern banks of the great river, but a flood in 1753 wiped out the homes and public buildings on the Kentucky side. A few residents rebuilt, but most relocated to the northern banks, leaving Kentucky's rich bottomlands for agriculture.[8]

These Indians of the Ohio River valley relied on their French allies to help hold British colonists east of the Appalachians. When the French lost Fort Duquesne in 1758, the Shawnees and other Native Americans decided to consolidate their villages, abandoning exposed communities such as lower Shawnee Town and moving northwestward along the Scioto River, joining Chillicothe, Cornstalk's Town, Maquachake, and other communities. A generation later, the son of Chief Bluejacket remembered his father's version:

> After a time the white people got too many for red men and then we followed the best hunting toward the north. The Al-wa-ma-ke [bottom land] was good for the corn, and the M-vuegh-ke [hills] full of game. The Mean-e-lench [young men] hunted and ran on the war-path. The Pash-e-t-the [old men] caught A-ma-tha [fish] in the Bo-with-e [small streams] and the E-qui-wa [women] worked in the da-ne [corn]. Then many seasons passed, the tribe always going to the north, to when Black-Hoof was a Meen-e-lench [young man] and they were all north of the Great Se-pe [Ohio River]. Here we were given much land by our brothers, the Wyandots. We built many towns and lived long time in pease [*sic*], till the white men behind the Great Se-pe tried to drive us away.[9]

No more than a generation after reclaiming the valley of the Great Sepe as a traditional homeland, the Shawnees faced a new threat to their security and autonomy: American encroachment.

The woman giving direction in the cornfields is Nonhelema Hokolesqua, and her life epitomized the Shawnee frontiers of the eighteenth century. Born in 1718 into the Chalakatha (Chillicothe) division of the Shawnee nation, she spent her early youth in Pennsylvania, where the Shawnees lived under the careful watch of the Iroquois Confederacy. She, her brother Cornstalk, and her métis mother Katee accompanied her father Okowellos to the Alabama country in 1725, but the family returned to Pennsylvania within five years. In 1734 she married her first husband, a Chalakatha chief with whom she later had two daughters. By 1750 Nonhelema was herself a Chalakatha village chief. Four years later, when her husband died, she wedded Moluntha, a cousin from her mother's

Maquachake division. She bore two more daughters and a son, and the family migrated with the Maquachakes into the Ohio country, where she rejoined Cornstalk, who had relocated earlier.[10]

Nonhelema became a wife, a chief, an overseer of domestic productions, and a warrior—all made possible through the Shawnees' view of the world as a system of balance: war/peace, hunting/farming, the above world/the underworld, men/women. As in most other Native American cultures, such balance among the Shawnees assured prosperity, and while not ensuring gendered equality, it made gendered hierarchy difficult. Men's and women's arenas of influence and responsibility were complementary: in contrast to killing, which was at the heart of men's primary responsibilities of protecting villages and providing game, women exerted life-power as producers of crops, clothes, domestic goods, and children.[11]

Life-power was grounded in Shawnee cosmology. While a supreme being was male, the creator of life was Kohkumthena or Old Grandmother. Forming the Shawnee from the red clay and breathing life into them, Kohkumthena represented the essence of the Shawnee woman as producer and nurturer. She spoke a unique language that was intelligible to young children, at least until they began to learn Shawnee. The conceptualization of a female creator and caregiver not only reflected women's spiritual strength within Shawnee culture but also reinforced the respect accorded them. One tale relates how Kohkumthena created Corn Woman, protected her when she was raped by a Shawnee man, and returned her to the Shawnees when they were in need. Importantly, corn as a giver of sustenance and life-power was represented as a woman, and the relationship of women as the producers of corn gave them economic power. Ritualistically, in springs and summers, Shawnees celebrated women's activities: the Bread Dance (actually a set of rituals and dances) honored women's roles as providers, followed by the Green Corn Dance (also more than a singular dance), which acknowledged women's relationship to the fertility of the earth. During the latter, following the passing of the pipe, an opening address by a chief, and several sporting contests, the Shawnees ate until "each man and woman as they finished their dinner setting down their bowl saying, 'Ooway, nelah, netape hooloo'; literally, 'I have done; my stomach is full.'" During such feasts, participants consumed the life-power of women's work, ritualistically connecting women to sustenance and agricultural fertility.[12]

Women's elevated status is particularly notable because, unlike other eastern Native Americans, the Shawnees practiced patrilineality (tracing lineage through fathers) and patrilocality (in residence with the husband's clan). Nonhelema took her father's clan identity and migrated first with her father's group and then with her husband's. Still, in the absence of a strong gendered hierarchy, Shawnee women wielded authority similar to women in matrilineal and matrifocal societies. Their close relationship to the matrilineal Lenni Lenapes certainly influenced Shawnee gender ways. More important, however, may be that Shawnees revered women's life-power as the spiritual counterbalance to men's kill-power. Another Shawnee story told of a woman who, having removed herself from the village during her menstrual cycle, confronted a great horned serpent. She related her meeting to the village, and during her next seclusion, the warriors accompanied her, intent on trapping the serpent and killing it. But before the men could attack, the woman struck down the serpent with her clothes soiled with menstrual blood, evidencing to all "of what power it is." Both phallic and representative of the otherworldly powers that warriors sought when they went into battle (they carried medicine bundles filled with fragments of dead snakes), the serpent proved powerless against woman's life-power.[13]

Some women such as Nonhelema, typically relatives of the male chief, served alongside men as war chiefs and peace chiefs. Whichever role they assumed, women sustained their primary responsibilities as producers and nurturers. In times of peace, female chiefs exercised leadership over domestic affairs, directing the planting and harvesting of the fields, and organizing feasts: peace chiefs cooked corn and vegetables, representative of agriculture; war chiefs cooked meats, representative of hunting. When Shawnees from Maquachake arrived at Fort Finney in 1785 to negotiate with the Confederation Congress's representatives, the village's women under the leadership of Cawechile accompanied Chief Moluntha and the warriors. The American commissioners sought out the women as sources of information, and the Shawnees did not mind because "some Women were wiser than some Men." When war chief Kekewepellethe had a violent confrontation with commissioner Richard Butler, Cawechile interceded as peace chief to implore Kekewepellethe to reconsider his threat of continued war. The Shawnee women "all seemed very uneasy in Expectation that there would be a War."[14]

In times of war, female chiefs sought foremost to prevent the unnecessary spillage of blood, but if war was inevitable, they joined the battle. As the French and Indian War ended in 1763, Ottawa chief Pontiac led a rebellion against the British, and Nonhelema joined a warring party of Lenni Lenapes, Mingos, Shawnees, and Hurons who targeted Fort Pitt (formerly Fort Duquesne). On August 5–6 they clashed with British troops at the Battle of Bushy Run. Though the British eventually won, several Shawnees made their reputations, including Nonhelema, who became known among whites as the "Grenadier Squaw."[15]

As daughter to one chief, sister to another, and wife to a third, Nonhelema assumed the role of female chief throughout her adult life, but standing at six feet six inches, her success as warrior must also be attributed to her physical presence and strength. Warrior women exerted tremendous cultural power because through war and menstruation they evinced both male and female relationships to blood. They embodied the blurring of genders and consequently were viewed as extraordinarily powerful and potentially dangerous. As a warrior, a chief, and a leader of Shawnee women, Nonhelema wielded tremendous influence; she did not live with Moluntha but had her own village, which Americans called "Grenadier Squaw's Town." Still, despite her early warring, Nonhelema abandoned her warrior status by the mid-1770s, warning the Americans of an impending attack on Fort Randolph in 1778 and spending most of the 1770s and 1780s as a peace chief instead.[16]

Unlike Nonhelema, most Shawnee women did not go to war but participated when war came to them. After the Battle of Sandusky in 1782, Shawnees tortured and burned Col. William Crawford in retaliation for the slaughter of ninety Christian Lenni Lenapes at Gnadenhutten, Ohio, earlier in the year. For two hours, Shawnee women and men prodded Crawford with firebrands while he begged for death. When he finally collapsed, they scalped him. The ritual death tested Crawford's spiritual power against their own; their success in breaking and scalping him symbolically thrust his soul into the underworld. That women joined in the torture related not only their spiritual power in Shawnee society but also their investment in defeating the invaders. Crawford represented a specific threat to Shawnee women. As farmers bound to the earth and mothers bound to their children, they were less mobile than hunters and warriors and, consequently, far more vulnerable to invasion. The greatest threat to Shawnee stability was when whites, as George Bluejacket remembered, "sent their Shen-a-nees [Big Knives] to our lodges and killed our E-qui-we and A-po-te-the [women and children]." Women's deaths disrupted agriculture and food preparation, and eliminated voices of peace that occasionally moderated the war cries of grieving fathers, husbands, and sons.[17]

War was not the only threat to Shawnee culture. For rituals such as the Green Corn Dance, Shawnee women prepared traditional foods. But since their return to the Ohio River valley in the 1740s, Shawnee interaction with European traders had introduced new foods and material culture. Cabbage, turnips, and cucumbers supplemented corn, beans, and pumpkins as common staples. Use of wooden bowls faded as iron kettles, creamware, and glazed earthenware became popular. Shawnees' assimilation to European material culture, however, may have been more a consequence of the large number of captives who lived among them than European trade. Captive European and African American women exchanged foodways by introducing new recipes and demonstrating usage of the cookware sold by traders. As Shawnee women assessed the clothing of female captives, they purchased more European clothes. In 1773 a visitor found every Shawnee woman in one village garbed in black, blue, or red petticoats heavily adorned with trade silver trinkets. On one woman, he counted "near five hundred silver brooches stuck in her shift, stroud and leggings."[18]

Clothing and kettles symbolized a deeper transformation under way. By the 1770s European goods were transforming not only Shawnee material culture but also the gendered balance that characterized their society. Although Shawnee women engaged with women captives, they more often interacted with European men who traded with or warred against them. But European men expected to interact with other men, requiring Shawnee women to give up many traditional roles—a pattern found among the Cherokees, Choctaws, and Creeks during the era. It is plausible that Nonhelema's abandonment of the war-chief role resulted from Europeans' dismissal of her in a "man's" role. Some Shawnee men, those who became wealthier through trade with British and American colonial traders, began to revise their ideas of gender; and some Shawnee women, most often those married to traders or daughters of such marriages, accepted the new hierarchical notions of patriarchy. In trade, diplomacy, and war between the 1770s and 1810s, kill-power would exert greater cultural influence than life-power in Shawnee society. The gender balance that characterized Shawnee culture waned as men became more important as protectors, warriors, and negotiators, resulting in the weakening of Nonhelema's status, voice, and authority, as well as that of other Shawnee women.[19]

Nonhelema's life embodied the transformations under way in Shawnee culture. As war came to the Ohio River valley, the Shawnees abandoned Chillicothe, "Grenadier Squaw's Town," Maquachake, and other villages along the Scioto River. The Maquachakes again migrated northwestward, establishing a new village where Nonhelema joined Moluntha. As American colonials attempted to settle Kentucky, tensions increased between the Americans and the Shawnees, and among the Shawnees themselves. Divisions and villages splintered as Shawnees elected to either fight the threat or seek peace and accommodation. Nonhelema and the Maquachake village chose peace, but kill-power won out. Hoping to preserve her way of life, she petitioned the Confederation Congress in 1785 for a two-thousand-acre grant in Ohio, as compensation for her warning about the attack on Fort Randolph, her subsequent activities to bring peace to the Ohio country, and loss of livestock. Congress responded with "one suit or dress of Cloaths including a blanket per annum, and one ration of provisions each day during her life." The following year, Benjamin Logan's American army raided the Shawnee villages. In the new Maquachake, they found Moluntha flying an American flag as evidence of his alliance with the Confederation. He surrendered peacefully, but an enraged Kentuckian took up a hatchet and hacked Moluntha to death. The Kentuckians took Nonhelema and her daughters captive and returned to Kentucky. Shawnee oral tradition continues that they cut off the fingers on her right hand, disabling the great Grenadier Squaw. And then Nonhelema disappeared from history.[20]

Stand on the edge of the woods outside Boonesborough on the southeastern edges of the Bluegrass region and watch the white women masquerading as soldiers. It is September 9, 1778. Shawnee chief Blackfish's force—more than four hundred Shawnees, Cherokees, Wyandots, Miamis, Lenni Lenapes, and Mingos and a dozen French Canadian militiamen—has been waiting for two days to escort Daniel Boone and the fort's other residents into captivity, as Boone had promised Blackfish months earlier. Our vision is not set on the men traditionally situated at the center of this story, however. There, atop the wall, through the cracks in the fort's chinking, and occasionally in the small windows of the blockhouses, we catch a glimpse of men who look a bit like women, locks of hair occasionally falling from under their beaver hats, the bosoms of their vests and jackets fuller than those of the other men. As one colonist recalled, Col. Richard Callaway told the women "to put on hats and hunting shirts and to appear as men and git up on the top of the walls and as they might appear as a great many men"—a tactic that, combined with faulty intelligence from British governor Henry Hamilton in Detroit, reinforced the illusion of a greater fighting force behind the walls of Boonesborough than there actually was. Among those cross-dressers is a sixteen-year-old woman named Jemima.[21]

Born in 1762 in North Carolina's Yadkin River country, Jemima was the fourth child of Daniel and Rebecca Boone. On returning from one of his long hunts into Kentucky, Daniel found his wife nursing an infant. Frontier rumors circulated that the child was not his, and according to one version, Rebecca responded to her husband: "You had better have staid [*sic*] at home and got it yourself." Daniel's response? "Oh well, the race will be continued."[22]

White men, led by the intrepid Boone, had been wandering Kentucky for more than a decade before the first white women traversed the Appalachians to settle. In 1775 Jemima arrived with her family, marking a significant shift in the frontier process. Previously, Americans understood Kentucky as off-limits: Indian territory on the far side of the Proclamation Line (1763) in which backcountry men had risked their lives to extract deer and buffalo skins, meat, and salt. The arrival of families transformed Kentucky's frontier into an extension of American settlement. Women and children required a more aggressively defensive posturing and forced men to commit to settling. As whites arrived in Kentucky in the 1770s and 1780s, therefore, they faced a peculiar paradox: the presence of white women required greater protection but, as the women in hats and hunting shirts evinced, those women had to risk their lives by participating actively in that defense.[23]

Like Native American women, white women faced the existential threat of frontier warfare. They often found themselves placed in dangerous situations, usually unarmed and occasionally through white men's insistence. One group of migrants, after being attacked by Indians, forced the women to "wear big coats . . . and made them ride with sticks on their shoulders." During the siege of Boonesborough in 1778, the Shawnees demanded to see Boone's daughters, and the white men behind the fort walls complied, sending Jemima and two other women outside where "they took out their Combs" and "let their hair flow over their Shoulders." The Indians laughed—whether at the women or at their men's willingness to sacrifice them we will never know—and left. During the 1782 siege of Bryan's Station, the men induced the women to wander out to the spring and retrieve water, despite their pleading that "*they* were not bullet-proof, and that the Indians made no distinction between male and female scalps!" The difference could not have been starker. Shawnee society permitted women to serve in defensive roles, but in most cases Shawnee men sought to protect Shawnee women during war; white men pushed white women to participate in their own defense, often without the resources to actually protect themselves.[24]

In contrast to Shawnee women, white women did not live in a world that understood gender in a balanced manner. In the colonies, white women had been dependents within their husbands' patriarchal spheres, confined to the domestic realm and with authority solely over lesser dependents—children and slaves. Men were credited with being the warriors and negotiators, producers and consumers, and they exerted patriarchal authority over their wives and daughters. As with the Shawnees, however, whites' gender ideals were in transition in the 1760s and 1770s. Colonials' political and military conflicts with Great Britain resulted in new ideas about gender and the appropriate roles for women in a republican society. During the American Revolution, as white women participated in economic boycotts and the war effort, white men had little choice but to reimagine patriarchal notions about relegating women to the domestic sphere, disconnected from the public sphere. Republican womanhood reframed white women's roles: they became the keepers of conscience—their husbands', their families', and the embryonic nation's. Assuming responsibility for the traditional male commitment to the common good, white women sacrificed themselves to family and society, providing men the opportunities to pursue individualistic endeavors. Intent on being good republican wives and mothers like their sisters in the East, white women who migrated to Kentucky worked and harvested the fields, sheared sheep, milked cows, plucked chickens, prepared food, spun and dyed thread and yarn, wove cloth, made clothes, and birthed, nursed, reared, and educated children as part of their civic duties, forfeiting their lives to their husbands' and fathers' pursuits.[25]

Unlike eastern republican women, however, white frontier women also assumed what had been considered traditional male responsibilities such as defense, consequently forcing reassessment of gender roles. Beyond dressing as men, some women fought like men. Esther Whitley impressed white and Native American men alike as among the best shooters on Kentucky's frontier, telling one group of visiting Cherokees that she had learned "in order to kill them should occasion ever make it necessary." She was not alone: "Hugh Luper's, Samuel Daviess', General Logan's, Whitley's wives, kept rifles, and were mighty hard to beat, 100 yards." When one group of settlers migrating down the Ohio River suspected a threat, the "women who were armed, as most of them were with pistols, took positions with their husbands." When widely reviled British general Henry Hamilton (known to American colonials as the "hair-buyer general" because he paid Indians for scalps) arrived as a captive at Logan's Station in 1779, Jane Menifee took up a tomahawk that arrived alongside him and threatened to scalp him, remarking that the weapon had certainly been used on women and children. After John Merrill was shot during an Indian attack, his wife took an axe to four Indians as they tried to breech the cabin door, killing two and wounding two others. Then, as two came down the chimney, she stoked the fire, and when they fell, she chopped them up. During a Shawnee attack on McConnell's Station, an Indian crawled under the cabin and "was trying to lift the slabs, and one of these, a very heavey [*sic*] woman, would always jump upon it, and he hadn't purchase enough to throw her off." A couple of women then poured boiling water through the floor planks: "Twas said he made a dreadful howling." When Shawnees attacked her family's cabin near Saint Asaph, Hannah Woods took up an axe and severed the arm of an Indian attempting to push open the door, then she assisted her mother in "finishing" him with a "Broad Ax & Bar of Iron." During the siege of Boonesborough, Jemima Boone ran among the men, carrying ammunition and loading their guns. As she entered a doorway, she felt what she thought was someone slapping her backside, but she soon realized she had been hit. The ball lodged in the folds of her petticoat, only superficially breaking the skin and falling out when she tugged her clothes. Years later, in conversation with an elder Cherokee chief, Cephas Washburn recalled a woman who "moulded bullets and loaded the rifles for her husband" as he held off the attacking Indians. His Cherokee acquaintance concluded, "*She* was a *man*, and worthy to sit at the council fire with the wisest chiefs." Indeed, by acting as soldiers, all of these women acted as men. Among the Shawnees, women assumed warrior status through familial connections and physical prowess. Among white Kentuckians, women became soldiers out of desperation and necessity.[26]

But it is noteworthy that, despite examples of white women soldiers, the pretense remained that as dependents reliant on the protection of white men, they were not *supposed* to be soldiers. Unlike Nonhelema, who engaged in battle as a war chief, and other Shawnee women who joined in torturing and burning William Crawford as part of a ritual of vengeance and condemnation of his spirit, white culture did not license women to kill. They were, instead, to be spectators of men's heroic actions, serving as arbiters of frontier manhood. As Nathanial Hart recalled, "The women could read the character of a man with invariable certainty. If he lacked courage, they seemed to be able to discover it, at a glance." Particularly, "if a man was found to be a coward, he stood a poor chance to get his washing, or mending, or anything done." During the siege of Boonesborough, Elizabeth Callaway forcefully coaxed Tice Brock from his hiding place to go fight, even as he pleaded, "I was not made for a fighter—I was not made for a fighter." Jane Sprowl sternly reprimanded her brothers who talked a good game: "It is easy to fight Indians sitting in the chimney corner, with your bellies' full of mush and milk." One pioneer remembered how, at Moore's Station, "the men had gotten very careless, and while the guards were out, they would all go out and play at ball, and those that were not playing, would go out and lie down, without their guns." The women sneaked outside the station, fired some rifles, and ran back inside, startling the men who "were in so great haste, they run right through the pond. They were all exceeding mad, and wanted, some of them, to have the women whipped." Even as the women laughed about their prank, however, they had made a point about vigilance and security. Because white women supposedly depended on men for protection, their best weapon against Native Americans was the bolstering of manly heroism and the ridicule of cowardice.[27]

All this is to say that in acting as good republican women, migrating westward for the good of family, community, and even nation, and enabling their husbands' and fathers' wanderlust, white women were complicit in the settler colonialism under way in Kentucky and determined to make it succeed. Susannah Johnson recalled her father's decision to move from South Carolina to Kentucky. Her mother consented so that "her children, when arrived at maturity, might seek homes in new counties, and for the sake of keeping the family together, she consented to remove." Women were drawn to Kentucky by visions of a new home, a fertile garden, and the perpetuation of family. In making that decision, white women such as Mrs. Johnson transformed Kentucky from an extractive frontier to a settler colony, one that required the elimination—through death, removal, or assimilation—of Native Americans in order to secure protection of self and ownership of land. With guns, axes, and moral authority in hand (and a vision of permanent colonization in mind), white women were as great a threat to Indian lives and culture as any white man. Consequently, Indian warriors targeted white women as enemies, scalping them, killing them, taking them captive, and exposing the inability of white men to protect white women.[28]

Women such as Jemima Boone knew the threat before moving westward. They had heard stories like that of Mary Draper Ingles, taken captive and escaped in 1755, and some had read *A True History of the Captivity and Restoration of Mrs. Mary Rowlandson* (1682). White women imagined the terrors of Indian attack—the deaths of their children and husbands, their own captivities and permanent separation from families, the possibilities of torture, death, and sexual violation. Yet, because Indian men considered sexual intimacy with any woman as ritually impure during wartime, the threat of rape was fantastical. Indian trader James Adair told of Shawnee captain Jack, who "did not attempt the virtue of his female captives, lest (as he told one of them) it should offend the Indians' God." Torture and death, of course, were certainly plausible.[29]

Consequently, Kentucky's white women confined themselves to the limited geography of forts, stations, and their immediate environs. "A woman dare not go 40 yards to pick beans without a guard," remembered John Dyal. Women who did wander learned the lessons of terror in the most direct way. In 1784 eleven-year-old Keturah Leitch witnessed the horrors as she migrated into Kentucky: mangled bodies, a scalp with beautiful blonde ringlets hanging from a tree limb. She lived the next eleven years behind the walls of Bryan's Station and Leitch's Station. Like Leitch, most white women bunkered down for years on the defensive behind the walls. They called it being "forted," the psychological consequences of which were summed up by Daniel Trabue: "They was a coruagus [*sic*] people but yet I will say they all looked very wild. You might frequently see the women a walking around the fort looking and peeping about seeming that they did not know what they was about but would try to incourage [*sic*] one another and hopt [*sic*] for the best." For what were they looking? When Rachel McCutchens wandered beyond the fort walls with her son, Shawnees captured her and killed the boy. She escaped and "was crazy after she returned" and "went about with a rake, turning over the leaves in the fence corners, looking for her son."[30]

In the white imagination, Indian captivity was transformative, and white women who survived captivity, however brief the captivity may have been, were considered damaged and often were ostracized, devalued as wives and mothers, and occasionally just left to roam about, turning over the leaves in the fence corners. When rescued in 1785, Mrs. McClure was presumed to be psychologically scarred from having cooked for her captors beside a rack on which hung "six scalps stretched in hoops"—four of which had been her children's. The circumstances of her captivity and escape affected Mary Draper Ingles so much that "she appeared absorbed in a deep melancholy, and left the arrangement of household concerns & the reception of strangers to her lovely daughters." Hannah Sovereigns had been captive for six years and, when she returned to Kentucky, was considered ill suited for marriage to all but another former captive, Ben Linn. In some cases, the returned captives were considered sexually compromised. After Jenny Wiley's return, rumors circulated that she gave birth to a dark-skinned, dark-complexioned daughter.[31]

Jemima Boone, too, experienced captivity. In July 1776 she and Elizabeth and Frances Callaway left the security of Boonesborough to canoe on the Kentucky River. Floating too close to the far banks of the river, the girls were grabbed by two Cherokees and three Shawnees. Their screams alarmed the settlers, including the girls' fathers, who quickly formed a rescue party and took pursuit. Richard Callaway worried that the Indians would "violate his daughters," despite Daniel Boone's assurances that that was not the way of the Native Americans. Jemima took an active role in her own defense, breaking branches and disturbing rocks in order to mark her trail, spending much of the time trying to reach a small penknife in her pocket, and even flirting with the Cherokee Hanging Maw. When they stopped for the first night, the Native Americans "cut their clothes off to the knees, took off their shoes and stockings, and put on moccasins." Their journey continued for another day and night; not until the third day did the rescue party catch up and save the girls.[32]

The girls' return to Boonesborough was certainly upsetting to their families and other settlers: they *looked* like Indians. In fact, one of the Callaway girls had been misidentified during the rescue and almost shot. Their clothes were torn, suggesting physical violation despite Boone's guarantee otherwise. The girls were traumatized by the episode, of course, forming strong emotional bonds with their rescuers. Within eighteen months, all three married members of the rescue party. At fifteen years of age, Jemima wed Flanders Callaway, a cousin of the Callaway girls, and had her first child two years later.[33]

Unlike many other white women who experienced captivity, however, Jemima Boone Callaway seemed to recover rather quickly from the experience and even expressed a quirky humor about it. A few years later, as she attempted to ford a river, Jemima fell from her horse. On being saved, she announced that "a ducking is very disagreeable this chilly day but much less so than capture by the Indians." Still, her brief captivity had an important effect on her. Jemima pointed to that episode as a significant bonding moment with Daniel. When he was captured and presumed dead in 1778, the rest of the family returned to North Carolina, but Jemima remained at Boonesborough, waiting for him. When he decided to move to the Missouri frontier, she persuaded her husband to join the migration. Her father lived his later years with Jemima, and when he died in 1820, she perpetuated his myth until her own death nine years later. As with Jemima's experience, the greatest consequence of whites' success against the Indian threat was the strengthening of patriarchy.[34]

Stand by a cabin on Kentucky's western plateau in 1808 and watch the enslaved black girl preparing the new ground. Her name is Matilda, she is nine years old, and she has only recently arrived as part of a larger migration group led by her owner, Randolph Lewis. In the distance is the Tennessee River, and beyond are the Chickasaw lands from which occasional raids are made on the American settlement at Eddyville and the farms cropping up in Kentucky's westernmost territory. As Matilda pulls rocks and weeds from the soil, she is watched by an elderly slave couple hoeing the ground nearby—Sarah and Frank, who have acted as her parents since leaving Virginia.

Despite her youth, Matilda's story is like that of so many other African American women who came to Kentucky before her. Whites' decisions to move westward directly affected slaves' lives. A few years earlier, when Robert and Ann Cabell Harrison decided to transfer their Virginia plantation to Kentucky in two separate migrations, an observer noted, "Tomorrow the negroes are to get off and I expect there will be great crying and morning [*sic*], children Leaving there [*sic*] mothers, mothers there [*sic*] children, and women there [*sic*] husbands." Historians have made much of white women's distress at leaving kin networks behind as their husbands dragged them westward, but they did have husbands and in most cases children to mitigate their loneliness. Their trials pale in comparison to slave women's anxieties about leaving behind not only extensive kin networks but husbands and children as well. For many black women like Matilda, life on the Kentucky frontier was a truly solitary experience.[35]

While most black women saw their families disrupted by migration, there is evidence that some managed to sustain family. Molly, slave to Benjamin Logan, brought her three young sons to Saint Asaph in 1776. Five years later, Peter Durrett and his wife arrived as part of Joseph Craig's household. Fanny, Betsy, Nisey, and their children accompanied seven slave men in an advance group for John Breckinridge's plantation in the 1790s. In most cases, the ability of a family to remain intact depended largely on the generosity of the owner. Of course, children who accompanied their mothers did so because they assumed the slave status of their mothers and, consequently, were property of the mother's owner. Slave women also negotiated with masters to either avoid or join a migration so as to stay with their children or husbands. "You mention Old Tener she is a nother shak bag," wrote a Virginia relative to new Kentucky settler and slave owner Polly Breckinridge in 1801, "the Lazy slut that went out [to Kentucky] last was so intent on going that she made her self out to be pregnant."[36]

Having family, then, was a significant achievement for an enslaved black woman; it was critical to developing a sense of stability and security. Given the fragility of life on the frontier, slave women constructed new families, even if they successfully migrated with a husband or children. In 1795, as he met with Shawnees, a white man recognized an African American woman who had been taken captive years earlier. He tried to secure release, but she refused to leave without the four children to whom she had given birth while living among the Shawnees. The negotiator claimed that "She wo'd rather live w white people," but her actions demonstrated that she wanted to live with family.[37]

Like most other black women, Matilda migrated to Kentucky without any family. Early in 1808 she traveled down the Ohio River with three white families and more than twenty slaves from Virginia's Shenandoah Valley to Kentucky's westernmost Livingston County. Although her father was part of the migration group, it seems her mother was not. Her father was Charles Lewis, the brother of her owner, whose act of miscegenation in 1799 had apparently brought shame on his family. Whether the slave woman with whom he slept had died in childbirth or been sold off is unknown, but she quickly disappeared from memory. Matilda assumed the slave status of her mother and became a ward of the slave community on Randolph Lewis's plantation. When the Lewis brothers decided to relocate en masse to the western frontier, she left behind a mother she never knew and traveled with a father who did not care.[38]

She found a new mother in Sarah, who held significant status and most likely was the matrifocal center of a small slave community: Matilda, Sarah and Frank, and three other blacks occupied the Lewis farm. We should not be surprised to find strong women within frontier slave families. Slave owners displaced slave men's authority over family, deprived them of the type of power that emanated from property ownership, and refused to acknowledge them as fathers. Not only did children stay with mothers, but their mothers were often the only immediate family they knew. Additionally, slave women outnumbered slave men in preparing frontier Kentucky's new grounds, digging ditches, hoeing, weeding, and working the fields. West African women traditionally cleared new grounds for agriculture, including uprooting trees and removing rocks, but cultural tradition carried less weight in trans-Appalachia: instead, because female slaves cost less than male slaves and therefore were more expendable, owners hesitated little to put enslaved women to hard labor in dangerous frontier circumstances. Given the obstacles constructed against black male authority and the number of enslaved women, a picture of relative gender equality among blacks emerged in Kentucky, allowing for women such as Sarah to become family and community leaders.[39]

Still, while Matilda and other black women toiled hard in the fields, they also were expected to be domestic laborers. In contrast to Native American women, who produced and reproduced out of a spiritual understanding of the balance of genders, and to white women, who performed domesticity to sustain the patriarchal structures they inhabited, black women had to abide by the gendered regimens dictated by their owners. Their chores—producing cloth and clothing, dairying, cooking and serving meals, household cleaning, and child care—kept them in contact with white families, and specifically the white women who oversaw their work. Their domestic work made them critical members of the farm family, black and white. One enslaved man complained in 1778 that "we have no women to wash for us, on Sundays we stalk about without being able to talk to any one." Women's domestic skills not only empowered them within the households but also provided a bit of independence as well. For three years William Hardin left a slave woman tending his Green River farm. Hunters regularly visited the cabin, delivering meat to her while she prepared their skins for trade: "She had nothing to do but to dress the deer skins. . . . She got to be an excellent hand." And a few years after her arrival in Kentucky, when she had honed her domestic skills, Matilda became a hired-out domestic servant, making additional money for her owner and herself. Because of their talents, black women became vital to whites' development of the frontier.[40]

They also faced the same existential threat on Kentucky's frontiers as did white and Indian women. Whites claimed land and often sent "a parcel of poor slaves where I dare not go myself" to tend those claims while they returned eastward to gather families and supplies. John Bruce left two slaves behind at his Bourbon County cabin and arranged for hunters to supply them with meat in his absence. The man was scalped and the woman taken hostage. Four slaves—two men, a woman, and a girl—accompanied Nathaniel and William Ewing to their new Kentucky claim. When the brothers returned to Maryland for supplies, one of the slaves panicked. Unable to persuade the others to leave with him, he wandered to a nearby fort for help, returning a few days later to find the other man and the women slaughtered: "It was believed from the sign, that the Negro man had fought, and that with an axe. The wall was seen bloody . . . off a little piece from where the Negro lay." The Bruce and Ewing slaves were largely defenseless; they did not have weapons to guard against attack. In 1798 a new set of slave laws codified the restriction already in place: slave owners could not arm their slaves with "any gun, powder, shot, club, or other weapon, whatsoever, offensive or defensive," although exception was made for slaves in dangerous frontier conditions but only with "license from the justice of the peace of the county." The slaves themselves could not apply for a license, and if the slave owner had yet to migrate and apply for the license, then his or her slaves remained defenseless.[41]

Black women, like white women, shared the geography of fort life. While they lived behind the fort walls, they also routinely went beyond them to herd livestock, tend and harvest gardens, and gather water or milk. In 1775 Benjamin Logan's slave Molly joined Esther Whitley and Anne Logan in milking the cows while the fort was under siege. The Shawnees shot and killed one of the guards, scurrying the women back into the fort. Not surprisingly, black women were occasionally among the first to be sent beyond the walls for help when a fort or station came under attack, as when "a black woman was poked thro' [the station wall] and told to go and alarm the nearest station" during an attack in Tygart's Valley. In 1774 Shawnees captured a black woman near Shelby's Fort, tortured her in view of the settlement to get her to tell the number of men and guns inside, and then let her go.[42]

Like other black women on the frontier, Matilda survived the Indian threat without the benefit of weapons to which white women had access, and she performed arduous field labor just as black men did. In 1811 Randolph Lewis died, leaving Matilda to his wife, who subsequently hired her out. That same year, Randolph's brothers Lilburn and Isham murdered George, a member of Matilda's extended slave community. They caught him running away and, in order to teach the other slaves a lesson, bound him and used an axe to chop him up in front of the other slaves and burn him in the fireplace. The New Madrid earthquake hit, collapsing part of the chimney and interrupting their attempt to destroy the evidence. Even though they hid George's bones in the fireplace as their slaves reconstructed it, an aftershock revealed the grisly murder. As the murder trial unfolded, Mary Lewis died and Matilda was sold along with Sarah and Frank to Andrew Threlkeld as part of the Lewis estate settlement. With the end of the Civil War some fifty-three years later, she became free and lived out her life in Marion, Kentucky, as "Aunt Matilda," a minor celebrity for her memories of George's murder.[43]

Nonhelema Hokolesqua, Jemima Boone Callaway, and Matilda Lewis Threlkeld never met, but as women, their lives were similar in many ways. They shared experiences of migration and resettlement, agricultural work and domestic production, and the responsibilities of childbirth, child raising, and sustaining family relationships. Such experiences may have defined their worlds as "female," but they were hardly the markings of a female frontier: white women in Massachusetts, black women on Georgia's Sea Islands, and native women in Hawaii performed gender similarly. The primary factor defining social norms for frontier women cannot be just gender. In order to find Kentucky's female frontier, we must give "frontier" as much weight as "female."

Historian David Hackett Fischer once wrote, "Whenever a culture exists for many generations in conditions of chronic insecurity, it develops an ethic that exalts war above work, force above reason, and men above women." For three generations, from the 1750s through the War of 1812, the peoples who lived in and around Kentucky were immersed in such a culture. Every person regardless of race, gender, or age faced the threat of attack and possible death on a daily basis. Shawnee women watched their authority as peacemakers erode just as white women, inspired by republican womanhood, joined white men in colonizing trans-Appalachia, forcing black women to accompany them as laborers to clear lands and establish claims. By the 1770s all women—red, white, and black—lived in an increasingly patriarchal frontier that was characterized foremost by terror and war.[44]

If we search for women in that violent, male-oriented culture, we soon recognize that Kentucky's female frontier was defined not by women's shared responsibilities but by women's shared vulnerability. Cultural strictures in native and white cultures inhibited women's abilities to defend themselves, and legal constrictions hindered black women's self-defense. Among the Shawnees, unless a woman achieved status as a war chief, she relied on warriors for protection. Only occasionally did a Nonhelema have the opportunity to fight for herself. White women such as Jemima also depended on men for defense, regularly ridiculing cowards who failed to do so, and, when frustrated by lack of protection, often abandoning cultural standards of womanhood and taking up guns and axes to protect themselves. Black women were most vulnerable, often without defenders or weapons. Slave owners exposed Matilda and other African American women to the threat of Indian attack without much concern for their well-being. And while death was the immediate threat, captivity also shaped women's shared vulnerability. Jemima Boone's capture and rescue became famous as frontier lore, but other white women were not so fortunate, losing their families and even their identities to native assimilation. Nonhelema too was a captive, taken from Maquachake to Kentucky after the death of Moluntha. Did she die in captivity? Some traditions have her returning to Ohio to die, more a reflection of the myth of the "noble savage" than historical fact. Matilda was a captive as well, albeit not of Indians but of whites' enslavement. Because frontier farmers were often desperate for money, they readily sold slaves, separating mothers from children. Not even Matilda's identity was her own: her surnames—first Lewis and then Threlkeld—were those of her owners. All three women and the thousands whom they represent lived under the constant threat of violent disruption from families, communities, and their own conceptualizations of self.

Stand at Cumberland Gap and watch the procession of civilization, marching single file—the wives and daughters, white and black, who abandoned kin in the East to construct new lives in the West, the Shawnee woman wielding a tomahawk with a warring party, the captive being forced northward to the Indian towns along the Ohio River where she will live out the rest of her life, the white woman pushing aside the leaves in search of her lost children, the enslaved black woman sent ahead to create a small farm and secure her master's property claim, the Native American women advocating for peace, the white women dressed as men and carrying sticks, the woman of any race who will die within the month and be buried in an unmarked grave—and Kentucky's female frontier has passed by.

NOTES

1. Frederick Jackson Turner, "The Significance of the Frontier in American History," *Annual Report of the American Historical Association for 1893* (Washington, D.C.: Government Printing Office, 1894), reprinted in Frederick Jackson Turner, *The Frontier in American History* (New York: Holt, 1920), 12.

2. Humphrey Marshall, *The History of Kentucky*, 2 vols. (Frankfort: S. Robinson, 1824); Thomas D. Clark, ed., *The Voice of the Frontier: John Bradford's Notes on Kentucky* (Lexington: University Press of Kentucky, 1993); Timothy Flint, *Biographical Memoir of Daniel Boone* (Cincinnati: N. & G. Guilford, 1833); John A. McClung, *Sketches of Western Adventure* (1832; Covington, Ky.: Richard H. Collins, 1872). For a discussion of the erasure of women from Kentucky's frontier narrative, see Craig Thompson Friend, *Kentucke's Frontiers* (Bloomington: Indiana University Press, 2010), 281–83.

3. Etta DeGering, *Wilderness Wife: The Story of Rebecca Bryan Boone* (New York: David McKay, 1966), xii, xiv; Thomas D. Clark, *Frontier America: The Story of the Westward Movement* (New

York: Charles Scribner's Sons, 1959), 244–45, 492–93. For studies that neglected women, see R. S. Cotterill, *History of Pioneer Kentucky* (Cincinnati: Johnston & Hardin, 1917); Thomas Perkins Abernethy, *Three Virginia Frontiers* (Gloucester, Mass.: Peter Smith, 1962). For examples of studies that looked at "exceptional women" as participants in the male process of civilization or as foils for demonstration of male character-building, see Thomas D. Clark, *Kentucky: Land of Contrast* (New York: HarperCollins, 1968), 9–10; idem, *Three American Frontiers: Writings of Thomas D. Clark*, ed. Holman Hamilton (Lexington: University of Kentucky Press, 1968), 10–12; George Morgan Chinn, *Kentucky: Settlement and Statehood, 1750–1800* (Frankfort: Kentucky Historical Society, 1975), 110; Otis K. Rice, *Frontier Kentucky* (Lexington: University Press of Kentucky, 1993), 14–15. Ironically, in presocial history descriptions of "culture"—an arena usually associated with women and in which the study of women made early inroads—no women are mentioned in relationship to early Kentucky. See Louis B. Wright, *Culture on the Moving Frontier* (Bloomington: Indiana University Press, 1955); Arthur K. Moore, *The Frontier Mind: A Cultural Analysis of the Kentucky Frontiersman* (Lexington: University of Kentucky Press, 1957). Mary Holley, wife of an early president of Transylvania University, made brief appearances in John D. Wright Jr., *Transylvania: Tutor to the West* (Lexington: Transylvania University, 1975), but only in regard to how her pregnancy affected her husband's decision to migrate westward.

4. Joan E. Cashin, *A Family Venture: Men and Women on the Southern Frontier* (Baltimore: Johns Hopkins University Press, 1991), 6; Dee Brown, *Gentle Tamers: Women of the Wild West* (Lincoln: University of Nebraska Press, 1958); Paul Petrick, "Gentle Tamers in Transition: Women in the Trans-Mississippi West," *Feminist Studies* 11 (1985): 677–84; Margaret Ripley Wolfe, "Fallen Leaves and Missing Pages: Women in Kentucky History," *Register of the Kentucky Historical Society* 90 (1992): 66. For evidence of the persistence of the "gentle tamers" paradigm, see Robert Morgan, *Boone: A Biography* (Chapel Hill, N.C.: Algonquin, 2007), 62–63, 187–88; Ellen Eslinger, *Running Mad for Kentucky: Frontier Travel Accounts* (Lexington: University Press of Kentucky, 2004), 37–38.

5. Helen Deiss Irvin, *Women in Kentucky* (Lexington: University Press of Kentucky, 1979), 1; Glenda Riley, *Female Frontier: A Comparative View of Women on the Prairie and the Plains* (Lawrence: University Press of Kansas, 1989), 5; Stephen Aron, *How the West Was Lost: The Transformation of Kentucky from Daniel Boone to Henry Clay* (Baltimore: Johns Hopkins University Press, 1996), 3; Ellen Eslinger, *Citizens of Zion: The Social Origins of Camp Meeting Revivalism* (Knoxville: University of Tennessee Press, 1999), 232.

6. Elizabeth A. Perkins, *Border Life: Experience and Memory in the Revolutionary Ohio Valley* (Chapel Hill: University of North Carolina Press, 1998), 143; Craig Thompson Friend, *Along the Maysville Road: The Early American Republic in the Trans-Appalachian West* (Knoxville: University of Tennessee Press, 2005), 24–25; also Randolph Hollingsworth, "'Mrs. Boone, I Presume?' In Search of the Idea of Womanhood in Kentucky's Early Years," in *Bluegrass Renaissance: The History and Culture of Central Kentucky, 1792–1852*, ed. James C. Klotter and Daniel Rowland (Lexington: University Press of Kentucky, 2012), 93–130. A promising first step in discovering Kentucky's female frontier is forthcoming in Honor Sachs's *Home Rule: Households, Manhood, and National Expansion on the Eighteenth-Century Kentucky Frontier* (New Haven, Conn.: Yale University Press, 2015).

7. Friend, *Kentucke's Frontiers*, xxii; Cashin, *A Family Venture*, 6; Antonia Casteñeda, "Women of Color and the Rewriting of Western History: The Discourse, Politics, and Decolonization of History," *Pacific Historical Review* 61 (1992): 515. For efforts at integrating women of color into frontier Kentucky's narrative, see Aron, *How the West Was Lost*; Margaret Ripley Wolfe, *Daughters of Canaan: A Saga of Southern Women* (Lexington: University Press of Kentucky, 1995), 66–70; Friend, *Kentucke's Frontiers*. On the evolution of women's frontier history, see Joan M. Jensen

and Darlis A. Miller, "The Gentle Tamers Revisited: New Approaches to the History of Women in the American West," *Pacific Historical Review* 49 (1980): 173–214; John Mack Faragher, "History from the Inside-Out: Writing the History of Women in Rural America," *American Quarterly* 33 (1981): 537–57; Glenda Riley, "Frederick Jackson Turner Overlooked the Ladies," *Journal of the Early Republic* 13 (1993): 216–30; Margaret Walsh, "Women's Place on the American Frontier," *Journal of American Studies* 29 (1995): 241–55; Margaret D. Jacobs, "Getting Out of a Rut: Decolonizing Western Women's History," *Pacific Historical Review* 79 (2010): 585–60; Karen J. Leong, "Still Walking, Still Brave: Mapping Gender, Race, and Power in U.S. Western History," *Pacific Historical Review* 79 (2010): 618–28.

8. A. Gwynn Henderson, "The Lower Shawnee Town on Ohio: Sustaining Native Autonomy in an Indian 'Republic,'" in Craig Thompson Friend, ed., *The Buzzel about Kentuck: Settling the Promised Land* (Lexington: University Press of Kentucky, 1999), 25–56; William E. Sharp, "Fort Ancient Farmers," in *Kentucky Archaeology*, ed. Barry Lewis (Lexington: University Press of Kentucky, 1996), 175.

9. George Bluejacket, "A Story of the Shawnoes: Wapaughkonnetta, October 19, 1829," trans. John Allen Raynor, typewritten copy, c. 1930s, Ohio Historical Society, Columbus.

10. Don Greene and Noel Schultz, *Shawnee Heritage I: Shawnee Genealogy and Family History*, 2nd ed. (n.p.: Lulu.com, 2008), 173.

11. Theda Perdue, *Cherokee Women: Gender and Cultural Change, 1700–1835* (Lincoln: University of Nebraska Press, 1998), 13; Natalie Zemon Davis, "Iroquois Women, European Women," in *Women, "Race," and Writing in the Early Modern Period*, ed. Margo Hendricks and Patricia Parker (New York: Routledge, 1994), 248–49.

12. James H. Howard, *Shawnee! The Ceremonialism of a Native American Tribe and Its Cultural Background* (Athens: Ohio University Press, 1981), 43–44, 164–70, 175, 225; C. F. and E. W. Voeglin, "The Shawnee Female Deity in Historical Perspective," *American Anthropologist* 46 (1944): 370–75; Milo Milton Quaife, ed., *The Indian Captivity of O. M. Spencer* (Chicago: R. R. Donnelley, 1917), 106–7.

13. Howard, *Shawnee!* 100–101; Albert S. Gatschet, "Shawnee Texts, Myths, with Interlinear English Translation," c. 1878–79, National Anthropological Archives, Smithsonian Institution, Washington, D.C., in Gregory Evan Dowd, *A Spirited Resistance: The North American Indian Struggle for Unity, 1745–1815* (Baltimore: Johns Hopkins University Press, 1992), 7.

14. Howard, *Shawnee!* 109; Journal of General Butler, in *The Olden Time*, ed. Neville B. Craig, 2 vols. (Pittsburgh: Wright & Charlton, 1848), 2:522; John Robinson Harper, "Revolution and Conquest: Politics, Violence, and Social Change in the Ohio Valley, 1765–1795" (PhD diss., University of Wisconsin–Madison, 2008), 1–4; quotations from Colin Calloway, "Maquachake: The Perils of Neutrality in the Ohio Country," in Calloway, *The American Revolution in Indian Country: Crisis and Diversity in Native American Communities* (New York: Cambridge University Press, 1995), 164.

15. Joan R. Gunderson, "Nonhelema (or Grenadier Squaw) (ca. 1720–1786)," in *Women and War: A Historical Encyclopedia from Antiquity to the Present* (Santa Barbara: ABC-CLIO, 2006), 434.

16. Colin Callaway, *The Shawnees and the War for America* (New York: Penguin Library of American Indian History, 2007), 65–66, 80, 84.

17. Dowd, *A Spirited Resistance*, 14–15; Bluejacket, "A Story of the Shawnoes"; Dark Rain Thom, *Kohkumthena's Grandchildren: The Shawnees* (Indianapolis: Guild Press of Indiana, 1994), 47–48.

18. Michael N. McConnell, *A Country Between: The Upper Ohio Valley and Its Peoples, 1724–1774* (Lincoln: University of Nebraska Press, 1992), 211, 213, 215–16; Rev. David Jones, *A Journal of Two Visits Made to Some Nations of the Indians on the West Side of the River Ohio in the Years 1772 and 1773* (Fairfield, Wash.: Galleon Press, 1973), 84.

19. "The Infant Tecumseh," *The New-York Mirror, and Ladies' Literary Gazette*, May 15, 1824, 332; Perdue, *Cherokee Women*, 61–64; Claudio Saunt, "'Domestick . . . Quiet Being Broke': Gender Conflict among Creek Indians in the Eighteenth Century," in Andrew R. L. Cayton and Fredricka J. Teute, *Contact Points: American Frontiers from the Mohawk Valley to the Mississippi, 1750–1830* (Chapel Hill: University of North Carolina Press, 1998), 151–74; Greg O'Brien, "Trying to Look Like Men: Changing Notions of Masculinity among Choctaw Elites in the Early Republic," in *Southern Manhood: Perspectives on Masculinity in the Old South*, ed. Craig Thompson Friend and Lorri Glover (Athens: University of Georgia Press, 2004), 49–70.

20. Callaway, "Maquachake," 159, 169; Gunderson, "Nonhelema," 434; Papers of the Continental Congress, reel 69, item 56: 169–70, National Archives, Washington, D.C.; Green and Schulz, *Shawnee Heritage I*, 194; Callaway, *Shawnees and the War for America*, 84; Harper, "Revolution and Conquest," 4.

21. Chester Raymond Young, ed., *Westward into Kentucky: The Narrative of Daniel Trabue* (Lexington: University Press of Kentucky, 1981), 58.

22. John Dabney Shane interview with Stephen Cooper, 1889, Draper Manuscript Collection, University of Wisconsin, Madison (hereafter DMC), 11CC101; John Dabney Shane interview with Nathaniel Hart, c. 1843–44, DMC 17CC195.

23. John Dabney Shane interview with Sarah Graham, c. 1840s, DMC 11CC51; Friend, *Kentucke's Frontiers*, 65; Richard Phillips, "Settler Colonialism and the Nuclear Family," *Canadian Geographer* 52 (2009): 239–53; R. C. Harris, "The Simplification of Europe Overseas," *Annals of the Association of American Geographers* 67 (1977): 469–83.

24. Elizabeth L. Cushow to Lyman Copeland Draper, March 14, 1885, DMC 21C24; and March 28, 1885, DMC 21C27; McClung, *Sketches of Western Adventure*, 68–69.

25. Mary Beth Norton, "The Evolution of White Women's Experience in Early America," *American Historical Review* 89 (1984): 616–17; idem, *Liberty's Daughters: The Revolutionary Experience of American Women, 1750–1800* (New York: Little, Brown, 1980), 155–272; Linda K. Kerber, *Women of the Republic: Intellect and Ideology in Revolutionary America* (Chapel Hill: University of North Carolina Press, 1980), 69–114, 199–200; Ruth H. Bloch, "American Feminine Ideals in Transition: The Rise of the Moral Mother, 1785–1815," *Feminist Studies* 4 (1978): 101–26.

26. John Dabney Shane interview with Levisa McKinney, DMC 9CC12; John Dabney Shane interview with William McBride, c. 1840s, DMC 11CC262; "Autobiography of Allen Trimble," *Old Northwest Genealogical Quarterly* 9 (1906): 206–7; Irvin, *Women in Kentucky*, 9, 15; John Dabney Shane interview with Martin Wymore, c. 1840s, DMC 11CC130; Isaac Hite to Abraham Hite, April 26, 1783, Filson Historical Society, Louisville, Kentucky; John Mack Faragher, *Daniel Boone: The Life and Legend of an American Pioneer* (New York: Henry Holt, 1992), 131; Cephas Washburn, *Reminiscences of the Indians*, ed. J. W. Moore (1869; New York: Johnson Reprint, 1971), 206.

27. John Dabney Shane interview with Capt. Nathaniel Hart, c. 1843, DMC 17CC207; John Dabney Shane interview with John Gass, c. 1840s, DMC 11CC13; Jane Sprowl, in Donald F. Carmony, ed., "Spencer Records' Memoir of the Ohio Valley Frontier, 1766–1795," *Indiana Magazine of History* 55 (1959): 357; John Dabney Shane interview with Mrs. Samuel Scott, c. 1840s, DMC 11CC225–26; Perkins, *Border Life*, 143–46; Robert Morgan, *Boone: A Biography*, 187–88; Annette Kolodny, *The Land Before Her: Fantasy and Experience of the American Frontiers, 1630–1860* (Chapel Hill: University of North Carolina Press, 1984), chap. 2; Faragher, "History from the Inside-Out," 555–56.

28. Patrick Wolfe, *Settler Colonialism and the Transformation of Anthropology: The Politics and Poetics of an Ethnographic Event* (New York: Cassell, 1999), 2; Susannah Johnson, *Recollections of the Rev. John Johnson and His Home: An Autobiography*, ed. Rev. Adam C. Johnson (Nashville, Tenn.: Southern Methodist Publishing House, 1869), 16–17.

29. Kolodny, *The Land Before Her*, 10–11; Irvin, *Women in Kentucky*, 18–30; James Adair, *Adair's History of the American Indian, 1775*, ed. Samuel Cole Williams (Johnson City, Tenn.: Watauga Press, 1930), 168–72.

30. John Dabney Shane interview with John Dyal, c. 1840s, DMC 13CC228; John Dabney Shane interview with Mrs. Mary Perkins, vol. 7, box 2, John Day Caldwell Papers, Cincinnati Historical Society, Cincinnati, Ohio.

31. Bayless Hardin, "Whitley Papers, Vol. 9—Draper Manuscripts—Kentucky Papers," *Register of the Kentucky Historical Society* 36 (1938): 198–99; Henry Hamilton quotation on Mary Draper Ingles in Irvin, *Women in Kentucky*, 30, also 21, 24, 28.

32. Faragher, *Daniel Boone*, 131–40; John Dabney Shane interview with Robert Wickcliffe Sr., 1859, DMC 15CC84; Elizabeth L. Cushow to Lyman Copeland Draper, March 31, 1885, DMC 21C28.

33. Faragher, *Daniel Boone*, 140; Irvin, *Women in Kentucky*, 13.

34. Narrative of Peter Houston, manuscript, 13–14, c. 1830s, DMC 20C84.

35. Unknown to Polly Cabell Breckinridge, October 12, 1804, Breckinridge Family Papers, Manuscript Division, Library of Congress, Washington, D.C.; Eslinger, *Running Mad for Kentucky*, 37.

36. Ira Berlin, *Generations of Captivity: A History of African-American Slaves* (Cambridge, Mass.: Harvard University Press, 2003), 190–91; Irvin, *Women in Kentucky*, 2, 7; Friend, *Along the Maysville Road*, 36; Gail S. Terry, "Sustaining the Bonds of Kinship in a Trans-Appalachian Migration, 1790–1811: The Cabell-Breckinridge Slaves Move West," *Virginia Magazine of History and Biography* 102 (1994): 455; Boynton Merrill Jr., *Jefferson's Nephews: A Frontier Tragedy* (1976; Lexington: University Press of Kentucky, 1987), 85; Marion B. Lucas, *History of Blacks in Kentucky*, Vol. 1: *From Slavery to Segregation, 1760–1891* (Frankfort: Kentucky Historical Society, 1992), 20; Mary Hopkins Cabell to Polly Cabell Breckinridge, August 12, 1801, Breckinridge Family Papers.

37. John Dabney Shane interview with John Graves, c. 1840s, DMC 11CC122.

38. Merrill, *Jefferson's Nephews*, 49, 85; Berlin, *Generations of Captivity*, 190–91.

39. Ellen Eslinger, "The Shape of Slavery on Virginia's Kentucky Frontier, 1775–1800," in *Diversity and Accommodation: Essays on the Cultural Composition of the Virginia Frontier*, ed. Michael J. Puglisi (Knoxville: University of Tennessee Press, 1997), 180; Frederick C. Knight, *Working the Diaspora: The Impact of African Labor on the Anglo-American World, 1650–1850* (New York: New York University Press, 2010), 47–48; Eugene D. Genovese, *Roll, Jordan, Roll: The World the Slaves Made* (New York: Vintage Books, 1972), 500–501; Philip D. Morgan, *Slave Counterpoint: Black Culture in the Eighteenth-Century Chesapeake Lowcountry* (Chapel Hill: University of North Carolina Press, 1998), 533; Merrill, *Jefferson's Nephews*, 208–9, 417.

40. Berlin, *Generations of Captivity*, 178–79; Michel Sobel, *The World They Made Together: Black and White Values in Eighteenth-Century Virginia* (Princeton, N.J.: Princeton University Press, 1987), 44; Morgan, *Slave Counterpoint*, 196, quotation on 670; John Dabney Shane interview with Col. John Graves, c. 1845, DMC 11CC125.

41. Thomas Hart to Nathaniel Hart, August 3, 1780, in "Shane Collection of Documents: The Hart Papers," *Journal of the Presbyterian Historical Society* 14 (1931): 343–44; John Dabney Shane interview with James Wade, DMC 123CC38; "Slaves," February 14, 1798, in William Littell and Jacob Swigert, *A Digest of the Statute Law of Kentucky*, 2 vols. (Frankfort, Ky.: Kendall & Russell, 1821), 1:1150–51; Friend, *Kentucke's Frontiers*, 194–95.

42. Lucas, *History of Blacks in Kentucky*, 1:xiii; John Dabney Shane interview with Jesse Kennedy, 1852, DMC 11CC37; John Dabney Shane interview with David Crouch, c. 1843, DMC 12CC47.

43. Merrill, *Jefferson's Nephews*, 316, 352.

44. David Hackett Fischer, *Albion's Seed: Four British Folkways in America* (New York: Oxford University Press, 1989), 680. For the terror context, see Friend, *Kentucke's Frontiers*.

Anne Pogue McGinty and Anne McCarty Braden

(c. 1735–1815; 1924–2006)

The Power of Place across Four Centuries

CATHERINE FOSL

This is a story of two Annes—separated in Kentucky history by centuries but united by blood ties, family folktales, and a common name, as well as by the partiality with which their contributions to the Bluegrass State are remembered. One is Anne Pogue McGinty, an early settler who followed Daniel Boone into the territory in 1775, bringing the first spinning wheel across the Cumberland Gap, operating what appears to have been the first tavern in Harrodsburg, and becoming one of the more prosperous women in frontier Kentucky.[1] The other is McGinty's five times great-granddaughter, Anne McCarty Braden—a social-justice activist born in Louisville in 1924—whose radical reputation as a communist civil rights agitator earned her two sedition charges for trying to bring down the government of the commonwealth. In the post–World War II era, Anne Braden could hardly have been situated more differently from her illustrious ancestor in public memory: the mere mention of Braden's name pumped adrenaline into the veins of segregationists across Kentucky and the South, and more than one candidate for office in the 1960s promised if elected to drive her and her husband from the state.[2]

This essay explores the biographies of each of the two Annes through their points of intersection and discontinuity. Sources tell us far fewer details about the eighteenth-century Anne than they do about her twentieth-century namesake. Apart from their blood kinship, the ties that bind the two women may seem slender and tenuous. Yet it is important to note that even their common genealogy would remain largely unknown today were it not for investigations

ANNE MCCARTY BRADEN AND CARL BRADEN

At the gravesite of her ancestor, Ann [*sic*] Pogue McGinty, June 1951.

Courtesy of the Wisconsin Historical Society, ID #99909.

using methods such as oral history and family history to expand what more traditional political histories may not tell us about women's lives. Both women were public figures of their times, and while the later Anne was the more overtly political of the two, both were political in the more expansive sense that includes not simply the formal institutions of government but a wider set of symbolic, normative, and everyday practices that give shared meaning to communities. While both Annes have received some commemoration in state public history sites, what is known of them more broadly also reflects the persistent gaps—what an earlier scholar has called the "fallen leaves and missing pages"—in knowledge of Kentucky women's history.[3]

The two Annes are linked by a family tradition of female storytelling that kept the earlier one's memory alive as a quintessential pioneer woman for later generations of her family, who took great pride in her "womanly" contributions to the early settlement of Kentucky. Her tale seemed to hold special import for the young Anne McCarty (later Braden)—a dreamy, religious child given to writing diaries and poetry—growing up in the 1930s under the tutelage of a mother who had hopes of producing a great novelist. To that child, the pioneer ancestor who had helped build the community at Fort Harrod while the men were off fighting Indian wars seemed a kind of mythic figure, more dashing and brave than the women in her own midst. Most of the nineteenth century and the first two decades of the twentieth separated the two Annes, and the grandmothers who kept the eighteenth-century Anne's history alive in the interim likely sentimentalized it in keeping with the southern Victorian culture of which they were a part. Their tales, as young Anne McCarty later remembered them, tended to soften the violence and crudeness of pioneer life while embellishing its charm and courage and highlighting Anne Pogue McGinty's importance as what a mid-twentieth century scholar called a "gentle tamer" of the frontier Kentucky wilderness.[4]

Both frontier Kentucky and the slave South became centerpieces of the family legend, topics whose importance was impressed again and again on Anne McCarty as a child by many of her relatives, but most especially by her maternal great-grandmother, Mattie Owen Crabb, known fondly as "Mammy Crabb," a widow who lived alone in a tiny house in the central Kentucky town of Eminence, site for much of the family memory. A young slaveholding woman at the time of the Civil War, Crabb lived into her nineties, and she recalled being regaled herself by some of the same frontier folktales while seated at the knee of her own great-grandmother, Mary Pogue, Anne Pogue McGinty's daughter.[5]

Perhaps because they shared a name, the pioneer Anne who had helped settle Kentucky and had outlived four husbands loomed larger than life in the mind of her imaginative namesake in the 1930s. Like the earlier Anne, Anne McCarty Braden would become a highly resilient woman who would upend the life into which she was born. As an adult she would become one of the most committed whites in U.S. history to the cause of African American freedom. To do so at that time made her a "race traitor" in the minds of many whites throughout Kentucky and the South, and—unlike the earlier Anne—a heretic to many in her own family. While many civil rights activists were dismissed and criticized as "outside agitators," the example of Braden—about as far from an outsider to Kentucky as one could be—demonstrates that dissent and resistance to injustice often arise from within a given system, in part from its own collective memory. Albeit by a very different path, Anne McCarty Braden would ultimately join Anne Pogue McGinty as part of a lineage of strong Kentucky women who turned hardship into creativity and who helped forge a new social order amid difficult circumstances.[6]

Just as Anne McCarty Braden's childhood was enlivened by stories of her frontier ancestor, Anne Pogue (as she was always known to her descendants) would likely as a young woman on the western Virginia frontier have heard scores of swashbuckling tales of the danger and allure of the land to her west long before she ever set foot there. While traders passing through spoke of Kentucky as a virtual paradise, all on the frontier were equally alert to the rugged mountain barrier between themselves and the new land and to the threats from native people disturbed by the prospect of white interlopers.[7]

Little is known of the early life of Anne Pogue, born Anne Kennedy in about 1735 to a father, John or Joseph Kennedy, who according to family genealogies was "kidnapped on the shores of Ireland as a lad of six or seven years, brought to America and indentured for 10 years." No record remains of Anne's mother except that she bore other children. Anne's brothers William and Thomas Kennedy also became early Kentucky settlers. As was the custom in colonial Virginia, Anne did not marry until well into her twenties, yet before she was twenty-seven, she was widowed and had lost her firstborn child. In 1762, in old Augusta County, Virginia, she then married William Pogue, who according to lore was also her cousin. Pogue would become father to all six of Anne's children. For thirteen years the two lived in various parts of western Virginia, during which she bore five children in several western settlements.[8]

Women on the western frontier worked exhaustively, pregnant as much as not, and often tended their cabins alone on isolated homesteads while their husbands were off hunting or trading for supplies. In addition to caring for her young children and keeping house, Anne Pogue may well have been responsible for chopping wood, hauling water, milking cows, spinning yarn, making the family's clothing, cultivating crops, and hunting and harvesting game. The couple's frequent moves westward must have made for additional work, denying her a sense of stability and continuity. The historical record is silent on how Anne Pogue felt about the family's moves. In the patriarchal culture of which she was a part, it is impossible to know if she welcomed adventure and the search for fortune, or if, as was the case for many frontierswomen, she longed for the familiarity and community of those left behind. It may have been both. Still, the kind of determination she exhibited later in life does not square easily with the idea of utter subordination, and the 1770s Revolutionary era was a period of flux for American women. As conflicts with Britain spread ideas of liberty more widely across the colonies, women—while remaining largely subordinate to men in families and in public life—enlarged their civic responsibilities with the new work of rearing and educating sons and daughters prepared for liberty. Collectively, women of this period now became what historian Linda Kerber has called "republican mothers," a transition that represented a small but significant advance into politics. Anne Pogue's specific self-understanding with regard to revolutionary ferment remains unknown, but she went on to make a variety of civic contributions to what became Kentucky.[9]

In March 1775, only weeks after the birth of their fifth child, Mary (who would become the great-grandmother to Mattie "Mammy" Crabb in Eminence), Anne and William Pogue moved 140 miles north from Abingdon on the southwest Virginia frontier in search of reprieve from the bloody, constant struggles with native people that had punctuated their stay there. The Pogues also stocked up on supplies, for they would cross the Cumberland Gap before year's end and join Daniel Boone in Kentucky, then still the western end of the Virginia colony. Boone, under whose command William Pogue had served in the Shawnee battles that became Dunmore's War, had already been on several expeditions into Kentucky and was aggressively recruiting acquisitive-minded settlers to go back with him. So far, Kentucky settlements had been short-lived due to the ferocity of Indian resistance, but the treaty ending Dunmore's War created a peace that, while uneasy and temporary, emboldened more settlers to move the frontier west of the Alleghenies and extend Virginia into what became Kentucky.[10] Land was increasingly scarce in western Virginia, and men such as William Pogue were land hungry and always on the lookout for opportunity. Both he and his wife, Anne, had brothers who had already gone into Kentucky on exploratory expeditions.[11]

Very few white women had ventured into Kentucky by the time Anne Pogue arrived in Boonesborough in late September 1775 with her husband and five children. Boone had brought his own family there earlier in September, and four other families had recently arrived in nearby Harrodstown. The entry of women and children into the settlements transformed that immigration into what historian Joan Cashin has called a "family venture," signaling both the permanence of the endeavor and the mass influx about to begin.[12]

The delegation of forty or so, of which the Pogues were a part, found only the crudest of settlements on the banks of the Kentucky River, with no fort at all. Boone's men had just dug the Wilderness Road that summer, and it was fit only for foot travel or pack animals. While these early migrants might begin with wagons, they would be reduced to riding pack animals, and most walked hundreds of miles. The narrow path would not accommodate wagons for three years to come. The Pogues—reported to have brought to Kentucky the first hogs and chickens—were lucky enough to secure one of the five or six rough cabins already standing. Their abode was said to have been built by one John Kennedy, possibly Anne's brother or father. Living conditions at Boonesborough were harsh even by pioneer standards. Cleanliness was an impossibility; sufficient food was hard to come by; more settlers crowded into the one-room cabin as the weather worsened; and there was a constant fear of attack from native tribes. Flooded out after only a few months, the family departed for better opportunities in Harrodstown, a marginally more developed settlement thirty miles west. Along the way, a snowstorm forced the travelers to camp for several days under a rock shelf. According to the reminiscences of one of the Pogues' children years later, a party of ten Cherokee men and one woman passed by and shared food with them.[13]

In the context of ever greater white encroachment, the friendliness of those Cherokees was not indicative of general pioneer/native relations, however. In early 1776 raids by various tribes became so pervasive that about one-third of the three hundred settlers to Kentucky packed up and left. Those who stayed were "dirty, lousy, ragged, and half starved," one pioneer later recalled of that year.[14]

What the Pogues found in Harrodstown, consequently, was not much better than what they had left. The early settlers did not live together in a fort; instead they dwelled in their own cabins and simply packed household goods and rushed into the fort under threat of attack. The first Harrodstown residents' preoccupation with staking out their own lands for clearing and planting had left the community without adequate fortification in spite of constant threats. Construction of a log fort remained unfinished, and the Pogues allegedly worked on building the fort on the very night of their arrival. This project would likely have included Anne and her daughters as frontier demands blurred gendered divisions of labor.[15]

Harrodstown was better situated than its sister communities in Kentucky because it had three nearby springs for drinking water and washing. An Anglican minister had come in with the first settlers, and the abundance of women and children was thought to provide a "civilizing" influence. That influence, however, extended only so far in an era when Kentucky settlers struggled not only with the elements and the Native Americans but also with one another and with the eastern establishment to assert their land claims. Slavery, too, was a fixture in Harrodstown from its inception. Whether or not the Pogues brought slaves with them into Kentucky—and there were slaves in the group with whom they came over the Alleghenies—it was certainly a commonplace activity to do so. A traveler passing through early Fort Harrod noted that more than a tenth of its residents were slaves.[16]

As soon as the weather would allow, the Pogues cleared ground, built a cabin, and planted corn on acreage about two miles northeast of the fort on Gore's Spring. The Pogue family contributed a variety of skills to the fledgling town. Anne Pogue allegedly brought the first spinning wheel west of the Alleghenies, and her husband, a woodworker renowned for his fashioning of churns and other furniture that supplied neighbors and created a regional trading commodity, soon crafted a crude loom for her weaving. She is credited with developing the "linsey-woolsey" cloth that soon became the mainstay of pioneer clothing. She allegedly experimented with several native plants to find a fiber that could substitute for flax, then she wove the new fabric from a blend of nettle and wool made from buffalo hair. In August 1777 Anne Pogue gave birth to a daughter and named her Anne; the child was said to be the fourth white child born in Kentucky.[17]

Birth and mortality rates in frontier Kentucky were extremely high, with a violent death rate that surpassed that of the coastal colonies many times over. By early 1777 Harrodsburg, as it became known, was one of only two remaining settlements. One of the settlement's casualties was William Pogue, shot in a conflict with native peoples in September 1778, less than three weeks after Anne gave birth to their seventh child, who also died soon thereafter.[18]

At age forty, Anne Pogue was not a young woman when she came west, but unlike many whom the new land claimed or repelled, she found that the venture unleashed her creative potential. We know nothing of Anne Pogue's marksmanship or to what extent she may have resorted to the female violence that historian Craig Friend describes in the previous essay. Yet merely surviving multiple childbirths in such harsh conditions was an indicator of pluck, and she appears to have not only survived but thrived. Despite the hardships she must have faced trying to raise six children, at times alone, on the Kentucky frontier in an era punctuated by struggles over land and resources, her fortunes grew along with those of the Bluegrass. She outlived two more husbands (also casualties of settler conflicts with Native Americans) and became a successful businesswoman, operating the region's first "ordinary"—a combination hotel, restaurant, and tavern—in her home from at least as early as 1787. Whether or not she and William had been slaveholders earlier in Virginia, she became one now. While slaves and bound laborers probably did the harshest labor, she must also have been a hard worker. Meal preparation in that era was time and labor intensive for one's own family, let alone for paying customers.[19]

After 1785 native peoples of the Ohio valley, having once labeled Kentucky "the dark and bloody ground," increasingly found it so as they lost their momentum against settler encroachment. The population of immigrants now swelled to more than twenty thousand. The pace of community development quickened in places such as Harrodsburg. Following up on her initial success with linsey-woolsey, Anne Pogue established a fulling mill outside the town, which she operated with the labor of at least three slaves whom she owned, as well as several other servants apprenticed to her to learn weaving. No records remain to suggest the size of the mill, but neighbors allegedly sued its proprietor after a dam she built as a power source flooded adjoining lots in 1805.[20]

Multiple marriages and widowhood were commonplace experiences for early American frontierswomen. Extensive commerce and financial management, while not unknown, were less ubiquitous. Although English common law held that widows could claim only a lifetime or partial interest in their husbands' property, the fluidity of frontier legal and social relations seems to have worked in Anne Pogue's favor. She also appears to have been a literate woman, a skill that set her apart from probably half or more of her peers and likely proved helpful in advancing her status in Harrodsburg. Anne claimed title to several thousand acres, in part from her various husbands' estates and in part from her own residential claim. At least one husband (her third), Joseph Lindsay, willed her all he owned, and records suggest that his wishes were honored.[21]

Early Kentuckians were a fairly litigious lot, and Anne Pogue appeared over the years in dozens of court actions, with or sometimes without a male "security" standing in with or for her. When the Lincoln County court ordered development of the Wilderness Road in such a way as to bypass Fort Harrod, she appealed personally to the court to reroute so as to include the town—and her ordinary. It did so.[22]

Not all of her legal appearances had to do with her business interests. Her prominent roles in the community suggest a complex persona, one that was both resourceful and assertive. Such qualities, particularly in a woman, were bound to evoke ire and envy as well as praise. In accordance with the customs governing colonial women's behavior, Anne went to great lengths to ensure her good reputation. She was seemingly adept at the "moral coercion and public shaming" that historian Elizabeth Perkins has identified as a norm in women's public lives in frontier settlements. In 1788, for example, Anne and her fourth husband, James McGinty, came before a magistrate to defend her character against one Polly Dennis, who had allegedly defamed Anne in public, "falsely, maliciously, scandalously" accusing her of behavior such as adultery and incontinence. Again the court ruled in Anne Pogue's favor. A year later, perhaps in retaliation, Anne gave information resulting in court actions against Dennis for "having a bastard child" and against another resident, William Monrony, for "breaking the Sabbath." Later in life she became known, perhaps not surprisingly, as "keeper of the public morals" in Harrodsburg.[23]

Anne Pogue clearly flourished in the expanded gender conventions that frontier conditions and revolutionary ideologies propelled, and she managed, it seems, not to incur lasting community disapproval. The ingenuity and competence that she possessed in great abundance were prized qualities on the frontier, and she combined those traits—at least in the historical record—with the high moral character that was widely seen as virtuous in women. Besides promoting her own economic interests, she appears to have enlarged her maternal function to embrace the community at large. Like other "republican mothers" of the period, she helped advance an expanded notion of citizenship for women by her own prominent works at shaping a new settlement, at the same time acting largely within traditional, preindustrial understandings of womanhood.[24]

Yet the social order Anne Pogue helped establish in early Kentucky was changing, diminishing the leeway the frontier had offered in terms of traditional patriarchal relations for women scrappy enough to meet its harsh physical and emotional challenges. There is little further evidence of Anne in the public record as the nineteenth century opened. Kentucky's frontier era was remarkably brief. In less than a generation the frontier had moved on westward, and with that passage the tidewater aristocracy was moving swiftly into the Bluegrass. Kentucky society was still rough at the edges, and some tribes of Native Americans continued their resistance, but stores and houses dotted the landscape once filled with deer and elk. The great herds of buffalo that had so dominated the meadows of "Kanta-ke" for the Ohio Indians were eliminated completely by the 1790s. Planters and merchants assumed the mantle of leadership, and many of the earlier pioneers were dispossessed or simply opted (Boone among them) to move on westward toward Ohio and Missouri.[25]

Anne Pogue was not one of those. While she had achieved an economic foothold in early Harrodsburg, that footing was shaky for any settler, never mind a woman. Like many other mothers of the era, Anne left her surest legacy to Kentucky in the form of the six surviving children she had with William Pogue. She appears to have equipped them with the social and economic skills for prosperity as part of the new economic elite that was emerging in central Kentucky. All of the Pogue children eventually married and left Harrodsburg, fanning out to surrounding counties and beyond, accumulating considerable property among them and providing Anne with a total of fifty-nine grandchildren.[26]

The next generations found struggles over slavery to be the ascendant political controversy, not the conflicts with native peoples and the physical environment that had punctuated much of Anne Pogue's adulthood. Her third daughter, Mary Pogue Thomas—along with husband Morris Thomas, a Quaker originally from Pennsylvania—migrated to Shelby County, Kentucky, after 1799 to become part of the Fox Run Baptist Church, a congregation with sizable abolitionist sentiment. As the eighteenth century drew to a close, emancipation became a hot local political topic, engendering a broad, church-based movement against slavery. After the loss in 1792 of a constitutional battle that resulted in Kentucky's becoming the fifteenth state, with the first Constitution to give legal standing to slavery, antislavery activists in the commonwealth turned their attention to freeing slaves and returning them to Africa. To this end, Morris Thomas joined the American Colonization Society and on his death in 1853 provided for the emancipation of his slaves and their travel expenses to Liberia. The historical record is silent as to Mary Pogue Thomas's views on slavery or her participation in her husband's antislavery activities, but southern gender conventions demanded tolerance on her part if not agreement. The two had thirteen children, most of whom settled around Shelby and Henry Counties; at least one granddaughter—Mary Ann Owen, grandmother of Mattie Owen Crabb, who lived in Eminence—owned eight slaves. It was this line of Anne Pogue's family that generations later produced Anne McCarty Braden, though no family storyteller ever uttered a peep to her of Morris Thomas's or any other relative's abolitionist sympathies.[27]

No records exist to determine if the pioneer Anne was absorbed into one of her children or grandchildren's households in the final years of her life, although that would have been common practice for a widow in her position. Anne Kennedy Wilson Pogue Lindsay McGinty died at age eighty in 1815 and was buried in the old Fort Harrod cemetery next to her children's father.[28]

More than a century later, probably in the early to mid-1930s, Anne McCarty Braden's parents took her to visit her ancestor's graveside marker at what is today the Old Fort Harrod State Park. The park was established as Pioneer Memorial State Park in 1927, when Anne Braden was only three years old, and it may still have been under construction when she visited, because it was not completed and dedicated until 1934. Both parents, but especially her mother, found pride in their ancestors' place in early Kentucky, especially the centrality of Anne and William Pogue. The family routinely stopped on road trips around the state and region to read historical highway markers, and visits to Fort Harrod and other historic sites became opportunities to underscore the family folktales with which both Anne and her mother had grown up.[29]

Twenty-first-century visitors to the Fort Harrod historic site in Mercer County in central Kentucky will still find Anne Pogue McGinty memorialized there—one of the few Kentuckians of her gender and era to find even this limited fame. At the site of her grave is a historical marker, and a stone sarcophagus on which sits a bronze plaque bearing the words "Revolutionary Patriot 1775–1783," placed there probably around 1930, by a local chapter of the Daughters of the American Revolution named for Anne Pogue. Her life is revisited in the "Ann [*sic*] McGinty Blockhouse," where during visitors' hours women in colonial dress weave period fabric, display quilts, cook, or make candles. The historical interpretation devoted to her and other Fort Harrod pioneer women's contributions to colonial Kentucky has grown at the site over the years as women's and gender movements and scholars have uncovered and legitimated new and expanded options, visibility, and knowledge. A 1995 park brochure proclaimed Anne Pogue the "epitome of a pioneer woman," for example, but still did not take note of her role as proprietor of the town ordinary. Revised park literature circulated in 2013 identifies her as "the first home economics demonstrator" and describes her experiments with fabrics, mentioning the ordinary she operated without discussing her work as a tavern keeper. According to one park historian, interpreters at the site have long elaborated on Pogue's work in the ordinary. Details of the earlier printed omission could not be verified and may be attributed to incomplete research or to gender stereotyping, vestiges of which are still apparent in the site's extensive depiction of women's domestic contributions to early Kentucky alongside only a brief mention of female commercial management. What is clear is that the public presentation of Anne Pogue is still evolving along with the status of women in Kentucky history.[30]

The park inscribes only Anne Pogue's positive contributions to the culture of the emerging state and nation. County records and the historiography on colonial women suggest that she was a much more complicated presence two centuries ago, and that remains the case for her descendant Anne McCarty Braden, who was scorned by many as a communist and a race traitor until the closing decades of her life. Even today, more than a few Kentuckians would probably be loath to liken Anne Braden to her illustrious forbear, Anne Pogue McGinty.[31]

Yet it is impossible to make sense of Anne Braden's choices in the twentieth century without first understanding the depth of her roots in Kentucky and the origins of her steadfast claim, as a Kentuckian, to a southern identity. The point of genesis for that identity lies in long hours spent at her grandmothers' storytelling sessions. Braden recalled later that although her mother had been fascinated by the family's prominence in the founding of Kentucky, Braden "was fascinated by this five-times-great grandmother of mine for a different reason. I think she was a very strong woman. What I always heard—and this must have been word-of-mouth through the family—was that she sort of ran the fort. She was considered something of a tyrant by the men, even though they kept marrying her, because she insisted that they stick around the fort and till the land, whereas their inclination was to go out and fight Indians. I really think I would have liked her."[32]

Those family history lessons, although sentimentalized, led the namesake Anne to a keen attentiveness to history throughout her adult life even as she interpreted events somewhat differently than intended. While she was fascinated by the strength and resiliency of this ancestor whose name she bore, Anne McCarty Braden also lay awake at night as a child, troubled by the Indian massacres that were laced into those early settlement narratives. Reared in the Episcopal Church, Anne was a deeply religious child, and her reaction to these stories represented one of her earliest remembered pangs of conscience at injustice. Later she would come to realize they were also her first dim awareness of the color prejudice that as an adult she came to excoriate as part of a system of white supremacy.[33]

In April 1963, at the height of the post–World War II African American freedom movement, the Rev. Martin Luther King Jr. sat in a jail cell and furtively scrawled on concealed newsprint what would become his famous "Letter from Birmingham Jail." In the letter he criticized the widespread silence of white southern moderates and called by name a mere six white southerners who "have recognized the urgency of the moment and sensed the need for powerful 'action' antidotes to combat the disease of segregation." One name on that list was that of a Kentuckian: Anne Braden.[34]

In including her on his short list of whites fully dedicated to civil rights, King acknowledged Braden's race radicalism as extraordinary, and he clearly viewed it as heroic. Not so for her family of origin. By that time she had been shocking them for fifteen years with her immersion in racial-justice causes, which often landed her in the headlines both in Kentucky and in Alabama, where her parents lived. Most outrageously perhaps, from their perspective, she and her husband Carl Braden had risked prison and had stared down a sedition indictment for a dramatic act of housing desegregation in 1954 in their native Louisville. No one in Anne McCarty Braden's family of origin could have anticipated that as an adult, she would commit her life to notions of racial and social justice they would find somewhere between odd and abhorrent. Yet many of the sources of that transformation in her values arose within her family during her childhood and adolescence. She was born Anne Gambrell McCarty at Louisville's Saint Anthony's Hospital on July 28, 1924, the second child and only daughter of parents Gambrell and Anita (Crabbe) McCarty, both of whom were also native Kentuckians.[35] Gambrell, son of a pharmacist, came from Owensboro, and the couple married soon after World War I at Anita's family home in Eminence. The McCartys were Democrats who, while not politically active, accepted wholeheartedly the racial segregation that was a fixture of life for their generation in Kentucky and the South. Both descended from families that had held slaves and had fought for the Confederacy in the Civil War, even though Kentucky had been a deeply divided state that had sent nearly four times as many soldiers to the Union army as it did to the Confederate side.[36]

Anne's mother, Anita (meaning "little Anne") Crabbe McCarty—whose family had found nineteenth-century prominence in the distillery business—was especially proud of her long-standing Kentucky background, feeling that her pioneer heritage helped legitimize the family as aristocratic however modest their present economic circumstances. The many moves to different parts of Kentucky and Mississippi required by Gambrell McCarty's job as a traveling salesman during the early Depression years also strengthened Anita's connection to Eminence, even after they settled in Anniston, Alabama, when Anne was seven. The McCartys saw themselves as part of what their daughter later called the "southern aristocracy," and they encouraged her from early childhood to see race as a natural dividing line placing her and her kind in a superior stance in relation first to Native Americans and later to African Americans, whom they knew only as servants.[37]

Part of what sustained that thinking was the family legendry as it was passed down to Anne's mother Anita, and then on to Anne herself through their grandmothers' stories. As those sagas moved past the frontier era and into the nineteenth century, white supremacy emerged as a more overt centerpiece of their plotline. Mattie "Mammy" Crabb glorified "Old South" Kentucky through tales of her own slaveholding years growing up in Eminence, and of the Confederate Lost Cause that her husband, William Crabb, had served loyally. Crabb reified for younger family members the "moonlight and magnolias" imagery of her youth, sentimentalizing an upper-class lifestyle that tended to exaggerate the ornamental aspects of white southern womanhood to which, in reality, relatively few were privy. Her reminiscences also recreated tales of the post–Civil War

Reconstruction era in Kentucky history in much the same distorted way it was viewed by many elite whites of Crabb's time in Kentucky and across the South—a bad dream in which traditional race relations were turned upside down by Yankee "carpetbaggers" who profited from the proud but defeated white southerners, setting up corrupt governments kept afloat only by manipulating black voters eager for revenge against their former masters.[38]

Although family members in the several generations before her liked to think of themselves as highly distinct from African Americans, Anne McCarty's family mythologies of race—punctuated perhaps because they were set in the rigidly, sometimes brutally segregated framework of her Alabama upbringing—touched her in a profoundly different manner than they had her forebears. Having to "turn myself inside out and upside down" was how Braden described the painful process she went through to uproot those powerful, deep-seated lessons of her youth and transform them into what became her life's passion for racial and social justice.[39]

Two other elements of her young life also proved instrumental in shaping the activist she became. One was her religious faith, encouraged through her family's involvement in Grace Episcopal Church in Anniston. The church congregation was mostly financially comfortable, even elite—a quality that appealed to Anita McCarty's class consciousness and part of why she chose it. Yet the church was pastored by a social gospel–oriented minister, Jim Stoney, who encouraged his parishioners to grapple with and ameliorate the Depression-era wretchedness and poverty in their midst. The church was not involved in any interracial efforts (although a few southern Protestant churches were). But as an early teen, Anne participated in a church youth group through which she discussed topics such as socialism. The group also allowed her to meet children of local mill families who represented virtually her only close contact with poverty and suffering in those years.[40]

Despite a keen intellect and the kind of sensitivity that caused her to weep at seeing a modest country schoolhouse burn—because children would be deprived of schooling, her senior prom date recalled—Anne McCarty nonetheless seemed upon finishing Anniston High School a fairly ordinary young woman of her class, race, place, and time. Ironically, a second crucial influence took shape then with her decision to accede to her mother's wishes and attend not the customary universities of Alabama or Kentucky (Anita's own alma mater) but one of the "better" southern women's colleges—first Stratford Junior College and then Randolph-Macon Woman's College, both in Virginia.[41]

Anne was in college from 1941 to 1945, the same years as U.S. involvement in World War II, making her part of a transitional generation of American women who came of age as the war ended. Her political transformation began on those elite single-sex college campuses. An intellectual awakening happened as she discovered what she considered "the world of ideas"—reading classic works of literature and meeting an earlier generation of feminists who were now professors or alumnae and became mentors to her. She also discovered theater, dance, and her first independent taste of politics. For Anne that included a vague awareness that segregation was wrong, prompted by the racialized crusade of Nazi fascism and by meeting for the first time southern liberals who criticized her region's racial arrangements.[42]

When Anne graduated from Randolph-Macon in May 1945, she left with an English degree and a determination to become a famous newspaperwoman. She took advantage of wartime opportunities for women in journalism, becoming a staff writer for the *Anniston Star*. A brief stint covering the courthouse for the *Birmingham News and Age-Herald* followed, and it soon became apparent to her dismay that African Americans had no hope of justice there amid racial violence and a rigid racial hierarchy—both of which were extreme even by southern standards. Sickened by the harsh divisions of segregation and the limiting feel of southern white culture, where well-to-do women seemed destined for lives hosting bridge parties and going to the country club, Anne fled the Deep South at age twenty-three. She "ran away," as she described it, only as far as to the city of her birth, where she took a reporting job at the *Louisville Times*, afternoon companion to the region's most respected newspaper, the *Louisville Courier-Journal*. Drawn initially by her family ties there, she also thought the newspaper's prestige would be a good stepping stone for a job with one of the nation's leading papers outside the region.[43]

Although its buses and streetcars were desegregated and African Americans retained voting rights, Louisville was only marginally less segregated than Alabama in 1947 when Anne flew there alone to live. Yet one important difference at the South's northern border lay in its feeling of possibility, particularly in the visibility of dissent from the racial status quo. Her arrival coincided with a new crusade headed by the Louisville chapter of the National Association for the Advancement of Colored People (NAACP) to integrate public parks. By chance Anne was assigned to cover the legal challenge that ultimately desegregated the University of Kentucky. Farther north and out of her parents' oversight, she sought out civil rights activists on her own and tentatively began to make friends across the color line. In doing so, she had to unlearn old habits: even pronouncing "Negro" properly took work after growing up in a household that had tossed around racial epithets casually.[44]

The final catalyst, perhaps, for Anne McCarty's turning inside out the values of her upbringing was her relationship with coworker Carl Braden, a Marxist-oriented journalist who had grown up poor in Louisville's Portland neighborhood with parents who were Socialist Party members and staunch trade unionists (even naming him after Karl Marx). Carl covered labor for the *Times*, and he introduced Anne to local unionists, both black and white, active in the left wing of the postwar upsurge of labor activism. Ten years her senior and far more politically informed than she, Carl became her closest friend and political mentor during her early months in Louisville as she began to see Kentucky and southern culture in an increasingly uncomfortable new light. Friendship turned to romance, and her feelings for him provided what was perhaps the critical impetus for the wrenching changes she underwent that year. "It took something as strong as the emotional pull to him to shake me loose from my past," she later reflected with some embarrassment about what a "savior" he was for her in their early days together.[45]

Something in Anne responded deeply to the vigor that emanated from the labor and civil rights organizers she met in 1947. As that year ended she changed profoundly; as she later wrote, "I had to come to terms with the fact that my whole society—one that had been very good to me—my family, friends, the people I loved and never stopped loving—were just plain wrong—wrong on race. It's a searingly painful process, but it's not destructive, because once you do it, you are free." When she defied familial gender norms by moving in with Carl in the spring of 1948 and then marrying him three months later, she also thought of herself as "changing sides in the class struggle." Both wanted from the partnership not only personal fulfillment but also a way to enact their shared ideals. Anne later described "a real sense . . . that we were joining our lives to bring about a new world. . . . The idea of being a successful newspaperwoman didn't even appeal to me anymore." She had returned to Louisville with a vaguely liberal sensibility, and, unlike peers she met in Birmingham, she now found many liberal gradualists for civil rights in her midst. Yet those were not the currents that appealed to her sharpening sense of injustice. Instead, her metamorphosis into a political activist was molded more from the working-class, militantly interracial, anticapitalist, and internationalist ideology of the postwar left she discovered there. Such initiatives were often led by members of the Community Party (CP), which had been a prime vehicle for battles against southern segregation since the Depression era. These people and ideas seemed to Anne to mesh more closely with Christian ideals she had first absorbed in the Episcopal Church.[46]

Anne's marriage to Carl—who was most definitely not what her parents had hoped for in a son-in-law—strained her relationship with them and created a distance that, while cordial, would soon widen to a chasm. Over the next few years the Bradens left mainstream journalism and worked in the left wing of the labor movement through the Farm and Equipment Workers Union Local 236 (FE) and in a variety of national organizations that faced increasing stigmatization as "Communist fronts."[47]

Although the "Popular Front" left-liberal alliance that had propelled social reforms throughout the 1930s and 1940s was still vibrant in 1948, Anne was conscious enough of the gathering domestic Cold War in her midst to know she was joining an increasingly controversial movement. Yet those emotionally difficult months set her life course on social change. Just as the family mythology had peppered her imagination as a girl, this period of her young adulthood remained vivid for her for the rest of her life as a formative "turning point." She explained later, "I hope I've grown since then, but for me the real change was from being a woman of the white privileged class in the South to being what I consider a revolutionary." As she grew more confident in her politics and became more immersed in what remained of the interracial subculture of the post–World War II left, opposing segregation became more of a "compulsion" for her, and she urged her husband toward greater racial activism, too.[48]

She no longer wished to leave the city and region of her birth but to transform them. Ending the Jim Crow racial hierarchy that had been so extolled by both family folktales and the larger culture in her youth seemed the key ingredient for wider social justice. "I hadn't rejected the people in that white world, but I had rejected its values, its standards," she explained much later. "I had this feeling that I had been liberated from a world that was wrong, and that I needed to share that vision with others."[49]

Anne McCarty Braden spent nearly six subsequent decades doing just that. Remaining in Louisville for the rest of her life in the same house she and Carl bought early in their marriage, she could have become one of the many rank-and-file activists, black and white, female and male, who never "make history," had it not been for one fateful occurrence in the spring of 1954. Mere days before the U.S. Supreme Court issued the death knell to legal segregation in its landmark *Brown v. Board of Education* ruling on May 17, Anne and Carl Braden acted as the "fronts" for African Americans Andrew and Charlotte Wade to buy a new home in an all-white Louisville suburb.

Andrew Wade was an electrician and World War II veteran fed up with racial hierarchy and eager as so many Americans were in that era to move to the suburbs. Repeatedly rebuffed by racial barriers in making such a purchase himself, he sought the advice of a realtor who recommended white assistance, and early that spring Wade turned to the staunchest pro–civil rights whites he knew. As

Anne wrote later of the events that unfolded that year, “any other answer would have been unthinkable” in reply to Wade’s request for help, and they readily agreed to buy the house and then transfer its deed to the Wade family. On completion of the purchase in the suburban Shively neighborhood the Wades had selected, white neighbors who realized blacks were moving in burned a cross in front of the new home and shot out its windows the very night of their arrival. Six weeks later, amid criticism from the local press and constant community tensions, the Wades’ new house was dynamited one evening while they were out.[50]

More than anything else, it was the crime, controversy, and trial stemming from those actions (what became known as the “Wade-Braden case”) that catapulted the Bradens into statewide and national headlines and gave them a kind of fame that, in that era, was more aptly considered infamy. What began as a dramatic challenge to Louisville’s housing desegregation turned into a local variation of the anticommunist hysteria known nationwide as McCarthyism when Commonwealth’s Attorney A. Scott Hamilton began theorizing that the purchase and subsequent dynamiting had all been a communist plot to destabilize local race relations. In a region rife with tension over the racial changes that *Brown* portended and a nation on its guard against the threat of internal subversion, the Bradens’ act of open defiance to segregation looked to many like treason, especially once their many left-wing associations became public. In October 1954 Anne and Carl Braden and five other white supporters of the Wades were charged with sedition, a vaguely defined charge that had lain inert in Kentucky law since its adoption in 1919 during the first Red Scare. The Bradens were jailed, and their two young children were sent to Alabama to live temporarily with Anne’s parents in spite of the family’s differences.[51]

That December, after a sensationalized trial in which even their closest friends shunned them, Carl Braden—the perceived ringleader—was convicted of sedition and sentenced to fifteen years’ imprisonment. A paid FBI informant had connected him to the Communist Party, though not to the violence or any plot. As Anne and the other defendants awaited a similar fate, Carl served eight months and was out on a $40,000 appeal bond when a U.S. Supreme Court decision invalidated state sedition laws because of their capricious use. Anticlimactically, it seemed at the time, Anne Braden and the other codefendants were never tried, and the remaining sedition charges were dropped—although the Wades were never able to return to their dream house to live, and residential segregation continued uninterrupted.[52]

Carl was ultimately freed and the Bradens were able to reunite with their children, but those events of 1954 made pariahs of the pair. Blacklisted from local employment, they were on the verge of leaving Louisville for a new start. But Anne Braden felt impelled to stay in the region and the city of her birth, and the two found work as regional organizers for a New Orleans–based civil rights organization, the Southern Conference Educational Fund (SCEF), with a mission to solicit greater white southern support for the blossoming African American freedom movement. From 1957 to 1973 Anne edited SCEF's monthly newspaper, the *Southern Patriot*, one of the few regional news organs to give sympathetic coverage to the emerging movement. For decades, nonetheless, the Bradens were repeatedly lambasted as radicals, subversives, and communists in any social advocacy campaign of which they were a part—especially by southern politicians in Kentucky and across the South in the years from 1955 to 1968 known by historians of the civil rights movement as the "Montgomery to Memphis" period. Part of their civil rights work became, necessarily, a defense of civil liberties, or the right to dissent. To counter the claim of being an "outside agitator," Anne Braden took some measure of comfort in those years in being able to claim, rightfully, that she descended from Kentucky's first settlers.[53]

Besides hurling her into regional notoriety, the sedition charges "burned my bridges to a privileged past," Braden wrote in her 1958 memoir. *The Wall Between*, one of the few books of its time to unpack from within the psychology of white southern racism, became a finalist for the National Book Award and was praised by the likes of Eleanor Roosevelt and Dr. Martin Luther King Jr. Yet in the eyes of many in her family of origin—and indeed many of her white peers in Louisville and Alabama—it merely reaffirmed what the last few years had already established: how much she had diverged from her family's ideas of right and wrong. Her only brother cut off all contact with her for decades as a result of the sedition case.[54]

Yet Anne's commitment to racial justice as part of a broader agenda of ending poverty and war remained unwavering. It continued through the southern sit-ins of the early 1960s when a new generation of black and white youth reclaimed the Bradens as mentors and Anne in particular as an icon of a white southern woman who defied racism. It continued when she became one of the few whites of her generation to endorse the call for Black Power later in the 1960s, and when civil rights campaigns led to economic justice drives in the eastern Kentucky coalfields, resulting in a second sedition indictment against the Bradens, this one in Pike County in 1967.[55]

Like her ancestor Anne Pogue, Anne Braden lived a considerable part of her adulthood as a widow. Only fifty years old when Carl Braden died suddenly of a massive heart attack in 1975, Anne never remarried but remained immersed in social and racial justice campaigns until her own death at age eighty-one. Her commitment to ending segregation and to what she called "being on the right side of history" outlasted the violent opposition to civil rights. By the end of her life in 2006, having received many community service awards, Anne Braden was more a heroine than the pariah she had been for so long. By that time, her life had touched nearly all of the social movements that had swept Kentucky and the nation over the previous half century. In each of them, her emphasis was on racial justice as a task for whites.

Instead of outright rejection, Anne Braden turned upside down and inside out the mythology of whiteness that had been imparted to her from the treasured family tales she grew up with, including the stories of white frontier bravery against the alleged savagery of native peoples and of plantation gentility. From them she remained attuned to the power of history even as she crafted a new narrative that renounced many of the values her family of origin held dear, while holding fast to the emotional ties of family and place from her Kentucky and southern past. She never lived in Eminence, but she buried both Carl and one of their daughters there, and her attachment to Louisville flavors any interview ever done with her. Her own racial conversion narrative, retold in *The Wall Between* and in decades' worth of speeches and journalistic writings, suggests that she cherished key moments and people from those family tales even as she discarded or reformulated others.

Neither the eighteenth-century Anne nor her twentieth-century descendant was a campaigner for women's rights, but both possessed an expansive sense of female agency that made possible a great many achievements. To what extent Anne Braden "inherited" that from Anne Pogue, or the idea of Anne Pogue, is debatable, but what seems clear is that the stories of strong, independent women stayed with Braden her entire life and had a shaping influence on who and what she became. While both Annes had a deep attachment to Kentucky and the place it might become, any suggestion that Anne Braden followed in her five times great-grandmother's footsteps would be too simplistic, however. After all, Anne Braden's activist passions were in many ways diametrically opposed to the movement of which the earlier Anne had been a part. Civic minded though she may have been, Anne Pogue McGinty was part of a colonizing population that denied, displaced, or exterminated the existing peoples and cultures they encountered in Kentucky, and did so out of what were at that time unexamined assumptions of white supremacy. In that process, Pogue sought to stabilize a new social order, whereas Braden, who inherited that order generations later, devoted her efforts to transforming it by destabilizing the white supremacy that undergirded it. Civil rights laws achieved in the 1960s by the social movements of which she was a part, as well as the subsequent widespread decline of the most overt forms of racism, suggest a measure of success in that transformation.

While both Annes sought adventure through their husbands, both were ambitious, autonomous, political women who lived much of their adult lives outside of marriage. Each possessed a powerful moral presence that made them controversial figures in their respective times. Both left their marks—albeit very different ones—on the state they came to call home, and the multiple, still-evolving ways the earlier Anne is remembered suggest that her more contemporary descendant may likewise become subject to more complicated reinterpretations in public memory in the years to come.

NOTES

1. The spelling of the name "Pogue" is somewhat inconsistent in the historical record. It appears in various sources as "Poage," "Poague," "Poag," and "Pogue." One family historian has explained that in Virginia the family spelled their name "Poage" but that some confusion surrounded the will of Anne's husband William Poage in Kentucky in 1778, resulting in a change of spelling by all his heirs to "Pogue"; other spellings were simply mistakes, according to Andrew Woods Williamson et al., *Descendants of Robert and John Poage*, vol. 1 (Staunton, Va.: McClure, 1954), 931–91. On this matter, see also *Calendar of the Kentucky Papers of the Draper Collection of Manuscripts* (Madison: State Historical Society of Wisconsin, 1925). Lyman Copeland Draper Manuscripts, Calendar series, vol. 2, 4CC, 113–14 (hereafter cited as Draper Papers). Anne Braden knew the family name spelled as "Pogue," consistent with the heirs of William Pogue, and I am therefore choosing to spell the name "Pogue" in this manner throughout the essay for ease of reading. There are similarly multiple spellings of Pogue McGinty's first name, and although it is spelled "Ann" at Old Fort Harrod State Park, I am spelling it here as "Anne," consistent with most family histories, with the early scholarship on her, and with the artifact of a personal signature attributed to her (Harrodsburg Historical Society).

2. For more on this aspect of Braden's story, see my biography of her: Catherine Fosl, *Subversive Southerner: Anne Braden and the Struggle for Racial Justice in the Cold War South* (Lexington: University Press of Kentucky, 2006), 307.

3. Ideas of the symbolic and the everyday defined as "political" derive from many sources in social history since at least the 1970s (see the many examples in women's history listed in n. 9 below), but my particular ideas here were shaped by Rosemary Zagarri's *Revolutionary Backlash: Women and Politics in the Early Republic* (Philadelphia: University of Pennsylvania Press, 2007), esp. introduction. Public history sites that recognize Braden include a painting as part of the "Kentucky Women Remembered" exhibit that hangs in the state capitol, a Kentucky highway marker in front of her former home, a plaque at the University of Louisville's Freedom Park, and an institute containing her book collection and bearing her name in the university's College of Arts and Sciences. The quoted phrase is from Margaret Ripley Wolfe, "Fallen Leaves and Missing Pages: Women in Kentucky History," *Register of the Kentucky Historical Society* 90 (1992): 64–89.

4. Anne Braden, multiple interviews by author, Louisville, Kentucky, especially March 10, 1989 (tape 5), and June 11, 1996, Oral History Collection, University of Kentucky Libraries, Lexington. The most complete account of the role of family storytelling and of depictions of Anne Pogue

McGinty in particular in the shaping of Anne Braden's identity is found in a series of interviews she did with Sue Thrasher, Louisville, Kentucky, April 18, 1981, esp. tape 1, side 1, transcript available in Highlander Center Library, New Market, Tennessee (copy also in author's possession). This quoted point is not intended to suggest that Braden's grandmothers used these words, only that this kind of account would have been commonplace during her 1920s–1930s childhood, and that her seemingly traditional grandmother and great-grandmother would have been influenced by southern Victorian cultural norms highlighting gender differences and female domesticity, in which even reform efforts frequently located women as "moral guardians," or by the twentieth century as "social housekeepers." The classic work situating Kentucky and southern women in these larger currents of American culture of this era is Anne Firor Scott, *The Southern Lady: From Pedestal to Politics, 1830–1930* (Chicago: University of Chicago Press, 1970); for a more current and readily applicable example, see Joan Marie Johnson, *Southern Women at the Seven Sister Colleges: Feminist Values and Social Activism, 1875–1915* (Athens: University of Georgia Press, 2008). A considerable body of scholarship examines women's "civilizing" influence on Kentucky and other western settlements of the colonial era. Among the most foundational—and source of the quotation here—is Dee Brown, *Gentle Tamers: Women of the Wild West* (Lincoln: University of Nebraska Press, 1958).

5. Braden, interview with Thrasher, tape 1, side 1, 14–16 of transcript; Braden, interview by author, March 10, 1989 (tape 5).

6. On Braden as a race traitor, see Catherine Fosl, "Anne Braden and the Protective Custody of White Southern Womanhood," in *Throwing Off the Cloak of Privilege: White Southern Women Activists in the Civil Rights Era*, ed. Gail Murray (Gainesville: University Press of Florida, 2004), 101–30. Murray discusses the "outside agitator" dynamic in her introduction to the collection.

7. John Mack Faragher, *Daniel Boone: The Life and Legend of an American Pioneer* (New York: Henry Holt, 1992), 68.

8. Williamson et al., *Descendants of Poage*, 1:930 (quotation); George M. Chinn, *The History of Harrodsburg and the Great Settlement Area of Kentucky, 1774–1900* (Harrodsburg: Harrodsburg Historical Society, 1985), 189.

9. For more on the lives of colonial American women, see, for example, Joan Jensen, *Loosening the Bonds: Mid-Atlantic Farm Women, 1750–1850* (New Haven, Conn.: Yale University Press, 1986). More recent treatments of women and gender in the Ohio valley can be found, among others, in Elizabeth A. Perkins, *Border Life: Experience and Memory in the Revolutionary Ohio Valley* (Chapel Hill: University of North Carolina Press, 1998), and in Craig Thompson Friend's essay in this volume, "Nonhelema Hokolesqua, Jemima Boone Callaway, and Matilda Lewis Threlkeld: Searching for Kentucky's Female Frontier," 8–32, building on and revising his discussion of women in his earlier *Along the Maysville Road: The Early American Republic in the Trans-Appalachian West* (Knoxville: University of Tennessee Press, 2005). (Readers will also find a far more extensive examination than I include here of historiography on frontier women, especially those of Kentucky and the Ohio valley, in Friend's new essay.) Although substantial scholarship has appeared in the past twenty-five years on women and the American Revolution, Mary Beth Norton's *Liberty's Daughters: The Revolutionary Experience of American Women, 1750–1800* (New York: Little, Brown, 1980) is the classic work situating eighteenth-century American women within patriarchy (see esp. chaps. 1–5). In another groundbreaking work on early American women, Linda Kerber coined the phrase "republican motherhood," which remains highly influential in understanding women in relation to the coming of the American Revolution. See Kerber, *Women of the Republic: Intellect and Ideology in Revolutionary America* (Chapel Hill: University of North Carolina Press for the Institute of Early American History and Culture, 1980).

10. Elizabeth Poage Thomas autobiographical statement, in Draper Papers, 4cc85, 344; Lewis Preston Summers, *History of Southwest Virginia, 1746–1786, Washington County, 1777–1870* (Richmond: J. L. Hill, 1903), 156–57.

11. M. L. Cook and Bettie A. Cummings Cook, *Fincastle and Kentucky Counties, Va.-Ky. Records and History*, vol. 1 (Evansville, Ind.: Cook Publications, 1987), 147.

12. Draper Papers, 4cc85, 344. The quoted phrase is from Joan E. Cashin, *A Family Venture: Men and Women on the Southern Frontier* (Baltimore: Johns Hopkins University Press, 1991).

13. Draper Papers, 4cc85, 344; Faragher, *Daniel Boone*, 113; details of the journey can be found in Helen Deiss Irvin, *Women in Kentucky* (Lexington: University Press of Kentucky, 1979), 2–3. Chinn, *History of Harrodsburg*, 189; *Harrodsburg's National Historic Pre-Eminence* (Harrodsburg, Ky.: Daniel Mac-Hir Hutton, n.d.), pamphlet, n.p., in Anne Pogue McGinty Folder, Harrodsburg Historical Society, Harrodsburg, Kentucky (hereafter cited as McGinty Folder, HHS). Sometime after I conducted research there in the 1990s, documents in this folder disappeared from the Harrodsburg Historical Society. Copies of some of the documents are in my possession, while others, about which I merely took notes, are to my knowledge no longer available at HHS.

14. Faragher, *Daniel Boone*, 130–31.

15. Thomas D. Clark, *A History of Kentucky* (New York: Prentice-Hall, 1937), 97; Draper Papers, 4cc85, 344. On women settlers and work, Joan Jensen offers an expansive view of farm women's labor in *Loosening the Bonds*, as does Perkins in *Border Life*.

16. Alonzo Willard Fortune, *The Disciples in Kentucky* (Lexington: Convention of Christian Churches in Kentucky, 1932); Irvin, *Women in Kentucky*, 15–17; Ellen Eslinger, "Slavery on the Kentucky Frontier," *Register of the Kentucky Historical Society* 92 (1994): 3.

17. W. H. Perrin, J. H. Battle, and G. C. Kniffin, *History of Kentucky, Illustrated: General History* (Louisville: F. A. Battey, 1887), 212; S. V. Nuckols, "History of William Poage and His Wife, Ann Kennedy Wilson Poage Lindsay McGinty," *Register of the Kentucky Historical Society* 11 (1913): 101–2; Irvin, *Women in Kentucky*, 13–14; "The Reminiscences of Gen. John Poage," Draper Papers, 4cc113, 468. In numerous interviews, Anne Braden recalls having been told as a child that this birth was of the first white child born in Kentucky, but records show it to have been the fourth.

18. Violence and high mortality rates are discussed in many Kentucky histories. I drew these findings from Z. F. Smith, *History of Kentucky* (Louisville: Courier-Journal Job Printing Co., 1886), 127; Faragher, *Daniel Boone*, 144; Williamson et al., *Descendants of Poage*, 1:930–31.

19. Friend, "Searching for Kentucky's Female Frontier," 8–32; M. L. Cook, *Mercer County, Kentucky Records*, vol. 1 (Evansville: Cook Publications, 1987), 15; "Mercer County Tax Books, 1789–1812," Microform #008156, Kentucky Department for Libraries and Archives, Frankfort; Grace Stephenson Linney Hutton, *Old Taverns* (Harrodsburg, Ky.: Harrodsburg Herald Printing, 1957), 3, pamphlet in possession of HHS. The travails of frontier life for Kentucky women, including childbearing and domestic work, are detailed in several sources; among the early ones are Irvin, *Women in Kentucky*, and Wolfe, "Fallen Leaves and Missing Pages."

20. Perrin et al., *History, Illustrated*, 225; "Anne Poague McGinty," unpublished paper prepared by Ms. Green Johnson, n.d., in McGinty folder, HHS, 8–9.

21. An extensive historiography has emerged over the past several decades surrounding premodern women's property rights. These insights are drawn primarily from one of the foundational works that propelled this literature: Marylynn Salmon, "Women and Property in South Carolina: The Evidence from Marriage Settlements, 1730–1830," *William and Mary Quarterly*, 3rd ser., 39 (1982): 656. "Interesting Historic Document," clipping from *Harrodsburg Herald*, May 22, 1925, found in McGinty Folder, HHS (this document shows a sample alleged to be Anne Pogue McGinty's signature;

copy in author's possession); *Marriage Bonds and Consents, 1786–1810, Mercer County, Kentucky*, compiled by Alma Rae Ison and Rebecca Conover (Harrodsburg, Ky.: HHS, 1970), 52; "Excerpts from *The Certificate Book of the Virginia Land Commission, 1779–1780*," *Register of the Kentucky Historical Society* 21 (1923): 162; Green Johnson paper, McGinty Folder, HHS, 7–9.

22. "Excerpts from *The Certificate Book*," 162; Green Johnson paper, McGinty Folder, HHS, 7; Hutton, *Old Taverns*, 3.

23. Perkins, *Border Life*, 143; M. L. Cook, *Mercer County, Kentucky Records*, vol. 1 (Evansville, Ind.: M. L. Cook, 1987), 136; Green Johnson paper, McGinty Folder, HHS, 7.

24. This interpretation of Anne Pogue McGinty's role in shaping a new settlement while acting largely within traditional, preindustrial understandings of womanhood is consonant with Kerber's well-known thesis on women and "republican motherhood" during the American Revolution, as discussed above in n. 9.

25. Wolfe discusses this greater flexibility in gender conventions due to fluid social relations in the frontier era in "Fallen Leaves and Missing Pages," 74–75; Stephen Aron, "The Significance of the Kentucky Frontier," *Register of the Kentucky Historical Society* 91 (1993): 315; Faragher, *Daniel Boone*, 263. Aron's book *How the West Was Lost: The Transformation of Kentucky from Daniel Boone to Henry Clay* (Baltimore: Johns Hopkins University Press, 1996) explores this transition fully.

26. Williamson et al., *Descendants of Poage*, 1:930–32.

27. Ibid., 1:931, 991; Joan Wells Coward, *Kentucky in the New Republic: The Process of Constitution-Making* (Lexington: University Press of Kentucky, 1979), 38–62. For a sampling of the historiography on southern white women's relationships to slavery, see, for example, two competing depictions in Elizabeth Fox-Genovese, *Within the Plantation Household: Black and White Women of the Old South* (Chapel Hill: University of North Carolina Press, 1988), and Catherine Clinton, *The Plantation Mistress: Woman's World in the Old South* (New York: Pantheon, 1982). A more recent study of antebellum southern slaveholding women that, like Clinton, suggests some commonalities between black and white women's experiences is V. Lynn Kennedy, *Born Southern: Childhood, Motherhood, and Social Networks in the Old South* (Baltimore: Johns Hopkins University Press, 2009). Braden repeatedly emphasizes the storytellers' omissions in her interview with author, June 11, 1996.

28. Williamson et al., *Descendants of Poage*, 1:931–32.

29. Braden, noted in various interviews by author. The park's history derives from several sources, including Federal Writers' Project, *Kentucky: A Guide to the Bluegrass State* (Lexington: University of Kentucky, 1939), 171–72; www.parks.ky.gov/parks/recreationparks/fort-harrod/history.aspx (accessed December 3, 2013); David Coleman, email correspondence with author, December 6, 2013.

30. David Coleman, email correspondence with author, March 27, 2013; "Old Fort Harrod State Park," Kentucky Department of Parks brochure, 1995, in author's possession (the DAR chapter spelled their mentor's name "Ann Poague," but I have preserved the more widely used spelling in this essay); 2013 park brochure, copy in author's possession; David Coleman, email correspondence with author, December 4 and 6, 2013. This email correspondence revealed his and other staff members' uncertainties about the history of Anne Pogue's connection to the ordinary, the omission of which I observed in a visit to the park in 1995. The site and brochures also discuss the pioneer Jane Coomes and her early educational efforts, which I do not mention in this essay since Coomes is tangential to its focus. In my exchanges with Coleman, I also observed that representations and literature for the site are and have historically been dependent in part on volunteer labor, which may be responsible for the variations in interpretation and consistency in the 2013 brochure; for instance, the name "Pogue" is spelled "Pogue" in relation to William, but "Poague" when applied

to Anne (spelled "Ann"), the latter possibly to comply with the spelling used by the DAR chapter named in her memory.

31. A personal anecdote illustrates the vestiges of notoriety surrounding Braden. After writing a column for the *Louisville Courier-Journal*, published August 26, 2012, that spoke positively of her activism, I received a threatening message on my voicemail later that day warning me that she was "not a good American" and that cautioned me against memorializing her.

32. Braden, interview by Thrasher, tape 1, side 1, and transcript, 15–16.

33. Ibid. According to Braden (conversation with the author, June 11, 1996, notes in author's possession), pinpointing this memory as her first awareness of color prejudice happened only in the 1990s when she attended an experiential workshop on racism.

34. Martin Luther King Jr., "Letter from Birmingham Jail," April 16, 1963, http://mlk-kpp01.stanford.edu/index.php/resources/article/annotated_letter_from_birmingham/ (accessed June 27, 2013).

35. For an unknown reason, Lindsay Crabbe, son of William and Mattie Crabb and later a prominent distiller, added an "e" to the end of the family surname sometime in the 1880s. See Williamson et al., *Descendants of Poage*, 1:991; *Biographical Cyclopedia of the Commonwealth of Kentucky* (Chicago: John Mg. Gresham Co., 1896), 304–5, 437–38.

36. Braden, interviews by author, March 5, 1989, and June 11, 1996.

37. Ibid.; the phrase "southern aristocracy" is from page 2 of Reminiscences of Anne Braden, told to Lenore Hogan, June 23, 1972, in the Columbia University Oral History Research Office Collection, New York City (hereafter cited as Braden, interview by Hogan, CUOHROC).

38. Braden, interviews with author, March 5, 1989, June 11, 1996 (the quotation marks are mine, but these word choices pepper the interviews); for more on Kentucky women of this era, see Richard Sears, "Working Like a Slave: Views of Slavery and the Status of Women in Antebellum Kentucky," *Register of the Kentucky Historical Society* 87 (1989): 1–19, and Wolfe, "Fallen Leaves and Missing Pages." An especially relevant essay that draws a line between representations of nineteenth-century southern women's experiences in 1930s-era American popular culture is Elizabeth Fox-Genovese, "Scarlett O'Hara: The Southern Lady as New Woman," in *Half Sisters of History: Southern Women and the American Past*, ed. Catherine Clinton (Durham, N.C.: Duke University Press, 1994), 154–79. In fact, Reconstruction in Kentucky was so removed from those stereotypes that some historians have nicknamed this era in the state as "Confederate supremacy"; see, for example, Ross A. Webb, *Kentucky in the Reconstruction Era* (Lexington: University Press of Kentucky, 1979), 25, 59.

39. Braden referred to the process in this manner in many interviews, speeches, and conversations with the author and others. See especially June Rostan, "Inside-Out and Upside-Down: An Interview with Anne Braden," *Colorlines*, March 15, 2001, http://colorlines.com/archives/2001/03/insideout_and_upsidedown_an_interview_with_anne_braden.html (accessed June 27, 2013).

40. Anne Braden, interview by author, November 18, 2001, Louisville, Kentucky.

41. Allen Draper, conversation with author, June 14, 1989, Anniston, Alabama, notes in author's possession.

42. I have borrowed the phrase "transitional generation" from Susan Hartmann, "Women's Employment and the Domestic Ideal in the Early Cold War Years," in *Not June Cleaver: Women and Gender in Postwar America, 1945–1960*, ed. Joanne Meyerowitz (Philadelphia: Temple University Press, 1994), 84; Anne Braden, interview by author, March 10, 1989 (tape 6), Louisville, Kentucky.

43. Braden, interview by author, March 10, 1989 (tape 6); this odyssey is also described more fully in Anne Braden, *The Wall Between* (New York: Monthly Review Press, 1958; Knoxville: University of Tennessee Press, 1999).

44. For more detail on postwar Louisville civil rights campaigns, see Tracy E. K'Meyer, *Civil Rights in the Gateway to the South* (Lexington: University Press of Kentucky, 2009); Wade Hall, ed., *The Rest of the Dream: The Black Odyssey of Lyman Johnson* (Lexington: University Press of Kentucky, 1988), esp. 127; Patrick McElhone, "The Civil Rights Activities of the Louisville Branch of the NAACP, 1914–1960" (MA thesis, University of Louisville, 1976), iii; Kentucky Commission on Human Rights, *Kentucky's Black Heritage* (Frankfort: Commonwealth of Kentucky, 1971), 92–93; the point about language is from Braden, interview by author, March 8–9, 1989 (tape 3).

45. These points are made in several Braden interviews by author, esp. March 8–9, 1989 (tape 3); quotation is from Braden, interview by Thrasher, tape 7, side 1, and transcript, 184–85.

46. First quotation is from Anne Braden to author, June 11, 1997, personal correspondence in author's possession; Braden to author, December 28, 2001, 15–17, personal correspondence in author's possession, explicates her view of liberalism; in our final conversations as *Subversive Southerner* went to press, Braden elaborated on her differences from liberals and discussed her view on religion in some depth: see the book's epilogue, 338; for a fuller history of the Communist Party in the South during and after the Great Depression, see Robin D. G. Kelley, *Hammer and Hoe: Alabama Communists in the Great Depression* (Chapel Hill: University of North Carolina Press, 1991).

47. Braden, interview by author, June 17, 1999; Braden interview by author, March 8–9, 1989 (tape 3); Braden, interview by Thrasher, April 18, 1981, tape 7, side 1, and transcript, 184–85; the Farm and Equipment Workers' (FE) Local 236 is discussed at length in chapter 5 of Toni Gilpin's "Left by Themselves: A History of the United Farm Equipment and Metal Workers Union, 1935–1955" (PhD dissertation, Yale University, 1981); Braden's participation in so-called "communist front" groups such as the Civil Rights Congress (CRC) and the Committee to Save the Rosenbergs is detailed in Fosl, *Subversive Southerner*, esp. chap. 5.

48. The quotation is from Braden, interview by Thrasher, tape 6, side 1, and transcript, 161; Braden mentions her compulsion to end segregation in *The Wall Between* (1999), 34.

49. This material is discussed at length in Braden, interview by Hogan, December 7, 1978, Interview 2, on 105 in transcript, CUOHROC; quotation is from Braden, interview by author, Louisville, November 18, 2001.

50. Quotation is from Braden, *The Wall Between* (1999), 3; for a full examination of this case, see Catherine Fosl, "The Dynamite Was Fear: Segregation, Anticommunism, and Sedition in Louisville, Kentucky, the South's Northern Border" (which also contains extensive historiographical references to Cold War anticommunism), in *Making a New South: Race, Leadership and Community after the Civil War*, ed. Paul Cimbala and Barton Shaw (Gainesville: University Press of Florida, 2007), 147–70.

51. Fosl, "Dynamite Was Fear," esp. 154–61. Both of the sources in n. 48 elaborate on these details.

52. Material not specifically cited is drawn from my biography of Braden.

53. A full account of her marginalization during this era is found in Anne Braden, "A View from the Fringes," *Southern Exposure* 9 (Spring 1981): 68–73.

54. Anne Braden quoted in *The Wall Between* (1999), 337.

55. For a detailed discussion of that case, see Fosl, *Subversive Southerner*, chap. 11, 293–310.

Mary Jane Warfield Clay
(1815–1900)

Wifely Devotion, Divorce, and Rebirth in Nineteenth-Century Kentucky

WILLIAM KUBY

The case of Mary Jane Warfield Clay offers a compelling example of both the challenges and rewards of women's history. Public knowledge of Clay's life derives primarily from the memoirs of her estranged husband, prominent emancipationist Cassius Marcellus Clay, who wrote of their 1874 divorce with great bitterness. Cassius Clay's narrative depicts Mary Jane as a cold and selfish wife, whose greed and laziness led to the deterioration of a forty-five-year marriage and whose financial ineptitude caused great angst for her abandoned husband. A close examination of the few personal documents left behind by Mary Jane, however, paints an entirely different picture. Mary Jane's personal writings reveal her to be a woman beleaguered by her absent husband's debts and fighting to achieve financial stability for her family as Cassius pursued his political ambitions. While her husband spent seven years in Saint Petersburg as American minister to Russia, Mary Jane reared the couple's children; withstood attacks from Confederate troops; oversaw the construction of White Hall, the family's Richmond, Kentucky, estate; and increased her family's income through the cultivation and rental of land. This is hardly the story of an idle plantation mistress.

Although we do not have a firsthand account of the divorce from Mary Jane, we know enough about her role in the marriage to question the unflattering portrayal that her husband provided. Her writings suggest that her devotion to marriage and family took precedence over all other personal interests and

WHITE HALL

Home of Mary Jane Warfield Clay. Richmond, Kentucky.

affairs. While she displayed no particular affection for bookkeeping, the construction of ponds, or the sale of cattle, she embraced these tasks, and many others, during her husband's absence, with the consistent goal of providing for her family. When disagreements and rumors of Cassius's infidelity pushed her to a breaking point, she gave up on her marriage, leaving Richmond in 1868 for an independent life in Lexington. In truth, she had already lived as an independent woman in her years as head of White Hall. As a female divorcée, however, she lost any financial claims to the estate, and she left her reputation vulnerable to public attacks by her ex-husband. In many ways Mary Jane was fortunate; she had inherited sufficient income from her family to live out the rest of her years comfortably. But her story nonetheless reminds us of women's legal and financial dependence in nineteenth-century Kentucky, and it reveals the unsteady social position that divorcées were forced to occupy.[1]

Mary Jane Warfield was born in Lexington in 1815 into a family of strong women. She was the second daughter of Elisha Warfield, a medical doctor and breeder of thoroughbred horses, and Maria Barr Warfield, who managed a market-garden business and oversaw the family's land and slaves. Mary Jane had six sisters: Ann Elizabeth, Ellen, Rebecca, Julia, Caroline, and Laura.[2] The Warfield parents valued the education and the intellectual development of their children. They sent the young Mary Jane to Shelby Female Academy, a new institution for young women in Lexington, also attended by Mary Todd Lincoln.[3] Given that only a few thousand women had the opportunity to receive more than four years of formal education in this era, Mary Jane's access to schooling illustrates both the Warfields' upper-class status and their belief in the necessity of education for their daughters.[4]

In 1831 the sixteen-year-old Mary Jane met the twenty-year-old Cassius Marcellus Clay, then a student at Lexington's Transylvania College. Clay was instantly smitten with the young woman, and a brief courtship ensued.[5] Yet Clay's writings indicate that another woman occupied his mind at this time and that his interest in Mary Jane—though strong—was not exclusive.[6] Not prepared to commit to lifelong romance at age twenty, Clay left Kentucky later in 1831 to complete his undergraduate education at Yale University, where he devoted himself to antislavery causes. Though he was legally unable to free the slaves his father had entrusted to him, Clay and his brother Sydney emancipated all of the family's unentailed slaves shortly before Cassius began college; he would succeed in liberating his remaining slaves in 1844. Clay graduated from the university with honors, and on February 22, 1832, he spoke out publicly against slavery for the first time in a ceremony commemorating the centennial of George Washington's birth.[7]

After his graduation from Yale, Clay returned to Kentucky to enroll in the law school at Transylvania.[8] He also rekindled his nascent romance with Mary Jane, making many visits to the Warfield estate to call on the attractive and affluent young woman.[9] If Clay had not at first been certain of his compatibility with Mary Jane, he was soon convinced that she was the match for him. Years later, Clay would reflect on the young Mary Jane's charms, recalling her fair, smooth skin, her long auburn hair, and her large gray-blue eyes. He would also emphasize her beautiful singing voice, noting, "She was the best amateur-singer I ever heard; and, as I have been familiar with the voices of Jenny Lind, Lucca, Patti, and all the most celebrated singers of my day, I venture to say that hers was, in compass and tone, unsurpassed." Though his perceptions of Mary Jane would evolve as he aged, the young Clay believed her to be "the most amiable of women," and he valued her ability to command the attention of crowds. He was thrilled to learn that Mary Jane harbored equally strong feelings.[10]

Not all observers approved of the burgeoning romance between Cassius and Mary Jane. After witnessing flirtation between the young couple, Mrs. John Allen, the mother of Clay's brother-in-law Madison Johnson, voiced her disapproval. Calling Cassius aside, she implored, "Cousin Cash, I see that you are much taken with Mary Jane. Don't you marry her; *don't you marry a Warfield!* There are the Misses W. W——, E. B——, C. H——, and E. R——, fine and cultured women of large fortunes and good families, but in all these things you are at least their equal." She then exhorted, "You can marry one of them, who will make you a good wife, and you will be happy."[11] One wonders why Mrs. Allen felt so strongly that Mary Jane's family name made her an unworthy bride. Elisha Warfield's financial success suggests that it was not monetary wealth that rendered the Warfields unequal to the Clays.[12] Perhaps this warning against the Warfield family derived in part from distrust of Mary Jane's older sister Ann, whom Clay referred to as "a scandalmonger" who "terrorized all of Lexington" with an inclination for gossip and a vindictive attitude.[13] Or possibly Mrs. Allen's concern derived from an understanding of the power that Maria Barr Warfield held within her household, and a corresponding anxiety that Mary Jane would take on a similarly dominant role in her marriage to Clay. Whatever the case, Cassius would later claim that Mrs. Allen had been correct to caution him against the union.[14]

For the time being, however, Clay paid the warning no heed. He sent a letter to Dr. Elisha Warfield requesting consent for Mary Jane's hand in marriage. He would later realize the error of this approach, for if Dr. Warfield served as the family's primary breadwinner, the more outspoken Maria Barr Warfield was its unofficial leader, and she expected to be consulted in such matters. The Warfields ultimately consented to the arrangement, but Clay's faux pas would lay the foundation for decades of conflict with his in-laws, and in Clay's view, it would poison his marriage to Mary Jane.[15] Though Cassius and Mary Jane announced their engagement in 1832 and set a wedding date for February 1833, Maria Barr Warfield chose to complicate the proceedings. A few days before the wedding, Mrs. Warfield, still irritated that Clay had not consulted her about his upcoming nuptials, showed Cassius a letter that John P. Declarey had sent to Mary Jane. In the letter Declarey, a Louisville physician who had formerly courted Mary Jane, attacked Clay's character and suggested that Mary Jane would be making a mistake should she follow through with the wedding. Clay was enraged, and he traveled to Louisville to confront Declarey for his impudence.[16] When he encountered his rival, Clay demanded an apology. On receiving none, Clay struck the older man repeatedly with a hickory cane. The furious Declarey then challenged Clay to a duel, which Clay accepted. But after the men failed to reach an agreement over the time and venue at which the fight would occur, Clay departed from Louisville. Meanwhile, the anxious bride-to-be awaited her fiancé's return to Lexington, uncertain whether he would arrive in time for the wedding, or if he was even still alive.[17]

Clay did make it to Lexington in time to exchange vows on February 26, 1833. His war with Declarey did not end there, however. On learning that Declarey had called him a coward for not following through with the duel and had pledged to beat him with a cowhide whip should they ever come face to face, Clay determined to settle the score. After a postwedding visit with friends and Mary Jane's kin, Clay returned to Louisville to finish the duel. When Declarey spotted Clay in his hotel, he turned pale and fled. Though Clay remained in Louisville for a few days after this brief encounter, he eventually returned to Lexington. The following evening Declarey committed suicide by cutting his arteries. Clay blamed Maria Barr Warfield for Declarey's death, claiming that her actions had "sowed the seeds of alienation and distrust in her own household, which in time bore fruit."[18] Whether or not we attribute this death to Mrs. Warfield's acts, the inauspicious events surrounding Cassius and Mary Jane's wedding portended a tumultuous union.

But their early years together appear to have been harmonious enough. The couple made a home at Clermont, Cassius Clay's estate outside Richmond, and began to raise a family. In 1835, the year her husband was first elected to the Kentucky legislature from Madison County, Mary Jane gave birth to Elisha Warfield Clay. She would bear eight other children over the course of the next sixteen years—Green in 1837, Mary Barr in 1839, Sarah (Sallie) Lewis in 1841, Cassius Marcellus Jr. in 1843 (this child died in infancy), a second Cassius Marcellus Jr.

in 1845, Brutus Junius in 1847, Laura in 1849, and Flora in 1851 (this child died after six weeks). Eight years later, in 1859, Mary Jane bore a tenth and final child, Anne (Annie) Warfield Clay.[19] Childbearing brought its share of hardships and sorrow, including the deaths of two infants, whom Cassius believed were poisoned by their nurse Emily, one of the Clays' remaining slaves.[20] But Mary Jane was a devoted mother, committed to educating and nurturing her children. She was often required to perform this work alone, as her husband's political and military service led him outside of Kentucky on a regular basis.[21]

In 1838 Cassius Clay purchased Morton House, a grand $15,000 Lexington home that, in reality, he could not afford. The Clays' move to Lexington gave Mary Jane closer access to her family and allowed her husband to foster his political career. He served as a delegate to the national Whig convention in December 1839, and he grew into an increasingly vocal opponent of slavery in subsequent years. He was elected to the state legislature from Fayette County in 1840, but his unabashed emancipationism would prevent his reelection the following year.[22] Mary Jane must have held some reservations about her husband's political ambitions and the violent confrontations he seemed to court. She remained ignorant of her husband's 1841 duel with political rival Robert J. Wickliffe, who had provoked Clay by insisting publicly that Mary Jane and her family were supporters of slavery.[23] But she did know about her husband's 1843 fight with Samuel M. Brown, an assassin from New Orleans who was hired to kill Clay for his emancipationist rhetoric. After Brown struck Clay with a club, Clay fought back with a bowie knife. Though Brown shot Clay with a revolver, Clay proved the more effective fighter in mauling his opponent with his knife. He walked away from the fight mostly unscathed.[24] Incidents like this made Mary Jane all the more aware of the physical and emotional dangers that her husband's outspoken opposition to slavery brought to her family.

In spite of these threats, Mary Jane supported her husband's antislavery activism, and she was initially willing to accompany Cassius on political trips. In 1844 the twenty-nine-year-old Mary Jane traveled alongside Cassius on a journey through the North in support of his cousin Henry Clay, the Whig Party's presidential candidate. Leaving their three children with relatives, the couple set out on a tour of the Midwest and Northeast. While Mary Jane appreciated the exposure to new cities and cultures, she remained detached from the political purposes of her husband's trip. Her correspondence provides commentary on the long buggy rides from town to town, the people she met, the cities she visited, and the ways she occupied herself while her husband was giving speeches. She was struck by the number of people who rushed to greet Cassius and to shake his hand—many of them mistaking him for his more famous cousin.

But above all, she seemed interested in the food found in each locale. In one letter to a friend, she described in detail the meals served in the homes of her midwestern hosts, offering her general approval of the food's preparation. She was most enthusiastic in her descriptions of fruit, providing vivid accounts of the color, size, and taste of the plums, peaches, and grapes she encountered.[25] In a way, this fascination with fruit signaled the important role that horticulture and gardening would soon play in her life.

Less than two years after Henry Clay's presidential defeat, Mary Jane's new role as de facto head of the family would commence. At this point, cracks in the marriage seemed to be forming—in 1845 an unspecified quarrel had led Cassius Clay to throw away his own wedding ring.[26] Perhaps this tension played into Clay's decision in 1846 to serve in the U.S. Army in the Mexican War. It was here that Mary Jane's anxious mail correspondence with her brother-in-law Brutus began. Pregnant and already mother to five living children, Mary Jane took on the additional burden of controlling the Clay family finances and paying off her husband's debts, which resulted primarily from the production and circulation of Clay's antislavery newspaper, the *True American*.[27] Her letters to Brutus reveal unease over an endless stream of bills and the frequent appearance of local debt collectors. They also reflect a pragmatic mind, a genuine desire to restore all money to its rightful owners, and a schematic system for settling her husband's debts as efficiently as possible.[28] Despite the fact that Mary Jane became solely responsible for addressing the family's economic concerns, she never held full knowledge or control over the family finances, or even a key to her husband's desk—inside of which, she was convinced, there might be important papers pertaining to even more debts.[29] While she did not complain publicly of her situation, she suffered the regular indignity of writing her husband with pleas for money and groveling for contributions from her brother-in-law. One can only imagine the emotional toll this took on a woman who believed in her heart that wives should not have to rely on the goodwill of men to sustain themselves and their children.

Between June 1846 and December 1847, Mary Jane's letters teem with anxiety. In addition to the question of the *True American*'s finances, Mary Jane was responsible for the upkeep of the Clays' Lexington house and Madison County farm.[30] She debated the most effective ways to cultivate fruits and vegetables on these two properties, and she worried about the sale of cattle, which she hoped would ease the family's debts. Consequently, many of her letters go into detail about the price and condition of the Clays' supply of hogs, cows, and mules.[31] Her role as a temporary single mother also occupied considerable time during these solitary months. On top of caring for and educating her own sons and daughters, she adopted a motherly role toward other children in the community, at one point taking the children of an ailing friend into her home for an extended period of time, in spite of her own son's illness.[32] Her letters reflect no resentment or stress over the challenges that single parenting must have brought, and they often minimize the responsibilities of mothering. Though she briefly mentioned the birth of her son Brutus in a letter sent on March 1, 1847—the infant had been born just nine days prior—the primary focus of this missive remained the sale of cattle.[33]

Read together, these letters depict a woman committed to maintaining her family's economic stability, sometimes at the expense of her own physical and emotional well-being. In October 1846 she relocated the family from its home in Lexington to the farm outside Richmond in hopes of saving money, and she sold her carriage in an effort to pay off debt. "It is impossible to live in town on the same means that I can in the country and I have determined to go," she declared before leaving Lexington. "It may be but a drop in the bucket towards liquidating Mr. Clay's debts, but many drops fill the bucket after a while and debt oppresses me."[34] She vowed never to leave the farm until every debt was paid.[35] It is easy to dismiss these sacrifices as the problems of rich folk—indeed, the choice of which home to inhabit is not a decision frequently granted to the truly impoverished. But her willingness to surrender her own comfort for the good of the family stands in stark contrast to the picture that Cassius Clay would later paint of his wife as a leech whose very survival was indebted to her husband's magnanimity.[36] Meanwhile, though Mary Jane never wrote an unkind word against her husband during his time in Mexico, she acknowledged that his indebtedness posed great inconvenience to creditors, including her own brother-in-law. To Brutus she wrote, "You do not know how disturbing it is to me that Mr. Clay is so troublesome to you concerning his business and with how much gratitude I receive your kind attentions."[37] Perhaps this sense of distress accounts for some of the later tensions that would develop between Mary Jane and her husband.

Any frustration Mary Jane Clay felt was replaced by concern when she learned in April 1847 that her husband had been taken prisoner by Mexican forces. Though she received word from Cassius that his captors were treating him well, she could not suppress her anxiety over his safety and her fear that his imprisonment would delay his return to Kentucky.[38] Meanwhile, Cassius embraced this forced estrangement from his wife as an opportunity to form a new romantic bond. After eight months of captivity in Mexico City, Clay and his fellow American prisoners were transferred to a guarded monastery in the town of Toluca. While in Toluca, Clay became acquainted with a charming eighteen-year-old woman named Lolu, whom he sneaked out of the monastery to see as often as he could. Knowing he would be killed if his identity as a captive American became evident, he took to disguising himself in a sombrero and a serape, slipping away to visit his paramour and her pet parakeet.[39] This romance came to an end when Clay was released from the monastery in September 1847. He returned to Kentucky on December 6 and was welcomed back by Mary Jane, who knew nothing of Lolu. At this point, Cassius reclaimed his responsibilities as social and financial head of household, and Mary Jane's anxious correspondence with her brother-in-law came to a temporary halt.[40]

Few records account for Mary Jane Clay's experiences during the next fifteen years, which the family spent at Clermont. Mary Jane bore three more infants and continued to rear the elder children. While she ceased to function as head of the Clays' Lexington and Richmond properties in these years, she continued to oversee various horticultural and agricultural pursuits on the grounds, including yard work, the construction of an arbor, and the production of food items such as apple cider and pickled fruits and vegetables. She also sewed articles of clothing for her children, several of whom studied at boarding schools in Lexington. In spite of her children's absence, she took an active role in their education, correcting the misspellings in the letters they sent her and encouraging them to seek extra assistance in their writing skills. She also fostered their spiritual development, encouraging them to follow Christ, to say their prayers, and to strive to be moral and decent individuals. In the meantime, she found time for some personal leisure activities, including music and riding lessons.[41]

There is reason to suspect, however, that beneath her active daily routine, Mary Jane Clay was suffering from malaise, if not depression. In 1853 the fourteen-year-old Mary Barr Clay expressed concern that her mother was severely unhappy in her day-to-day existence. In a letter from school the younger Clay depicted her mother as a woman struggling to fend off loneliness and idleness. "I see you going about with a sad face, seeing to the servants [*sic*] work trying to take some pleasure in their work but cannot," the daughter wrote. She continued, "I see you go to the house it is all desolate, there is no sound to be heard, there is no one there, the two children are out playing and you are by yourself." She proceeded to discuss Mary Jane's apparent longing for her absent children and to suggest that Cassius was rarely present at Clermont to keep his wife company.[42] We know that during these years Cassius Clay traveled frequently for speaking engagements, and at times he endured physical threat and attack for his antislavery views.[43] Perhaps Mary Jane's sadness derived in part from feelings of isolation due to her husband's regular absences and from the knowledge that someday he might not come home at all.[44]

Also adding to Mary Jane Clay's stresses were Cassius's ongoing monetary woes. A Cincinnati banking company he had organized collapsed in late 1854, and his finances spiraled downward from there. Two years later he announced his economic failure, and he was forced to auction off his possessions in a private sale. While several of his family members stepped in to help him pay off his debts, his wealthy father-in-law, Elisha Warfield, refused to assist him, only deepening Cassius's resentment toward his wife's kin.[45] When Mary Jane's father died in 1859, Clay refused even to attend Warfield's funeral. One can only imagine the impact this symbolic act would have had on his relationship with his grieving wife.[46] That said, their marriage seemed fairly steady in 1860, perhaps due in part to the $200,000 Mary Jane had inherited from her father.[47]

This harmony did not last. In 1861 President Abraham Lincoln appointed Cassius Clay to the position of American minister to Russia. Mary Jane expressed ambivalence about her husband's impending relocation overseas. She knew that her daughters craved a change of scenery, but she herself had great fondness for Clermont and country living. "This place grows more beautiful and more dear to me continually and if I consulted my own pleasure I would remain here," she wrote to a friend. In spite of her personal desires, however, Mary Jane accompanied her husband to Russia, as did their school-aged children. The family left Kentucky in April 1861. Before setting off across the Atlantic, Mary Jane and the children were detained in Philadelphia and New York for three weeks, as Cassius helped protect Washington from a Confederate attack. Due to hotel and travel costs, the family exhausted its immediate financial resources, and Mary Jane had to withdraw $5,000 from her inheritance. After this costly three-week diversion, the Clays set sail for Saint Petersburg.[48]

While Mary Jane appeared to be settling into her new life in Russia, her large furnished house and the stream of invitations to diplomatic events did not cure her longing for home. Though the precise reason for her decision to leave Russia with her children in January 1862 is not clear, historians have theorized that she worried about her daughter's fragile health during the cold winter and that she grew tired of her husband's flirtations with other women. Cassius Clay was displeased about his wife's departure, insisting that Mary Jane left "contrary to my wishes, and regardless of my protest."[49] When he was reappointed to the position in 1863, Mary Jane was unwilling to join him in Saint Petersburg, opting instead to stay at Clermont to oversee the renovation of the Clays' estate.[50] In spite of his frustration with his wife's departure, Cassius gave Mary Jane power of attorney to manage the family's property. She played an instrumental role in converting Clermont into White Hall, a much larger estate, which Cassius hoped would lend itself to the entertainment of local and national political figures. He seemed eager to put Mary Jane to work on the construction of the new property, informing his brother Brutus that on her return to Madison County, Mary Jane would "devote all her spare time to improve the farm, and build the house."[51]

At home in Kentucky, Mary Jane Clay commenced another round of intense communication with her brother-in-law over her family's practical and financial affairs. In spite of her responsibility for managing the construction of White Hall, she was left in the dark when it came to questions of money. In one letter, after describing the construction of White Hall's foundation, she asked Brutus for money. Clearly uncomfortable to be back in this position of having to beg for funds, Mary Jane seemed to have no other option, apart from once again accessing her inheritance. She wrote, "I understood Mr. Clay to say, you would furnish all our necessities, naming the amounts and the supplies. I knew nothing of his arrangements and asked no questions."[52] Subsequent letters discussed the technical elements of estate construction—from brickwork and stonework to the costs of hired labor.[53]

On top of dealing with the intricacies of the White Hall project, Mary Jane had to face the realities of life as a single woman in Civil War–era Kentucky, a state that experienced military raids and guerrilla terror.[54] Mary Jane took an active role in seeing to the safety of the Union army. She offered lodging to Union soldiers and allowed thousands of government horses and mules to graze on White Hall's grasslands. She also contributed much of her own livestock. As a result of this aid to Union forces, Mary Jane was vulnerable to Confederate aggression. In late July 1864 her carriage house and lumber house were burned to the ground. Mary Jane was convinced that this was an act of arson, and it caused her to worry for her own safety.[55] Meanwhile, Cassius made many references to the turmoil in Kentucky in the letters he sent from across the Atlantic. As he caroused with the czar and other Russian royals, he assured his wife that the military activity occurring in the South would subside, and he expressed hope that Confederate guerrillas would be driven out of the state.[56] In spite of these concerns, his distance from the situation shows in his ongoing efforts to minimize the threat that his family faced. In one letter to daughter Mary Barr Clay, he voiced relief that White Hall was safe following the incursion of rebel troops into Richmond. Moreover, he was pleased to learn that his family was "getting on cheerfully at home, under the difficult circumstances of the war." He continued, "I am glad you don't allow your spirits to be depressed—but make the best of it. I am hopeful that you will be spared any more raids: as they are becoming more and more bitter in the warfare."[57]

Despite her dangerous surroundings, Mary Jane was very productive during these years. She embraced her role as head of household, declining to visit Brutus during the summer of 1864 due to her realization that "home is the only proper place for heads of families."[58] Cassius, however, was not willing to surrender his claim to this role. From Russia he continued to assert control over all goings-on at White Hall, instructing his wife through letters on what crops to grow, how to dig ponds, and how to go about creating a "very pretty bridge" on the property.[59] He also provided Mary Jane with parenting instructions, forbidding her from sending their daughter Laura to boarding school and consenting to Mary's baptism after an initial resistance.[60] Blending her own parental instincts with remote instructions from her husband, Mary Jane saw to her children's proper upbringing. Above all, she valued their education, and she encouraged her daughters to defy the southern convention of early matrimony and to postpone marriage until they had completed their schooling.[61] On top of her achievements in childrearing, Mary Jane managed White Hall with much success until her husband's return to Kentucky in 1869. At the same time that she oversaw the 2,500-acre farm, Mary Jane also paid off a great portion of her husband's debts through property rental and the sale of livestock and crops; it has been estimated that she raised $80,000. She also saw to the construction of the $30,000 house and supported her family with money she made from the farm.[62]

While her husband served in Russia, Mary Jane harbored growing suspicions of his infidelity, perhaps due to rumors of an extramarital affair with a Russian ballerina.[63] Mary Jane also heard the allegations of indecency leveled against her husband in 1867 by Eliza Chautems, a poor Irish mother raising her children in Saint Petersburg. Clay had helped rescue Mrs. Chautems from poverty by lending her enough money to open a boardinghouse. When Clay realized that the woman had no real intention of paying the loan back, and that she was in fact selling the furniture he had purchased for her, he initiated legal proceedings against her. In retaliation, Mrs. Chautems sent a petition to Congress, alleging that Clay had physically assaulted her after making inappropriate advances toward her fourteen-year-old daughter. While Eliza Chautems's charges against Clay proved unfounded, the scandal nonetheless damaged his reputation in Kentucky and drove a wedge between him and his wife. Already suspicious of her husband's infidelity, Mary Jane believed the rumors, drawing Cassius's ire and creating a lapse in their correspondence.[64]

When Cassius Clay returned to the United States in 1869, he and Mary Jane were on icy terms. Nearly four decades into their marriage, the rift began to appear insurmountable. Mary Jane, already disturbed by rumors of her husband's dalliances, was further aggravated by Cassius's decision to visit friends and conduct political activities in New York City for nearly a year before he returned to his family at White Hall.[65] During her husband's stay in New York, Mary Jane sent him a letter stating her desire to purchase the cemetery lot in Lexington where their children were buried—the clear implication here being that she had no intention of being buried with her husband, who himself planned to be interred alongside relatives in Richmond. Clay viewed this request as a "proclamation of perpetual war," which he "sternly accepted," selling her the lot without protest.[66]

When Cassius returned to Kentucky, he was alarmed to find that his children did not know him, and that whatever impressions they *did* have of their father had been influenced negatively by the Warfield family, whom Clay described as his "inveterate enemies." Unimpressed with the White Hall renovations, he believed that Mary Jane had overspent his money on the home's construction and had failed to pay him any of the income she had received through its rental.[67] Meanwhile, Mary Jane told him that he was no longer welcome in their home. She banished him to a separate room of the new house, and when winter came she moved his belongings yet again into a room with an unfinished fireplace. Clay complained of cold "so intense that icicles froze on my beard."[68]

One night, Mary Jane called Cassius into her room and offered to pay him back all of the money he had sent her in his absence. He refused out of pride. This response seemed to unleash the torrent of anger that Mary Jane had been holding back. Suddenly, according to Cassius's recounting of events, fury replaced cold silence, and Mary Jane castigated Cassius bitterly for "all the faults and escapades of a life-time." Her husband responded coolly. Of the event, he wrote, "The scene was closed by my asking her if she had any thing more to say; and I finally, with suave tones, bade her goodnight, and returned to my room, and locked the door after me ever afterward during her stay in my house."[69] This final phrase—"during her stay in my house"—in many ways encapsulates the reasons for Mary Jane's bitterness. After nearly forty years of marriage to Clay, during which time she supported his political career, accompanied him on the campaign trail and for a short time in Russia, raised their children as a frequently single parent, and oversaw the renovations of the family's house, she still held no legal, economic, or social claim to that very house. In asserting sole financial responsibility for the construction of White Hall, Cassius Clay failed to acknowledge that his wife's time and labor had been at the heart of its renovation and that her lone parenting had allowed for the preservation of the family housed within. Under southern coverture laws, which denied married women the right to their own wages and real-estate holdings, the state supported Clay's assumption that the family's property belonged to him alone.[70]

Mary Jane left White Hall soon after this fight, and with daughters Laura and

Annie—the only two children still living at home—she took up temporary lodging in her sister's Lexington residence.[71] As historian H. Edward Richardson has noted, however, she and Cassius seem to have maintained a "marriage of convenience" in the months following her departure. Under this arrangement, Mary Jane would return to White Hall on occasion to help her estranged husband entertain his political allies and to maintain the appearance of matrimonial harmony before guests. During one such event, a carriage arrived on the premises. A woman exited the carriage, accompanied by a four-year-old boy. When Clay greeted her, she responded, "General Clay, I have brought your son from Russia." After inspecting the boy in the light, Clay escorted him through the front entrance of White Hall and introduced him to guests as "my adopted son from Russia." The party broke up shortly after Clay's dramatic announcement.[72]

The actual parentage of this child is not certain, but he was born Leonide Petroff in Saint Petersburg in 1866. Clay sent for the child in 1870 and adopted him shortly thereafter, changing his name to Launey Clay and raising him as his own. Many have speculated that the child was indeed Clay's biological son, and Clay never denied this charge. Mary Jane was among this camp, and she left White Hall after the incident, relocating permanently to Lexington, where she bought a house of her own.[73] Clay claimed that Mary Jane made an attempt at reconciliation after this final rupture, an offer that he rebuffed.[74] In December 1877 he filed for divorce on grounds of desertion. Mary Jane had been occupying a separate residence at this point for more than the five years required by Kentucky law to procure a divorce. She did not contest the suit, and thus the forty-five-year marriage was terminated on February 7, 1878.[75] Because Kentucky law then ensured that married women held no legal title to their husbands' property, and because Mary Jane had signed away her right of dower on the couple's initial separation, she was not eligible for any financial support from her former husband.[76]

As historian Paul E. Fuller has indicated, Mary Jane fared better than other Kentucky divorcées might have in her position. Since fathers held guardianship rights over their children in the case of divorce, Cassius had the full legal right to separate daughter Annie, the couple's remaining minor child, from her mother.[77] He chose not to take this action, however, and Annie remained with Mary Jane until she reached adulthood. Moreover, Mary Jane was fortunate to have come from a wealthy family and to have inherited a trust fund from her parents that would allow her to live out her years in a comfortable manner. Because she was not entitled to any holdings in the estate whose construction she had overseen, one wonders how she would have sustained herself had it not been for this inheritance.[78] In addition to receiving no compensation for her many years of physical and emotional labor on her family's behalf, Mary Jane had her reputation tarnished by the publication of her husband's memoir in 1886. In an extended rant, Clay exposed the cruelties he had allegedly incurred in marriage and insisted that his wife owed him the $80,000 she had raised by renting the property during his time away; he made no mention of the work she had put into the property's development and upkeep.[79] His short-lived marriage to the fifteen-year-old Dora Richardson, whom he wed in 1894 at age eighty-four, was not enough to temper his enduring wrath toward his former wife. Clay complained that conflicts with Mary Jane contributed to the deterioration of his second marriage, and he referred to the "vendetta" that his ex-wife waged against him in personal correspondence sent after his second divorce.[80]

Mary Jane Warfield Clay did not leave behind written commentary to support or counter her husband's angry words. While we need not assume that she was faultless in the decline of her marriage, we should also be wary of accepting Cassius's claims without reservation. Questions of blame aside, Mary Jane moved on from the drama within the walls of White Hall, and she lived out her remaining decades in peace, investing her time in agriculture and feminist politics. Even into her seventies and eighties, Mary Jane Warfield Clay maintained her own 350-acre farm in Richmond. She profited from sales in wheat, cattle, and sheep, generating several thousands of dollars annually.[81] In addition to her business success, Mary Jane devoted herself to the cause of women's rights. While direct accounts of her decades in activism are scarce, it is clear that Mary Jane took an energetic role in the movement alongside daughters Mary, Sallie, Laura, and Annie. The Clay daughters—disgusted by the unjust financial price their mother had paid for her divorce—became central actors in the women's rights movement, both in Kentucky and on the national level.[82] Three decades after the Seneca Falls Conference of 1848, woman suffrage remained an unfulfilled goal, and this denial of female citizenship rights motivated the Clay women to action. In 1879 the sixty-four-year-old Mary Jane made her Lexington home a headquarters for suffrage activism, and she and her daughters went door-to-door to enlist supporters for women's rights activities. While the Clays encountered some success in recruiting participants, all too many women resisted because, in Mary Jane's view, they were "afraid of displeasing their husbands." This was a feeling to which the former Mrs. Clay could relate, as it was not until her marriage to an antisuffragist dissolved that she was able to take a public role in denouncing gender inequality.[83]

In addition to suffrage work, Mary Jane Clay took part in postbellum initiatives to protect wives from abusive marriages. While women's rights leaders held varied opinions on the morality of divorce, many believed that wives should be able to choose divorce in order to escape drunken husbands, physical and verbal abuse, and patriarchal control.[84] The right to divorce was likely not a priority for Mary Jane, as Kentucky already permitted women to terminate their marriages if their husbands abused them, drank excessively, or committed adultery.[85] But Mary Jane and her daughters did seek to protect married women from economic exploitation, joining other women's rights activists in a quest to grant wives the right to their own wages and property holdings. Collective efforts to overturn laws of coverture swelled in the postbellum South, as more and more women—many of whom had functioned without male protection during the Civil War years—laid claim to the material possessions that marriage denied them. Mary Jane Clay, who had left her own marriage without any compensation for her physical and financial labor, thus pushed for fairer property laws for married women and for the overturning of coverture laws.[86] The Clay women's efforts contributed to the 1894 passage of the Married Woman's Property Act in the Kentucky state legislature, which gave wives control over their own landholdings, wages, and personal property. This act permitted married women to maintain their legal and economic identities, and it likely spared future wives from the uncertain circumstances that Mary Jane faced should their marriages crumble.[87]

Mary Jane Warfield Clay died on April 29, 1900, following a long illness. She was eighty-five years old. Among the prominent figures to grieve her loss was women's rights activist Susan B. Anthony, who wrote these words to Mary Barr Clay a week before her mother's death: "My love and respect for your dear mother and all of her girls have grown with the years—so that today I am dipped into sympathy with all of you—almost as if it were my very own mother whose ebbing life-tide were going out. The world is indeed the poorer to us who can no longer say mother!"[88] It is time to incorporate these loving words into our record of Mary Jane Warfield Clay's life. They do not erase the angry narrative that Cassius Clay presented in the wake of the couple's separation, but they do remind us of Mary Jane's dedication to family, her unfaltering work ethic, and her commitment to the cause of women's rights. These contributions are equally central to Mary Jane Warfield Clay's biography, and they reveal the meaningful life that one nineteenth-century Kentucky woman was able to forge for herself in the face of legal and cultural barriers to her independent existence. We deprive ourselves of this complex story when we view Mary Jane Warfield Clay merely as the estranged wife of Cassius Marcellus Clay. The many roles she filled both inside and outside of that marriage entitle her to a richer legacy.

NOTES

1. For seminal works on nineteenth-century divorce, see Jane Turner Censer, "'Smiling through Her Tears': Ante-bellum Southern Women and Divorce," *American Journal of Legal History* 25 (1981):

24–47; Glenda Riley, *Divorce: An American Tradition* (New York: Oxford University Press, 1991); Norma Basch, *Framing American Divorce: From the Revolutionary Generation to the Victorians* (Berkeley: University of California Press, 1999); Hendrik Hartog, *Man and Wife in America: A History* (Cambridge, Mass.: Harvard University Press, 2000); Loren Schweninger, *Families in Crisis in the Old South: Divorce, Slavery, and the Law* (Chapel Hill: University of North Carolina Press, 2012).

2. Paul E. Fuller, *Laura Clay and the Woman's Rights Movement* (Lexington: University Press of Kentucky, 1975), 2; Betty Boles Ellison, *A Man Seen but Once: Cassius Marcellus Clay* (Bloomington, Ind.: Author House, 2005), 25, 33–34.

3. Ellison, *A Man Seen but Once*, 25. The Shelby Female Academy was more frequently called Ward's Academy, in reference to its director, Dr. John Ward. See Jean H. Baker, *Mary Todd Lincoln: A Biography* (New York: Norton, 1987), 37.

4. Baker, *Mary Todd Lincoln*, 37. While Baker provides no statistics for Kentucky, she notes that only a quarter of the teenage girls in Massachusetts were still in school in 1860. One can assume that the number of female teenage pupils in 1820s and 1830s Kentucky would have been even lower.

5. H. Edward Richardson, *Cassius Marcellus Clay: Firebrand of Freedom* (Lexington: University Press of Kentucky, 1976), 15–17.

6. Cassius Marcellus Clay (hereafter CMC), *The Life of Cassius Marcellus Clay: Memoirs, Writings, and Speeches* (Cincinnati: J. F. Brennan, 1886), 62–63.

7. Richardson, *Cassius Marcellus Clay*, 17–24; David L. Smiley, *Lion of White Hall: The Life of Cassius Marcellus Clay of Kentucky* (Madison: University of Wisconsin Press, 1962), 66, 71.

8. Ellison, *A Man Seen but Once*, 32. As Ellison notes, Clay did not pursue a comprehensive legal education, but instead he enrolled in a six-month course. He never applied for a license to practice law.

9. Clay was not alone in this endeavor, as Mary Jane had a number of suitors at the time. Richardson, *Cassius Marcellus Clay*, 26.

10. CMC, *Life of Cassius Marcellus Clay*, 65–68.

11. Ibid., 68.

12. On the significance of wealth in nineteenth-century southern courtship, see Bertram Wyatt-Brown, *Southern Honor: Ethics and Behavior in the Old South* (New York: Oxford University Press, 1982), 217–22.

13. Richardson, *Cassius Marcellus Clay*, 26–27; CMC, *Life of Cassius Marcellus Clay*, 64.

14. CMC, *Life of Cassius Marcellus Clay*, 549. On courtship and gendered expectations within marriage in the Old South, see Anya Jabour, *Scarlett's Sisters: Young Women in the Old South* (Chapel Hill: University of North Carolina Press, 2007); Steven M. Stowe, *Intimacy and Power in the Old South: Ritual in the Lives of the Planters* (Baltimore: Johns Hopkins University Press, 1987); Jane Turner Censer, *North Carolina Planters and Their Children, 1800–1860* (Baton Rouge: Louisiana State University Press, 1984); Charlene M. Boyer Lewis, *Ladies and Gentlemen on Display: Planter Society at the Virginia Springs, 1790–1860* (Charlottesville: University of Virginia Press, 2001); Catherine Clinton, *The Plantation Mistress: Woman's World in the Old South* (New York: Pantheon, 1982), 59–86; Wyatt-Brown, *Southern Honor*, 199–225; Brenda Stevenson, *Life in Black and White: Family and Community in the Slave South* (New York: Oxford University Press, 1996), 37–94.

15. CMC, *Life of Cassius Marcellus Clay*, 69–71; Ellison, *A Man Seen but Once*, 25, 33–34; Fuller, *Laura Clay*, 2. Clay looked askance at the unconventional power dynamic within the Warfield household. He did not support the quest for women's rights and suffrage, and he deemed the granting of property rights to women a "fatal mistake." See Smiley, *Lion of White Hall*, 31.

16. CMC, *Life of Cassius Marcellus Clay*, 71; Richardson, *Cassius Marcellus Clay*, 28–29.

17. Thomas Bodley to William A. Bodley, February 24, 1833, Bodley Family Papers, Filson His-

torical Society (hereafter FHS), Louisville, Kentucky; CMC, *Life of Cassius Marcellus Clay*, 71–72; Ellison, *A Man Seen but Once*, 34–35. On the culture of dueling between southern men, see Wyatt-Brown, *Southern Honor*, 327–61.

18. CMC, *Life of Cassius Marcellus Clay*, 72–73.

19. Richardson, *Cassius Marcellus Clay*, 31; Smiley, *Lion of White Hall*, 257–58n10; Zachary F. Smith and Mary Rogers Clay, *The Clay Family* (Louisville: John P. Morton, 1899), 122. As Laura F. Edwards notes, in 1850 the average number of children born to free women of childbearing age across the country was 5.4, while southern women bore an average of seven children. Edwards, *Scarlett Doesn't Live Here Anymore: Southern Women in the Civil War Era* (Urbana: University of Illinois Press, 2000), 40.

20. CMC, *Life of Cassius Marcellus Clay*, 565; Smiley, *Lion of White Hall*, 71. Two of the Clays' other children died of diphtheria as adolescents: Elisha in 1851 and the second Cassius Jr. in 1857. See Richardson, *Cassius Marcellus Clay*, 31; Fuller, *Laura Clay*, 3. As the Clay family's case indicates, rates of childhood mortality were high, even among affluent families. In her study of the planter class in antebellum North Carolina, Jane Turner Censer estimates that at least one child in four did not reach its fifth birthday, and she argues that the mortality rate would have been much higher among poorer families. Censer, *North Carolina Planters*, 28.

21. Southern men's careers often took them away from their families for extended periods of time, a practice that most wives did not question or challenge. See Jabour, *Scarlett's Sisters*, 209–10.

22. Richardson, *Cassius Marcellus Clay*, 32–34; Ellison, *A Man Seen but Once*, 39; Smiley, *Lion of White Hall*, 43–53.

23. CMC, *Life of Cassius Marcellus Clay*, 80–81; Smiley, *Lion of White Hall*, 51–52; Richardson, *Cassius Marcellus Clay*, 34–35; Ellison, *A Man Seen but Once*, 42–43.

24. Richardson, *Cassius Marcellus Clay*, 34–37.

25. Mary Jane Clay (hereafter MJC) to Caroline Tarleton, Paynesville, August 28, 1844, Cassius M. Clay Papers, FHS, Louisville, Kentucky (hereafter Cassius M. Clay Papers). For example, in one descriptive passage Mary Jane wrote, "About ½ after nine we went up to Mrs. Matthews and there found dishes of the plums abovementioned, the color of the egg plum, round not so large as a bantum [*sic*] egg quite, almost tasteless, which she said was caused by the rain which had been falling almost continually for ten days. Fine looking peaches with little flavor, which she attributed to the rain, most delicious grapes deep, deep purple, and the blue plum smaller than our common plum but very sweet. I have no idea in the world that their peaches ever compare with ours in flavour."

26. CMC, *Life of Cassius Marcellus Clay*, 540; Smiley, *Lion of White Hall*, 116–17.

27. On the volatile history of the *True American*, see Smiley, *Lion of White Hall*, 80–106. Accounts of the number of children in the Clay family vary. While David Smiley writes that Cassius left Mary Jane with three children, H. Edward Richardson's more precise accounting of the family's birth order puts the total of living children in 1846 at five: Elisha, Green, Mary, Sallie, and the second Cassius Jr. (The first Cassius Jr. was born and died in 1843.) Richardson, *Cassius Marcellus Clay*, 31; Smiley, *Lion of White Hall*, 116–17.

28. In one letter she asked Brutus for a detailed list of every sum that Cassius owed to him, the bank, or any other creditor: "I have made a rough calculation of the amount of money necessary to carry on the farm and pay *all* expenses of Town & Country. All things included, it amounts to $3,000 or, thereabouts used economically. All other income, to whatever amount as long as I have a word to say in the matter, shall be exclusively devoted to the payment of Mr. Clay's debts." She also asked her brother-in-law for a monthly allowance for incidental expenses so that she would not have to receive it from outside lenders. MJC to Brutus Clay (hereafter BC), November 8, 1846, Clay Family

Papers, 1780–1959, Special Collections and Archives, University of Kentucky Libraries, Lexington (hereafter Clay Family Papers).

29. Ibid. Laura Edwards uses the phrase "deputy husband" to describe a wife's domestic responsibilities when her husband fought in wars. She writes, "When men left for the front, women stepped into this traditional female role and took over the difficult task of plantation management under particularly demanding circumstances. Husbands wrote lengthy letters full of agricultural advice about such things as planting, harvesting, milking, slaughtering, marketing, and negotiating relations with overseers and slaves. But an irregular mail service brought advice sporadically. Basically, women were on their own." While some women thrived in this position, others struggled mightily. Edwards, *Scarlett Doesn't Live Here Anymore*, 77–78.

30. Cassius Clay ceased to edit the paper when he departed for Mexico, but Mary Jane continued to receive letters containing money for subscriptions. She also had to pay for a final edition of the newspaper after her husband discontinued his involvement, as the publisher did not receive notification until after he had begun production. MJC to BC, October 18, 1846; Paul Seymour to BC, October 22, 1846, Clay Family Papers.

31. MJC to BC, November 30, 1846, January 10, 1847, Clay Family Papers.

32. MJC to BC, September 28, 1846, Clay Family Papers.

33. MJC to BC, March 1, 1847, Clay Family Papers.

34. MJC to BC, October 11, 22, 1846, Clay Family Papers.

35. MJC to BC, November 8, 1846, Clay Family Papers.

36. CMC, *Life of Cassius Marcellus Clay*, 540–45.

37. MJC to BC, July 9, 1846, Clay Family Papers.

38. MJC to BC, April 25, May 3, 1847, Clay Family Papers.

39. CMC, *Life of Cassius Marcellus Clay*, 159–62; Smiley, *Lion of White Hall*, 127–28; Ellison, *A Man Seen but Once*, 70.

40. Smiley, *Lion of White Hall*, 128–29.

41. Mary Barr Clay (hereafter MBC) to MJC, November 4, 1853; MJC to MBC, October 19, 1854, Cassius M. Clay Papers; Fuller, *Laura Clay*, 5.

42. MBC to MJC, November 4, 1853, Cassius M. Clay Papers.

43. See Ellison, *A Man Seen but Once*, 75–82.

44. Cassius Clay acknowledged that his speaking engagements and business trips kept him away from his children, and he would later complain that his sons and daughters did not really know him. Smiley, *Lion of White Hall*, 157.

45. CMC, *Life of Cassius Marcellus Clay*, 538; Ellison, *A Man Seen but Once*, 94; Richardson, *Cassius Marcellus Clay*, 75–76; Smiley, *Lion of White Hall*, 156.

46. CMC, *Life of Cassius Marcellus Clay*, 538–39.

47. Ellison, *A Man Seen but Once*, 99.

48. Ibid., 101, 107–13.

49. Ibid., 118–19; Richardson, *Cassius Marcellus Clay*, 97; CMC, *Life of Cassius Marcellus Clay*, 539.

50. Richardson, *Cassius Marcellus Clay*, 97–98.

51. Indeed, Clay saw Mary Jane's departure as an opportunity for an expedited renovation project. In a letter to Brutus, Clay wrote that his wife hoped "to save enough money thus out of our salary to build the new house in four years, or sooner: if the rebels will allow us." He then proceeded to describe the plans she would oversee—plans that would have been much delayed had Mary Jane remained in Saint Petersburg. CMC to BC, January 11, 1862, Clay Family Papers. On the architectural reconstruction of the property, see Ellison, *A Man Seen but Once*, 103–5.

52. MJC to BC, March 23, 1862, Clay Family Papers. Mary Jane also displayed her discomfort with the situation by insisting that Brutus ignore her request should it cause him any trouble. She wrote, "Now if it inconveniences you *at all* do not send it, I beg of you."

53. MJC to BC, April 8, 1862, June 21, 1864, Clay Family Papers.

54. Fuller, *Laura Clay*, 5. See also Brian D. McKnight, *Contested Borderlands: The Civil War in Appalachian Kentucky and Virginia* (Lexington: University Press of Kentucky, 2006); Lowell H. Harrison, *The Civil War in Kentucky* (Lexington: University Press of Kentucky, 1975). For additional work on southern women's dealings with Union troops, see Drew Gilpin Faust, *Mothers of Invention: Women of the Slaveholding South in the American Civil War* (Chapel Hill: University of North Carolina Press, 1996), 196–219; Edwards, *Scarlett Doesn't Live Here Anymore*, 79–81.

55. Fuller, *Laura Clay*, 5–6; MJC to BC, July 21, 1864, Clay Family Papers. Mary Jane mentioned that another cabin had been burned the year before. Initially she had assumed that this conflagration was an accident, but now she realized it was a deliberate wartime act.

56. CMC to MJC, July [n.d.] 1863, Cassius M. Clay Papers.

57. CMC to MBC, May 20, 1863, Cassius M. Clay Papers. On the experiences of female-run southern families during the Civil War era, see Faust, *Mothers of Invention*, 129–34; Stephen V. Ash, *When the Yankees Came: Conflict and Chaos in the Occupied South, 1861–65* (Chapel Hill: University of North Carolina Press, 1995).

58. MJC to BC, July 21, 1864, Clay Family Papers.

59. CMC to MJC, October 9, 1863, Cassius M. Clay Papers. He closed this patronizing letter by stating, "With these hints, and some invention, a great many pretty, and cheap ornaments may be made."

60. CMC to MJC, December 26, 1863, Cassius M. Clay Papers. Despite his interest in his children's upbringing, Cassius Clay remained in Russia during daughter Mary's 1866 wedding in Kentucky to John Francis Herrick. In a letter written to his wife on October 2, 1866, Clay expressed delight over their daughter's nuptials before moving quickly on to a description of Princess Dagmar of Denmark's visit to Moscow. Clay also missed his daughter Sallie's wedding on June 3, 1869. CMC to MJC, October 2, 1866, Cassius M. Clay Papers; Fuller, *Laura Clay*, 13.

61. Fuller, *Laura Clay*, 9. As Fuller notes, all three Clay daughters married late by the standards of their time: Mary and Annie at age twenty-seven and Sallie at twenty-eight. On the social pressures placed on nineteenth-century southern women to marry early, see Jabour, *Scarlett's Sisters*, 90.

62. Fuller, *Laura Clay and the Woman's Rights Movement*, 3; Ellison, *A Man Seen but Once*, 141.

63. Richardson, *Cassius Marcellus Clay*, 114–15; Ellison, *A Man Seen but Once*, 142.

64. Clay expressed his indignation over Mary Jane's refusal to believe his innocence; see CMC, *Life of Cassius Marcellus Clay*, 540. He described the scandal in detail on 463–78. See also Smiley, *Lion of White Hall*, 205–8; Ellison, *A Man Seen but Once*, 144–45; Keven McQueen, *Cassius M. Clay: Freedom's Champion* (Paducah, Ky.: Turner Publishing Company, 2001).

65. McQueen, *Cassius M. Clay*, 28; Fuller, *Laura Clay*, 14–15.

66. CMC, *Life of Cassius Marcellus Clay*, 547.

67. Ibid., 540. Clay noted that his son Green was the only one of his children with whom he retained close ties. He suggested that Mary Jane later punished Green for his continued loyalty to his father by selling the land on which Green and his wife lived, thus dismissing her son from her home. According to Cassius, this act had a detrimental effect on Green's nervous system, and as a result, "the remainder of his life was but a slow descent into the unknown forever." Ibid., 544. As is the case with so many other elements of the marriage, Mary Jane's side of this story is unavailable.

68. Ibid., 547.

69. Ibid., 547–48.

70. As Loren Schweninger explains, under the laws of coverture, a married woman "was subordinate to her husband in her person and property" in southern states throughout the antebellum and Civil War eras. He writes, "As a result of this absorption of the legal entity of a wife into that of her husband, wives could not, until the late antebellum era, except in Louisiana or where protected under marital agreements, use state laws to claim as their separate property either what they possessed before their marriages or what they had received afterward through bequests or gifts." *Families in Crisis in the Old South*, 82. On laws of coverture, see also Amy Dru Stanley, *From Bondage to Contract: Wage Labor, Marriage, and the Market in the Age of Slave Emancipation* (Cambridge, UK: Cambridge University Press, 1998); Nancy Cott, *Public Vows: A History of Marriage and the Nation* (Cambridge, Mass.: Harvard University Press, 2000); Peter W. Bardaglio, *Reconstructing the Household: Families, Sex, and the Law in the Nineteenth-Century South* (Chapel Hill: University of North Carolina Press, 1995), 31–32; Norma Basch, *In the Eyes of the Law: Women, Marriage, and Property in Nineteenth-Century New York* (Ithaca, N.Y.: Cornell University Press, 1982); Marylynn Salmon, *Women and the Law of Property in Early America* (Chapel Hill: University of North Carolina Press, 1986); Hartog, *Man and Wife in America*.

71. Fuller, *Laura Clay*, 15.

72. Richardson, *Cassius Marcellus Clay*, 117–18.

73. Ibid., 117–18; Ellison, *A Man Seen but Once*, 147.

74. CMC, *Life of Cassius Marcellus Clay*, 541, 549.

75. Case Files, 1803–1914, Court of Justice Fayette County Circuit Court, Kentucky Department for Libraries and Archives, Frankfort; Fuller, *Laura Clay*, 15. For Kentucky's divorce laws at this time, see Carroll D. Wright, *A Report on Marriage and Divorce in the United States, 1867–1886* (Washington: Government Printing Office, 1889), 96–97.

76. CMC, *Life of Cassius Marcellus Clay*, 548; Fuller, *Laura Clay*, 16–17. On the financial struggles that divorced southern women faced, see Schweninger, *Families in Crisis*, 80–97.

77. Fuller, *Laura Clay*, 16. On the complexities of gender and child custody in nineteenth-century America, see Michael Grossberg, *Governing the Hearth: Law and the Family in Nineteenth-Century America* (Chapel Hill: University of North Carolina Press, 1985), 234–85; Bardaglio, *Reconstructing the Household*; Riley, *Divorce*; Hartog, *Man and Wife in America*; Clinton, *The Plantation Mistress*, 84–85.

78. Fuller, *Laura Clay*, 16–17.

79. CMC, *Life of Cassius Marcellus Clay*, 540–41.

80. "Petition to the President, Senate and House of Representatives," January 18, 1899, Cassius M. Clay Papers. This petition claimed that Richardson had been a "loving, pure and loyal wife," who had been "broken in body and mind by the 'Vendetta' waging war against them." One assumes that this petition refers to the same "vendetta" that Clay referenced in an 1898 letter to Colyer Meriwether, in which Clay stated, "My eyes are weak from the criminal 'vendetta' waged against me by my divorced wife Mary Jane Warfield Clay." Clay to Colyer Meriwether, July 8, 1898, Manuscripts and Folklore Archives, Western Kentucky University, Bowling Green. See also Richardson, *Cassius Marcellus Clay*, 126–36, on Clay's short-lived second marriage.

81. MBC, "Kentucky," in Elizabeth Cady Stanton, Susan B. Anthony, and Matilda Joslyn Gage, eds., *History of Woman Suffrage*, 3 vols. (Rochester, N.Y.: Charles Mann, 1886), 3:820.

82. For major works on the social, political, and intellectual origins of the women's rights movement, see Eleanor Flexner, *Century of Struggle: The Woman's Rights Movement in the United States* (Cambridge, Mass.: Belknap Press of Harvard University Press, 1959); Sylvia D. Hoffert, *When Hens*

Crow: The Woman's Rights Movement in Antebellum America (Bloomington: Indiana University Press, 1995); Lori D. Ginzberg, *Untidy Origins: A Story of Woman's Rights in Antebellum New York* (Chapel Hill: University of North Carolina Press, 2005).

83. Fuller, *Laura Clay*, 23. Meanwhile, Cassius Clay spoke out publicly against woman suffrage in a June 28, 1887, speech at Yale University. Misc. Mss. Collection, FHS, Louisville, Kentucky. Other major works on woman suffrage activism include Aileen Kraditor, *The Ideas of the Woman Suffrage Movement: 1890–1920* (New York: Columbia University Press, 1965); Ellen Carol Dubois, *Feminism and Suffrage: The Emergence of an Independent Women's Movement in America, 1848–1869* (Ithaca, N.Y.: Cornell University Press, 1978); Marjorie Spruill Wheeler, *New Women of the New South: The Leaders of the Woman Suffrage Movement in the Southern States* (New York: Oxford University Press, 1993); Elna C. Green, *Southern Strategies: Southern Women and the Woman Suffrage Question* (Chapel Hill: University of North Carolina Press, 1997); Sally G. McMillen, *Seneca Falls and the Origins of the Women's Rights Movement* (New York: Oxford University Press, 2008).

84. Riley, *Divorce*, 71–74; Elizabeth B. Clark, "Matrimonial Bonds: Slavery and Divorce in Nineteenth-Century America," *Law and History Review* 18 (1990): 25–54.

85. Wright, *Report on Marriage and Divorce*, 96–97.

86. Fuller, *Laura Clay*, 38–39. For additional work on efforts to secure married women's access to earnings and property, see Suzanne Lebsock, "Radical Reconstruction and the Property Rights of Southern Women," *Journal of Southern History* 43 (1977): 195–216; Basch, *In the Eyes of the Law*; Faust, *Mothers of Invention*, 251–52; Cott, *Public Vows*, 52–55. On the limitations of married women's property acts, see Sara L. Zeigler, "Wifely Duties: Marriage, Labor, and the Common Law in Nineteenth-Century America," *Social Science History* 20 (1996): 63–96.

87. Fuller, *Laura Clay*, 38–50. For a summary of Sallie, Annie, Laura, and Mary Barr Clay's additional contributions to the women's rights movement, see Lynn E. Niedermeier, *Eliza Calvert Hall: Kentucky Author and Suffragist* (Lexington: University Press of Kentucky, 2007), 54–55.

88. Susan B. Anthony to MBC, April 21, 1900, Cassius M. Clay Papers.

Emilie Todd Helm and Mary Todd Lincoln

(1836–1930; 1818–1882)

"We Weep Over Our Dead Together"

ANGELA ESCO ELDER

A lifeless slip of paper delivered the news. "Atlanta, Ga.," the telegram read. "Mrs. General Helm is in Griffin. Find her and send her up in train today. The General is dead." After receiving the message, Emilie Todd Helm, wife of Confederate brigadier Benjamin Hardin Helm, felt so heartbroken that, she recalled, the "days and weeks after I scarcely remember at all." She was a twenty-six-year-old mother of three children under age six. She had been married just seven years, and now she was a Confederate widow. Eighteen months later, lingering wartime hostilities also made a widow of Emilie's older sister, Mary Todd Lincoln. Mary's husband famously died in 1865, when an actor slipped behind him, raised a gun, and pulled the trigger. In the crowded backroom of a boardinghouse, Mary's heart broke before a hushed assembly as she wailed for her husband to "take her with him."[1]

The Civil War wrecked many American families but made particularly harsh work of the Todds. Of the fourteen children, eight sided with the Confederacy and six with the Union. Two Todd boys were killed, and the rest were left with deep emotional wounds. Two Todd sisters, Emilie and Mary, had to mourn dead husbands *and* dead brothers. In their respective sections, Emilie and Mary were war widows and public figures, having survived the bloodshed to walk as human embodiments of sacrifice. Everyone in the nation had to pick up the pieces and march on, but as famous widows, Emilie and Mary had to don their dark uniforms and perform their roles on a public stage.[2]

EMILIE TODD HELM

From the Lincoln Financial Foundation Collection, courtesy of the Indiana State Museum and Historic Sites.

MARY TODD LINCOLN

1861. Library of Congress.

The Todd sisters were but two of two hundred thousand white women widowed by the war. Mary, somewhat infamously, became a diva of grief, inconsolable and insufferable. This essay focuses primarily on her sister Emilie's very different "career" as a Confederate widow. While her quick tongue, famous family, and stint as a visitor in the Civil War White House make her a fascinating figure, Emilie's experience as a young widow in a war-torn Confederacy is a broadly typical example of a Confederate widow who performed her part perfectly. "Mother" to her husband's "Orphan" Brigade, organizer for the United Daughters of the Confederacy, author of unpublished Lost Cause fiction, unswerving puffer of her husband's memory, Emilie achieved a kind of professional fame as a widow—and through her we can more clearly see the society that created her role, built her stage, and applauded her performances. Ultimately, it was Emilie, not Mary, who became exactly what her society demanded she be. Seven years married, she would be for almost seventy years the public widow of Benjamin Hardin Helm. Suffering like hers would be rewarded, not merely by her region but, ironically, by her nation, who found room not only to pity and thank her for her sacrifice but also to erect on the foundation of such southern suffering a narrative of *national* reconciliation.[3]

By the early 1830s a grand brick home on Main Street in Lexington, Kentucky, swarmed with Todd babies, toddlers, and teens. Emilie was the eleventh of fourteen children born into the family, and her birth on November 11, 1836, brought the number of children living within the Todd home to nine. The fourteen-room house was more hive than home, buzzing with the comings and goings of siblings, guests, and slaves. Quick tongues, fiery tempers, and rowdy antics burst forth daily, and in a sea of children attempting to distinguish themselves, Emilie always had her beauty. "I think you were too young to remember it," Elizabeth Norris wrote, describing the time when Emilie and her good looks "turned the City of Lexington upside down." While out with her enslaved nurse, a young Emilie strayed into the street and disappeared. "The day dragged slowly with untold agony" for Emilie's mother, while Emilie's father, the police, and Lexington's men made every effort to find her. Late in the afternoon, Emilie's father discovered her in the house of a childless couple. "The man and his wife were considered good people," Norris explained to Emilie, "but your uncommon beauty overcame his sense of right."[4]

One week before Emilie's seventh birthday, her older sister married Abraham Lincoln. Mary, a self-described "ruddy pine knot," was not as pretty as Emilie, but then her betrothed was no looker, either. Abraham's gangly frame and misshapen face were the subject of common comment; even Mary's sister Frances called him "the plainest man" in Springfield, Illinois. The couple had met in the

Springfield home of eldest sister Elizabeth, and over the course of two years they courted, got engaged, got disengaged, courted, and got engaged again. On November 4, 1842, just hours after their most recent decision to wed, they took their vows in Elizabeth's parlor. In the rush of events, the cake turned out poorly and rain beat loudly against the windows throughout the ceremony, but in spite of it all, Abraham slipped onto Mary's finger a ring engraved with the words "Love is Eternal." Together, they made a home in Springfield and immersed themselves in Abe's political career.[5]

When discussing their marriage, Mary acknowledged their "opposite natures." Mary had a feisty personality, a penetrating yell, and an ungovernable temper. Abraham had his uncouth appearance and underdeveloped manners. She could be physically and emotionally abusive, he emotionally absent. And yet Mary and Abraham, for all their individual faults, complemented each other in ways few others could. She smoothed out his country appearance and polished his manners. He tolerated her wild moods and unstable emotions. For better or worse, they grew together as a pair. As Abe joked, "My friends, this is the long of it," he said, pointing to himself. Then, with a hand on Mary's head, he would add, "And this is the short of it."[6]

In 1846, four years into the Lincoln marriage, the Prairie State's voters elected Abraham to the U.S. House of Representatives. Mary and Abraham packed their belongings and their two young sons and began the lengthy trek to the nation's capital. Along the way, they planned a visit to the Todd home in Lexington. It was a cold November day when they arrived at the brick house, a home Mary had not seen in seven years. For Abe, both the house and the people within it were new. He had met Mary's father but none of his other Todd relatives. Then again, Mary had yet to meet her two youngest sisters as well. When she left home, Emilie was the second youngest of the family, just three years old. Now Emilie was ten and caught up in the excitement of the preparations for the Lincolns' arrival.

Crowded in the wide hall with the rest of her family, Emilie watched as the door burst open and Mary glided in, carrying her youngest son Eddie. "To my mind she was lovely," Emilie recalled. With "clear, sparkling, blue eyes, lovely smooth white skin with a fresh, faint wild-rose color in her cheeks; and glossy light brown hair, which fell in soft, short curls behind each ear," Mary seemed nearly angelic. Despite being awestruck by her older sister, Emilie had quite a different opinion of her new brother-in-law. "I remember thinking," Emilie said, "of Jack and the Beanstalk, and feared he might be the hungry giant of the story, he was so tall and looked so big." With a full black cloak and a fur cap with ear straps, little of his face could be seen. "Expecting to hear the 'Fee, fi, fo, fum!'

I shrank closer to my mother and tried to hide behind her voluminous skirts," she explained. Abe, after shaking hands with the adults in the hall, retrieved Emilie from her hiding place, lifted her high into his arms, and exclaimed, "So this is little sister." His voice and smile banished her fear of the gentle giant. "I was always after that called by him 'little sister,'" Emilie remembered. Emilie never knew Mary without Abraham, and of all Mary's many sisters, Abe was especially fond of Emilie.[7]

Over the following decade, Emilie would blossom into adulthood and marry. Once a beautiful child, Emilie grew into "one of the handsomest and loveliest women in the world," with dark hair, petite frame, and "happy smile." Her marital choice, Benjamin Hardin Helm, was a dashing young West Point graduate and rising lawyer-politician. Six feet tall, with brown hair, clear blue eyes, and "an expression of countenance that no single term can describe," he was handsome. As important, his family was wealthy and well connected. Benjamin's grandfather had been a U.S. senator and his father Kentucky's governor. Benjamin was the firstborn child, and at age twenty-five, he fell completely in love with nineteen-year-old Emilie, describing her as "absolutely essential to my very being" eighteen months into their relationship. While few details of their courtship are known, Benjamin would later comment on the profound mystery of falling in love with her. "What a wonderful change we undergo in this world," he mused to his young wife. "One year we will have nothing particularly to care for or live for—when the next will find us united in the dearest and holiest ties, of which the heart is capable of enjoying—and life is dear for the sake of the lovely being who has linked her fate with yours."[8]

On March 26, 1856, six months after their first meeting, the couple married in Frankfort, Kentucky. Almost immediately, Benjamin returned to shaking hands and giving speeches across the commonwealth, serving as the district attorney for three counties and stumping for politician Millard Fillmore. "A lawyer's business is no child's play if he attends to it properly," he had advised his younger sister years earlier, informing her that a lawyer's "leisure time should be devoted to his profession." But now, not even three months married, he found the work more trying, writing to Emilie, "I cant keep your image out of my mind, all the time, nearly." He wrote his letters with her daguerreotype before him, feeling simply "foolish" about his young bride. Benjamin desired to alter the laws of physics for their love, hoping "time will pass off rapidly, untill we meet and then it may linger." When he traveled, Emilie returned to live with her mother in Lexington. Benjamin loved the "excitement of speaking and the active exercise" of his career, but complete satisfaction eluded him while apart from Emilie. "If I could only see your happy face at the end of each day I would be perfectly contented. . . . I never wanted to see any body half so bad in my life as I do you," he sighed. Wishfully dreaming, Benjamin promised, "I shall fly on the wings of love to see you."[9]

Emilie's society not only brought him happiness, Benjamin believed, but also aided his career. "My love for you, dear wife will cause me to be a man of fame if by energy and industry I can ever reach it; it is true that the hill is a high and rugged one to climb, and I may often feel like fainting by the way side," he wrote, "yet when I have your love to cheer me on, and your smiles to reward my exertions, [I feel] redoubled energy and rigor." Her love sustained him, encouraged him, and filled him with hope. "Love in married life is as essential to happiness as the congenial rays of the sun," he believed. "Without love in a man's life he would be enshrouded in utter darkness and misery and selfishness." In his mind, love and ambition intertwined, for "the love of so pure a wife is enough to urge me on to fame and fortune." Benjamin, consumed with feelings of affection, thought Emilie could not possibly love him as he loved her. "I think I can hear you say 'Ah! Man cant love like a woman,'" he wrote, "but you know not the heart of old Kentucky's son."[10]

Five years later, the Civil War intruded on Emilie's marriage. Before joining the Confederacy, Benjamin visited the White House and received an offer from Abraham for a high-ranking position within the U.S. Army. It was all Benjamin had ever wanted. "I never had such a struggle," he told a friend, "and it almost killed me to decline." The Todd family was tearing in two. Benjamin publicly aligned himself with the Confederacy and by October 1861 wrote Emilie that he was "getting up my regiment very rapidly and think I will soon be in the field again." Despite his success with his regiment, he worried about the future. "This separation I sincerely hope will not continue long," he assured Emilie, but "I have gone in for the war and if God spares my life I expect to battle to the end of it."[11]

Separation was not something they did well, as Emilie and Benjamin had discovered in their newlywed years. "I wish I was able to live at home all the time or to carry you around with me," Benjamin wrote typically. During the war years, they chose the latter option. As often as possible, Emilie followed Benjamin to his various posts; whenever they did separate, Benjamin fretted constantly. "I have not recd a letter from you for some time. I hope the yankees have not frightened you so that you have lost the power of writing," he half-jokingly teased in 1863. In addition to being an affectionate husband, Benjamin was a doting father who constantly asked about his children and requested that Emilie "kiss the dear little children for me and tell them Papa is very anxious to see them." Of his first daughter, he believed her to be "the prettiest baby that was ever born." When Emilie and the children were close by, Benjamin would visit as often as his position allowed. The traveling contained potential dangers for Emilie, which she described in her wartime diary. After checking into a hotel in Atlanta, she requested the clerk search her rooms before she was willing to stay in it. She described herself as "not a timid woman" and carried a gun, but she would rather be safe than sorry. Emilie claimed that under one bed, the clerk "drew out by his boots a negro—he pretended to be asleep and was kicked unceremoniously down stairs." After putting her children to bed, Emilie could not sleep. Thinking about "the peril I had escaped," Emilie read by candlelight until her "beloved H" arrived "in a new uniform looking so fresh." His handsome appearance caused her to forget her fright as she enjoyed the "delight to feast my eyes on him" before drawing him into the adjoining room to gaze lovingly on his sleeping children.[12]

On September 20, 1863, Emilie's husband found himself in a "perfect tornado of bullets" at the Battle of Chickamauga. Amid the cutting storm of minié balls, dirt, and powder was one small lead mass that punctured his liver, ending his life before sunset and shattering Emilie's forever. A young captain from Kentucky received news of the Confederate victory and celebrated in his diary with, "It is glorious news. It makes a fellow feel taller, stouter, fatter, better, lighter, heartier, saucier, braver, kinder, richer, and everything good & great. Hurra for hurra!!" He then turned to what the victory meant: "Gen Helm of Ky is killed. So the wail comes up with the shout of victory."[13]

As the news spread throughout the South, a steady stream of condolence letters came to Emilie, revealing the hopes and expectations placed on widows. Letters encouraged Emilie to devote herself to religion, to receive physical assistance, to accept empathy graciously, and to understand that her loss was not her own. An ideal widow did these things. Family and friends prayed for Emilie to turn to God, believing that "every tendril of your anguished heart that reached unto Him, will be greatly bound and healed." Writers also urged her to turn to them, assuring that "any thing or all I have would I most cheerfully yield for the relief of yourself or Hardin's children." All writers sympathized with Emilie, but several also emphasized that her loss was Kentucky's loss. "A great nation will bear on you its struggling heart," wrote one, "and millions of hearts will vibrate with your sorrow. Your loss has been theirs." Though her husband had died, as the wife of a Confederate officer Emilie's loss could not simply be her own. These letters cast Emilie in the role of a widow, and in them she found her script. In the coming decades Emilie would prove to be "as good a wife as any man on earth could desire," both "pure and lovely," even without her husband present.[14]

Before this work could begin, Emilie sought a return to her old Kentucky home. After Emilie boarded a boat to Baltimore, Union officials informed her that she would have to take an oath of allegiance to the United States before proceeding. Emilie refused. Her husband had just sacrificed his life in opposition to the United States, so how could she promise to uphold it? As her daughter would later explain, "It was treason to her dead husband [and] to her beloved Southland." Unable to persuade her, the Union officers telegraphed the White House for instructions. Abraham Lincoln, her brother-in-law, supposedly responded with one line: "Send her to me."[15]

When Emilie approached the White House in 1863, she was "a pathetic little figure in her trailing black crepe." Her trials transformed the once-beautiful and joyous woman into a "sad-faced girl with pallid cheeks, tragic eyes, and tight, unsmiling lips." Reunited with Abe and Mary, Emilie wrote, "We were all too grief-stricken at first for speech. . . . We could only embrace each other in silence and tears." Certainly, the war had not been easy on the Lincolns, either. The Todd sisters had lost two brothers, Mary had lost a son, and Emilie's loss of Benjamin gave them much to grieve over together. Emilie and Mary found comfort in each other's company, but their political differences divided them. "Sister and I cannot open our hearts to each other as freely as we would like," Emilie wrote. "This frightful war comes between us like a barrier of granite closing our lips." Not everyone who encountered Emilie would do so with a tongue thus tied. She was, after all, a widow of the enemy. "Well, we whipped the rebels at Chattanooga and I hear, madam, that the scoundrels ran like scared rabbits," jabbed Senator Ira Harris of New York when he visited the White House. Answering "with a choking throat," Emilie retorted, "It was an example, Senator Harris, that you set them at Bull Run and Manassas." After a failed attempt to get a rise from Mary, Harris returned to prodding Emilie and informed her, "If I had twenty sons they should all be fighting the rebels." Forgetting where she was but not her Confederate loyalties, Emilie replied, "And if I had twenty sons, Senator Harris, they should all be opposing yours." When the incident was relayed to Abe, he chuckled that "the child has a tongue like the rest of the Todds." "You should not have a rebel in your house," shouted General Daniel Sickles, who had accompanied Harris and overheard the conversation. Drawing himself to his full height, Abraham replied in a quiet voice, "Excuse me, General Sickles, my wife and I are in the habit of choosing our own guests. We do not need from our friends either advice or assistance in the matter." Longing for home and believing "my being here is more or less an embarrassment," Emilie decided it was time to complete her journey to Kentucky. "You know Little Sister I tried to have Ben come with me," Abraham reminded Emilie before she left. Emilie answered that her husband had followed "his conscience and that for weal or woe he felt he must side with his own people." After embracing Mary and Abe, Emilie returned to Lexington to live with her mother, enjoy her "sweet little brood" of children, and grieve.[16]

Approximately a year and a half later, Abraham Lincoln's death sent Mary into a mental spiral that ended only with her own death seventeen years later. In the days immediately following Abraham's murder, Mary filled the White House with "the wails of a broken heart, the unearthly shrieks, the terrible convulsions." She stayed in bed, refused visitors, and seemed "more dead than alive—broken by the horrors of that dreadful night as well as worn down by bodily sickness." The loss of Abe was one from which she would never recover. Mary did not mourn with grace as Emilie did but instead dissolved into a puddle of self-pity. Overtaxed and mentally unstable, she felt unable to do anything else. To make matters worse, Mary broadcast her self-pity publicly and demanded sympathy from the world. In the months and years to come, her overwhelming grief, shopping sprees, and constant need for attention would suffocate those around her. Her older sister Elizabeth described Mary best, explaining that she "had much to bear though she don't bear it well; She has acted foolishly—unwisely and made the world hate her." And hate her they did, without sympathy for her loss or her grief, for she was unable to bear her loss as a widow should.[17]

Meanwhile, her sister Emilie succeeded in playing the part perfectly. She may have lost her husband, but Emilie had a new role, and new opportunities, to enjoy in the latter part of the nineteenth century. And enjoy them she did. Unlike Mary, as a widow Emilie did not retreat to the gloomy confines of her mind or home; she remained active in her community and state. She joined bustling crowds in 1883 for the gubernatorial inauguration, continuously crisscrossed Kentucky visiting friends and family, joined the Filson Club, and served as a postmistress in Elizabethtown for twelve years. Her movements appeared in newspapers across the nation. In July 1895 Emilie unsuccessfully politicked for state librarian, but if newspapers were any measure of public opinion, the public adored her still. "Mrs. Emily Todd Helm, the late postmaster of Elizabethtown and widow of the gallant leader of the Orphan Brigade," reported a paper in Stanford, Kentucky, "is the latest entry and we will wager dollars to doughnuts that in the final count the excellent and deserving lady will be there or thereabouts."[18]

Though many in the public loved Emilie, Benjamin's Orphan Brigade nearly worshiped her. During the war, she had cared for, camped with, loved, and verbally defended the men. In 1863, her husband not yet two months dead, she wrote a letter to commander John C. Breckinridge after some Kentuckians felt "hurt" by Breckinridge's reported remark that their brigade "was one of the worst and but a band of thieves and robbers," prompting him to assure her that "I never uttered such language." After the war, soldier George W. Quarles, who hoped to become the deputy warden of his county, asked for Emilie's "aid and influence." "I don't want the parties to know I solicited your support," he explained, so "write as though unsolicited and having known me through your husband." In addition to recommendations, Emilie also sent pictures of her husband to those who requested them, such as Frank Lyon, who promised, "I shall treasure it very highly." In 1868 Edwin Porter Thompson approached Emilie to gather information about her husband for his history of the Orphan Brigade, vowing that "when I get a copy of the General's biography, I will take time to transcribe and send you a copy for examination and approval, or suggestions." Additionally, the Elizabethtown Volunteers company changed its name to the Helm Guards, not in memory of her husband but "in honor of Mrs. E. T. Helm, the widow of the late General Hardin Helm."[19]

Veterans formally invited Emilie to reunions of the Orphan Brigade, which began in 1882. While her status as the widow of their general earned her a place on the invitation list, her relationship with the brigade caused men to genuinely desire her attendance, for she was "especially invited." In 1884 the reunion committee not only consulted Emilie about their plans to move Benjamin's remains but also forwarded the program to her "for approval or amendment." J. D. Pickett, the chaplain Emilie requested to give the eulogy, also wrote to Emilie for advice, desiring that she write "frankly and fully" because he wanted the eulogy "to be precisely what will gratify you." At a later reunion, Emilie "announced her desire to shake hands with every member of the command," and the veterans, in turn, voted to bestow on her the title "Mother of the Brigade." In the 1920 reunion outside of Paris, Kentucky, Emilie's own portrait "appeared on the badges of red, white and blue, worn by the veterans of the Brigade," and "beautiful tributes were paid to her." As a part of their yearly ritual, Emilie symbolized all they hoped a wife and woman could be. Never remarrying and faithful to her husband decades after his death, her actions implied that a Confederate soldier was irreplaceable.[20]

Emilie also served within Kentucky's United Daughters of the Confederacy (UDC). "We meet in session," she insisted, "not for the purpose of keeping alive the prejudices, acrimonious feeling and hatred of the past" but rather to "cherish the memory of our dead heroes, to devise ways and means to make their graves, to re-entomb as many of them as possible in their native state," and to "prevent a fake record of our heroes['] deeds being brought down as History." Emilie called for a "history equally fitted for use North and South, divested of all passion and prejudice," for Kentucky's schools. Northerners might not approve of her version of the "plain unvarnished truth," however. Emilie believed and repeatedly wrote that "the men of the South fought for a just cause and that in an unequal struggle they were the bravest of the brave." Histories that spoke of southern men as "rebels" or a "rebellion" did not please Emilie. Kentucky's UDC grew rapidly and gained thousands of white, middle- and upper-class members across the South, encouraging Emilie in what she believed to be a "sacred duty."[21]

To create her version of history, Emilie also urged members to gather up letters and preserve "all [the] war relics" of Confederate soldiers. She hoped "to perpetuate the glorious memories of the most unselfish devotion to home and country." Additionally, she called for women to conduct interviews with soldiers. Women should be "gathering details now from survivors," she wrote, for they were the "noblest and bravest people that ever suffered and died for a principle." Emilie believed that women should be included in this version of American history. "God bless the Confederate women of our dear Southland—They are the pride and the glory of our country and this Kentucky division to all Kentuckians," she insisted. For her work within the UDC, a chapter was named after her beloved husband. When the organization met in 1901 to decorate graves, "a life sized portrait of Gen. Ben Hardin Helm occupied a conspicuous place." Emilie thus continued to shape the memory of her husband, bringing recognition and honor to him decades after his death.[22]

The longer Emilie lived, the more organizations clamored for her attendance and participation. The Chickamauga Park Commissioners, the *Confederate Veteran* magazine, and the UDC historian all sought her. In addition to the yearly Kentucky reunions of the Orphan Brigade, Emilie was invited to reunions across the South. In 1898 the Louisiana division of the United Confederate Veterans encouraged her to attend their ceremonies and promised her "a seat upon the platform" and the opportunity to "make any remarks you may see fit." Despite the many invitations, Emilie remained closest with her husband's command. Forty years after her husband's death, she still served as a living representation of their general. A letter from her, even in the twentieth century, was "like a message of approval from Gen Ben Hardin Helm."[23]

Emilie also devoted time to penning fictional and nonfictional accounts of the war and postwar era. While she would never become a published author, Emilie wrote on a variety of topics, including several stories featuring a white woman's interaction with African Americans in the postwar South. In one, a former enslaved woman assured her widowed master that she would never leave her. "Now Old Miss," said Chloe, the formerly enslaved character in Emilie's tale, "Whar is [it] I got to go—I am gwine to stay right whear I is—my white chillen expects me to stay and tak car of you. . . . I aint gwine to leave you." This happy slave narrative conformed to the Lost Cause themes developing throughout the South and hints at the darker side of the reunification project, one that does not include equality for African Americans.[24]

While compiling a genealogy of the Todd family, Emilie wrote hundreds of letters to relatives and strangers across the nation to gather information. "You must not be discouraged in your undertaking," replied one relative. "It is not characteristic of the Todds, to give up any thing fairly began." As Emilie became increasingly consumed with her project, her older sister Elizabeth teased, "Do not exhaust yourself in your researches, it will be impossible to trace beyond Adam and Eve." In documenting the honorable deeds of her ancestors, Emilie perhaps believed she could repair the present reputation of the shattered Todd family. After all, of the fourteen Todd siblings, Emilie stood alone in 1920. In fact, Emilie had been the only Todd alive for nearly sixteen years, surviving her three younger siblings by more than forty years, a lonely fact not lost on the public. "Mrs. Helm is the only member of her family living to-day," wrote the *Adair County News* when announcing Emilie's visit to the county in February 1905.[25]

As a living relic of the Todds, Emilie both represented them and shaped how they would be remembered. Better yet, Emilie's wild siblings could not undermine or challenge her efforts from their graves. She worked tirelessly to salvage the image of her sister Mary, who passed away in 1882. In 1898 the *Saint Paul [Minnesota] Globe* reported that Emilie denied that there had ever been two marriage ceremonies arranged for Mary and Abraham and rejected "the existence of that inharmony to which so many allusions have been made." The paper concluded, "It would be better for the world to accept these statements, bury rank gossip in the dark pit in which it belongs and henceforth regard Mrs. Lincoln only as the honorable and honored helpmeet of the greatest American of the century." Of course, as Emilie knew, Abraham and Mary had two engagements (but the first ended prior to the choosing of a wedding date) and marital discord, but this was not the image of the Todds or the Lincolns that Emilie wanted remembered.[26]

While Emilie strove to shape the memory of the Todds, another project was taking place. In 1909, "while ten thousand people stood in reverence with bared heads . . . a veiling of the stars and stripes fell gracefully away" to reveal a statue of Abraham Lincoln in Hodgenville, Kentucky. One paper reported "the canopy that hid the statue from view was drawn away by the hand of Mrs. Ben Hardin Helm, a sister to the wife of Lincoln, and cheer after cheer went up." "Your Minnie bullets have made us what we are," Emilie had written bitterly to Abraham in the final years of the war. Now she honored him before a crowd of ten thousand Americans, as a widow of the war and nation, not simply the South. Instead of rehashing the political divisions of the Todd family, reporters instead emphasized their familial ties. It was as Emilie had written: "We should revive no memories that may embitter the future." To the nation, the reunification of the Todd family represented the reunification of white America, and Emilie's suffering had redeemed them all. Union widows had lost a husband but won a war; Confederate widows had lost it all. If a Confederate woman could honor the man responsible for the deaths of her husband and two brothers, could not the nation also become one again?[27]

As a war widow, Emilie had lost a husband but gained a powerful role in her society. The Civil War existed as a transformative force in many women's lives, but this was especially true for widows. Both during and after the Civil War, Emilie had a specific role to play—bound not merely to patriarchy but to nationalism—first to Confederate nationalism and then to national reconciliation. Through Emilie, we see how the emotional, human experience of losing a husband could be channeled, contained, and reinvested. Through her loss she earned social capital, which she spent wisely, shaping the terms of reunification. Instead of an embarrassment, the Todd family became a sacrifice; instead of traitors, they became national heroes. Emilie herself became southern pride and American patriotism personified in one little widow. She served as the unelected spokesperson of the Todds and a symbol of reunification, and as the years marched on, Emilie increasingly became a living monument to the official American past. In short, she succeeded in doing what the Confederacy failed to do: she survived and shaped the nation, until her heart finally stopped on February 20, 1930, sixty-six years and five months after her husband's. "We ought not to grieve over anyone who has to live until they are feeble and unable to enjoy life," wrote Emilie, adding, "I hope every one will feel this if I live to be old." After devoting a lifetime to the cultural politics of mourning, Emilie did not want anyone to grieve over her.[28]

NOTES

1. I refer to historical figures in this essay by last names, unless their spouses also appear in the narrative. In those cases, notably Benjamin/Emilie Helm and Abraham/Mary Lincoln, I use their first names for clarity's sake. This essay keeps all spelling and phrasing quoted from documents in original form, except for occasions when punctuation has been converted to modern-day notations for clarity. Readers may also notice that within some quotations Emilie's name was spelled differently; I refer to her as Emilie for consistency. Despite her lengthy career as a Confederate widow, little has been published about Emilie Helm. Only one biography, just fifty-two pages long, has been published in the eighty years since her death: Dorothy Darnell Jones's *Emilie Pariet Todd Helm: Abraham Lincoln's "Little Sister"* (Lexington, Ind.: Deer Trail, 2007). Other studies on the

Lincolns and the Todds, such as Stephen Berry's *House of Abraham: Lincoln and the Todds, a Family Divided by War* (Boston: Houghton Mifflin, 2007), and Jerrold M. Packard's *The Lincolns in the White House: Four Years That Shattered a Family* (New York: St. Martin's, 2005), include valuable discussions on Emilie and her relationships with Abraham and Mary. Her widowhood has not been analyzed. Elizabeth Dixon, quoted in Catherine Clinton, *Mrs. Lincoln: A Life* (New York: HarperCollins, 2009), 245; Emilie Todd, undated Civil War reminiscence, Emilie Todd Helm Collection, Kentucky Historical Society (KHS), Frankfort. Unless otherwise indicated, all primary source materials noted in this essay, including correspondence, diaries, and newspaper clippings, are contained in the KHS collection.

2. The loyalties of some of the Todds shifted throughout the war, the Copperheadism (if not treason) of Margaret Todd and her husband, Charles Henry Kellogg, being a key example. See Berry, *House of Abraham*. The topic of Civil War pensions is the only aspect of Civil War widowhood that historians have explored in detail. For excellent articles on Civil War widows, the pension system, and financial support, consult one of the following: Jennifer Lynn Gross, "'Good Angels': Confederate Widowhood in Virginia," in *Southern Families at War: Loyalty and Conflict in the Civil War South*, ed. Catherine Clinton (New York: Oxford University Press, 2000); Jennifer Lynn Gross, "'And for the Widow and Orphan': Confederate Widows, Poverty, and Public Assistance," in *Inside the Confederate Nation: Essays in Honor of Emory M. Thomas*, ed. Lesley J. Gordon and John C. Inscoe (Baton Rouge: Louisiana State University Press, 2005); Jennifer L. Gross, "The United Daughters of the Confederacy, Confederate Widows, and the Lost Cause: 'We Must Not Forget or Neglect the Widows,'" in *Women on Their Own: Interdisciplinary Perspectives on Being Single*, ed. Rudolph M. Bell and Virginia Yans (New Brunswick, N.J.: Rutgers University Press, 2008), 180–94; Robert Kenzer, "The Uncertainty of Life: A Profile of Virginia's Civil War Widows," in *The War Was You and Me: Civilians in the American Civil War*, ed. Joan E. Cashin (Princeton, N.J.: Princeton University Press, 2002).

3. The number of women widowed by the Civil War is difficult to determine. J. David Hacker provides the most recent number, suggesting that approximately 750,000 men lost their lives in the Civil War, and that if 28 percent of the men who died in the war were married at the time of their death, the resulting number of widows would have been 200,000. J. David Hacker, "A Census-Based Count of the Civil War Dead," *Civil War History* 57 (2011): 311. A map illustrating the tremendous numbers of widows created by the Civil War can be found in J. David Hacker, Libra Hilde, and James Holland Jones, "The Effect of the Civil War on Southern Marriage Patterns," *Journal of Southern History* 76 (2010): 65.

4. Jean H. Baker, *Mary Todd Lincoln: A Biography* (New York: Norton, 1987), 45, 74; Elizabeth L. Norris to Emily Todd Helm, March 7, 1895, in Elizabeth L. Norris Collection, Abraham Lincoln Presidential Library, Springfield, Illinois.

5. An excellent book on the twists and turns of Mary and Abraham's engagements is Douglas L. Wilson's *Honor's Voice: The Transformation of Abraham Lincoln* (New York: Knopf, 1998); Carl Sandburg and Paul M. Angle, *Mary Lincoln: Wife and Widow* (New York: Harcourt, Brace, 1932), 43; Frances Todd, as quoted in Baker, *Mary Todd Lincoln*, 83; Clinton, *Mrs. Lincoln*, 61.

6. The "long of it/short of it" joke is one Abraham would use in many different circumstances, including with fellow politicians and speakers. It was perhaps most amusing, however, with his wife, whose differing heights and shapes made quite an impact. Mary Lincoln to Eliza Stuart Steel, Chicago, May [23, 1871], in *Mary Todd Lincoln: Her Life and Letters*, ed. Justin Turner and Linda Turner (New York: Knopf, 1972), 200; Abraham Lincoln, as quoted by Daniel J. Ryan, *Lincoln and Ohio* (Columbus: Ohio State Archaeological and History Society, 1923).

7. This story comes from Emilie's daughter's book on Mary Lincoln. Historians should read this

text with a critical eye, as it was written and published decades after the war. Emilie, as I discuss later in this paper, carefully crafted the image of the Todds and Lincolns that she showed the world in the postwar period. Some stories in this book, when compared to other sources and historical fact, ring true; others do not. Katherine Helm, *The True Story of Mary, Wife of Lincoln* (New York: Harper & Brothers, 1928), 99–100.

8. Benjamin Hardin Helm (hereafter BHH) to Emilie Helm (hereafter EH), July 4, 1856; Edwin Porter Thompson, *History of the First Kentucky Brigade* (Cincinnati: Caxton, 1868), 346–47; BHH to EH, March 15, 1857; BHH to EH, March 15, 1857.

9. BHH to Lucinda Helm, October 28, 1855; BHH to EH, June 20, 1856; BHH to EH, July 12, 1856; BHH to EH, March 15, 1857; BHH to EH, June 18, 1856; BHH to EH, June 25, 1856.

10. This degree of lovesickness is one that Abraham and Mary would never experience or, at the very least, write about. Their marriage was never known for its affection. For more on southern manhood, see Stephen Berry, *All That Makes a Man: Love and Ambition in the Civil War South* (New York: Oxford University Press, 2003); Craig Thompson Friend and Lorri Glover, eds., *Southern Manhood: Perspectives on Masculinity in the Old South* (Athens: University of Georgia Press, 2004); John Mayfield, *Counterfeit Gentlemen: Manhood and Humor in the Old South* (Gainesville: University Press of Florida, 2009); Stephanie McCurry, *Masters of Small Worlds: Yeoman Households, Gender Relations, and the Political Culture of the Antebellum South Carolina Lowcountry* (New York: Oxford University Press, 1995); BHH to EH, March 15, 1857; BHH to EH, June 3, 1857; BHH to EH, June 25, 1856.

11. BHH to EH, October 10, 1861.

12. This diary is missing. Most historians believe that Emilie burned it just before she died because it contained "too much bitterness." BHH to EH, October 19, 1856; BHH to EH, June 26, 1863; BHH to EH, April 20, 1862; BHH to EH, June 3, 1857; Emilie Hardin Helm, diary excerpt.

13. Nineteenth-century etiquette books also prescribed how a woman should mourn, from her dress to her actions. See *How to Behave: A Pocket Manual of Republican Etiquette, and Guide to Correct Personal Habits* (New York: Fowler & Wells, 1856), or Emily Thornwell, *The Lady's Guide to Perfect Gentility* (New York: Derby & Jackson, 1856), 217; Edward O. Guerrant, *Bluegrass Confederate: The Headquarters Diary of Edward O. Guerrant*, ed. William C. Davis and Meredith L. Swentor (Baton Rouge: Louisiana State University Press, 1999), 331.

14. Within Emilie's papers at the KHS are condolence letters from ten different people, and many individuals sent Emilie multiple letters. The quotations included in this paragraph are but a tiny sampling of the themes in these letters. Mrs. E. Pickett, Maysville, Kentucky, to EH, December 31, 1863; H. M. Bruce, Richmond, Virginia, to EH, September 22, 1863; E. Pickett, Maysville, Kentucky, to EH, December 31, 1863; BHH to EH, March 18, 1857.

15. This telegram has not survived, so we have to take Emilie's word on Abraham's response. Katherine Helm, *True Story of Mary*, 221.

16. Ibid., 221, 224, 229, 230, 231, 233; John L. Helm, Frankfort, Kentucky, to EH, January 20, 1864.

17. Perhaps Mary could not play the part of a perfect widow, given her mental issues. We will never know for certain if her mental health debilitated her to the point where she cannot be held responsible for her actions. Elizabeth Keckley, *Behind the Scenes, or, Thirty Years a Slave and Four Years in the White House* (New York: G. W. Carleton, 1868), 191; as quoted in Baker, *Mary Todd Lincoln*, 249; Elizabeth Todd Edwards in *Herndon's Informants: Letters, Interviews and Statements about Abraham Lincoln*, ed. Douglas L. Wilson and Rodney O. Davis (Urbana: University of Illinois Press, 1998), 444.

18. With three children, no money, no job skills, and an extended family financially ruined by

the war, Emilie did have some difficult times immediately following the war. Evidence from this period of her life is more limited, but it appears she taught music in Indiana for a period of time and visited her father and in-laws frequently. T. W. W. Gilkeson, Brownsburg, Virginia, to Elizabeth Todd Helm, February 7, 1867; *Frankfort (Ky.) Roundabout*, September 8, 1883; John Helm, Frankfort, to EH, February 23, 1867; William E. Bates, Madison, Indiana, October 14, 1874; Filson Club Membership Certificate for Emilie Todd Helm, October 6, 1890; *Stanford (Ky.) Semi-Weekly Interior Journal*, July 23, 1895.

19. John C. Breckinridge, before Chattanooga, Tennessee, to EH, October 31, 1863; George W. Quarles to EH, May 8, 1880; Frank G. Lyon, Alabama, to EH, August 30, 1888; Ed. Porter Thompson, Saint Stephen, Nebraska, to EH, February 25, 1868; "Helm Guards," undated newspaper clipping.

20. Rodger Hanson's widow was the first "Mother" of the Orphan Brigade. Emilie was the second, filling the role after Mrs. Hanson's death. W. O. Bullock, Lexington, to EH, Elizabethtown, Kentucky, August 30, 1883; John H. Weller, Louisville, to EH, September 9, 1884; J. D. Pickett to EH, September 14, 1884; "Mrs. Helm Made Mother of the Orphan Brigade," *Louisville Courier-Journal*, unidentified newspaper clipping; *Paris (Ky.) Bourbon News*, October 5, 1920.

21. A better determination of Emilie's exact role within the UDC will require additional research within the organization's records. While Emilie wrote extensively about the purpose of the organization, her personal papers do not indicate if her main function was as a figurehead invited to speak for publicity or as a more substantial worker within the organization. The most complete history of the UDC is Karen Cox's *Dixie's Daughters: The United Daughters of the Confederacy and the Preservation of Confederate Culture* (Gainesville: University Press of Florida, 2003). EH, undated writing that begins with "Ladies and Daughters of the Confederacy."

22. EH, undated writing that begins with "A third of a century"; EH, undated writing that begins with "God bless the Confederate women"; EH, undated writing that begins with "The duty of a Historian"; EH, undated writing that begins with "Ladies and Daughters of the Confederacy"; *Louisville Courier-Journal*, November 22, 1901.

23. J. Y. Gilmore to EH, January 11, 1898; R. Cobb, Wichita Falls, Texas, to EH, November 26, 1904.

24. EH, "The Spirit of 1860." The concept of the Lost Cause has a long history. Important works that discuss women's roles in crafting this ideology include Charles Reagan Wilson, *Baptized in Blood: The Religion of the Lost Cause, 1865–1920* (Athens: University of Georgia Press, 2009); Gaines M. Foster, *Ghosts of the Confederacy: Defeat, the Lost Cause, and the Emergence of the New South, 1865–1913* (New York: Oxford University Press, 1987); Caroline E. Janney, *Burying the Dead but Not the Past: Ladies' Memorial Associations and the Lost Cause* (Chapel Hill: University of North Carolina Press, 2008).

25. John Todd to EH, December 5, 1880; Elizabeth to EH, April 30, 1880; *Adair County News*, February 22, 1905.

26. Newspapers throughout the country, including northern papers such as the *Pittsburgh Dispatch* and New York City's *Sun*, reported on Emilie's activities, which speaks to her popularity and national fame. Thanks to the papers, her fame spread, and households far beyond her state and region could read about her beliefs and actions. In many ways Emilie's postwar actions are similar to those of George Pickett's widow, LaSalle Corbell. Like Emilie, LaSalle shaped the way her husband would be remembered in history, ignoring and denying facts that did not match the image she desired to create. See the excellent essay by Lesley J. Gordon, "'Cupid Does Not Readily Give Way to Mars': The Marriage of LaSalle Corbell and George E. Pickett," in *Intimate Strategies of the Civil War: Military Commanders and Their Wives*, ed. Carol K. Bleser and Lesley J. Gordon (New York: Oxford University Press, 2001), 69–86; *Saint Paul (Minn.) Globe*, September 4, 1898.

27. Nina Silber argues that a sentimental rubric took hold of the reunion process and that "southern women became the domestic and morally refined exemplars of true womanhood." Nina Silber, *The Romance of Reunion: Northerners and the South, 1865–1900* (Chapel Hill: University of North Carolina Press, 1993), 23; *Louisville Courier-Journal*, June 1, 1909; EH to Abraham Lincoln, October 30, 1864, Lincoln Papers, Library of Congress, as quoted in Berry, *House of Abraham*, 174; EH, undated writing that begins with "Ladies and Daughters of the Confederacy," Helm Papers.

28. Stephanie McCurry contends that the Confederacy became answerable to poor whites and women in ways the Old South never had been. My research leads me to believe that the Confederacy is, in fact, even more answerable to its widows and that emotions play a powerful role in this history. Stephanie McCurry, *Confederate Reckoning: Power and Politics in the Civil War South* (Cambridge, Mass.: Harvard University Press, 2010); EH to Albert Edwards, August 15, 1899, Abraham Lincoln Presidential Library, Springfield, Illinois.

Josie Underwood and Frances Dallam Peter

(1840–1923; 1843–1864)

Two Union Women in Civil War Kentucky

ANDREA S. WATKINS

In October 1861 Josie Underwood wrote: "Nothing new has happened today. The same trying intrusions and annoyances. . . . But tonight as I looked out from my window at the tents shining white in the moonlight, with here and there a camp fire, and hear the various bugle calls from far off and near—there is something thrilling and beautiful in it all, in spite of the underlying and ever abiding sadness."[1] The sentiment Underwood expressed in her diary demonstrated the divided nature of her war experience in Bowling Green, Kentucky. While the war brought dramatic and exciting experiences to Kentucky women, the division in the state over the conflict led to disrupted relationships, arrests, relocations, and tragic loss of the lives of friends and family members. For Josie Underwood and Frances Dallam Peter, two young Union women, the Civil War introduced tension, excitement, and sacrifice. These two women expressed themselves in different ways, but their writings document how each faced the political division of the state, enemy occupation, and widespread suffering caused by the fighting. Through their personal diaries Josie Underwood and Frances Dallam Peter reveal the nature of the home front for Union supporters in a commonwealth torn asunder.

Kentucky in the Civil War was a state divided, which was reflected in the diaries of Underwood and Peter. These women with strong Union sentiments faced challenges related directly to occupation by enemy forces, and their experiences demonstrate the depths of emotion and sacrifice that the war brought to women in a Union state under attack. Former friends were now suspect, family members were "lost" to the other side, and terrain that was once familiar and comforting was forever changed by invading troops. Their writings also provide a look at the war from the point of view of young, unmarried women who understood the larger political, social, and economic aspects of the military struggle, while at the same time reflecting on beaus, music, and friendship as would any young girl in the nineteenth century. The unique experiences of Underwood and Peter as Union women in divided communities show how the war altered the lives of young, unmarried women as powerfully as it did their married sisters, mothers, and older friends.[2]

Johanna Louisa "Josie" Underwood was born on November 5, 1840, to Warner Lewis and Lucy Underwood. Warner was a lawyer in Bowling Green who had spent several years as a land agent in Texas in the 1830s. Well respected in Warren County, he was elected as a representative to the state legislature (1848–53) and to the U.S. House of Representatives (1855–59) as a member of the American (Know-Nothing) Party. In 1839 he purchased the Underwood family home and farm, Mount Air. The property was located at the northeastern end of Bowling Green and provided a good income for the family, who were considered wealthy by community standards. At the time of the Civil War, Josie and three younger brothers and a sister lived at Mount Air with their mother and father, and an orphaned niece and nephew of Lucy Underwood. Three older sisters were married but visited the home throughout the war years.[3]

The family also held twenty-eight slaves, of whom ten were small children. Having inherited several slaves, Warner Underwood seemed to have little to say about the institution other than to worry about how the slavery question created problems for national unity. The writings of his daughter Josie reveal few internal struggles she may have had with slavery, though she commented frequently on the role of various slaves in family life. Despite this benign view of slavery, the Underwood family members were strong Union supporters in a divided Bowling Green. Warner Underwood campaigned for the John Bell/Edward Everett Constitutional Union presidential ticket in 1860. After Abraham Lincoln's victory, Underwood traveled in southeastern Kentucky to encourage support for the Union against secessionist demands. Josie's mother vowed never to "be driven out of the Union and give up the Flag and all it stands for, for which her father and forefathers fought."[4] This strong sentiment permeated Josie's own views and led her to several heated exchanges and contentious actions in the early years of the war.

Josie had attended local private schools and finished her education at the Russellville Female Institute in 1860. She was a member of a local literary club, and she enjoyed teaching her younger brothers and sister lessons. Her diary is remarkably open on her views of secession and the war, but it also contains the descriptions of daily activities, attendance at parties, the theater, and several marriage proposals. The diary's first entry was in December 1860 as she embarked on a journey to visit her sister Juliette ("Jupe") and her husband, William Western. A visit with her friend Jane Grider was the first taken after finishing school and she "became a full fledged 'Young lady.'"[5] It ended in September 1862, when the family traveled to Glasgow, Scotland, after Warner Underwood was appointed consul by Abraham Lincoln.

Frances Dallam Peter, born January 28, 1843, in Lexington, was the daughter of Dr. Robert Peter and Frances Paca Dallam. Dr. Peter was a native of Cornwall, England, who came to the United States in 1817 and arrived in Lexington fifteen years later. A chemist, geologist, and physician, he received an MD in 1834 from Transylvania University. He married Frances Paca Dallam at the Lexington Episcopal Church the following year, and the two had eleven children. Before the Civil War, he served as the chair of the chemistry and pharmacy departments, the dean of faculty, the librarian of the medical school, and the editor of the medical school journal at Transylvania. When the war began, Dr. Peter held the post of senior surgeon of the U.S. Army in Lexington. The family lived in Lexington during the war, at the corner of Market Street and Mechanics Alley across from the Little College Lot, where troops camped while stationed in the city.[6]

Frances, called "Frank" by her family, had epilepsy. Because of the illness Frances spent less time in the public eye, but her family did not attempt to hide her away. She attended the Sayre Female Institute and expressed herself in creative writing, sketching, and the diary she kept from January 1862 to April 1864. Her diary entries represent observations of what was going on outside the home rather than inside, reflecting her greater interest in knowing what was happening outside her close circle of friends and family. Unlike Josie Underwood, Frances rarely mentions beaus and marriage proposals, parties, and visits to friends. Frances wrote more on the news of events in Lexington, military actions, and ongoing activities of local secessionists. Her diary illuminated how much information was passed through an informal network of women residents in Lexington and through the newspapers when available. Neither diary provides a full account of the war years, for Josie's writings end with the beginning of a long overseas journey in 1862, and Frances's entries stopped four months before her death from epileptic seizures at age twenty-one in 1864.[7]

Josie Underwood's diary began in late December 1860 with a trip to Memphis, Tennessee, where she visited friends, shopped, and sat with her sister Jupe reading, writing, and sewing. She also attended her first "big *full grown* ball."

Secession talk entered almost all of these events, and Josie compared it to Banquo's ghost that "*will not [die] down* but will come up—no matter what the place or time." Josie found herself drawn into many of these conversations, and she used the information gleaned from her father to make an impassioned case against secession. At the ball held on January 1, 1861, the governor of Mississippi, Henry Foote, approached and commended her for presenting her father's views so well and nobly. Warner Underwood repeatedly articulated that the South would suffer if it left the Union. According to Josie, her father stated, "If there is war—it will surely be in the South and the whole land desolated and laid in waste and slavery will certainly go if the Union is dissolved." The answer was for the South to fight for its rights from inside the Union.[8]

Even amid the political talk, life continued for the young southern woman. While in Memphis, Josie received three different offers of marriage. But she found that none of the young men elicited a feeling of deep love. She desired a match that she loved "with my whole heart and soul." Thomas Grafton, a Mississippi lawyer working in Memphis, attracted Josie's attention; he asked if she might love him despite his commitment to follow the views of his home state. But Josie was a Union girl, and although she respected him, she did not love him. The two agreed to continue a writing correspondence once they left Memphis.[9] This is the first of many friendships that faced the difficulty of divided views on politics and later the actual war. When Josie returned to Bowling Green, she found tensions heightened. Some of her friends no longer went out with one another, and fist fights occurred among the younger boys such as her brother Warner. Josie wrote that "unpleasant feelings between old friends" had arisen, and she exchanged words with Lizzie Wright in February 1861, though "we have never had a disagreeable word pass between us in all our lives before." The words and actions continued to build, and Josie wrote again in May 1862 that she and Lizzie exchanged "merely the coldest bows and never a visit now." She had written a year earlier: "The excitement grows greater and every day seems bringing war nearer and friends farther and farther apart."[10]

Divisions such as this are reflective of the citizenry at large in Kentucky, a border state with economic and social ties to the North and the South. After the war began, both sides wanted Kentucky to declare for their cause, but Kentucky's official stance was neutrality. As the most important of the four border states, its farm values ranked seventh in the nation; livestock, fifth; and population, ninth. President Lincoln resisted a push to force the state's people to make a decision in the early months of the war, and his patience was rewarded. Despite Confederate propaganda efforts and the entrance of troops across the southern border, the Kentucky Unionist legislature effectively ended neutrality on September 11, 1861, when it passed a resolution ordering Confederate troops from the state. Yet Southern sympathizers remained, and many men crossed the border to Tennessee to join the Confederate army. Such sympathies divided not only friends but also families. U.S. senator John J. Crittenden, who promoted a peace compromise in 1860–61, saw his oldest son, George, resign a commission in the U.S. Army to join the Confederacy, while Lincoln's extended family through his wife, Mary Todd Lincoln, had three brothers serve in the Confederate army.[11]

Such divisions reached into the Underwood family as well. William Western, the husband of Josie's sister Juliette, believed in the maintenance of slavery, states' rights, and secession. This led him to volunteer for the Southern army in August 1861. The family was upset by the news, and Josie expressed disgust at his joining Nathan Bedford Forrest's brigade. Forrest only months before was the owner of a "Negro Yard" in Memphis and "no decent people had anything to do with him." But the greater shock came a few weeks later when word reached them that Josie's uncle, Matthew Winston Henry, known as Wint, had resigned from the U.S. Army. Wint, who was a cadet at West Point when the war began in April, had graduated three months early and been sent to Missouri in June 1861. A bout of rheumatism caused him to travel to Hot Springs, Arkansas, for treatment, and on his way there he visited the Underwoods at Mount Air. Josie's father spent hours talking with Wint about his service, and the young man promised that his desire to serve the Union was great. Yet Warner Underwood believed the secessionist members of the family in the South "will be too strong for him." It was just ten days after this visit that a letter arrived from Wint explaining that he had learned the "true conditions of conflict" and that he "could not conscientiously fight any longer against the South." He had resigned his commission and joined the Confederate army. Josie's mother was heartbroken and wept bitterly, "Oh! If he had only died or been killed defending the flag and the country for which his fathers fought—before he turned traitor." She decreed that his name was never to be uttered in her presence and that he should be treated as if he were dead. In her diary that day, Josie contrasted the harshness of her mother's pronouncement with the natural beauty of the world she saw from her window, and she pondered how humanity had so spoiled the peaceful creation of God. "I can't understand why God permits it so to be for the Angel song of 'Peace on Earth, good will to man' seems forever hushed."[12]

The Peter family was not divided on the issue of which side to support, but the family had a falling out with friends and neighbors once the war began. Henrietta Morgan lived at Hopemont a block from the Peter home across the Little College Lot. She was the mother of John Hunt Morgan, who would rise to fame during the war in Confederate circles as a cavalry general who used guerrilla tactics most effectively. Prior to the war, the families had close ties, but once the Morgan family supported secession and the Confederacy, relations grew strained. Frances took particular interest in the happenings at the Morgan house and was preoccupied with the visitors to Hopemont as well as the actions of John Hunt Morgan on the battlefield. The first entry in the diary, dated January 19, 1862, recorded the arrest of a secessionist hiding at Mrs. Morgan's house.[13] Frances expressed contempt for Henrietta Morgan's sheltering of Southern sympathizers and how her home appeared to be part of a network of communication for Confederates in the area. One man "carrying the secesh mail" was arrested after he "inquired for Mrs. Morgan & thus betrayed himself." The strained relations between Union supporters and secessionists in Lexington led to swings in morale and rumors concerning the fortunes of both sides. In March 1862 Frances reported, "The secesh are getting pretty high here." When a train carrying Confederate prisoners of war passed through the city, a large crowd of secessionists met it at the station, where they "hurrad for Jeff Davis and made a great fuss over the scamps."[14]

Frances's diary highlighted the dangers for supporters of both sides throughout the war in Lexington. She wrote of the burning of a Mrs. Castleman's outbuildings, slave cabins, farm equipment, and lumber one night in October, stating, "She is a secesh & that is the 5th fire since the rebels came." In 1862 Union store owners were forced to open their businesses for Confederate troops and were paid in scrip or not at all. The following year, when Union control was cemented in central Kentucky, the secessionists had a harder time. One diary entry related how five "secesh ladies" were arrested on the train to Nicholasville for expressing "treasonable sentiments." The women appeared at the provost's office. The federal government had appointed a provost marshal in every Kentucky county, and such officials were authorized to arrest those suspected of aiding the Confederacy. Individuals under suspicion had to take an oath of allegiance, and often they were required to purchase a bond for loyal conduct or face arrest and imprisonment. The five women arrested in Nicholasville were sentenced to go south, but they protested. The choice was given to them to go south or go to jail, at which time the women took the oath of allegiance and went their own way.[15] When a group of Confederate prisoners arrived in Lexington from the Cumberland Gap on September 21, 1863, Frances wrote that a "secesh lady (or rather a rebel individual of the feminine gender, for she disgraced the name of lady)" met the group and talked with them and sang rebel songs. The guard made an effort to move her away from the prisoners but was accosted by the woman with "insolent language." When she finally left for home, the guard followed her because a group who watched her display had gathered with stones "and would have mobbed her . . . had [they] not been prevented."[16]

Both young women provide a firsthand account of the Civil War home front—a home front that as Unionists they experienced under occupation for a time. Bowling Green and Lexington were controlled by both Union and Confederate forces during the early years of the war. Bowling Green, founded in 1798, started as a small incorporated town but grew in size and importance with the steamboat era. Lock and dam construction allowed the shallow draft boats to travel up the Green and Barren Rivers, and a portage railroad built in 1832 sent goods to the heart of the town. In 1859, when the Louisville and Nashville (L&N) Railroad was completed, it made a stop in Bowling Green and was a key junction for the Memphis line. The town had grown significantly by the start of the Civil War, and command of the hills that surrounded it gave a distinct advantage to the side that controlled the area. The Confederate army arrived on September 17, 1861, and fortified the city. In November it was chosen the capital of Confederate Kentucky. But after Union victories at Forts Henry and Donelson, the Confederates evacuated on February 14, 1862, and destroyed the railroad depot, several buildings, and the bridges over the Barren River.[17] Lexington, called the Athens of the West, was the cultural center of early Kentucky and was second only to Louisville in commerce by 1860. Well known for Transylvania University and its medical school, the city had been home to Henry Clay and was home to the family of Abraham Lincoln's wife, Mary. A significant portion of the population supported the Confederate cause; when Confederate troops marched into the city on September 2, 1862, they were hailed as heroes by many. They held the city until after the Battle of Perryville when Confederate forces pulled out of the state, and Federal troops reoccupied the city on October 16, 1862.[18]

Both women described wartime life in the beginning as exciting. Underwood wrote in June 1861: "The times are so exciting I can't half describe anything—all thought of ordinary things is upset—and we are living in a state of nervous tension that makes everybody excited and restless." She found that "even the negroes—naturally too—can't half do their work. They, poor souls, have more reason perhaps than anybody to be anxious and eager for news." And then, on September 17, 1861, Confederate troops under the command of Kentuckian Simon Bolivar Buckner arrived in Bowling Green by railcar from Camp Boone in Tennessee. Josie's father watched through a looking glass at Mount Air as the troops lowered the Union flag and raised a Confederate one in its place. He comforted the family with a call to take courage. The men of the family left for town to see what was happening, and the women waited nervously at home. After a few hours, soldiers appeared in their yard asking for food. Josie's mother ordered their slave Jake to give the men cold ham, biscuits, fruit, and milk, saying, "I will never refuse a hungry man food—but you must excuse me from asking into my house, men who have helped pull down our country's flag." The soldiers laughed and remarked as they left, "Yanks."[19]

Four days later, Josie and her brother Warner were out for a ride on horseback when they met a line of soldiers on the road. The pair believed the men involved in a drill but quickly returned home when they saw their front gate opened and the "thousands of men" march into Mount Air's front yard. Mount Air's location on the northeastern end of Bowling Green was a key location for Confederate troops, and within a week men were pitching tents in the front fields of clover and behind the main house in the barn lot and orchard. Destruction of the family's property included troop use of rail fences for fires, fruit taken from the orchard, milk stolen from the cows, and other items pilfered from the family stores. One soldier came to the house early one morning and took the family's breakfast when the slave cook turned to retrieve eggs from the pantry. The incidents left Josie with the observation, "We are humiliatingly helpless." Josie knew several of the Confederate officers, and the men sent letters or came to the house requesting permission to visit her. One captain wrote her a letter expressing his "intense devotion," but Josie suspected he only wished to break the monotony of camp life with "a flirtation with the enemy—a sort of sham Romeo and Juliette [*sic*] affair." She refused all such invitations on principle, her father's and her own, although at times she stopped to talk with an officer on the road or in town, saying, "I do enjoy the chance talks with them even though we give and take pretty sharp thrusts in defending our different principles."[20]

The soldiers gave the family little privacy in the main house and used the hall from the front door to the back door as a thoroughfare instead of walking around the house. One day two soldiers entered Josie's mother's room to warm themselves by the fire even as her mother lay in the bed sick. In mid-October a group of soldiers marched through the house after breakfast carrying axes with orders to cut down all the walnut and oak trees near the barn because they blocked the sight range of a planned new fort. Then the slave Uncle Todd ran to the house looking for Warner Underwood, upset that the soldiers ordered him to leave his cabin immediately because they were going to tear it down. Underwood went to the slave's cabin, but it had already been removed; he had time only to organize the young boys and slave children to bring Uncle Todd's possessions to the main yard. Josie wrote that the slaves "can't yet understand that it is possible for their 'Marster' to be so 'run over,'" and for Uncle Todd to see that Underwood was "powerless . . . to prevent the destruction of his cabin." The following month another home that Underwood owned and rented was taken apart by soldiers despite protests from the family. "Instead, the knowledge that the property belongs to Pa, the man who has opposed secession so strongly, makes them more anxious to destroy anything they can belonging to him," Josie wrote.[21]

Frances Peter experienced no destruction of her family property or deprivation of resources during the war, but there was a change in atmosphere in Lexington when Confederate troops marched through the streets on September 4, 1862. That day the church bells rang "in a doleful way & the secesh ladies paraded about with the stars and bars in their hands & streamers of red white & red on their dresses and bonnets." The Peter family watched as a company of men brought their horses to the lot across from their house, which was kept "shut & doors locked . . . because we were afraid of the house being searched." One evening after the company left for patrol, Dr. Peter asked Frances's sister Lettie for some music. With the soldiers gone from the lot the family no longer worried about attracting attention, but while Lettie played there was a knock at the door. Two "rough dirty fellows" stood at the door asking to come in and hear the music. Lettie refused them and said, "If they wanted to hear her play they could stand by the window & listen." Peter's father was arrested and asked to take an oath for the Confederacy, which he refused. The family was offered the opportunity to leave the state, but Dr. Peter remained steadfast that his home was in Lexington and he wanted to stay. His position as a doctor helped the family's situation. The Confederates initially offered him a parole in exchange for a pledge not to pass information to any Unionists. Later they restricted his movements to the short distance between his home and the hospital.[22]

A few days into the occupation, a Confederate soldier from Florida stopped at their door and explained how "he & a good many others had been 'poked' into the army at the point of the bayonet." Stricken with the measles after departing and not fully returned to health, the young man said that he never expected to get so far and that all he wanted was to go home. Frances's mother asked him if he had anything to eat at the hospital and if he had taken something for his cough. Patients had plenty of bread and mutton, he replied, but he did not have medicine for the cough. The steward had reserved medical supplies left by local women for the severely ill. The soldier hoped to find some chicken soup or milk and believed this would make him better. Mrs. Peter said she would gladly offer him some milk, but the cow had already been "milked & maltreated" by the soldiers quartered in the area. When she later spoke a word against the Confederacy, he warned, "I heard there was an order out that any one who spoke against the Confederacy was to be arrested & I wouldn't like to see that happen to you after you have been kind to me." On September 24 a soldier encamped across from their home came to the door asking for a bucket to water the horses. Mrs. Peter refused to provide one with the explanation that the last bucket she had lent was not returned. She told him to go to "one of those secesh houses," indicating two homes across the lot, and ask for help. The young man asked if Mrs. Peter was the enemy, to which she replied that she was a Union supporter. He walked away pointing at the house and saying to his friends, "Why if that there isn't a damned union house."[23]

The Unionists were heartened to learn of the retreat of Confederate forces from Covington and northern Kentucky days after the army took Lexington. Gen. Henry Heth's division had marched out of Lexington in the hope of capturing Newport, Covington, and Cincinnati. But on seeing the Union fortifications on the hills south of Covington and Newport, and skirmishing with enemy pickets for two days, the Confederates returned to Lexington without a fight. One soldier from Texas told the Peters that "we didn't retreat we only came back to get water," and that story made the rounds within the secessionist circles in town. When one young woman was asked by a neighbor if she had heard of the retreat from Covington, she replied that the Confederates "fell back for want of water" and she had seen a letter from an officer noting he had breakfast within four miles of the Ohio River. The neighbor retorted, "Why did the[y] come back to Lexington for water instead of going on to the Ohio?" The next day a soldier at the door of the Peter house "admitted he thought they [Confederates] were in a bad fix here." Other reports from towns throughout central Kentucky recounted the movements of both armies, and the citizens had to rely on these word-of-mouth accounts given that the Confederates controlled the distribution of mail and newspapers. Frances wrote that Gen. Edmund Kirby Smith had issued an order to imprison anyone caught reading a northern newspaper.[24]

Despite the tensions and uncertainty of life during wartime, both families looked for ways to help those less fortunate than themselves. Lucy Underwood, Josie's mother, prepared broths, soups, and horehound syrup for the soldiers who were ill at the hospital. When she received a note of thanks from the attending doctor and surgeon, according to Josie, her mother commented to the doctor, "I am very glad to do anything I can for *sick* men, no matter who or what they are; but when they are well enough to fight against their country, I want nothing more to do with them."[25] In December nineteen men were arrested in nearby Hart County recruiting for the Union, and the group was jailed in Bowling Green. Lucy Underwood and Mary Ann Hodge requested permission to provide warm clothing for the accused, who had arrived with few coats and hats. The women gathered coats, pants, and underclothing that were checked by the guards before given to the imprisoned men. Later the women asked

Gen. William J. Hardee if they might deliver the prisoners "something nice for Christmas." The general denied their request for Christmas but suggested that they come on New Year's Day with the items. The Union women prepared cakes, ham, turkey, soup, biscuits, pickles, jellies, and "real coffee" and served the men, who "were almost too overcome to thank us." Prisoners from the Confederate army came to the doors of their rooms as well and asked for food, which the ladies generously shared. The women agreed that they hoped their gesture showed the "Rebels" that Union people were the kindest.[26]

The aid offered by women throughout the war drew on female networks established in the antebellum years as sewing groups, church associations, and reform societies. Such activities allowed women a chance to participate in the war effort, express their own patriotism, and play upon their domestic skill.[27] One request to the Lexington Ladies Aid Society was from Capt. James Dudley, who described how his men had "no socks, nor good clothes," and the women set immediately to work to remedy the situation. Frances related how Union women visited the sick in one of the local hospitals on October 4, 1862, and the Confederate soldiers who were there asked if they might have some of the goods the women brought. When the ladies asked if the women from their own side did not bring them such items, the men replied that such donations had stopped. Frances wrote, "Poor wretches! The Confederacy hasn't done much for them!"[28]

Throughout her diary Frances also commented on the local concerts held to raise funds for soldier aid. Such concerts in support of Union troops were held before and after the Confederate occupation in Lexington. Frances provided a description of one event she attended six months after the Confederate occupation had ended. Beginning March 5, 1863, a tableau was held for two nights for the Aid Society. The "very pretty" scene featured a performance that opened with a song from "Thirty Four Stars" with "the 'stars' being so many little girls dress[ed] in white with red and blue scarfs, with black velvet bandeaus on their heads with each a large silver star in front." The song, a parody of the Southern song "The Bonnie Blue Flag," contained the line:

> The rebel forces say Hurra!
> For the hated Stars and Bars,
> But we will make them feel the stripes
> And make them see the stars . . .[29]

Concerts and fairs were common throughout the war and the most successful way to raise funds. Such events were designed to attract a wide audience and funnel public money to soldier support. Frances reported that one concert had made $166 after expenses.[30] Of course, these events also offered a welcome diversion. In 1864 a Sociable Club was started by the young ladies of Lexington for "dancing & amusement." The group was for ladies only, but the members could bring one gentleman with them to their meetings, and three kinds of refreshments of the host's choosing were served. While this was designed as a party, in consideration of the times the dress code prohibited evening wear but encouraged "promenade or 'at home' villetes." The second of weekly meetings was held in the Peter house on March 18.[31]

As the Confederate occupation of Bowling Green continued, the celebration of Christmas in 1861 was quiet for Josie Underwood, with none of her married sisters present and younger brother Warner enlisted in the Union army. The family celebration included stockings for the children and slave children, and handmade gifts of dolls, wraps, and gloves. One young slave exclaimed, "Old Santy Claus got through with his pack [in] spite [of the] secesh." The planned turkey dinner was denied when the slave Uncle Lewis discovered the hidden bird had been stolen. Josie complained that "no doubt some Army men had our Christmas dinner." Later that evening she and her parents reflected on the situation in their home and country, and the three prayed for peace. "Alas! how the song of the Angels is mocked by the present condition of the country," Josie wrote. The next day she recorded how the difficulty of obtaining goods had affected the family; she was taking old dresses apart to make over, and their coffee was almost gone. But the hardest was yet to come, when on December 28, 1861, Warner Underwood was called to headquarters with no reason given.[32]

Underwood spent three hours at the Confederate headquarters meeting with Gen. Albert Sidney Johnston. Johnston spent the time attempting to persuade Underwood, whom he knew, to join the secessionists to prevent further trouble and to improve his situation. Warner refused to do what he believed was wrong, and he returned home. The reality of Johnston's warning came on January 1, 1862, when three soldiers arrived at Mount Air with a military order for the family "to vacate the premises immediately." Josie's father protested that "immediately is a quick word, gentlemen, to a man who has lived at a place 40 years," and he went to headquarters and acquired a two-day extension. Warner Underwood secured a cabin fifteen miles away in Allen County for the family and several of the slaves, while the remaining slaves moved to local farms owned by Union men. The family worked quickly to pack not only what they needed but also what they valued, not knowing when or if they would return. Books, some furniture, and the piano were sent to a friend's home in town, while other goods were packed into wagons for the move. A colonel from a Missouri regiment came into the home examining the rooms with plans to bring his wife to the camp. He offered to purchase the bedroom furniture and furnishings in Lucy Underwood's room. Deciding that the extra money was more desirable, she agreed. The family left on a cold, rainy morning with the slave Aunt Sis crying, "My Lord! I knowed poor white trash got themselves into fixes—but I never did expect—men and my master to cum to sich a fix as this." The following day, the slave Uncle Lewis and Josie's younger brother Henry returned to Mount Air for a locked cabinet left the day before and to collect the money owed from the Missouri colonel for Lucy Underwood's furniture. When they arrived, the cabinet had been broken into and the colonel laughed, "Did your mother think I was going to pay Union people for anything. That's a good joke. This is only a *small confiscation* we call it." Henry responded, "I call it a big steal," and the two departed empty-handed.[33]

Their new home was two small cabins connected by a dogtrot. The Underwoods lived in one cabin, and the other served as the kitchen and living quarters for the slaves Aunt Dams, Uncle Lewis, Jake, and three children. The remote location marked a change from their home in the middle of an army encampment, and the local residents visited them with gifts of turnips, beans, and hazelnuts. To make better use of their resources, the family decided to send Lucy's orphaned niece and nephew to live with her sister in Russellville, and Lucy, Henry, and Uncle Lewis took the pair to the train station on January 20, 1862. After the children's departure, the trio stopped at headquarters to request a pass to show the pickets they would meet on their return journey. Josie later wrote that she believed this request betrayed her father's location to the secessionists in town who wanted to further harass Warner for his Union views. Late at night on January 22, a knock was heard at the door, and John Burnam stood there with a warning. Burnam was a member of the Council of Ten, a citizen group "who manage and suggest local meanness to the rebels in command," according to Josie. He informed Warner that the council had met that afternoon and decided to have him arrested for his Unionism and sent south. Burnam attempted to stop the action, but when he failed he rode through the evening to the cabin to urge Warner to leave immediately. Thanking the man for his help, Josie's father gathered a few items of clothing and biscuits, kissed the family good-bye, mounted his horse, and left. The next day after dinner, six soldiers and a lieutenant arrived at the cabin and asked if this was where Mr. Underwood lived. Josie replied that Mrs. Underwood and his children were here, but he was not present. Four of the men asked to come into the cabin to warm themselves, as the others remained at the fence holding their horses. Josie invited them in knowing that they were inspecting the room for signs of her father. Satisfied that he was not hidden on the premises, the lieutenant said, "I'm glad your father isn't here, Miss, I don't like this kind of job." They rode off and waited in the woods for a time to see if Underwood reappeared, but soon after they left. The family continued at the leaky cabin with dwindling resources, but happy with the knowledge that Warner had made it to Union lines and was now with his son Warner and son-in-law Benjamin Grider.[34]

The situation for the Confederate army changed in February 1862, with losses at Forts Henry and Donelson, and an evacuation of Bowling Green was ordered. The family received a letter on February 12 that informed them the troops were leaving Mount Air and they needed to return to prevent "evil persons" from destroying it. They left the next morning but arrived too late. The house was a charred ruin, set on fire by the retreating troops the night before. The house, orchards, trees, and fences were all gone. "Ruin, devastation and desolation everywhere!" Josie exclaimed. Unsure about what to do, the family went to Nancy Hall's residence in Bowling Green for dinner and to contemplate their next action. That night more buildings were burned as the Confederate troops continued their evacuation. Around eleven o'clock the next morning, as the Underwoods prepared to return to the cabin, they heard cannon fire. Word reached them that Union troops were firing from Bakers Hill to prevent Confederates from further destroying the town. Everyone went to the cellar with blankets, comforters, and a few chairs to wait out the attack. Hugh Gwynn, a local Confederate soldier on his way out of town, arrived at the house concerned about their situation and offered to help Mike Hall with all the women and children. Sitting below ground, they watched through the cellar doors as shells exploded around the town square. Josie was nearly hit in the face by a ball when she and Gwynn returned to the house for food and sewing supplies. When the firing ended, Gwynn left them to look for his regiment, and the citizens waited for the Union troops' arrival. Josie was reunited with her father and younger brother on February 16 when they returned to Bowling Green. The family moved into sister Frances "Fanny" Grider's home in town, and they were "thankful to be together once more—even with the sorrow of having our dear old home left us in ruins."[35]

The evacuation of Lexington by Confederate troops in October 1862 was part of the larger retreat from Kentucky ordered by Gen. Braxton Bragg in the wake of his defeat at the Battle of Perryville on October 8 and the absence of widespread Southern support from the Kentucky population at large. Frances Peter wrote on October 8 that when the ceiling in the parlor of Henrietta Morgan's home collapsed, the local ladies believed "it was a very bad omen." Many of the Southern sympathizers left with their slaves that day, and "rebel officers at the Phoenix [Hotel] when packing up told their wives not to stop to pack large trunks as they couldnt wait for much baggage." As the Southern troops continued to move south, Frances reported that it seemed few arrangements had been made for Confederate soldiers in the local hospitals, and the army's wagons were filled with "stolen goods." A few days later the order came to the sick men to "make their way to Knoxville the best way they can." By October 17 Frances wrote how she and others discussed who should take down the rebel flag when the retreat was complete, and it was agreed that the action should fall to "the meanest man in town," Jack Keiser. "And sure enough the other night when the secesh left they paid Keiser to take their flags down for them."[36] But the excitement was not over. As John Hunt Morgan and his men were guarding the retreat of Gen. Kirby Smith and his men south of Richmond, with Smith's approval, Morgan's men doubled back to Lexington for a strike at the L&N Railroad to cut Union supply lines. Frances noted that on the morning of October 18, "Morgans guerilla [*sic*] came galloping in & they surprised our men who were camped at James Clays."[37] But by October 25 life returned to normal with the renewed publication of the local *Observer and Reporter* and plans to reopen the schools the following week.[38]

After life under enemy occupation ended, both young women continued in a daily routine dotted with the realities of war. Josie Underwood's younger brother was wounded at Shiloh in April 1862, and her parents rushed to Pittsburgh Landing to help him and the Kentucky wounded. They missed finding their son, as a friend had put him on a boat for home ahead of their arrival. Josie met her brother in Bowling Green with his arm in a sling, his coat sleeve split, and dirty bandages wrapped around the wound. She gathered warm water and clean bandages to redress the injury, and when she removed the dirty bandages maggots fell from the wound and the rotten smell nearly knocked her over. She praised the bravery of her brother, who said, "God pity the poor fellows who are wounded so much worse and couldn't come home."[39] After Lucy Underwood received an appointment as the "receiver and distributor of sanitary stores," a back room of the house was assigned to hold the boxes of food, wine, clothing, comforters, and bandages that arrived. As local doctors requisitioned materials, Lucy with several other women filled their requests. The amount of material led some in the community to question if items were not used for purposes other than intended. One "secesh woman" said to Lucy, "I expect you live very high at your house since *your northern friends* have sent so many good things for their soldiers." Josie's mother responded, "We live very well, thank you—but not nearly so well as you would—under the same circumstances." Josie testified that her mother was so scrupulous with the supplies she would not allow Josie and a friend to have a small box of dried cherries even when they claimed they would share them with her wounded brother Warner.[40]

In Lexington, Frances Peter continued in 1863–64 to report on events at the local hospitals, troubles with local secessionists, and some political news involving the Copperheads.[41] She noted in January 1863 that her brother Bob was recovering from diphtheria, which had swept the city in recent days and had led to the death of a cousin whose husband and five children still suffered from it. She also expressed several harsh views of Confederates and the end of slavery as a war aim. On July 25 she relayed a story from the newspapers in Richmond, Virginia, that suggested the killing of dogs in the South because they ate too much bread. Frances wrote, "It would be a good thing if they would kill all the two legged as well as the four legged ones." She offered a dislike for abolitionists, explaining, "I always understood that this war was undertaken merely to put down rebellion, and that the government was forced to resort to arms to save the Union . . . not for the purpose of abolishing slavery though, the latter has been greatly undermined and broken up by the war." She was bothered by the urging of Henry Ward Beecher to keep fighting until slavery was abolished. Frances held that when the rebels laid down their arms and returned to the Union, the war should stop and "then let the ballot box decide the slavery question if there are any slaves left."[42] Like Josie Underwood, Frances Peter vehemently opposed Southern secession and questioned whether some of Lincoln's actions as president were constitutional. But after two years of war and measured leadership, in an entry dated December 19, 1863, she wrote of Lincoln that "the more we see of him the better we like him," and if he ran for reelection, "I know a good many people here will vote for him."[43]

Josie Underwood also experienced a transformation of opinion concerning Abraham Lincoln. In January 1861 she chafed at the words of her friend Thomas Grafton, who teased that the secessionists would fight under a banner with the motto "Sic Semper Tiranus" and a picture of "*your* friend Lincoln." Josie wrote that Grafton knew she disliked Lincoln and that it "is one of the hard things for the Unionists to contend with—so many of them don't approve Lincoln's course and have to fight his extreme views as well as the secessionists." But a visit to Washington, D.C., in the summer of 1862 produced a change in Josie's attitude toward the president. In recognition of his loyalty and suffering for the Union, her father was invited to go to the capital to meet with Lincoln about an appointment, and he asked Josie to accompany him. During their stay Josie dined with Mary Todd Lincoln, whom she described as "a handsome gentle woman" and not "the course, loud, common woman the papers had made her out to be." After leaving the first lady at Soldier's Home, the party encountered a lone horseman on the road from the city. Josie's father stopped his carriage; as the rider pulled up, Warner introduced Abraham Lincoln. He shook hands with all those present and talked with them for ten to fifteen minutes. Josie wrote,

"Lincoln in appearance certainly falls far short (though he is so long) of my idea of how a President should look. In fact a very common-looking man he is—but I must confess there was a kindliness in his face—that does not fit the tyrant—unfair man I have been thinking him." The following day, Warner Underwood met with Lincoln at the White House, where he was offered the position of American consul to Glasgow, Scotland. Underwood told the president that he had been a Bell man in 1860 and had worked against him and his policies in the past, but Lincoln responded that he knew all of this and wanted him because he was a good lawyer, a southern Union man, and a strong Presbyterian. Josie wrote that the position "comes like a God-send in the gloomy outlook," and the pair returned to Bowling Green to prepare for the journey to Scotland once the Senate confirmed the appointment.[44]

As the family made the necessary arrangements to leave, Josie decided that she did not want to part from her secessionist friend Lizzie Wright on bad terms. She surmised that with her side now victorious in Bowling Green and Lizzie's fiancé fighting and unable to send word, "I believe I have been the ungenerous one." On the evening of September 1, 1862, Josie walked across the street from her sister Fanny's house to the porch where Lizzie was sitting, taking the chance that her old friend might snub her. She quickly told Lizzie that she was leaving and could not go without saying good-bye. Lizzie stretched out her hand and said, "I am glad you can't and I was just sitting here wishing you would come over." The two sat holding hands and talked not of war and differences, but of Scotland and the many scenes from novels and poems that Josie might see when there. At the end of the evening, Josie wrote that she felt better and possessed a "lighter heart." The diary's last entry on September 8, 1862, read, "And now, good-bye, poor war dilapidated little Bowling Green with friends—associations and estrangments [*sic*], good-bye."[45]

The Civil War diaries of Josie Underwood and Frances Peter differ in their nature, but they represent a universal experience for both. Josie Underwood stood firm on her father's principles through the war and never backed down from her support in any situation. Her diary was reflective and contained personal details, from rejected marriage proposals to the destruction of her family home by enemy troops. Josie struggled as friends chose the opposite side, and she labored to adjust to various living situations as dictated by wartime dislocations. There was a sense of excitement in the early pages of the diary as secession talk escalated, but the horrors of war took their toll on the author by the end. Josie saw the cost the war exacted, and for her the burden was high. For Frances Peter, whose epilepsy kept her from fully engaging in public life, a network of relatives and friends passed her information that led to an accounting of activities throughout Lexington and central Kentucky. The view out her window onto the Little College Lot and her own keen observational skills added detail to her descriptions of soldiers' comings and goings throughout the war. The lack of personal examination and reports on family activities within the home reveals that Frances's desire may have been to participate more in the world around her, but there is no evidence of self-pity in the text. The focus of her diary entries on what happened outside her home provides readers with a thorough look at the operations of two armies, several hospitals, soldiers' aid societies, and informal networks of communication through civilian eyes.

While the two women recorded their war experiences in different tones and different locations, both demonstrated that the Civil War was an experience that deeply divided the commonwealth. As the leaders in Kentucky addressed the reality that the citizenry was of two minds, Josie Underwood and Frances Peter lived through lost friendships, lost loved ones, and a shared sense of community that would not soon return. Josie described the situation succinctly on October 16, 1861: "I never dreamed it possible we could have war in this country, brother against brother, friend against friend, as now."[46]

NOTES

1. Nancy Disher Baird, ed., *Josie Underwood's Civil War Diary* (Lexington: University Press of Kentucky, 2009), 113.

2. For other published Civil War diaries or memoirs by Kentucky women, see Martha McDowell Buford Jones, *Peach Leather and Rebel Gray: Bluegrass Life and the War, 1860–1865, Farm and Social Life, Famous Horses, Tragedies of War, Diary and Letters of a Confederate Wife*, ed. Mary E. Wharton and Ellen F. Williams (Lexington: Helicon, 1986); G. Glenn Clift, ed., *The Private War of Lizzie Hardin: A Kentucky Confederate Girl's Diary of the Civil War in Kentucky, Virginia, Tennessee, Alabama, and Georgia* (Frankfort: Kentucky Historical Society, 1963); Mary Julia Neal, ed., *The Journal of Eldress Nancy: Kept at the South Union, Kentucky, Shaker Colony, August 15, 1861–September 4, 1864* (Nashville: Parthenon, 1963).

3. Baird, *Josie Underwood's Civil War Diary*, 2–5; *The Kentucky Encyclopedia*, s.v. "Underwood, Warner Lewis." The original Underwood diary has not been found, but a typed photocopy of the work is located in the Kentucky Library at Western Kentucky University, Bowling Green.

4. The slave count is from the 1860 census. Baird, *Josie Underwood's Civil War Diary*, 3–7, 78.

5. Ibid., 2, 24.

6. John David Smith and William Cooper Jr., eds., *A Union Woman in Civil War Kentucky: The Diary of Frances Peter* (Lexington: University Press of Kentucky, 2000), x–xiii; *The Kentucky Encyclopedia*, s.v. "Peter, Robert." Little College Lot today is the site of Gratz Park.

7. Smith and Cooper, *Diary of Frances Peter*, xiii–xviii, xxvii.

8. Baird, *Josie Underwood's Civil War Diary*, 33, 39.

9. Ibid., 33, 27, 51–52. Underwood and Grafton continued a correspondence until October 1861, when she decided to write for the last time. Grafton was killed at the Battle of Fair Oaks (Seven

Pines), Virginia, in 1862. She wrote when learning of his death, "Poor fellow! poor fellow! how, I wish I had loved him! . . . All my patriotism is gone tonight." See Baird, *Josie Underwood's Civil War Diary*, 200.

10. Ibid., 62, 68, 175, 81.

11. James A. Ramage and Andrea S. Watkins, *Kentucky Rising: Democracy, Slavery and Culture from the Early Republic to the Civil War* (Lexington: University Press of Kentucky, 2011), 289–90; Lowell H. Harrison and James C. Klotter, *A New History of Kentucky* (Lexington: University Press of Kentucky, 1997), 190–92. For more on the divisions of the Crittenden and Todd families, see Damon R. Eubank, *In the Shadow of the Patriarch: The John J. Crittenden Family in War and Peace* (Macon, Ga.: Mercer University Press, 2009); Stephen Berry, *House of Abraham: Lincoln and the Todds, a Family Divided by War* (Boston: Houghton Mifflin, 2007).

12. Baird, *Josie Underwood's Civil War Diary*, 69–70, 89–90, 86–87, 92.

13. Smith and Cooper, *Diary of Frances Peter*, xix–xx, 3–4. For more information on the Morgan family and the Civil War action of John Hunt Morgan, see James A. Ramage, *Rebel Raider: The Life of General John Hunt Morgan* (Lexington: University Press of Kentucky, 1986).

14. Smith and Cooper, *Diary of Frances Peter*, 22, 10–11.

15. Ibid., 48, 31–32, 124; Ramage, *Rebel Raider*, 100.

16. Smith and Cooper, *Diary of Frances Peter*, 163.

17. *The Kentucky Encyclopedia*, s.v. "Bowling Green"; Harrison and Klotter, *New History of Kentucky*, 130–32.

18. Ramage and Watkins, *Kentucky Rising*, 292–94; *The Kentucky Encyclopedia*, s.v. "Bowling Green"; Harrison and Klotter, *New History of Kentucky*, 199-202; James Lee McDonough, *War in Kentucky: From Shiloh to Perryville* (Knoxville: University of Tennessee Press, 1994), 148–49.

19. Baird, *Josie Underwood's Civil War Diary*, 85, 94, 99–101.

20. Ibid., 102–7, 121–22, 117–18.

21. Ibid., 128–29, 114–15, 121.

22. Smith and Cooper, *Diary of Frances Peter*, 30–32, 33–34. Frances wrote that he was arrested three times, but he was never placed in jail or forced to take the loyalty oath.

23. Ibid., 35–36, 43. Mrs. Peter pointed across the lot to Mrs. George Woolley's and Mrs. Henrietta Morgan's homes as the "secesh houses."

24. Ibid., 40–41, 35.

25. Baird, *Josie Underwood's Civil War Diary*, 107. Horehound is a plant used for treatment of the common cold and cough in folk medicine.

26. Ibid., 130, 133, 137–38.

27. Jeanie Attie, *Patriotic Toil: Northern Women and the American Civil War* (Ithaca, N.Y.: Cornell University Press, 1998), 33. For more information on women's activities during the Civil War, see Nina Silber, *Daughters of the Union: Northern Women Fight the Civil War* (Cambridge, Mass.: Harvard University Press, 2005); Judith Giesberg, *Army at Home: Women and the Civil War on the Northern Home Front* (Chapel Hill: University of North Carolina Press, 2009); Drew Gilpin Faust, *Mothers of Invention: Women of the Slaveholding South in the American Civil War* (Chapel Hill: University of North Carolina Press, 1996).

28. Smith and Cooper, *Diary of Frances Peter*, 93, 51.

29. Ibid., 106.

30. Attie, *Patriotic Toil*, 95; Smith and Cooper, *Diary of Frances Peter*, 84.

31. Smith and Cooper, *Diary of Frances Peter*, 200.

32. Baird, *Josie Underwood's Civil War Diary*, 133–35.

33. Ibid., 135, 138–39, 141–44.

34. Ibid., 146–51, 153–54.

35. Ibid., 154–61, 164–65. The Confederates burned all the bridges across the Barren River. With the river high it took the Union troops until the morning of February 15 to enter the town.

36. Smith and Cooper, *Diary of Frances Peter*, 56–57, 59, 61, 65.

37. Ibid., 66. The skirmish involved was a surprise attack on the Fourth Ohio Cavalry camp on the grounds of Ashland, Henry Clay's estate in Lexington. See Ramage, *Rebel Raider*, 124–25.

38. Smith and Cooper, *Diary of Frances Peter*, 71.

39. Baird, *Josie Underwood's Civil War Diary*, 173–74. Warner Underwood obtained an appointment for his son Warner to West Point, and the young man left for the academy on June 18, 1862. See ibid., 177, 180.

40. Ibid., 178–80.

41. Copperheads were also known as Peace Democrats. It is believed the term "Copperheads" was first used in 1861 by Ohio Republicans to disparage antiwar Democrats by comparing them to the poisonous snake. It became widely used by late 1862, and some Republicans applied the term to all northern Democrats. See James M. McPherson, *Battle Cry of Freedom: The Civil War Era* (New York: Oxford University Press, 1988), 494n8; Jennifer L. Weber, *Copperheads: The Rise and Fall of Lincoln's Opponents in the North* (New York: Oxford University Press, 2006), 2–4.

42. Smith and Cooper, *Diary of Frances Peter*, 144, 170.

43. Ibid., xviii–xix, 176.

44. Baird, *Josie Underwood's Civil War Diary*, 51, 184–85.

45. Ibid., 199, 201.

46. Ibid., 116. Josie Underwood married Charles Nazro of New York in 1870 and had four children. She lived in New York, Denver, and San Diego, where her husband died in 1898. She returned to Bowling Green in 1912 and participated in community activities until her death in 1923. Frances Peter died from epileptic seizures on August 5, 1864, and is buried in the Lexington Cemetery. See ibid., 21–22; Smith and Cooper, *Diary of Frances Peter*, xxvii–xxviii.

Laura Clay
(1849–1941)

States' Rights and Southern Suffrage Reform

MARY JANE SMITH

Progressive Era reformer Laura Clay was known nationally for her more than three decades of tireless effort to win woman suffrage, especially for southern women. The Kentuckian spent more than a decade on the board of the National American Woman Suffrage Association (NAWSA). Yet in 1920 Clay, along with her fellow southern suffragist and friend Kate Gordon, actively lobbied against the organization's ultimate goal: the ratification of the Nineteenth Amendment to the U.S. Constitution granting universal female suffrage. Although this position confused, confounded, and irritated her longtime national and state allies in the movement, it was perhaps foreshadowed by an October 21, 1893, headline in the *Cincinnati Enquirer* describing her suffrage work as "Miss Laura Clay's Plan for White Supremacy." This headline depicting Clay plotting to ensure white supremacy in the South as her primary political reform agenda illustrates the paradox of Clay's career as a national woman suffrage Progressive reformer who often allowed the regional demands of southernness and white supremacy to trump her more principled, albeit elitist, call for educated woman suffrage open to all women who qualified.[1]

Laura Clay's family wealth and political history were integral to her ideological commitment to and her financial ability to devote much of her adult life to suffrage work. Her father, Cassius Marcellus Clay, was one of the largest landowners in Madison County and active in politics, serving in the Kentucky state legislature and as minister to Russia for six years. Her mother, Mary Jane Warfield, was the daughter of a prosperous businessman. After they married, Cassius Clay and Mary Jane Warfield Clay settled in an Italianate mansion, Clermont (later renamed White Hall), on the Madison County estate—more

LAURA CLAY

Laura Clay Photographic Collection, Special Collections,
University of Kentucky Libraries, Lexington.

than two thousand acres—that Clay had inherited from his father, Green Clay.[2] In the mid-1850s, however, Cassius Clay suffered a serious financial setback that lasted almost a decade, and, according to Laura Clay's biographer, Paul Fuller, her mother was primarily responsible for putting the family back on a sound financial footing. Although Mary Jane Clay had kept the Clays' business affairs in order while her husband was in Russia, when they divorced following his return, she was left with no financial recompense for her business efforts or her contributions to the family income. Even though her deceased father's wealth allowed her to maintain a middle-class standard of living for the rest of her life, Mary Jane Clay's experience of the financial and political gender inequities of the time played a role in her daughters' interests in women's rights.[3] And while Cassius Clay did not provide for his wife on their divorce, he did provide for his children, allotting Laura Clay, for example, three hundred acres that she managed as a successful farming enterprise that made possible her financial independence and stability throughout her life.[4]

Laura Clay also seems to have inherited her parents' commitment to political activism. Cassius Clay was a fervent antislavery advocate whose views often made him unpopular in a slaveholding state. He was well known for traveling armed and ready to fight to defend his and other antislavery advocates' rights to free speech.[5] Clay favored the gradual emancipation of slavery through "free discussion and the ballot" in accordance with the Kentucky state and U.S. constitutions so as to avoid extralegal means such as slaves running away or armed rebellion.[6] Indeed, his antislavery ideology often seemed more concerned with the welfare of white Kentuckians than of enslaved blacks, as he believed that slavery limited the economic opportunity of nonslaveholding white Kentucky farmers and their voice and power in the state.[7] Clay evidenced a strong belief in the structures of the political system to advance the cause of emancipation, which led some abolitionists to accuse him of relying too much on "expediency" and compromise with the existing political framework. These beliefs and his denunciation of federal intervention in the South during Reconstruction to protect the rights of newly freed slaves foreshadowed the later inability of his daughter, Laura, to see beyond the limitations of the existing southern political system to secure woman suffrage for all women, including African American women.[8]

Laura Clay's diary, which she kept sporadically between 1864 and 1880, outlines the trajectory of her ideological commitments and points to her determination from a relatively early age to achieve those commitments. The first set of entries, from 1864 to 1865, began when she was fifteen years old and displayed much of the obsession with piety, obedience, and submission that historian

Anne Firor Scott has described as typical of young southern elite women at the time.[9] Clay's entries primarily chronicle her fear that she did not have the requisite faith, repentance, and will toward God that she believed she needed to be a good Christian. But rather than give up her desire to feel her faith more deeply and sincerely, Clay determined instead to work harder at the outward signs of faith until her inward faith caught up.[10] These early diary entries also demonstrate characteristics she would manifest throughout her long career as a woman's rights activist. For instance, the opening of her entry dated May 15, 1864, reveals her spirit of rebelliousness, her faith in reason, and her belief in her own abilities, especially in her intelligence: "I wish to reason with myself. I feel rebellious sometimes about the difference in intellectual power between men and women." Although Clay recognized that these feelings challenged traditional gender norms, later in the entry she consoled herself through her faith in the rewards of heaven, where she believed men and women would be equal. Yet she steadfastly refused to deny her faith in herself: "I think I have a mind superior to that of many boys my age, and equal to that of many more. Therefore when we get to heaven, we will be equal. If I am not perfectly submissive hereafter, I will pray God to make me so. Except for this feeling of inequality, I think I prefer being a woman to a man."[11]

When Clay resumed her diary ten years later, she reflected on the entries made by her younger self. She specifically returned to the use of the term "rebelliousness" and acknowledged that her entry a decade earlier perhaps represented "some of the first stirrings of the feelings and opinions which now I believe to be the main motives next to the general desire for the spread of God's kingdom for my activity in life. I allude to my Woman's Rights opinions." In 1874, rather than attempting to console herself with the possibility of gender equity in the "hereafter," Clay now asserted that God had called her to work for woman's rights, "both through my feelings which call me that way and the education of life which has fixed . . . my thoughts and opinions." She reiterated that she was not jealous of men but only wanted women to "awake to the higher life which God through the advance of Christian civilization has opened to them." By this time Clay's parents had separated and her father had welcomed a boy who was possibly his illegitimate son into his home at White Hall, circumstances Clay acknowledged when she wrote, "Our own unhappy domestic life has left my eyes unblinded to the unjust relations between men and women and the unworthy position of women." And, in perhaps her most unrestrained reflection on gender and her "education of life," Clay continued: "When I consider the unspotted chastity, the temperance, the unselfishness, the daily ruling of life by duty of women, and compare it to the sensual and selfish lives of men, it seems to me marvelous that their virtues should be overlooked by the world and all the great evolutions in the moral world should be imputed to men."[12]

By 1878 Clay had set herself on a path dedicated to extraordinary personal achievement and service to other women. Although she was uncertain exactly what her profession would be, she felt a clear responsibility to use her "more than ordinary intellect" in the service of others. She would go on to use that intellect for more than three decades in the fight for woman suffrage.[13]

In the late 1870s Laura Clay, her mother, and her sisters—Mary Barr Clay, Sallie Bennett Clay, and Annie Clay—all became involved in the woman suffrage movement. In 1869 the national woman suffrage movement had split into two factions—the National Woman Suffrage Association (NWSA) led by Elizabeth Cady Stanton and Susan B. Anthony, and the American Woman Suffrage Association (AWSA) led by Lucy Stone and Henry Blackwell—owing largely to tensions over the passage of the Fourteenth and Fifteenth Amendments to the U.S. Constitution granting provisions for suffrage to African American men. The suffragists who formed the NWSA had argued that the amendments should not be ratified unless they included provisions for woman suffrage, while those who formed the AWSA regretted that the amendments did not include provisions for woman suffrage but believed that including women would jeopardize their passage. The two groups also differed over the question of how best to obtain woman suffrage legislation. The NWSA worked for the passage of a federal amendment, whereas the AWSA argued that suffragists should work to enfranchise women through individual states.[14] Although the Clay sisters had worked with both organizations before they united in 1890, the issues of African American suffrage and of federal versus state enfranchisement would continue to haunt Laura Clay and other southern white suffragists until the ratification of the Nineteenth Amendment in 1920.[15]

In 1888 Clay helped organize and served as president of two suffrage groups in Kentucky, first the Fayette County Equal Rights Association and then the statewide Kentucky Equal Rights Association (KERA).[16] Like other prominent southern suffragists at the time, she tried to use her involvement in the Woman's Christian Temperance Union (WCTU) to further the cause of woman suffrage. Under the leadership of Frances Willard, the national WCTU made a concerted effort to organize southern women. In 1881 Willard undertook her first extended and well-publicized tours of the South during which she organized ten southern states, including Kentucky. At its annual convention that year, under pressure from Willard, the national WCTU adopted a franchise department to agitate for woman suffrage, although Willard, recognizing the conservatism of the South on the issue, emphasized a policy of "states' rights" to keep the newly organized southern states from bolting.[17] (The Kentucky WCTU would not adopt a franchise department until 1892.) WCTU members did provide Clay and other southern suffragists a network through which they could get their message to the general public. In 1892 Clay wrote to Mollie McGee Snell, former corresponding secretary of the Mississippi WCTU and national evangelist for the WCTU, urging her to also write and advocate on behalf of equal rights for women. Although Snell declined, citing her other commitments, she professed her commitment to the cause ("I too make equal rights a part of my religion") and agreed to help expand the network of southern white suffragists. "I will promulgate the principle of equal rights as I go throughout the state, will also sound around and give you [a] list . . . of the suffragists I discover in the different places," she vowed.[18]

In the decade following its founding, Laura Clay and the KERA worked tirelessly to improve the legal and social conditions of women in Kentucky. In 1890 Kentucky called a convention to rewrite its state constitution. Clay and a delegation of women from the KERA went to Frankfort to lobby for women's rights to be included in the new document. The delegation asked for full suffrage for women, property rights for wives, and the extension of full school suffrage to all women. Although the delegates appointed a special Committee on Woman's Rights and granted Clay the right to speak before the convention, the only woman suffrage clause written into the new constitution was one giving the general assembly the right to grant women school suffrage. Nonetheless, the KERA later managed to win two significant victories during the 1894 general assembly: the passage of the Married Woman's Property Rights Bill, which gave women control of their personal property and real estate after marriage, and legislation granting women the right to vote for and hold positions on school boards in the cities of Covington, Lexington, and Newport. Two years later, working with the Kentucky WCTU, the KERA secured funding for a separate girls' juvenile home with funding equal to the boys' home and equal representation for women on the board of trustees. And after ten years of submitting petitions, in 1898 the KERA successfully lobbied the general assembly to pass a bill requiring at least one woman physician in state mental institutions.[19]

On the national level, the NAWSA, largely owing to Clay's prodding, in 1892 formed a special committee on southern work with the Kentuckian as chair.[20] Using this committee to further develop a network of southern suffragists, Clay maintained a steady correspondence with women throughout the South. Working through state presidents, she asked her correspondents to send her names of women who might be interested in the suffrage movement. She then sent them national suffrage material, including the *Woman's Journal*, and various state suffrage newspapers to aid their recruiting and organizing efforts. Illustrating her deep commitment to the South and her determination that her native region would lead the nation in the fight for woman suffrage, Clay also used this committee to solicit funds from other members across the nation to support the southern work by purchasing literature and sponsoring speakers to tour southern states.[21] At the 1894 NAWSA convention, however, after Clay had made a direct appeal for funds, a New York delegate intimated that donating funds for the southern committee took money away from other states' efforts and asked that New York delegates "hold on to their hearts and purses" until their own work was sufficiently funded. In response, Clay passionately argued that success in the South was more important because it would spur other regions, especially the North, to enact woman suffrage. If Democratic states in the South granted woman suffrage, Clay declared, Democratic politicians in New York would "fall over themselves to give the women of New York suffrage." Indeed, Clay said that she would "go further" and assert that the "North cannot be carried until you have the South with you." To bolster her point, she predicted: "Every Southern organized state helps Kansas and New York to win and when the whole South is organized the tone of the press all over the country will have changed, and no one can estimate the past effect and the present effect and the continuous effect upon every state in the United States." Clay's response set off a miniregional debate that had to be calmed by Susan B. Anthony, who declared that the NAWSA "shall know no North, no South, no East, no West, no Kansas, no New York, as above each and every other state in the Union."[22] Although a small regional dustup, this episode illustrates Clay's vision and the tenacity of her faith in the South's power to lead the national movement.

At the same 1894 NAWSA convention, Clay argued that had Mississippi had a state woman suffrage association in 1890, its constitutional convention that year might well have granted woman suffrage because, according to Clay, two-fifths of the convention delegates had voted to support a proposal to grant woman suffrage with an educational qualification. Anthony quickly agreed with Clay, noting that "it was out of our bitter experience of 1890 that the Southern Committee was formed."[23] Therefore, when South Carolina called a convention in 1895, like Mississippi's 1890 gathering, primarily to disfranchise black male voters, Clay joined a delegation of suffragists in attempting to persuade its convention to enact woman suffrage with an educational qualification.

Clay and her colleagues were well received in the Palmetto State. Her speeches during the South Carolina campaign contained the arguments that she would use to support the vote for women during the rest of her suffrage career. Clay based her case on Christianity, industrialization, and maintenance of white supremacy. Harkening back to her earlier years when she had comforted herself that men and women would be equal in the afterlife, Clay now argued that because the souls of men and women were equal before God, they should be equal before the law. Clay also insisted that because industrialization had forced many women to work outside the home, they needed the vote to protect their rights in the marketplace.[24] Yet Clay's final argument that woman suffrage with an educational and property qualification would ensure white supremacy is the most difficult to confront.

In the late nineteenth- and early twentieth-century South, Clay would have been considered a racial moderate. She believed that whites were intellectually and morally superior to blacks and better suited to guide the political affairs of the region. Like many other southern white suffragists, she resented that black males had been enfranchised before what she considered better qualified white women.[25] Unfortunately for Clay, though, woman suffrage and African American suffrage were inextricably and negatively linked in the minds of many white southerners. As W. E. B. DuBois wrote in 1912, "Any agitation, discussion or reopening of the problem of voting must inevitably be a discussion of the right of black folk to vote in America. . . . Essentially the arguments for and against are the same in the case of all groups of human beings."[26] Therefore, Clay's racially moderate views must be considered in the context of not only her time and region but also their ideological and principled consistency and the limitations that they placed on her goal of extending the franchise to women.

Five years before the South Carolina convention, in 1890, Clay wrote a response to a call to disfranchise southern black men that, had she consistently hewed to her arguments, would have made her one of the few southern white suffragists who advocated explicitly or implicitly the equitable treatment of southern African Americans and the vote.[27] However, it is unclear whether Laura Clay was arguing from principled ideology or political expediency to further the cause of woman suffrage. In her editorial, Clay insisted that a "sense of justice" would prevent the "wholesale disenfranchisement of a race." The complaint of southern whites was not that African American males had the vote, she said, but rather that the numerical impact of their vote was out of proportion to the "intelligence and virtue that they bring to the support of Republican government."[28] The real problem, Clay maintained, was how to restore what she viewed as the necessary white supremacy without "corrupting the ballot box, or repudiating the principles of true Democracy, which defends the right of every class to representation."

As a solution to this problem, Clay advocated giving educated women the vote regardless of race. This would have been a racially progressive position for a white southerner in 1890; however, Clay's logic was predicated on the fact that woman suffrage with an educational qualification would ensure white supremacy while preventing the addition of an "enormous number of ignorant negro women to the mass of ignorant negro men voters." Clay acknowledged that two states—Mississippi and South Carolina—had black majorities but assured her readers that the enfranchisement of "educated women" would give the whites a majority and "the white men, reinforced by the educated white women, could 'snow under' the negro vote in every state."[29] Clay's use of the term "ignorant negro vote" was a common discursive trope among white suffragists in the late nineteenth century, designed to not only denigrate black male voters but also discredit the very idea of most African Americans being suited to responsible citizenship. Clay ended her editorial with a gesture toward democracy and national reconciliation that nonetheless highlighted how inextricably intertwined the woman suffrage and race questions were in the South: "The race question of the South must ultimately be settled by the statesmen of the South, and in a manner approved by the sense of justice of the whole nation," she insisted. "It would be a noble and honorable thing for the south if for its settlement they should inaugurate the next great triumph of Democratic principles for which the world watches and waits,—woman suffrage."[30]

Three years later, in 1893, Clay wrote a letter to the editors of the *Woman's Journal* that further muddled her principles regarding the woman suffrage question and race. Her letter was in support of an earlier editorial written by H. Augusta Howard, a suffragist from Georgia, on noted Massachusetts senator and abolitionist Charles Sumner and the enfranchisement of women. Clay agreed with Howard's conclusion that Sumner's willingness to advocate the enfranchisement of African American men before the enfranchisement of white women diminished his stature and claim to greatness as an advocate of democratic principles and equality. Granting that Sumner's role in the abolition of slavery was honorable, Clay argued that "his part in conferring political privileges on the negro men, while he left the enfranchisement of all women 'to the future and to themselves' is a blot on his fame that I . . . [and] . . . any future generation of both men and women can . . . but regard as a flaw in the man whom they will honor for his other worth."[31]

As in her 1890 editorial, Clay evidenced unusually democratic principles for southern whites of the time when she declared that "the ultimate political enfranchisement of the negro man was right, none wishes to dispute." She concluded, however, with the caveat that with the laws, physical force, and the "bias of sex always pleading for him," African American men could have been "left 'to the future' and to himself." Clay asserted that politicians first should have helped women, whose case, she said, was "harder and whose ability for self-help was less." Indeed, not only did Clay argue that black men's enfranchisement could have waited; she also insisted that "every principle of justice demanded that the rights of women should have taken precedence." (It is unclear if Clay meant to include black women in her demand for justice.) Clay overshadowed her earlier democratic gesture toward the justice of enfranchising black men by her later assertion that Sumner had actively injured women by enfranchising black men because, she maintained, black men's stage of "mental and moral development" made them "hostile to the rights of women." Clay ended with the lament that the greatest affront Sumner and his colleagues imposed on women was that they had added the word *male* to the Constitution for the first time in the passage of the Fourteenth Amendment, which happened solely to confer the vote on black men.[32] Although making some concessions to the justice of enfranchising black men, Clay seemed unable to concede that point without ultimately questioning the legitimacy of black men as worthy of the franchise.

When in South Carolina, in the interest of political expediency, Clay further compromised the more democratic principles she expressed in her editorials.[33] As noted above, Clay argued that woman suffrage with an educational qualification would guarantee white supremacy in South Carolina because there were more educated white women than black women, thereby yielding a majority of white voters.[34] However, Clay did not hold to her position of educated suffrage for South Carolina women voters. She shifted her position when some delegates to the constitutional convention questioned whether an educational qualification would prove restrictive enough to ensure white supremacy. Rather than standing by her principled support of an educational qualification applied equally to black and white women, Clay instead wrote to South Carolina officials and other suffragists to find out the number of black and white women owning taxable property of at least three hundred dollars in each county. Mrs. M. A. Conley of Lexington, South Carolina, reported that there were 8 black women and 426 white women with taxable property in that amount. Conley added: "So you see there is no danger of losing white supremacy by the exception of those eight votes provided that they all vote. Probably not one of them would attempt to vote if they had the chance."[35]

In South Carolina Clay did not refuse to support a property qualification in addition to an educational qualification for woman suffrage, although it clearly violated her ideological principle that woman suffrage was needed to protect the interests of women who had been forced to work outside the home. The racial calculus here is underlined by Clay's refusal a decade later to support a similar property qualification for woman suffrage in the Oregon campaign. Clay's biographer, Paul Fuller, does not address the contradiction of Clay's willingness to accept a property qualification for women in South Carolina but not in Oregon. Yet he does argue that the seeming contradiction in Clay's willingness to accept an educational qualification in Kentucky but not a property qualification in Oregon (and later Pennsylvania) rested in her assumption that the majority of women disfranchised by an educational qualification alone would be African American, while almost all (additional) women disfranchised by a tax-paying qualification would be native-born white women.[36] Fuller maintains that Clay was typical of nineteenth-century white suffragists who were willing to disfranchise blacks and immigrants while fighting for the right of native-born white women to vote. In fact, he argues that Clay so strongly opposed a tax-paying qualification for woman suffrage in Oregon that she threatened to pull her support if it was adopted.[37] Yet in South Carolina, with its larger proportion of blacks, Clay was apparently willing to disfranchise native-born white working women if necessary to ensure a white majority vote.

In the decade and a half following the South Carolina constitutional convention, Clay became a national leader in the suffrage movement. In 1896 she was elected first auditor of the NAWSA, an office she would hold for almost sixteen years. From 1902 to 1907 Clay also chaired the NAWSA Increase of Membership Committee, where, according to Fuller, she almost tripled the membership of the national organization from 17,000 in 1905 to 45,501 in 1907, when she resigned as chair. Fuller states that Clay's reforms during her tenure as chair of the membership committee were key to the continued growth of the NAWSA, which by 1915 would claim more than a hundred thousand members. During this period Clay also led or played major roles in suffrage campaigns in Oregon (1906) and in the statehood constitutional conventions of Oklahoma (1906–7) and Arizona (1909).[38]

As in South Carolina, Clay's work in the Oklahoma campaign again highlighted the link between woman suffrage and black suffrage. In a speech before the Oklahoma constitutional convention, Clay advocated for woman suffrage based on a collective statement issued by the Conference of Southern Women Suffragists, who had convened in Memphis, Tennessee, in December 1906 at the request of Belle Kearney, a well-known national WCTU lecturer and Mississippi suffragist. Clay was elected president of the conference, whose "Statement of Purpose" called for the "enfranchisement of all women who can read and write" but added the familiar appeal to white supremacy: "We ask for the ballot as a solution of the race problem. There are over 600,000 more white women in the southern states than all the negro men and women combined."[39] In a telling exchange of letters, Clay was chastised by a Kentucky suffragist, Laura White, who wrote that she was "sorry to see that you had used the race problem argument in Oklahoma." White argued that in addition to angering blacks and aligning them against woman suffragists, the argument was a "very poor" one. She cited a letter in her hometown newspaper that claimed that blacks had held the swing vote in thirty-two elections in Kentucky and that temperance advocates who "controlled" the black vote in thirty-one elections had lost only the one in which they did not "get the negro vote." White closed by suggesting to Clay that attempting to appeal to black voters as had the prohibitionists would be a more effective strategy than alienating them. She expressed her hope that Clay's argument would "do no harm."[40]

Clay's response to White demonstrates the fine line that Clay walked between her personal principles, her regional loyalty, and her political goals. Clay began by assuring White that the NAWSA was not responsible for the "race argument" but that it had been used at the behest of the Oklahoma suffragists. Marshaling other southern suffragists to bolster her position, she noted that the newly formed Tennessee Equal Rights Association had also chosen to use the argument in a thousand leaflets it recently had printed. Furthermore, Clay reminded White that the argument had originally been proposed by social activist Henry B. Blackwell, a founder of the AWSA, whom she described as a "very warm friend of the negro race." Like Blackwell, she believed it provided the best protection for black voters because the only "dignified position" southern opponents of black suffrage would allow was for blacks to be a "minority vote, where his vote is not feared, and therefore not fraudulently cast out." This echoed Clay's own 1890 editorial and the southern suffragists' reassurance that "a large white majority dispenses with the necessity of doubtful expedients for minimizing the negro vote." Thus, like many southern Progressives, Clay argued that integrity could be restored to southern politics by eliminating the influence of black male voters. In reply to White's possibly rhetorical question as to whether the race problem had been solved in Kentucky, where, she noted, whites outnumbered blacks by a large majority, Clay replied that no problem existed in her native state because whites so far outnumbered blacks that they did not fear blacks' having the franchise; therefore the black vote was "as free and uninhibited as that of any other ignorant and venal class."[41] This assessment of African Americans and their fitness for the privileges and prerogatives of responsible citizenship could explain why by 1907 Clay had moved considerably away from her principled advocacy of suffrage for educated women, both white and black.

Shortly after the Conference of Southern Women Suffragists' meeting in 1906 that produced the Statement of Purpose that Clay defended, Belle Kearney proposed launching a campaign to petition the Mississippi state legislature for suffrage for women in presidential elections. After consulting with other Mississippi suffragists and with NAWSA officials including Laura Clay, Louisiana's Kate Gordon, and Henry Blackwell, Kearney acceded to Gordon's demand that she ask for full suffrage but for white women only. Like Clay, Gordon was deeply loyal to the South. Both women constantly lobbied the NAWSA to provide more resources for southern efforts and consistently warned the national organization that woman suffrage could not be won nationally without southern support. Clay approved of Kearney and Blackwell's original proposal to ask for presidential suffrage. Gordon, however, refused to support the effort, believing that it was useless given the two-dollar poll tax in many southern states and the dominance of the Democratic Party, which meant that most general elections were, according to Gordon, a "foregone conclusion."[42] Blackwell acquiesced to the southern suffragists' demand to ask for suffrage for white women only; after all, Mississippi women had a right to direct a Mississippi campaign as they saw fit.[43] Gordon lobbied Anna Howard Shaw and the NAWSA to endorse the effort, but Clay and Blackwell agreed that the organization should stay out of the campaign if it sought suffrage for white women only.[44]

Clay's role in the discussions reveals a contradictory mix of political principle and expediency that ultimately demonstrates how Clay's democratic impulses concerning woman suffrage were restricted and restrained by her paramount concern for southern states' rights and its ideological and political commitments to white supremacy. Kate Gordon instigated and insisted that Kearney make her request for woman suffrage explicitly and exclusively for white women only. Clay appears to have embraced the idea as a politically expedient opportunity to test its constitutionality and to advance Gordon's plan to challenge *Minor v. Happersett* (1875), a Supreme Court decision that ruled that the Fourteenth Amendment did not confer the right to vote on women when it bestowed citizenship on those born or naturalized in the United States.[45] In opposition to Gordon, Clay explained to Anna Howard Shaw that although she was personally willing to aid the effort, she did not want the NAWSA to become involved; she doubted the constitutionality of requesting suffrage for white women only and was afraid that the national organization would appear to lack "sound judgment" if it supported a measure that was subsequently ruled unconstitutional. Clay further explained that she looked on the Mississippi effort as an "experimental venture" that should not be endorsed "at present" by suffragists nationally.[46] Clay had expressed to Gordon her belief that Mississippi was a likely state in which to test the principle of white women's suffrage because it and South Carolina were the only two states with African American majorities. Clay firmly believed that southern politicians in states with large numbers of blacks would not reopen the suffrage issue unless they could be assured that no additional African American voters would be added to the rolls and that the black vote would be of no consequence in elections.[47] Yet Clay continued to insist that she herself believed in the principle of equal suffrage: "Personally, I desire to see every fit person endowed with the ballot, as the rightful expression of the inalienable right of self-government."[48]

Treading a fine line between political expediency and principled ideology, Clay drew a distinction between the abstract principle of the individual's "inalienable right of self-government" and the actual right to "help govern others" that comes with the franchise. In a letter to Catherine Waugh McCulloch, Clay insisted that "the southern people . . . do not indulge in any delusions about a childlike and irresponsible race." She continued: "Their circumstances force them to see that a ballot for every man and a fair count means, where there are more negroes than whites, as in Mississippi, an abandonment of civilization as white Americans have maintained it, and a decline to a state of society suited to the mental and moral development of negroes." Although Clay reiterated that she did not want the Democrats or the South to "advocate qualification of color," she hoped that there would be no "constitutional bar to an individual state's regulating woman suffrage by such qualifications as it feels is necessary for its own prosperity."[49]

Clay seemed either unable or unwilling to confront the contradiction or the irony in her position. If a state were permitted to regulate woman suffrage as it saw fit, then it was unlikely that most southern states would allow the "inalienable right of self-government" to African American women. Additionally, Clay seems not to have considered that a state might think its "prosperity" dependent on restricting the franchise to male voters. But Clay did attempt to mitigate the harm that her position posed for potential African American women voters. Harkening back to her 1893 Charles Sumner editorial, Clay argued that the legal position of women was far inferior to the position of blacks; therefore it was more important that some white women be enfranchised than for black women or black men to be able to vote. Besides, Clay reasoned, if white women had the vote and improved laws for women, black women would share in the improved conditions.[50]

The debate over the Mississippi campaign for white woman suffrage moved Laura Clay farther from her principled position of educated woman suffrage. After traveling to Mississippi to meet with Gordon and the Mississippi suffragists, Clay reported to Henry Blackwell that the women had decided that they would ask for a constitutional amendment granting white women the vote on the same terms as men only if the word "white" was upheld as constitutional by legal experts and only if politicians confirmed that there was no possibility that reopening the suffrage question would jeopardize white supremacy. For Clay this represented the limits of woman suffrage within the confines of white supremacy. "You see," she told Blackwell, "not even for woman suffrage would these southern suffragists jeopardize white supremacy."[51]

By 1911 Clay's work both inside and outside southern states had made her a leader in the national woman suffrage movement. But that year, as a result of a growing rift on the NAWSA board of directors between Clay and her allies, mainly from western states, and Anna Howard Shaw and her mostly eastern allies, Clay was defeated for reelection to the position of first auditor that she had held in the NAWSA for fifteen years. The disagreements between the two factions ranged over a number of issues, including the location of national headquarters, the frequency of board meetings, and auxiliary membership quotas. Although the convention was held in Louisville, in Clay's home state, she was defeated for four positions on the board. Paul Fuller argues that Anna Howard Shaw and her friends on the board had prearranged a strategy to defeat Clay and her allies.[52] The Kentuckian was gracious in defeat and accepted the chairmanship of the membership committee, a position she would hold for the next two years. Immediately after the NAWSA convention, Clay engineered her own removal from office as president of the KERA, a position she had occupied since its 1888 founding, and chose as her successor Madeline McDowell Breckinridge of Lexington. Between 1911 and 1917 Clay continued to work in various state suffrage campaigns and speak at state suffrage conventions in eastern and midwestern states.[53] And she remained an influential voice in the KERA until her resignation in 1919, when she could no longer countenance the organization's support for ratification of the Nineteenth Amendment.

Scholars of the southern suffrage movement generally agree that Laura Clay never actually supported women's enfranchisement through federal legislation. Paul Fuller and fellow historian Marjorie Spruill Wheeler maintain that Clay was willing to work within the NAWSA as long as the possibility of a federal amendment was remote and the national organization continued to support work for state suffrage amendments.[54] With the election of Carrie Chapman Catt as president of the NAWSA in 1915, the prospects for the federal amendment were revitalized. In September 1916, at a special convention meeting of the NAWSA in Atlantic City, Catt introduced and received the endorsement of more than thirty-six state presidents for her "Winning Plan" to work for woman suffrage through a federal amendment. The plan called for highly organized and centralized woman suffrage work that would be directed by the national organization; state suffrage societies were to subsume their goals to the wishes of the NAWSA. Although Catt had already determined that the NAWSA would concentrate its work on the federal amendment, during the convention, the delegates held a three-cornered debate as to whether the national should work solely for state amendments, solely for the federal amendment, or for both state and federal legislation as set forth in the organization's constitution and bylaws. Unsurprisingly, Laura Clay and Kate Gordon took the position that the association should work solely for the passage of state amendments. When Catt put the question to the delegates, they voted not to change the constitution. Catt then ingeniously proposed a resolution stating that the debate had determined that "Article II of the constitution, which provides that suffrage shall be secured by appropriate National and State legislation, shall be interpreted to mean that the immediate and principal object of the association is to secure the submission of a Federal amendment and that State campaigns are preparedness to that end."[55] Although Clay and Gordon protested this resolution, it passed the convention by a wide margin.

Clay continued to believe that the federal amendment was a long shot given that the House of Representatives had defeated the amendment in January 1915, the party platforms of both the Republicans and Democrats recommended woman suffrage by state action, and the South would never support the federal amendment.[56] By this time, Clay had begun to vigorously advocate for her U.S. Elections Bill, which would give women the right to vote for U.S. congressmen and senators. Although the U.S. Elections Bill had to be passed by federal legislation, Clay argued that it did not violate the principles of states' rights because, in matters other than gender, states could determine qualifications for voters. Clay believed that southern women could use the political leverage afforded by federal suffrage to press their states for state suffrage amendments. Under Anna Howard Shaw's leadership, the NAWSA had endorsed Clay's bill at its 1914 Nashville convention (and would do so again in 1916), but the bill did not fit into Carrie Chapman Catt's Winning Plan for concentrated work on the federal amendment and thus languished without real organizational support.[57]

In addition to moving farther away from her colleagues in the NAWSA, Clay was also becoming more at odds with the KERA. The majority of Kentucky suffragists, like the majority of southern suffragists, decided to follow Catt's Winning Plan. According to Madeline McDowell Breckinridge, although there had been a good chance the Kentucky state legislature would have passed woman suffrage in 1918, the KERA decided to abide by the wishes of the NAWSA and concentrate on passing the federal amendment. Clay was one of only two executive board members who voted to oppose the NAWSA plan and instead work for the state amendment. In June 1918, when Catt visited Lexington, Clay cast the only negative vote on a resolution to ask the Kentucky legislature to endorse the federal amendment. When the U.S. Senate approved the Anthony amendment, she resigned from the KERA and helped organize and fund the Citizen's Committee for a State Suffrage Amendment. This group's intent was to lobby Kentucky legislators and the delegates to the state Democratic convention to pass a state suffrage amendment and to oppose the Anthony amendment.[58]

Laura Clay continued to insist that her opposition to the federal amendment was based on states' rights principles, particularly the enforcement clause of the amendment, which, she contended, would give Congress power over state elections. At one point, calling the proposed federal amendment the "Anthony Force Bill," Clay argued that the South was not the only vulnerable section. All states, she said, would lose power over their state governments, especially less populous and far western states. As an example, she suggested that the Japanese would be able to gain any concession they desired from Pacific states, if, through their "diplomacy" and their "friends" among U.S. voters, they could "win a party in the western states or other states favorable to them."[59] Clay consistently denied that her opposition to the Anthony amendment was because it would enfranchise black women. However, in her appeals to western congressmen, she was making a race-based argument that echoed the earlier statements that she made to try to persuade southern politicians to support woman suffrage as a way to guarantee white supremacy.

Although Clay did not lobby against the amendment in her home state, which ratified it on January 6, 1920, she acquiesced to her friend Kate Gordon's request to travel to Tennessee to work against the amendment. Both she and Gordon were extremely disappointed that a southern state provided the necessary ratification vote when Tennessee approved the Anthony amendment on August 18, 1920.[60]

After ratification, Clay continued to be active in Kentucky politics. She helped organize the Democratic Women's Club of Kentucky, but, adhering to her faith in local control of political issues, she refused to join the League of Women Voters. "In my judgment the glory and the strength of our government is the large measure of local self-government which is given to the people," she declared, "and I am therefore jealous of any movement which endeavors to centralize power in Washington and to diminish the people's watchfulness over the legislation which effects their own peculiar requirements."[61] Likewise, despite her long years of membership in the WCTU, Clay in the 1920s came to support the repeal of the Eighteenth Amendment. Although she favored temperance, she claimed never to have supported federal prohibition, again citing states' rights as the preeminent reason why the "noble experiment" should be repealed. In

1928 she campaigned for the "wet" Democratic presidential nominee Al Smith. She remained active in the Episcopal Church—and its politics—until her death in Lexington on June 29, 1941. She was ninety-two.[62]

Laura Clay was a steadfast advocate of woman suffrage who devoted much of her mental, physical, and financial resources to the cause. She was also an ardent and consistent defender of the doctrine of states' rights. Only briefly wavering in her commitment to states' rights, she opposed the federal suffrage amendment that achieved the goal for which she had worked for more than thirty years. Clay was a southern suffragist who said that she upheld the right of all qualified educated women to vote. However, she seemed unable or unwilling to confront the political reality that during her lifetime, in most southern states, her advocacy of equal suffrage for educated women regardless of race could not be realized under the doctrine of states' rights and its concomitant commitment to white supremacy.

NOTES

1. *Cincinnati Enquirer*, October 21, 1893, Laura Clay scrapbook, box 18, folder 1, Laura Clay Papers, Special Collections and Archives, Margaret I. King Library, University of Kentucky Libraries (hereafter cited as Clay Papers).

2. For information on Cassius Clay, see Harold Richardson, *Cassius Marcellus Clay: Firebrand of Freedom* (Lexington: University Press of Kentucky, 1976), and David L. Smiley, *Lion of White Hall: The Life of Cassius M. Clay* (1962; Gloucester, Mass.: Peter Smith, 1969). See also William Kuby's essay in this volume, "Mary Jane Warfield Clay: Wifely Devotion, Divorce, and Rebirth in Nineteenth-Century Kentucky," 59–80.

3. Paul E. Fuller, *Laura Clay and the Woman's Rights Movement* (Lexington: University Press of Kentucky, 1975), 16. Fuller's excellent biography remains the most in-depth treatment of Clay's life and work. Marjorie Spruill Wheeler covers Clay's involvement in the suffrage movement in her comprehensive and indispensable study of the southern suffrage movement, *New Women of the New South: The Leaders of the Woman Suffrage Movement in the Southern States* (New York: Oxford University Press, 1993). For an earlier brief discussion of Laura Clay, see Clavia Goodman, *Bitter Harvest: Laura Clay's Suffrage Work* (Lexington, Ky.: Burr Press, 1946).

4. Laura Clay paid her father rent for the land until his death. See Fuller, *Laura Clay*, 17.

5. David L. Smiley, "Cassius Clay and John G. Fee: A Study in Southern Anti-Slavery Thought," *Journal of Negro History* 42 (1957): 204–8.

6. Cassius Marcellus Clay, *The Life of Cassius Marcellus Clay: Memoirs, Writings, and Speeches*, vol. 1 (Cincinnati: J. Fletcher Brennan, 1886), 106–7, 571–72; Smiley, *Lion of White Hall*, 48–51; Richardson, *Firebrand of Freedom*, 20–23.

7. Smiley, "Cassius M. Clay and John G. Fee," 203, 205; Richardson, *Firebrand of Freedom*, 19.

8. Cassius Marcellus Clay, *Life of Cassius Marcellus Clay*, 572. On Cassius Clay and Reconstruction, see ibid., 511–19.

9. Anne Firor Scott, *The Southern Lady: From Pedestal to Politics* (Chicago: University of Chicago Press, 1970).

10. Laura Clay Diary, n.p., box 1, folder 1, Clay Papers. By 1874, when Clay began her second set of diary entries, she decided that she had, indeed, become a better Christian but resolved to continue to monitor her "besetting sin" of indolence. See Clay Diary, July 26, 1874, Clay Papers (hereafter cited as Clay Diary).

11. Clay Diary, May 15, 1864.

12. Ibid., July 26, 1874, October 25, 1874.

13. Ibid., July 15, 1878.

14. Aileen Kraditor, *Ideas of the Woman Suffrage Movement, 1890–1920* (New York: Norton, 1981), 3–4; Carol Ellen Du Bois, *Feminism and Suffrage: The Emergence of an Independent Woman's Movement* (Ithaca, N.Y.: Cornell University Press, 1999); Eleanor Flexner, *Century of Struggle: The Woman's Rights Movement in the United States* (New York: Atheneum, 1971), 140–55.

15. Mary Barr Clay, "Kentucky," in *History of Woman Suffrage*, ed. Elizabeth Cady Stanton, Susan B. Anthony, and Matilda Gage, 3 vols. (Rochester, N.Y.: privately published, 1887), 3:819.

16. Laura Clay, "Kentucky," in *History of Woman Suffrage*, ed. Susan B. Anthony and Ida Husted Harper, 6 vols. (Rochester, N.Y.: privately published, 1902), 4:665.

17. On the WCTU and the South, see Ruth Bordin, *Woman and Temperance: The Quest for Power and Liberty, 1873–1900* (Philadelphia: Temple University Press, 1981), 76–85.

18. M. M. Snell to Laura Clay, March 24, 1892, box 1, folder 6, Clay Papers.

19. Laura Clay, "Kentucky," 665–73. For a detailed discussion of the activities of the KERA during these years, see Fuller, *Laura Clay*, 41–48.

20. Harriet Taylor Upton, ed., *Handbook of National American Woman Suffrage Association, 1893* (Washington, D.C: Stormont & Jackson, 1893), 76.

21. Box 1, folder 7, Clay Papers; Fuller, *Laura Clay*, 57–59.

22. Upton, *Handbook of NAWSA*, 1894, 51, 53.

23. Ibid., 48–49. According to A. Elizabeth Taylor, Clay's assessment of the support for woman suffrage among the Mississippi delegates was optimistic. Although various proposals were offered, the issue never came to a vote. Even Hala Hammond Butts, who wrote the Mississippi section for Anthony and Harper's *History of Woman Suffrage*, vol. 4, concluded her section on the 1890 convention by stating: "All these noble efforts resulted in no action whatever to enfranchise women." See A. Elizabeth Taylor, "History of Mississippi Woman Suffrage," *Journal of Mississippi History* 30 (Spring 1968): 5; Hala Hammond Butts, "Mississippi," *History of Woman Suffrage*, ed. Anthony and Harper, 4:787.

24. Fuller, *Laura Clay*, 64–65.

25. On southern suffragists generally, see Wheeler, *New Women of the New South*. On southern suffragists and the spectrum of their racial positions specifically, see ibid., 102–12.

26. W. E. B. DuBois, "Editorial," *The Crisis*, September 1912, 243.

27. For a detailed treatment of southern white suffragists and their racial views, see Wheeler, *New Women of the New South*.

28. Laura Clay, "The Race Question Again," Laura Clay scrapbook, box 18, folder 28, Clay Papers.

29. Ibid. On black male voting and the idea of the corruption of southern politics, see Dewey W. Grantham, *Southern Progressivism: The Reconciliation of Progress and Tradition* (Knoxville: University of Tennessee Press, 1992), 112–16.

30. Laura Clay, "The Race Question Again," box 18, folder 281, Clay Papers.

31. Laura Clay, "Laura Clay on Charles Sumner," Laura Clay scrapbook, box 18, folder 281, Clay Papers.

32. Ibid.

33. For an overview of the South Carolina constitutional convention and race, see George B. Tindall, "The Question of Race in the South Carolina Constitutional Convention of 1895," *Journal of Negro History* 37 (1952): 277–303; on the South Carolina constitutional convention and woman suffrage, see Antoinette Elizabeth Taylor, "South Carolina and the Enfranchisement of Women: The Early Years," *South Carolina Historical Magazine* 77 (1976): 115–26.

34. Fuller, *Laura Clay*, 65.

35. [First name unknown] Finley, Auditor, Laurens County, South Carolina, to Laura Clay, October 23, 1895; Mrs. M. A. Corley to Laura Clay, September 28, 1895, box 1, folder 11, Clay Papers; Fuller, *Laura Clay*, 66.

36. Fuller, *Laura Clay*, 101.

37. Ibid.

38. Ibid., 82–86, 98–106.

39. "Statement of Purpose," December 6, 1906, box 3, folder 47, Clay Papers.

40. Laura White to Laura Clay, April 5, 1907, box 3, folder 51, Clay Papers.

41. Laura Clay to Laura White, May 7, 1907, box 3, folder 52, Clay Papers.

42. Kate Gordon to Laura Clay, October 11, 1907; Kate Gordon to Anna Howard Shaw, October 15, 1907, box 4, folder 57, Clay Papers.

43. Henry Blackwell to Laura Clay, October 17, 1907, box 4, folder 57, Clay Papers.

44. Kate Gordon to Anna Howard Shaw, October 15, 1907; Laura Clay to Henry Blackwell, October 14, 1907; Laura Clay to Anna Shaw, October 30, 1907, all in box 4, folder 57, Clay Papers.

45. Kate Gordon to Laura Clay, August 2, 1907, box 4, folder 55; Laura Clay to Kate Gordon, September 17, 1907, box 4, folder 56, Clay Papers. In her letter to Gordon, Clay was still advocating the idea of presidential suffrage, but she endorsed Gordon's "scheme" (laid out to Clay in her letter of August 2) to find a way to reopen the question of the Minor-Happersett case and the Fourteenth Amendment. On Gordon and the *Happersett* decision, also see Kraditor, *Ideas of the Woman Suffrage Movement*, 175–76.

46. Laura Clay to Anna Howard Shaw, October 30, 1907, box 4, folder 57, Clay Papers.

47. Laura Clay to Kate Gordon, September 17, 1907, box 4, folder 56; Laura Clay to Laura White, May 7, 1907, box 3, folder 52; Laura Clay to Henry Blackwell, October 14, 1907, box 4, folder 57; Laura Clay to Anna Howard Shaw, October 30, 1907, box 4, folder 57; Laura Clay to Henry Blackwell, December 15, 1907, box 4, folder 59, Clay Papers.

48. Laura Clay to Anna Howard Shaw, October 30, 1907, box 4, folder 57, Clay Papers.

49. Laura Clay to Catherine Waugh McCulloch, December 13, 1907, box 4, folder 57, Clay Papers.

50. Laura Clay to Henry Blackwell, October 14, 1907, box 4, folder 57, Clay Papers. In a letter to Anna Howard Shaw, Clay provided a rather convoluted justification for her position on white woman suffrage only. Clay wrote: "I am in favor of obtaining the right of white women to vote, if I can, even if the negro women will have to wait awhile for the fit ones to vote. I do not think their chances for enfranchisement is [*sic*] delayed by this procedure, but to the contrary. This move may be the speediest for the enfranchisement of all women, north and south." See Clay to Shaw, October 30, 1907, box 4, folder 57, Clay Papers.

51. Laura Clay to Henry Blackwell, December 15, 1907, box 4, folder 59, Clay Papers. The Mississippi campaign did not come to fruition; see Kate Gordon to Laura Clay, January 15, 1908, box 4, folder 60, Clay Papers.

52. Fuller, *Laura Clay*, 125. For a detailed account of the growing dissension on the NAWSA board and Clay's defeat at the 1911 Louisville convention, see ibid., 113–27.

53. Ibid., 136.

54. Ibid., 140–41; Wheeler, *New Women of the New South*, 135, 138–40. Both Fuller and Wheeler discuss the brief period when Clay supported the federal amendment. This occurred from approximately mid-January 1918, after President Woodrow Wilson came out in support of the federal amendment, to June 1918, when she renewed her opposition. See Fuller, *Laura Clay*, 149–51; Wheeler, *New Women of the New South*, 165.

55. Hannah J. Patterson, ed., *The Handbook of the National American Woman Suffrage Association and Proceedings of the Forty-Eighth Convention* (New York: National American Woman Suffrage Publishing Co., 1916), 26–27.

56. For insider views of the woman suffrage movement, see Carrie Chapman Catt and Nettie Rogers Shuler, *Woman Suffrage and Politics: The Inner Story of the Suffrage Movement* (New York: Charles Scribner's Sons, 1926).

57. Clay wrote numerous letters advocating the United States Elections Bill. See Laura Clay to [first name unknown] Finnegan, February 15, 1915, box 12, folder 200; Laura Clay to Kate Gordon, October 28, 1915, box 12, folder 207; Laura Clay to Nellie Nugent Sommerville, November 24, 1915, box 12, folder 208, Clay Papers. See also Fuller, *Laura Clay*, 143–44; Wheeler, *New Women of the New South*, 138.

58. Madeline McDowell Breckinridge, "Kentucky," in *History of Woman Suffrage*, ed. Ida Husted Harper, 6 vols. (New York: National American Woman Suffrage Association, 1922), 6:211–12; Fuller, *Laura Clay*, 150–51, 154–56.

59. Box 16, folder 275, Clay Papers; Fuller, *Laura Clay*, 156.

60. Wheeler, *New Women of the New South*, 175–76; Breckinridge, "Kentucky," *History of Woman Suffrage*, ed. Harper, 6:213.

61. Laura Clay to Miss Scrugham, December 8, 1920, box 15, folder 249, Clay Papers.

62. Fuller, *Laura Clay*, 163–66; Wheeler, *New Women of the New South*, 191.

Sophonisba Preston Breckinridge
(1866–1948)

Homegrown Heroine

ANYA JABOUR

❀ ❀ ❀

In 1927 Cecilia Razovsky, one of the organizers of the upcoming National Conference of Social Work, to be held in Memphis, Tennessee, wrote to University of Chicago social work professor Sophonisba Breckinridge to solicit her assistance with the program. "Can you suggest someone from the South who can intelligently present the so-called 'Nordic' point of view" on the "immigrants invad[ing] the country with their own different cultural values?" she inquired. "I am very anxious to have your suggestions as you know the South so well." Breckinridge politely rebuffed Razovsky's request. Although born and reared in Kentucky, she explained, "I have lived in Chicago for thirty years now, and I know the South almost not at all." Distancing herself from the South both geographically and ideologically, she urged the planning committee to reject the proposed forum on the immigrant problem, at least as currently framed. Although she regretfully conceded that "I am afraid we are pretty much 'Nordic' in that part of the world," she explained, "I see no reason why we should discuss loss" in terms of "Nordic" values. "I should certainly put the question in the other way," she remarked.[1]

Although in this exchange Breckinridge appeared to have left her southern roots behind, other evidence indicates that she maintained important connections to her home state. Indeed, Breckinridge remained acutely aware of—if also sometimes uncomfortable about—her southern origins. When she warmly congratulated a fellow University of Chicago employee who challenged racial segregation in the residence halls, she also called attention to their shared southern roots. "I am so grateful too that you are a southerner," she enthused. "You have given new evidence of southern independence and genuine social and public spirit."[2] Throughout her long life, Breckinridge sought ways to reconcile her southern and "Nordic" background with her commitment to "genuine social and public spirit." In the process, she became a homegrown heroine, a role model for southern progressivism.

Sophonisba Preston Breckinridge was born in 1866 in Lexington. The second child of Issa Desha and William C. P. Breckinridge, "Nisba," as her friends and family fondly nicknamed her, was profoundly influenced by the Breckinridge family's tradition of public service. Her family tree included prominent politicians such as John C. Breckinridge, who ran for the presidency against Abraham Lincoln in 1860 on the Southern Democratic ticket, and public figures such as Robert Jefferson Breckinridge, an outspoken opponent of the secession movement. Her own father, W. C. P. Breckinridge, was a Confederate officer, a successful lawyer, and a Democratic congressman.[3]

Nisba enjoyed a close relationship with her father. After the deaths of both his first wife and their infant daughter and then being denied the opportunity to enjoy his first living child's infancy while he served in the Confederate army, W. C. P. Breckinridge claimed his "Peace Baby," as he called his second-born, as his own. "You were my baby from the hour of your birth," he asserted, backing up his claim with a detailed account of his early care for his favorite child: "I put you to sleep; I walked you when you were sick." In her never-completed draft autobiography, Nisba described her father as "wonderfully patient and kind" as well as closely involved in her upbringing; it was her father who taught her how to tie her shoes, and it was also her father who taught her the alphabet by pointing the letters out in his law books.[4]

Nisba's later recollections suggest that she had an attenuated relationship with her mother. Issa's health was poor, largely as a result of her constant childbearing. Although a gap of four years separated the eldest, Ella, from the second child, Nisba, the next three children—Desha, Campbell, and "Little Issa"—were born at intervals of only fifteen months, and there were still more "babies and babies to come," Robert and Curry. The illness and death of two children—Campbell in 1870 and Little Issa in 1872—also consumed Issa's attention and sapped her strength. Although she fostered a close relationship with her eldest child, Ella, that built on the strong bond mother and daughter had forged during W. C. P.'s wartime absence, Issa had little time or energy to devote to her younger children. Instead, she relied on African American servants to perform basic domestic tasks, from preparing meals to bathing and dressing the children.[5]

From the beginning, the Breckinridges seem to have tacitly assumed that Nisba would never marry. Several factors probably contributed to this expectation. Observing her mother's nonstop childbearing and chronic health

SOPHONISBA BRECKINRIDGE

In her office at the University of Chicago.

Edith and Grace Abbott Papers, Archives & Special Collections, University of Nebraska–Lincoln Libraries.

problems may well have led Nisba to reject marriage and motherhood at an early age. Although the slightly built young woman with masses of thick hair and striking dark eyes attracted at least two serious suitors, Nisba, unlike her outgoing older sister Ella, always was more interested in books than beaux. As her mother once remarked, "I fear you [are] Papa's sole [and] only hope for an educated daughter." W. C. P. also encouraged Nisba to seek alternatives to what he called the "aimless life" of the southern belle. Like many elite but impoverished whites in the uncertain economy of the postbellum South, he hoped that higher education and "honest toil" would enable his daughter to support herself rather than depending on either her father or a husband.[6]

In addition, both parents expected their precocious daughter to perpetuate the family legacy—to do "noble things," as Issa put it. "The [Breckinridge] name has been connected with good intellectual work for some generations—for over a century," W. C. P. counseled. "You must preserve this connection for the next generation." Disappointed with their sons' performance—Robert wrestled with drinking and gambling problems, while Desha initially struggled to find a professional identity—the Breckinridges encouraged their unmarried daughters, Nisba and Curry, to continue their educations with the intention of pursuing professional careers. (Ella, the oldest, married in 1889.) "If God gave our girls more purpose than our boys," pronounced Issa, "He intended they should do more."[7]

Eager for his favorite daughter to pursue higher education, W. C. P. persuaded the trustees of Kentucky Agricultural and Mechanical College (now the University of Kentucky) to admit women, and in 1880, at age fourteen, Nisba became a member of the first entering class of women. Although A&M allowed women to attend classes, it by no means treated them as equals. Female students could only earn certificates, not diplomas, and there was significant resistance to their presence on campus. Although Nisba completed four years of coursework and excelled in all her classes, she did not obtain a degree.[8]

Dissatisfied with the educational opportunities for women in Kentucky, Nisba enrolled at Wellesley College in 1884. She later observed that "the great charm that Wellesley had for me was that it was made or established for me or the likes of me." Indeed, the Massachusetts college was an ideal place for an intelligent woman in Victorian America to develop confidence in her abilities and find a context for her ambitions. In this "Adamless Eden," a women's college with an all-female faculty, students and teachers alike forged strong personal and professional bonds that fostered female achievement and social reform. Nisba did not exaggerate when she described Wellesley as her "natural sphere."[9]

For Nisba, the sense of mission common to first-generation collegiate women merged with her eagerness to carry on the family tradition of public service to produce a strong sense of being destined to make a difference in the world around her. Although she reveled in her years at Wellesley, she also was anxious to begin her life's work, even though she was not yet clear what that might be. "I am fairly pining to get to work," she confided to her mother, "to do something, somehow—somewhere." During her time at Wellesley, while studying mathematics and classics, Nisba pondered future possibilities for a career as a teacher, a classics scholar, a mathematician, a scientist, or—most frequently—a lawyer. What remained constant, however, was her desire to do more than simply support herself; she wanted to "go out and fight" to make the world a better place.[10]

Attending Wellesley not only reinforced Nisba's commitment to public service but also challenged her views on race. She had been born in the heyday of Radical Reconstruction, when the Republican-dominated U.S. Congress passed constitutional amendments freeing slaves, granting African American civil rights, and guaranteeing black men's right to vote. Yet southern whites fought to maintain white supremacy in both legal and extralegal ways. As her father put it, "We want a white man's State and we intend to have it."[11]

The Breckinridges were strong advocates of "redemption," by which white Democrats reclaimed political dominance from black Republicans and their northern allies. Indeed, W. C. P. owed his political success as a longtime member of the House of Representatives (1885–95) to southern whites' desire to regain their former superiority. When W. C. P. first attained office, Issa hastened to share her ecstasy with her daughter: "I remember the good old days when Democrats 'ruled the land'—when our friends & kindred were in power. I thank God there is a chance for our children to see such times."[12]

Although both of her parents celebrated self-rule and white supremacy, Nisba also received mixed messages about race from her father, whose emphasis on reason and fairness ran counter to his beliefs in racism and segregation. As Breckinridge later observed, "He was always for fair play." Although W. C. P. characterized African Americans as "savages" incapable of self-government, he also supported African American education in his home state—even sharing the speaker's podium with black civil rights advocates at times—because he believed that since African Americans paid taxes, those taxes should be used to fund African American schools. Although he helped orchestrate and defend laws that denied African American men the right to vote, he also insisted that blacks be allowed to give testimony against whites in Kentucky courts, even when this unpopular stance lost him a race for district attorney of the tenth circuit court. And although he insisted that the "Teutonic race" was destined to "dominate the world," he also asserted that African Americans were entitled to "fairness, justice and protection," if not to equal rights. However, W. C. P.'s commitment to "fair play" did not translate into social equality.[13]

Nisba's parents shared responsibility for training her in racial etiquette, a code of conduct intended to reinforce white supremacy by demanding deference from African Americans. When Nisba enrolled at Wellesley, one of the few colleges to admit African Americans, both parents expected her to maintain social distance from her black classmates. Nisba's mother emphasized the importance of racial etiquette in her letters. "How do you treat them—I hope there will be no necessity for you to come in contact with them, but I have no fear of your contamination or of your not doing what is becoming a lady," she wrote. "I have such faith in your good breeding—good sense & true lady hood that I have not concerned myself about it. It is a hard thing for people raised with our prejudices to ever treat them as equals," she added, but reassured herself—and reminded Nisba—to use racial etiquette to maintain social distance: "I can trust you to treat them properly—I suppose Papa wrote you how."[14]

For his part, W. C. P. counseled "forbearance." Although he opined that it would be impossible to regard African Americans as equals, he remarked, "to a gentleman or lady there need be no personal embarrassment." Presumably, W. C. P., like Issa, assumed that Nisba could and should treat the African Americans with whom she came in contact with polite distance. As to the larger question "of what ought to be done with the race," he confessed, "the problem of the colored race in America is a very troublesome one," but one that need not affect interpersonal relationships.[15]

The Breckinridges' adherence to white supremacy was apparent in letters Nisba and her parents exchanged early in her college career. Although, like most elite white southerners, Nisba had grown up in close contact with blacks as inferiors and employees, interacting with African Americans as peers and equals was a new and unwelcome experience, and she did her best to avoid contact with "the colored girls" at her school. Ultimately, however, attending a northern college in the company of African Americans would transform Nisba's views on race relations and racial equality.[16]

In her unpublished autobiography, Breckinridge related several incidents that challenged her southern upbringing. When an African American choir from Fisk University performed at Wellesley during Nisba's first term at the school, President Alice Freeman invited the singers to dine with the students and faculty. Sharing a meal was a potent symbol of equality. Although white family members and black domestic workers necessarily shared household space, white southern parents taught their children to maintain physical and thereby social separation in a variety of ways, especially by taking meals separately from African Americans. For Nisba, encountering African Americans at the dinner table amounted to an existential crisis, and she was unable to eat her own meal.[17]

Two years later, the Junior Promenade proved to be a test case for Nisba's evolving attitudes about racial equality. As she later described it, the event was "the occasion of my working through the problem of racial relationships." In her first three years at Wellesley, Nisba had become friendly with Ella Smith, an attractive and intelligent member of her entering class and a fellow classicist. The African American student wanted to invite guests to attend the Junior Promenade, but her white classmates objected. With the president's backing, however, Nisba persuaded her classmates to allow Ella Smith's guests to attend the event. Nisba entered Wellesley College skeptical about African American equality; she left committed to advancing African American rights.[18]

After graduating at the head of her class in 1888, Nisba, like many first-generation women college graduates, suffered from a period of indecision and melancholy. Despite studying for and passing the Kentucky bar in 1892, she was unable to establish a successful practice. She taught high school in Washington, D.C., and Staunton, Virginia, traveled in Europe, and kept house for her father, who was widowed in 1892. Like many of her contemporaries, Nisba found her choices constrained by the power of "the family claim" on single women.[19]

Although W. C. P. soon remarried, his new relationship only increased his daughter's difficulties. Less than a year after Issa's death, W. C. P. married a cousin, Louise Wing. Almost immediately, another woman, Madeline Pollard, filed suit in a Washington, D.C., court alleging breach of promise, claiming that W. C. P. had reneged on his promise to marry her. She further averred that she and the congressman had engaged in a lengthy extramarital affair that began shortly after their first meeting on April 1, 1884—immediately prior to Nisba's first year at Wellesley—and continued into 1893, during Issa's final illness. Testifying that the affair had resulted in the birth of two children, one in 1885 and another in 1888, Pollard also presented evidence that after conceiving a third time, shortly after Issa's death, she secured a promise of marriage, only to miscarry and then learn that her lover had married another woman.[20]

Unable to deny the affair in the face of overwhelming evidence, W. C. P. instead fought the suit by defaming the plaintiff's character, assembling a team of lawyers and detectives to collect incriminating evidence to suggest that at the time of the initial encounter—when he was forty-seven and Pollard was seventeen years old—Pollard was a sexually experienced seductress rather than the innocent schoolgirl she claimed to be. Despite herculean efforts to cast aspersions on Pollard's character and veracity, the judge ruled in Pollard's favor and ordered W. C. P. to pay her $15,000 in compensation. The public also found W. C. P. guilty, and he lost his bid for reelection to Congress—an outcome that further weakened his already shaky finances and made it impossible for him to pay Pollard.[21]

Nisba was "an infinite comfort" to her father during and after the trial. She packed his belongings in Lexington in preparation for his return to the capital city for the trial and then moved to Washington for several months to care for his new wife, "Cousin Louise," who suffered a nervous breakdown as a result of the publicity accompanying the scandal. In addition, Nisba assisted her father both by taking statements from witnesses about the Pollard affair and by copying his speeches for his unsuccessful bid for reelection.[22] Turning down a sociology fellowship at the University of Wisconsin and giving up her plans to attend law school at the University of Michigan, she renounced what she called "a false desire for independence," devoted herself to "home matters," and became, in her father's words, "the mainstay—the cement of the family."[23]

Yet the loss of her mother, the shock of her father's infidelity, and her own self-denial took a toll on Nisba. She sank into a deep depression. Concerned for his daughter's health, W. C. P. urged her to take a vacation. Her decision to visit a Wellesley classmate in Chicago in 1894 marked a major turning point in her life. Deciding to pursue advanced degrees at the newly established coeducational University of Chicago, she later claimed that she never journeyed home to Kentucky without a return ticket to Chicago in her possession.[24]

In Chicago Breckinridge met Marion Talbot, dean of women at the fledgling University of Chicago, who encouraged her to pursue graduate studies and helped finance her education with a graduate fellowship and a part-time job. Within three years Breckinridge fulfilled the requirements for her master's degree in political science with Ernst Freund, a legal scholar, and in 1897 she defended her thesis on "The Judicial System of Kentucky." She promptly began work on her PhD in political economy, earning the degree with high honors in 1901 with a dissertation on "Legal Tender: A Study in English and American Monetary History," under the supervision of J. Laurence Laughlin. When she was passed over for faculty appointments in favor of her male colleagues, she enrolled in the University of Chicago's law school, which opened in 1902. In 1904, as the highest-ranked member of the first graduating class, Breckinridge also became the first woman to earn a doctor of jurisprudence degree at the University of Chicago.[25]

Still unable to find a faculty position in any of her fields of expertise, Breckinridge stayed on at the University of Chicago as assistant dean of women and head of Green Hall, a women's dormitory. She also accepted an appointment as assistant professor in the new Department of Household Administration, created and chaired by her mentor, Marion Talbot. Although today associated with conventional gender roles and conservative values, in its early years home economics—also known as domestic science—was both a new profession for women and a product of Progressive reform. Building on the other new "social sciences," early domestic science programs more closely resembled present-day graduate programs in public health and public policy than high school "home ec" classes. Moreover, unlike the fields of political science, economics, and sociology, which were hostile to women, domestic science allowed female faculty to create and define "a department of their own." Breckinridge took full advantage of the possibilities, offering a course that arguably might be described as one of the first courses in women's studies, "The Legal and Economic Position of Women."[26]

One of the students in this course was Edith Abbott, a former schoolteacher and brilliant statistician who came to the University of Chicago in 1903 to pursue a doctorate in political economy. Breckinridge and Abbott immediately formed a close emotional and intellectual bond. Recalling a classroom interaction that would prove to be a turning point in both women's lives, Breckinridge wrote: "Among the students who took the course on women was Edith Abbott. I shall never forget the fright she caused me when I said something about the way in which women had carried the work of the world while men were doing the fighting and hunting. 'Do you mean to say?' she asked. 'I thought I did,' I replied. 'I must look into that,' she replied."[27]

Abbott's dissertation on women's work became a classic text, *Women in Industry*, and Breckinridge proposed that the pair collaborate on a statistical study of women's work in the United States. Local settlement house workers, including Hull House founder Jane Addams, enthusiastically supported the study. University of Chicago settlement leader Mary McDowell solicited support from Breckinridge's sister-in-law, Madeline McDowell Breckinridge, a Kentucky suffragist and settlement house advocate. Ultimately, the nineteen-volume report, published between 1910 and 1913, provided the basis for the establishment of two new federal bureaus, the U.S. Children's Bureau and the U.S. Women's Bureau.[28]

In the meantime Breckinridge accepted a temporary appointment as inspector of yards, investigating the working conditions of women in the infamous stockyard district and reporting her findings to the federal Bureau of Labor to provide ammunition for their request for funding for a full-scale investigation.[29] In addition, Breckinridge and Abbott coauthored a long article in the January 1906 *Journal of Political Economy*, largely based on Abbott's doctoral research, that offered an overview of women's industrial employment based on census data from 1890 and 1900 and included the then-startling assertion: "Women have always worked."[30] In the very next issue, Breckinridge contributed a short piece on "Legislative Control of Women's Work" in which she advocated so-called protective legislation for women workers.[31]

Breckinridge and Abbott's studies captured the attention of the Chicago branch of the Women's Trade Union League (WTUL). Both the premise that women's work was an inescapable fact of life and the argument that women merited treatment as a "protected class" of citizens meshed well with the priorities of the league, an organization of working-class "wage-earners" and middle-class "allies" that endeavored to improve the position of women in the workforce by promoting protective legislation. Breckinridge became a sought-after speaker on women's labor issues. In October 1906, along with speakers such as Agnes Nestor of the WTUL, Breckinridge demanded legislation to require safety guards on dangerous machinery and workplace insurance to compensate employees injured on the job.[32]

In 1907 Breckinridge and Abbott's work on women's labor garnered an invitation to live at Hull House, granting both women an entrée into what one scholar has dubbed "a female dominion in American reform."[33] Although her responsibilities at the University of Chicago only permitted her to be in residence at Hull House during vacation quarters (approximately three months of each year), Breckinridge was listed as an official resident, and while on site she shared fully in the life of the settlement. Edith Abbott and her sister Grace, who also had pursued graduate studies at the University of Chicago, became full-time residents.[34]

At Hull House Breckinridge, inspired by the "settlement spirit," founded the Immigrants Protective League, joined the WTUL, and served on the board of directors of the Juvenile Protective League—all organizations that met at Hull House. With Addams, Breckinridge also helped create the Chicago Urban League, a local civil rights organization, as well as joining the fledgling National Association for the Advancement of Colored People.[35]

In addition to introducing her to a panoply of Progressive reforms, Hull House also offered Breckinridge new professional opportunities. Impressed by Breckinridge's research, resident Julia Lathrop invited her first to deliver lectures at the Chicago School of Civics and Philanthropy and then to direct research funded by the Russell Sage Foundation as the head of the Chicago School's Department of Social Investigation. As director of research, Breckinridge raised funds from philanthropic agencies that allowed her to hire Abbott, with whom she collaborated on numerous coauthored volumes on immigration, housing, women's work, juvenile delinquency, and compulsory education.[36]

Like their initial studies of women's work, Breckinridge and Abbott's subsequent books used social science as the basis for social reform. For instance, at the request of the city's sanitary inspector, Charles Ball, the pair conducted a major study of housing in Chicago, resulting in numerous articles and pamphlets and ultimately a book. To facilitate the housing study, Ball appointed Breckinridge "Tenement Inspector in the Department of Health, without salary," in which capacity she reported to the City of Chicago's Sanitary Bureau and conducted research with the assistance of students at the Chicago School of Civics and Philanthropy.[37]

To conduct the study, Breckinridge and Abbott divided the city into districts and sent teams of students to investigate conditions in each one and record their observations. Although Ball recommended that the study exclude "the negro districts," Breckinridge insisted on including them. Canvassing the selected neighborhoods residence by residence, students carefully summarized the conditions they found on cards, which were then transcribed before being tabulated and analyzed.[38]

The resulting book, *The Housing Problem in Chicago* (1910), a study that fairly bristled with social scientific data about the city's immigrant slums, revealed "flagrant cases of overcrowding and disregard of regulations concerning air space and lighting" in Chicago's working-class dwellings, leading Breckinridge to become an early advocate for minimum-wage legislation. The research also had a major impact on housing and sanitation in the Second City. As a direct result of the study, the city changed some of its waste-disposal practices, such as designing a new plan for treating wastewater and adopting new regulations on dumping waste in the stockyards.[39]

Another major research project that advanced social reform was a longitudinal study of Chicago's wayward youth. With funding from the Russell Sage Foundation, Breckinridge and Abbott devoted five years to research in the court records and the public schools, which resulted in the 1912 publication of *The Delinquent Child and the Home*, a study of the juvenile court system in Chicago, and the 1917 publication of *Truancy and Non-Attendance in the Chicago Schools*, which addressed both compulsory education laws and child labor legislation. For these studies, Breckinridge and Abbott conducted research in the records of the Chicago Juvenile Court, the nation's first such judicial entity, which had been established in 1899, for its first ten years of operation. They also designed detailed "schedules," or forms, that posed questions about each youthful offender's conduct and habits, physical and mental condition, nationality and language, housing conditions and family life, and socioeconomic status.[40]

Based on this research, Breckinridge in 1910 presented a proposal for public assistance for single mothers at the Illinois State Conference of Charities and Corrections. Pointing out that a substantial proportion of juvenile delinquents came from single-mother families in which widowed or deserted women struggled in vain to meet their families' financial obligations, manage their poverty-stricken households, and supervise their young children, she argued that it was in the public interest to provide single mothers with financial support. The following year Illinois enacted the Fund-to-Parents Act, which established the nation's first "mothers' pensions" program.[41]

Like "mothers' pensions," Chicago's first public child welfare agency originated as a research project. Despite the promise of the Fund-to-Parents program, its funding was too limited—and the guidelines too restrictive—to provide meaningful assistance for poor mothers. In particular, never-married African American women encountered so much discrimination that they effectively were excluded from the program. To address the needs of African American children, Breckinridge and Abbott again turned to research as an avenue to reform.[42]

Beginning in 1920 the pair drew on private agencies, individual philanthropists, and university funding to launch a research project on social services for black families and establish a foster care placing agency for African American children. In addition to child placing, the innovative program provided a boardinghouse for unwed mothers and their children, financial support for poor families as an alternative to the separation of parents and children, and services for children with physical disabilities and behavioral problems. Breckinridge later explained the logic of offering services for children with funds earmarked for research: "So little was known about the needs of the negro child and the problem presented by their care that it was felt necessary to do the work for them after the method of a research project."[43] Despite constant fundraising efforts, the program was perennially short of cash. In 1932, after more than a year of repeated requests from both Abbott and Breckinridge, who each served on the advisory board of the Cook County Bureau of Public Welfare, the county assumed responsibility for the program, financing it through state and federal emergency relief funds and renaming it the Children's and Minors' Service, which served children regardless of race.[44]

At the same time that Breckinridge used social scientific data to promote social welfare legislation, she coordinated a seven-year effort to transform the privately funded Chicago School of Civics and Philanthropy into the university-affiliated Graduate School of Social Service Administration (SSA). As the nation's first graduate school of social work associated with a research university, the school represented the coming of age of a new profession for women. After years of part-time, temporary, and grant-funded work, the new school offered Breckinridge and Abbott greater professional status and job security as full-time university faculty. It also provided them with a platform from which to promote a distinctive approach to professional social work that used social scientific research as the basis for public policy recommendations. Finally, the new school allowed them to expand the scope of their academic activism from the local to the national level.[45]

Breckinridge and Abbott's relationship strengthened, and in turn was strengthened by, their work together at first the Chicago School of Civics and Philanthropy and then at the School of Social Service Administration. Although the two women did not share a residence until the last years of Breckinridge's life (Breckinridge lived at Green Hall, and Abbott at Hull House), they were clearly life partners. After Breckinridge's death, Abbott received a flood of condolence letters acknowledging—if not naming—the significance of their forty-year relationship. Secretary of Labor Frances Perkins reflected on how much Abbott would miss "the daily contact, the faithful loyalty, the shared experiences, [and] the tender friendship" that she and Breckinridge had enjoyed for so long.[46]

Like many other women educators, activists, and professionals in the early twentieth century, Abbott and Breckinridge seamlessly merged their personal and professional lives. Indeed, their personal relationship and their professional careers were mutually reinforcing. Moreover, Abbott and Breckinridge transformed their personal and professional partnership into a political powerhouse. They worked together closely in local, state, and national advisory committees and public agencies on crime and law enforcement, child welfare, and public welfare administration. Ultimately, the power couple helped shape both the Social Security Act of 1935 and the Fair Labor Standards Act of 1938. Paying tribute to the women's political effectiveness as well as their personal and professional partnership, Frank Bane of the American Public Welfare Association reflected: "In setting up the various relief administrations and Social Security, it was Edith Abbott with Sophonisba and a few others . . . who gave us the greatest help in organizing government for the administration of welfare programs. Edith and Sophonisba—as the University of Chicago called them, A and B.—what a pair!"[47]

Much of Breckinridge and Abbott's work was related to a new government agency located in the Labor Department, the U.S. Children's Bureau. The bureau's modus operandi—investigate, educate, legislate—meshed well with the pair's emphasis on social science scholarship as the basis for social welfare legislation. Breckinridge, Abbott, and their students conducted numerous studies on behalf of the Children's Bureau, headed successively by Breckinridge's former employer, Hull House veteran Julia Lathrop; University of Chicago graduate and Hull House resident Grace Abbott, Edith's sister; and Katharine Lenroot, Grace Abbott's former assistant. Both by giving their students the opportunity to conduct research for the bureau and by modeling the SSA curriculum on the bureau's civil service exams, Abbott and Breckinridge gave their students a significant advantage in seeking postgraduate employment with the Children's Bureau, which functioned practically as an employment service for SSA graduates. At the same time, their research buttressed the bureau's efforts to promote child welfare through public policy. For instance, at the Second White House Conference on Children in 1919, Breckinridge contributed to the formulation of "Minimum Standards of Child Welfare," including the federal government's responsibility to ensure or subsidize "an adequate economic level" for every family.[48]

Together with other women associated with the Children's Bureau and women's organizations such as the National Consumers' League, Breckinridge was an integral part of an influential network of New Deal women who shaped the emerging welfare state. Breckinridge's innovation of "mothers' pensions" and her notion of "minimum standards" informed the U.S. welfare state in the form of the aid to dependent children program (later AFDC) in the Social Security Act. As a member of the section on the care of children with disabilities at the 1930 White House Conference on Children, Breckinridge also helped design these programs under the Social Security Act. Her decades of agitation for child labor laws finally came to fruition with the adoption of the 1938 Fair Labor Standards Act. Breckinridge also played an active role in the administration of the Social Security Act, serving on numerous advisory committees regarding the Children's Bureau's administration of key New Deal programs. Finally, by collaborating with Federal Emergency Relief Administration officials on a social-work training program, she established professional standards for public welfare administration that were incorporated into the 1939 amendments to the Social Security Act, which implemented civil service merit hiring throughout the new federal welfare system.[49]

Breckinridge not only helped create the U.S. welfare state but also trained the nation's first generation of public welfare employees. However, her interest in social welfare extended beyond national borders. Both her commitment to feminist pacifism and her involvement in an international movement to promote child welfare led Breckinridge to become one of the United States' best-known women internationalists. Breckinridge's involvement with internationalist efforts began with the Woman's Peace Party (WPP), which in turn grew out of the U.S. woman suffrage movement. A prominent suffragist, she in 1911 was elected, with Jane Addams, vice president of the National American Woman

Suffrage Association (NAWSA). Together with the NAWSA president, Carrie Chapman Catt, Breckinridge and Addams cofounded the WPP in 1915. Addams was chair of the new organization; Breckinridge was treasurer.[50]

Later that year Breckinridge and Addams traveled to The Hague as U.S. delegates to the International Congress of Women, the first international meeting of women to discuss the ongoing war in Europe. Ultimately, the congress adopted a series of resolutions protesting "the madness and the horror of war," calling attention to the particular dangers war posed to women, including sexual assault; proposing an International Court of Justice and a Council of Conciliation and Investigation to mediate international disputes and "establish a just and lasting peace"; and demanding national self-determination, continuous mediation, universal disarmament, free commerce, and woman suffrage—a set of demands that would later inform both the League of Nations and its successor organization, the United Nations.[51]

Following the congress, two delegations made a total of thirty-five visits to political and religious leaders of both neutral and belligerent nations. When Addams, who participated in the visits, returned home, she did so as the first president of the new International Committee of Women for Permanent Peace, later the Women's International League for Peace and Freedom (WILPF). Meanwhile, back in Chicago, Breckinridge continued to serve as treasurer of the WPP, which became the U.S. chapter of WILPF. Although WILPF allowed member branches considerable latitude, there were two fundamental requirements for membership: support for woman suffrage and a commitment to peaceful resolution of international disputes.[52]

The U.S. entry into World War I in 1917 was a critical moment for the nation's feminist pacifists, who disagreed among themselves about what position to take on war service. When Carrie Chapman Catt committed NAWSA to the war effort, Breckinridge objected. Together with Addams and other members of the WPP, she insisted on a commitment to both woman suffrage and world peace.[53]

Pacifism, however, was not a popular stance in wartime America. Indeed, pacifist feminists who were openly critical of the war found themselves sentenced to five to ten years in federal penitentiaries for violations of the Espionage and Sedition Acts. Breckinridge sought ways to engage in war service without supporting the war effort. Building on her earlier efforts on behalf of protective legislation for women workers, she joined the Woman's Division of the Council of National Defense, serving on that organization's Committee on Women in Industry. The committee conducted in-depth investigations of conditions in defense industries, such as the factories that produced navy uniforms, where women made up a majority of the workforce. Their final report called attention to poor working conditions and racial discrimination in war industries and argued that wartime conditions did not justify relaxing workplace regulations. Serving on the Committee on Women in Industry was a form of patriotism that was consistent with both the official stance of the Chicago WPP and Breckinridge's longtime interest in improving women's labor conditions.[54]

While Breckinridge engaged in her own form of patriotic pacifism, her younger sister Curry served as a Red Cross nurse in France. Breckinridge was very close to Curry. She had tutored her when her dyslexia caused her to fall behind in her studies, and she assumed primary responsibility for her after their mother's untimely death, when Curry was only sixteen years old. Curry had followed in her older sister's footsteps by seeking advanced education in Chicago, acquiring her nursing degree from the Presbyterian Hospital Training School in 1908. After working in a state hospital for the mentally ill in Illinois and in a tuberculosis sanitarium in Michigan, she spent twenty-six months in France working in Red Cross hospitals. Exhausted, she returned to the United States to seek treatment for heart problems. Despite the best medical care and her sister's personal attention, she died at Chicago Presbyterian Hospital, the same hospital where she had completed her nurse's training, in June 1918.[55]

The loss of her beloved sister only reinforced Breckinridge's adamant opposition to militarism. As a founding member of the American Union Against Militarism, she protested civil liberties violations such as legal harassment of conscientious objectors and deportation of suspected subversives. The union's Bureau of Conscientious Objectors evolved into the Civil Liberties Bureau and eventually, in 1920, into the American Civil Liberties Union. The national organization, under the leadership of Roger Baldwin, coordinated the civil liberties efforts and legal defense of a wide range of pacifist, socialist, and even anarchist groups and individuals.[56]

Breckinridge was executive director of the Chicago branch of the Civil Liberties Bureau. In addition, through her work with the Chicago Immigrants Protective League, she provided similar legal assistance to immigrants whose civil rights were in jeopardy in wartime. As cofounder, longtime secretary, executive board member, and trustee of the league, Breckinridge exerted considerable influence over its activities. Although not officially a civil liberties organization, the league was committed to seeking asylum for political refugees, assisting immigrants to gain entry to the United States, and preventing the deportation of immigrants under the restrictive Immigrant Act of 1917, which allowed for denial of entry or deportation of a wide range of "undesirables," including those suspected of opposing the war. In addition, the league provided interpreters for non-English speakers at Selective Service Bureaus and helped foreign nationals gain exemptions from military service.[57]

Despite vicious red-baiting that targeted Breckinridge and her colleagues at

Hull House and the Children's Bureau, Breckinridge remained an active member of WILPF throughout the 1920s, 1930s, and 1940s.[58] In 1940, on the brink of U.S. involvement in another international conflict, she used a book review of a history of the WPP as an opportunity to defend opponents of U.S. entry into the war against "the charge of lack of patriotism" and to celebrate pacifism as "true patriotism."[59]

By the 1930s, however, the focus of Breckinridge's internationalist work had shifted to an emerging international child welfare movement. Although this movement was also active in Europe, it is perhaps best exemplified by the Pan American Child Congresses. Breckinridge, who had previously attended European child welfare gatherings, began to attend the Latin American congresses in 1927, the same year that the United States joined nine other nations in Montevideo, Uruguay, in establishing a Pan American Institute for the Protection of Children. Three years later, Breckinridge was an official U.S. Children's Bureau representative to the Sixth Pan American Child Congress, held in Lima, Peru. At that congress, several streams of child welfare advocacy converged to produce a demand for a strong welfare state that provided health care, education, financial assistance, and legal protection for children. The congress thus represented the culmination of several decades of child welfare reform in the United States, Europe, and Latin America and the coming of age of a truly international child welfare movement.[60]

Participants in the congress regarded the gathering as a way to advance international understanding as well as promote child welfare. The opening statement of the final report pronounced: "Cooperation in safeguarding the health and well-being of children truly has been said to afford one of the soundest means of promoting understanding and harmony among nations."[61] Immediately after the Sixth Pan American Child Congress, Breckinridge helped establish the U.S. Committee on Cooperation in Pan American Child Welfare Work. Like the Pan American Congress from which it grew, this group emphasized the advantages of hemispheric child advocacy both for children's welfare and for international relations.[62]

Breckinridge's national and international visibility led to her selection, in 1933, as the United States' first woman delegate to an international diplomatic meeting. At this historic gathering, the Seventh Pan American Conference, held in Montevideo, the United States formally announced its "Good Neighbor" policy (which opposed U.S. armed intervention in Latin America), and assembled delegates from nineteen countries adopted the Convention on the Rights and Duties of States, which established the declarative theory of statehood as international law. In addition to ratifying the convention, Breckinridge participated in drafting language upholding international law, peace treaties, free trade, and continuous mediation, thereby bringing the priorities of WILPF to a new venue.[63]

At the Pan American Conference, Breckinridge also took a leading role in debating women's independent citizenship rights. Her work in this area brought her into conflict with Doris Stevens of the National Woman's Party (NWP) and her organization, the Inter-American Commission of Women. When U.S. feminists engaged in transnational activism in the 1920s and 1930s, they brought the debate between former suffragists who supported protective legislation and opposed the Equal Rights Amendment (such as Breckinridge) and those who criticized protective legislation and supported the Equal Rights Amendment (such as Stevens) into the international arena. After the failure of the Equal Rights Amendment in the United States—largely due to opposition from women's groups such as the League of Women Voters (LWV) that were concerned about the future of protective legislation—the Inter-American Commission crafted the Equal Nationality Treaty. Although at the conference she supported the aims of the treaty, which was intended to ensure that women would not lose their citizenship status as a result of marrying a foreign national, Breckinridge vociferously protested the international measure. Like her fellow LWV members, she feared the Equal Nationality Treaty would open the door to another Inter-American Commission proposal, the Equal Rights Treaty, modeled on the NWP's Equal Rights Amendment. Many activist women believed that such a measure would invalidate the very reforms they had dedicated decades to promoting. Although the delegates at the Pan American Conference adopted the Equal Nationality Treaty, they tabled the Equal Rights Treaty, allowing both feminist factions to claim a qualified victory.[64]

For all her commitment to social justice in Chicago, the United States, and the world, Breckinridge never abandoned her Kentucky connections. Rather, she found ways to integrate her southern origins with social justice. At a personal level, Breckinridge remained close to her Kentucky kin and promoted their educational opportunities and economic security. At a political level, she used her local contacts to keep informed about and advance policy regarding race relations and social welfare both in her home state and at the national level.

Of her siblings who remained in Kentucky, Breckinridge maintained the most regular contact with her brother Desha. Desha shared his sister's commitment to Progressive reform. His wife, Madeline McDowell, who advocated for woman suffrage, child welfare, and settlement work, was one of Breckinridge's regular correspondents; she also visited Breckinridge in Chicago and modeled her own Lexington settlement after Hull House. Breckinridge so admired her sister-in-law that she wrote a laudatory biography of her after her premature death from tuberculosis in 1920. Desha supported his wife's work by allowing her space in the newspaper he edited, the *Lexington Herald*, and he continued to advocate the causes she and Breckinridge promoted until his own death.[65]

After Desha's death in 1935, Breckinridge worked to keep the *Lexington Herald* faithful to her brother's vision, resisting other family members' attempts to take over control of the newspaper and instead working closely with editor Thomas R. Underwood, who shared Desha's progressivism. Indeed, Breckinridge became Underwood's mentor and muse. One of her first actions after Desha's death was to write to birth control advocate Margaret Sanger to have Underwood added to Sanger's mailing list. "He is a very able young person, very open-minded, and on the whole rather radical," Breckinridge explained, adding: "He and the paper need to be informed, and I am anxious to have the paper approach these new topics in a way that will be rather persuasive to the community than give rise to any spirit of antagonism." On another occasion, Breckinridge asked a Kentucky Works Progress Administration official for "any suggestions or ways in which the *Herald* could be more serviceable. I know that Mr. Underwood wants to do everything in his power," she confidently asserted. In addition to suggesting editorials on a variety of topics, including birth control, Breckinridge also planted editorials in the *Herald*. "I should like to have them unsigned just as though they were done in the office there," she explained, in order to appeal to local readers. Breckinridge's anonymous editorials addressed a wide range of social issues, including the Social Security Act of 1935 and federal antilynching legislation.[66]

Breckinridge also exploited her contacts with Kentucky legislators, several of whom were "old personal friend[s] of my family," to advance social justice. For instance, in 1937 she wrote to Senator Alben W. Barkley, a friend of Desha's, to urge him to support a federal child labor amendment. "I think that nothing would have given my brother such satisfaction as to know that something was being done constructively to cure that particular evil," she closed her letter. "I know that you will sympathize with me in my feeling about this." Indeed, Breckinridge's lobbying was effective. After receiving a letter from Underwood encouraging him to vote in favor of a bill on public works, Kentucky congressman Fred Vinson responded that he always was "more than glad to give anything that Miss Nisba Breckinridge is interested in my most careful thought and consideration. I start off on her side."[67]

In addition to using her Kentucky connections to promote national programs, Breckinridge also maintained a special interest in social justice in her home state. She corresponded regularly with Kentucky residents about labor organizing, race relations, and public welfare. As University of Louisville professor Margaret Strong interjected in a 1932 letter about the commonwealth's welfare programs, "You see I am passing on our troubles to you because I do not forget that Ky. is your home & that Ky. problems are yours."[68]

Indeed, although Breckinridge never again made her home in Kentucky, she continued to deal with problems there. After a dissipated youth that culminated in his boarding an ill-fated schooner bound for Calcutta that sank en route to India in 1891, Breckinridge's brother Robert resurfaced in 1914. He had spent the intervening twenty-three years working as a merchant marine in the South Seas, investing in a gold mine in South Africa, participating in the Boxer Rebellion in China, and running a gambling operation in Australia, among other exploits. Following his return to the United States, he married and moved back to his hometown, where he assisted Desha with the *Lexington Herald* before again falling prey to alcoholism and gambling in the 1930s, leading him to borrow and steal from his brother to support his addictions.[69]

Robert's marriage to Ann Clair Harringer produced three children: his sister's namesake, Nisba Desha (b. 1916), known as "Nim"; another daughter named Clair (b. 1921) for her mother; and a son, Robert, known as Bobby (b. 1925). Nisba assumed responsibility for all three children's schooling and health care in the early 1930s, when Robert's marriage ended in divorce.[70] "I do not try to tell you again how wonderful you are and what a comfort and a help you have been," Desha wrote his sister in 1932. "God knows what we would have done without you." Nim spent a year at the University of Chicago settlement before attending college in Wisconsin, while Bobby went to boarding school in Illinois. Breckinridge also arranged and financed a stay at a boys' camp in Wisconsin for Bobby, who exhibited behavioral problems. She also subsidized Clair's education, and she maintained contact with all the children and their teachers. "I don't know what the future of those children will be," Desha confessed. "I do know that if it is good it will be because of you, that you have saved them and made it possible for them to be self-sustaining, self-respecting citizens."[71]

Apparently reformed, Robert began corresponding regularly with Breckinridge in the 1940s. He collected materials of their father's, which she intended to use as the basis for a biography; she paid for his medical bills and living expenses. Like other members of the family, Robert suffered from a heart condition. By midsummer 1944 he required around-the-clock care and alternated between living in a hotel and staying in the hospital. Breckinridge covered all the expenses of her brother's care, including expensive oxygen treatments and private-duty nurses to supplement those on the hospital staff, prompting him to confide to his hired caretaker, "I never knew Nisba loved me so much. I've always loved and admired her, but I thought she didn't care much for me—I wish I had known sooner." She also wrote frequently to her ailing brother. To his sister, Robert wrote: "I am so very grateful to you. Your letters are, of course, the biggest part of my life." Robert died on July 10, 1944.[72]

Robert's death came just a year after Ella's, leaving Nisba the only surviving child of W. C. P. and Issa Desha Breckinridge.[73] Breckinridge continued to capitalize on family connections to promote social justice. During World War II, for instance, she corresponded with her cousin, Department of State official Breckinridge Long, about easing immigration and naturalization procedures for war refugees.[74] Although she never completed either the biography of her father or her own autobiography, she ensured that her family's legacy would remain intact by donating their papers to the Library of Congress. Breckinridge died in 1948, the same year that the United Nations adopted the Universal Declaration of Human Rights, which incorporated many of the measures she had promoted throughout her life. She was buried in the family plot in the Lexington Cemetery. After a lifetime dedicated to family service, public welfare, and social justice, Sophonisba Preston Breckinridge, a homegrown heroine, came home to Kentucky.

NOTES

1. Cecilia Razovsky to Sophonisba Preston Breckinridge (hereafter SPB), August 16, 1927; SPB to Cecîlia Razovsky, August 25, 1927, Sophonisba Preston Breckinridge Papers (hereafter SPBP), Library of Congress, Washington, D.C. This essay is based on my ongoing research for the first full-scale biography of Breckinridge. I thank the Women's and Gender Studies Program at the University of Montana for providing time and space to work on this essay at the 2012 WGS Writing Retreat and the National Endowment for the Humanities for supporting full-time work on this project with a 2012 summer stipend. The University of Montana's Department of History, College of Arts and Sciences, and Faculty Professional Enhancement Program also helped support my research.

2. SPB to Hasseltine Byrd, March 14, 1932, SPBP.

3. For useful treatments of Breckinridge's childhood, education, and early career, see Ellen Fitzpatrick, *Endless Crusade: Women Social Scientists and Progressive Reform* (New York: Oxford University Press, 1990); Melanie Beals Goan, "Establishing Their Place in the Dynasty: Sophonisba and Mary Breckinridge's Paths to Public Service," *Register of the Kentucky Historical Society* 101 (2003): 45–73; Joan Marie Johnson, *Southern Women at the Seven Sister Colleges: Feminist Values and Social Activism, 1875–1915* (Athens: University of Georgia Press, 2008); James C. Klotter, *The Breckinridges of Kentucky* (Lexington: University Press of Kentucky, 1986), chap. 14.

4. W. C. P. Breckinridge (hereafter WCPB) to SPB, March 30, 1885; and Sophonisba Preston Breckinridge Autobiography (hereafter SPB Autobiography), n.p., Sophonisba P. Breckinridge Papers, University of Chicago. On other Confederate fathers' close relationships with their children, see also James Marten, "Fatherhood in the Confederacy: Southern Soldiers and Their Children," *Journal of Southern History* 63 (1997): 269–92.

5. SPB Autobiography; SPB Autobiographical Notes, in Miscellany: Speeches and Articles by and about Breckinridge Family, SPBP.

6. Issa Desha Breckinridge (hereafter IDB) to SPB, April 6, 1885; and WCPB to SPB, March 30, 1885, SPBP. On changing expectations for this generation of southern white women, see Jane Turner Censer, *The Reconstruction of Southern White Womanhood, 1865–1895* (Baton Rouge: Louisiana State University Press, 2003); Anya Jabour, *Scarlett's Sisters: Young Women in the Old South* (Chapel Hill: University of North Carolina Press, 2007), chap. 6.

7. IDB to SPB, January 22, 1885, May 11, 1892, SPBP; WCPB to SPB, November 16, 1902, quoted in Klotter, *Breckinridges of Kentucky*, 317.

8. SPB Autobiography; see also *Annual Register of the State College of Kentucky* (Lexington, Ky.: Transylvania Printing, 1881), 8, 12; *Annual Register of the State College of Kentucky* (Frankfort, Ky.: Major, Johnston & Barrett, 1882), 8; *Annual Register of the State College of Kentucky* (Frankfort, Ky.: Major, Johnston & Barrett, 1883), 8; *Annual Register of the State College of Kentucky* (Frankfort, Ky.: Major, Johnston & Barrett, 1884), 7; and State of Kentucky Matriculators Book (1869–1889), 106, 122, 136, 156, all in Special Collections and Archives, University of Kentucky Libraries, Lexington.

9. SPB Autobiography; SPB to IDB, January 11, 1886, Issa Desha Breckinridge Papers (hereafter IDB Papers), Breckinridge Family Papers, Library of Congress; and Patricia Ann Palmieri, *In Adamless Eden: The Community of Women Faculty at Wellesley* (New Haven, Conn.: Yale University Press, 1995).

10. SPB to WCPB, n.d., W. C. P. Breckinridge Papers (hereafter WCPB Papers), Breckinridge Family Papers, Library of Congress; SPB to IDB, n.d. (Friday Eve), IDB Papers; SPB to WCPB, March 20, 1887, WCPB Papers. See also SPB to IDB, Wednesday, n.d. [1884–1885], and January 11, 1886, IDB Papers; SPB to WCPB, March 9, 1887, March 20, 1887, June 10, 1887, WCPB Papers; WCPB to SPB, October 8, 1884, SPBP. See also Emily Mieras, "Latter-Day Knights: College Women, Social Settlements, and Social Class in the Progressive-Era United States," in *The Educational Work of Women's Organizations, 1890–1960*, ed. Anne Meis Knupfer and Christine Woyshner (New York: Palgrave Macmillan, 2008), 101–19.

11. Quoted in Klotter, *Breckinridges of Kentucky*, 147.

12. IDB to SPB, November 6, 1884, SPBP.

13. W. C. P. Breckinridge, "Who Were the Confederate Dead?" address at the unveiling of the Confederate monument at Hopkinsville, Kentucky, May 19, 1887, quotations on 3, 16, 28–29, copy in Miscellany: Speeches and Articles by and about Breckinridge Family, SPBP; SPB Autobiography.

14. IDB to SPB, September 19, 1884, SPBP. On racial etiquette and white supremacy, see Jennifer Ritterhouse, *Growing Up Jim Crow: How Black and White Southern Children Learned Race* (Chapel Hill: University of North Carolina Press, 2006), especially chaps. 1 and 2; and Kristina DuRocher, *Raising Racists: The Socialization of White Children in the Jim Crow South* (Lexington: University Press of Kentucky, 2011). For more on the intimate but unequal interracial relationships between the Breckinridge children and their black servants, see Eleanor Breckinridge Chalkley, "Magic Casements," Part I, 12, 20, 33, 39–41, and 49, Mss. Autobiography, c. 1940s, transcript by James C. Klotter, Special Collections and Archives, University of Kentucky Libraries.

15. WCPB to SPB, October 3, 1884, SPBP.

16. IDB to SPB, September 26, 1884, SPBP.

17. SPB Autobiography.

18. SPB Autobiography; see also Johnson, *Seven Sister Colleges*, 104; Fitzpatrick, *Endless Crusade*, 8.

19. On the first generation of women college graduates, see especially Joyce Antler, "After Col-

lege, What? New Graduates and the Family Claim," *American Quarterly* 32 (1980): 409–34; Roberta Frankfort, *College Women: Domesticity and Career in Turn-of-the-Century America* (New York: New York University Press, 1977); Patricia A. Palmieri, "Patterns of Achievement of Single Academic Women at Wellesley College, 1880–1920," *Frontiers: A Journal of Women Studies* 5 (1980): 63–67. On Breckinridge, see SPB Autobiography; "Ready for the Bar," *New York Times*, November 29, 1892.

20. Louise Breckinridge, Statement, July 3, [1894]; John Lancaster to WCPB, May 23, 1894, WCPB Papers; Klotter, *Breckinridges of Kentucky*, 161–63, 352 n. 27.

21. William Rose to M. Totten, December 7, 1893; William Rose, "Report," January 18, 1894; WCPB to Charles Meng, January 18, 1894, WCPB Papers; Fitzgerald, *Endless Crusade*, 11–12; Klotter, *Breckinridges of Kentucky*, 163–69; "Madeline Pollard and Cong. Breckinridge: The Story of a Famous $50,000 Love Suit," *Chicago Daily Tribune*, April 7, 1940.

22. WCPB to Mr. Mitchell, May 10, 1894; SPB to WCPB, January 8, 1894; SPB to WCPB, May 4, 1894; see also May 5, 7, [July 20], July 21, 1894; WCPB to DB, July 11, 1894, WCPB Papers.

23. WCPB to Curry Breckinridge, December 15, 1896; and WCPB to SPB, December 28, 1896, both in SPBP; SPB to WCPB, November 20, 1894, WCPB Papers. See also SPB to WCPB, September 6, 1893; WCPB to DB, January 22, 1894; and SPB to WCPB, January 27, 1894, all in WCPB Papers.

24. WCPB to DB, January 22, 1894, WCPB Papers; WCPB to SPB, November 21, 1897, SPBP; SPB Autobiography.

25. See n. 3.

26. Beverly B. Cook, "Sophonisba P. Breckinridge," *Women and Politics* 3 (1983): 95–102; Megan J. Elias, *Stir It Up: Home Economics in American Culture* (Philadelphia: University of Pennsylvania Press, 2008); Sarah Stage and Virginia B. Vincenti, eds., *Rethinking Home Economics: Women and the History of a Profession* (Ithaca, N.Y.: Cornell University Press, 1997).

27. SPB Autobiography.

28. Memorandum, marked "Recommended by President in Feb. 1905"; Mary McDowell to M. M. Breckinridge, February 17, 1907, Madeline McDowell Breckinridge Papers, Child Labor Correspondence, 1906–1915, folder 9, Special Collections and Archives, University of Kentucky Libraries; "University Girl Upholds Toilers," *Chicago Daily Tribune*, October 17, 1906; Mary McDowell to SPB, December 27, 1906, SPBP; Louise C. Wade, "The Heritage from Chicago's Early Settlement Houses," *Journal of the Illinois State Historical Society* 60 (1967): 411–41, esp. 419–20. See also Edith Abbott (hereafter EA), *Women in Industry: A Study in American Economic History* (1910; New York: Arno Press, 1969).

29. Charles P. Neill to JA, January 29, 1906, Jane Addams Papers Project (hereafter JAPP), reel 6; Daniel Ross to SPB, February 26 and April 11, 1906, SPBP; "Woman Puts O.K. on O'Neill Report," *Chicago Daily Tribune*, June 11, 1906.

30. EA and SPB, "Employment of Women in Industries: Twelfth Census Statistics," *Journal of Political Economy* 14 (1906): 14–40 (quotation on 14).

31. SPB, "Legislative Control of Women's Work," *Journal of Political Economy* 14 (1906): 107–9.

32. "University Girl Upholds Toilers," *Chicago Daily Tribune*, October 17, 1906. See also Nancy Schrom Dye, *As Equals and as Sisters: Feminism, the Labor Movement, and the Women's Trade Union League of New York* (Columbia: University of Missouri Press, 1980).

33. Robyn Muncy, *Creating a Female Dominion in American Reform, 1890–1935* (New York: Oxford University Press), 1991.

34. Russell Ballard, "The Years at Hull House," *Social Service Review* 22 (1948): 432; see also *Hull House Year Books* and List of Residents, both in Hull House Collection, box 32, folder 294, University of Illinois at Chicago (UIC).

35. Muncy, *Creating a Female Dominion*, 14.

36. Robyn Muncy, "Gender and Professionalization in the Origins of the U.S. Welfare State: The Careers of Sophonisba Breckinridge and Edith Abbott, 1890–1935," *Journal of Policy History* 2 (1990): 290–315.

37. Charles Ball (hereafter CB) to SPB, November 4, 1909, SPBP.

38. CB to SPB, November 8, 1909; SPB to Jane Addams (hereafter JA), December 23, 1909; SPB to Kate Holliday Claghorn, March 24, 1910; see also CB to EA, October 4, 1909; CB to SPB, October 6, 1909; SPB to CB, November 1, 1909; SPB to Dora Allen, April 22, 1910; Harris Franklin Hall to SPB, January 13, 1915; SPB to Harris Franklin Hall, January 15, 1915, all in SPBP.

39. "Will Ask Parties for Living Wage," *Chicago Daily Tribune*, June 14, 1912; SPB to W. A. Evans, February 11, 1910, and W. A. Evans to SPB, February 14, 1910, SPBP.

40. Dr. Sarah Brayton to SPB, May 19, 1908; Leonard Ayres to SPB, October 7, 1910; Pauline Goldmark to SPB, November 5, 1909; Ethelbert Stewart to SPB, October 5, 1910; J. W. Glocker to SPB, November 15, 1910; D. P. MacMillan to SPB, November 16, 1910, and enclosed schedules, SPBP.

41. SPB, "Neglected Widowhood in the Juvenile Court," *American Journal of Sociology* 16 (1910): 53–87; Joanne L. Goodwin, *Gender and the Politics of Welfare Reform: Mothers' Pensions in Chicago, 1911–1929* (Chicago: University of Chicago, 1997).

42. Goodwin, *Gender and the Politics of Welfare Reform*, 148–49.

43. SPB to Jacob Kepecs, May 4, 1929 (quotation); SPB to Mrs. Anita Blaine, March 1, 1928; SPB to L. D. White, March 17, October 15, 1928; Memorandum to Mr. White and Members of the Sub-Committee on Research Projects for 1929–30, February 28, 1929, all in SPBP; Sandra M. Stehno, "Public Responsibility for Dependent Black Children: The Advocacy of Edith Abbott and Sophonisba Breckinridge," *Social Service Review* 62 (1988): 485–503.

44. SPB, Letter to Editor, draft [January 17, 1932]; Advisory Board of Cook County Bureau of Public Welfare to Board of County Commissioners, February 10, 1932, all in SPBP; Stehno, "Public Responsibility," 491.

45. See especially Lela B. Costin, "Edith Abbott and the Chicago Influence on Social Work Education," *Social Service Review* 57 (1983): 94–111; Anya Jabour, "Relationship and Leadership: Sophonisba Breckinridge and Women in Social Work," *Affilia* 27 (2012): 22–37; Muncy, "Gender and Professionalization." See also Michael Reisch and Janice Andrews, *The Road not Taken: A History of Radical Social Work in the United States* (Ann Arbor: Sheridan, 2001); Leslie Leighninger, "Social Work: The Status of Women in a 'Female Profession,'" in *Women and Minorities in American Professions*, ed. Joyce Tang and Earl Smith (Albany: State University of New York, 1996), 111–33; Roy Lubove, *The Professional Altruist: The Emergence of Social Work as a Career, 1880–1930* (Cambridge, Mass.: Harvard University Press, 1965); Daniel Walkowitz, "The Making of a Feminine Professional Identity: Social Workers in the 1920s," *American Historical Review* 95 (1990): 1051–76.

46. F. Perkins to EA, August 19, 1948, SPBP; see also Jabour, "Relationship and Leadership."

47. Frank Bane to Arlien Johnson, copy enclosed in Frank Bane to Wilma Walker, October 24, 1957, Abbott Papers, University of Chicago. See also Blanche Wiesen Cook, "Female Support Networks and Political Activism: Lillian Wald, Crystal Eastman, Emma Goldman," in *A Heritage of Her Own: Toward a New Social History of American Women*, ed. Nancy F. Cott and Elizabeth H. Pleck (New York: Simon & Schuster, 1979), 412–44; Megan Elias, "'Model Mamas': The Domestic Partnership of Home Economics Pioneers Flora Rose and Martha Van Rensselaer," *Journal of the History of Sexuality* 15 (2006): 65–88; Lillian Faderman, *To Believe in Women: What Lesbians Have Done for America—A History* (Boston: Houghton Mifflin, 1999); Trisha Franzen, *Spinsters and Lesbians: Independent Womanhood in the United States* (New York: New York University Press,

1996); Thomas R. Sedgwick, "Early Hospital Social Work Practice: The Life and Times of Janet Thornton," *Affilia* 27 (2012): 212–21; Susan Ware, "Unlocking the Porter-Dewson Partnership: A Challenge for the Feminist Biography," in *The Challenge of Feminist Biography: Writing the Lives of Modern American Women*, ed. Sara Alpern et al. (Urbana: University of Illinois Press, 1992), 51–64.

48. SPB, "Family Budgets," *Standards of Child Welfare: A Report of the Children's Bureau Conferences, May and June, 1919* (Washington, D.C.: U.S. Department of Labor, 1919), 34–43 (quotation); see also Kriste Lindenmeyer, *"A Right to Childhood": The U.S. Children's Bureau and Child Welfare, 1912–1946* (Urbana: University of Illinois Press, 1997); Molly Ladd-Taylor, "Hull House Goes to Washington: Women and the Children's Bureau," in *Gender, Class, Race and Reform in the Progressive Era*, ed. Noralee Frankel and Nancy S. Dye (Lexington: University Press of Kentucky, 1991); and Muncy, *Creating a Female Dominion.*

49. SPB, "New Horizons of Professional Education for Social Work," in *National Conference on Social Welfare, Official Proceedings of the Annual Meeting, 1936*, 119–32, http://quod.lib.umich.edu/cgi/t/text/; Josephine Brown, "What We Have Learned about Emergency Training for Public Relief Administration," *National Conference on Social Welfare, Official Proceedings of the Annual Meeting, 1935*, 237–45, http://quod.lib.umich.edu/cgi/t/text/; *The Children's Bureau: Yesterday, Today and Tomorrow* (Washington, D.C.: Government Printing Office, 1937), 42–43, 52–53; *White House Conference of Child Health and Protection: Directory of Committee Personnel, July 1, 1930*, in reel 33, box 47, folders 3–4, Lillian Wald Papers, New York Public Library; Alice Kessler-Harris, "Designing Women and Old Fools: The Construction of the Social Security Amendments of 1939," in *U.S. History as Women's History: New Feminist Essays*, ed. Linda K. Kerber, Alice Kessler-Harris, and Kathryn Kish Sklar (Chapel Hill: University of North Carolina Press, 1995), 87–106; Lindenmeyer, *"A Right to Childhood,"* 179–98; Landon R. Y. Storrs, *Civilizing Capitalism: The National Consumers' League, Women's Activism, and Labor Standards in the New Deal Era* (Chapel Hill: University of North Carolina Press, 2000); Susan Ware, *Beyond Suffrage: Women in the New Deal* (Cambridge, Mass.: Harvard University Press, 1981).

50. Harriet Hyman Alonso, *Peace as a Women's Issue: A History of the U.S. Movement for World Peace and Women's Rights* (Syracuse, N.Y.: Syracuse University Press, 1993), 57–58.

51. Jane Addams, Emily G. Balch, and Alice Hamilton, *Women at The Hague: The International Congress of Women and Its Results* (New York: Macmillan, 1915), 9, 150–59; Lela B. Costin, "Feminism, Pacifism, Internationalism, and the 1915 International Congress of Women," *Women's Studies International Forum* 5, nos. 3–4 (1983), 300–315.

52. Ibid.

53. [Harriet P. Thomas] to JA, March 24, 1917, reel 11, JAPP; Erika A. Kuhlman, *Petticoats and White Feathers: Gender Conformity, Race, the Progressive Peace Movement, and the Debate over War, 1895–1919* (Westport, Conn.: Greenwood Press, 1997).

54. Pauline Goldmark to Members of the National Committee on Women in Industry, November 2, 1917; Ashley Hughes to Members of the National Committee on Women in Industry, November 19, 1917; M. Edith Campbell to SPB, December 18, 1917, with enclosed reports; Ashley Hughes to EA, January 19, 1918, with enclosed reports, SPBP. See also Kathleen Kennedy, *Disloyal Mothers and Scurrilous Citizens: Women and Subversion during World War I* (Bloomington: Indiana University Press, 1999); Margaret Vining, "War and Peace 101: The University of Chicago, Sophonisba Breckinridge and Applied Sociology in the Great War," *Icon: Journal of the International Committee for the History of Technology* 14 (2008): 106–22.

55. "War Work Takes the Life of Miss Breckinridge," *Chicago Daily Tribune*, June 24, 1918; see also SPB to "My dear Miss Crandall" [1918], SPBP.

56. JA to Harriet P. Thomas, May 30, 1916; SPB to JA, August 30, 1916, September 4, [1917], JAPP, r9; Frances H. Early, "Feminism, Peace, and Civil Liberties: Women's Role in the Origins of the World War I Civil Liberties Movement," *Women's Studies* 18 (1990): 95–115.

57. "The Immigrant and the War, Being the Ninth Annual Report of the Immigrants' Protective League for the Year Ending December 31st, 1917," Immigrants Protective League Records, supplement II, box 4, folder 60A, UIC. See also Robert L. Buroker, "From Voluntary Association to Welfare State: The Illinois Immigrants' Protective League, 1908–1926," *Journal of American History* 58 (1971): 643–60, esp. 656; and Vining, "War and Peace 101," 110–11, 115, 118, and 121n22.

58. SPB to Ida Curry, November 26, 1934, SPBP; Lucia Maxwell, "Spider Web Chart: The Socialist-Pacifist Movement in America Is an Absolutely Fundamental and Integral Part of International Socialism," *Dearborn Independent*, March 22, 1924, 11, http://womhist.alexanderstreet.com/wilpf/doc3.htm#spiderweb; Carrie A. Foster, *The Women and the Warriors: The U.S. Section of the Women's International League for Peace and Freedom, 1915–1946* (Syracuse: Syracuse University Press, 1995), 36; Elizabeth Dilling, *The Red Network: A "Who's Who" and Handbook of Radicalism for Patriots* (Chicago: privately published, 1934); Kim E. Nielsen, *Un-American Womanhood: Antiradicalism, Antifeminism, and the First Red Scare* (Columbus: Ohio State University Press, 2001), 124–30; appendix B, 147.

59. SPB, review of Mary Louise Degen, *The History of the Woman's Peace Party*, in *Social Service Review* 14 (1940): 383.

60. On the European context, see especially Seth Koven and Sonya Michel, eds., *Mothers of a New World: Maternalist Politics and the Origins of Welfare States* (New York: Routledge, 1993); on Breckinridge's involvement, see Martha Branscombe, "A Friend of International Welfare," *Social Service Review* 22 (1948): 436–41. For the Latin American gatherings, see Donna J. Guy, "The Pan American Child Congresses, 1916 to 1942: Pan Americanism, Child Reform, and the Welfare State in Latin America," *Journal of Family History* 23 (1988): 272–92.

61. *Sixth Pan American Child Congress, Lima, July 4–11, 1930: Report of the Delegates of the United States of America* (Washington, D.C.: Government Printing Office, 1931), 1.

62. Neva Deardorff to Lillian D. Wald, January 12, 1931; "Constitution of the United States Committee on Cooperation in Pan American Child Welfare Work"; and "United States Committee on Cooperation in Pan American Child Welfare Work," folder 5, box 41, Lillian Wald Papers, Columbia University.

63. "Women and the Seventh Conference, Prepared by S. P. B. for the Delegation"; and *Final Act Seventh International Conference of American States*, both in Miscellany, 1933, SPBP. See also Harriet Hyman Alonso, "Suffragists for Peace during the Interwar Years, 1919–1941," *Peace and Change* 14 (1989): 243–62; Anne Marie Pois, "The U.S. Women's International League for Peace and Freedom and American Neutrality, 1935–1939," *Peace and Change* 14 (1989): 263–84; Christy Jo Snider, "The Influence of Transnational Peace Groups on U.S. Foreign Policy Decision-Makers during the 1930s: Incorporating NGOs into the UN," *Diplomatic History* 27 (2003): 377–404.

64. Candice Lewis Bredbenner, *A Nationality of Her Own: Women, Marriage, and the Law of Citizenship* (Berkeley: University of California Press, 1998), chap. 6; Beatrice McKenzie, "The Power of International Positioning: The National Woman's Party, International Law and Diplomacy, 1928–34," *Gender and History* 23 (2011): 130–46; Megan Threlkeld, "How to 'Make This Pan American Thing Go?': Interwar Debates on U.S. Women's Activism in the Western Hemisphere," in *Women and Transnational Activism in Historical Perspective*, ed. Kimberly Jensen and Erika Kuhlman (Dordrecht, The Netherlands: Republic of Letters, 2010), 173–91.

65. SPB, *Madeline McDowell Breckinridge: A Leader in the New South* (Chicago: University of

Chicago Press, 1921); Melba Porter Hay, *Madeline McDowell Breckinridge and the Battle for a New South* (Lexington: University Press of Kentucky, 2009).

66. SPB to Thomas Underwood (hereafter TU), August 13, 1936, April 30, 1937, Thomas Underwood Papers, Special Collections and Archives, University of Kentucky Libraries; SPB to Mary, Mr. McDowell, and Thomas Underwood, February 25, 1935; SPB to TU, April 9, 14 (quotation), 18 (enclosing "The Emergency Relief and the Birth Control Movement"), 1935, January 16, 1939; SPB to Margaret Sanger, April 9, 1935; TU to SPB, April 10, 15, 17, 1935; SPB to George Goodman, March 11, 1936; SPB to TU, November 20, 1939, SPBP. Breckinridge began feeding editorials to Underwood even before Desha's death. See SPB to TU, July 22, 1933, SPBP.

67. SPB to Senator James Byrnes, March 18, 1936; Fred Vinson to TU, March 25, 1936; SPB to Walter West, March 30, 1936; SPB to Senator Harry Byrd, March 30, 1936; SPB to Hon. J. Hamilton Lewis, March 30, 1936; SPB to Hon. Fred Vinson, February 8, 1937; SPB to Sen. Robert Wagner, January 23, 1939, SPBP; SPB to Hon. Alben W. Barkley, April 30, 1937, Underwood Papers.

68. Margaret K. Strong to SPB, January 17, 1932, SPBP.

69. On Robert's departure for Calcutta, see WCPB to SPB, April 26, 1892, SPBP; on his return, see L. Polk and Co.'s Lexington (Kentucky) Directory, 1925, ancestry.com, U.S. City Directories (Provo, Utah, 2011); SPB to Herford Breckinridge Porter, March 27, 1931; Desha Breckinridge (hereafter DB) to Robert Breckinridge (hereafter RB), May 7, 1932; Clinton Harbison to SPB, August 24, 1933, SPBP. On the intervening years, see "Believed Dead during 23 Years, He Visits Chum: Son of Late Congressman Breckinridge, Thought Lost at Sea, Is Alive," *Chicago Daily Tribune*, December 17, 1914; "Breckinridge's Son a Globe Trotter: Spends Three Years in Tramping around the World and Suffers Many Hardships," *Chicago Daily Tribune*, December 29, 1896.

70. 1920 U.S. Federal Census, Martin, Floyd, Kentucky; 1930 U.S. Federal Census, District 6, Fayette, Kentucky; Commonwealth of Kentucky Certificate of Death, Kentucky Death records, 1852–1953, ancestry.com.

71. It is unclear where Clair lived or attended school. Clair's schooling: Clair Breckinridge to SPB, August 8, 1937, SPBP. General child supervision: SPB to Grace Abbott (hereafter GA), October 19, 1932, SPBP. Nisba Desha's school and dentistry: DB to SPB, August 24, 27, 1927; Mary D. Sharpe to SPB, August 15, 1931; Account of Nisba Breckinridge, April 28, 1932; Nisba Desha Breckinridge to SPB, January 6, 11, 1932, SPBP; see also SPB to Marion Talbot (hereafter MT), August 30, 1935; MT to Nisba Desha, May 16, 1946 (penciled draft), Marion Talbot Papers, University of Chicago (hereafter Talbot Papers). Bobby's schooling and medical expenses: DB to SPB, July 25 (quotation), 27, 1932, July 8, 1933 (quotation); SPB to Dr. W. J. Monilaw, July 25, 1932; Dr. W. J. Monilaw to SPB, July 27, August 4, 1932; S. Satterfield to SPB, September 7, 1934; SPB Secretary to Murray Drug Company, September 22, 1934; Charles L. Street, St. Alban's School, Sycamore, Illinois, to SPB, October 12, 1934, all in SPBP. Breckinridge also subsidized more distant kinfolks' education. See Jessica [Pickett] to SPB, April 6, 1928; SPB to Jessica Pickett, January 16, 1929, SPBP. All three children married. Robert F. Breckinridge enlisted in the U.S. Army in 1945 after one year of college and was stationed in California. National Archives and Records Administration, *U.S. World War II Army Enlistment Records, 1938–1946*, ancestry.com; original at World War II Army Enlistment Records, RG 64, NARA. Nisba Desha married Ernest Nielsen, and Clair married Vincent Pearson. Breckinridge evidently felt she had fulfilled her family obligations. At her death, she left her entire estate ($10,000 in stocks and bonds after expenses) to Edith Abbott. Although Robert F. Breckinridge retained a lawyer to attend the probate hearing and challenge Abbott's claim, Abbott remained both sole legatee and executrix. See Will of Sophonisba Breckinridge, 1948; Probate Records, "In the Matter of Sophonisba P. Breckinridge," no. 48–P-7605, docket No. 478, page No. 46 (inventory, hearing transcript, and receipts),

Cook County Circuit Court Archives, Richard J. Daley Center, Chicago. According to Marion Talbot, who chaperoned her at the women's college in Constantinople, Turkey, Nisba Desha had been an ungrateful recipient of her aunt's generosity. See MT to Nisba Desha, May 16, 1946 (penciled draft), Talbot Papers.

72. RB to SPB, March 10, 1943, February 24, March 19, 25, 28, April 12, 21, June 6, 11, 26, 30, July 5 (quotations) with enclosed bills from Dr. A. O. Sisk, 1944; Mary Drummy to SPB, March 30, June 23, 26, July 5, 1944, with enclosed bills from St. Joseph Hospital; SPB to Mary (Mrs. W. J. Drummy), May 24, 1944 (telegram); SPB to RB, June 12, 1944, with guest statements from Phoenix Hotel and Good Samaritan Hospital; Dr. W. O. Bullock to SPB, June 23, 1944; Wally (Mrs. Henry) Wilder to SPB, June 23, 1944; SPB to Mrs. Ernest Harper (telegram), July 10, 1944; SPB to Lila W. Steele, July 10, 1944 (telegram); "Data of Activities of Hon. Wm. C. P. Breckinridge, Prepared for Dr. S. P. Breckinridge by Robert J. Breckinridge and Mary C. Drummy, March 22, 1941," Miscellany, 1940–1941; bill from Good Samaritan Hospital, July 11, 1944; D. M. Lowe Funeral Home Statement, July 28, 1944, Miscellany, 1942–1945, all in SPBP.

73. RB to SPB, March 10, 1943; Kate M. Jaquette to SPB, March 3, 1943, SPBP. Breckinridge evidently had a strained relationship with her older sister, with limited contact except when Ella, Lyman, and their daughter Lyssa came to stay at the summer cottage Breckinridge shared with Talbot in New Hampshire in September 1917. See Pine Tree Cove Guest Books, box 10, Talbot Papers. Ella Breckinridge Chalkley mentioned Breckinridge by name only twice in her draft autobiography, written in the 1940s, which runs to more than two hundred transcribed pages (multiple parts and paginations). See "Magic Casements," Part 1, 72, 75. Ella was survived by a daughter, Lyssa Chalkley Harper, and a son, Lyman Chalkley. See Will of Sophonisba Breckinridge.

74. SPB to Hon. Breckinridge Long, March 21, 1944, SPBP.

Katherine Pettit and May Stone

(1868–1936; 1867–1946)

The Cultural Politics of Mountain Reform

SARAH CASE

In a 1900 appeal addressed to the Kentucky Federation of Women's Clubs (KFWC), Katherine Pettit summed up her goal for a social settlement in the mountains: "To live among the people, in as near a model home as we can get, to show them by example the advantages of cleanliness, neatness, order, study along both literary and industrial lines, and to inspire them to use pure language and to lead pure, Christian lives." The mountain people "stand ready, willing and waiting to do their part, if we do ours."[1] Pettit's plea on behalf of a rural mountain social settlement revealed several assumptions of mountain reformers such as herself: the belief that education encompassed not only literacy but also lessons in housekeeping, farming, and hygiene; that women from the "level lands" could uplift as well as educate mountain communities; and that the mountain people looked eagerly to outsiders for help. Her appeal was successful, and two years later Pettit, May Stone, and two other women founded a settlement school at Hindman, Knott County's seat, forty-five miles from the nearest railroad stop. In 1913 Pettit went on to found another school on Pine Mountain in nearby Harlan County.[2]

Industrial education was the heart of the curricula of both schools and was what the founders believed made them modern and relevant. To Pettit and Stone, industrial education had several meanings, the most important being the teaching of "habits of industry" and personal morality. Progressive Era southern educators believed that African Americans and mountain whites—traditional outsiders in southern society—would benefit from schooling that emphasized discipline, industriousness, and social graces. Hindman and Pine Mountain demonstrated a particular interest in reshaping gender norms: the schools educated both boys and girls, seeking to create respectable mothers and responsible fathers, in addition to providing services to adult women. By teaching mountain people modern ways of working and living, reformers sought to uplift individuals and also to aid the mountain region and the South generally in combating stereotypes of feuding, illiteracy, poor health, and poverty, which increasingly had become a source of embarrassment as New South promoters worked to portray their region as progressive. Reformers' attempts to "uplift" mountain people contributed to this effort and underlined the links between mountain work and broader southern concerns.

Mountain whites were especially attractive to reformers as well as philanthropists because of their racial identity. Folklorists, anthropologists, and ballad collectors labeled the mountaineers "100 percent Anglo-Saxons," racially pure even if culturally backward, and therefore redeemable. As home missionaries, social reformers, and donors began to lose interest in the plight of the freedmen in the post-Reconstruction era, white mountaineers seemed ideal recipients for uplift efforts.[3] In this way the increase of interest in mountain reform, like "Blue-Gray" reunions of Civil War soldiers, federal acquiescence to segregation, and romantic historical and literary portrayals of the antebellum plantation, contributed to national reconciliation grounded in white supremacy.[4] By the early twentieth century, mountain reformers acquired financial support from not only private contributors but also state and federal governments hoping to aid white mountaineers.[5]

Although they viewed some aspects of mountain life as backward, the faculty of both settlement schools also admired and sought to preserve the folk music, handicrafts, language, and customs—the premodern "survivals" that made mountain culture distinctive and valuable. Mountain folk art and music seemed to demonstrate the continuity of a native white folk culture in the face of industrial development, immigration, and urbanization. Educators hoped that Hindman and Pine Mountain's students would combine the aspects of folk culture they admired with industriousness and modern manners to embody ideals of Progressive mountain motherhood and manliness. The competing desires of reformers—to bring Progressive values of efficiency, faith in science, temperance, and greater gender equality to mountain people, while at the same time preserving their "old-timey" handicrafts and music and celebrate them as pure Anglo-Saxon folk—point to the ambivalence with which mountain reformers, and Americans generally, regarded modernity and progress. Pettit and Stone offer useful ways to explore this ambivalence and the contradictions of New South mountain reform.

The moving force behind both the Hindman and Pine Mountain schools was

KATHERINE PETTIT

Courtesy of Hindman Settlement School.

MAY STONE

Courtesy of Hindman Settlement School.

native Kentuckian Katherine Pettit. Born in Lexington in 1868, Pettit grew up on a Bluegrass farm. Her parents, Benjamin F. and Clara Mason Pettit, came from "pioneer stock," and one of her ancestors reportedly carried a printing press across the mountains from Virginia, founding Kentucky's first newspaper, the *Kentucky Gazette*. She attended the prestigious Sayre School in Lexington and then remained in the city, joining the Women's Christian Temperance Union (WCTU) and other women's clubs.[6] By all accounts, Pettit was a candid, energetic, serious-minded woman whose forcefulness and sense of purpose could sometimes make her overbearing.[7] Yet her strong will and dedication aided her in her pursuit of founding a mountain settlement.

Like other educated, privileged women of her day, Pettit felt a powerful sense of wanting to be useful, and also like many of her peers, she felt especially attracted to social settlements. In the 1880s educated middle-class women with few career opportunities and a desire to improve the lives of the disadvantaged began founding settlement houses in working-class or poor urban neighborhoods, and the settlement became one of the major institutions of middle-class women's social activism. Although the best-known settlement advocate, Jane Addams of Chicago's Hull House, considered the settlement particularly suited to urban reform, Pettit believed that the settlement principle also could be successfully applied to rural areas.[8]

For a native Kentuckian, the rural mountainous area of the eastern section of the state seemed a logical place to exercise the reform impulse. Contemporary interest in the mountainous areas of the upper South that became known as Appalachia almost certainly sparked Pettit's attraction to the region.[9] In the late nineteenth century "local color" writers began using the southern mountains as an exotic setting for their novels, part of the "romance of reunion" that imagined national reintegration after the Civil War as a marriage between a feminized (weakened and docile) South and a masculine (powerful but generous) North.[10] The mountain narratives helped create the perception of Appalachia as a distinct and unique region. In these stories Appalachia functioned as a "domestic preserve," a pristine, isolated, and feminized area that served as the symbolic opposite of the industrial, progressive, masculinized nation. The area therefore served a psychic need for middle-class Americans who, dependent on but uncomfortable with industrial development, urban growth, and broadening consumerism, sensed a loss of authenticity and human values.[11] In this way Appalachia became an important symbol of an older America of ethnic homogeneity and agrarianism.

Immigration, in particular, disrupted beliefs about American identity. Increasing numbers of people associated with overcrowded cities, strange religions, and "un-American" ideologies such as socialism and communism poured into the country from southern and eastern Europe. Reacting to the perceived threat of these "alien" peoples, American scientists and social scientists articulated a hierarchy of the races, topped by "Anglo-Saxons." At the same time, southern whites sought to legislate racial privilege through segregation laws. Appalachia, lacking a large antebellum slave population as well as urban areas with teeming "ethnic" slums, became celebrated for its "pure Anglo-Saxon" racial and cultural heritage. The actual presence of both European immigrants and native African Americans was symbolically erased from the landscape.[12]

Significantly, the representation of Appalachia as isolated, premodern, and "100 percent Anglo-Saxon" became especially popular just as the area itself underwent profound economic and social changes including land shortages, outmigration, and industrial coal mining. Following these changes, accounts of the southern mountains began to focus on a more menacing aspect of the region's lack of sophistication, depicting it as depraved and violent, plagued by feuds and moonshining. Exaggerated and sensational press coverage of mountain violence, epitomized by the now-iconic Hatfield-McCoy feud, gave Appalachia and its people a more frightening cast.[13]

Sensationalized media accounts of mountain life attracted social and religious reformers who viewed the region's inhabitants as desperately in need of moral uplift and education. One of these, Edward Guerrant, a native of the Kentucky Bluegrass and friend of Katherine Pettit's family, may have encouraged the future settlement founder to consider mountain social work. Having read and heard stories about feuds and other violence in the region, Pettit was already curious about the problems of the mountains.[14] In 1895 she visited Hazard, a town of six hundred, and other eastern Kentucky communities. The following year she helped found and took part in the KFWC's traveling library program, distributing books and periodicals to mountain homes.[15] By February 1899 Pettit began trying to win sponsorship for a permanent mountain settlement school. Although not able to raise enough money to found a year-round school, she did persuade the KFWC and the WCTU to fund three summer camps in the mountains. In summer 1899 Pettit and three other club members spent six weeks teaching sewing, cooking, and reading near Hazard.[16] The next summer the clubwomen relocated to Knott County, in the county seat of Hindman, a town surrounded by "thickly settled country," and the following year to an area described by Pettit as "the most remote spot in all the southern mountains." The three camps consisted of large tents, ringed by hammocks and outdoor tables, and decorated with Japanese lanterns and pictures from magazines.[17]

Of Pettit's coworkers, only May Stone joined her for all three summers. Although Stone did not initially share Pettit's familiarity with the mountains or her long-term goals—she evidently joined the 1899 settlement only after an original volunteer pulled out—she soon became strongly committed to rural settlement work.[18] Stone was more reserved and genteel than Pettit, as her nickname, the "Ladyest," suggests. She came from a more elite background than her coworker; at various times her father served as a Confederate cavalryman, Kentucky state representative, Louisville city attorney, general counsel of the Louisville and Nashville (L&N) Railroad, and Kentucky state senator. Like Pettit and many other white female activists of her time, Stone chose education and club work rather than marriage, attending Wellesley College and joining the WCTU, the Daughters of the American Revolution (DAR), and the KFWC.[19]

The pair endeavored to integrate the summer camps into the community, and according to their own reports, they largely succeeded. The camps received so many visitors, even during inclement weather, that Pettit remarked wearily, "Settlement workers should not indulge in visions of ease." Local people invited them to events such as political gatherings, funerals, and religious "meetings" and expected them to honor the invitation. In addition to holding cooking, sewing, kindergarten, and Sunday school classes, Pettit, Stone, and their coworkers joined the annual teachers' institute, dispensing books, decorations, and advice. Visits to local homes to hand out books and magazines, check if their cooking and housekeeping lessons had taken hold, or just talk with local people took up a great deal of their time. Community members often turned to the settlement workers to help aid the sick or dying, and the women treated everything from snakebites to serious illnesses, once even preparing the body of a young girl for burial as her family displayed intense grief.[20] Pettit and Stone endured difficult travel, isolation, physical deprivations, and painful accidents.[21] Despite these hardships, Pettit and Stone returned home that summer determined to open a permanent school in the mountains.

After another year of fund-raising, the two secured the sponsorship of the WCTU for a year-round mountain institution. After considering several communities, the pair chose the town of Hindman, site of their second camp, for the new school.[22] Although rich in coal, the extremely rugged terrain of Knott County prevented much excavation until adequate roads were built in the 1930s, and in 1900 the county remained primarily agricultural.[23] Community residents donated nearly two acres of land on the banks of Troublesome Creek as well as their labor to help build the school. Others gave a few dollars toward the $2,600 needed to purchase an additional acre and a school building. By merging their project with the existing public school, Pettit and Stone received extra income from the county, although not nearly enough to cover their expenses. The new school, known as the WCTU school or the "Log Cabin Settlement," for its twenty-eight-room central log building, opened in August 1902, with 162 students.[24]

Pettit and Stone looked to established social workers for guidance, staying for several months at various settlements. They also gained advice from Stone's Wellesley classmate, Kentuckian Sophonisba Breckinridge, the nationally known social reformer, settlement advocate, and Hull House veteran. Her younger sister Curry Breckinridge joined the 1900 summer camp at Hindman. Their sister-in-law Madeline McDowell Breckinridge, associated with public health work in the area, founded her own mountain school thirty miles from Hindman.[25] Through the Breckinridge family, Pettit and Stone participated in a nationwide network of social settlement workers.

Although Hindman's founders regarded themselves primarily as settlement workers, their interests reflected the influence of other female reform traditions, especially the values of the WCTU. The two women found local people's use of alcohol and tobacco deeply troubling, and they were shocked to observe the inhabitants indulging openly at community gatherings. The women blamed alcohol for the widespread violence and feuding that plagued the region and believed that it led men to neglect or physically abuse their families. Sales of "moonshine," they noted with disapproval, funded the local Ku Klux Klan.[26] Drinking and the use of tobacco by teachers, women, and children as young as five years old especially disturbed the settlement workers. To combat these evils, the women gave lectures, taught songs, and distributed pledge cards. Several Knott County residents renounced alcohol, tobacco, and swearing, taking the "triple pledge," and reported to Pettit and Stone that they had stuck with it.[27] On the other hand, there is evidence that at least one producer of homemade spirits resented the settlement enough to engage in vandalism and perhaps even arson, acts that did little to deter the temperance advocates.[28]

Pettit and Stone's attempt to reach out to local women also indicated the influence of the WCTU. Reflecting the organization's interest in promoting sisterly ties across class and ethnic lines, Pettit and Stone viewed mountain women oppressed as *women* and strove to improve their physical health and social status.[29] The reformers identified constant and debilitating pregnancy as the major factor in mountain women's physical frailty, lack of education, and emotional exhaustion. They were appalled to encounter very young mothers or women with six, eight, even ten children. Although surviving documents are silent about any advice Pettit and Stone may have shared on techniques for limiting fertility, they clearly hoped that the education they provided would encourage women to have fewer children.[30]

They also viewed mountain women as overworked and exploited. Appalachian men were depicted as lazy, violent, and prone to alcohol or drug abuse; they, in Pettit's words, "seemed to think their duty consists in hunting, fishing, and sitting on the fence talking politics."[31] Women, on the other hand, had to "plow the fields or hoe them . . . put in the crops, tend them, build and repair fences, [and] make the garden," on top of housekeeping, cooking, washing, milking, sewing, and "everything else done at all." As a result of their unrelenting labor and multiple childbirths, Pettit reported, "Those 18 and 20 looked 30, those 25 looked 35, and those over 30 looked as old as they ever get."[32] In some of their writings, Pettit and Stone could be very critical of mountain women; they occasionally described them as neglectful, ignorant, and superstitious, and beholden to backward notions of childcare completely at odds with modern, scientific advice.[33] The personal behavior of some women, such as use of tobacco and alcohol, overly emotional religious worship, and poorly kept homes, also made them suspect. Still, settlement workers generally viewed mountain women as victims of poverty and male abuse and believed themselves obligated to assist their unfortunate sisters. As Pettit asserted, "It is the deplorable condition of the women that appeals so strongly to me."[34]

Inappropriate gendered division of labor, particularly women working in fields, has long symbolized a society's backwardness, and Pettit and Stone, consciously or not, may have been drawing on this trope when they characterized mountain women as overworked and men as lazy. In any case, for Hindman teachers, the limitations put on mountain women underscored the premodern nature of Appalachian society. No wonder, then, that a major focus of the school was teaching mountain children the "correct" way of gendering labor as a means of molding responsible fathers and husbands who would be protectors and providers instead of patriarchs and who shared family life with respectable and knowledgeable mountain mothers.

Their concern with the welfare of children, also a reflection of the WCTU's agenda, led Pettit and Stone to decide to create a school that would also offer extension classes for adults rather than a typical social settlement.[35] The choice also stemmed from need, as the area lacked a coordinated, comprehensive school system.[36] Mountain people themselves hoped for more educational opportunities for their children, as letters sent by leaders and schoolchildren from Hindman and other communities testified.[37] Additionally, Pettit and Stone believed that a "real school" would give mountain boys and girls "the right kind of foundation" for a modern, Progressive future.[38] Knott County children, despite evidence of poor parenting and their own shocking use of tobacco and alcohol, remained "wide awake, quick and ambitious"—capable of improving with good examples and careful instruction, according to Pettit and Stone.[39]

By 1908, four years after its founding, 279 pupils attended Hindman, ranging from young kindergartners to near-adults beginning school in their late teens or early twenties.[40] The settlement claimed the only kindergarten in "all the mountain region." A few students were able to board, but others walked several miles each day to attend. Nonetheless, the school boasted unusually high rates of daily attendance. Most students enrolled in the eight standard grades, but a few took advanced classes, usually as preparation for teaching or attending college.[41] Despite setbacks, including fires in 1905, 1906, and 1910, the school continued to add new buildings, including a small hospital, boarding homes, and a library. Even so, the school could not accommodate all interested children; in 1910 the waiting list contained more than seven hundred names. Pettit and Stone regularly had to turn away whole families who showed up pleading to be allowed to enroll.[42]

The mostly female faculty had attended women's colleges, most often Smith or Stone's alma mater, Wellesley, or midwestern state universities.[43] Several teachers found the difficulties of living in an isolated rural community overwhelming, such as one who reportedly wrote her mother: "I shall be glad to leave here, for of all Godforsaken spots, this is one of them."[44] Yet others stayed for decades, among them Wellesley graduate and poet Ann Cobb. Novelist Lucy Furman spent more than ten years at Hindman as housemother for young boys and wrote several books based on the school, which acquainted national audiences with its work.[45] Elizabeth Watts arrived at age nineteen intending to stay at most a year; she spent the next forty-seven years at Hindman, as a teacher, assistant director, and director, remaining on the board of directors until her death in the 1980s.[46]

Like other contemporary southern schools, Hindman combined modern academic pedagogy with industrial education. Influenced by John Dewey's theories of experiential and participatory education, Stone and Pettit hoped to create a lively, interesting classroom and replace the neglectful and incompetent teaching they reported observing in local schools with active class participation. Instead of harsh discipline and rote memorization, the school emphasized "spontaneity"; as a teacher wrote: "The spirit of the child, rather than such petty details as folded hands and correctly placed feet counts here."[47] Additionally, as was typical in southern schools, industrial training made up a major aspect of the curriculum.[48] All Hindman students took industrial classes as well as traditional subjects, the "Academic and Industrial Departments meeting and merging," according to boys' housemother Lucy Furman.[49] By January 1908 the school could boast industrial resources such as a workshop, power house, blacksmith's forge, lathe, and drill press. Boys learned to make furniture, forge steel, and repair equipment, while all female students took classes in homemaking, including sanitation, cooking, and laundering. These courses would prepare young women to fulfill "the needs of the mountain home."[50] Courses in homemaking and metalworking were useful, but faculty believed that boarding students received "the chief benefit" of the school's industrial instruction.[51] Live-in students did extra chores that maintained the facility, provided practice in various skills, and helped create a democratic atmosphere. Male students grew several acres of vegetables, raised livestock, and ground dried corn for storage in the school's silo. They also shoveled coal to run the school's furnace, erected new school buildings, and drilled wells. Girls prepared food, washed laundry, and scrubbed floors and windows.[52]

As it did for many other schools founded in the late nineteenth and early twentieth centuries, Booker T. Washington's Tuskegee Institute served as an inspiration for Hindman. In 1899 Pettit and Stone visited Tuskegee and Margaret Washington's Elizabeth Russell Settlement for the first of several times, incorporating at Hindman several of Washington's approaches for promoting morality, discipline, and physical health. As Stone wrote almost twenty years later, "What Tuskegee has done for the colored race, the Hindman School is doing for the mountain people."[53] It may seem ironic that an institution that promised to educate 100 percent Anglo-Saxon folk would model itself on Tuskegee, but it points to the enormous influence of Washington on southern, not just African American, education.[54] Hindman, like Tuskegee, hoped to uplift its students by destroying the legacy of a backward past. The school sought to combat what it perceived to be cultural practices that kept the region mired in poverty and served as obstacles to joining the economic and social progress of the New South.

Cooking exemplified the approach of the settlement workers. Dismayed by the unhealthfulness of the "fat bacon, corn bread and a few vegetables, all cooked in the most unwholesome way" that they observed as making up the mountain diet, settlement workers gave special attention to food preparation. Pettit had spent time studying at John Harvey Kellogg's Battle Creek Sanitarium, and the settlement's interest in nutrition reflected that influence. Mountain women learned to make beaten biscuits instead of cornbread, to use more vegetables and less grease, and to cook with vegetable oil instead of lard.[55] This attention to cooking might seem to support critics' contention that settlement workers were interested primarily in frivolous matters.[56] Yet for Appalachian women, food preparation absorbed a significant amount of time and effort. By improving the work of mountain women, reformers believed that they helped promote improved ways of living in mountain communities.[57] Settlement workers' concern with both health and women's heavy workload led them to promote new, more efficient, and more "modern" ways of preparing food.

The settlements also hoped to treat the perceived backwardness of the mountain people through better health care. On their earliest trips to the mountains, Pettit and Stone reported prevalent "stomach trouble and risings" and "dreadful sores" among the mountain people, made worse by consumption of greasy food, tobacco, and alcohol. They also observed crowded and dirty homes and unsanitary cooking and cleaning practices. Most troubling to the settlement workers, parents appeared unconcerned about their children's sicknesses or accidents, leaving everything from broken limbs to snakebites untreated. The settlement workers understood a direct link between moral and physical health, making the illness and neglect they observed more disturbing. "Without any regard to the laws of health," Pettit wrote, "how can the people be strong, mentally or morally?"[58] Poor health symbolized the "diseased" state of mountain society itself.

In response, Pettit and Stone set about providing more modern health care. Hindman opened a small "hospital," staffed by a licensed nurse who also taught classes for all the school's pupils.[59] In 1910 Pettit and Stone tackled eradicating trachoma, a painful and debilitating eye infection, at the urging of Pettit's friend Linda Neville.[60] By 1916, with the aid of the Kentucky and U.S. Departments of Health, the disease had been virtually wiped out in Knott County.[61] The health clinic at Hindman resembled other public-private hybrid institutions of the Progressive Era, created by activist women able to gain state support for their interests in the years prior to the suffrage amendment.

Pettit's belief in the connection between physical and moral health, and her attempt to control her students' exposure to negative influence, contributed to her decision to found a new school, accepting boarders only. Her years at Hindman confirmed Pettit's belief that even small towns offered young people too many temptations and distractions. Day students who returned to their homes each night did not show the dramatic improvements that boarding students did, she lamented.[62] In 1910 a devastating fire had prompted Pettit and Stone to consider leaving Hindman to create a new school elsewhere, but the local outpouring of support for rebuilding the school in Hindman convinced them to stay.[63] Early in the following year, Pettit began thinking seriously again about leaving the town.[64] Although there is little direct evidence to suggest so, Pettit's choice may have had something to do with a personal rift between herself and Stone; in any case, her decision to break a promise to stay at Hindman until it had secured the goal of a $100,000 endowment engendered resentment from Stone.[65]

In 1913 Pettit, along with former Hindman principal Ethel de Long, founded a private, independent school that accepted boarding students only and did not have to conform to public school requirements. They chose the Pine Mountain area of Harlan County because of its remote setting. Like its sister institution, Pine Mountain School emphasized industrial education. Students helped construct the school, kept it clean, and prepared meals. Much like at Hindman, the purpose of this instruction was both to save money and to create better mountain farmers and homemakers.[66]

At Pine Mountain, too, Pettit remained determined in her work improving the health of the community. In a 1913 letter to John C. Campbell, a reformer writing an extensive survey of mountain life with a grant from the Russell Sage Foundation, Pettit attributed the high rate of disease among the mountain people to bad sanitation, pointing out common problems such as locating wells near grave sites or privies. Within a year, Campbell helped secure funding that allowed Pine Mountain to create a modern sanitary system.[67] It would take, however, an embarrassing and deadly typhoid epidemic at Hindman before the settlement updated its sanitation system. Although Stone was aware that the school's primitive sewage system threatened its water supply, she could not find room in the school's tight budget to upgrade. In fall 1914 typhoid broke out, infecting more than fifty students and teachers and killing one child. Although the school took effective measures to stem the outbreak, damage was already done. Because only the settlement was affected, the incident hurt the image of the school, and donations, which had suffered after the founding of Pine Mountain, declined further.[68] Yet even with this setback, Hindman continued to promote itself as a resource for public health, offering clinics and funding traveling nurses.[69]

Like Hindman, Pine Mountain incorporated health care into its curriculum and extension work. Students could study general family care or prepare to become trained nurses.[70] The school had a clinic to service the community, and in 1916 Ethel de Long, Pettit's partner at Pine Mountain, reported that its doctor "inspired such affection" that the community voted for a tax to pay her salary.[71] In 1919 Dr. Grace Huse and Harriet Butler, formerly the nurse at Hindman, founded an affiliated "medical settlement" four miles from Pine Mountain.[72] Two years later the school reported that two more workers had joined the clinic and that the dedicated Dr. Huse, the only certified MD in a radius of twenty-five miles, reached her patients on horseback. By 1923 a "Health House" was completed, with material and labor donated by the community.[73] In all of these efforts, Pine Mountain and Hindman sought to revitalize both the physical bodies of mountain people and the communities as a whole.

Despite their sustained efforts to reform the health care, foodways, gender roles, and work patterns of Knott and Harlan County residents, both schools also endeavored to preserve the folk crafts and music that gave the area nostalgic appeal. Fund-raising material emphasized the old-fashioned lifestyle of the mountains, noting, "In many ways we are living a hundred years ago. Our children come to us from pioneer homes, where the language of Shakespeare is spoken, and custom and sentiments of mediaevel [*sic*] days still survive."[74] Students gave frequent concerts of traditional music, and ballad collectors visited the schools.[75] The major focus of the cultural programs at Hindman and Pine Mountain was handicrafts. Pettit and Stone expressed admiration and respect for the textiles, carpentry, baskets, and other products made in mountain homes. To support and promote these skills, the settlements taught them in their industrial programs.[76] The settlement schools looked to Berea College in Madison County for guidance.[77] With its emphasis on serving mountain whites, Berea became a resource for Hindman, providing practical advice to the settlement school, and many of Hindman's industrial arts instructors received degrees from Berea. In addition, Pettit and Stone encouraged their graduates to attend the college.[78]

Much of the appeal of mountain crafts produced at Berea and the settlement schools came from its association with the Scottish, English, and Scotch-Irish heritage of the mountain people. Settlement workers sought to connect weaving designs with a British source, noting cultural or linguistic patterns that seemed to indicate a link to the British past. Their journals are peppered with quotes of the old-fashioned speech of their neighbors, and they appended a list of quaint or unusual expressions to the summer camp diary. Still, despite their fascination with the British heritage of Appalachians, and unlike contemporary descriptions of the region celebrating its racial purity, Pettit and Stone acknowledged the existence of African American Appalachians. The earliest journals described and named the several women whom they employed to do the washing and ironing at one of the summer camps, even joking that their settlement work extended to teaching them proper ways of doing laundry. More meaningfully, Pettit made a point of including Knott County African Americans in her visits to local homes.[79] In a 1908 newsletter she wrote that local blacks were "highly respected by their white neighbors" and praised the children's willingness to walk eight miles each way to school, noting, "We have never yet heard of any white children walking sixteen miles a day to get to school." Pettit boasted that the school distributed Christmas gifts donated by Hampton and other black institutions to African American neighbors.[80] Ten years later, after a Pine Mountain teacher was raped and murdered, Pettit defied local leaders by insisting on the innocence of a black convict laborer accused of the crime.[81]

Many fund-raising newsletters, however, did not shy away from the idea that mountain people shared a racial bond with potential donors.[82] Over time, the tendency to highlight mountain people's racial identity became more pronounced, and by the World War I years, the language of fund-raising materials became openly nativist. In 1920 teacher Susanne Gregory praised the "racial vigor and virility" of mountain people and declared, "Let us lift our eyes unto the hills and fear not an industrial revolution."[83] The timing of this shift suggests a link to widespread anti-immigrant and antisocialist feeling of the Red Scare. Belief in mountain Anglo-Saxon racial stock, along with the related phenomenon of interest in the area's "old-timey" folk crafts, made Appalachia a symbolic "haven" from the immigration-related problems, labor unrest, and race riots troubling urban America.

Urban Americans could even own a piece of this rural haven by purchasing folk crafts made at Berea, Pine Mountain, and Hindman by mail order. Through Fireside Industries' catalogues, the schools promoted the sale of textiles, woodwork, baskets, and other goods made by students or older community members.[84] Mountain crafts makers testified to appreciating the new influx of cash brought about by selling their work. One Hindman woman claimed to have made enough money from her baskets to feed and clothe her family with extra funds left to hire help for her farm. In Pine Mountain textile weavers reported purchasing new stoves or paying for dental care.[85] Not all of the textiles, woodwork, and baskets produced for Fireside Industries were strictly traditional. Sometimes local people adapted their crafts to appear more attractive to their national audience, and in this sense the market, in the guise of middle-class urban taste, generated adaptations that changed the very mountain folk culture celebrated for its old-fashioned authenticity. There is, of course, some irony that this self-conscious attempt to preserve Appalachian culture brought mountain people directly into a national marketplace.

The crafts programs, in fact, actually served to modernize mountain life no less than did the settlements' work in reforming labor, cooking, and health care. Like contemporary interest in memorializing the Confederacy, the crafts programs of the settlement schools celebrated a dying past while looking ahead to a more prosperous future. Yet whereas New South promoters enthusiastically supported industrial development as crucial to southern success, Pettit and Stone expressed ambivalence about the economic changes taking place in the mountains. Railroads, timber companies, and mines, they maintained, deeply threatened mountain life. At the same time, the settlement workers believed that mountain people could benefit from economic development. Their attempt to reform social practices and welcome some aspects of development while also preserving a rural, agricultural economy underlines the complexity of attitudes with which mountain workers regarded modernization.

The dramatic changes created by economic development became increasingly evident over the first two decades of the twentieth century. By the mid-1920s, large numbers of railroads, coal mines, lumber companies, and textile mills had transformed eastern Kentucky.[86] Ownership of coal mines became increasingly concentrated, and proprietors often lived outside of the region, sometimes as far away as New York or London.[87] As a consequence of the increase in mining and lumbering, many mountain people lost their land, selling their farms or the mineral rights to them to speculators. By 1930 agriculture was no longer the chief source of income in Knott County, and even families on farms earned more from wage work than from agricultural production. As the mountain South became increasingly developed, residents migrated to communities, often company towns, surrounding centers of extractive industries.[88]

Stone and Pettit expressed uncertainty about mountain industrialization and worried about the effect that social and economic dislocations would have on the character of mountain people. In the last fund-raising letter they wrote together, in 1913, Pettit and Stone noted that coal and timber development had led to the expansion of the railroad. Hindman was now "only" twenty miles from the nearest rail station. Despite their critical views of a society once marked by "violence and utter recklessness," they feared that the end of isolation would destroy the "solid values" of mountain life.[89] They lamented that in mining camps, towns, and cities mountain people were taking up with "the most no-account element" and losing their simple virtues. Pine Mountain faced the dislocations of coal mining and timber removal more directly than did Hindman. Although Pettit had chosen the area because of its extreme isolation, Harlan County became one of the prime coal-producing areas of Kentucky.[90] Ethel de Long Zande asserted that coal-mining camps presented greater danger to mountaineers' character than did the traditional honest, if poor, rural life.[91] Like other Progressive Era educators, Pettit, Stone, and Zande took seriously threats to their students' character, viewing morality as key to progress.

The vast difference in wealth between these industries and small local landowners also troubled the settlement workers. Stone asserted that mountain farmers sometimes sold land worth $50,000 for as little as $700 to coal and timber developers, a process she labeled "commercial exploitation."[92] Zande also referred to the enormous disparity between the prices paid for land and trees and their value to developers. In her view, the process of "capital" carrying away "the coal and timber that constitute the material resources" of the region constituted an "emergency."[93] During Pettit's first summer at Pine Mountain she sent Campbell a list of thirty-four questions about mountain society and educational work in the region. Several questions focused on the impact of economic development: "Are the mountain people who have sold their lands or resources getting adequate returns?" and "Are the companies who own the mining towns organizing them with any view for the welfare of the mountain people?"[94] Newsletters from both schools, however, often tempered such sharp criticism with praise. Stone stepped back from calling mining and lumber companies "ruthless," noting that they sent the school donations and "the most sympathetic letters." Surely the school's financial dependence—not to mention her father's position with the L&N Railroad—blunted her criticism, at least in this sort of fund-raising document.[95] Yet, despite Stone's forgiving tone, the exploitation of the mining and timber industries concerned her, as it clearly did Pettit and Zande.

Still, both settlements primarily focused on individual uplift. Historians have rightly called into question the effectiveness of the mountain reformers' approach, especially in light of the persistent poverty of the mountain region.[96] In fact, both schools identified success primarily as reforming local residents' character.[97] Pettit delighted in the "nice homes" and "clean, well-behaved children" of former students, who themselves had become "prosperous" and "good fathers and mothers."[98] Pointing to the "industriousness" of her male students, Lucy Furman wrote that they no longer wasted their time "lying around idle as many of the boys in this country do."[99] A local woman told Pettit that "Hindman boys made the nicest husbands that she had ever known . . . so considerate of their wives, so helpful in their homes and careful with the children."[100] Settlement schoolteachers claimed credit for the marked decline in shooting and drinking on the streets of Hindman.[101]

Additionally, they could boast of success in expanding educational opportunity and improving health care. Hindman educated many more local students than the previous public schools had been able to do and more effectively. Many alumni of the settlements went to college and, according to teacher Lucy Furman, "outdistance[d] the other students."[102] A few Hindman graduates ventured to northern colleges, although most attended in-state schools such as the University of Kentucky, Transylvania College, and Berea.[103] Settlement teachers also pointed to the productive classrooms of Hindman-trained teachers. Graduates became judges, doctors, and lawyers. One alumnus, Josiah Combs, received a PhD from the Sorbonne and became a well-known folklorist specializing in the ballads of the southern mountains.[104]

Although very little actually written by local residents survives, there were indications that at least some community residents genuinely welcomed the schools. From the first summer camps, the settlements were well attended, and many local families invited the "quare wimmen" into their homes.[105] One prominent local jurist, a "Judge Combs," showed special interest in education and wanted his girls to attend school rather than "settle down at the head of the hollow with some man and go to hoeing corn and building fences." Pettit and Stone helped arrange for one of his daughters to receive a scholarship from the KFWC to attend high school in Harlan.[106] Local leaders in mountain communities often supported institutions associated with modernization and progress, including schools, railroads, and extractive industries, seeing in them hope for an end of isolation and poverty.[107] But less prominent residents also showed an interest in the camps and later the schools. Isolated rural families especially appreciated donations of reading material. One man declared after receiving a book, "Wall, they'll be no sleeping at our house tonight" as "everybody will stay up to hear this read."[108] Even young men prone to drinking and violence attended classes at the camps.[109] As the settlement became established, at least some residents found it a valuable part of their community, as the long waiting lists for entrance to Hindman attest. After a devastating fire in 1910, local residents raised $6,000 in a matter of weeks for the new building, and in addition they donated the labor required to rebuild.[110] Garden clubs, sewing clubs, cooking classes, mothers' clubs, and other extension courses remained well attended into the 1920s.[111]

Despite their confidence that Knott County residents "understood exactly why we were there," it is clear that some mountain people did not wholly assent to the settlement workers' critique of their society. While some such as the jurist Combs may have viewed the school as a chance for social modernization, other local people embraced only the aspects of the settlement that they found advantageous. Reading material, medical attention, and kindergarten classes generally were welcomed. Some women may have found the settlement's instruction in sewing and cooking useful, or they enjoyed the sociability offered by the classes. Others might have found Pettit and Stone's views on gender inequalities attractive. Yet their approval of some of Pettit and Stone's criticisms of local men did not always mean that they agreed that mountain society required complete reform. Many local women took what they considered of practical use from the settlements without giving up what they considered their family duty—fashioning their own version of Progressive mountain motherhood.

A few Knott County residents openly rejected the idea that the settlement camps' "ways of doing things" were superior. Some found their plan to send Judge Combs's daughter to school in Harlan strange or questioned how "old maids" could give sound advice on child rearing.[112] Others brushed off the exhortations to give up alcohol and tobacco, and settlement workers recognized that those who made temperance pledges received pressure from friends to ignore them.[113] Rumors circulated after a 1905 fire destroyed a brand-new building that the blaze had been set by a homemade distiller upset with loss of revenue as a result of the settlement's temperance message.[114] The reformers especially encountered resistance to Sunday school as many mountaineers, especially older men and local preachers, rejected the practice as an unorthodox innovation not sanctioned by the Bible.[115]

To Pettit and Stone these grumblings represented the challenges they faced in reforming mountain society and offered no real discouragement. Both women devoted significant years of their lives to mountain work. By the end of the 1920s, however, they both spent less time actively running their respective institutions. In 1930 Pettit retired from Pine Mountain but continued to be active in mountain work, especially conservation projects, until her death from cancer in 1936. Stone remained officially Hindman's director until her death in 1946; however, after 1920 she increasingly relied on other staff members, especially assistant director Elizabeth Watts. By 1924 Stone spent only summers at Hindman. She continued to aid the school financially, dipping into her personal savings during the Depression years and leaving the school a large portion of her substantial estate.[116]

The legacy of these women and institutions is complex. Drawn to the romance of the "simple" and "authentic" life of the mountains, they nonetheless sought to bring modern, Progressive values to the mountain people. Hoping to preserve mountain handicrafts, they made them available to a national market. Sympathetic to mountain women, they viewed themselves as best able to care for their children, away from the corrupting influence of the home. And while shrinking from the virulent racism of the time, they were central to creating the mythology of Appalachians as "100 percent Anglo-Saxon," American folk. Pettit and Stone demonstrated the ambiguous, complex, and even contradictory impulse of mountain reform and southern Progressivism.

NOTES

The author would like to thank the editors for their work preparing this volume. Additionally, many thanks to Jane De Hart, Carl Harris, Elvin Hatch, and John Majewski for reading multiple versions of this essay and offering extensive comments and critiques. Thanks also to Deborah Blackwell for her encouragement and for fascinating conversations about mountain reform, and to John Inscoe for suggesting that I submit this essay to this volume. Additionally, I would like to express my appreciation of the late Mike Mullins, the extremely dedicated executive director of Hindman Settlement School, for his generosity and hospitality during my stay there.

1. Katherine Pettit, "Camp Industrial at Hindman, Knott County, Kentucky, June 12 to August 31,

1900," in *The Quare Women's Journals: May Stone and Katherine Pettit's Summers in the Kentucky Mountains and the Founding of the Hindman Settlement School*, ed. Jess Stoddart (Ashland, Ky.: Jesse Stuart Foundation, 1997), 67–133, quotation on 94.

2. Jess Stoddart, "Introduction," in Stoddart, *Quare Women's Journals*, 17–57; James S. Greene, "Progressives in the Kentucky Mountains: The Formative Years of the Pine Mountain School, 1913–1930" (PhD diss., Ohio State University, 1982); David E. Whisnant, *All That Is Native and Fine: The Politics of Culture in an American Region* (Chapel Hill: University of North Carolina Press, 1983), chap. 1; Nancy Forderhase, "Eve Returns to the Garden: Women Reformers in Appalachian Kentucky in the Early Twentieth Century," *Register of the Kentucky Historical Society* (1987): 237–61; David Whisnant, "Old Men and New Schools: Rationalizing Change in the Southern Mountains," in *Folklife Annual 1988–89*, ed. James Hardin and Alan Jabbouz (Washington, D.C.: Library of Congress, 1989), 74–85; Rhonda England, "Voices from the History of Teaching: Katherine Pettit, May Stone and Elizabeth Watts at Hindman Settlement School, 1899–1956" (PhD diss., University of Kentucky, 1990); Deborah L. Blackwell, "The Ability to 'Do Much Larger Work': Gender and Reform in Appalachia" (PhD diss., University of Kentucky, 1998); Karen Tice, "School-work and Mother-work: The Interplay of Maternalism and Cultural Politics in the Educational Narratives of Kentucky Settlement Workers, 1910–1930," *Journal of Appalachian Studies* 4 (1998): 191–224; Jess Stoddart, *Challenge and Change in Appalachia: The Story of Hindman Settlement School* (Lexington: University Press of Kentucky, 2002).

3. James C. Klotter, "The Black South and White Appalachia," *Journal of American History* 66 (1980): 832–49.

4. Nina Silber, *The Romance of Reunion: Northerners and the South, 1865–1900* (Chapel Hill: University of North Carolina Press, 1993); David Blight, *Race and Reunion: The Civil War in American Memory* (Cambridge, Mass.: Harvard University Press, 2001); Alice Fahs and John Waugh, *The Memory of the Civil War in American Culture* (Chapel Hill: University of North Carolina Press, 2004).

5. This was especially true of health care, such as the eye clinic established at Hindman, discussed later in this essay. John McMullen, *Results of a Three-Year Trachoma Campaign Begun in Knott County, Ky., in 1913* [Public Health Service Report] (Washington, D.C.: GPO, 1923); Stoddart, *Challenge and Change*, 75–77.

6. Lucy Furman, "The Work of the Fotched-On Women. Originator of Mountain Settlements Got Land from Patriarchs," unidentified newspaper clipping, c. September 1936, Katherine Pettit Biographical Folder, series 3, Hindman Settlement School Archives, Hindman Settlement School, Hindman, Kentucky (hereafter HSS Archives); Frances Jewell McVey, "The Blossom Woman," *Mountain Life and Work* 10 (April 1934): 1–5; Stoddart, *Challenge and Change*, 27–28; Nancy K. Forderhase, "Katherine Pettit," and F. Kevin Simon, "Sayre School," in *Kentucky Encyclopedia*, ed. John E. Kleber (Lexington: University Press of Kentucky, 1992), 719, 799.

7. Elizabeth Watts to Mrs. Henry Boynton, January 13, 1913, quoted in Stoddart, "Introduction," 37; Elizabeth Watts, "Katherine Pettit," Hindman Settlement School newsletter, Katherine Pettit Biographical Folder, HSS Archives. For a sense of Pettit's strong personality, see also her letters to William Frost of Berea College on behalf of Hindman and Pine Mountain students requesting admission or scholarships, in folders 1 and 2, box 1, Katherine Pettit Papers, Hutchins Library, Berea College, Berea, Kentucky (hereafter Hutchins Library); and the letters to John C. Campbell in series 1, John C. and Olive Dame Campbell Papers, Southern Historical Collection, University of North Carolina, Chapel Hill (hereafter Campbell Papers).

8. Robyn Muncy, *Creating a Female Dominion in American Reform, 1890–1935* (New York: Oxford University Press, 1991); Kathryn Kish Sklar, "The Historical Foundation of Women's Power in

the Creation of the American Welfare State," in *Mothers of a New World: Maternalist Politics and the Origins of Welfare States*, ed. Seth Koven and Sonya Michel (New York: Routledge, 1993), 43–93; Allen F. Davis, *Spearheads for Reform: The Social Settlements and the Progressive Movement, 1890–1914* (New York: Oxford University Press, 1967). For Addams's identification of settlements with urban needs, see Muncy, *Creating a Female Dominion*, 11.

9. Historian John Alexander Williams notes that the term "Appalachia" resists clear definition and that scholars have interpreted the term both very broadly (as did the Appalachian Regional Commission of 1964, which included counties from New York to Mississippi) and quite narrowly. He observes that scholars have used cultural, environmental, and sociological boundaries of the region. John Alexander Williams, "Appalachia," *Encyclopedia of Social History*, vol. 1 (New York: Charles Scribner & Sons, 1993), 1031–44.

10. Silber, *Romance of Reunion*, 143–52.

11. Henry Shapiro, *Appalachia on Our Mind: The Southern Mountains and Mountaineers in the American Consciousness, 1870–1920* (Chapel Hill: University of North Carolina Press, 1978); T. J. Jackson Lears, *No Place of Grace: Antimodernism and the Transformation of American Culture, 1880–1920* (New York: Pantheon Books, 1981); Allen Batteau, *The Invention of Appalachia* (Tucson: University of Arizona Press, 1990); Jane S. Becker, *Selling Tradition: Appalachia and the Construction of an American Folk, 1930–1940* (Chapel Hill: University of North Carolina Press, 1998).

12. Durwood Dunn, *Cades' Cove: The Life and Death of a Southern Appalachian Community* (Knoxville: University of Tennessee Press, 1988); Batteau, *Invention of Appalachia*; Whisnant, *All That Is Native and Fine*; Silber, *Romance of Reunion*; Shapiro, *Appalachia on Our Mind*; John C. Inscoe, ed., *Appalachians and Race: The Mountain South from Slavery to Segregation* (Lexington: University Press of Kentucky, 2001); George Fredrickson, *The Black Image in the White Mind: The Debate on Afro-American Character and Destiny, 1817–1914* (New York: Harper & Row, 1971); Joel Williamson, *A Rage for Order: Black-White Relations in the American South since Emancipation* (New York: Oxford University Press, 1986).

13. David Whisnant, *Modernizing the Mountaineer: People, Power, and Planning in Appalachia* (Boone, N.C.: Appalachian Consortium Press, 1980); Ronald Eller, *Miners, Millhands, and Mountaineers: Industrialization of the Appalachian South, 1880–1930* (Knoxville: University of Tennessee Press, 1982); Altina Waller, *Feud: Hatfields, McCoys, and Social Change in Appalachia, 1860–1900* (Chapel Hill: University of North Carolina Press, 1988); Batteau, *Invention of Appalachia*; Dwight B. Billings and Kathleen M. Blee, "Agriculture and Poverty in the Kentucky Mountains: Beech Creek, 1850–1910," and Alan Banks, "Class Formation in the Southeastern Kentucky Coalfields, 1890–1920," in *Appalachia in the Making: The Mountain South in the Nineteenth Century*, ed. Mary Beth Pudup, Dwight B. Billings, and Altina L. Waller (Chapel Hill: University of North Carolina Press, 1995), 233–69, 321–46; John C. Hennen, *The Americanization of West Virginia: Creating a Modern Industrial State, 1916–1925* (Lexington: University Press of Kentucky, 1996); Ronald L. Lewis, *Transforming the Appalachian Countryside: Railroads, Deforestation, and Social Change in West Virginia, 1880–1920* (Chapel Hill: University of North Carolina Press, 1998).

14. May Stone, "Hindman Settlement School, 1902–1945," 2, HSS Archives; Watts, "Katherine Pettit"; Furman, "Work of the Fotched-On Women," 1; Whisnant, *All That Is Native and Fine*, 37–38.

15. Stone, "Hindman Settlement School, 1902–1945," 1–2; Whisnant, *All That Is Native and Fine*, 24–25, 34–37; England, "Voices from the History of Teaching," 121, 126–28; Stoddart, "Introduction," 32.

16. Stone, "Hindman Settlement School, 1902–1945," 1–2; Stoddart, "Introduction," 19, 34–35. Pettit and the others kept accounts of each of the summer camps, in order to report back to the KFWC

and to show the importance of future settlements. The journals, "Camp Cedar Grove at Hazard, Kentucky, 1899"; "Camp Industrial at Hindman, Knott County, Kentucky, June 12 to August 31, 1900"; and "Daily Record of the Social Settlement in the Mountains of Kentucky, Sassafras, Knott County, June 25 to October 4, 1901," are collected in Stoddart, *Quare Women's Journals*. The author of the Camp Cedar Grove journal is uncertain, and it may be true that, as England argued, neither Pettit nor Stone wrote it. Although the journal is much briefer and perhaps more critical than later accounts, I do not find the differences in focus or tone as sharp as she asserted, and therefore assume that Pettit is its author. England, "Voices from the History of Teaching," 47–54.

17. Pettit, "Camp Industrial," 71–73, 81 (first quotation); Pettit and Stone, "Sassafras," 169–70, 168 (second quotation); photographs in Stoddart, 136, 138, 144.

18. In her own account, Stone indicates that she was interested from the start, but apparently she joined the camp after original volunteers left or were unable to go. Stone, "Hindman Settlement School, 1902–1945," 1–2; England, "Voices from the History of Teaching," 47; Stoddart, "Introduction," 35.

19. "Henry Lane Stone," from the *National Cyclopedia of American Biography*, and "Miss May Stone Dies at Louisville," *Hindman News*, February 1, 1946, both in May Stone Biographical Folder, series 3, HSS Archives; Stone, "Hindman Settlement School, 1902–1945"; Nancy K. Forderhase, "May Stone," in Kleber, *Kentucky Encyclopedia*, 857. As Linda Gordon has shown, prominent white female Progressive reformers were much less likely to marry than the population as a whole. Linda Gordon, "Black and White Visions of Welfare: Women's Welfare Activism, 1890–1945," *Journal of American History* 78 (1991): 559–90. Southern white women from elite backgrounds of Pettit and Stone's generation, as Jane Censer has found, sought self-support and independence much more often than usually assumed. Jane Turner Censer, *The Reconstruction of White Southern Womanhood, 1865–1895* (Baton Rouge: Louisiana State University Press, 2003). Joan Marie Johnson asserted that southern women who attended the "Seven Sisters" colleges, as Stone did, were often on the forefront of southern women's clubs and disproportionately involved in social activism. Joan Marie Johnson, *Southern Women at the Seven Sister Colleges: Feminist Values and Social Activism, 1875–1915* (Athens: University of Georgia Press, 2010).

20. Pettit, "Camp Industrial," 68–69, 85, 87, 91; Pettit and Stone, "Sassafras," 163, 190–93, 200, quotation on 213.

21. Pettit, "Camp Industrial," 67–69; Pettit and Stone, "Sassafras," 215–17, 250, 267–68.

22. Knott County's population in 1900 was 8,700, with 2,151 living near Hindman and 331 in town. The county's residents were 97.9 percent native-born white of native-born parentage, 1.9 percent African American, and 0.1 percent white of "foreign or mixed heritage." "Knott County Enumerated Census, 1900" (typed and bound as a booklet at the Knott County Public Library, Hindman, Ky.). See also U.S. Department of Commerce, Bureau of the Census, *Compendium of the Eleventh Census of the United States, 1890* (Washington, D.C.: Government Printing Office, 1895), 488; U.S. Department of Commerce, Bureau of the Census, *Thirteenth Census of the United States, 1910: Supplement for Kentucky* (Washington, D.C.: Government Printing Office, 1913), 579, 608.

23. In 1926 Ruth Huntington reported on a bond just passed that would fund a "good road" from the two nearest railroad stops into Hindman. Huntington, Hindman Settlement School newsletter, 1926, folder 3, box 1, Hindman Settlement School Collection, Hutchins Library. The Knott County enumerated census of 1900 listed farming as by far the most common occupation. "Knott County Census, 1900." But the census also shows that not all of the county farmers were the independent yeomen of rural mythology; in 1900, 31 percent (432) of farms were operated by tenant farmers, and by 1910, 881 (49.7 percent) were. *Thirteenth Census, Supplement for Kentucky*, 660.

24. Stone, "Hindman Settlement School, 1902–1945," 3, and Stone, "Katherine Pettit's First Trips," HSS Archives; *Hindman Settlement School*, pamphlet, 1928, 2, Appalachia Collection, Special Collections and Archives, University of Kentucky Libraries, Lexington (hereafter UK); "Hindman Settlement School," in *History and Families: Knott County Kentucky* (Paducah, Ky.: Turner, 1995), 59–60. Stoddart reports that in 1910 the county provided less than $1,000 annually, at a time when teachers' salaries required $5,000 a year and the school's overall annual receipts totaled more than $38,000. Stoddart, *Challenge and Change*, 51, 81.

25. Breckinridge, who held a JD as well as a PhD in political science from the University of Chicago, helped define the profession of social work through her position in the university's School of Social Service Administration. England, "Voices from the History of Teaching," 62–63; Whisnant, *All That Is Native and Fine*, 38–39; Stoddart, "Introduction," 32–33; Muncy, *Creating a Female Dominion*, 69–70, 79–82; Mary Breckinridge, *Wide Neighborhoods: A Story of the Frontier Nursing Service* (1952; Lexington: University Press of Kentucky, 1981); Stoddart, *Challenge and Change*, 1, 49. Like Sophonisba Breckinridge, Stone may have been influenced by the example of Vida Scudder, a Wellesley professor active in Boston's Denison House. See Vida Scudder, "Settlement Past and Future," in Lorene M. Pacey, *Readings in the Development of Settlement Work* (Freeport, N.Y.: Books for Libraries Press, 1971), 42–43, 69–70.

26. Unlike many other white southern women who approved of the "protection" offered by the Klan, Pettit blamed the Klan for some of the region's problems with violence, accusing it of "degrading" local boys and involving them in the criminal traffic of alcohol and stolen cattle. Pettit, "Camp Industrial," 87, 88; Pettit and Stone, "Sassafras," 198–99.

27. Pettit, "Kentucky Mountain Folk," 7–8; Pettit, "Camp Industrial," 89–90, quotation on 101; Pettit and Stone, "Sassafras," 160, 166, 180, 245, 257.

28. Stoddart, *Challenge and Change*, 63.

29. The WCTU linked not only the debilitations of alcoholism but also domestic violence, poverty, child abuse (including sexual abuse), prostitution, and other threats to the home with indulgence in liquor. Ruth Bordin, *Women and Temperance: The Quest for Power and Liberty, 1873–1900* (Philadelphia: Temple University Press, 1981); Barbara L. Epstein, *The Politics of Domesticity: Women, Evangelicalism, and Temperance in Nineteenth-Century America* (Middletown, Conn.: Wesleyan University Press, 1981); Glenda Gilmore, *Gender and Jim Crow: Women and the Politics of White Supremacy in North Carolina, 1880–1920* (Chapel Hill: University of North Carolina Press, 1996), 48; Anastatia Sims, *The Power of Femininity in the New South: Women's Organizations and Politics in North Carolina, 1880–1930* (Columbia: University of South Carolina Press, 1997), 58–59, 68–72.

30. Comstock laws criminalizing abortion and contraception were in effect during this time, which of course would have discouraged Pettit and Stone from advocating them. The two apparently found it improper to discuss publicly widely practiced techniques such as withdrawal and planned abstinence. Janet Farrell Brodie, *Contraception and Abortion in 19th-Century America* (Ithaca, N.Y.: Cornell University Press, 1994).

31. Pettit, "Kentucky Mountain Folk," 3.

32. Pettit, "Camp Cedar Grove," 63–64.

33. Tice, "School-work and Mother-work."

34. Pettit, "Kentucky Mountain Folk," 3.

35. Ibid., 3–4; Pettit, "Camp Industrial," 94.

36. Joseph F. Kett, "Women and the Progressive Impulse in Southern Education," in *The Web of Southern Social Relations: Women, Family, and Education*, ed. Walter J. Fraser Jr., R. Frank Saunders Jr., and Jon L. Wakelyn (Athens: University of Georgia Press, 1985), 166–80, esp. 172–74.

37. Sarah Howard to Katherine Pettit, 1900; Roy Baker to Katherine Pettit, 1900; Willie Fugate to Katherine Pettit, 1900; French Combs to Katherine Pettit, 1900; G. P. Combs to "The Hope of the Mountains," c. 1900, all bound with the summer camp diaries in Katherine Rebecca Pettit Papers in the Bullock/Pettit Family Papers, UK. Hindman did have a county-funded school, but with only two teachers for two hundred students of all ages, it was unable to meet the area's educational needs. Pettit, "Camp Industrial," 81.

38. Stone, "Hindman Settlement School, 1902–1945," 3.

39. Pettit, "Camp Industrial," 91. On female reformers targeting children and teens, see Alison Parker, *Purifying America: Women, Cultural Reform, and Pro-Censorship Activism, 1873–1933* (Urbana: University of Illinois Press, 1997), especially chap. 2; Gwendolyn Mink, *Wages of Motherhood: Inequality in the Welfare State, 1917–1942* (Ithaca, N.Y.: Cornell University Press, 1995).

40. May Stone and Katherine Pettit, WCTU Settlement School newsletter, January 1908, 3, 4, 6, box 1, HSS Archives.

41. C. F. Huhlein to William Frost, September 15, 1902, and Katherine Pettit and May Stone, WCTU Settlement School fund-raising letter, September 1, 1902 (quotation), both in folder 1, box 1, Hindman Settlement School Collection, Hutchins Library; Stone and Pettit, WCTU Settlement School newsletter, January 1908, 3.

42. Hindman Settlement School Chronology, HSS Archives; *Hindman Settlement School* (pamphlet), 1928, 2–4, Appalachia Collection, UK; Stone and Pettit, WCTU Settlement School newsletter, January 1908, 1, 4; Lucy Furman, WCTU Settlement School newsletter, January 1910, 9, box 1, HSS Archives.

43. Stoddart, "Introduction," 36.

44. "At the Post Office" (Hindman Settlement School newsletter), 1916, 3, box 1, HSS Archives.

45. Lucy Furman, *Mothering on Perilous* (New York: Macmillan, 1913); Furman, *Sight to the Blind* (New York: Macmillan, 1914); Furman, *The Quare Women: A Story of the Kentucky Mountains* (Boston: Atlantic Monthly Press, 1923); Furman, *The Glass Window* (Boston: Little, Brown, 1923).

46. Stoddart, *Challenge and Change.*

47. Grace Hatch, "The Hindman Settlement School," *Kentucky Magazine* 1 (September 1917), quoted in England, "Voices from the History of Teaching," 109 (quotation); Greene, "Progressives in the Kentucky Mountains"; Stoddart, *Challenge and Change*, 20–21.

48. Wayne J. Urban, "Educational Reform in a New South City: Atlanta, 1890–1925," in *Education and the Rise of the New South*, ed. Ronald K. Goodenow and Arthur O. White (Boston: G. K. Hall, 1981), 114–30; William A. Link, *A Hard Country and Lonely Place: Schooling, Society, and Reform in Rural Virginia* (Chapel Hill: University of North Carolina Press, 1986), 177–79; James L. Leloudis, *Schooling the New South: Pedagogy, Self, and Society in North Carolina, 1880–1920* (Chapel Hill: University of North Carolina, 1996), 100; Ann Short Chirhart, *Torches of Light: Georgia Teachers and the Coming of the Modern South* (Athens: University of Georgia Press, 2005), 89.

49. Furman, WCTU Settlement School newsletter, January 1910, 3.

50. May Stone and Katherine Pettit, WCTU Settlement School newsletter, January 1908, 3, box 1, HSS Archives; May Stone and Ruth Huntington, WCTU Settlement School newsletter, January 1914, 2, box 1, HSS Archives (quotation).

51. Lucy Furman, WCTU Settlement School newsletter, 1910, 3. This idea is echoed elsewhere, including Stone and Pettit, WCTU Settlement School newsletter, January 1908, 3.

52. Furman, WCTU Settlement School newsletter, January 1910, 3–5; Stone and Huntington, WCTU Settlement School newsletter, January 1914, 2; May Stone, Hindman Settlement School newsletter, January 1921, box 1, HSS Archives.

53. Stoddart, "Introduction," 41; Pettit and Stone, "Sassafras," 264; Stone and Huntington, Hindman Settlement School newsletter, January 1918, 4, box 1, HSS Archives (quotations).

54. Louis Harlan, *Booker T. Washington: The Wizard of Tuskegee* (New York: Oxford University Press, 1983); W. Fitzhugh Brundage, *Booker T. Washington and Black Progress: Up from Slavery 100 Years Later* (Gainesville: University Press of Florida, 2003); David H. Jackson Jr., *Booker T. Washington and the Struggle against White Supremacy: The Southern Educational Tours, 1908–1912* (New York: Palgrave Macmillan, 2008).

55. Pettit, "Kentucky Mountain Folk," 2; Pettit, "Camp Cedar Grove," 63 (quotation); Pettit, "Camp Industrial," 106–7; Stoddart, *Challenge and Change*, 49.

56. Scholars critical of mountain settlements, especially David Whisnant, have argued that the heart of the reformers' agenda was an attempt to change the mountain people's culture, which the schools narrowly defined as "manners," cooking, and clothing. Reformers such as Pettit and Stone, critics contend, squandered their attention on such matters, ignoring the major economic changes taking place in the mountains. It is true that the settlements, like many Progressive Era schools for urban immigrant children, taught students to set tables, use napkins, excuse themselves from the table, and even "Fletcherize" (the careful chewing associated with the Progressive Era health food movement). Such social skills could hardly help poverty-stricken families, yet reformers' interest in creating better-behaved mountain children did not negate an interest in engaging in large issues of modernity and poverty. In their minds, instruction in scientific farming, medical improvements, and genteel manners all represented a modern, progressive, and enjoyable way of life. Whisnant, *All That Is Native and Fine*, 46–47, 66–68.

57. Additionally, as cultural anthropologists, food historians, and others have shown, the techniques, taboos, and rituals surrounding cooking and eating offer profound insight into cultures. Mary Douglas, ed., *Food in the Social Order: Studies of Food and Festivities in Three American Communities* (New York: Russell Sage Foundation, 1984); Carole Counihan, *The Anthropology of Food and the Body: Gender, Meaning, and Power* (New York: Routledge, 1999).

58. Pettit, "Camp Cedar Grove," 63 (first and second quotations); Pettit, "Camp Industrial," 85, 89 (third quotation). Also see Sandra Lee Barney, *Authorized to Heal: Gender, Class, and the Transformation of Medicine in Appalachia, 1880–1930* (Chapel Hill: University of North Carolina Press, 2000).

59. Furman, WCTU Settlement School newsletter, January 1910, 5.

60. Judy Gail Cornett, "Angel for the Blind: The Public Triumphs and Private Tragedy of Linda Neville" (PhD diss., University of Kentucky, 1993).

61. Lucy Furman, "The Clinic at Hindman," September 1911, and J. A. Stucky, "Dr. J. A. Stucky's Visit to Hindman," April 1911, box 6, Linda Neville Papers, UK; "Abstract of the Report of Dr. J. A. Stucky," *Bulletin of the State Board of Health of Kentucky*, November 1911; McMullen, *Three-Year Trachoma Campaign*; Stoddart, *Challenge and Change*, 75–77. See James Duane Bolin's essay in this volume, "Linda Neville: 'The Lady Who Helps Blind Children See,'" 251–73.

62. Pettit justified her insistence on boarders only at Pine Mountain: "For many, many reasons—not the least among them the parent's view that if whiskey gives him pleasure he should not deny it to his tiny child—we know it is wise to keep the children in our school home for eight or nine months out of the year." Pine Mountain Settlement School newsletter, October 1, 1913, 2, box 1, HSS Archives.

63. Katherine Pettit and May Stone, Hindman Settlement School newsletter, January 26, 1910, box 1, HSS Archives; John C. Campbell to Katherine Pettit, March 2, 1910, folder 18, series 1, Campbell Papers; Helen V. Rue, WCTU Settlement School newsletter, 1913, 2, box 1, HSS Archives; *Hindman Settlement School* (pamphlet), 1928, 3, Appalachia Collection, UK.

64. Katherine Pettit to John C. Campbell, April 21, 1911, folder 22, series 1, Campbell Papers.

65. Whisnant, *All That Is Native and Fine*, 30–31; Stoddart, *Challenge and Change*, 70–71.

66. Katherine Pettit to John C. Campbell, April 21, 1911, folder 22, series 1, Campbell Papers; Pine Mountain Settlement School newsletter, October 1, 1913, 2; Ethel de Long, Pine Mountain Settlement School newsletter, November 14, 1914, box 1, HSS Archives; Evelyn Wells and Alice Cobb, "Pine Mountain School, 1913–1945," 1–2, HSS Archives; Ethel de Long, "The Far Side of Pine Mountain," *Survey*, March 13, 1917, 627–30 (quotation on 629); Ethel de Long, "The Pine Mountain School: A Sketch from the Kentucky Mountains," *Outlook*, February 21, 1917, 318–20; Tice, "School-Work and Mother-Work," 195.

67. Katherine Pettit to John Campbell, June 19, 1913, folder 31, series 1, Campbell Papers; John Campbell to John M. Glenn, June 24, 1913, folder 31, series 1, Campbell Papers.

68. Stoddart, *Challenge and Change*, 79–81.

69. Ibid., 89.

70. *Notes from the Pine Mountain School* 11 (April 1926), 3, folder 3, box 2, Pine Mountain Settlement School Collection, Hutchins Library (hereafter PMSS Collection); Wells and Cobb, "Pine Mountain Settlement School, 1913–1945," 4.

71. Pine Mountain Settlement School newsletter, April 13, 1916, folder 3, box 1, PMSS Collection.

72. Pine Mountain Settlement School newsletters, May 1919 and February 1919, both in folder 3, box 1, PMSS Collection.

73. Pine Mountain Settlement School newsletter, November 1923, folder 3, box 1, PMSS Collection.

74. Furman, WCTU Settlement School newsletter, January 1910, 1.

75. Evelyn K. Wells, "Folk Songs and Folk Dances at the Pine Mountain Settlement School," folder 2, box 1, PMSS Collection.

76. Pettit, "Camp Industrial," 68–69; Pettit and Stone, "Sassafras," 273–79; Wells and Cobb, "Pine Mountain School," 7; *Notes from the Pine Mountain Settlement School* 1 (February 1923), 1, folder 3, box 2, PMSS Collection; Whisnant, *All That Is Native and Fine*, 19, 51–57; Becker, *Selling Tradition*, 60, 67.

77. The distance between Berea and Hindman, in a straight line, is 74 miles. Today the driving distance is close to 115 miles. Berea College had been founded in the 1850s by abolitionists, closed during the war, and reopened in 1866 as "a utopian experiment," an integrated and coeducational school advocating full racial and sexual equality. The experiment proved short-lived. Even before Kentucky state law mandated segregation in education in 1904, specifically targeting Berea, President William Frost reinvented Berea's mission as preserving white mountain folk culture through industrial training in old-fashioned handicrafts. Richard Sears, *A Utopian Experiment in Kentucky: Integration and Social Equality at Berea, 1866–1904* (Westport, Conn.: Greenwood, 1996); Klotter, "Black South and White Appalachia," 846–48.

78. Letters in folders 1 and 2, box 1, Hindman Settlement School Collection, Hutchins Library.

79. Pettit and Stone, "Sassafras," 177, 201, 217–18, 230, 232.

80. Katherine Pettit and May Stone, "Christmas in a Remote Part of the Kentucky Mountains," WCTU Settlement School newsletter, undated (c. 1908), box 1, HSS Archives.

81. The convict laborer never stood trial. The man that Pettit and Zande believed had killed their colleague, a traveling veterinarian and a native of a neighboring county, was acquitted twice, and the crime was never officially solved. Deborah L. Blackwell, "A Murder in the Kentucky Mountains: Pine Mountain Settlement School and Community Relations in the 1920s," in *Searching for Their Places: Women in the South across Four Centuries*, ed. Thomas H. Appleton Jr. and Angela Boswell (Columbia: University of Missouri Press, 2003), 196–217.

82. Newsletters signed by Pettit and Stone seemed to be less prone to using this language.

83. Gregory, Hindman Settlement School newsletter, c. 1920, 8. Notably, in early material Pettit called mountain people "thin and unhealthful," not "the strong vigorous individuals we are taught to believe." "Kentucky Mountain Folk," 2.

84. Katherine Pettit to Eleanor Frost, December 11, 1901, folder 1, box 1, Hindman Settlement School Collection, Hutchins Library; Furman, WCTU Hindman Settlement School newsletter, January 1910, 3; Stone and Huntington, WCTU Hindman Settlement School newsletter, January 1914, 4; *Hindman Settlement School* (pamphlet), 1928, Appalachia Collection, UK; Blackwell, "The Ability to 'Do Much Larger Work,'" 75; Whisnant, *All That Is Native and Fine*, 61–68; Becker, *Selling Tradition*, 56–71.

85. May Stone and Katherine Pettit, WCTU Settlement School newsletter, January 1913, 5, box 1, HSS Archives; Rue, WCTU Settlement School newsletter, 1913, 3; *Notes from the Pine Mountain Settlement School* 1 (February 1923), 1–2, folder 3, box 2, PMSS Collection.

86. Between 1909 and 1919 the number of wage earners in the Kentucky extractive industries (mines, quarries, and gas wells) more than doubled to 43,563 (coal miners made up 39,769 of these). Kentucky contained 240 coal enterprises worth $12,100,075 in 1909; by 1919 the number rose to 635 and their worth to $98,486,910. *Thirteenth Census of the United States, 1910: Supplement for Kentucky: Mines and Quarries*, 710; U.S. Department of Commerce, Bureau of the Census, *Fourteenth Census of the United States, 1920: Supplement for Kentucky: Mines and Quarries*, 151. See also Eller, *Millhands, Miners, and Mountaineers*, 140–49.

87. Between 1909 and 1919 the number of "proprietors and firm members" increased by only about 50 to 386, although the number of mines rose from 442 to 864 and petroleum wells rose from 1,109 to 5,214. *Fourteenth Census of the United States, 1920: Supplement for Kentucky: Mines and Quarries*, 155–57. See also John Gaventa, "Land Ownership, Power, and Powerlessness in the Appalachian Highlands," in *Cultural Adaptation to Mountain Environments*, ed. Patricia D. Beaver and Burton L. Purrington (Athens: University of Georgia Press, 1984), 142–55.

88. Nonagricultural income averaged $342, farm $215. Eller, *Millhands, Miners, and Mountaineers*, xviii–xx, 53–55.

89. Stone and Pettit, WCTU Settlement School newsletter, January 1913, 1 (quotation), 2, 6.

90. In 1928 thirty-six of the students' fathers claimed primary occupations as loggers, miners, or railroad employees, and forty made a living from the land. *Notes from the Pine Mountain Settlement School* 3 (December 1928), 3–4, folder 3, box 2, PMSS Collection; Batteau, *Invention of Appalachia*, 116.

91. She became Ethel de Long Zande after marrying Luigi Zande, an Italian immigrant who taught at Pine Mountain. Ethel de Long Zande, Pine Mountain Settlement School newsletter, October 28, 1918, and Pine Mountain Settlement School newsletter, April 1, 1924, 2, both in folder 3, box 1, PMSS Collection.

92. May Stone, Hindman Settlement School newsletter, September 1920, 3, box 1, HSS Archives.

93. de Long, "The Far Side of Pine Mountain," 628.

94. Katherine Pettit to John Campbell, June 19, 1913, folder 31, series 1, Campbell Papers.

95. Stone, Hindman Settlement School newsletter, September 1920, 4. Her father, general counsel for the L&N Railroad, also served on Hindman's board of directors. Whisnant, *All That Is Native and Fine*, 76.

96. Whisnant, *All That Is Native and Fine*, 263–66; Batteau, *Invention of Appalachia*, 168–75; Becker, *Selling Tradition*, 221–23.

97. May Stone, Hindman Settlement School newsletter, October 1922, 4, box 1, HSS Archives.

98. Katherine Pettit, untitled and undated newsletter (c. 1924), 1 (first, second, and third quotations), 3 (fourth quotation), box 1, HSS Archives.

99. Furman, WCTU Settlement School newsletter, January 1910, 7.

100. Pettit, untitled and undated newsletter (c. 1924), 3.

101. Within the first eleven years of the school's founding, the crime rate in Knott County dropped from 137 felonies and 16 murders to 17 felonies and 1 homicide. Rue, WCTU Settlement School newsletter, 1913, 2; Stone and Pettit, newsletter, January 1913, 1–2; Lewis H. Kilpatrick to Marion Williamson, August 1924, box 1, HSS Archives; Elizabeth Watts to Mrs. Henry Boyston, 1912, quoted in England, "Voices from the History of Teaching," 147.

102. Lucy Furman, WCTU Settlement School newsletter, January 1911, box 1, HSS Archives.

103. Letters in folders 1 and 2, box 1, Hindman Settlement School Collection, Hutchins Library.

104. May Stone, Hindman Settlement School newsletter, September 1921, 1–2; May Stone, Hindman Settlement School newsletter, January 1923, 3; and Pettit, untitled and undated newsletter (c. 1924), describing trip to Hindman, 2, all in box 1, HSS Archives; Eunice Slone, "Our Alumni Association and What It Has Done for Our School," box 9, HSS Archives; Whisnant, *All That Is Native and Fine*, 90–92.

105. Pettit, "Cedar Grove," 61–62; Pettit, "Camp Industrial," 71, 85, 87, 91–92, 94, 129–33; Pettit and Stone, "Sassafras," 204, 271.

106. Pettit and Stone, "Sassafras," 180–81 (quotation), 219, 234.

107. Robert S. Weise, *Grasping at Independence: Debt, Male Authority, and Mineral Rights in Appalachian Kentucky* (Knoxville: University of Tennessee Press, 2001).

108. Pettit, "Camp Industrial," 81.

109. Pettit and Stone, "Sassafras," 245; Pettit, "Camp Industrial," 88.

110. Stoddart, *Challenge and Change*, 69–70.

111. May Stone and Ruth Huntington, Hindman Settlement School newsletter, January 1917, 3–4, box 1, HSS Archives; Stone, Hindman Settlement School newsletter, January 1923, 1.

112. Pettit and Stone, "Sassafras," 260; Furman, *Quare Women*, 167–68. Furman's work is fictional, but she claimed to have based it on her observations of mountain women.

113. Pettit and Stone, "Sassafras," 199, 228, 248, 257.

114. Stoddart, *Challenge and Change*, 63.

115. Pettit and Stone, "Sassafras," 226, 240–41, 257.

116. *Hindman Settlement School* (pamphlet), 1928, Appalachia Collection, UK; Stoddart, "Introduction," 38–39; England, "Voices from the History of Teaching," 114–15, 132, 147, 155.

Enid Yandell
(1869–1934)

Kentucky's Frontier Sculptor and "Bachelor Maid"

JUILEE DECKER

Enid Bland Yandell was born on October 6, 1869, in Louisville. She was the eldest child of Louise Elliston Yandell (1844–1908) and Lunsford Pitts Yandell Jr. (1837–84), a surgeon, Civil War veteran, and medical professor. The future artist was followed by siblings Maud, Elsie, and Lunsford Pitts Yandell III. Family influence in the field of art may be attributed to the passing of a torch from mother to daughter, as dilettante arts were practiced by young girls of her status. However, a female was not assumed to be a serious practitioner but rather a dabbler in paint—that is, one with a fancied interest even if skill were present. A second track of familial influence came from the technical side, that is, the dexterity of working with one's hands—requisite for a sculptor's craft—which Enid later attributed to her father's surgical skill.[1]

Within three years of undertaking serious art studies, Enid's fame as a talented daughter of Kentucky was established thanks to her achievements in the field of large-scale sculpture associated with the Columbian Exposition. Yandell traveled to Chicago in 1891 to take up a position at the fair, an international exhibit aimed at attracting tourists and showcasing achievements in arts, science, and industry. Enid worked alongside other young female sculptors who had been assigned tasks of reproducing works designed by male contemporaries, such as Lorado Taft. At the same time she also completed works on commission, most notably the sculpture of Daniel Boone she created for the Kentucky State Building at the exhibition, on commission from the Filson Club, Louisville's historical society. The suggestion to sculpt Boone as *the* emblem of the state originated with Enid, who knew and corresponded with Col. Reuben T. Durrett, a lawyer and amateur historian who served as the first president of the Filson Club, an organization dedicated to preserving Kentucky history through the collection of genealogy and rare, unpublished materials. In May 1892, after working for a year on projects related to the Woman's Building, the artist corresponded with Durrett, who fancied having a large-scale sculpture of Kentucky's male founders in the city—a desire that he had expressed to Enid on more than one occasion. She remarked,

> Perhaps I have discovered a plan for the accomplishment of your pet scheme, now mine also, of having a statue of [George Rogers] Clark made and put in one of our parks. The different states are having figures of their great men made to go in their State buildings and Kentucky can boast of greater forefathers than any of them. Now should the park Commission join with the Fair commission they could have Stat[u]es of Clarke [*sic*], [Daniel] Boone, etc. made in Staff and sent to the fair, then afterward they could be cast in Bronze and marble and donated to the parks. . . . Now this is the time to arrange this thing and as the time is short it should be done as quickly as possible.[2]

Durrett agreed with Yandell's suggestion and established a subscription fund through the Filson Club to pay her to create a statue of Daniel Boone.[3] Yandell, having learned firsthand how states were marketing themselves at the fair, applied what she had observed to her native state and, more broadly, to her own sculptural practice, thereby creating an opportunity for herself.

Through her work in Chicago, Yandell associated herself with the image of a Kentucky frontiersman and, further, with such ambition, persistence, and accomplishment of pioneerism that she thrived as a sculptor in the male-dominated genre of public statuary. This notion was not lost on her contemporaries or the press, who often associated Yandell with the entire state of Kentucky. Just as Boone was emblematic of the frontier and, specifically, Kentucky, Yandell was emblematic of the female sculptor and of the Kentucky sculptor, even though she left the state as a teen and only returned for brief visits. Her ties to the Bluegrass State remained strong, however, even until her last significant commission, the Pioneer Monument at Harrodsburg, which she designed in 1924.

Throughout her life, Yandell was celebrated as an accomplished artist and praised also for her philanthropic work, particularly related to World War I. Little is known about her private life, though details emerge through her association with close companions Jean Loughborough and Laura Hayes, who coauthored with Yandell a semiautobiographical narrative of women's work at

For my friend Col R. T. Durrett. –

ENID YANDELL AND FREDERICK MACMONNIES

With Daniel Boone statue, Chicago, 1892–93.

Individual Photograph Collection, the Filson Historical Society, Louisville.

the World's Fair titled *Three Girls in a Flat*, and the Baroness Geysa Hortense de Braunecker, who lived with Enid in Paris from around 1895 through 1902.[4] From 1891 on, Yandell seemed to live the life of a "bachelor maid"—a single woman in the late nineteenth and early twentieth centuries who operated independently of men and managed her own business affairs.[5] The term was officially applied to Yandell in 1949, fifteen years after her death, though her status as an unmarried working woman in the field of sculpture would have made the association apparent to her contemporaries after her first departure from Louisville to take up artistic practice full time.[6]

Accounts of Yandell's public life are recorded in reviews of her work, news of sculptural competitions, self-promotion material, and philanthropic work that appeared in the periodical press from 1891 through her death in 1934. Nonetheless, a thorough examination of Yandell's personal and private life has yet to be written.[7] This is due in part to the dearth of extant primary documents written by Yandell, as a number of the letters written by Enid were collected by her grandmother at the family estate in Nashville only to perish in a fire.[8] The largest collection of letters and documents concerning Enid's life, however, is housed in the Yandell Family Papers and the Enid Yandell Collection at the Filson Historical Society in Louisville.[9] Certainly, individual letters written by Yandell and associated ephemera may be found in other autograph collections or records; however, no complete list of such documentation exists, thus making the search for details of Yandell's personal life a difficult task. Complicating the research is the frequent misspelling of her first and last names (variations of Enid include Enie and Ella, while numerous variations of Yandell include Tandell, Yandle, Yandel, and Yardell). Thus, constructing such a narrative is an endeavor that must chiefly focus on Yandell's artistic accomplishment as an integral part of, if not inseparable from, her private life.

The earliest known letter from Enid's hand—dated June 17, 1878, and written in Louisville—details the eight-year-old's affection for her grandmother. Two years later, Enid tells her grandmother of her visit to Lexington in August 1880, writing how the city was "a large place" where she enjoyed the company of her siblings and the Desha and Breckinridge families. By 1883 she detailed her studio work and the effort she put forth: "I went to a time[d] sketch at the studio on Saturday. I worked very hard and got very tired."[10] This earliest personal account of a studio practice evidences her serious pursuit of art by age thirteen, the result of persistence and accomplishment as much as a reward for praises bestowed on her thus far.

Despite this artistic ability, her role within the family seemingly increased with her age and as a result of her father's death in 1884. Nonetheless, letters from these early years written to her mother and grandmothers indicate her interest in art and sports rather than familial responsibility. For instance, a letter from August 16, 1886, recounts a family visit to Michigan where Enid rowed two miles and spent the afternoon in the woods and on a fishing expedition, where she caught five bass.[11] Narratives of her creative life evidence her transition from early works done in mud as a toddler to molding in wax and clay and negotiating the reductive work of carving.[12] Following these artistic interests, Enid matriculated at Hampton College in Louisville, a small, private, female academy with 14 instructors and approximately 280 students.[13] There she excelled in both academics and art, with success bolstering her interest in further study.

After graduating from Hampton, she took a significant step in her artistic pursuits by moving to Cincinnati to undertake serious study in sculpture and carving in 1887, an opportunity that her mother facilitated by making an inquiry to the Cincinnati Art Academy on Enid's behalf in September of that year.[14] By October Enid was residing with other young art students at a Walnut Hills boardinghouse run by a Miss Foster; the situation was adequate, although certainly not up to her mother's standards.[15] Evidence from letters indicates that Enid's move away from the family caused anxiety in her mother, who cautioned her young girl—only eighteen when she moved north of the Ohio River—to act in a manner becoming of her father's daughter and on behalf of her mother's love.[16] Enid's mother also asked her daughter to write and account for every detail in her room, including furniture and bed, so that she could imagine her (actually, "picture" her) as "[she] sit[s] in there at work."[17]

At Cincinnati instruction was delivered in a coeducational setting, with drawing a requisite and electives offered in painting, sculpture, and woodcarving. Advanced students could take anatomy and dissection, although we do not have evidence that Yandell enrolled in these; at minimum, she participated in life drawing (drawing from the nude or a partially draped figure) as a measure of learning how to craft the human form in three dimensions.[18] An eager student, Enid covered a four-year program in two years, bearing witness to her ambition and focus. Attending the academy also afforded her opportunity to view works of art firsthand.[19] Yandell graduated in 1889, setting sail for Europe with her mother and two sisters.[20]

On her return, Yandell had intended for her star to rise because of her artistic abilities, rather than her wealth or beauty. These latter qualities were ascribed to her as Queen of the Satellites of Mercury, a role she played for the eponymous pageant, an unusual and short-lived social event held in Louisville.[21] Clearly, Enid attracted attention as a young lady of the city during 1890, the year that she reigned as queen. This attention came despite her interest in, and pursuit of, art as a career. She forged a change of position within this social milieu by asserting her occupational identity as a practicing artist and her constitution as a bachelor maid.

Coming on the heels of her degree from Cincinnati and her notoriety as a pageant queen, Yandell determined to take up her own practice and get her name out to clients. She sent invitations for a July 3, 1891, viewing of her work at her newly established Louisville studio.[22] The family's big, comfortable Victorian house on Broadway served as her home, studio, and exhibit venue during these early years.[23] Having a space reserved for her work, Enid brandished business cards and offered viewing hours for her pieces, which led to increasing interest in her work. One of her earliest commissions was a bust of Colonel Durrett "which faithfully portrays the massive head and broad, strong brow of that scholarly gentleman. The work is accurately executed and the features wonderfully portrayed."[24] This claim for authority came through Yandell's attention to detail in portraiture and veristic handling of form.

Beyond its critical acclaim, the bust of Durrett is significant in Yandell's *oeuvre* because he played a key role in her development as an artist and bachelor maid. After Enid's father died, Durrett took care in writing to Enid while she was away in Cincinnati, and it seems his interest in her career may have led to her selection as an artist for the Columbian Exposition in 1891. He recommended Yandell to Bertha Honoré Palmer, a businesswoman, socialite, and philanthropist originally from Louisville, who served as president of the Board of Lady Managers for the event. This organization of women served as part of the governing body of the fair and, particularly, authorized the creation of a separate building for women's exhibits, which came to be known as the Woman's Building.[25]

Durrett's recommendation, along with Enid's education and travels, secured a position for her in Chicago. She was not alone, as several women artists were employed there in the service of art. Janet Scudder, one of Yandell's classmates from Cincinnati, recounted the circumstances of their employment. The sculptor Lorado Taft told Daniel Burnham, the chief architect of the fair, that he wanted to employ women among his assistants in order to complete the work on one of the fair structures, the Horticulture Building, on time. In response, Burnham requested that Taft employ "anyone who could do the work . . . white rabbits, if they would help out." Thus, the group of female assistants to Taft became known as the White Rabbits.[26] Their task was "pointing up" the statuary sent to Chicago, meaning the works were sent in model form to be enlarged on site by these assistants. Accounts of Enid's experiences may be gleaned from letters sent to Durrett, as the two continued to correspond once Enid had moved to Chicago. On September 24, 1891, Enid recounted how she had settled into her work in Chicago: "Mrs. Palmer has been most kind to me and taken really a personal interest in me—I have made many charming friends here & some of them very influential. . . . I am very nicely fixed with some other girls who are also workers." In this same letter, Enid also mentioned her invitation from Palmer to address the women of the Board of Lady Managers on the topics of women's work, and Enid's own work in particular. Such a request seems to have established the young artist's authority, early on, as competent among her peers.[27] Yandell, likewise, wrote to Durrett about her work ethic and drive: "I am studying hard and I hope daily becoming a better and big[g]er woman—if not a greater sculptor—But I know it is only by work one ever becomes great so I labor on steadily."[28] In addition to offering encouragement to Yandell, Durrett also supplied the artist with cider that he had prepared and shipped to her while she was in Chicago.[29]

While they were "pointing up," female sculptors were permitted to secure other independent work for the Woman's Building at the same time. In this capacity, Enid was awarded a contract to create unique work for the roof of the building. For this, she designed two dozen caryatids, column supports taking the form of a female in classical drapery. These were her largest works to date at nine feet tall, and they earned her a Gold Medal, one of only three given to women at the fair.[30] Such statuary were aesthetic and functional, but they also demonstrated artistic integrity inasmuch as the reference to Greek sculpture as source material—specifically, the Porch of the Maidens at the Erechtheion, an ancient temple on the north side of the Acropolis in Athens. Selecting such a subject demonstrated Yandell's thorough knowledge of classical subject matter and her academic training as well as her independent pursuit of the arts while living in Louisville. While growing up, Enid had no access to public collections of art; however, she frequently attended public spectacles such as the Southern Exposition, an annual event held from 1883 to 1887 in her home city. At the exposition, the art gallery exhibited works from finer collections along with curios and art of the past.[31] In the absence of a city art museum, this exposition would have functioned as a major exhibition venue for the budding artist in her hometown.

While in Chicago, Yandell, Scudder, and others were free to take on other commissions and, by extension, made significant contributions to the sculptural work at the entire fair complex. Enid's role extended beyond the Horticulture Building to work on the caryatids for the Woman's Building and, significantly, the commission mentioned at the beginning of this essay—the Daniel Boone sculpture that truly established her name among artists, patrons, and the public and cemented her association with her home state of Kentucky. To fulfill this commission, Yandell used artifacts to prepare an authentic rendering by securing Boone's hunting shirt, flintlock rifle, tomahawk, knife, and powder horn, which were in the possession of Colonel Durrett, a descendant of Boone.

By the end of 1892 Yandell had accepted the commission to prepare the large Boone sculpture for the Kentucky Building. The contract was written with her intentions in mind, allowing her the option of creating two busts—one of Boone and one of Kentucky frontiersman George Rogers Clark—or producing a single, life-sized statue of either man. Pledges were secured by December 1892 and the final contract was signed on January 28, 1893, between the Filson Club's committee and Enid Yandell, who was identified as "Sculptor, also of Louisville, Ky."[32]

Yandell's commitment to the Boone project brought confidence: she was proud of the work, and her peers likewise provided positive feedback on it. Moreover, the Boone commission contributed toward her growth as an independent woman employed in sculpture. In explaining this success to Durrett, Enid recounted that she had created a "sketch" or model in clay and had intended for him to see the work before she committed it to plaster. Promising to send photographs of the work to him, she remarked, "This is by far the best thing I have done and I hope it will meet with your approval. The gun & coat I have copied exactly and will return this week—The face is a combination of all the portraits and about 40 years old—in his prime—The artists who have seen it like it and I have new courage to go on working learning & doing better—I have made a great stride in my profession this year and am grateful to the Filson Club for this opportunity to show what I can do."[33]

Published accounts leading up to the unveiling recorded, with anticipation, what was forthcoming:

> Miss Enid Yandell's . . . Boone, which has just been completed in clay and which will be modeled in staff within a few days . . . is certain to win the praise of every son and daughter of the Blue Grass State, who will thus pay tribute to the memory of one of Kentucky's pioneers and add to the living glory of one of the State's fairest daughters. But not Kentucky alone will admire the splendor of Miss Yandell's latest and greatest achievement; for the work is one of such artistic and historic worth as to make it the theme of the praise of art students and connoisseurs from all over the world, who will find in this statue a new evidence of the ability of an American woman.

The article describes the sculpture, noting Boone's clothing, gun and tomahawk, watchful pose, and silent step.[34] Such exquisite handling and authentic lifelikeness demonstrated Yandell's skill. As the Chicago newspaper *Inter Ocean* reported: "Miss Yandell has performed her task with fidelity, rare talent and grace, in, no sense, however betraying the woman's art. It is the best thing [she] has thus far done.... It shows a decided advance upon all her previous efforts and is a happy indication of what may be expected of her as the years advance and her art progresses. Ere long the figure will be cast in bronze and given a position in [Louisville's] Cherokee Park."[35]

Corresponding with Durrett about her successes and the Boone sculpture, Yandell expressed competence and also sought intellectual stimulation from him: "I am sure you are right and very wise about my choosing American History as my field in Sculpture—and when I come home I hope you will give me some interesting history & biographies to read up—The Boone is cast and in place at the Ky Building—and I await further—instructions for the committee in regard to unveiling.... Awaiting your commands—Faithfully."[36] The sculpture was completed and arrived at the corner of the yard surrounding the Kentucky Building at the World's Fair on June 2, 1893.

Yandell's depiction of Daniel Boone brought all those present into deeper association with Kentucky. As the *Chicago Herald* claimed, "Everybody present was a Kentuckian by birth, adoption or education and in the gathering was a goodly number of people whose progenitors made a considerable part of Kentucky history." Politician William O'Connell Bradley offered the oration, which was followed by Governor John Y. Brown's address. After speaking, he grasped the ropes to loosen the American flag that had draped the statue. A great shout went up, including calls for Enid, who appeared for a moment on the balcony overlooking Boone and the crowd surrounding her work. The *Chicago Herald* identified her as a "Kentucky Belle," reporting: "She was jauntily attired in a tailor-made suit of blue serge, wearing a white vest, standing collar, four-in-hand tie and black derby hat. Her eyes danced with pride, but she could not be induced to speak. She bowed her acknowledgments and, with Mrs. Potter Palmer, who accompanied her to the building, left the balcony and joined friends below."[37]

The *Louisville Courier-Journal* recorded even more detail in its remark that as the flag covering the statue fell away "there stood Boone in the coat he wore and the gun he carried when he first saw the Kentucky River." After the unveiling, the band struck up "Dixie," a rather unusual anthem to honor a pioneer and frontiersman, but a suitable salute to postbellum Kentuckians, many of whom shared a Confederate past, as Enid had.[38] From that moment forward, Enid Yandell was associated with Daniel Boone, pioneer and frontiersman.

This Boone commission reflects how aptly Enid Yandell, a twenty-three-year-old bachelor maid, succeeded in accomplishing an artistic feat and closely associating herself with her state. The *Louisville Commercial* noted, "It was reserved for the genius of a young Kentucky girl to have such a conception of the old pioneer and to embody it in a statue. The faithful young artist, trusting as little as possible to imagination, has reproduced the identical hunting shirt and rifle and tomahawk and scalping-knife and powder-horn used by Boone in life. We are reminded by the statue of the cautious step which makes no noise as the light foot touches the ground."[39]

The plaster cast of Boone debuted at Chicago to great acclaim and was subsequently shown at several exhibitions. As a result of this commission, Yandell became known as Kentucky's female sculptor. While Yandell was born and raised in the state, she trained in Cincinnati, entered the profession in Chicago, and further trained and worked in studios in New York, Massachusetts, and France. She created public statuary and private works in the United States and Europe from the 1890s and managed an art school on Cape Cod from 1908 until her death. However, throughout her lifetime she was adamantly claimed by southerners and praised by fellow artists and critics in relation to her Kentucky connection. For instance, she was featured in an article on "American Women Sculptors" in 1899, associating her with the state.[40] Fellow artist Janet Scudder referred to Yandell in her autobiography as "Kentucky's representative sculptor," an act that clearly associated the artist with her native state.[41]

Yandell was from Kentucky, retained her ties to the state, and also depicted Kentuckians without abandoning Kentucky themes in her work—taking on sculptures of Boone until the end of her lifetime. Moreover, she had hoped to secure patronage from the South, which would be articulated through her southern roots. The article "A Southern Girl at the World's Fair" pointed out her lineage, her father having served as a staff surgeon and medical inspector of Confederate commander William J. Hardee's corps. The article further commented on her pride "of being the daughter of a Confederate soldier" who had hoped "for her greatest patronage from the South."[42]

During the 1890s Yandell was characterized in publications as a "gifted sculptor, an American and Southern young woman."[43] The *Louisville Courier-Journal*, shortly after Yandell's award at Chicago, called her a "Louisville sister of the Muses . . . going from triumph to triumph" and acknowledged that "the proudest leaf in Enid Yandell's wreath" was a measure of praise given by noted sculptor Augustus Saint-Gaudens, instructor at the Art Students League in New York, who remarked, "If at her age I had done what she has done, I would have considered my title to fame assured." Such a statement attested to Yandell's accomplishment at a young age and the prospect for future successes. In closing, the paper called on the public to watch her star rise by decreeing, "So let all men know that the climax of Enid Yandell's career is yet to come."[44]

Simultaneously, Yandell garnered attention through her writing. Her name was listed first on the title page of *Three Girls in a Flat*, written with friends Jean Loughborough and Laura Hayes.[45] The text provided readers with a contemporary account of young women living in the city and working for the fair. It gave insight into the life of a bachelor maid, even if partially fictionalized. A second literary effort appeared a few months later when Yandell recounted her description of sculpture at the fair.[46] Together these works demonstrated Enid's interest in writing, a pleasure and skill that she carried with her throughout her life. They also demonstrate her interest in both authorizing the fair experience through the eyes of an artist and documenting the work of artists for a wider population.

As a narrative, *Three Girls in a Flat* introduced characters who closely resembled actual women working at the Columbian Exposition. Adding a layer of truth and immediate relevance, the text situated itself in relation to the fair through its dedication "To that noble body of women which is acting as advance guard to the great army of the unrecognized in its onward march toward liberty and equality—THE BOARD OF LADY MANAGERS of the WORLD'S COLUMBIAN EXPOSITION." The president of this board, Bertha Honoré Palmer, played a role in the story just as she did at the fair. The three central characters of the work (Marjorie, Virginia or Gene, and Duke or the Duke) took their cues from each of the three coauthors. Each held a profession, though the Duke was the most adamant and independent of these. Marjorie's profession was defined in the context of writing, making her a parallel to Laura Hayes, Palmer's private secretary. Gene's profession at a desk job is recounted in chapter 12, while the story refers frequently throughout to her social engagements; this character paralleled Jean Loughborough, Palmer's record keeper and file clerk. The third of these, the Duke, was employed as a sculptor. Her association with Yandell even extended to attire and physical qualities, including moderate build and long, dark hair.[47] Also of note was the similarity in her last name, Wendell, which bore resemblance to Enid's surname.[48]

The majority of the text offered accounts of the experiences of the three and a primer on the active, social, professional, independent woman. Telling passages in the narrative contrasted a married woman's role (as a slave to one's husband) with the freedom of women who could go out of the home to work, travel to Europe, enjoy social outings, entertainments, and spectacles—even an attempt to visit a Turkish bath—and organize events in their flat. The book showcased the antics of young women living on their own. The text also gave a bird's-eye view of gendering the fair and the associated occupational identity, particularly through the Duke's Kentucky roots.[49] By way of introduction to the character Colonel Rogers, a connection is made between the Duke and Yandell's own home state. In fact, Rogers bore resemblance to Colonel Durrett, a figure whom Yandell revered. While the Duke was not commissioned to make a bust of Rogers, Yandell did undertake such a task by preparing a bust of Durrett, a painted plaster completed in 1891 that was exhibited at the Art Institute of Chicago that year.[50] Gendered perspectives emerge throughout *Three Girls in a Flat*, not only in terms of its bachelor maid framework but also in terms of its shorter narratives. For instance, in chapter 2, the Duke asks Marjorie to open her diary and read about her time abroad. Marjorie obliges and selects a passage from June 29, 1891, which recounts a time when Mrs. Palmer received Mr. Theodore Stanton, who inquired as to the part women were to play in the World's Fair. His success in making this inquiry led the narrator to assume that he had skill in handling "the woman question with an ease and fearlessness that could only have come from deep conviction or early training." The narrator further discloses that Stanton, in addition to being a journalist, was the son of reformer Elizabeth Cady Stanton. Inclusion of such personalities and details thus served to illustrate the feminist approach taken in the text.[51]

In addition to such narratives that are external to the fair yet greatly inform the story, passages recounted the history of the Woman's Building and other signal elements to be celebrated through the fair, which would open a year after the book's publication, in 1893. For instance, chapter 5 offered a history of the Woman's Building and served as homage to its architect, Sophia Hayden. After this, attention turned to Enid Yandell, the creator of the caryatids and also a coauthor of this work of literature: "The clay models for these figures were designed and molded by Miss Enid Yandell, of Louisville, Kentucky, who at the early age of twenty-two has much reputation as a sculptor. This roof garden is one of the most charming places imaginable, with its high, arching palms, and the various ferns and flora that have been contributed through members of the Board of Lady Managers all over the country." This passage continued with an explanation of the building's purpose, which might also serve as one of the purposes of *Three Girls in a Flat*: "The Board of Lady Managers wished to emphasize particularly the progress of women in a business and professional way, and in this connection will show the finest work they have done in the various lines, such as illustrating, wood-engraving, painting, sculpture, wood-carving, designing for wall paper, carpets, fabrics, etc., as well as a complete showing of journalistic and literary work."[52] Yandell duly contributed to both the visual and literary arts—contributions that greatly enrich our understanding of the bachelor maid and her world in the early 1890s.

Enid's persona, in the form of the fictional Duke, also embodied the burgeoning pioneering spirit with which Yandell would come to be associated. On the occasion of the unveiling of Chicago's Grant monument in Lincoln Park, a stone and bronze sculpture by Louis Rebisso, the Duke and the others encounter President Ulysses S. Grant's widow, Julia Dent Grant, and come into contact with older perspectives on women and women's work.[53] Despite being a guest of Mrs. Palmer on this day of celebration in honor of the Civil War general and former president, the Duke argues with Mrs. Grant, the lady of the hour, over the role of women. As author, Yandell tells this story to assert the right of women to be employed. The thrust of the discussion, however, is the right of women to be employed *as sculptors*. Grant admittedly knew one other female sculptor, Lavinia (Vinnie) Ellen Ream, who worked in Washington. Despite this, Grant simply disliked her due to her particular profession and her holding a job: "I don't approve of women sculptors as a rule. . . . Every woman is better off at home taking care of husband and children. The battle with the world hardens a woman and makes her unwomanly." Perhaps this can be read in terms of northern-southern distinctions—in light of Grant's understanding of the South through her father, "Colonel" Frederick Dent, who gave service to the Confederacy, and through her husband's embattled war service for the Union, which led to his election to the presidency. However, it seems more likely that the distinction comes from Grant's age and position in the limelight as a first lady during Reconstruction. Confronting Julia Grant and convincing her that perhaps there is room for women within professions, including sculpture, the Duke contends that cutting marble would enable a woman to develop "muscle to beat biscuit" when she keeps house.[54]

In addition to such a significant authorial debut with *Three Girls in a Flat*, Yandell also wrote an article, "Sculpture at the World's Fair," that appeared in *Current Topics* in April 1893, just prior to the exhibition's opening. Unlike the semiautobiographical yet fictionalized account of gendered politics and women's professions at the time, this essay served to document the works on view, and in doing so it demonstrated Yandell's personal understanding of art at the time.[55] Thus, her work for the Woman's Building and the Kentucky Building at the Columbian Exposition, when paired with her authorial debut with *Three Girls in a Flat* and her review of the women's work at the fair, reveal robust beginnings as a professional. These contributions assured broad exposure for Yandell's work, as such avenues offered the opportunity for women (and other publics) to identify with one another, showcase their work, and communicate with a mass public.

Yandell was triumphant in her effort to participate as an active agent at world's fairs and became known primarily for her large public sculptures and monuments, which were on view in Louisville and Nashville, as well as Providence, Rhode Island; Albany, New York; and New Haven, Connecticut. From the 1890s until her death, Yandell oscillated between smaller works in bronze and clay and the large-scale commissions. Evidence throughout Yandell's career bore witness to her success across media, size, and scale, as well as audience. She exhibited regularly in Paris and New York and was celebrated for her public statuary, being awarded medals at Chicago and Nashville, in addition to the World's Fairs in Buffalo in 1901 and Saint Louis in 1904. Yandell was known for giving exquisite form and mastering lifelikeness—both in terms of physiognomy and also patination and coloring. Her education and early fame as a sculptor and her family connections may have provided the opportunity to secure the commissions, but she quickly moved beyond these associations to generate an occupational identity on a national scale.

Yandell achieved recognition within her peer group, that is, through her election in 1899 to the National Sculpture Society, the first organization of professional sculptors formed in the United States. In announcing her award, particular mention was made of her Boone sculpture for the Columbian Exposition—which attracted the admiration of not only Kentuckians but also art critics from every part of the world—and the enormous figure of Athena she constructed for the replica of the Parthenon erected for the Tennessee Centennial in Nashville in 1897. Recalling the Athena, in particular, Yandell commented: "It brought me into such prominence . . . that I was represented in the newspapers with a tiara on my head. The tiara and the photograph, however, belonged to Mrs. Van Leer Kirkman, president of the Nashville Centennial Woman's Board." To correct any perceptions that she might be feminized by wearing the crown jewels of a queen, Yandell remarked blandly, "I assure you I do not own a tiara." Such prescriptive crafting of her own image worked to distance these bachelor maid days from earlier events in her life, particularly the occasion when she had worn a crown as Queen of the Satellites in 1890. Thus, the characterization of Yandell that emerged during the 1890s was tied to her accomplishments in the field of public statuary and, as a result, forged a self-image of independence and agency.[56]

Yandell began to identify herself as a sculptor by profession shortly after her election to the National Sculpture Society. Enid's claims of being a sculptor, backed by her successful record of commissions and purchases, as well as her recognition by her peers, afforded her the opportunity to publicly claim her authority. The City Directory of New York from 1900 includes her listing as such. And from 1908 forward her letterhead also identified her as a sculptor.[57] Those outside of the art world questioned, as Julia Grant had, Enid's right to work at all but particularly within the field of sculpture. In response, Yandell's mother had grown used to answering such questions with a quip: "People ask me so often how you happened to be a sculptor & I always make the same reply you were just born that way."[58]

While negotiating a studio practice in Louisville, Chicago, New York, and Paris from 1891 through 1907, Yandell's association with Boone and frontierism remained fixed and offered evidence of Kentucky's artistic heritage. Following the 1893 exhibition of the statue of Boone, Yandell reduced the sculpture to a traditional bust and a miniature form that could be used as promotional material. She also made several life-sized plaster casts of the original Boone and exhibited these for thirteen years—from the 1893 debut in Chicago to the Nashville Centennial Celebration in 1897 to the Louisiana Purchase Expo in 1904.[59] The permanent placement of Kentucky's frontiersman did not materialize until Charles C. Bickel, manufacturer of the "Daniel Boone" brand cigar, donated $10,000 for the work to be cast in bronze. The dedication of this life-sized Boone emerging from the trees atop stone planks was held on June 15, 1906, a feature event of Kentucky Home-Coming Week. An estimated fifty thousand people went to Cherokee Park in Louisville to see the statue's unveiling, which was delayed by rain. Bickel's granddaughter pulled the ribbons that removed the drape over the form. The crimson covering landed in a puddle at Boone's feet, a reminder, perhaps, of Kentucky's "dark and bloody ground," which referred to the fierce battles between the Indians and frontiersmen passing through the Alleghenies into this wilderness.[60] John Breckinridge Castleman of Louisville made the presentation address for Bickel, and the acceptance speech was made by Colonel Durrett, who had expressed to Enid some fifteen years earlier his desire to have such a work on view in the city.[61]

From the plaster cast of Boone to this later bronze statuary, Yandell's work was associated with the pioneer. In fact, *her depiction* of Daniel Boone became a representation of the frontier, more broadly. For instance, the work was used as an illustration for an article on expansion that appeared in *The Outlook* on January 25, 1908. At the head of the article was a full-page image of Boone—in cap and fringed jacket with rifle in tow—that leads off the article on "The Romance of American Expansion."[62] In addition to a full-page photographic reproduction of Yandell's Boone, the article was supplemented with engraved images of source material that Enid had used to model her sculpture, namely, the rifle, hunting shirt, powder horn, tomahawk, and hunting knife from Durrett's collection. Thus, the Boone legacy followed Yandell into this middle phase of her artistic career.

In 1908, the same year as the publication noted above, Yandell settled at Edgartown, Massachusetts, where she would head the Branstock School of Art for nearly thirty years.[63] She focused especially on summer classes for aspiring artists, akin to the summer schools that were becoming popular among American modernists. In addition to classes, Branstock offered exhibition of small paintings, works on paper, and sculpture.[64] The environment proved to be a crucible of artistic activity for Yandell. Here she completed smaller works that were derived from literary and historical subjects, including sundials as well as public and private fountains. While Enid's pre–World War I years were dominated by sculptures for the World's Fairs and monuments to individuals—including women's education proponents Emma Willard and J. J. Rucker—her postwar production diminished, as it did for many artists, due to the economic depression and the poor reception for artists at the time. During and after the war, Yandell grew committed to improving the lives of others by undertaking significant humanitarian work both at home and in France. It remains unclear, however, if Yandell created art while giving service to the war effort.[65]

Given her age and diversified interests in teaching, exhibition, and small-scale commissions, Yandell pursued one significant large-scale composition after World War I: the Pioneer Memorial Park Monument at Harrodsburg, Kentucky. This monument was commissioned by the Kentucky Pioneer Association, a local group of citizens, to memorialize the early settlers of the state. Such a heroic commission was garnered through competition, drawing the most prized American sculptors of the day. Yandell submitted her design and was awarded a contract for the project in 1924, beating out sixteen male competitors for the design of the monument. Her selection was noted in the press, which called on her fame without explicitly stating her own roots as a pioneer sculptor: "ENID YANDELL, a woman famous in the art of sculpture, has been selected to design the monument of the Kentucky pioneer which will overlook the grounds dedicated to the memory of the early settlers of this 'back door of the nation.'"[66]

It is no wonder that Yandell was selected to design the monument at Harrodsburg—not only for her abilities as an artist but also for her association with her home state. Leading the praise was her native city, whose newspaper announced her victory in securing the commission. As told by the *Louisville Herald*, "A Woman Three Times a Pioneer in Art Is Chosen to Do a Pioneer Monument at Harrodsburg, Kentucky." Yandell was proclaimed a pioneer in Chicago; among the first women elected for membership to the National Sculpture Society, "therefore a pioneer for the second time"; and for the third time with her design of the gnomon/sundial *The Four Seasons* using "a wing of a bird held in the hands of summer," a commissioned piece that Yandell had completed in 1900.[67]

For the Pioneer Memorial Park Monument, Yandell returned to Kentucky—

literally and figuratively. Working on the project renewed her pioneer spirit while expanding its physical manifestation. Photographs annotated by her detail the site and, when coupled with her typed description of the monument design, offer an understanding of her authority as Kentucky's frontier sculptor.[68] Yandell's monument was intended to go beyond a personal likeness—a milestone she had achieved years earlier with the Boone sculpture for the Kentucky Building at the Chicago World's Fair. Here, back in her native state, her work could convey the pioneer spirit of those who first encountered the wilderness in 1767 and helped develop a settlement in 1775. Boone, along with frontier military leader George Rogers Clark and nameless other individuals who served as pathfinders and trailblazers, were to be heralded for their expansion into what would become Kentucky and points westward. They were the early settlers of a state that, a century and a half later, still merited celebration.

For this project, Yandell attempted to branch out from her earlier pioneer depiction. According to the artist's visual and verbal renderings, the work would function more as an installation consisting of several components. On that measure alone, it was a departure from her previous projects—singular works taking on the forms of a bust, a life-sized figure, or a colossal statue, monuments conceived with one focal point. Among these were the Carrie Brown (Bajnotti) Fountain in Providence, Rhode Island, which contains allegorical figures representing "The Struggle of Life" amidst a granite basin of more than two hundred spray outlets, and the monument and relief sculpture to John W. Thomas in Nashville, consisting of a bronze, full-length portrait atop a stone base with four rectangular bronze reliefs.

At Harrodsburg Yandell intended to exhibit reliefs of Daniel Boone; James Harrod, who settled the first site in the state in 1774; and Meriwether Lewis and William Clark, who led the Corps of Discovery Expedition that began near Louisville in 1803.[69] These were to have been supplemented with the verse "Kentucky Homecoming 1924." But Enid's ambition extended beyond likeness in order to expand the conception of the pioneer and to create what she referred to as the "Pioneer Unit." The components were a pioneer man in the typical Boone fashion—a hunting shirt—though he was not to be considered Boone but rather *every man*. According to Yandell's notes, "the Pioneer will be typical but not a portrait." In addition, women were to play a role in this commemoration: "The woman Pioneers, who had equal hardships and more uninteresting labor than the men, have never before been recognized." Yandell further acknowledged their work in tanning the buffalo and elk skins that created the garment—the very hunting shirt of Boone's fame.[70] Such a vast array of perspectives required more than a series of medallions or, even, a cluster of relevant figures. Yandell rose to the challenge and, accordingly, conceived of her most ambitious work to date: a platform, set amid a landscaped park area, with several figures consisting of a pioneer man, a woman pioneer holding a baby in her arms, and a youth carrying the flintlock rifle. She even went so far as to claim that through her work she could immortalize the woman who also served as a pioneer: "The Pioneer Man went to the trackless forest primeval, his woman followed her mate. It shall be my joy to sing in bronze the epic of these women and children."[71]

On receiving the commission for this project, Yandell met with critical acclaim. Lawrence F. Abbott wrote in his January 1925 article, "The Gate of the West," of the 150th anniversary of Kentucky's founding, merging the historic event with American westward expansion in general: "Kentucky is celebrating, therefore, the prowess, not of one man, but of a dauntless host whose names we do not know. The statue by Enid Yandell which will be unveiled at Harrodsburg will stand as a monument not only to Boone, but also to those who, by the wilderness and the Natchez of all other westward-running trails, fared on into the unknown wilds to lay the stepping-stones for civilization across a continent."[72] The *New York Sun* acknowledged Yandell's "gaining for her sex recognition in the field" of sculpture: "It was not many years ago that any statement concerning the work of a woman in sculpture was made with apologies, which, however unnecessary, were rather expected by a public unused to the sight of women laboring in this distinguished field." This public had included the generation of Julia Dent Grant, with whom the Duke in *Three Girls in a Flat* had exchanged words thirty years earlier. Yandell demonstrated the promise of women in the field of sculpture, and when asked about this, she remarked, "Yes, I think it is a lovely occupation for women, if they have love for form. It requires much study and is wonderful for developing the mentality. It requires a great deal of physical strength and, of course, one must have talent before entering the field. The field is not overcrowded for art is still much unappreciated in this country, but every year I see it advance."[73]

Yandell's plan would have transformed the Pioneer Memorial State Park from rustic forts, fortifications, and the old spring into a landscaped area accentuated by figural and relief sculpture recognizing Lewis and Clark, Boone, and Harrod as well as the unfamiliar citizens embodied as unforgettable types bearing witness to the hardships and unintended consequences of Manifest Destiny. But Yandell's conception never materialized, as the project was aborted for reasons unknown. No extant correspondence to or from her, scrapbooks, or newspaper clippings detail the rationale, although a few possibilities exist. First, Enid's focus had shifted to teaching in New England; while she did travel to Fort Harrod in 1924 to visit the site for the memorial, it was one of the few visits she made back to her native state in her later life. By this time she had established her school and practice and devoted much of her time to its development as well as her numerous, if smaller, commissions. Second, and more likely, the death of her architect brother-in-law, Donn Barber, on May 25, 1925, dealt a blow to the project, as he was to be her principal collaborator.[74]

Despite Yandell's presumed withdrawal from this project, a commission to complete park renovations and bolster the attractions in Harrodsburg was managed. On June 16, 1927, the Pioneer Memorial Park—later renamed Old Fort Harrod State Park—was opened as a reconstructed replica of the first fort on that site.[75] Over the next several years, additional enhancements were made with federal funding, including the *First Permanent Settlement of the West*, the Pioneer Memorial conceived by sculptor Ulric Ellerhusen and architect Francis Keally to replace Enid's winning design.[76] This sculpture was dedicated by President Franklin Delano Roosevelt on November 16, 1934.[77] Today, the monument is more commonly known as the George Rogers Clark Federal Monument, thus diminishing the Boone connection—though he is represented on the far right side of the monument, along with Harrod. A third grouping depicts an unsettled family of man, woman, and child. An inlay map outlines the routes of the early pioneers.

Enid Yandell was an artist first and foremost, as well as a noted author and humanitarian. Artists of her sort—those who worked on large-scale projects associated with temporary events such as the World's Fairs—made names for themselves both through their work and through their association with peer sculptors. Yandell's reach throughout her lifetime was broad, richly complex, and varied by virtue of her connections with well-known male artists, including Daniel Chester French, who proposed her name as a member of the National Sculpture Society; Philip Martiny, at whose studio Yandell had worked in Chicago and under whom she studied at the Art Students League; Lorado Taft, whose personality is revealed in manuscript letters and wonderfully detailed in *Three Girls in a Flat*; and Frederick MacMonnies and Auguste Rodin, with whom she studied and corresponded in Paris. Her fame came through initiative and ambition in both large-scale commissions and smaller works. Even with the accolades and praise Yandell earned as a medalist at Chicago and Nashville, for her humanitarian work in France and the United States during the war, and her notoriety as a pioneer on multiple occasions and in several contexts, her complete story has not yet been given its due. Scholars have suppressed the history of Enid Yandell, perhaps due to her apparent regional appeal, specifically her persistent and celebrated depiction of Daniel Boone. The claim by previous scholars that Yandell withdrew from art late in life casts a dim shadow on a brilliant career that bore witness to oscillations between temporary and permanent public sculpture; statuary in parks, squares, and at fairs; and private works for domestic spaces. When taken together, Enid Yandell's body of visual art as well as her letters and literary works reveal the complexities of Kentucky's frontier sculptor and bachelor maid.

NOTES

1. "How an American Girl Has Astonished the Art World," clipping in the Filson Historical Society (Louisville), Enid Bland Yandell (1870–1934) Papers, 1875–1982, Mss A/Y21b/Folder 105 (hereafter FHS Mss A/Y21b/Folder #).

2. The Filson Historical Society, Reuben T. Durrett (1824–1913) Added Papers, 1883–1910, FHS Mss A/D965c/Folder 97 (hereafter FHS Mss A/D965c/Folder #).

3. See FHS Mss A/Y21b/Folder 59 for the agreement between the members of the Filson Club.

4. Enid Yandell, Jean Loughborough, and Laura Hayes, *Three Girls in a Flat* (Chicago: Bright, Leonard, 1892). Letters from Enid's mother, Louise, to Enid, while she was in Paris, often included mention of Geysa (or Geyza) and their "bohemian" lifestyle. See, for instance, FHS Mss A/Y21b/ Folder 23, esp. correspondence from 1897. In fact, Louise remarks on her gratitude for Geysa in a letter to Enid dated February 21, 1898: "Love to dear Geysa—I really do not know how to express to her all my appreciation of what she does for you." FHS Mss A/Y21b/Folder 24. In 1898 Yandell sculpted a bust of the baroness; its whereabouts are unknown.

5. The term was popularized through a novel written in 1894 by Constance Cary Harrison, whose tale discloses the dilemma between Marion Irving and her betrothed Alexander Gordon. See Constance Cary Harrison, *A Bachelor Maid* (New York: Century, 1894).

6. Melville O. Briney, "Enid Yandell, Louisville's Gifted Bachelormaid," *Louisville Times*, July 28, 1949.

7. Yandell has been the subject of three biographical studies over the past thirty years. Scholarly treatment of the artist has focused on her life and works more than constructions of personal and occupational identity. These include Desiree Caldwell's exhibition and catalogue, "Enid Yandell and the Branstock School," Museum of Art, Rhode Island School of Design (1982); historian Nancy Disher Baird's comprehensive article, "Enid Yandell: Kentucky Sculptor," *Filson Club History Quarterly* 62 (1988): 5–31; and Stephanie Darst's exhibition and catalogue, "The Sculpture of Enid Yandell," J. D. Speed Museum, Louisville (1993), which built on Baird's narrative.

8. According to Nancy Baird, a family descendant on Enid's mother's side remembered hearing that three generations of correspondence and ephemera were burned in the 1920s as a means of simplifying the process of clearing the estate before sale. See Baird, "Enid Yandell: Kentucky Sculptor," 6n2.

9. The Yandell Collection has been microfilmed and is available through the Smithsonian's Archives of American Art. For access to this collection, see http://www.aaa.si.edu/collections /enid-yandell-papers-6900. This collection of autograph items gives some evidence of her experiences through accounts of her art and pictorial musings as well as visual and verbal source material richly supplemented by correspondence between her and members of her family, friends, and professional colleagues.

10. FHS Mss A/Y21b/Folder 1.

11. FHS Mss A/Y21b/Folder 2.

12. Enid's left-handed nature is described in a handwritten note by her niece, Elsie Barber Trask, who also includes genealogical information about the Yandell family. E. B. Trask, July 31, 1981, FHS Mss A/Y21b/Folder 71.

13. *American College and Public School Directory*, vol. 16 (Chicago: C. H. Evans, 1893), particularly the section on "Colleges, Female Seminaries, Academies," 31. The listing includes the president's name and the number of instructors at the school: "Hampton College, Louisville. L. D. Hampton, 14."

14. Newspaper clipping (n.d.), Enid's scrapbook, 49, FHS Mss A/Y21b/Folder 94.

15. Louise Yandell to Enid Yandell, October 27, 1888, FHS Mss A/Y21b/Folder 12.

16. Louise Yandell to Enid Yandell, October 12, 1887, FHS Mss A/Y21b/Folder 5.

17. Louise Yandell to Enid Yandell, c. October 18, 1887, FHS Mss A/Y21b/Folder 5.

18. Information on classes and general experience comes from Janet Scudder, a classmate of Enid's, whose autobiography offers a glimpse into the studio. See Janet Scudder, *Modeling My Life* (New York: Harcourt, Brace, 1925), 90–108. From Scudder we learn that female students were able to draw from the nude, but we have no affirmation that Enid learned in this way, although Nancy Baird states it in "Enid Yandell," *Kentucky Women: Two Centuries of Indomitable Spirit and Vision*, ed. Eugenia K. Potter (n.p.: Big Tree Press, 1997), 190. See also Mary Bryan Hood, *Kentucky Women Artists: 1850–2000, A Collaborative Exhibition* (Owensboro, Ky.: Owensboro Museum of Art, 2001).

19. The Cincinnati Museum Association was established in 1881, and a permanent art museum was founded in May 1886. The building was completed in Eden Park and was heralded worldwide as "The Art Palace of the West." See http://www.cincinnatiartmuseum.org/visit/info/history.

20. See Darst, "Sculpture of Enid Yandell," 2; Baird, "Enid Yandell: Kentucky Sculptor," 9, supported by letters in FHS Mss A/Y21b/Folder 16.

21. Scrapbook compiled by Yandell, FHS Mss A/Y21b/Folder 94.

22. Yandell's scrapbook contains a white calling card of her studio and a clipping dated July 3 [1891]: STUDIO. 315 WEST BROADWAY. MISS YANDELL. PRIVATE VIEW FRIDAY, JULY THIRD. AFTER TEN O'CLOCK A.M., FHS Mss A/Y21b/Folder 94, p. 49.

23. On her home setting, see Briney, "Enid Yandell, Louisville's Gifted Bachelormaid." Regarding her use of her home as a studio as early as 1891, see FHS Mss A/Y21b/Folder 94, p. 49, along with entries around 1891.

24. Clipping c. 1891, FHS Mss A/Y21b/Folder 94, glued on p. 49.

25. FHS Mss A/D965c/Folder 73.

26. Scudder, *Modeling My Life*, 58.

27. FHS Mss A/D965c/Folder 81.

28. Letter, April 15, 1892, in FHS Mss A/D965c/Folder 97.

29. FHS Mss A/D965c/Folders 81 and 97.

30. The other two females earning gold medals were Mrs. Bertha Palmer and Sophia Hayden, architect of the Woman's Building.

31. Bryan S. Bush, *Louisville's Southern Exposition, 1883–1887: The City of Progress* (Charleston, S.C.: History Press, 2011).

32. The Filson Club members' agreement, FHS Mss A/Y21b/Folder 59. Pledges were received from nineteen participants whose contributions ranged from $25 to $100 each.

33. Yandell to Durrett, April 29, 1893, FHS Mss A/D965c/Folder 114.

34. *Louisville Commercial*, June 2, 1893, clipping in FHS Mss A/Y21b/Folder 66.

35. *Chicago Inter Ocean*, April 30, 1893.

36. Yandell to Durrett, May 20, 1893, FHS Mss A/D965c/Folder 114.

37. "By Kentucky Belles," *Chicago Herald*, June 2, 1893.

38. *Louisville Courier-Journal*, June 2, 1893. For the deeper cultural context on how "Dixie" could be played in Chicago to honor both a young female artist and a frontier Kentucky hero, see Anne E. Marshall, *Creating a Confederate Kentucky: The Lost Cause and Civil War Memory in a Border State* (Chapel Hill: University of North Carolina Press, 2010).

39. *Louisville Commercial*, June 2, 1893, clipping in FHS Mss A/Y21b/Folder 66.

40. Pauline King, "American Women Sculptors," *Harper's Bazaar*, March 4, 1899, 180–82.

41. Scudder, *Modeling My Life*, 58. Also see scrapbooks in FHS Mss A/Y21b/Folders 76–78 and 94–97.

42. "A Southern Girl at the World's Fair," clipping in FHS Mss A/Y21b/Folder 69. The article also remarks on Enid's work on a Confederate monument, presumably a commission for Louisville that was later revoked, and notes, "She has a special gift for portraiture, and has made successful busts of Dr. D. W. Yandell, Mr. A. V. Dupont, Col. Durrett, Mrs. Locke, of New York, Mrs. F. S. Peabody of Chicago, and many others."

43. See article by "C." titled "The Bachelor Maid in Art," *Southern Magazine*, February 1895, 504.

44. See clipping from the publication *Chat-Nash*, hand dated by Enid Yandell, June 14, 1894, and affixed in a scrapbook about her career. The *Chat-Nash* clipping recounts the *Louisville Courier-Journal* story about Enid's rising fame, including the quotation from Saint-Gaudens. The *Chat-Nash* appears to have been associated with the Nashville and Chattanooga (N&C) Railroad, which had service connecting Nashville and Louisville. See FHS Mss A/Y21b/Folder 66.

45. Yandell et al., *Three Girls in a Flat.*

46. Enid Yandell, "Sculpture at the World's Fair," *Current Topics*, April 1893, 251–55.

47. Such identifiers may be confirmed with a simple glance into the photographic records of Yandell's youth. See Enid Bland Yandell, Enid Yandell Photo Collection, Collection number 987PC52x.1–284, the Filson Historical Society (Louisville).

48. The Duke was also known as Miss Wendell. The family's genealogy reveals an uncle, Dr. David Wendel Yandell, who lived in Louisville.

49. Yandell et al., *Three Girls in a Flat*, chap. 3.

50. This association between Durrett and Rogers is first observed here, in this essay, and merits further investigation. For the provenance and exhibition history of the Durrett bust, see Darst, "Sculpture of Enid Yandell," 15.

51. Yandell et al., *Three Girls in a Flat*, 27–28.

52. Ibid., 65–66, 75.

53. Louis T. Rebisso (1837–1899) was a Cincinnati-based artist whom Yandell certainly knew from her training at the academy. The sculpture was dedicated in 1891, and more than two hundred thousand people attended the ceremony, including Yandell, as noted in this account. See Yandell et al., *Three Girls in a Flat*, 101.

54. Yandell et al., *Three Girls in a Flat*, 104–5.

55. Enid Yandell, "Sculpture at the World's Fair," *Current Topics*, April 1893, 251–55.

56. Clipping, c. 1900, FHS Mss A/Y21b/Folder 105.

57. New York City Directory, 1900, p. 1396, top. For the letterhead, see FHS Mss A/Y21b/Folder 75.

58. FHS Mss A/Y21b/Folder 27. While the intent is unclear in this passage from Enid's mother to the sculptor, there is no other context to indicate praise or acclaim, as had been issued to Enid a decade earlier by several family members in their correspondence to her while she was at the academy in Cincinnati.

59. Caldwell, "Yandell and the Branstock School," 4.

60. *Louisville Courier-Journal*, June 16, 1906.

61. *Chicago Inter Ocean*, June 16, 1906.

62. H. Addington Bruce, "Daniel Boone and the Opening of the West," *Outlook*, January 25, 1908.

63. She purchased this property in 1907.

64. FHS Mss A/Y21b/Folder 75.

65. "Americans Aid French Artists," *New York Times*, May 30, 1915. See also Darst, "Sculpture of Enid Yandell," 9.

66. "To Restore Harrod's Fort," *New York Sun*, March 26, 1925, clipping in FHS Mss A/Y21b/ Folder 67.

67. This information comes from a typed document that appears to be a press release for the *Louisville Herald*, April 30, 1924, titled A WOMAN THREE TIMES A PIONEER IN ART IS CHOSEN TO DO A PIONEER MONUMENT AT HARRODSBURG, KENTUCKY. See FHS Mss A/Y21b/Folder 61 and 62. Erroneously, documents refer to Yandell as the first woman to be elected to the National Sculpture Society. She was among the first. Theo Alice Ruggles Kitson was elected in 1893; Yandell and Bessie Potter Vonnoh were elected in 1899.

68. FHS Mss A/Y21b/Folder 62.

69. See Yandell's sketchbook in FHS Mss A/Y21b/Folder 96.

70. Undated typed manuscript about the Pioneer Monument that also includes plans for collaboration on a park at this site with Donn Barber, her brother-in-law. FHS Mss A/Y21b/Folder 62.

71. Yandell, undated typed manuscript about America and Kentuckians, FHS Mss A/Y21b/ Folder 73.

72. "The Gate of the West," *Outlook*, January 10, 1925. The article does not mention the form of the work, although from Enid's sketchbook we know that she had intended to have roundels or profiles of Lewis, Clark, Harrod, and Boone. See FHS Mss A/Y21b/Folder 96.

73. "Bronze and Marble Worker Sun Dial's Enthusiastic Sponsor: Miss Enid Yandell, Sculptor, has done Meritorious Work, Gaining for Her Sex Recognition in this Field. Many of Her Best Known Pieces are Designed for the Out-of-Doors," *New York Sun*, March 12, 1924, in FHS Mss A/Y21b/ Folder 95, between pp. 4 and 5.

74. "Obituary: Donn Barber, F.A.I.A.," *Journal of the American Institute of Architects* 13 (July 7, 1925): 274.

75. Bobbi Dawn Rightmyer and Anna Armstrong, *Harrodsburg*, Images of America Series (Charleston, S.C.: Arcadia, 2011).

76. In some documentation about this monument, Ulric Ellerhusen's name is alternatively spelled "Ulrich" and "Ellerhausen," while the name of Francis Keally, of the firm Trowbridge and Livingston in New York, is often misspelled "Kelly."

77. "Harrodsburg" in John E. Kleber, ed., *The Kentucky Encyclopedia* (Lexington: University Press of Kentucky, 1992), 414.

Madeline McDowell Breckinridge
(1872–1920)

A Sense of Mission

LINDSEY APPLE

Despite the fact that she could neither vote nor hold political office until the last year of her life, Madeline McDowell Breckinridge became Kentucky's foremost Progressive Era reformer. Like many other young women at the beginning of the twentieth century, she sought the means to use her abilities more actively than women traditionally had been allowed to do and found it in the new reform movement. She worked to alter the poverty that characterized not only the Appalachian region of the state where she first saw it but also the underbelly of her prosperous and elitist hometown of Lexington. Though her reform mentality developed in her family's sense of noblesse oblige, she introduced a method called "scientific charity," also called the case-work approach, to Kentucky. Madeline Breckinridge revolutionized education, limited child labor, and helped create a juvenile-justice system. Lobbying for better health care, particularly in the treatment of tuberculosis, a disease that had reached epidemic proportions in the commonwealth, brought her national recognition. Through all these reforming efforts she demanded more responsible and responsive government and revealed an eye for detail that few male politicians had shown. Best known for her role in formulating a plan to convert Kentuckians to the cause of woman suffrage and for serving as an officer and tireless spokesperson of the National American Woman Suffrage Association (NAWSA), Breckinridge merited a lion's share of the credit when Kentucky ratified the Nineteenth Amendment.

Considered one of the most liberal of southern woman suffragists, Breckinridge actually represented the border-state mentality. Rather than reject her heritage, she chose instead to use or manage the traditions and skills taught in

MADELINE MCDOWELL [BRECKINRIDGE]

Age 19. Courtesy of Ashland, the Henry Clay Estate, Lexington, Kentucky.

her youth to accomplish important reforms. Like many Progressive reformers in the South, she sought to blend tradition and progress, yet she used methods singularly and in combinations that added a feminist dimension to Kentucky politics.[1] This descendant of the statesman Henry Clay came very close to filling the shoes of her illustrious ancestor, an accomplishment historians and nineteenth-century moralists smugly suggested could not be done by those who followed him.[2]

Madeline McDowell's youth gave little indication of the reforming zeal that would characterize her as an adult. Born on May 20, 1872, in Franklin County, she moved at age ten to Ashland, Henry Clay's stately home just east of Lexington. Her father, Maj. Henry Clay McDowell, had raised horses at Woodlake in Franklin County, but he purchased Ashland, he said, because it had been such an important part of his wife's youth. The granddaughter of Henry Clay, Anne Clay McDowell had been orphaned as a child and spent a great deal of time in her grandparents' home.[3]

The move placed Madge, as the family called her, in the social center of the Bluegrass region during her most formative years. Since frontier days Lexington had styled itself the "Athens of the West." Because of the rich soil it was a prosperous town, for a time larger even than Cincinnati and Louisville. Landowners bred thoroughbred horses in an era when horses were as important for transportation as for sport. Lexington was also a commercial center. Mules, pork, and hemp for rope and cotton bales anchored the southern trade and filled the coffers of the wealthy. Though horse farms were not plantations, Lexington's elite patterned their society after that of the American South. Madge could easily have grown up to be a refined society matron. In the best sense of the term she did.[4]

Madge received her formal education at Miss Higgins' School and Miss Butler's Day School, Lexington girls' schools that emphasized social skills more than academic ones. Though not finishing schools in the traditional sense, they taught young ladies the manners and conduct required in Bluegrass society. The girls learned to dance, serve tea, and converse politely. They also studied the lives of famous women such as Marie Antoinette and Mary, Queen of Scots, though more as models of style and grace than for their historical roles. Mark Twain labeled the South's fascination with honor, valor, and romance as "Sir Walter's Disease." Young women studied literature and poetry; they saw the beauty in the world around them and were protected from all that was ugly or base. The husband of one of Madge's many Clay "cousins" called it an education in "King Arthur and rainbows."[5]

Lexington's gentry also provided opportunities for the McDowell daughters to develop and exhibit social skills. As with the planter class of the South, a social season brought together the "right" young men and women. Cotillions, kermises, luncheons, and other events highlighted the time. Young women learned to avoid controversy in conversation, hopefully even in thought, and honed other skills intended to make them charming hostesses or guests. There was a purpose to it all more important than entertainment. Society matrons spoke of acceptable matches and "good" marriages. Young women had to be accomplished enough to attract an acceptable male, then to oversee his home and rear children to accept the same values they practiced. When Elizabeth Murphey Simpson claimed in *The Enchanted Bluegrass* (1938) that Lexington had an abiding interest in pedigree, she was not writing about thoroughbred horses.[6]

Most young women moved directly from their fathers' homes to those of their husbands. Others well into the 1920s could teach or hold minor positions, at least until they married. Upper-class women had servants, though it took some effort to manage them properly. Lexingtonians, at least those of the gentry, expected things to remain very much the same. As in the South, women were placed on a pedestal where they would be admired. Barbara Welter's cult of true womanhood has been shown to be a myth rather than the reality of southern life, but that is not to say that the traits of domesticity, piety, submissiveness, and purity were not the bases for a young woman's education.[7]

Madge McDowell enjoyed Lexington's social setting. Tall and slender with large captivating eyes, she had a countenance that suggested a gentleness, an intellectual bent, or perhaps a naïveté, though the latter would have been a misleading impression. She read widely, but she also loved to play tennis and golf. Like most Kentuckians of the gentry class she learned to ride horses, but she did it better than most. Her father on one occasion wrote that Madge "did everything well."[8]

Major McDowell provided the means for his family to live the traditional southern lifestyle. James B. Clay's widow had been forced to sell Ashland in the aftermath of the Civil War, but McDowell brought it back into the family in 1882 and turned it into a showplace of southern hospitality. McDowell epitomized the border-state mentality. A veteran of the Union army, he was an astute businessman. He owned large blocks of commercial and residential property in Louisville, and he participated in, often leading, myriad companies building railroads and exploiting the natural resources of the Kentucky-Virginia mountain region. His sons called him "the Capitalist"; one historian has called him a Kentucky robber baron.[9] Quite harsh at times in his business practices, he resembled in appearance that image of a soft, genteel, and aristocratic figure that came to be called the "Kentucky Colonel." Though a lifelong Republican, he paid lip service to the Lost Cause, contributed to the erection of southern monuments, and socialized with former rebels as if there had been no war. It was also to his business advantage to open Ashland to guests. Northerners and southerners wanted to see the home of Henry Clay, and he welcomed those of the right social classes. The *Lexington Leader* described Ashland as "typical of the South's best enlightenment and gracious hospitality." Major McDowell was "the very prince of entertainers." The *Atlanta Constitution* declared the estate a charming reminder of the Old South and proclaimed Madge's sister Nettie a true southern belle. When tennis became popular in Lexington, the major had a court constructed and Ashland became a gathering place for his children's friends. It also became something of a literary center. The artist and novelist Robert Burns Wilson and writer John Fox Jr. visited regularly. Another frequent guest, the southern apologist Thomas Nelson Page, claimed Ashland was like "getting back to before the war."[10]

The McDowells taught their children by action as well as words the importance of their position in society. Noblesse oblige carried not only responsibilities of charity but also an understanding of one's own importance. The children learned that they were descendants of two significant families. Mrs. McDowell's father had fought and died with honor in the Mexican War, and everyone knew Henry Clay. Madge's great-great-grandfather on her father's side, Samuel McDowell, served in the Revolutionary War and led Kentucky in its earlier efforts toward statehood. Even today, a McDowell and a Clay are Kentucky's representatives in the U.S. Capitol's Statuary Hall. Noblesse oblige required giving back to the community and the nation. Major McDowell almost singlehandedly kept the Lexington mental asylum operating, and virtually no charitable request went begging. The children learned early; on holidays and birthdays they gave small gifts to the family servants.[11]

McDowell also provided the means for his children to live the lifestyle of the elite. His sons were sent to Yale and the University of Virginia, and, though he grumbled about it occasionally, he gave them large allowances. When her brother Thomas Clay McDowell seemed about to become a millionaire, Madge wrote to their mother jokingly that now she had a child "who knows how to make money as well as to spend it." All the children received substantial clothing allowances, and McDowell established a trust from which they received monthly checks throughout their lives.[12]

The charms of life on the pedestal could be quite alluring; it could also become a prison. Madge could easily have taken her place there. Her two sisters did so to some degree until Madge's reform efforts gave them new direction. However, there were other lessons, ones that did not conform to the broad contours of Welter's cult of true womanhood. Madge's heritage created self-confidence. What historian Bertram Wyatt-Brown argued about the antebellum South held true for postbellum southern elites: they continued to seek aggressiveness and confidence in their children, girls as well as boys. Their class would continue to lead southern society, so they had to have confidence. George H. Clay put the concept in Kentucky terms when he advised his sister-in-law on how to rear her daughter, one of Madge's "cousins": "Give the little filly her head, so she'll have spirit."[13] Madge McDowell had spirit, more perhaps even than her father would have appreciated.

The education of the McDowell daughters conformed to the prejudices that generally limited women in the late Victorian era. Like many southern males, Major McDowell wanted his daughters to become socially accomplished, enough so to attract husbands who would provide for them as he did. Proud of Madge's ability, he let her spend the 1889–90 school term at Miss Porter's School in Farmington, Connecticut, but he warned her not to overtax herself in deep study. Then he brought her home after one year because of the risk of separating her during "four impressionable years" from "the community in which she expected to live out her life."[14] That year, however, proved to be an important one. She gained some independence away from family, and she met bright young women who were not completely satisfied with their traditional roles. Probably without the knowledge of their instructors—Miss Porter's School was also rather traditional—the young women were reading Darwin and Spencer, studying socialism, and raising questions about traditional religion.[15]

Although often overlooked, limits also existed to the submissiveness of southern women. Women of Madge's social class were socially superior to the majority of men and owed them nothing more than politeness. In a poem patterned on a Lexington "belle," Madge's cousin Susan Clay described the type as a social butterfly, a flirt, a flower that bloomed in brilliance but faded rapidly. Madeline McDowell never fell into that trap. Letters from two suitors, both prominent journalists—Harrison Robertson and W. W. Thum—reveal males who groveled before a woman in charge. When their letters became too intimate she unceremoniously dumped them. Madge enjoyed intellectual discussion with men and needed escorts to parties or the country club, but she did not play the role of the belle. In fact, none of her relations with men seemed overly romantic. She allowed much more intimacy, at least in correspondence, from her schoolmates at Miss Porter's School than from the men who pursued her.[16]

Madge felt comfortable among the leadership class. Her friends at Miss Porter's came from families of wealth and importance. At Ashland she met business leaders such as William Vanderbilt, Benjamin Helm Bristow, and Milton H.

Smith. At Ashland Madge helped receive the Duke of Marlborough, delegations from Japan, Belgium, and France, and New York bankers. She used her traditional skills, but she also learned to feel comfortable in the presence of important people.[17]

Returning from Farmington, Madge McDowell faced a quandary. Like many young women of the era, she wondered what she could do with her life. Her decision did not come easily. She maintained a full social calendar, entertaining friends, attending parties, and traveling. An occasional class at the university and meetings of a literary group called the Fortnightly Club provided intellectual exercise. She also had a fascination with foreign languages, studying German, French, and Greek on her own. Yet it was not enough. Writing to her mother as late as 1898, she said she had been to the country club three nights in a row, with different escorts, but she complained that her days were "uncommonly long and dull."[18]

In 1895 Madge published an article on Henry Clay in *Century* magazine.[19] The outpouring of praise and encouragement suggests she had shared her lack of direction with others. A good friend from Lexington, Sophonisba Breckinridge, had already broken the traditional bonds. She attended Wellesley and then studied law in her father's office. She and Madge had talked about studying law together, but for some reason Madge did not pursue it. After being admitted to the bar, Nisba (as family and friends called her) then earned a PhD in political economy and taught at the University of Chicago. She communicated regularly with Madge, urging her to focus her talents. She praised Madge's article as an example of her intellect, writing ability, and potential for significant contribution, but she also hinted that the study of sociology and economics should replace that of German literature.[20] Later, she invited Madge to Chicago hoping she would consider attending the university. Several university catalogs in Madge's papers suggest that she thought about pursuing a degree. Nisba introduced her to reform-minded women such as Grace and Edith Abbott, Marion Talbot, and Julia Lathrop, and she arranged a visit to Hull House, the settlement house created by Jane Addams.[21]

Another member of the Breckinridge family played an instrumental role in Madge's life. Lexington's gentry class was small enough that Madge had known Desha, Nisba's brother, most of her life. In 1895 he wrote a congratulatory note when she published the article on Henry Clay. They began to share opinions about books. On one occasion Breckinridge secured books on socialism for her, though noting that he did not agree with the philosophy.[22] As in most small towns, local gossips suspected Desha and Madge shared more than an interest in books. Madge's close friend, Stites Duvall, wrote in December 1895 that there was "talk" of a marriage. Jokingly, perhaps, Duvall said that she did not want Madge to marry Desha nor any other Breckinridge, or even any other man "at least just yet."[23] Duvall enjoyed company on that score; Major and Mrs. McDowell were not pleased with the budding relationship either.[24] They did not need to worry, at least for a time. When Desha began to write too intimately, Madge suggested he cool his ardor. Politically astute, he apologized, and she did not dismiss him as she had Robertson and Thum.[25]

The marriage of Madge and Desha did not take place for several years. Nor did Madge attend the University of Chicago. In late 1890 she suffered what was thought to be a sprained ankle. In fact, it was much worse. Numerous remedies and two surgeries provided only temporary relief over the next five years, and physicians finally diagnosed it as tuberculosis of the bone. It was a turning point in Madge's life. Both McDowells and Clays knew the disease all too well. Her mother and two brothers suffered with it. On the Clay side, Henry Clay died of the illness in 1852, preceded in death from tuberculosis by daughter Lucretia and grandson Martin Duralde III and followed by son James and at least three grandsons who died of it in the 1860s. On June 22, 1896, Dr. Virgil P. Gibney, an orthopedic surgeon, amputated Madge's foot.[26]

Two lessons stood out above all others in the Clay family legacy. First, there was the duty to make a contribution, and second, that contribution had to be made quickly. Not only tuberculosis but other diseases had taken many promising young members of the family. Henry and Lucretia Clay buried seven children and several grandchildren. Anne Clay McDowell's two brothers died of disease during the Civil War, her youngest child when he fell into a fire. Within the extended family a spoken, or unspoken, moral lesson was that one's contribution should be made early because death, "ruthless death," as Henry Clay called it, stalked the family. Madge saved a six-page list of quotations of well-known writers regarding the length and purpose of life. The most poignant one read: "It matters not how long we live but how." Nisba Breckinridge would have to worry about Madge's focus no longer.[27]

Madge and Desha married on November 17, 1898. Traditional values appear to have been the motivation for her decision. It was apparently not romance. Even after agreeing to marry Desha she wrote tellingly: "I do believe that he is worth trying. You know that I didn't feel a bit certain in the beginning—for that matter I don't suppose I am certain right now for I never am certain of anything in the world—but . . . I have come to respect and admire and believe in him more. I have tried doing without him and it is almost too hard—and he does love me very truly." James C. Klotter, biographer of the Breckinridge family, says they both bore hidden scars that may have brought them together: Madge's tuberculosis and a scandal that devastated Desha's family. His father, a man he loved dearly and who influenced him deeply, became involved in a public sex scandal that cast a shadow over the Breckinridge family. Yet a strong intellectual bond also developed that Madge could not and did not want to deny. Desha also felt that union. Initially more conservative than Madge, he grew to accept many of her views, and together they became a major force in Progressive Era Kentucky.[28]

Madge became a public figure in the cause of reform with two issues almost simultaneously. On February 11, 1899, a local thug named "King" McNamara shot and killed Jacob Keller, a railroad cashier. McNamara, several brothers, and their father posed a constant threat to peace in Lexington. It was not an uncommon situation. The Civil War left the entire state a victim of lawlessness. The commonwealth had one of the highest homicide rates in the country, but few paid adequately for their crimes. Juries valued manliness above justice, and political officials seemed unconcerned or susceptible to pleas for clemency. Madge had personal knowledge of such events. In 1884 her cousin, Harry I. Clay, had been shot and killed by Andrew Wepler, a saloonkeeper and city alderman in Louisville. After a jury sentenced Wepler to two years, leading Louisville politicians immediately inundated the governor with appeals for clemency.[29] In Lexington the police arrested McNamara then released him, allegedly on bond. On the same day, his brother William McNamara wounded another man. When King McNamara fled, the police made little effort to track him down. Lexington's citizens decided it was time to act. It was not merely the violence that enraged them but the corruption of the police and political leaders. Not only had the authorities made little effort to bring McNamara to trial, they had released him without collecting the $1,000 bond. Madge rallied the women of the community and raised funds to offer a reward for his capture. According to the *Herald*, the women shamed the men of Lexington into rejecting the status quo of violence and political corruption.[30]

Thirteen years after the murder the state finally brought McNamara to justice, which reveals Breckinridge's ability to continue fighting for her cause in the face of obstacles. Reform did not come easy in Kentucky or the nation, but defeat for her served merely as a temporary setback and a source of frustration with the men who controlled government. She continued to present additional evidence, to rally reform-minded people, and to play politics herself. Her tenacity became legendary in the state.

In being married to a newspaper man, Breckinridge had an advantage most reformers did not enjoy: a means for keeping issues in the public arena. In early 1897 Desha became the editor and publisher of the *Lexington Herald*, and he asked Madge to write book reviews for the paper. The reviews revealed a growing interest in the problems of poverty, the abuse of immigrants, and the plight of the working class. Among the books she reviewed were Jacob Riis's *A Ten Years' War* and John Jay Chapman's *Practical Agitation*. She was impressed by Riis's belief that progress had been and could be made and Chapman's emphasis on government action. Desha gave her freedom to advance her causes in the newspaper; when he was away she wrote editorials, and in 1905 she developed a woman's page far different from those found in other papers. A true woman's page, she argued, should be more than discussions of fashion or "squaw talk." Her goal was to advertise whatever came within the scope of the intelligent woman's interest, and few issues, political or social, fell outside that definition. Madge used the section to educate women and to move them along toward her definition of women's interests. The column employed, in fact, a subtle blend of "squaw talk" and education to reform. Other papers praised her efforts, and the "Woman's Page" gained national attention.[31]

At the same time she struggled with the McNamara case, Madge resurrected a church group active in charity. Affiliated with Christ Church Episcopal Cathedral in Lexington, the Gleaners mirrored religiously affiliated women's organizations throughout the South that dedicated themselves to charitable training and action. The group provided Breckinridge an opportunity to exercise the sense of noblesse oblige learned from her parents. Interest in the organization had waned, but Madge revived it, opened it to members of other denominations, and used it to launch a social settlement program in eastern Kentucky.[32]

Lexington's mayor, Henry Duncan, provided another outlet for the women of the city. In the harsh winter of 1899–1900 he asked them to revive a benevolent society to administer city relief to the poor. Breckinridge helped create two organizations that became the backbone of the Progressive movement in Lexington. On February 14, 1900, she helped found the Associated Charities of Lexington, and in April reformers organized the Civic League.[33]

Sharing the name of organizations in other American cities, the Associated Charities reflected the connection between Madge and women reformers of the University of Chicago. The group sought to establish a sound and constructive process for distributing aid to the poor. While emergencies made relief essential, the organization worked to correct the causes of systemic poverty. It also sought to differentiate between the deserving poor and those merely looking for a handout. That approach has been criticized as based in class prejudice—a charge that has merit. The language of the movement was often paternalistic and patronizing. Claiming an intent to make charity scientific, the organization created detailed files on those who received aid and used a work requirement to weed out the unworthy. Madge adamantly opposed indiscriminate handouts, even challenging the Salvation Army at one point. Charity, she maintained, should work toward ending poverty. Yet many of the organization's methods remain today—the case-work method, the removal of religious tests, and the employment office—and so do the philosophical differences in attitudes about how to address the issues of poverty.[34]

The Civic League was a more traditional organization. It sought to educate public opinion to society's needs by collecting and disseminating information. To help do that it sponsored nationally known speakers on specific reform issues. Perhaps at no time in Lexington's history did it experience such an array of distinguished visitors. Jane Addams came several times; reformer Max Eastman, Judge Ben Lindsey, suffragist Emmeline Pankhurst, and women's rights advocate Carrie Chapman Catt spoke in Lexington along with other authorities on parks, education, child labor, tuberculosis, and woman suffrage. The Civic League also lobbied government entities for change. Its broad mission boiled down to determining problems, educating the public and government officials, and reminding government of its duties.[35]

Much has been written about the elitist and nativist motivations of Progressive Era reformers, but the era was also one of those periodic occasions in American history when public excitement coalesced around both the need for and the ability of citizens to affect reform. Resembling the movement that occurred in the 1960s, many citizens awoke to the inequities of society and believed that through government action, wrongs could be corrected. The result was a "convulsive" reform movement seeking to remodel society. Progressives worked to rid government of corruption and make it more democratic and more responsive to society's needs. They also acted to regulate the large corporations and alleviate the inequities that had been produced in a period of rapid industrial growth.[36]

The experiences working with the Gleaners and on the McNamara case produced that awakening in Breckinridge. She embraced the reform movement with a fervor few could match, but she remained constantly aware not only of the traditional values of Kentuckians but also of her own. Like most southern women, her reforms remained largely in that area of progressivism that Dewey W. Grantham called "social justice" or Robert H. Wiebe termed "humanitarian progressivism." Involvement in reform of government or regulating corporations resulted from her concerns about poverty, abuse of the poor, and the needs of education. She also could leave to Desha and the *Herald* political issues such as the direct election of senators, the income tax, and the direct primary. Madge occasionally criticized corporations but always in relation to working-class conditions and the plight of the poor.

If Breckinridge had a blind spot it involved corporations. One of her best friends was the daughter of Milton H. Smith, the antilabor leader of the Louisville and Nashville (L&N) Railroad. Many of the girls from Miss Porter's School came from wealthy industrial families, and she successfully solicited those friends for funds to support her reforms. Finally, her loyalty to her own family limited her ability to see clearly. Not only did her father exploit the natural resources of eastern Kentucky with little regard for its people; he also owned rental property in Louisville that the city condemned because of its state of disrepair. The trust fund that paid Madge's expenses when she traveled for reform causes primarily derived from that exploitation—and she seldom questioned it.[37]

Breckinridge's reforming efforts fall into four general categories—the eradication of the causes of poverty, education, health care, and finally suffrage—but they were like a tree with many connecting branches. Each reform seemed to take years to work through a head-in-the-sand legislature, so Madge labored in all four areas simultaneously. Often one reform effort revealed additional needs. Confronting poverty, she saw the failures of the education system in Kentucky and the South. Struggles in education made her aware of the poor job male politicians had done and convinced her that women were better informed on the needs of children. Lack of action by male-dominated government on education, food quality, health issues, and legal protection of women led her to embrace the cause of woman suffrage.[38]

A series of reforms, under the auspices of the Civic League, began with the establishment of a playground in Irishtown, one of the poorest sections of Lexington. Initially settled by Irish immigrants, the section had become a slum not unlike those Madge had encountered in Chicago. Dilapidated, closely packed houses created a fire hazard. To socialize, men went to the saloons, and alcoholism led to desertion and abuse. Children played in the dirty, unpaved streets when not augmenting the labor force of Lexington businesses. It proved almost impossible to keep houses or people clean; no source of clean water existed. The Civic League established a summer playground on a vacant lot there in 1901 and incorporated settlement house programs for adults. The residents gathered in the evenings to sing patriotic music and hear speakers discuss personal and community improvement. To everyone's delight, including the local police, the experiment became immensely successful.[39]

The Civic League created another playground the next summer and encouraged city government to build a permanent park. The Irishtown summer program proved the beginning of a modern park system and a beautification program for Lexington. Local florists planted trees and shrubbery throughout the city, and the Civic League cooperated with city government to bring in Frederick Law Olmsted to plan the parks. Madge persuaded the government to purchase the property for Woodland Park. In the black community, Douglass Park provided similar open spaces and a healthy place for people to gather on warm evenings and weekends. Madeline Breckinridge's name is indelibly linked to that system.[40]

The success emboldened the reformers to create longer-lasting programs. They established a permanent kindergarten, and the Civic League hired a young woman who had worked in a similar New York program. She taught sewing and other domestic skills. They installed playground equipment, and Madge enticed city government to fund the continuation of the kindergarten throughout the year.

Irishtown confronted Madge with the problems of education. In Fayette County students often completed only the third grade. The Kentucky school year was short, and fewer than half of the school-age children attended. Teachers were treated horribly by trustees who saw the school systems as their fiefdoms. Madge noted that in 1907 Fayette County spent only $2,000 out of a budget of $185,000 on schools. The Kentucky Federation of Women's Clubs, already involved in educational reform, became an ally in the struggle for compulsory education and better schools. As a member of the organization's legislative committee, Madge urged better training of teachers, improved methods for hiring instructors, and protection against arbitrary dismissal. Recognizing the control local trustees had on Kentucky education, the reformers supported changing the school districts to county systems in order to lower the number of school trustees and improve the qualifications of those officials. On the university level they lobbied for better conditions for female students (including a women's dormitory), a dean of women, and a home economics department.[41]

While visiting a Colorado tuberculosis sanatorium in 1903, Madge learned of a progressive juvenile justice system created by Judge Ben Lindsey. Even before returning to Lexington she submitted articles to the *Herald* on how such a system could redeem young people, limit juvenile crime, and thereby improve conditions in the city. The juvenile system was more than a court. In a four-year period thirty-five investigations of prostitution occurred. The court forced police to close bars and dance halls selling liquor to minors, attacked gambling halls, and cooperated with the school system to decrease truancy.[42]

Breckinridge and the Civic League courted and received the support of Kentucky's professional educators in their efforts. State superintendents such as James H. Fuqua and John Grant Crabbe sought allies in education reform wherever they could find them. Additionally, the Kentucky Development Commission, seeking economic benefits for the state, saw the need for education reform. Breckinridge rarely missed an opportunity to enlist help. In 1906 she became a board member of the Educational Improvement Commission of Kentucky, though she had to shame the all-male group who formed the organization before they would choose a woman as a member.[43]

The blending of government and private efforts characterized Breckinridge's approach to reform. She had shown an interest in government as early as the year she spent at Miss Porter's School. Marion Houston, a classmate there, claimed that Madge believed in "a slowly approaching socialism." Though hardly a socialist, she and Desha shared with other Progressive reformers the belief that government action would be required because the problems of poverty were too large for private efforts alone and the corporations that were partially responsible were too powerful to be curbed by any other entity.[44] From Mayor Henry Duncan's call for the women of Lexington to administer public relief funds, Madge pursued a close cooperation between the private and public sectors. The Associated Charities administered government and private funds to create playgrounds, kindergartens, and a school in Irishtown. On several occasions Madge noted that if citizens showed the way government would eventually respond.[45]

The best example of public-private cooperation was the creation of the Abraham Lincoln model school, a project that took nearly a decade to complete. Irishtown convinced Breckinridge that education provided the best way out of poverty, but achieving education at any level in Kentucky presented a host of problems. Poor parents resisted sending their children to school because they needed the income child labor provided. Businessmen claimed ending child labor would make it difficult to compete with neighboring states that allowed it. Breckinridge worked with both the Kentucky and national child labor organizations. Ever the pragmatist, she suggested that government could pay the lost wages to parents. To corporations, she argued a moral position, a civic responsibility, to improve society.[46]

Leaning on the knowledge she gained from Chicago reformers, she recognized that a school could also serve many of the functions of the settlement house. In 1907 she brought Jane Addams to Lexington to speak on child labor, compulsory education, and self-help programs. The next year, again with public-private cooperation, planning began for the model school. When completed it incorporated many Progressive educational principles, and it contained a gymnasium and swimming pool, carpentry shop, laundry, and bath and shower facilities that could be used by people in the community year-round. Classes for adults were created in woodworking, cooking, sewing, hygiene, and home care.

Madge not only helped plan the curriculum but also led the Civic League in raising money for the project. Though she did not like raising funds, her aristocratic bearing and her family's history in the community made her very good at it. She challenged Lexington's upper class by appeals to noblesse oblige. Breckinridge also sought help from her former schoolmates at Miss Porter's and from wealthy ex-Kentuckians. Robert Todd Lincoln, the surviving son of the martyred president, donated a large sum in memory of his father. The league raised $35,000 for the project, and the school board provided $10,000. Her ability to raise funds, combined with her successful work in organization and community education, led to her successful efforts in Lexington.[47]

On December 6, 1911, Sophonisba Breckinridge spoke at the laying of the cornerstone of the Lincoln School. The school, which met many of the needs of the Irishtown community, truly was a model. Its educational philosophy spread to other schools reaching children across the city and state, and it brought national attention to Lexington and to Madeline Breckinridge.[48]

Historians have argued that many upper- and middle-class reformers of the Progressive Era were attempting to impart their values to immigrants and the poor. In a period of rapid change the "established" classes feared the deterioration of the nation as they knew it. Breckinridge's arguments for reform, unfortunately, gave credence to that charge. In appealing to Lexington's citizens to build playgrounds and schools, she placed most emphasis on character building and values—American values. Her articles and speeches also made use of nostalgic episodes from the nation's history that would appeal to the white middle and upper classes. Her insistence on manual training in the schools also suggests a traditional attitude toward the poor. Breckinridge believed the poor needed work skills to pull them out of poverty. The study of Latin or Greek would do them no good at all. Breckinridge probably suffered from some class bias; there is little reason to believe she expected to have lunch with such people at the local country club within her generation. However, her ability as a politician must be considered in any assessment of her motivation. Uncannily gifted at evaluating the mindsets of both those who would help her and those she wanted to persuade, she believed that rural Kentuckians cared deeply about traditional values even if few immigrants settled in Kentucky. As a good politician, Breckinridge used that to her advantage. An idyllic picture of American history and the moral lessons she and her class believed it taught appealed to the people whose support she needed. Kentuckians would also be more inclined to accept a program of self-help for the poor than to entertain a critique of capitalism.[49]

Closely associated with class in the Progressive Era is the question of race. Many "well-meaning moderates" condemned lynching, stressed self-help, and supported manual training. Historian Dewey Grantham called the position an updated version of paternalism. Breckinridge fits in that group, but the fact that she was as adept at telling an audience what it wanted to hear as was her illustrious ancestor makes it difficult to assess her position. She must be placed in the context of her time. In 1896 the Supreme Court in *Plessy v. Ferguson* had upheld the principle of separate but equal. When the playground opened in Irishtown, African American children were barred from it. Madge did not object openly. Her biographers argue pragmatism as a justification, claiming any objection in that era would have been futile. Recognizing the political landscape, she worked quietly and behind the scenes for improvements in the African American community. The Civic League funded training for African American teachers and paid playground supervisors. In the midst of creating a park system, Madge encouraged the city to develop Douglass Park within the black community. Many of her educational reforms appear to conform to the "trickle down" theory. As change proved successful in white schools, the segregated African American schools usually benefited, even if belatedly and only partially. Madge advocated manual training for blacks as well as poor whites, seeing the development of a skill as self-help. She also urged the school system to purchase land around the African American schools and attempted to raise money for playground equipment. She sought grants from northern philanthropists to support those schools, and both she and her mother contributed from their own funds. Pictures of black and white children on the grounds at Ashland also indicate an attitude more advanced than most. Lexington's African American community saw her as a hero. Nevertheless, she stood far closer to Booker T. Washington than to W. E. B. DuBois. Madge appeared to share her great-grandfather's view that African Americans were capable of intellectual equality but history and culture had created inferiority. In that sense, race was an element of class. The potential for equality was so remote she did not seem to contemplate it.[50]

In 1905 the Civic League and the Associated Charities opened a campaign in her third area of reform, the treatment of tuberculosis, or what had been called consumption in the early nineteenth century. It was not the first effort in the cause of better health. Nurses had taught hygiene in Irishtown and provided home visits for sick schoolchildren. Madge, of course, knew the pain, psychological and physical, of tuberculosis. A new urgency appeared in 1903 when doctors discovered what they called a "weakness" in one of her lungs. It seems likely that she suffered tuberculosis in not just her bones but in her lungs as well.[51]

Robert Koch's 1882 discovery of the tubercle bacillus led to the use of the modern term "tuberculosis." Medical authorities and the public believed there was a familial susceptibility, but while several modern studies have suggested a genetic basis for it, no gene has been identified.[52] It would have been difficult to convince McDowells or Clays that no connection existed. Too many young family members had been lost to tuberculosis for it to be seen as anything less than a sentence of death. Increasingly, Madge had to take time for treatment, but she continued to work at a furious pace.

Despite her personal knowledge of tuberculosis, Breckinridge studied the prevailing literature, sought advice from foremost authorities, assessed the needs, then launched an effort to educate the public and the political leadership.[53] The Civic League led the way in establishing the Fayette Tuberculosis Association and proposed legislation to the state legislature for its 1906 session. When that measure failed, Madge, as usual, merely doubled her efforts. Fighting against the tradition of individual freedom and responsibility, she insisted that government had to be given additional powers to fight the disease. The Board of Health needed the legal authority to quarantine and to disinfect the houses of the sick. A new measure was presented to the state legislature in 1908, but Breckinridge could not lobby for it. Her own bout with tuberculosis forced her to the sidelines.

Resuming her efforts after the obligatory period of treatment, she helped found and direct the Kentucky Association for the Prevention and Relief of Tuberculosis. In 1912 the Kentucky General Assembly passed a tuberculosis bill that established a state tuberculosis commission. Madge served from 1912 to 1916 as a member of the commission. On November 15, 1916, a ceremony was held to lay the cornerstone of the Blue Grass Sanatorium. She not only served as the chief lobbyist for the effort but also raised $50,000 to fund it. Much of the money came from her own family, Aunt Mag giving $10,000 in honor of her father, Dr. William Adair McDowell, and other family members donating in the memory of Major McDowell.[54]

As usual, persuading the political establishment proved the biggest hurdle. However, by 1905 she had developed a technique that was difficult for politicians to evade.[55] Using the evidence she collected, Breckinridge educated the public through the pages of the *Herald*. Most important, she knew her audience. She sought help from those organizations and individuals who preferred to work in a particular area. The Kentucky Federation of Women's Clubs undertook the challenges of educational reform. Initially, the "thoroughbred women" of the women's clubs were not prepared to seek the vote for women (though that would come later), but throughout the state they carried the battle for better education. Breckinridge also worked with church groups, the YWCA, the temperance union, business leaders, educators, even the Daughters of the American Revolution and the Daughters of the Confederacy. The cause was more important than the politics of her allies.

Breckinridge worked the state the way Henry Clay had worked Congress a half century earlier. Small towns and ruling elites tended to emphasize the positive aspects of their communities and to be quite defensive in the face of criticism. Lexington and Kentucky seemed particularly so. Madge carefully balanced criticism with praise, knowing just how she could use her social standing and heritage and the pressure she could exert because of it. She used the history of Lexington, from the frontier women who helped save Bryan's Station when Native Americans attacked to those involved in churches and charitable institutions, to show the city it could do the right thing. In the newspaper she detailed the efforts of other states and challenged Kentucky leadership to keep up, scoffing at the comparisons made to southern states instead of looking at national progress. She blended praise of Lexington and Kentucky as great places to live with criticism of complacency and the threat of being outpaced by other areas that, she hinted, had far less potential. She was not above using archrival Louisville as an example of what Lexington should do, and she frequently wrote about reforming efforts in New York, Chicago, Denver, and San Francisco as if Lexington and Louisville would fall behind if its citizens remained complacent. A difficult tightrope to walk, she had more room for error and considerable skill in walking it.[56]

Madge Breckinridge also shared with her great-grandfather a charisma and an ability to lead. There was clearly a sense of dignity about her. Historian Anne Firor Scott noted in *From Pedestal to Politics* (1970) that southern women sought to maintain their social position even as they agitated for the vote. While true, the concept belies the fact that many of those women were willing to work even if proper etiquette frowned on rolling up one's Victorian sleeves. While Madge sometimes became frustrated with the pace at which southern women embraced change, she recognized the desire to stay within the regional value structure. She personally tested the boundaries but diplomatically led those who followed.

Breckinridge asked no one to do what she was unwilling to do herself. The fact that she did so much made it difficult for others to refuse when she asked for their help. She galvanized members of her family; both of her sisters set aside their southern training to help, and at Madge's request Anne Clay McDowell often appeared at meetings so that Henry Clay would be associated with the cause of reform. Throughout Kentucky and the nation, she used the name of her celebrated ancestor to lend legitimacy to her cause. Her mother and Aunt Mag donated money to many of her causes, while her sister-in-law Elsie Clay traveled with her and sponsored speaking events in southwestern Virginia, even though her husband was lukewarm, at best, to their efforts. Kinsmen Thomas and Annie Gratz Clay were active in the Civic League. Robert A. McDowell, a cousin, helped draft legislation that Madge's various organizations submitted to the state legislature, and his wife served as a member and officer in the Kentucky Equal Rights Association (KERA). Kentucky's elite most often were impressed enough to follow the example.[57]

Perhaps her greatest strength was her ability to organize the reform effort. She galvanized women to recruit workers, distribute literature, and pressure politicians; she enlisted speakers and sought aid in drafting legislation; she organized speaking tours for herself and others; she inspired an ever-growing army of reformers. Contemporaries called her the "guiding hand," the "heroic mold," the "flame," the "fire," the "moving spirit" of the movement.[58]

Madeline McDowell Breckinridge is best known for her work for woman suffrage. She served as president of the KERA from 1912 to 1916 and again in 1919–20. She also served on the board of the NAWSA from 1913 to 1915 and spoke for the organization throughout the country. The struggle for the vote was a logical progression from her other reform efforts. Increasingly frustrated by the inaction of legislators and the excuses given by the men who controlled government, she publicly blamed men for the pitiful state of education. Women, she argued, raised children to school age, and then, in their infinite wisdom, men controlled the educational decisions that affected those children. As a result, Kentucky schools ranked forty-seventh in the nation. Madge played on the role of women as the keepers of morality to emphasize the skills they could bring to educational planning if their path were not blocked by men.[59]

The turning point came in 1902, when state representatives Billy Klair and J. Embry Allen pushed through legislation to revoke an 1894 law that allowed women in second-class cities, including Lexington, to vote in school board elections. Indeed, the event may mark the radicalization of Kentucky women. Such a slap in the face to women who had labored to improve the schools moved those who had avoided the question of suffrage to change their minds. Madge led a decade-long struggle to recover the school vote, and in the process the attitudes of Kentucky women evolved to include support of full suffrage.[60]

Madge's rhetoric became sharper, no doubt because she was angry but also because her base of support was more accepting. She continued to be polite and "lady-like" when the circumstances called for it, but politicians learned that she would not play the submissive role they preferred. In an address to the National Woman Suffrage Association held in Louisville, she lashed out at male dominance: "Kentucky women at present have no greater political rights than the women of Turkey; for we have none at all." She continued: "It is simply stupid of [Kentucky men] still to class us poetically and oratorically with whiskey and horses, and legally and politically with criminals and idiots." She is perhaps most famous for her retort to Governor James B. McCreary: "Kentucky women are not idiots—even though they are closely related to Kentucky men." Others felt the sting of her sarcasm. A politician who reneged on a promise faced not only public humiliation but also a threat to his career. At a conference in Louisville in 1918, the KERA created a public display titled "Lest We Forget." It was a list of the names of legislators who had not supported woman suffrage. When Ollie James and J. Campbell Cantrill, two old-line politicians, attempted a ruse to defeat the suffrage issue in the state legislature, Breckinridge discovered their falsehood and publicized it. She also began a movement among KERA members to challenge both men in the next election. A challenge proved unnecessary; the thought that women would mount opposition sent a clear message.[61]

Breckinridge also made effective use of a tactic most commonly associated with a later period of reform. Her biographers have suggested that she would have condoned violence like the English suffragists had it proved necessary to win the vote. It did not because she understood the nuances of politics. She merely had to hint at its possible use, all the while remaining the lady. Madge clearly admired Emmeline Pankhurst, the English suffragist, and defended her use of violence in England. No politician could escape the message when Breckinridge invited Pankhurst to Louisville and Lexington to speak. The Kentuckian compared revolution in Ireland to the woman's cause. Rebellion of men against government was respectable, she said, but men were aghast at the thought that women might react in similar fashion. Again the message was unmistakable. She understood that moderation is defined by the extremes. Politicians of the 1960s viewed Martin Luther King Jr. as far less "radical," and therefore much more approachable, after Malcolm X and more impatient civil rights figures emerged. Madge brought to Lexington the socialist leader Max Eastman, Pankhurst, and others who at least appeared radical to conservative Kentucky politicians. Even the national suffrage leader Carrie Chapman Catt wondered if Madge might put off Kentucky politicians by championing Pankhurst. But suddenly, politicians decided they should talk to one of their own. Combining such tactics with a campaign to rally the people, she persuaded Kentucky's politicians, including her old nemesis J. Campbell Cantrill and the influential Alben W. Barkley, to embrace the cause in time to support the Nineteenth Amendment.[62]

It was not just men who caused problems for the suffrage movement. In a state that compared woman suffrage to agnosticism, it took significant planning and effort to recruit a force of women that would get the attention of the politicians. Breckinridge borrowed literature from other states, and her cadre of workers created Kentucky-specific materials as well. She organized automobile trips, parades, and essay contests in schools. In her first term as president of the KERA she raised the membership from 1,779 to 10,577.[63]

She also had to walk a narrow line between the factions that threatened to destroy the NAWSA. She was truly a border-state figure in that organization. Elected to the NAWSA board in 1914, she essentially filled the southern slot vacated when Kate Gordon and Laura Clay left over NAWSA's support of a federal amendment. Recognized as an excellent speaker, Breckinridge traveled extensively throughout the southern and western states drumming up enthusiasm and helping recruit support for NAWSA. She lobbied governors, congressmen, and President Woodrow Wilson. However, two issues threatened to divide the movement. Most southern delegates, including Kentucky's Laura Clay, wanted NAWSA to support only state amendments granting suffrage. They argued that it was a states' rights issue. In reality, it had more to do with the second stumbling block—race. Southern leaders did not want a federal measure because it could call attention to southern efforts to disfranchise African Americans. Madge had to tread carefully because many Kentuckians shared the South's views. She again seemed to share one of the traits of her great-grandfather: knowing when to say different things to different audiences. If there is consistency it is that she would take suffrage any way she could get it. However, she tried not to burn bridges in the process. When Kate Gordon created the Southern States Woman Suffrage Conference, she attempted to recruit Breckinridge. Madge refused to join, but she continued to work with Gordon, invited her to speak at a KERA conference, and raised no objections to state suffrage legislation when speaking in the South. In an effort to convince southern women that the vote was essential, she was most inclined to attack chivalry and the traditional views that undervalued women.[64]

In the South she attempted to keep the issue of race from dividing the members of NAWSA. Long after NAWSA dropped the argument, Breckinridge continued to claim in her southern speeches that women's votes would assure an Anglo-Saxon majority in the South, and she peppered her speeches with quaint stories more worthy of Uncle Remus. Nor did she invite African American women's groups into the KERA. It is difficult to determine whether she was endeavoring to find common ground or expressing her class bias when she advocated educational qualifications for those allowed to vote. When she spoke in western states, however, other issues dominated. Moreover, she was far too astute not to know that large concentrations of African Americans in some areas would in fact alter the "Anglo-Saxon majority." At least in this case, political spin trumped her usual emphasis on solid evidence. Though careful where she said it, she feared that the racial question was a false issue intended to derail the suffrage movement.[65]

Breckinridge also tried to avoid the power struggle involved in Alice Paul's creation of the National Woman's Party. Just as Gordon's group objected to

NAWSA's advocating a federal suffrage amendment, Paul opposed NAWSA's compromising with the southern position. Madge did not join the National Woman's Party, but she refused to criticize the group as others in NAWSA did. In fact, she did a masterful job in avoiding the personal animosities that developed between many of the leaders of the movement. Once again Kentucky, or a Kentuckian, tried to play border-state compromiser in an American crisis.[66]

A personal animosity Breckinridge could not avoid involved Dr. Anna Howard Shaw, the president of NAWSA. Because of the dissention within the organization and Shaw's weak leadership, a movement developed to replace her. Madge had created strong relationships with state suffrage leaders throughout the country, impressing them with both her willingness to lend her support and her clear, precise arguments in favor of suffrage. A group led by Gertrude L. Leonard asked her to be a candidate for the NAWSA presidency. Madge consulted with Nisba Breckinridge and Jane Addams, but ultimately she refused the candidacy. Dr. Shaw was reelected, and Madge remained as second vice president. That did not satisfy Shaw. An early draft of Nisba Breckinridge's biography of Madge, now in the Breckinridge family papers, suggests that Shaw could never quit evaluating Madge as merely a descendant of Henry Clay. Though Breckinridge left that out of the published biography, it indicates a lingering pettiness over the potential challenge to leadership. The wounds continued to fester when Addams refused to accept an honorary vice presidency in the organization. Madge forced Shaw's hand in an executive board meeting when Shaw withheld a letter from Addams. Shaw then blamed Breckinridge for Addams's rather public refusal. Madge's popularity with the membership certainly did nothing to soothe Shaw's feelings. In February 1915 Madge resigned. She cited overwork as the cause, but the struggle with Shaw was obscuring the greater goal.[67] The decision was vintage Breckinridge.

The states' rights issue also led to tension between Breckinridge and Laura Clay. Slowly marginalized in the national movement, Clay felt increasingly isolated in KERA as well and resigned in 1919.[68] Madge admired Clay's record of service to women's rights and to both the state and national suffrage organizations and wanted to avoid an open break. The women were also related, and Madge's traditional values led her to recoil from a confrontation.[69] In addition, she found it discomforting to challenge a leadership figure who had earned respect. Although Madge questioned Laura Clay's actions publicly when the latter tried to influence Kentucky legislators against the national amendment, her efforts to keep the peace actually strained relations with Carrie Chapman Catt, by now the president of NAWSA. Breckinridge continued to insist that Clay should be honored for all the work she had done even if in the last days she "dissented from the policy of the National."[70]

The final years of the struggle for suffrage were not good ones for Madge. There can be little doubt that the pace she kept exacted a physical toll. She traveled extensively throughout the southern and midwestern states and even to San Francisco and Boston. Sometimes she spoke in a different city every day of the week. At home she wrote letters and speeches or held planning meetings. Tuberculosis also took its toll. Amazingly, her physicians pronounced her cured of the disease in the autumn of 1918. She clearly was not. From 1913 she sought treatment in a sanatorium in Colorado, New York, or North Carolina once or twice each year. She became edgy, even difficult, at times.[71]

Her personal life presented painful issues as well. In 1917 her mother died. The next year Curry, Desha's sister, and her Aunt Mag died. Also in 1917, rumors that Desha was having an affair with Mary LeBus, a woman involved in the suffrage movement and with whom Madge and Desha socialized, became prevalent in Lexington. For a woman of her dignity, the gossip that she knew occurred because she knew Lexington had to cause great pain, but, like the southern lady, she held her head high and buried herself in work. She referred to the affair only in a few letters to her sister Nettie, who also knew the pain of infidelity. Some family members have claimed an understanding existed between Madge and Desha about other women. If true, perhaps it originated in her health issues. Madge's biographer, Melba Porter Hay, suggests that there may have been others and that Madge at times even blamed herself, a not uncommon if lamentable trait in the lives of southern women.[72]

There would be no divorce. That was unacceptable in turn-of-the-century Lexington as well as to two proud individuals. More important, Madge and Desha felt an intense intellectual bond that each perhaps enjoyed with no other person. Desha owed to Madge much of his commitment to reform, and they had become a team, anticipating the thoughts of the other and sharing the daily struggle to motivate their city and state. After the ratification of the Nineteenth Amendment, Madge planned to attend the International Conference of Women in Europe. Desha was scheduled to accompany her, but while visiting a home owned by Mrs. LeBus, the couple had an argument and she refused to let him go.[73] However, even in the company of good friends, Madge missed him while in Europe. She reveled in the sights and experiences she had wanted to see since her teenaged years, but she wrote that she preferred seeing them with him. On her return in September 1920, they greeted each other with an enthusiasm that would normally be unexplainable given the circumstances of their marriage. At home they gave parties and continued to press for reform. She soon resumed her busy schedule, but even when physically apart they wrote in warm personal terms, longing for the time they could be together. Desha fretted about her health, and according to Madge, he met "her every need" with regard to it. He arranged her stays in sanatoria and often accompanied her.[74] If the family excuses for Desha are true, clearly there was a complex relationship between them that met important needs.[75] That relationship also met vital needs of Lexington, the state, and the women of the nation.

On November 25, 1920, Madeline McDowell Breckinridge died of complications from a stroke. She was forty-eight years old. "Death, ruthless death" had claimed another descendant of Henry Clay far too young. The city, the state, and the nation had reason to mourn.

The inevitable, though unanswerable, question is what she might have achieved had she lived a reasonable span of years. Yet she died having accomplished many of the tasks she set for herself. The Lincoln School proved a dramatic success. The juvenile court made a difference. State and local tuberculosis hospitals provided a monument to her efforts. And the Nineteenth Amendment had passed. Madeline McDowell Breckinridge cast a full ballot just weeks before her death.

Historians may continue to argue that no descendant of the great statesman Henry Clay has filled his shoes, but a case can be made that in her own arena Madeline McDowell Breckinridge came close. "The Great Compromiser" had a vision for the nation but found it impossible to convince his countrymen. Madge, in contrast, secured a great deal of her vision. She proved herself as astute politically as he was, measuring her city, her state, her allies, and those who stood in the way of change. The poor of Lexington, black and white, lived a little better because of her efforts. Students at the Lincoln School walked beneath her portrait and celebrated her life every year. Education, always a problem in Kentucky, took a step forward. Breckinridge provided much of the momentum. Government would wax and wane on its responsibility to public health, but the fact that it had a responsibility became a part of the political dialogue. And, of course, women received the right to vote. She could have been the leader of NAWSA when the vote was won if she had challenged Anna Howard Shaw and thus earned a national name for herself. Instead she is credited with elevating the state, its women as well as its men, to a level of equality too long denied.

Like her great-grandfather, she recognized the need for compromise. Some politicians complain that compromise is a lack of principle. Breckinridge knew her causes were just, but in a democracy one accepts half or quarter measures today with an eye on tomorrow. Compromise offers a means to an end, a necessary means when the voice of all citizens is respected. One educated the population until enough pressure could be brought to the side of justice. In 1910, a decade before ratification of the Nineteenth Amendment, few would have thought Kentucky would approve such a measure. Breckinridge and her cadre proved them wrong. Henry Clay's contribution occurred largely at the national level. Breckinridge realized that leadership is required at all levels of society, and she made contributions at the city and state as well as the national level.

Madge Breckinridge was not just a leader of women; she became a very good American politician. She knew her audience and became the master teacher, effective guide, and motivator. Historians have recognized southern women for their role in the Progressive movement, but there is a nagging implication that they could not quite escape the limitations of the cult of true womanhood. They wanted change without appearing to want change, to be a part of the political process without threatening the white knights to whom they paid homage. That comes dangerously close to saying they were inferior because they did not fully adopt the methods used by men. Madeline Breckinridge sought her own path to success, a woman's path. She could have played the role of southern lady to perfection, but she refused to grovel or bat her eyes to seduce male support. Throughout her life she gained intellectual and emotional support from other women: family women, the students at Miss Porter's, the University of Chicago reformers, and her fellow suffragists. She remained refined, genteel, and aristocratic; she was also informed, focused, and determined. Breckinridge did not escape her traditional upbringing. In fact, she did not try to escape it; it was a part of who she was. It became instead the basis of her understanding of the people and forces that had to be changed. Claude Bowers, a popular historian and politician, wrote after her death, "The story of Madeline McDowell Breckinridge should be studied by every woman who would serve her community."[76] Indeed, all Americans can learn from her efforts.

NOTES

1. Carey Olmstead Shellman, "Nettie Peters Black, 1851–1919," in *Georgia Women: Their Lives and Times*, ed. Ann Short Chirhart and Betty Wood, vol. 1 (Athens: University of Georgia Press, 2009), 313; Sara Alpern, Joyce Antler, Elizabeth Israels Perry, and Ingrid Winther Scobie, *The Challenge of Feminist Biography: Writing the Lives of Modern American Women* (Urbana: University of Illinois Press, 1992), 7–8; Dewey W. Grantham, *Southern Progressivism: The Reconciliation of Progress and Tradition* (Knoxville: University of Tennessee Press, 1990).

2. Harriet Martineau to Reverend Samuel Gilman, June 12, 1835, Special Collections and Archives, University of Kentucky Libraries, Lexington; *Lexington Observer and Reporter*, May 15, 1858. See David S. and Jeanne T. Heidler, *Henry Clay: The Essential American* (New York: Random House, 2010); Robert V. Remini, *Henry Clay: Statesman for the Union* (New York: Norton, 1991);

Glyndon G. Van Deusen, *The Life of Henry Clay* (Boston: Little, Brown, 1937); Sara Bearss, "Henry Clay and the American Claims Against Portugal, 1850," *Journal of the Early Republic* 7 (1987): 168–69. The elite citizens of Lexington enjoyed noting the failures and shortcomings of Clay's descendants. Many descendants felt a great deal of stress because of that pressure. See Lindsey Apple, *Cautious Rebel: A Biography of Susan Clay Sawitzky* (Kent, Ohio: Kent State University Press, 1997), 22, 63, 73, 119, 126, 212, 239; and Lindsey Apple, *The Family Legacy of Henry Clay: In the Shadow of a Kentucky Patriarch* (Lexington: University Press of Kentucky, 2011), 168, 172–74, 179, 238. The author's interviews with family members revealed a strong sense of responsibility to live up to Henry Clay's reputation and a belief that family members were always being compared to him to their detriment.

3. Anne's mother died in 1840; her father, Henry Clay Jr., died in the Battle of Buena Vista in 1847. Anne spent time in Louisville with a relative and at Ashland.

4. See James C. Klotter, "Central Kentucky's 'Athens of the West' Image in the Nation and in History," in *Bluegrass Renaissance: The History and Culture of Central Kentucky*, ed. James C. Klotter and Daniel Rowland (Lexington: University Press of Kentucky, 2012), 11–35.

5. Jo Della Alband, "A History of the Education of Women in Kentucky" (Master's thesis, University of Kentucky, 1934), 154–55; Gladys V. Parrish, "The History of Female Education in Lexington and Fayette County" (Master's thesis, University of Kentucky, 1932); Anne Goodwyn Jones, "Southern Literary Women as Chroniclers of Southern Life," in *Sex, Race, and the Role of Women in the South*, ed. Joanne V. Hawks and Sheila L. Skemp (Jackson: University Press of Mississippi, 1983), 356; Susan Clay to Mrs. Charles D. Clay, August 15, 1927, Henry Clay Memorial Foundation Papers, Special Collections and Archives, University of Kentucky Libraries (hereafter HCMF Papers).

6. Elizabeth Murphey Simpson, *The Enchanted Bluegrass* (Lexington, Ky.: Transylvania Press, 1938), preface.

7. Barbara Welter, "The Cult of True Womanhood: 1820–1860," *American Quarterly* 18 (1966): 151–74.

8. Henry Clay McDowell to Anne Clay McDowell, August 3, 1894, HCMF Papers.

9. Bill Marshall, former director of Special Collections and Archives at the University of Kentucky Libraries, referred to Major McDowell as a robber baron and suggested that a study should be made of his business interests. See Milton H. Smith to Henry Clay McDowell, January 3, 1891; Henry Clay McDowell to Buckner, Cummins & Co., November 16, 1897; R. A. McDowell to Henry Clay McDowell, August 20, 1898, all in HCMF Papers. McDowell was no relation to Henry Clay. Like many families of that era, they named their son after a famous person they admired. Henry Clay Frick, known for his business ventures and his art collection, is another example.

10. Maude Arthur, "A Visit to Henry Clay's Home," *Atlanta Constitution*, n.d., clipping, HCMF Papers; *Lexington Leader*, June 7, 1889, March 3, 1890, April 19, 1892; Harriet R. Holman, ed., "The Kentucky Journal of Thomas Nelson Page," *Register of the Kentucky Historical Society* 68 (1970): 13.

11. The HCMF Papers contains a folder on McDowell's work with the Lexington Lunatic Asylum. See also Henry Clay McDowell Jr. to Anne Clay McDowell, April 16, 1911, HCMF Papers; Melba Porter Hay, *Madeline McDowell Breckinridge and the Battle for the New South* (Lexington: University Press of Kentucky, 2009), 59.

12. The McDowell Papers in the HCMF collection contain large files of business records and McDowell's checkbooks. See also Apple, *Family Legacy of Henry Clay*, 202–8; Henry Clay McDowell Jr. to Henry Clay McDowell Sr., April 24, 1893; Madeline McDowell Breckinridge (hereafter MMB) to Anne Clay McDowell, July 9, 1901; William Adair McDowell to Henry Clay McDowell Sr., November 11, 1896; Nettie McDowell to Anne Clay McDowell, December 26, 1904, all in HCMF papers.

13. Bertram Wyatt-Brown, *Southern Honor: Ethics and Behavior in the Old South* (New York:

Oxford University Press, 1982), 144, 154, 232–33; George H. Clay to Mariah Pepper Clay, August 9, 1897, HCMF Papers.

14. Sophonisba P. Breckinridge (hereafter SPB), *Madeline McDowell Breckinridge: A Leader in the New South* (Chicago: University of Chicago Press, 1921), 15; Hay, *Madeline McDowell Breckinridge*, 18.

15. Marion Houston to Madeline McDowell, October 28, 1892, October 23, 1894, HCMF Papers.

16. Harrison Robertson to Madeline McDowell, December 2, 21, 1892, March 17, 1893; W. W. Thum to Madeline McDowell, December 20, 1892, January 1, April 10, 1893, July 20, 24, 1894, HCMF Papers. These letters resemble those by other men pursuing young women of the upper class, indicating that, at least until marriage, women had far more control over relationships than has been suggested. Mariah Hensley Pepper, for example, virtually toyed with Charles D. Clay before their marriage. See Mariah Hensley Pepper to Charles D. Clay, December 18, 1895, January 5, February 2, March 5, 11, April 18, August 18, 1896, HCMF Papers. Marion Houston wrote about marriage after a visit to Ashland, "Like you I don't much care who the man is provided he lives near Ashland." Marion Houston to MMB, May 25, 1892, HCMF Papers.

17. Hamilton Busbey to Henry Clay McDowell Sr., January 5, 1898; K. Fujinami to Henry Clay McDowell, January 26, 1898; Adolphus Busch to H. C. McDowell, April 15, 1897, all in HCMF Papers. Theodore Roosevelt was also a friend of McDowell's.

18. Nettie Belle Smith to Madeline McDowell, January 22, 1893; Henry Clay McDowell to Anne Clay McDowell, August 3, 1894; Madeline McDowell to Anne Clay McDowell, August 4, 1898, HCMF Papers; Apple, *Cautious Rebel*, 47, 50; Henry Clay Simpson Jr., *Josephine Clay: Pioneer Horsewoman of the Bluegrass* (Louisville: Harmony House, 2005), 72–79; Hay, *Madeline McDowell Breckinridge*, 6.

19. *Century* magazine was a publication aimed at America's middle and upper classes. Its editors sought to enhance people's knowledge of the national past. Madge's article accompanied a portrait of Henry Clay.

20. James C. Klotter, *The Breckinridges of Kentucky, 1760–1981* (Lexington: University Press of Kentucky, 1986), 193, 195; Madeline McDowell to Anne Clay McDowell, August 4, 1898; SPB to Madeline McDowell, September 20, 1893, October 3, 1894, [September 1895]; Desha Breckinridge to Madeline McDowell, [month unknown] 24, 1895, all in HCMF Papers.

21. There are in her papers catalogs from a number of universities, indicating that she considered pursuing a degree. Breckinridge published a biography of Madge after her death.

22. Desha Breckinridge to Madeline McDowell, June 24, 1894, HCMF Papers; *Lexington Herald*, June 18, 1900. She also reviewed John Jay Chapman's *Practical Agitation*, which encouraged the use of the political system and the need for pressure on both political parties. See *Lexington Herald*, May 26, 27, 1900.

23. Stites Duvall to Madge McDowell, December 1895, HCMF Papers.

24. The Clays and the McDowells did not think highly of the Breckinridges. In 1859 W. C. P. Breckinridge, Desha's father, married the daughter of Thomas Hart Clay. Clay wrote at the time, "There is an odor about R. J. Breckinridge I do not admire. The Sons are just commencing the practice of law with I think a poor prospect of success. . . . They are a coarse family." A year after the marriage Lucretia Clay Breckinridge and a son were dead. Breckinridge again ran afoul of the family in 1882, when Major McDowell sought to buy Ashland. Seeking to increase the price, Breckinridge tried to provoke a bidding war between the James B. Clay descendants and Major McDowell. Outright animosity developed in 1893, when Madeline Pollard sued Breckinridge for breach of promise. He had carried on an affair with Pollard, promising to marry her when his second wife died, but he married another woman. The scandal rocked Lexington, and McDowell

was encouraged by Democratic and Republican politicians to run against him for his seat in the U.S. House of Representatives. McDowell chose not to do so after receiving a letter mentioning scandals in which the McDowells were involved, including gambling debts and a paternity suit against Thomas Bullock, Nettie McDowell's new husband. The letter also noted a public dispute between one of McDowell's daughters and a Breckinridge daughter "which is providing a delicious morsel to scandal mongers." Though McDowell did not challenge Breckinridge politically, it did not help the strained relations. See Thomas H. Clay Diary in the possession of Dr. William Kenner, microfilm copy at Special Collections and Archives, University of Kentucky Libraries; Theodore Roosevelt to Henry Clay McDowell, May 7, 1894; Basil Duke to Henry Clay McDowell, June 14, 16, 1894; Benjamin Bristow to H. C. McDowell, June 2, September 13, November 28, 1894, all in HCMF Papers. For the scandal see Klotter, *Breckinridges of Kentucky*, 160–70. Basil Duke was a Confederate officer who, along with Breckinridge, rode with Gen. John Hunt Morgan. He was a Louisville lawyer and Democratic politician.

25. Desha Breckinridge to Madeline McDowell, June 24, 1894, HCMF Papers.

26. Madeline McDowell to Anne Clay McDowell, April (n.d.) 1891, HCMF Papers; Hay, *Madeline McDowell Breckinridge*, 44; Klotter, *Breckinridges of Kentucky*, 213.

27. For Henry Clay's statement see Henry Clay to Dr. George McClellan, September 24, 1846, in *The Papers of Henry Clay*, ed. Melba Porter Hay (Lexington: University Press of Kentucky, 1991), 10:280–81. There were also quotations from Milner, Tennyson, Carlyle, and others. See HCMF Papers.

28. Madeline McDowell to Henry Clay McDowell Jr., May 20, 1897, HCMF Papers; Klotter, *Breckinridges of Kentucky*, 213.

29. Lindsey Apple, "In Search of a Star: A Kentucky Clay Goes to the Arctic," *Filson Club History Quarterly* 71 (1997): 3–26; Robert M. Ireland, "Homicide in Nineteenth Century Kentucky," *Register of the Kentucky Historical Society* 81 (1983): 134–53; James C. Klotter, *Kentucky Justice, Southern Honor, and American Manhood: Understanding the Life and Death of Richard Reid* (Baton Rouge: Louisiana State University Press, 2003), 31–33. The Louisville newspapers—the *Courier-Journal*, the *Post*, and the *Commercial*—discussed the death of Harry Clay and the trial of Andrew Wepler throughout 1884 and 1885.

30. *Lexington Herald*, February 12, 17, 18, 1899.

31. Ibid., June 18, 1900, September 30, 1905; W. C. P. Breckinridge to SPB, May 7, July 9, 1900; Paul Kellogg to MMB, February 15, 1906; Annie A. Halleck to MMB, January 31, 1907, all in Breckinridge Family Papers, Library of Congress (hereafter BFP). The heading for the column carried the phrase "Whatever a woman can do, that, by divine ordination she ought to do, by human allowance she should be privileged to do, by force of destiny in the long run she will do." See example in *Lexington Herald*, February 18, 1906.

32. *Lexington Herald*, January 11, 1900; Grantham, *Southern Progressivism*, 15; Nell Irvin Painter, *Southern History across the Color Line* (Chapel Hill: University of North Carolina Press, 2002), 200–202.

33. *Lexington Herald*, January 8, April 25, 1900.

34. Ibid., April 15, December 16, 1900, September 8, 1901. Breckinridge would wage a lengthy war with the Salvation Army because she believed its methods encouraged people to depend on the dole rather than developing means to escape it. She also objected to the lack of accountability in regard to the organization's use of government funds. She was largely unsuccessful in her efforts.

35. *Lexington Herald*, August 25, 1900.

36. For the Progressive Era see Edward L. Ayers, *The Promise of the New South: Life after Reconstruction* (New York: Oxford University Press, 1993); Eldon J. Eisenach, *The Lost Promise of*

Progressivism (Lawrence: University Press of Kansas, 1994); Lewis L. Gould, ed., *The Progressive Era* (Syracuse, N.Y.: Syracuse University Press, 1974); Peter Levine, *The New Progressive Era: Toward a Fair and Deliberate Democracy* (New York: Rowman & Littlefield, 2000); Richard Hofstadter, *The Age of Reform* (New York: Vintage, 1955); Arthur S. Link, *Woodrow Wilson and the Progressive Era, 1900–1917* (New York: Harper, 1954); Grantham, *Southern Progressivism.*

37. The records of McDowell's varied business interests are preserved in HCMF Papers.

38. Fannie H. White Price to MMB, May 1, 1919; Paul V. Smith to Civic League, May 5, 1919, BFP.

39. *Lexington Herald*, September 8, 1901.

40. Ibid., September 8, 1901, May 4, 1902; H. F. Hillenmeyer to MMB, August 20, 1901; D. J. Thomas to Desha Breckinridge (hereafter DB), May 18, 1901, BFP.

41. E. R. Jones to MMB, November 25, 1907, BFP; *Lexington Herald*, February 27, 1906; *Lexington Leader*, May 30, 1909.

42. *Lexington Herald*, March 6, 1902, December 21, 1913.

43. Again, Madge had the advantage of her husband's newspaper to fight for her causes. She used a basic argument of the Progressive movement against the Educational Improvement Commission. Who knew most about the needs of young children? Within the family, who were the teachers, and guardians, of morality? How could the commission voice such concepts, then omit women from its board? See also Nancy K. Forderhase, "'The Clear Call of Thoroughbred Women': The Kentucky Federation of Women's Clubs and the Crusade for Educational Reform, 1903–1909," *Register of the Kentucky Historical Society* 83 (1985): 19–35; William E. Ellis, *A History of Education in Kentucky* (Lexington: University Press of Kentucky, 2011), 157–58.

44. Marion Houston to Madeline McDowell, October 23, 1894; DB to Madeline McDowell, June 30, 1895, HCMF Papers; *Lexington Herald*, December 26, 1907.

45. *Lexington Herald,* June 24, 1902; SPB, "Southern Pioneers in Social Interpretation," *Journal of Social Forces* 2 (1921): 107; MMB to Samuel H. Bailey, December 8, 1908; J. H. Simrall, Lexington Public Schools, to MMB, April 15, 1910; MMB to Lexington Public School Board, [1910], all in BFP.

46. *Lexington Herald,* January 10, 24, 1907; Richard W. Knott to MMB, February 14, 1907, HCMF Papers. The papers also include information on her work with the state and national child labor organizations. Breckinridge's work on child labor and a compulsory education law give ample evidence of the care with which she prepared her argument. She sought information from Jane Addams and Florence Kelley on compulsory education. She then gained the support of key people such as James McGill, the president of the Kentucky State Federation of Labor, and Andy Ludwig of the Department of Agriculture, Labor, and Statistics. She also worked with friendly politicians in an effort to pass legislation and joined national organizations interested in the cause. See Jane Addams to MMB, [n.d.] 1903; Florence Kelly to MMB, August 8, 1903; James McGill to MMB, May 10, 1903; Andy Ludwig to MMB, June 25, 1903; John L. Whitehead to MMB, February 28, 1902, all in BFP.

47. Carl E. Schultzer to DB, December 16, 1909; J. K. Mitchell to MMB, November 24, 1909; James A. Allen to MMB, December 15, 1909; R. A. Long to MMB, December 16, 1909, all in BFP.

48. See J. B. Cassity, Report to Board of Commissioners, City of Lexington, December 31, 1913; Mary McDowell to MMB, January 12, 1914, BFP. McDowell asked Breckinridge to speak on the use of schools in neighborhood development at a meeting of the National Conference of Charities and Correction.

49. *Lexington Herald*, April 29, 1900, May 5, 1907.

50. Grantham, *Southern Progressivism*, 231. See also HCMF Papers; Civic League Minutes, October 4 1918, BFP.

51. W. C. P. Breckinridge, Desha's father, wrote to his daughter Sophonisba that because of the

"hereditary disposition" to tuberculosis, the diagnosis caused "great anxiety." See letter of October 19, 1903, vol. 3, BFP; Hay, *Madeline McDowell Breckinridge*, 92–93.

52. Irwin W. Sherman, *Twelve Diseases That Changed Our World* (Washington, D.C: ASM Press, 2007), 125. See also Thomas M. Daniel, *Captain of Death: The Story of Tuberculosis* (Rochester, N.Y: University of Rochester Press, 1997); Frank Ryan, *The Forgotten Plague: How the Battle against Tuberculosis Was Won—and Lost* (Boston: Little, Brown, 1992).

53. Pamphlets and journal articles on the subject can be found in her papers. See HCMF Papers.

54. Certificate, Kentucky Board of Tuberculosis, BFP.

55. Pamphlets and journal articles about treatments of tuberculosis sufferers from many states and nations appear in HCMF Papers. See also Arnold C. Kleb to MMB, November 17, 1905, BFP.

56. *Lexington Herald*, February 18, 1899, March 15, April 15, 29, 1900, September 8, 1901, May 4, 1902.

57. MMB to Anne Clay McDowell, October 18, 1913, HCMF Papers.

58. Nisba Breckinridge included at the end of her biography of Madge many of the tributes written in her honor by state and local organizations. See SPB, *Madeline McDowell Breckinridge*, 31–32, 252, 260, 263. Desha also devoted an entire issue of the *Herald* as a tribute to Madge. See *Lexington Herald*, December 5, 1920.

59. *Lexington Herald*, September 8, 1901, June 23, 24, 1902; Hay, *Madeline McDowell Breckinridge*, 86.

60. Ellis, *History of Education*, 158; Hay, *Madeline McDowell Breckinridge*, 80.

61. When Governor Augustus E. Willson vetoed Madge's tuberculosis bill, she responded in a newspaper column refuting his position point by point. The article was composed but certainly not demure. See "A State Sanatorium for Tuberculosis and an Answer to the Objections of Governor Willson," newspaper files, BFP. In a series of editorials Breckinridge used adult illiteracy in the state as evidence of the poor job men had done in education. "It seems," she wrote, "that the thing to be argued in Kentucky is not whether women are fit for school suffrage but whether men are fit for it." *Lexington Herald*, "Some Reasons for Granting School Suffrage to Kentucky Women," May 1910, clippings in HCMF Papers; "Kentucky: Forty Seventh," HCMF Papers; MMB, "The Prospect for Woman Suffrage in the South," an address to the National Woman's Suffrage Convention, October 29, 1911, HCMF Papers; quotation in Hay, *Madeline McDowell Breckinridge*, 184. State senator C. W. Burton promised to vote for a suffrage measure but reneged. Newspaper clipping, HCMF Papers.

62. Alben W. Barkley to MMB, December 17, 1919, BFP; MMB to Magdalen McDowell, October 22, 1913, HCMF Papers; *Lexington Herald*, April 12, 1913; Carrie Chapman Catt to MMB, December 15, 1919.

63. MMB, President's Report, Kentucky Equal Rights Association, 1916; Anna V. Becker to MMB, August 14, 1913; L. C. Obenchain to MMB, August 15, 1913, BFP.

64. Hay, *Madeline McDowell Breckinridge*, 154; Kate Gordon to MMB, October 2, 1914, BFP.

65. MMB, "The Prospect for Woman Suffrage in the South"; MMB, "Information from U.S. Census of 1910," BFP; Marjorie Spruill Wheeler, *New Women of the New South: The Leaders of the Woman Suffrage Movement in the Southern States* (New York: Oxford University Press, 1993), 104, 111; Hay, *Madeline McDowell Breckinridge*, 140, 155.

66. Jouett Shouse to MMB, September 24, 1914; MMB to Jouett Shouse, September 24, 1914, HCMF Papers. Shouse had worked at the *Lexington Herald* before moving to Kansas, where he was elected to the U.S. House of Representatives. He wrote to Madge to complain about the policy of holding the party in power responsible for the failure to pass a suffrage measure. Madge informed him that Alice Paul's group advocated such a policy, not NAWSA.

67. See SPB, "Notes," BFP; SPB to MMB, [1914]; SPB to MMB, November 14, 1914; MMB to Anna Howard Shaw, May 16, 1915; Josephine Weidler to MMB, November 25, 1915; Elizabeth Yates to MMB, November 25, 1915, BFP.

68. Laura Clay to MMB, June 5, 1919, BFP.

69. A characteristic of southern manners, respect for older and accomplished members of the extended family was very much a part of the training of youth in the Clay and McDowell families. Both Henry and Anne McDowell yielded to Susan M. Clay in family matters and showed her the utmost respect, though she could be extremely trying at times. Respect may also explain the relationship McDowell had with James B. Clay Jr., an unreconstructed Confederate, and with John M. Clay, whose eccentricities gave way at times to mania. When Major McDowell died, Henry Clay McDowell Jr., the eldest son, became the head of the family, overseeing the Ashland farming operation and directing the trust fund. The siblings accepted his decisions.

70. Laura Clay to MMB, May 7, 1919; MMB to Mrs. J. R. Judah, November 17, 1919; MMB to Carrie Chapman Catt, December 15, 1919; Carrie Chapman Catt to MMB, December 15, 1919; MMB to Carrie Chapman Catt, December 20, 1919, BFP.

71. Hay, *Madeline McDowell Breckinridge*, 246.

72. Ibid., 209–10, 224. Margaret Ripley Wolfe in *Daughters of Canaan* argues that women below the Mason-Dixon line were for too long "haunted by the specter of 'the southern lady.'" Broadening the concept, she noted that, like their "American sisters," southern women "were socially conditioned to speak not of their *rights* but of their *responsibilities*" (134). Modern scholarship generally studies those women who escaped the tenets of the myths that confined their gender, but those "myths" remain the backdrop against which even those women struggled. Some women broke free of southern, or Victorian, restrictions. Others struggled against those restrictions even as they failed or refused to break free. The threats of being ostracized, of getting a bad name, or ruining the family reputation were real in small southern communities. Those values, deeply instilled, proved difficult to overcome. Guilt is a trait taught not just to women but to children in general and to adherents of numerous religious sects. Though enforced by family and community, those values also hid within the minds and emotions of individual women. Confining values that may be rejected on an intellectual level can in times of emotional crises exploit the vulnerability of the individual, and that is true regardless of gender. Even as southern women demanded more equality, the old values often lurked in their subconscious. Madge's acceptance of even partial responsibility for her husband's infidelity, while disappointing, should not come as a complete surprise. She was sick and emotionally vulnerable, and she lived in a community that thrived on gossip. Overwhelmed, she began to question herself. Even today self-blame, particularly in spousal abuse cases, is a societal concern. See Apple's *Cautious Rebel* for another example within the Clay family. Works by Shirley Abbott, Lillian Smith, and Sallie Bingham and the fictional character Carol Kennicott in Sinclair Lewis's *Main Street* indicate the lingering impact of such values even as women rejected them. See also Carl N. Degler, *At Odds: Women and the Family from the Revolution to the Present* (Oxford: Oxford University Press, 1980), 162–63, 170; Anne Firor Scott, *The Southern Lady: From Pedestal to Politics* (Chicago: University of Chicago Press, 1970), 169, 180; Anne Firor Scott, *Making the Invisible Woman Visible* (Urbana: University of Illinois Press, 1984), 181; Wyatt-Brown, *Southern Honor*, 51–55, 173, 246, 238, 282–83; Virginia Kent Anderson Leslie, "A Myth of the Southern Lady: Antebellum Proslavery Rhetoric and the Proper Place of Women," in *Southern Women*, ed. Caroline Matheny Dillman (New York: Hemisphere, 1988), 23–32; Alpern et al., *Challenge of Feminist Biography*, 7. See also Lillian Smith, *Killers of the Dream* (New York: Norton, 1949); Shirley Abbott,

*Womenfolks: Growing Up Down South (*New York: Ticknor & Fields, 1983); Sallie Bingham, *Passion and Prejudice: A Family Memoir* (New York: Knopf, 1989); Sinclair Lewis, *Main Street* (New York: Harcourt, Brace & Howe, 1920).

73. MMB to DB, June 13, 29, 1920; MMB to Nettie Bullock, May 26, 1920, HCMF Papers.

74. MMB to Nettie Bullock, August 27, September 13, September 26, 1913, August 16, 1916; MMB to Anne Clay McDowell, August 15, 1916; MMB to DB, [1917], all in HCMF Papers.

75. DB to Curry Breckinridge, June 29, 1916; MMB to Nettie Bullock, 1917; MMB to DB, June 13, June 29, 1920, BFP.

76. Claude Bowers, newspaper clipping, HCMF Papers.

Linda Neville
(1873–1961)

"The Lady Who Helps Blind Children See"

JAMES DUANE BOLIN

The small mountain boy wanted to express his gratitude to the woman from so far away—at least she had seemed so far away to him—in the bustling city of Lexington. After all, she had cured him of the eye disease trachoma, a dreaded ailment that by the first decade of the twentieth century had blinded or threatened to blind more than thirty thousand of the residents in eastern Kentucky alone. The little boy did not know the name of the disease; all he knew was that he had been blind, and now he could see.

Nor did he know the name of the kind woman who had saved him. But he wanted to thank her. He wrote her the note of thanks himself in his child's hand and addressed the envelope simply, "To the Lady Who Helps Blind Children See, Lexington, Kentucky."[1] The postal carrier had no trouble directing the note to its intended recipient. She lived at 722 West Main Street, Lexington, Kentucky, from her birth on April 23, 1873, and throughout her life, except for four years of study at Bryn Mawr (1891–95), the elite college for women ten miles west of Philadelphia, and when she traveled from one end of the commonwealth to the other for the prevention of blindness and other causes, and finally three years in a Lexington nursing home before her death on June 2, 1961.

By the 1920s most everyone in Lexington, many across the state, and a widening circle of Progressive Era reformers around the nation knew Linda Neville, or Miss Linda as she came to be called. Her renown was hard won. Why is it, after all, that such women of accomplishment have often been the victims of personal sadness and tragedy even as they have healed and restored and made life better for thousands of strangers outside their own homes, outside those they love the most?[2]

LUCY FURMAN (LEFT) AND LINDA NEVILLE (RIGHT)

June 3, 1937. Courtesy of Special Collections, University of Kentucky Libraries, Lexington.

Like other Progressive reformers such as Theodore Roosevelt or, in Kentucky, Madeline McDowell Breckinridge, Linda Neville and her older sister Mary were reared by her father and mother in a home environment that stressed noblesse oblige. Because her family had been given much, the Nevilles were expected to help others unable to help themselves. Linda's father, John Henry Neville, a Greek and Latin scholar, began teaching at the State College in Lexington in 1880. Before he died in 1908, the school had promoted him to a vice presidency. Professor Neville became a legend among pupils and alumni. Two of his most successful students were the Kentucky writers James Lane Allen and John Fox Jr. Fox remembered that "every college man must confess that he was most affected, as regards his student career, his reading and the current of his future life, by some one of his professors, and for us, this was the man."[3]

Linda's mother, Mary Payne Neville, came from an ancestral line that could be traced back to the very first non–Native American settlers of the Bluegrass. Mrs. Neville had accumulated the wealth and status worthy of the descendant of one of the commonwealth's first families. With Professor Neville's ties to State College and Mrs. Neville's family wealth and social standing, Linda and Mary never wanted for anything that family, money, or Lexington society could provide.

Lexingtonians recognized Linda for her special qualities even as a small child, and at least one local newspaper article pointed out her headstrong determination. Family friend Susie M. Wilson wrote that "a lovely little daughter of Professor Neville, of this city, was induced to sit for a picture. But at the moment of execution, one of her chubby arms was thrown across her eyes, in the effort to conceal her face, and just as she had exclaimed, 'I won't' the photograph was made." The scene made such an impression on Wilson that she wrote the following lines in an eerie foreshadowing of the work of the future crusader:

> "I won't!" and up before the eyes
> The little arm went stealing,
> Obscuring their light from our view
> Yet beauty, still, revealing.[4]

No doubt about it. Linda and Mary Neville were special. As the sisters grew up, the educational institutions in the "Athens of the West" would not do for the Neville girls, despite the presence—albeit a diminished one—of the once-proud Transylvania University, a new A&M College (later State College), and Hamilton Female College, founded in 1869 as Hocker Female College.[5] Instead, Professor Neville saw to the education of his daughters at home for a time. Their mother died in 1886, when Linda had just turned thirteen, but even before her death, it was the girls' father who saw after their education. Linda learned to read before she was five and later recalled that her father insisted lessons be prepared before anything else. For the Nevilles, an education made one independent, ready for a life's calling. And women as well as men could be called to a vocation outside the home, certainly if one's last name was Neville. Dr. Neville made sure that "his daughters did not grow up ignorant." "They had to be self-supporting," he taught them. If they did decide to marry someday, the professor declared, "it would be for love, and the genuine desire to build a home, and not for security." As for the professor, he would be perfectly happy if his daughters devoted their lives to changing the world rather than to abiding by "the cult of true womanhood," an antiquated ideal that imprisoned women to husband and home.[6]

Professor Neville "was determined that they should never have to marry" because their education was inferior or because they could not support themselves. His private lessons in reading and writing and rudimentary Greek and Latin also carried heavy doses of the Neville philosophy of education and work. "As long as I retain memory of anything . . . the only solid, the only unalloyed pleasure I have ever found, I have found in doing what I could to help forward the young; for one lesson that my 80 years have taught me is this, that if a man work for himself the fruit of his work, like Dead Sea apples, will turn to ashes upon his lips." Both daughters, but especially Linda, would take their father's philosophy to heart. She would often quote her father's words and even had them engraved in bronze to hang on her parlor wall.[7]

A French governess taught the sisters French for three years, and then they went to an aunt's private school in Lexington to study "history, German, mathematics, more Latin, and other subjects." Soon after their mother's death, first Mary, and then Linda, took a train to Germantown, Pennsylvania, to attend the finishing school of Mary E. Stevens. Its close proximity to Bryn Mawr near Philadelphia surely played a role in the choice of the finishing school, not that the Mary Stevens School was any sort of feeder school for Bryn Mawr. Every young woman who matriculated at Bryn Mawr had to pass the Harvard entrance examination or an equivalent test given by Bryn Mawr.[8]

Both Mary and Linda had no trouble gaining admittance and flourished, although Linda seems to have clashed from time to time with the college's formidable dean, Martha Carey Thomas. Professor Neville, back home in Lexington, did not ease the tension. In letters to Mary and Linda, he criticized the Bryn Mawr curriculum. "My regret all along," he wrote to Mary, "has been that to become a graduate you had to carry so heavy and worthless a load in English and Science." To Linda, he centered his disdain on the dean herself: "Not a professor there, I am sure, likes a hair on [her] head, nor would I. Get along with her as well as you can but take not a syllable of insolence from her without instantly resenting it."[9]

As strict as Professor Neville must have been on his students in Lexington, he took pedagogical liberties to help his daughters across the miles in Pennsylvania. After all, he had overseen every aspect of their educations before Mary and then Linda left for the Mary Stevens School. He did not let distance deter an intimate involvement in helping his daughters succeed. His dislike of Dean Thomas only made him more determined.

"Let me know as soon as possible what letters of Pliny are assigned to you," the professor instructed Linda during the fall semester of her sophomore year. The next week, he advised her to "send me exact numbers of the Pliny letters." "I may send you some hints for the essay," he wrote. As a father, Professor Neville wanted to know just what he could do "to lighten the load or smooth the road." The professor thought nothing of translating Greek and Latin passages for his daughters. "I have helped you on the Cicero letters chiefly to keep you from breaking down your health," he explained. "Let me know what I can do further." And then he exhorted: "Help every girl you can."[10]

With her own hard work—and perhaps with her father's guidance, prodding, and long-distance assistance—Linda took a bachelor's degree in Greek and Latin at the end of the spring term in 1895. "Dear Papa," she wrote as graduation neared, "I think I shall never regret coming to college. Indeed I am very glad that I came and for many reasons am sorry to see the close."[11]

Surely Mary held the same sentiments when she graduated from Bryn Mawr with an identical Greek and Latin degree the year before. The fact that both daughters graduated with degrees in the field of specialty of their famous father should have surprised no one; nor should their coming directly back to 722 West Main Street in Lexington on graduation. As unconventional for the times as Bryn Mawr had been, as determined as Dean Thomas was—and in theory Professor Neville as well—to produce women of self-sufficiency, Linda came back home in 1895 to a household that included her father, her sister, "a cook, a maid and handyman, all of whom lived on the premises."[12]

Within two years, the sisters had established the Misses Neville School in their home, designed to prepare students for "Eastern college examinations." They maintained this school for more than a decade until the death of Professor Neville in 1908. In truth, the young women held two primary occupations in the years from their Bryn Mawr graduations until 1908: first, seeing to the care of their father; and second, teaching and administering the Misses Neville School.[13]

It was only after the death of John Neville, Linda's beloved but dominating father, that she was free to find her life's calling, a vocation she pursued for the rest of her days. Linda displayed the peripatetic lifestyle that would characterize her years as an advocate for the blind even as she worked at home as a teacher and dutiful daughter. Through Christ Church Episcopal she joined the Gleaners, a group that supported the Proctor Industrial School in Beattyville, Kentucky, from 1902 to 1908. In the Gleaners Linda worked with her friend Madeline McDowell "Madge" Breckinridge, who would later do so much good in Kentucky's woman suffrage movement and in other causes. Breckinridge's biographer, Melba Porter Hay, aptly described the Social Gospel movement in which Neville and Breckinridge were so actively involved when she wrote that the Gleaners "focused more on reforming this world than on preparing for the next."[14]

It should not be surprising, then, that Neville's friendship with Breckinridge and her admiration for Laura Clay, two leading lights of Lexington, brought her into the woman suffrage movement, at least on the local level, where she helped organize women in Fayette County. Neville also worked in Lexington's Civic League and Associated Charities, where she was elected to the board of directors and served as secretary and vice president.[15] During these heady years just out of college, Neville learned the importance of leadership and organization. She also saw various models of how women worked together to get things done.

Neville believed, for example, that it was Madge Breckinridge who wrote the Christmas Day editorial in Lexington's *Morning Herald* in 1903. Titled "A Plea for Children," the editorialist urged voters to back a child labor law for Kentucky. "Is it inappropriate on the Birthday of a Child to make an appeal for some of the children of the present day who are bearing the burdens of older people and missing the joys of children?" the writer asked. Even though Lexingtonians did not witness "the wretchedness of the factory and sweat-shop children" of larger cities, there were "nevertheless children who are hard at work while more favored children are at school or at play."[16]

That Neville clipped the column in 1903 and then carefully annotated it again in 1952 while preparing to turn over her papers to the University of Kentucky is an indication of how much the editorial expressed her own developing concern for children's welfare. A Charlotte Perkins Gilman poem, included by Breckinridge—for the editorial must surely have been written by her—proved prophetic for Neville and must have comforted the aging crusader greatly when she read it again in 1952. One verse of the poem, "Mother to Child," reads:

> My prayer has been answered. The pain thou must bear
> Is the pain of the world's life which thy life must share.

Thou art one with the world—though I love thee the best;
And to save thee from pain I must save all the rest—
Well—with God's help I'll do it![17]

So Linda Neville's reform inclination had been forged at home in Lexington, at Bryn Mawr, and back home again. John Henry Neville had succeeded in rearing two daughters who were at once beholden to him while he lived and self-sufficient when he had gone on to his reward. While teaching school and caring for their father in his declining years, the Neville sisters also found time to establish their own credentials as prominent Lexington club women, Linda more so than Mary.

At a 1907 Lexington luncheon, Neville learned of a Clay County woman named Lula Doyle who had been brought to Lexington after a year of blindness to be examined by three oculists, "each one of whom pronounced her blindness permanent." Neville remembered years later, in 1939, that it was on "that day I began to feel a concern for helpless eye-sufferers, a concern that has stayed with me almost thirty-two years and will stay with me till the end."[18]

The following year, in July 1908, Neville took a fateful trip with "three companions" into the deep, dark eastern Kentucky mountains for the first time. She went to visit her friend Katherine Pettit, who, along with May Stone, founded the Hindman Settlement School in Knott County in 1902. Pettit and Stone applied Jane Addams's urban settlement house model to a rural, mountain setting to provide education and social services for poor, destitute mountain families.[19]

The difficulty of the journey from Lexington to Hindman opened Neville's eyes to the isolation of the mountain people. Neville and her friends left Lexington on an early-morning train that would carry them ninety miles to Jackson in Breathitt County; they arrived in the afternoon. In Jackson they engaged "at a heavy cost" a driver with his springless uncovered wagon and two mules for the trip to Hindman, a distance of between forty and forty-five miles. They rode steadily until "long after dark," when they had to seek lodging in a farmhouse. Neville and the two ladies slept together in one bed, while the young boy accompanying them and the driver slept in the dogtrot of the dwelling. They continued on the next morning in a driving rain. Neville wrote in her journal: "Much of the trip that day like much of the trip the day before was along through the waters of creeks and when we were not in the creeks we were going over rough roads, up and around the mountains, then down and around the mountains. There were very few intervening stretches of roadway at all level."[20]

The group was forced to spend another night, this time at a "farm house which was known to travelers over night." Neville wrote simply that "the next day the drive was like what has been described above." By this third day, Neville "felt my muscles were sore from the jolting and my flesh was sore in many places from bruises made when I had been tossed back and forth on the wagon seat." Finally, on the evening of the third day, the contingent made it to Hindman in time for supper. According to Neville, "we had spent about 52 hours getting from Lexington to Hindman, a distance that is now in 1939 traveled by automobile in three hours."[21]

Neville stayed ten days at the settlement school, soaking in everything she could about the work. "I listened to some of the visitors who came; I listened to the young man when he asked Miss Stone, one of the heads of the school, how much it would cost him to get to a hospital to get his eye cut out." The young man thought he could somehow raise the twenty dollars it would take to get to Lexington. Neville heard about the application of a small girl with eye trouble to enroll in the Hindman Settlement School. She listened as "the very able, carefully trained nurse [told] about the great prevalence in that section of the state of a blinding, painful eye disease which the people called 'red sore eyes', but which this nurse was convinced was nothing else than Trachoma, a disease that the U.S. Government was trying to keep out of this country through elaborate efforts at various ports of entry."[22]

In 1907 an estimated 33,000 Kentuckians suffered from trachoma. Today the U.S. Centers for Disease Control and Prevention identifies trachoma as "the world's leading cause of preventable blindness of infectious origin." A bacterial disease caused by *Chlamydia trachomatis*, "trachoma is easily spread through direct personal contact, shared towels and cloths, and flies that have come in contact with the eyes or nose of an infected person. If left untreated, repeated trachoma infections can cause severe scarring of the inside of the eyelid and can cause the eyelashes to scratch the cornea (trichiasis)." The painful condition of trichiasis "permanently damages the cornea and can lead to irreversible blindness." Currently, some eight million people, almost exclusively in third-world countries, are visually impaired as a result of trachoma; half a billion others are said to be at risk.[23]

Linda Neville's labor of a lifetime would lead to the eradication of the disease in Kentucky by 1952. It was the ten-day visit to the Hindman Settlement School in 1908 that spurred her to action, prompting her long, arduous, yet fulfilling calling as "the lady who helps blind children see." Impressed with the dedication of Pettit and Stone, along with two nurses serving the Hindman school, Neville returned to Lexington, accompanied by a child, an orphaned twin, who referred to herself as a "bastard." With "eye trouble," as well as somewhat deaf, the child would be the first in a long line of children to journey to Lexington, either accompanied by Neville or with her aid, to be treated by the city's physicians.[24]

Folks at Hindman made a dress for the little girl for the trip, and Neville remembered that "just as we were about to get into the wagon May Stone, with a gentleness that I delight in recalling, handed me for the child's trip a permit authorizing surgery for her, three or four dollars in money towards the traveling expenses, and she gave me a 'poke' filled with the child's clothes, some of them still wet." Neville never forgot this child, "the first in the procession of sufferers that has been coming for the last 30 or more years, the first of nearly 700 and they are still coming; two more today," she wrote in 1939.[25]

Arriving at 722 West Main, thirty-five-year-old Neville walked the child onto her lawn, where her ailing father sat. She feared that the professor "would object to my having assumed so much responsibility." But her father did not object, nor did her sister Mary. "Both were gentle with the little girl," Neville recalled. Although this child did not in fact have trachoma, Dr. J. A. Stucky, a Lexington oculist, fitted her with glasses at no cost, and the girl returned to Hindman. The long collaboration between Linda Neville, Dr. Stucky, and trachoma sufferers, young and old, in Kentucky's eastern mountains had begun.[26]

Dr. Stucky offered his services immediately to Pettit and Stone at Hindman, but arrangements for a clinic there could not be made for another year. Undaunted, Neville promptly met with another Lexington specialist, Dr. William N. Offutt, and persuaded him "to conduct an eye clinic at Witherspoon College, a missionary institution maintained by Presbyterians in Perry County." She believed it to be "the first such eye clinic conducted by a visiting oculist in a remote mountain place in Kentucky."[27]

At the same time, Neville continued to remember the great need she had witnessed at the Hindman Settlement School in Knott County. When a Lexington socialite and friend, Carrie Hillenmeyer, contributed twenty-five dollars to bring suffering Hindman students to Lexington to be treated, Neville deposited the gift in a bank under the name "The Mountain Fund." From this meager beginning, the Mountain Fund, always under Neville's strict control, would finance the transportation and treatment of thousands of trachoma victims and sufferers of what the mountain people referred to as "sore eyes."[28]

With intelligent and energetic role models, Linda learned how to use her abilities and her connections to accomplish her goals. When her father died, she grieved her loss, of course, but she was also able to finally answer her calling in earnest. Along with the establishment of the Mountain Fund, Neville also contacted the head of the Lexington and Eastern Railway Company (L&E), asking him to give reduced rates for mountain patients traveling by rail to and from Lexington. The manager agreed to provide "one-half fare privileges" for Neville's patients, a policy that continued until the Louisville and Nashville Railroad (L&N) absorbed the L&E into its vast network. Even then, the L&N

gave Neville free passes annually for the rest of her life. The railroad also provided free passes for the workers at Neville's clinics and, as Neville put it in her journal, "for such Mountain Fund patients as I might declare to be indigent." While many reformers lashed out at the stranglehold of the L&N on Kentucky legislators and governors, Neville expressed only praise for the railroad and its "wonderful contribution through the years to the sufferers of Kentucky."[29]

The Mountain Fund kept growing, thanks to Lexington contributors, but as Neville's work became known more widely around the state, women such as Covington's Fannie Lovell began to give generously as well. Following that first little girl, Neville met ten patients at the Lexington railroad station in 1908, nine of them from the Hindman Settlement School. Each of the students carried a tin wash basin, because Pettit and Stone were trying to ensure that the disease would not be spread. Neville kept all but one of the students in her home until they could be seen by an eye doctor.[30]

A sixteen-year-old boy, having arrived accompanied by May Stone, had developed a sore throat, and after an examination, a Lexington surgeon suspected diphtheria. With no hospital in town set up for communicable diseases, however, the boy had nowhere to stay until the culture could determine if he did indeed have diphtheria. Neville suggested an empty cottage on the grounds of her home. She promptly tidied the place and set up a cot where the boy stayed for several days, taking his meals in Neville's home after the culture revealed that he did not have the dreaded disease. "I like to think about that young boy," Neville wrote years later in her journal, "about his gentleness in 1908. . . . I doubt if I have ever had a patient who felt greater gratitude for what we did for him and it was so little."[31]

Not every patient was as grateful as that young man. Later that year, a twelve- or thirteen-year-old boy, with a bad case of trachoma, came to Neville's house as others before him. The child was "untidy and ignorant," as well as terribly homesick. Neville tried to comfort him by telling the boy about Helen Keller and "how she had to stay away from home for so long." The boy interrupted Neville in the middle of the story and said, "You are laying a parable for me but I am aiming to go home tomorrow anyway." Not only was the diseased boy "untidy," homesick, and rude; Neville discovered that he had filled his pockets and the toes of his socks with her household treasures. Neville said she "held on for awhile longer," but when a Lexington oculist advised her to let the boy go home, she finally did let him go, knowing that his trachoma would only worsen. She encountered the same man six years later on a visit to the U.S. Public Health Service Hospital in Breathitt County, and his condition had indeed worsened. She never saw him again.[32]

The trachoma patient who was also a thief proved to be an anomaly. "Of the patients who were from time to time in my home," she wrote, "some were ill-bred, some well bred; some fairly well educated, and some densely ignorant; some neat and some not neat; some home-sick and some radiantly happy to be here; some with infected eyes and some with eyes damaged but not infected." She continued, "Most of the patients disposed to be honorable in their dealings with me." And then there was the one dishonest boy "with the paper dollar tucked in his sock, the electric wires that he had cut, and the silver spoon tucked in his pocket; most of the time groaning and moaning [who] stands out in my memory."[33]

Neville realized that she could not keep up the strain of caring for patients in her Main Street home. The day-to-day responsibility proved to be too much for two sisters, even with a cook, a maid, and a handyman. For rest and diversion, Neville decided to take a steamer to Europe in July 1909. She went, as she observed in her journal, "not knowing at all how long I was going to stay." As it turned out, Neville was simply unable to enjoy the trip "to the full," her "enjoyment often lessened by the thoughts which would come insistently about those pitiable eye sufferers whom I had come to know in Kentucky." She returned to Lexington in October.[34]

Once home, Neville went back to work immediately. And the work only intensified. By 1911 she confronted head-on the medical ignorance in the mountains regarding trachoma. She informed L. D. Lewis, the county judge of Leslie County, that a self-proclaimed "eye-doctor" had done "an immense amount of harm to the poor sufferers with eye trouble in the neighborhood of Hazard." "He has been protected in his practice by some of the local officials," Neville insisted, "and I am writing to appeal to you in the name of law, and as the natural guardian for these poor, ignorant, blind men of the mountains, that you protect them from his quackery."[35]

Neville also continued to expand her work beyond the elimination of trachoma to the tragedy of what the mountain people referred to as "baby's sore eyes," which in reality was blindness brought on by gonorrhea. In a bulletin written by Neville titled "Babies' sore eyes," the question is asked: "Who is to blame when a case of 'babies' sore eyes' occurs?" The answer? "Most often, the FATHER, for disease-producing immorality. Often, also, the DOCTOR, for failure to drop into baby's eyes disease preventing drops." And then another question: "WHO IS TO BLAME, when blindness follows?" The answer? "Often, the PARENTS and DOCTOR, for failure to call an oculist without one hour's delay." And then, "Also, you, the PEOPLE, for failure to get laws to protect babies from blindness."[36]

Neville's bulletin was actually printed for the Kentucky Society for the Prevention of Blindness, an organization she was instrumental in founding in 1910. Following the formation of the New York Committee for the Prevention of Blindness and the interest of Louisa Lee Schuyler of the Russell Sage Foundation in the work begun by Neville in Kentucky, a group from New York came to the commonwealth in June 1910 to encourage the formation of a similar, more formal organization in the state. Just a few days before the group's visit, Neville made an impressionable talk before a meeting of the Kentucky Federation of Women's Clubs in Frankfort about the need for the founding of a society in Kentucky.[37]

After meeting with the New York group in Neville's home, the Fayette Medical Society hosted a dinner in honor of Dr. Park Lewis, the head of the New York contingent, where the announcement was made of the creation of the Kentucky Society for the Prevention of Blindness. Neville accepted, as she put it, "what I thought would be the arduous duties of Executive Secretary, work without pay or expectation of pay." According to Neville, the first major task of the society would be to mount a "major attack" on trachoma.[38]

In 1910 Neville observed that she really knew "very little about health conditions in Kentucky" and that she "had few acquaintances outside of Fayette County." With a sure calling to treat adults and especially children with eye diseases, Neville realized she had much to learn; still, her Bryn Mawr experience coupled with the insight she gained as a member of the Associated Charities, the Fayette Tuberculosis Association, and the Board of the Fayette Juvenile Court all would serve her well as she assumed the duties of executive secretary of the new society. In addition, Neville did not discount her "good deal of valuable experience as a teacher and through [her] association with Lexington citizens of real social vision."[39]

Two legislative measures in 1910 helped Neville learn more. Although Governor Augustus E. Willson had vetoed the bill two years earlier, an act increasing the annual state appropriation to the Kentucky Board of Health from $5,000 to $30,000 became law. The Board of Health also secured the passage of a vital statistics law and the commonwealth's first pure food and drug act. Neville learned that Kentucky also had tuberculosis associations in Jefferson County and Fayette County. An "organization for the bedside nursing of the poor," managed by the "King's Daughters," existed in Louisville, and "some sort of City Board of Health" paid a salary to an executive director in Lexington. It became clear to Neville that despite the progress that had been made in Kentucky health care by 1910, almost nothing outside her own work had been done to advance eye care. The founding of the Kentucky Society for the Prevention of Blindness proved to be a pivotal moment in turning Neville's work into a statewide concern.[40]

As the newly minted executive director of the Kentucky Society for the Prevention of Blindness and as the sole caretaker of a growing Mountain Fund, Neville began her work in earnest. She did not labor in isolation, however. In 1911, for example, the ever-helpful Dr. Stucky, accompanied by four nurses, traveled "by mule and springless wagons through Clay, Breathitt, Knott, Laurel, Rockcastle, and Perry Counties" at a rate of "not more than three miles per hour," stopping at the Oneida School in Clay County and Witherspoon College in Perry County to lecture on trachoma prevention and to treat trachoma patients. Dr. Stucky continued on to Hazard and then spent ten days offering a prolonged clinic where it all began, at the Hindman Settlement School in Knott County.[41]

At Hindman, of the four hundred "natives" Dr. Stucky examined, 25 percent presented "infectious diseases of the eye." Most of these cases suffered from "serious complications of Trachoma" such as "trichiasis, entropion, panus, iritis, and perforation of the cornea." Stucky performed more than eighty operations, putting each patient under ether anesthesia.[42] Lucy Furman, who became Neville's close friend and who was at that time a member of the Hindman staff, described Stucky's methods and the conditions under which he worked: "In the operating room with incredible speed, one patient after another was etherized, laid on the table, and relieved of [their] trouble," she wrote. "In another room the sore eyes were being treated constantly by one of the nurses; in another, people were being examined for glasses." In all the surrounding rooms, except for Stucky's operating room, "cots holding patients stood thickly about." Tents set up outside the main building all filled up as well. Homes in the Hindman community accommodated patients receiving "only local treatments."[43]

Although at the first clinic reluctant mountain residents often refused free eye examinations, treatment, and especially surgical care, Furman noted that by 1911 reluctance on the part of parents had virtually vanished, along with a "noticeable lessening of prejudice against the surgeon's knife." Parents also willingly paid the drastically reduced fees for clinic services. For procedures that might normally cost "twenty-five or fifty dollars, they were permitted to pay from one dollar to ten dollars." Others having no money at all might bring "produce including chickens and eggs, gallons of honey, bushels of apples or beans and handwoven baskets."[44]

At the end of the ten-day clinic, Stucky seemed overcome with the medical condition of Kentucky's mountain people. "The solution of the great problem of the needs of the mountains, and this problem is as serious as it is great," the doctor said, "is only to be solved by arresting the diseases that now exist, as far as possible, and by education, especially the children." "The largest number of these cases of infectious eye diseases are in what are known as the pauper counties," he continued, "counties so poor that they have not even an alms-house."[45]

While Stucky and nurses served out in the field, Neville continued to take in as many patients as possible at her Lexington home. Increasingly, however, she traveled outside the Bluegrass to raise awareness of the plight of eye sufferers around the state. Neville persuaded a Louisville oculist to hold eye clinics in Breathitt County, where one-eighth of those examined during one clinic presented with trachoma. She also persuaded the Kentucky Medical Association to back legislation that would require compulsory notification of any "swelling in the eyes of young babies and for the requirement that Health Boards see that proper attention is then given to the babies, even if to do so requires the expenditure of money." In 1912 Neville delivered some forty addresses explaining the work before audiences in county courthouses, in "meetings especially called by me," in college classes and assemblies, and before groups of schoolteachers, women's clubs, and church societies. "I have traveled up and down this state," Neville wrote in her journal, "east and west, just to carry the message to audiences and also to have the opportunity of conferring with physicians in their offices about the conditions in their respective localities."[46]

On March 5, 1913, for example, Neville journeyed to Louisville to speak to a woman's club on the topic of "Preventable Blindness." "Kentuckians have reason to be distressed at the fact that their State, with the exception of two, has more blind people in it than any in the Union," Neville told those assembled. "And our distress becomes shame when we are told that one half the blindness is preventable, and the other half is the direct result of immorality," she continued. At that moment, Neville estimated, some 2,213 Kentuckians were totally blind, which meant that 1,107 might still have sight if they could receive the proper medical treatment. Neville urged members of the club to contribute to the Mountain Fund and to the Kentucky Society for the Prevention of Blindness, an organization that was started "at the suggestion of the Russell Sage Foundation, [but is] in no way financed by [them], and is in fact, so poor that its work is sometimes 'held up' for lack of postage stamps."[47]

Neville contrasted the plight of the blind with the life of a sighted person. "A person with normal sight has no possible means of imagining what it is to be blind," she said. "If you had seen, as I have, strong men break down and cry at being told that a portion of their sight was to be restored to them, you would feel impelled, as I am, to go out and do your mite to help the thousands for whom nothing is being done." She concluded: "The suffering from blindness is something that cannot be imagined." A *Louisville Herald* reporter covering Neville's address pointed out that while the U.S. government went to great trouble to keep out immigrants already having trachoma, agencies did nothing to treat the disease in the mountain counties of Kentucky "where it has already gained a foothold." He wrote that thousands of Kentuckians in the mountains already had trachoma and that the disease was "a menace not only to the people of that section but to the entire state," because it spread so rapidly. "Are we going to wait quietly while it comes down from the mountains into the cities, destroying the sight of thousands?" the reporter asked.[48]

Neville worked closely with Barksdale Hamlett, Kentucky's superintendent of public instruction, and Cora Wilson Stewart, the president of the Kentucky Education Association (KEA). Hamlett encouraged teachers around the state to cooperate with Neville by using cards to test students for eye troubles, and Stewart organized a vision committee of the KEA with Neville as chair. Having a presence in Kentucky's schools proved to be a breakthrough, and teachers regularly referred students with eye problems to Neville for treatment.[49]

"I realize that we must conserve the eyesight of school children, that we must check Trachoma so alarmingly prevalent among the mountain counties, and recently found among the pupils in the Lexington schools," Neville appealed to the Kentucky Federation of Women's Clubs in 1912. "We must insist that midwives and physicians use preventives against *Opthalmia Neonatorum*," she told the group, "that furthermore we must exert ourselves to wipe out the potent cause of *Opthalmia*, whether of infants or others, [that] we must lay aside all reticence and must cry out against the social evil [gonorrhea]. We must teach the adults and then we must teach the children that one of the frequent consequences of sin is blindness."[50]

Linda Neville, always so wrapped up in her work, never married. That is not to say that in her younger years she went unnoticed by men as she traveled and spoke and bargained with legislators and other state and county officials. After all, she would be quite a catch. From an old and prominent family, well educated at an elite eastern women's college, pretty, socially well connected, and socially conscious, Neville represented the very best of the Bluegrass, blue-blood elite. Herbert McConathy, of the tiny community of Nebo in Hopkins County in western Kentucky, certainly recognized in Neville something very special. In a September 1913 response to Neville's earlier letter, McConathy wrote, "You speak of finding something to cheer me with here at Nebo; well, your letter was just the right thing. There is one phrase of your letter, however, which I refuse to agree to; that is, a sort of underlying idea that I went to meet you out of charity or pity or some such sentiment. 'Far be it from such.'" "I met you because I wanted to do so; it was for my own gratification," he continued. "And please allow me to say that it was abundantly worth while. . . . I had far more interest in Miss Linda Neville than in the blind children or in 'votes for women.'" The suitor concluded: "I have been a believer in equal suffrage for something over a year, and my interest in afflicted children dates back much further, but a bright, modern, cultured woman is a rare luxury in this 'neck of the woods.'" Neville could not fail to mistake the intent of the last paragraph of McConathy's letter. "This life here is rather dull for me in a social way," he wrote. "There is not one person so far as I know, in the neighborhood who really cares for art or literature. . . . I should appreciate it greatly if you would let me hear from you now and then. Yours Very Truly."[51]

Despite such overtures from "cultured," unattached men she encountered on her travels, Neville had already made the decision that she would only be married to her work. Before Neville's father died, her aunt, Caroline N. Pearre, tried to encourage her interest in the "right," eligible young men of Lexington. Neville, however, seemed only interested in Dr. W. E. B. Smith, one of her father's former students and then a classics professor at Louisiana State University. According to Aunt Caroline, Professor Smith was "a brilliant, and I believe, a high minded, honorable man and sincere friend." At the same time, she continued, "He is more than old enough to be your father. So it is that you are very fond of him."[52]

Neville and Smith corresponded regularly with each other for eight years—from 1900 to 1908—but then in that one momentous year her father died, she made her first journey to the mountains, and Smith had to cancel a trip to Lexington when he was asked to represent the United States at the Pan-American Conference in Santiago, Chile. For both of these young idealists, their vocations took them away from each other, and although they wrote sporadically and cordially over the years, Neville's only flirtation with romantic love ended with that arduous trek on a rickety wagon to Knott County in 1908.[53]

And so it was that Linda Neville continued unwaveringly to concentrate on her first love and calling: to eradicate trachoma in the mountains of eastern Kentucky. The clinics remained open, Dr. Stucky and the nurses often traveled to the mountains, and Neville maintained a hectic speaking schedule to raise money for the Mountain Fund. Eventually, eleven more permanent clinics were founded throughout Kentucky's eastern mountains. And Neville found that her personal contact with the afflicted families, and especially the children, became more and more limited. In a February 14, 1935, letter to Dr. John McMullen, Neville waxed nostalgic about those early days when she first took up the struggle, or "those old Trachoma Days," as she called them. "Those mule-back rides, those court-room clinics,—how sad I feel at the realization that all that is so far in the past," she wrote. By 1935, however, Neville had turned her energies to "a new stage in Ky. . . . And we must rush to put syphilis on our map just as trachoma was there."[54]

As Evelyn Ashley Sorrell, author of a recent master's thesis on Neville makes clear, from the 1930s forward the Kentuckian "devoted as much of her life to venereal disease as she had trachoma and became obsessed with stopping its spread." Of course, Neville's work to combat "baby's sore eyes," a condition at birth passed on to the newborn from a mother infected by venereal disease from the father, had begun in 1908, almost as early as her trachoma work. As the decades passed, and after thousands of trachoma cases had been treated, Neville realized that the more pressing threat to clear sight came more from venereal disease than trachoma, so she increasingly turned her attention to "social diseases," though her trachoma work continued as well. Neville launched her "new crusade" primarily because of the "innocent victims" affected. Children always came first with her.[55]

According to Sorrell, Neville's upper-middle-class views and Victorian upbringing kept her from understanding completely the "working-class culture of women who freely mingled in gender-integrated places, such as factories, carnivals, and dance halls." Thus she "blamed the 1930s and 1940s outbreak of venereal disease on soldiers who were intimate with prostitutes while serving in World War I and World War II." For Neville, the only victims were the innocent children; she believed the "women were just as responsible for contracting these diseases, as were the husbands who brought them home after visiting prostitutes."[56]

Interestingly, the fathers, the individuals who infected the mothers and thus the children, "are missing from Neville's case files and from medical literature addressing the infected newborns." Clearly, Neville blamed the poor mountain women. As Sorrell puts it, "mothers shouldered the blame for becoming infected, becoming pregnant while infected, and giving birth to a child who inherited that infection." For Neville and other reformers, there were "bad" mothers and "good" mothers. "Bad" mothers allowed such a thing to happen, while seemingly "helpless" fathers stood by or more often were absent "throughout the course of conception, infection, pregnancy, and birth." Venereal disease became increasingly "a woman's problem."[57]

In *"Bad" Mothers: The Politics of Blame in Twentieth-Century America*, Molly Ladd-Taylor and Lauri Umansky argue that "mother-blaming" grew during the Progressive Era. Childbearing experts and middle-class women promoted a social reform movement historians call maternalism. These maternalists "used the concept of 'good' mothers, or those who had middleclass sensibilities and values." According to Ladd-Taylor and Umansky, maternalists became more critical of mothers whom they deemed "bad" because of "their class status or ethnicity." With her Victorian sensibilities, Neville's forthrightness in addressing the tragedy of venereal disease—in the 1920s she initiated a campaign for "premarital venereal disease testing"—is indicative of her determination to protect Kentucky's children at all costs.[58]

The 1920s and the 1930s proved to be years of great change and tragedy for Linda Neville, but not in the way of economic upheaval suffered by so many others of her era. Not only did she redirect her focus in her battle against blindness from trachoma to venereal disease, but she also shifted her reform work in other areas. Never, however, did Neville cease working. Indeed, her reform activities continued deep into the 1950s, until she could literally work no more because of declining health.[59]

In 1924 Neville resigned from a position in the Red Cross. The Kentuckian always had been in control, so it was natural that she had chafed in a situation where she had been controlled by others, in this case, the national leaders of the Red Cross. Likewise, in that same year, she resigned from the Kentucky Welfare Commission in order to accept an appointment from Governor William J. Fields to the State Board of Charities and Corrections. In making the appointment, Fields noted that Neville was "well known to the citizens of our state thru many splendid achievements." She had "devoted her life to the betterment of the conditions of the state's unfortunates."[60]

Neville's work on the State Board of Charities and Corrections surely would have overwhelmed a weaker, less experienced reformer. The board oversaw the Eastern State, Central State, and Western State mental hospitals; the State Reformatory and Penitentiary; the Houses of Reform; the State School for Girls; and what was called at that time the "Feeble-Minded Institute" in Frankfort. Neville embraced the work with her usual zeal. She toured facilities and demanded to see abused patients. In one instance she noticed that young boys at the Houses of Reform were not furnished with teaspoons at mealtime. On April 1, 1927, M. F. Conley, the commissioner of public institutions, wrote to Neville, assuring her that he had noted her complaint that the boys were "fishing bread out of their milk with a fork." The commissioner wanted Neville to know that he had taken the matter up with Dr. E. C. Hardin, the superintendent of the Houses of Reform. Superintendent Hardin explained that a former superintendent had taken spoons away so that the boys could not commit that breach of table etiquette of "crumbling bread into their milk." "Personally I believe," Hardin said, "that any adult who would deprive a boy of the pleasure of crumbling bread in milk should be prosecuted for cruelty." Hardin ended the cruelty and brought back the spoons.[61]

As Neville threw herself into her work more furiously than ever, she found that her closest coworkers were no longer there by her side for comfort and support. Her sister Mary died in 1931, and her first and most dependable oculist from "those old trachoma days," Dr. J. A. Stucky, was killed in an automobile accident that same year. Dr. J. N. McCormack, another supporter through the Kentucky Society for the Prevention of Blindness, died two years later, and Katherine Pettit, the first friend from the Hindman Settlement School who had made her aware of the great need, died in 1936. Neville worked on alone, passing from middle age into her twilight years.

A certain humility missing in the heady days of her youth now characterized her personality. As early as 1928, when a reporter sought out an interview, Neville responded that while she was honored to be asked, "for some years I have believed that I was no longer a matter of news." "When the things we were doing were actually novel [in the early days of our work] I even sought publicity," she explained. Now, she said, "I am personally of little interest even to my own neighbors. I am bent and gray and from long years of serious effort and too little play I have become, it seems to me, singularly unvivacious, singularly uninteresting as a personality." She suggested the writer interview Mary Breckinridge, the founder of the Frontier Nursing Service, instead.[62]

It seemed that Neville's humility grew despite prestigious awards lavished on her. In 1934 she became the first woman to receive the Lexington Optimist Club Trophy. Commonwealth's Attorney James Park, in presenting the award, commented that Neville had not made "any material contribution to the community." Instead, the award was for her "great spiritual contribution. Modest, unassuming and untiring, she has done noble things which richly deserve this recognition." In response, Neville said, "Man has missed the greatest pleasure if he works for self; he must not play to the galleries, and the ears that strain after the sound of applause will not hear the call of the distressed." Yet again, she repeated her father's words: "If a man work for himself, the fruit of his work, like Dead Sea apples, will turn to ashes upon his lips."[63]

A decade later, the Saint Louis Society for the Blind awarded Neville its Dana Medal "in recognition of her long meritorious service in the conservation of vision and in the prevention and care of diseases dangerous to eyesight." The presenter referred to Neville as an "angel of mercy," one who had worked for half a century for the blind in Kentucky. Newspapers in Saint Louis and Lexington called her "The Angel of Kentucky" and praised her work against trachoma and then against the threat to eyesight caused by venereal disease.[64]

Neville could not rest on her laurels, however. Her work was far from over. She had loved and healed the multitudes. Early in 1936 she had encountered a suffering infant "who would change the course of the rest of her life." The boy's mother died two days after giving birth, and when he was four days old, his father abandoned him forever. Neville would describe the boy named David as "homeless, motherless, fatherless, and blind." With her sister Mary and her closest friends gone, the child left completely abandoned, an operation to restore David's sight unsuccessful, Neville labored over what to do for him. Feeling, no doubt, a strong sense of a reformer's "maternalism," discussed by Ladd-Taylor and Umansky, and with her Victorian, upper-middle-class "good" mother sympathies coupled with decades of close regard for suffering babies just like David, Neville wrote her close friend Lucy Furman, "Tears are pouring down my cheeks now as I try to tell you." And then, "I have reasoned that thenceforward David's life will be intimately a part of mine, that my eyes must see for him."[65]

So Linda Neville, a sixty-three-year-old single woman, adopted David Devary into her family and home. Although he brought great joy to Neville's old age, he also brought many challenges. What Neville, the reformer, had seen among the multitudes for half a century was quite different from what "Mama Linda," the mother, experienced on a personal level each day. She sent David to the Arthur Sunshine School in New Jersey for a time, but when it closed, her son returned to Lexington. At home, he became a skilled pianist, but Mama Linda's micromanaging techniques did not work as well in parenting as they had seemed to work with the Mountain Fund. For example, David did not realize he was blind until at twelve years of age he overheard his mother mention the fact in a telephone conversation. His resentment mounted until Neville sent David at fourteen to the Kentucky School for the Blind, where the difficulties he had in adjusting to his new surroundings were understandable.[66]

Neville had envisioned a future for David where he would continue her crusading work after she was gone. She endeavored to prepare him for such work in the time she had him at home. She felt that the same determined techniques she had employed in her crusade against blindness would work in her education of David as well. They did not. David continued to have "emotional upsets" throughout the years he spent at the Kentucky School for the Blind. When at home, Neville spoiled him, dressed him in Victorian-era clothes, and carried with her an unrealistic ideal of David's future that proved injurious to him. Late in the 1950s, Neville, already unable to work productively, broke her hip and was forced to enter a Lexington nursing home. She died there on June 2, 1961. After his mother's death, David moved to a nursing home in Louisville.[67]

Linda Neville lived a life of great accomplishment. Because of her work, doctors and nurses labored in remote clinics to treat tens of thousands suffering from the eye disease of trachoma. She helped untold numbers of her fellow

Kentuckians through her direct work and the passage of legislation mandating premarital testing of couples for venereal disease. Most of all, as the nameless child had addressed his letter, she became simply "the lady who helps blind children see."

NOTES

1. The boy's letter has been perused by more than one historian in the Linda Neville Papers, Special Collections and Archives, University of Kentucky Libraries, Lexington (hereafter LNP).

2. Neville's reform work continued unabated until the 1950s, providing an example for Robyn Muncy's argument that progressivism, rather than being killed off by the Roaring Twenties, persisted for decades. See Robyn Muncy, *Creating a Female Dominion in American Reform, 1895–1935* (New York: Oxford University Press, 1991), xiv, as cited in Evelyn Ashley Sorrell, "'Obtuse Women': Venereal Disease Control Policies and Maintaining a 'Fit' Nation, 1920–1945" (Master's thesis, University of Kentucky, 2011), 11.

3. Quoted in D. Anthony Smith and Arthur H. Keeney, "Linda Neville (1873–1961): Kentucky Pioneer against Blindness," *Filson Club History Quarterly* 64 (1990): 361.

4. Susie M. Wilson, "I Won't," box 1, folder 10, LNP.

5. See William E. Ellis, *A History of Education in Kentucky* (Lexington: University Press of Kentucky, 2011), 121.

6. Judy Gail Cornett, "Angel for the Blind: The Public Triumphs and Private Tragedy of Linda Neville" (Ph.D. diss., University of Kentucky, 1993), 17. See also Barbara Welter, "The Cult of True Womanhood: 1820–1860," *American Quarterly* 18 (Summer 1966): 151–74.

7. Quoted in Cornett, "Angel for the Blind," 15, 16.

8. Smith and Keeney, "Linda Neville," 361; Cornett, "Angel for the Blind," 19, 20.

9. Quoted in Cornett, "Angel for the Blind," 23.

10. Ibid., 24, 25.

11. Ibid., 25.

12. Ibid., 26.

13. Ibid.

14. Melba Porter Hay, *Madeline McDowell Breckinridge and the Battle for a New South* (Lexington: University Press of Kentucky, 2009), 58.

15. Cornett, "Angel for the Blind," 34–36.

16. *Lexington (Ky.) Morning Herald*, December 25, 1903, in box 57, folder 2, LNP.

17. Ibid. As the reader will see, Neville suffered much when she adopted David Devary, a blind child, a few days after he was born. David was later institutionalized. The Gilman poem must have comforted Neville, especially toward the end of her life.

18. Neville Journal, box 1, folder 1, LNP (hereafter cited as Neville Journal).

19. Ibid.; http://www.hindmansettlement.org/about-us (accessed February 1, 2013).

20. Neville Journal.

21. Ibid.

22. Ibid.

23. Centers for Disease Control and Prevention, "Hygiene-Related Diseases," "Trachoma," http://www.cdc.gov/healthywater/hygiene/disease/trachoma.html (accessed February 9, 2013).

24. Neville Journal.

25. Ibid.

26. Ibid.

27. Ibid.

28. Ibid. Neville learned very quickly that "sore eyes" was the result of gonorrhea, passed down to the child from a mother who had been infected by the father. If treated immediately, the child could be saved from blindness.

29. For critics of the L&N, see Maury Klein, *History of the Louisville and Nashville Railroad* (Lexington: University Press of Kentucky, 2003), esp. chap. 17; Neville Journal.

30. Neville Journal.

31. Ibid.

32. Ibid.

33. Ibid.

34. Ibid.

35. Linda Neville to L. D. Lewis, January 28, 1911, box 58, folder 1, LNP.

36. "Bulletin No. 6 of the Kentucky Society for the Prevention of Blindness," box 58, folder 1, LNP.

37. Neville Journal.

38. Ibid.

39. Ibid.

40. Ibid.

41. Ibid.

42. Ibid.

43. Cornett, "Angel for the Blind," 76.

44. Ibid.

45. Neville Journal.

46. Ibid.

47. "Aid in Fight on Blindness Asked," *Louisville Herald*, March 6, 1913.

48. Ibid.

49. Neville Journal.

50. Ibid.

51. Herbert McConathy to Linda Neville, September 20, 1913, box 59, folder 7, LNP.

52. Caroline N. Pearre to Linda Neville, May 25, 1909, as quoted in Cornett, "Angel for the Blind," 30.

53. Ibid.

54. Linda Neville to John McMullen, February 14, 1935, as quoted in Sorrell, "'Obtuse Women,'" 12.

55. Sorrell, "'Obtuse Women,'" 12, 13.

56. See Joan Jacobs Brumberg, *The Body Project: An Intimate History of American Girls* (New York: Random House, 1997); Kathy Peiss, "'Charity Girls' and City Pleasures: Historical Notes on Working Class Sexuality, 1880–1920," in *Passion and Power: Sexuality in History*, ed. Kathy Peiss and Christina Simmons (Philadelphia: Temple University Press, 1989); both sources cited in Sorrell, "'Obtuse Women,'" 13, 14.

57. See Molly Ladd-Taylor and Lauri Umansky, eds., *"Bad" Mothers: The Politics of Blame in Twentieth-Century America* (New York: New York University Press, 1998); Sorrell, "'Obtuse Women,'" 33.

58. Sorrell, "'Obtuse Women,'" 33; Cornett, "Angel for the Blind," 163.

59. See Muncy, *Creating a Female Dominion*, xiv; Sorrell, "'Obtuse Women," 11.

60. Cornett, "Angel for the Blind," 163, 164.

61. Ibid., 164, 165; M. F. Conley to Linda Neville, April 1, 1927, box 71, folder 20, LNP.

62. Cornett, "Angel for the Blind,"169.

63. Ibid., 173.

64. Ibid.

65. Ibid., 180, 181. See Ladd-Taylor and Umansky, *"Bad" Mothers*, cited in Sorrell, "'Obtuse Women,'" 33.

66. Cornett, "Angel for the Blind," 209.

67. Ibid., 210.

Elizabeth "Lizzie" Fouse

(1875–1952)

Challenging Stereotypes and Building Community

KAREN COTTON MCDANIEL

On Saturday morning, April 5, 1925, following Gertrude Boulder's funeral, Mayor Hogan L. Yancey, Commissioner of Public Safety J. Morgan Gentry, and Acting Chief of Police Ernest Thompson were each presented with a signed petition from a delegation of Lexington's black women. In the petition the women extolled Gertrude Boulder as a "highly respectable member of the Evergreen Baptist Church, a member of the Y.W.C.A., active in the Woman's Council, community service and several fraternal organizations." The signed supplication further expressed the concern and disappointment of Lexington's best Negro women who "wish here to enter our protest, disgust and indignation against such treatment toward our law abiding citizens." The entreaty also sought an investigation into Boulder's death, chastised the police, and requested an amendment to local laws "so that the respectable women of our race would not have to die in a cell in the police station if found in an unconscious state on the street." After a full description of Boulder's appearance, conduct, and attire, the petitioners presented a scenario that the police should have followed to assist Boulder. Finally, the activists offered police their assistance in preventing similar incidents with black citizens in the future. At the top of the list of petition signers was the name of the woman who publicized and organized the protest: Mrs. L. B. Fouse.[1]

Elizabeth Beatrice Cook Fouse (1875–1952) serves as the quintessential example of black women's leadership in community-building endeavors in Kentucky during the early twentieth century. Her life provides an opportunity to explore the agency of an urban black woman in the Upper South, in a border state that initially rejected the Thirteenth Amendment and did not ratify it until 1976. As part of a southern society guided by white male privilege, Kentucky proved itself a difficult and often cruel place for black women. Elizabeth "Lizzie" Fouse defined herself and her life's work in this context. Her activism following the death of Gertrude Boulder reveals her organizational skill and fortitude in the face of Lexington's degradation of black women. Fouse not only raised the consciousness level of Lexington's black citizenry through her contestation for social justice, but she also helped bring about changes in the city police department's treatment of prisoners.

On March 31, 1925, Gertrude Boulder was found on a downtown Lexington street unconscious and unable to speak. The local police arrested her, charged her with drunkenness, and placed her in a jail cell. Although she appeared to be ill, the police neglected to seek medical attention for Boulder, who died as a result of their failure to administer care to a sick prisoner. What in Lexington's racial climate supported the untimely demise of Gertrude Boulder, a respectable citizen and devoted Christian who, it was later determined, suffered from a severe gastrointestinal condition?[2]

At the turn of the century, in spite of limited state segregation laws compared with those in many southern states, racial segregation existed throughout Kentucky. African Americans in the commonwealth had been enfranchised since the passage of the Fifteenth Amendment and were allowed to vote in most cities and towns without restrictions. However, in 1870 Lexington changed the date for the citywide election of offices to February, one month prior to the date the amendment became effective, thereby preventing blacks from voting in the first year of their eligibility.[3] In 1871 black Kentuckians were granted the right to testify against white people in trials and in 1882 the right to serve on juries.[4] Between 1890 and 1910 legislators deemed it necessary to pass laws to ensure that blacks remain "in their place." Legislation supported segregating people on interstate railroads and prevented racial integration in private as well as public institutions. Additionally, theaters, parks, libraries, welfare institutions, hospitals, restaurants, and many work sites remained segregated statewide.[5]

Census data verifies that the city of Lexington had the second-largest black population in Kentucky during the early years of the twentieth century. The largest concentration of African Americans in the state resided in central Kentucky in the counties surrounding Fayette, where Lexington was the county seat.[6] Like the rest of the state, black life in Lexington during the period 1890 through 1930 was characterized by Jim Crow indicators of racial segregation.

ELIZABETH FOUSE

"First Ladies of Colored America," *The Crisis*, October 1942.

However, the large percentage of African Americans in and around Lexington may have accounted for the more "fluid racial patterns" in the city.[7] In Lexington integration could be found in some restaurants, parks, theaters, and other amusement areas. But most accommodations were via Jim Crow sections, separate entrances, or other demeaning spatial arrangements. Historian George Wright attributes Lexington's fluid integration patterns to economic necessity. Businesses allowed African Americans service in these arenas due to the size of the black population and the financial resources they represented.[8]

Lexington's blacks were prohibited, however, from public libraries, hospitals, and other facilities. Both the local newspapers, the *Lexington Herald* and the *Lexington Leader*, provided a separate space titled "Colored Notes" for news from the black community. This column was always located in the back sections of both papers, sometimes among the classified ads. Housing patterns in Lexington indicate black neighborhoods in the city's east side and black hamlets (Davistown, Cadentown, Bracktown, Pricetown) surrounding the city. Within the city limits, some African Americans also lived on the same streets as European Americans.[9]

Lexington blacks were rarely appointed to local boards designed to remedy problems in the black community. Failure of the white community's leaders to work with blacks in stopping the spread of vice and crime in the black community led blacks to establish the Good Citizens League in 1905. The Colored Citizens Protective League of Lexington, which had been formed in the 1880s, also served to advocate social change, promote education reform, and fight for political and civil rights. Although Lexington had numerous black professionals and several businesses, the majority of black employment was in service to whites. These positions also provided the lowest wages. Blacks found employment in other occupations but in limited numbers. Unlike in most southern cities, several black individuals were employed as clerks in department stores.[10]

In Lexington racial relations were not as strained as in many rural areas, but racially motivated violence and brutality did occur in the city as well as in surrounding communities. African Americans who forgot "their place" were beaten, tortured, and/or lynched. From 1890 through 1940, 106 persons were lynched within fifty miles of Lexington.[11] The Ku Klux Klan was responsible for much of the racially motivated terrorism. But this violence also included local police brutality and other harsh conduct sanctioned by the authorities. The predominant police opinion defined all blacks as criminals with the exception of a few good "colored" citizens.[12]

Under these circumstances and amidst prevailing racist attitudes, black persons in the most innocent situations often suffered tragic and untimely deaths.

Such was the case of Gertrude Boulder, who became ill en route to her home in Lexington on March 31, 1925. Originally from Ohio, Boulder and her husband Bernard lived at 160 East 7th Street. They had paid off the debt for their house through their earnings; Bernard was a tinner in a local tin shop, and Gertrude worked as a private maid for a white family, who "spoke very highly of her services."[13] Gertrude, who was "subject to serious sick spells at times," had begun to feel ill at work on that March day and left early to go home.[14] She had refused her employers' offer to send her home in a taxicab.[15] Around 10:30 that evening Patrolman James Dunn found Boulder lying on Market Street near the intersection of Short Street in downtown Lexington.[16] Although there were "no signs of intoxication . . . no disorderly conduct, no scars to indicate quarrel, coupled with the fact that she was neatly dressed," the police assumed her unconscious state was the result of drunkenness and incarcerated her.[17] Considering police indifference to blacks' humanity and their well-being, it is not surprising that Gertrude Boulder was denied medical assistance and subsequently died in her jail cell. In Boulder's case, racial prejudice motivated white police officers to ignore her medical needs, and she died unnecessarily after "suffering from a severe attack of indigestion."[18]

But police indifference to ill black prisoners—illuminated by Boulder's death—would not be accepted by Lexington's black citizens. Elizabeth Fouse, a petite woman known as "Lizzie," stepped forward assuming a publicly confrontational posture and directly challenged the white power structure. At the time of the incident, Fouse served as the chair of the City Federation of Women's Clubs, through which she led an organized protest against the police department and called for an investigation into Boulder's death. Who was Lizzie Fouse that she could challenge the white establishment? Why would Fouse risk her livelihood and possibly her life to stand up for Gertrude Boulder? Fouse's personal friendships, community interactions, and civil rights' initiatives serve to reveal the values that structured her life, defined her character, and mandated her militant stance in the Gertrude Boulder incident.

Historian Darlene Clark Hine maintains that black women such as Lizzie Fouse played a significant role in establishing the local black communal infrastructures, the "religious, educational, health care, philanthropic, political, familial institutions and professional organizations that enabled our people to survive." Hine labels the process of building and shaping the black neighborhoods as "making community."[19]

Such community was built, in part, by black club women. Seeking a more public forum for their local social reform concerns, black women in 1896 established a national body, the National Association of Colored Women (NACW), to coordinate all local efforts nationwide. The national body encouraged all black women's groups to participate and did not look down on working-class women's efforts. The structure of the NACW did not call for a standardized social welfare program, although many common interests emerged, including concerns about the image of black women in the United States. In fact, the initial meeting that led to the formation of the NACW came about in response to a letter that had insulted black women.[20] On March 19, 1895, John W. Jacks, president of the Missouri Press Association, had sent a letter to Florence Balgarnie, honorable secretary of the Anti-Lynching Committee in London, England, in which he alleged that blacks were "wholly devoid of morality" and explicitly that black women "were prostitutes and all are natural liars and thieves." In response, Josephine St. Pierre Ruffin of the Woman's Era Club of Boston sent letters to black women across the country, along with a copy of Jacks's letter, encouraging them to recognize "the need of our banding together if only for our protection." While Jacks's attack may have been aimed at journalist and antilynching activist Ida B. Wells specifically, black women nationwide were outraged and felt compelled to address the letter's contents.[21] The women's meeting became known as the First National Conference of the Colored Women in America. Resolutions were adopted that denounced Jacks's letter and praised Wells for her work in spreading the truth about lynching to the world. Jacks's letter received little additional consideration at the meeting, although it served as the catalyst for mobilizing the nation's black women. The merging of the National Federation of Afro-American Women and the National League of Colored Women into the National Association of Colored Women allowed coordinated efforts in the quest for racial uplift.[22]

These club women were encouraged to maintain strong ties with the black church. It was through their church roles that Lizzie Fouse and other black women acquired their leadership, financial planning, and organizational skills. Historian Evelyn Brooks Higginbotham asserts that from 1880 to 1920 the church was "the most powerful institution of racial self-help in the African American community."[23] Tera Hunter indeed validates the church conventions' role in promoting the "leadership development, skills in governance, and religious education, and also applauding the most dedicated religious converts."[24] These opportunities placed women in roles that served to increase their self-esteem, promote racial identities, and define themselves as persons worthy of respect and emulation within the greater society. Likewise, the charitable activities of black women throughout Kentucky served to develop their black community's infrastructure. George Wright's studies of Kentucky reveal that similar benevolent clubs and societies emerged in cities such as Lexington and Louisville, among others.[25]

Lexington's black women were involved in numerous philanthropic activities.[26] In 1903 the Kentucky Association of Colored Women (KACW) was organized through the national body incorporating thirteen existing local clubs into the nationwide community building effort. The motto of the statewide association was "Looking upward, not downward; Outward not inward; Forward, not backward."[27] This defined goal fit the social reform model of improving the welfare of those who were, for whatever reason, in a less than desirable station in life. The emphasis on upward implies racial uplift, a self-help concept that sought to improve and refurbish the black image through moral and material improvements that often mirrored the larger society's definition of respectability and refinement.[28] The group's refusal to look downward recognizes that reform women were neither to pass judgment nor to look down on those they sought to assist. By looking outward they made a commitment to helping others instead of focusing on self-centered goals and programs. Recognizing that the final outcome of their uplift efforts was to move the masses into a new way of life through their programs, KACW members sought to forget the past and maintain focus on the race's future. The programs of KACW would incorporate aspirations for educational attainment, the adoption of Victorian ethics and behavior, and the maintenance of stable homes and families. Some Kentucky club members were actively involved in the national organization, holding prominent positions there. Lexington's Lizzie Fouse played a leadership role in both the state and the national women's club movements. Although she lived and worked in Corydon, Indiana, at the time the KACW was organized, Fouse attended the Louisville meeting at the Plymouth Congregational Church and gave remarks to the body assembled.[29]

She was born Elizabeth Beatrice Cook in Lancaster, Kentucky, the only child of William and Mary (Kennedy) Cook.[30] Lizzie's upbringing included the religious indoctrination of the Baptist Church, attending both Louisville's State University and Eckstein-Norton University in Cane Springs, Kentucky.[31] On August 10, 1898, Lizzie married William Henry Fouse (1868–1939) of Westerville, Ohio. At the time, she was employed as a teacher at the Constitution School in the Lexington colored school system.[32] Because Fouse was Methodist and Lizzie was a member of the Baptist Church, it is unlikely that they met in church. They most likely met through friends or at a teachers' convention, since William Fouse was also a teacher and had taught in the Colored High School in Corydon, Indiana, since 1893. Lizzie joined him as a teacher in that school system until 1904, when William was appointed principal of the Lincoln High School in Gallipolis, Ohio. Although she was an educator by profession, holding a lifetime membership in the American Teachers Association, Lizzie quit teaching that year.[33] When the Fouses moved to Covington, Kentucky, in 1908, so that William could assume the position of principal at William Grant High School, Lizzie could not have returned to teaching because Kentucky Revised Statute 161.1600 prohibited married women from teaching school.

Free from the constraints of teaching, Lizzie Fouse focused her attention on the problems of the black community. She became involved with the black women's clubs in Covington, joining both the Ladies Improvement and the Ladies Union clubs during her residence in that community. Prior to returning to Lexington, she was elected to serve as the president of the KACW. In 1913 William and Lizzie Fouse moved to Lexington where William would become the supervisor of Lexington's colored schools, a highly respected and important position in the black community.[34]

When Lizzie Fouse returned to Lexington she knew that she was returning to a community with a long history of black female activism, one that had met some of their community's needs since 1865 by establishing schools, supporting the poor, and caring for the aged. Having lived in this community at the beginning of her teaching career, she was probably attuned to many of the specific unfulfilled community needs. Fouse also was knowledgeable about the existence of specific benevolent and church clubs through her association with the KACW. Undoubtedly, Lexington's club women were familiar with the ideas and work of Lizzie Fouse due to her two-year term as president of the KACW in 1912–13. Women members of the First Baptist Church, which was affiliated with the General Association of Colored Baptists in Kentucky, knew Fouse from her regular attendance at the Baptist Women's Education Convention's annual meetings and similar Baptist functions. Additionally, Lizzie's mother, Mary P. Burnside, had lived in Lexington for many years and had probably discussed her daughter's career with fellow club members and church associates. Therefore, when Elizabeth Fouse returned to Lexington, her reputation as a respectable, religious, educated woman and club leader preceded her. This reputation, coupled with her husband's prestigious position in the city's black schools, predetermined a prominent position for her in Lexington's black community.

In the next twelve years Fouse worked in the secular and religious groups that had helped define her life. An active member of the First Baptist Church, Fouse's religious and personal convictions were evidenced in her lifestyle. With careful attention to their household resources, the Fouses were able to sustain a middle-class existence and permit Lizzie to engage in unpaid work through her club and church interests. She served on numerous church committees and gave generously of her time and financial means.[35] In 1920 Fouse established in Lexington the Phillis Wheatley branch of the YWCA. Motivated by a sense of racial self-definition and identification, Fouse never accepted the larger society's interpretation of a black woman's place and therefore took a leadership role in nurturing and maintaining the black community. Fouse always encouraged black women not to submit to an inferior posture, saying, "Don't look up and don't look down, look them straight in the eye."[36]

To secure liberties for African Americans and advance the race, black women recognized the need to mirror some of the attributes of the larger white society in order to gain those rights, challenge racism, and seek acceptance in mainstream culture. They believed that educational achievement, church membership, modest dress, healthy family relationships, marriage, the maintenance of proper homes, and work for worthwhile community causes were ways to achieve this acceptance. These standards were viewed as "the politics of respectability" among the women of the Baptist Church. Just as black women defined the standards for respectability, they also collectively critiqued the issues that limited progress in the black community, decided which ones to address, and determined the methods to achieve community strength and advancement.[37]

Baptist women's adoption of hegemonic values and behavior "did not constitute supine deference to white power," however. The black Baptist women's concern for proper behavior "served to reinforce their sense of moral superiority over whites." One Baptist Woman's Convention publication alleged that white behavior on streetcars was rude and reminded blacks, "Here is an opportunity for us to show our superiority. . . . Let us at all times and on all occasions, remember that the quiet, dignified individual who is respectful to others is after all the superior individual, be he black or white."[38]

Similar "racial uplift" values were generally accepted and promoted by other major black churches, including the African Methodist Episcopal (AME), the African Methodist Episcopal Zion (AMEZ), and the Christian Methodist Episcopal (CME), as well as smaller denominations. The racial uplift framework included obtaining higher education, adopting strict standards of ethical behavior, maintaining stable homes for family development, fostering the majority population's cultural ways, and becoming more charitable.[39] Through both the politics of respectability and racial uplift ideology, black women forged opportunities to control the economic growth of their community, the health of the race, the moral training of youth, and the general education of African Americans. Additionally, they exemplified the characteristics of respectability, generosity, marital devotion, and Christian living. Among these women, Lizzie Fouse was described by the *Indianapolis Freeman* in 1913 as "an excellent lady of much refinement."[40] The *KNEA Journal* wrote, "One cannot think of Prof. Fouse without the association of his fine wife," who was identified as "his constant companion."[41] Through her commitments to church values, temperance, and philanthropic works, as well as her educational attainments, modest dress, cleanliness, hard work, thrift, sexual propriety, and polished manners, Lizzie Fouse reflected both the "politics of respectability" and the "racial uplift" models.

African American women reinvented themselves through self-determination and the aid of extended families, kinship networks, and friendships whose mutually agreed-upon goals promoted the upward evolvement of the black community. They defined and transformed themselves and their communities by taking control of their working conditions, social structures, church activities, and personal spheres while attempting to uplift their entire race through benevolent programs. Darlene Clark Hine argues, "It was through 'making community' that Black women were able to redefine themselves, project sexual respectability, reshape morality, and define a new aesthetic." These ideas permeated the benevolent clubs, secret societies, and church organizations in all public and private spheres. "Uplifters" expected individuals with education, wealth, or social position to be involved in social welfare activities for the elderly, the poor, the uneducated, orphans and other children, and needy persons. The philosophies of the "politics of respectability" and "racial uplift" validated women's activist roles in the black community.[42]

However, respectable black women recognized that the dominant class in the United States viewed all African American women in terms of stereotypes, which these activists sought to challenge. Black women were viewed as sexual predators—as "immoral, insatiable, perverse; the initiators in all sexual contacts—abusive or otherwise."[43] Their bodies "epitomized centuries-long European perceptions of Africans as primitive, animal-like, and savage."[44] Perceptions of blacks as something other than human and their sexuality as different from that of whites had not only served to support slavery and sanction the sexual exploitation of black women; these notions had also created a definition of black women as carnal, savage, deviant, and promiscuous.[45] In 1902 a columnist for *The Independent*, a popular periodical, wrote, "I sometimes hear of a virtuous Negro woman but the idea is absolutely inconceivable to me. . . . I cannot imagine a creature as a virtuous Negro woman."[46] As a black woman in America, at a time when black women's virtue was widely contested, Fouse epitomized the "politics of respectability" model through her self-help, social reform, and behavioral choices. Her actions in response to Gertrude Boulder's death in 1925 confronted the stereotypes of African American women that had driven Lexington police to treat Boulder as they did. Fouse may also have understood the political nature of the event.

Fouse encouraged black women to work for political causes and political education, becoming involved herself in the Colored Women Voters League.

Early in 1919 the Lexington branch of the NAACP was established with one hundred charter members including Fouse and her husband. Of the group of forty women and sixty men, Lizzie Fouse was elected as the secretary.[47] Many of her organizational commitments were with interracial groups: the United Council of Church Women, the Southern Regional Council, and the YWCA. Participation in these groups provided opportunities for whites to interact with and recognize firsthand the commitment, dedication, and value of Lizzie Fouse to her community. Fouse persuaded local white leaders to assist in funding the Colored Day Nursery and the Phillis Wheatley YWCA through the Community Chest. Through her membership in the NACW and the NAACP, Fouse kept abreast of political and social movements, including the antilynching campaign. In 1918 Missouri congressman Leonidas Dyer proposed an antilynching bill that received Republican Party support during their 1920 national convention. In January 1922 the Dyer Anti-Lynching Bill was passed in the U.S. House of Representatives. Lizzie Fouse was a charter member of the Anti-Lynching Crusaders, an organization of women that raised money to support the Dyer bill. Its goal was to get one million women to support their cause. Fouse served as the Kentucky director of the organization, which began with sixteen members when it was established in 1922.[48]

Because of Jim Crow policies, most blacks, regardless of socioeconomic station, were confined to certain communities in Lexington. The Fouses lived at 219 North Upper Street and were very much ingrained in the black community. The close proximity of middle-class blacks such as the Fouses and working-class blacks provided opportunities for interaction and for Lizzie Fouse to better understand the plight of working people of different socioeconomic conditions than her own. When she was growing up Lizzie's father and stepfather were painters, while her mother was a dressmaker. Further, the national club ideology stressed the need for club leaders to be inclusive of working-class black women among their local clubs and state organizations, and the KACW membership complied. Within her own household, Lizzie was in daily contact with the working-class people who rented rooms from the Fouses. Over the years among their boarders were a tailor, a truck driver, and a waiter.[49]

In the Fouse family scrapbook, a note in Lizzie's handwriting reads: "Whoever engages in that which contributes to the welfare of society is engaged in business."[50] This note further articulates Fouse's understanding of her role in the community. She served as a catalyst for social and political change by mobilizing black women. Her most important actions in the community were those occasions when she risked her personal livelihood to publicly confront the white power structure and assert her claim for equitable rights and treatment for all citizens, especially those of color. Among her roles as a race woman was serving as an agent for change through the direct contestation of sexist attitudes and discriminatory racist policies that limited black people, especially black women. Gertrude Boulder could not have found a more highly respected and politically sagacious person than Lizzie Fouse to vindicate her ill-fated death.

The basic circumstances of Boulder's death were revealed in an article in the *Lexington Leader*, Lexington's evening newspaper, on April 1, 1925. The following day in the *Leader*'s "Colored Notes" column appeared a notice from L. B. Fouse, chairman of the City Federation of Women's Clubs, calling a meeting "to consider a very important matter relative to the death of Mrs. Gertie Boulder." The notice also requested "civic and charity organizations" to send a representative to the scheduled meeting. A similar message from Fouse appeared in the "Colored Notes" in the next morning's edition of the *Lexington Herald*, but Boulder's name was not mentioned. In the *Herald* notice "members of the city federation of women's clubs and other civic and charity organizations" were merely invited "to consider a very important matter."[51]

The meeting took place at the Phillis Wheatley YWCA on Friday night at eight o'clock, just hours after the Boulder funeral, which had begun at one o'clock that afternoon. In addition to Boulder's husband, two aunts, and other family members from Ohio and Kentucky, the funeral was likely attended by many local club women as well as lodge members of the Queen Victoria Court of Calanthe.[52] A few hours following what was doubtless an emotionally charged funeral service for their friend, neighbor, and relative—who had suffered a lonely, bitter death at the hands of racism—approximately a hundred black women met to discuss appropriate action in response to the injustice. They must have decided that an investigation into Boulder's death was warranted.

In response to Lizzie Fouse's appeal, more than eighty black female civic and club leaders and their representatives signed the petition that was printed in both Lexington newspapers. Following the name of each signer was the name of the organization that she represented along with the number of members. The first name on the letter was "Mrs. L. B. Fouse, City Federation, 40 clubs." The total number of members listed in these organizations surpassed nine hundred, in addition to the forty clubs that Lizzie Fouse's signature represented. The forty clubs of the City Federation included at least four hundred additional black women, since most clubs had a minimum of ten members. However, the actual number of persons represented on the petition is unknown, because many of these women were involved in more than one club.[53] The representation was varied and included civic organizations, religious clubs, parent-teacher organizations, secret societies, and social groups. All signatures on the petition were those of women, many of whom were like Gertrude Boulder—property owners, church members, club women, lodge members, married women—civic-minded black women trying to survive in a segregated world that often diminished their worth.

To the white establishment an organized protest from more than thirteen hundred law-abiding black women, bold enough to sign their names publicly protesting the actions of Lexington's police officers, must have been alarming. It was not a normal occurrence for the community's black women to take such a publicly militant stance challenging white authorities. These women were not simply confrontational but politically empowered; they now had the right to vote. Included in the petition was mention of Boulder's work at the polls during the previous year, which placed their concerns in a political context. Boulder, like most blacks in the city, was probably not known among whites other than her employers, and it is unlikely that she was a specific target of official neglect but rather suffered because of the preconceived notions of black women held by the city's law enforcement officers. The petition's specific reference to Boulder's political activities served to remind the elected officials who received those complaints that Boulder's colleagues were politically active as well. The recipients could neither ignore nor discount the issues presented by such a large number of voters.

Within a few days of the petition's appearance in the local papers, the activists received support from others in the community, including voices in the white community. Although some of Lexington's leading white establishments often supported black causes, they were particular about the efforts they chose to endorse. Both of Lexington's white newspapers supported the call for an inquiry into the death of Gertrude Boulder. On April 6 the editors of the *Lexington Leader* validated the Fouse group's grievance, calling it "a very proper request from leading Negro women" and asking that the investigation be "thoro [*sic*] and conclusive, this not only in justice to the dead woman, but to the end that such an occurrence may never again be repeated." The *Lexington Leader* editors also criticized the police for failing to follow commonly humane practices and laws "regardless of race, sex or station in life." *Lexington Herald* management complimented the women on their communication, which they concluded was "in spirit and in terms exceedingly restrained and in view of the facts stated most moderate." They agreed that an investigation should be forthcoming and that it "should be most rigorous and the full facts ascertained." Acting Police Chief Thompson and members of the police force also submitted a letter to the board of commissioners relinquishing their legal rights to notice and requesting a "public investigation of the recent death of Gertrude Boulder."[54]

The mayor agreed to an immediate public investigation scheduled for April 9 at 2:00 p.m. in the City Commissioners' Chambers of City Hall. City officials, the press, petitioners, and other black citizens attended the public examination of the circumstances surrounding Boulder's incarceration and subsequent death in the city jail. Testimony was heard from a number of police officers, medical personnel, and a black woman who served meals to the prisoners. At the conclusion of the inquiry, Mayor Yancey and the city commissioners issued an official report including a public acknowledgment that Gertrude Boulder was a person of "unimpeachable character thoroughly interested in the welfare of her community and her people, that she was a worker in all public drives for the benefit of the city, and contributed to all just causes both of her time and money." They concluded the report by calling Gertrude Boulder one of Lexington's "leading colored citizens" and extending their sympathy to the Boulder family. Additionally, the city introduced a policy change for handling prisoners perceived to be ill. This included calling physicians and providing treatment at hospitals.[55]

Why would so many black women stand up for this cause? At the turn of the twentieth century, black America—whose women had been raped as an acceptable and profitable practice during slavery—was castigated as immoral and unworthy of the rights allowed full citizens. Slanderous stereotypical images of immoral women led to judgments about the entire race, prompting middle-class black women to build and sustain the "politics of respectability" and racial uplift ideology. As Mary Church Terrell, the first president of the NACW, stated, "The world will always judge the womanhood of the race." Consequently, the fates of all black women from all socioeconomic classes were intertwined, thus requiring cooperative efforts from all to erase negative stereotypes. This idea was articulated in the NACW constitution's goals of "hoping to furnish evidence of moral, mental, and material progress . . . [and] to secure moral and civic harmony of action and co-operation among all women in raising to the highest plane home, moral and civil life."[56] Lizzie Fouse had worked for this progress.

In addition to her work with the KACW, Fouse was actively engaged in the work of the NACW serving in various years as the chair of the Scholarship Loan Board, statistician, chair of the Mother, Home and Child Department, and the organization's corresponding secretary. Many of Fouse's friends and followers were members of the KACW- and NACW-affiliated groups, which supported and valued black women's personal reputations and civil rights among their causes. Thus the white interpretation of Gertrude Boulder's morals and character in 1925 would inadvertently reflect on all of Lexington's black women. Lexington's club women had to correct the printed record regarding Gertrude Boulder in defense of their own reputations and so that all black women would not be viewed in the same light.[57] They had worked toward this goal for nearly thirty years.

Female solidarity in this situation also emanated from the long-standing relationships through kinship/friendship networks. These networks based on personal associations within the black community extended through family and friends and other communal associations. The process of "making community" brought together those who shared common goals to gain control over their own lives and communities. Black women learned that by pooling their physical energies and fiscal resources, they had increased power and could accomplish much more as a collective body than they could as individuals. This included the contestation of unequal treatment and facilities, where black women found themselves victimized by Jim Crow politics.[58]

Lexington's black women had a vested interest in redeeming Gertrude Boulder's reputation and disputing the persistent stereotypical opinion that most whites held of black women. Boulder represented them as morally principled, community-minded women, and to them she represented all black womanhood. Collective identity of black women with Boulder and the realization that the white authorities, if left unchallenged, could treat them in the same disrespectful manner, mandated that they contest the officials' actions. Allowing police officials to disrespect one of the community's honorable black women would serve to devalue the life of all its black women. Mobilized politically, recognizing their shared needs, limited resources, and alternatives, black women united in the struggle for social equality in a city whose police officers were determined to exclude, demean, exploit, or ignore them. In the process, Fouse and her followers were making community through political intervention tactics to eliminate the standards of Jim Crow. Lexington's black women were not strangers to civil rights protest activities in the state, and they eagerly followed Lizzie Fouse's lead.[59]

The mobilized effort of these women vividly demonstrates Fouse's commitment to and leadership in the fight for civil rights. The Boulder incident indicates that the white establishment still viewed black women according to generations-old stereotypes, as lewd and immoral persons unworthy of respect. Lizzie Fouse, one of Lexington's most respected black citizens, emerged to direct the contestation of city officials' racist treatment of women of color and demanded they be accorded the same level of respect and humanity as other citizens.

Over the years Lizzie Fouse's spheres of influence continued to expand beyond Lexington, through her NACW work and other organizations she joined. She was a delegate to the 1933 International Congress of Women in Chicago. In

1944 she was appointed to a statewide committee made up of black and white citizens; by executive order, Governor Simeon Willis had created the Kentucky Commission on Negro Affairs "to obtain and to study all the facts and conditions relating to the economic, educational, housing, health, and other needs for the betterment of Negro citizens of Kentucky." Fouse served on the housing committee.[60]

Fouse's influence in twentieth-century temperance efforts extended widely. In 1947 she represented the United States in England and Ireland at Women's Christian Temperance Union (WCTU) meetings, where she was the guest speaker at a banquet in Belfast Castle, Ireland.[61] Fouse was one of only three blacks in the U.S. delegation to Great Britain. Her international activities with the WCTU further garnered local attention as few blacks in Kentucky were involved in this association. Fouse served as president of Kentucky's eight WCTU Sojourner Truth Unions (black chapters) located in Ashland, Erlanger, Frankfort, Lexington, Louisville, Middlesboro, Paducah, and Richmond; in fact, she was instrumental in recruiting members and establishing chapters such as the one in Paducah, organized in 1947. The Kentucky Sojourner Truth Loyal Temperance Legion received the "State Membership Net Gain Certificate" from the national WCTU for adding ninety-four members in 1946. In 1947 the Sojourner Truth Loyal Temperance Legion earned the Anniversary trophy and the Faithful Union Certificate as well. Clearly committed to the work of the WCTU, Fouse was the only Sojourner Truth president who attended the seventy-fifth annual meeting in 1949 in Philadelphia. Members of both races knew Lizzie Fouse and respected her contributions to the city, the state, and the country.[62]

Her notoriety throughout Kentucky is evidenced by the publication of her obituary in the state's best-known newspaper, Louisville's *Courier-Journal*. It described her as a "Kentucky Negro leader" clearly reflecting her stature in the state.[63] The *Lexington Leader*'s announcement of her death in 1952 identified her as "Mrs. Lizzie B. Fouse, prominent Lexington citizen and Negro leader."[64] Whites as well as blacks understood that "if there was a worthy cause, Lizzie Fouse would be in the middle of it." She evoked the trust and respect of those with whom she worked.[65]

Fouse's life demonstrates the ways in which activist black women sought to shape their communities, control their own destinies, and leave an imprint on urban African American culture. She challenged the dominant culture's view of black women at the turn of the twentieth century and its lingering effects in the 1920s, when Gertrude Boulder was allowed to die in a Lexington jail cell. Fouse's lifelong activism represents the learned coping strategies, organizing traditions, and leadership training of several generations of black women.

NOTES

1. "Colored Women Make Protest: Delegation Appears before Mayor Yancey with Petition Asking Investigation into the Death of Gertie Boulder," *Lexington Leader*, April 5, 1925; "Complain of Police Action: Negro Organizations of City Send Open Letter to Mayor Yancey and Commissioner Gentry," *Lexington Herald*, April 5, 1925. The full text of the petition with names of the signers appears in both articles.

2. "Negro Woman Dies in Police Station Cell: Found Lying in Street," *Lexington Leader*, April 1, 1925.

3. *Kentucky's Black Heritage* (Frankfort: Kentucky Commission on Human Rights, 1971), 46.

4. Victor B. Howard, *Black Liberation in Kentucky: Emancipation and Freedom, 1862–1884* (Lexington: University Press of Kentucky, 1983), 106–7, 144, 155.

5. George C. Wright, *A History of Blacks in Kentucky*, Vol. 2: *In Pursuit of Equality, 1890–1980* (Frankfort: Kentucky Historical Society, 1992), 43–58.

6. U.S. Bureau of the Census, *Negroes in the United States, 1920–32* (Washington, D.C.: Government Printing Office, 1935).

7. Wright, *History of Blacks in Kentucky*, 2:63. In Wright's discussion on race relations in Kentucky, he refers to Lexington and Louisville in this manner. See 43–102 for a complete discussion of the state's racial climate during this period.

8. Ibid., 58–63.

9. Ibid., 59.

10. Ibid., 7–27.

11. Ibid., 80.

12. George C. Wright, *Racial Violence in Kentucky, 1865–1940: Lynchings, Mob Rule, and "Legal Lynchings"* (Baton Rouge: Louisiana State University, 1990), 294.

13. "Public Investigation Will Be Held into Circumstances Surrounding Death of Woman at Police Station," *Lexington Herald*, April 7, 1925.

14. 1920 U.S. Federal Census, Lexington Ward 4, Fayette, Kentucky Roll T625–569, 11A, ancestry.com (accessed September 1, 2012). While the census record lists her husband as Bernard, the funeral announcement in the April 2, 1925, *Lexington Leader* lists him as Burnet. "Colored Notes," *Lexington Herald*, April 3, 1925.

15. "Public Investigation," *Lexington Herald*, April 7, 1925.

16. "Negro Woman Dies," *Lexington Leader*, April 1, 1925.

17. *Lexington Herald*, April 5, 1925; *Lexington Leader*, April 5, 1925.

18. "Complain of Police Action," *Lexington Herald*, April 5, 1925.

19. Darlene Clark Hine, "Introduction," in *Hine Sight: Black Women and the Re-Construction of American History* (Bloomington: Indiana University Press, 1994), xxii.

20. Stephanie J. Shaw, "Black Club Women and the Creation of the National Association of Colored Women," in "*We Specialize in the Wholly Impossible": A Reader in Black Women's History*, ed. Darlene Clark Hine, Wilma King, and Linda Reed (Brooklyn, N.Y.: Carlson, 1995), 433–47.

21. NACW records, *A History of the Club Movement among the Colored Women of the United States* (Washington, D.C.: National Association of Colored Women, 1902), microfilm reel 1, frames 6–8.

22. Ibid., reel 1, frames 11, 12, 24; Charles Harris Wesley, *The History of the National Association of Colored Women's Clubs, Inc.: A Legacy of Service* (Washington, D.C.: National Association of Colored Women's Clubs, 1984), 28–39; Shaw, "Black Club Women," 433.

23. Evelyn Brooks Higginbotham, *Righteous Discontent: The Women's Movement in the Black Baptist Church, 1880–1920* (Cambridge, Mass.: Harvard University Press, 1993), 1.

24. Tera W. Hunter, *To 'Joy My Freedom: Southern Black Women's Lives and Labors after the Civil War* (Cambridge, Mass.: Harvard University Press, 1997), 67–68.

25. George C. Wright, *Life behind a Veil: Blacks in Louisville, Kentucky, 1865–1930* (Baton Rouge: Louisiana State University Press, 1985); Wright, *History of Blacks in Kentucky.*

26. Wright, *History of Blacks in Kentucky.* The activities included establishing schools and health camps, supporting the poor by furnishing clothing and paying for funerals, supporting missionary causes in Africa, and raising funds for a black orphanage, a local college, and a home for the elderly. In 1865 Lexington's black women established "Ladies Hall" on Church Street, which served as a school for black children. By 1892 Lexington's black women had established an orphan's home, and by 1903 they had founded a day nursery to support black working-class needs.

27. Lucy Harth Smith, ed., *Pictorial Directory of the Kentucky Association of Colored Women* (Lexington: Kentucky Association of Colored Women, 1946).

28. Kevin K. Gaines, *Uplifting the Race: Black Leadership, Politics, and Culture in the Twentieth Century* (Chapel Hill: University of North Carolina Press, 1996).

29. "Federation of Women's Clubs: Lifting as We Climb," *American Baptist* 26, no. 2 (January 8, 1904): 1.

30. "Lizzie Beatrice Fouse," in *Who's Who in Colored America: An Illustrated Biographical Directory of Notable Living Persons of African Descent in the United States*, ed. James G. Fleming and Christian E. Burckel (Yonkers, N.Y.: Burckel & Assoc., 1950), 193.

31. *The Crisis* 49 (October 1942), 321. The General Association of Colored Baptists of Kentucky established the Normal and Theological Institution in 1873 in Louisville, Kentucky. The name was changed to State University in 1884; finally, in 1918, the name was changed to Simmons University in honor of Dr. William J. Simmons. J. H. Ingram, *Religious Training in Education for Negroes in Kentucky* (Frankfort: Kentucky State College, 1940), 8. Eckstein Norton, founded by Dr. Simmons in 1890, was also a product of the black Baptists. It was located in Cane Springs (Bullitt County), twenty-nine miles south of Louisville. G. F. Richings, *Evidence of Progress among Colored People* (Philadelphia: George S. Ferguson, 1896), 218–221.

32. Fouse Family Papers (hereafter cited as FFP), box 2, folder 11 (reel 11), microfilm edition (1998), Special Collections, University of Kentucky, Lexington, Kentucky; also in Microfilm Collections, Paul G. Blazer Library, Kentucky State University, Frankfort; "After 45 Years of Service to Negro Education, Prof. W. H. Fouse, Pioneer, Will Retire in Spring," *Lexington Herald*, February 6, 1938.

33. FFP, box 1, folder 1 (reel 1). The specific reason that Lizzie Fouse quit teaching is not revealed in these sources. Perhaps her husband's income as a school principal was substantial enough to maintain the lifestyle that the Fouses desired. During their first ten years of marriage, the family account book offers evidence of accumulation of property, which no doubt provided them economic stability. Meticulous attention to their resources, coupled with his principalship, was enough to sustain a middle-class existence and permit Fouse to quit teaching. There are many other possibilities for her leaving paid work, including a lack of vacant positions in the school system. With William serving in a supervisory position as principal, her employment could have been frowned upon or may even have been illegal in the Ohio public school system.

34. Ibid.

35. Jennifer L. Pettit, "Consuming, Organizing, and Uplifting: Elizabeth B. Fouse and the Production of Class Identity" (MA thesis, University of Kentucky, 1998). Pettit's thesis provides a detailed description and analysis of the Fouses' consumerism, monetary donations, and middle-class lifestyle.

36. Karen C. McDaniel interview with Margaret Steward Cunningham, March 28, 1999, Lexing-

ton, Kentucky. Oral History Collection, Special Collections, Paul G. Blazer Library, Kentucky State University, Frankfort (hereafter cited Oral History Collection, KSU).

37. Higginbotham, *Righteous Discontent*, 14–15.

38. Ibid., 192–93.

39. Gaines, *Uplifting the Race*.

40. FFP, box 3, folder 23 (reel 23); *Indianapolis Freeman*, May 10, 1913.

41. "Tributes to the Late Prof. W. H. Fouse," *KNEA Journal* 16, no. 1, (January/February 1945), 7.

42. Hine, "Introduction," xxii.

43. Elsa Barkley Brown, "What Has Happened Here: The Politics of Difference in Women's History and Feminist Politics," in Hine et al., *A Reader in Black Women's History*, 47.

44. Evelyn Brooks Higginbotham, "African-American Women's History and the Metalanguage of Race," in Hine et al., *A Reader in Black Women's History*, 11; Winthrop Jordan, *White over Black: American Attitudes toward the Negro, 1550–1812* (Chapel Hill: University of North Carolina Press, 1968).

45. Higginbotham, "African-American Women's History."

46. Tullia K. Brown Hamilton, "The National Association of Colored Women, 1896 to 1920" (PhD diss., Emory University, 1978), 13, cited in Paula Giddings, *When and Where I Enter: The Impact of Black Women on Race and Sex in America* (New York: Morrow, 1984), 82.

47. John H. Bracey, August Meier, and Randolph Boehm, eds., *National Association for the Advancement of Colored People, Papers of the NAACP, Part 12, Selected Branch Files, 1913–1939* (Bethesda, Md.: University Publications of America, 1991), microfilm reel 11, frames 201–6.

48. "The Anti-Lynching Crusaders," *The Crisis* 25 (November 1922): 8; "A Movement against Lynching Organized by the Anti-Lynching Crusaders," *The Crisis* 25 (November 1922): 214. The southern white Democratic Party voting bloc in the U.S. Senate defeated the measure repeatedly, in 1922, 1923, and 1924.

49. *1870 United States Federal Census*, ancestry.com. Census record for William Cook family, Lancaster, Garrard, Kentucky; Roll M593_463, page 442B.; *R. L. Polk & Co.'s Lexington (Kentucky) Directory*, 1898, Special Collections and Archives,University of Kentucky Libraries, Lexington; *1920 United States Federal Census*, ancestry.com; *1930 United States Federal Census*, ancestry.com.

50. Scrapbook, FFP, box 3, folder 23 (reel 23).

51. *Lexington Leader*, April 1–2, 1925; *Lexington Herald*, April 3, 1925.

52. "Colored Notes," *Lexington Herald*, April 3, 1925. Calanthe was a black female benevolent society under the auspices of the Fayette Lodge of the Knights of Pythias. "Colored Notes," *Lexington Leader*, April 2, 1925.

53. Smith, *Pictorial Directory of the KACW*.

54. "A Justifiable Protest," *Lexington Leader*, April 6, 1925; "Let the Facts Be Known," *Lexington Herald*, April 8, 1925. The *Lexington Herald* and *Lexington Leader* offered full coverage of the Gertrude Boulder ordeal from April 1 through April 17, 1925.

55. "Official Report Made in Death of Gertrude Boulder," *Lexington Leader*, April 17, 1925; "Prisoners to Have Medical Examination: New Orders Are Issued to Police Department after Investigation of Woman's Death," *Lexington Herald*, April 18, 1925.

56. National Association of Colored Women, Constitution of the National Association of Colored Women (Louisville: W. H. Steward, 1904), 3.

57. NACW records (microfilm reel 14, frame 1249).

58. Hine, "Introduction."

59. S. E. Smith, ed., *History of the Anti-Separate Coach Movement of Kentucky* (Evansville, Ind.: National Afro-American Journal and Directory Publishing Co., c. 1895).

60. *The Report of the Kentucky Commission on Negro Affairs* (Frankfort, Ky.: Office of the Governor, 1945), 7, 36 (available at the Kentucky Department for Libraries and Archives, Frankfort).

61. *Records of the National Association of Colored Women's Clubs, 1895–1992*, ed. Lillian Serece Williams (Bethesda, Md.: University Publications of America, 1993), microfilm reel 14, frame 1249.

62. "The Kentucky White Ribbon: We Fight Alcoholic Drink" (newsletter of the Kentucky chapter of the WCTU), in FFP, box 3, folder 21; "National Women's Christian Temperance Union, 1945: August 31–1951: April 20," FFP, box 3, folder 21.

63. "Kentucky Negro Leader, Mrs. Lizzie B. Fouse, Dies," *Louisville Courier-Journal*, October 23, 1952.

64. "Heart Attack Proves Fatal to Mrs. Fouse," *Lexington Leader*, October 22, 1952.

65. McDaniel, Cunningham interview, Oral History Collection, KSU.

Mary Breckinridge
(1881–1965)

Kind Ambition and the Creation of the Frontier Nursing Service

MELANIE BEALS GOAN

As she wrote her autobiography toward the end of her life, Mary Breckinridge related in great detail the years of "aimless girlhood" that she endured before finally establishing the Frontier Nursing Service (FNS), the mission that would define her life's purpose and engage her full energies for more than forty years.[1] Like many young women who came of age in the late nineteenth century, Breckinridge's talents far exceeded the opportunities available to her. At the turn of the century, society celebrated blind ambition in men. Sons were encouraged to make something of themselves, while daughters who demonstrated similar determination often faced public disapproval and certainly limited professional prospects. Offered few avenues through which to develop her talents, Mary Breckinridge created her own opportunities. Through her public health work, she crafted a position of power for herself couched in a mission of humanitarianism. Like many of her contemporaries, she chose to apply her talents in socially acceptable ways that involved caring for others. Thus, we can say that her work with the FNS was fueled not by blind ambition but rather by kind ambition, a determination to find personal fulfillment through service to others.

When she established the FNS in Hyden in 1925, Mary Breckinridge created a protected space in which she and the women with whom she worked could gain nationwide recognition. The FNS eventually expanded to provide comprehensive, low-cost care to all members of its eastern Kentucky community, male and female, but initially its mission was to serve rural mothers and babies. The

FNS celebrated the work women performed in the home while simultaneously pushing the boundaries of society's gender expectations by enlisting an entirely female "army" of nurses.[2] Breckinridge's staff became famous for the heroic service they performed under challenging and often dangerous conditions. Through her leadership of the organization, Breckinridge found the adventure and won the acclaim she longed for as a young girl, but ultimately her investment in upholding traditional gender roles would limit the reach of her work.[3]

Born February 17, 1881, Mary Carson Breckinridge joined a dynasty of famous Kentucky social and political leaders. The family's achievements were heralded not only in the Bluegrass State but throughout the country. Her grandfather had served as U.S. vice president under James Buchanan before becoming Jefferson Davis's secretary of war and the highest-ranking U.S. official to command an army for the Confederacy. Other male members of the family distinguished themselves as congressmen, education reformers, and ambassadors. Possessing the Breckinridge name provided instant recognition and respect, but growing up in the celebrated family also carried with it a pressing duty to perpetuate this legacy. The idea was clear: a Breckinridge did not strive simply to succeed but to excel. For female family members, however, the message that Breckinridges must prove themselves as outstanding members of society could be contradictory and frustrating. Mary Breckinridge shared many of the gifts for which her male relatives were known; she was highly intelligent and possessed the public speaking abilities and charisma of a successful politician. She found, however, the path taken by her male relatives to be closed to her as a well-bred southern woman.[4]

Young girls coming of age in the late nineteenth century, particularly young southern women, were raised to understand that a proper woman belonged at home caring for her children and promoting the career of her husband. Mary's parents, Katherine and Clifton Breckinridge, enthusiastically upheld the ideals and customs of their Old South upbringing, and consequently the opportunities they offered their two daughters differed substantially from those available to their two sons. Mary later recalled that she regretted her inferior education, which was partly provided by governesses and then completed at "old-fashioned" Swiss and American finishing schools.[5] Her education centered on training her to be a good wife. Young women were attending college in increasing numbers during this period, but Mary's parents did not approve of such a choice. They assumed their daughters would marry respectable gentlemen who would provide financially for them. They certainly did not see their daughters' education as training for a future public role, and in keeping with late nineteenth-century

MARY BRECKINRIDGE

After suffering a broken back in a riding accident, she found working from her bed the most comfortable arrangement.

Courtesy of Special Collections, University of Kentucky Libraries, Lexington.

theories, they frequently expressed worry that Mary would weaken her body by overstimulating her mind.[6]

Internalizing two contradictory messages, the need to uphold the Breckinridge family's record of service and the competing demand to play the role of the properly submissive female, Mary spent her young adult years in turmoil. She shared her parents' respect for separate spheres, and she herself argued that women possessed a natural, God-given capacity to nurture and thus belonged in the home. Still, she constantly battled her craving for adventure and her desire to find her true purpose. The decade following Mary's graduation from finishing school left her, like many young women of her generation, struggling to reconcile "the life [she] longed to live" with the "life allowed [her]."[7]

Eager to have it all but raised in a period when this was not possible, Breckinridge chose the path society and her parents marked out for her. In 1904, after careful consideration, she decided to marry Henry Ruffner Morrison, a man who showed "high promise" in law and statecraft. She did not make this decision lightly; she only accepted her future husband's proposal after she felt sure that she could relinquish all of her own aspirations in order to promote his. The twenty-three-year-old bride looked forward to a long and happy marriage blessed with many children. When Morrison died shortly after their one-year anniversary, however, she was left to chart a new course for her life.[8]

Determined to learn a skill that would allow her to be useful to others, the young widow moved to New York City in 1907, where she enrolled at St. Luke's School of Nursing. Of all the careers she could have pursued, nursing seemed most appropriate because it fit well with her view of acceptable roles for women. Nursing capitalized on the qualities most Americans associated with women: self-sacrifice, patience, submission. Caring for others, whether in the home or in a hospital, was a duty women had long been expected to fulfill. By the twentieth century, nursing had grown significantly as a field of study, and its leaders consciously forged a professional identity. For women such as Mary, nursing provided the excitement, autonomy, and independence a profession could offer while still allowing its practitioners to preserve their softer, feminine side.[9]

Breckinridge did not seek paid employment following her graduation from St. Luke's in 1910. Instead, she remarried and turned her attention once again to starting a family. She joined her new husband, Richard Thompson, the president of a small women's college, in Eureka Springs, Arkansas. In 1914 she gave birth to a son, Breckinridge, or "Breckie," as he was known.[10] Mrs. Thompson emphasized that her family was her top priority, yet she carved out time to participate in a variety of social causes while living in Arkansas. Her husband embraced Progressive reform and encouraged his wife to do likewise. In the years before and after the birth of her son, Mary was quite visible in state and local reform movements, including the professionalization of nursing, woman suffrage, and child welfare, among others.[11]

Mary joined a new generation of women who invoked the traditional linkage between femininity, self-sacrifice, and moral superiority to justify taking on new responsibilities outside the home. Labeled "municipal feminists" or maternalists by historians, these women did not seek to escape the confines of separate spheres but instead used the special responsibility they had as women to care for others as a springboard to new forms of professional and voluntary service.[12] Mrs. Thompson viewed her activities outside the home as an extension of her natural domestic role. Stressing her position as a woman and as a mother to legitimize her public activities allowed her to use her talents in a meaningful way and to serve as she was taught a Breckinridge should do, while also protecting her from the scrutiny society often leveled against women who stepped beyond their proper sphere. The young mother justified her reform work by emphasizing the ways it would benefit her son and improve the world he would one day inherit.[13]

Mrs. Thompson had more advantages than most early twentieth-century mothers. She was financially secure, she lived in a home outfitted with modern conveniences, and she was a trained medical professional. Embracing the tenets of scientific motherhood, Breckinridge scrutinized every detail of Breckie's care, precisely regulating his diet and his sleep and bathroom habits. The devoted mother kept abreast of the most up-to-date child care literature and followed it faithfully. Still, in spite of every precaution, she could not protect her son when he suddenly developed a bowel obstruction just days after his fourth birthday. With no way to treat the infection that began to spread, Mary helplessly watched her son die.[14]

Breckie's death required Thompson to make a "complete readjustment."[15] She saw her main role in life to be a mother; any reform efforts on her part had simply been an extension of that. Now thirty-seven years old, Mary again had to choose a new path. One of her first steps was to initiate divorce proceedings against her husband, whom she would only say had committed "indignities."[16] Mary did not allow herself any time to grieve for her son but instead threw herself headlong into her work. Although there was "no longer any need for [her] in [her] nursery," she did not feel that her duties as a mother had ended.[17] Unable to care for her own babies, she committed herself to improving the health of disadvantaged children and educating their mothers. Unlike after her first husband's death, this time Mary could see clearly what she must do. Writing to her cousin Sophonisba four months after losing Breckie, she confided: "What an unspeakable blessing it is to be equipped with a profession of real use to which to turn at a time like this."[18]

In the years immediately following her son's death, Mary put her nursing skills and her rising stature within the child welfare movement to work, first by traveling the United States as an agent with the federal Children's Bureau and then by serving overseas in France with an American relief agency after the Great War. She traveled constantly over the next seven years, during which time she was struck by the number of poor rural women, both in Europe and in the United States, who lacked access to health care. She also witnessed a variety of approaches and plans designed to make health care more accessible. The ideas she collected during this period, especially her firsthand experience working with trained British nurse-midwives, would lay the foundation for the work that would consume the second half of her life.[19]

Having reclaimed her maiden name once her divorce finalized, Mary Breckinridge returned from France in 1921 with the general outline of a rural public health service in mind. While many details still needed to be set in place, she felt sure that the organization she envisioned, serving the many Americans who were "still living under primitive conditions of remoteness and isolation," would constitute the best use of her talents and energies. Billing her proposed service as a "demonstration," she intended to prove that the trained nurse-midwife, a type of caregiver new to the United States, could be the answer to America's growing health care gap. Her organization, she predicted, would become a model for others to replicate. She hoped to see similar services develop in "frontier" areas throughout the United States that lacked the "safeguards of life and health which the towns enjoy."[20]

Over the next four years, Breckinridge sought intensive preparation for the work that lay ahead. She attended Teachers College at Columbia University for a year, taking classes in public health, child psychology, nursing education, and statistics. Then, in the fall of 1923, she traveled to London, becoming certified to practice nurse-midwifery at the British Hospital for Mothers and Babies. From there, a visit to the Highlands and Islands Medical and Nursing Service in the Scottish Hebrides allowed her to witness in action a rural health service very similar to the one she hoped to create.[21] She outlined a plan for an organization that she tentatively called the "Children's Public Health Service" and began to solicit funding from several leading foundations.[22]

If she hoped to prove the validity of her methods and see her work copied in other locations, Breckinridge recognized she must choose very carefully the area in which to begin. She must prove that her ideas would work under the toughest of circumstances. Hoping to capitalize on the instant recognition that the Breckinridge name provided among both potential patients and donors, she zeroed in on eastern Kentucky. Following three months of travel through this mountainous region on horseback, meeting with reform leaders in the area, she ultimately decided to initiate her pilot project in Leslie County, which she described as a "poor little orphan of a county."[23] Leslie County fully met Breckinridge's three top priorities: it lacked trained medical care, it was home to individuals whom she believed would enthusiastically cooperate with her organization, and it was far removed from any form of modern transportation. Here, streambeds served as roads, electricity and indoor plumbing were unknown, and most families eked out a living through subsistence agriculture. Coal would not be extracted on a large scale in this area until the 1940s. As Breckinridge explained, "Nowhere were conditions more remote or more difficult."[24]

Employing a model that she had witnessed in Britain, Breckinridge intended to cope with the rugged terrain and the lack of good transportation by organizing nurses according to districts. Outpost centers, each staffed by two nurse-midwives, would be scattered across the organization's territory, ideally located nine to twelve miles apart so that a nurse was no more than an hour's horseback ride from any family in her district. Most care, including maternity services, would be offered in-home, with nurses providing the bulk of routine care. Breckinridge intended as soon as possible, however, to build a centrally located hospital, staffed by a physician who would serve as medical director. The hospital would act as a hub for her growing medical system, and the resident physician, who would advise nurses on complicated cases, would ensure patients the highest level of care.[25]

On May 28, 1925, in Frankfort, Kentucky, Mary Breckinridge called to order the inaugural meeting of the Kentucky Committee for Mothers and Babies. Twenty-one prominent men and women, many of them kin to Breckinridge, gathered that day to hear her outline her plan to bring medical care to Leslie County. Although she had already worked out the basic details of how her organization would function, Breckinridge sought approval from the committee on questions of location, staff, publications, and record keeping. As they would continue to do in the future, committee members enthusiastically rubber-stamped Breckinridge's suggestions. After securing the committee's permission to hire the organization's first two nurse-midwives, the group adjourned. Breckinridge had yet to identify a permanent funding source for her project, but she had a small inheritance from her mother that she could draw on initially. Breckinridge left Frankfort exhilarated. Her years of intense planning finally had come to fruition. The work could begin.[26]

The size and scope of Breckinridge's venture expanded quickly. By 1928, when she renamed her organization the Frontier Nursing Service, it operated four clinics, had two more under construction, and employed a staff of nine nurse-midwives and four registered nurses, the majority having been recruited from Britain.[27] By the end of the decade, frontier nurses served more than ten thousand patients in parts of four counties—Leslie, Clay, Perry, and Harlan. As reflected in the organization's name change, the mission moved beyond serving just mothers and babies to providing care to all members of the community. FNS nurses offered both acute care and a level of preventive care found in few places in the nation. Nurses spent much of their time in these early years inoculating patients against epidemic diseases and providing public health instruction. Ideally, each nurse tried to examine every infant (under one year old) twice a month. She visited preschoolers (children between one and six years) once a month. Schoolchildren were examined every three months and adults twice a year.[28] Later, during the Depression, the FNS would look beyond its patients' health care needs to address their economic constraints by establishing a social work department.

The FNS could not have grown as quickly as it did if it had not been for its director's herculean fund-raising efforts. Recognizing that the people of eastern Kentucky could not bear the costs of the care her nurses offered, Breckinridge emphasized the responsibility urban Americans had to join hands with their rural neighbors. Initially, she had expected that the federal government would underwrite a large portion of the costs, drawing on funding available through the 1921 Sheppard-Towner Maternity and Infancy Protection Act.[29] When federal funds were not forthcoming, she turned to industrialists operating in eastern Kentucky for support, but she found her efforts rebuffed.[30] Undaunted, Breckinridge hit the fund-raising circuit, creating a network of wealthy individual donors. She specifically targeted northeastern cities, relying on family and friends she knew there to introduce her to wealthy, philanthropic-minded individuals. She worked tirelessly to spread the word about the important work her nurses were doing, penning thousands of letters each year to donors and traveling in and out of the mountains on average every ten days.[31] Even after a riding accident in 1931 left her in almost constant pain with a broken vertebra in her back, she continued the exhausting speaking tours that underwrote the FNS's yearly budget.[32]

Donors responded enthusiastically to Breckinridge's appeals. During fiscal year 1926–27 alone, donations to the organization increased by more than 400 percent.[33] By the end of the decade Breckinridge's annual intake had surpassed $130,000.[34] The romantic reputation of the FNS's work attracted many contributors. The nurses' distinctive uniforms and their use of horses, at a time when cars were becoming the preferred mode of transportation for most Americans, made the organization seem quaint yet practical. Breckinridge won over supporters with her talent for public speaking. Like her famous male relatives who won acclaim for their ability to take the stump, Mary never failed to impress listeners with her "spellbinding stories."[35] In testament to her skill, she won praise from those who were accomplished public speakers themselves. Kentucky governor Happy Chandler commended her oratorical abilities, claiming that she could "charm the birds off the trees."[36]

By 1930 the FNS had become a household name. Thrilling tales of the FNS's work appeared frequently in mass-circulation magazines in the late 1920s. Journalists praised nurses' willingness to "leap into [their] saddle at a moment's notice and ride wherever duty calls," traveling "over mountain paths that hardly deserve the name even in the best of seasons." Once there, the nurses "safely usher a new being into the world" with no more than the light of an open fire and a lantern.[37] Breckinridge often compared FNS employees to soldiers bravely attacking death and disease. Not only did nurses risk their lives to provide care, their female patients similarly performed a patriotic duty by giving birth. "Maternity," Breckinridge wrote after the United States had entered World War II, "is the young woman's battlefield."[38] Since women placed their lives on the line, they, like the nation's soldiers, deserved the best care available, and the FNS was offering that care.

Breckinridge emphasized that FNS nurses were prepared to save mothers and babies at any cost, even if it meant sacrificing their own lives. The death of Nancy O'Driscoll, the first FNS nurse to die "in service," in 1931 proved her promise. The *Lexington Herald* printed a tribute to O'Driscoll soon after her death, praising the "Irish Heroine" for ignoring her own pain to tend to the needs of others. Even after her appendix ruptured, she refused to return to headquarters because she had not yet completed her rounds. The article concluded, "No soldier in the field of battle, no pioneer carrying the flag of civilization, ever died a more heroic death in a nobler cause than did . . . O'Driscoll."[39] Nancy O'Driscoll continued to serve the FNS long after she died; she became a mythic hero in Breckinridge's fund-raising appeals, illustrating nurses' bravery and commitment.

However, even as Breckinridge encouraged this masculine image of FNS nurses, she was careful to balance it by emphasizing their softer, feminine sides. Though she resisted using the term herself, she encouraged the media to describe her nurse-midwives as "angels on horseback."[40] She consistently stressed the attentive care her staff provided to society's most vulnerable members. Her nurses were brave, but they also remained wedded to women's traditional role as caregivers. Nurses themselves commented on these competing parts of their identity. After O'Driscoll "gave her life in the line of duty," one of her colleagues suggested that a nurse's tender nature, so much the core of her identity, survived even after death. She speculated that O'Driscoll was now "in the other land . . . mothering little ones passed on alone, or comforting the mothers who have gone on, leaving helpless babies to face life's problems here."[41] In life or in death, a nurse's first instinct was to care for others.

FNS publicity celebrated the essential work that women performed within the home and paid homage to Appalachian mothers who faced the most trying of circumstances. Early publications feature pictures of mothers who often appear weighted down by work and worry, surrounded by small children. Service literature stressed that mountain folk were hard-working, independent, and virtuous, and, importantly, they behaved as true men and women should. J. A. Stucky, a physician active in mountain health projects including the FNS, appreciatively noted that the Appalachian people were not "laborers, operatives, or salaried folk, but soil-owners and home-makers."[42] Breckinridge reinforced this reassuring image, stressing that the men they served still had "the utmost chivalry for women," while the mother remained "the heart of the household."[43] Separate spheres may have been breaking down in urban regions, but in Appalachia, men still knew how to be men and women still acted like proper women.

In no way did Mary Breckinridge intend to defy traditional gender norms when she created the FNS. Her decision to work with mothers and children fit nicely with society's understanding of the issues with which women should concern themselves. Locating the FNS in a rural area that, according to one observer, could "hardly be considered a woman's land," however, necessitated that Breckinridge and her nurses demonstrate a high degree of autonomy. They found it necessary to reshape gender expectations to fit the circumstances of their environment. The director quickly learned that her demonstration could not succeed unless she and the women she employed stopped designating duties as specifically men's or women's work and willingly tackled any task that confronted them.[44]

Breckinridge publicly stressed that her nurses deferred to doctors in all situations, but in reality their remote location often forced them to perform procedures that fell outside of the realm of nursing, including suturing wounds, administering anesthesia, and setting bones. In theory, nurse-midwives were supposed to conduct only normal deliveries and were instructed to call a physician in case of complications. Breckinridge granted, however, that often the frontier nurse-midwife had to "hold the fort" until the medical director arrived.[45] The FNS's Medical Routine plan acknowledged that a nurse-midwife on occasion had to overstep the boundaries of her position and authorized her to "act according to her own judgment," on the condition that she immediately report her actions to a supervisor.[46] Breckinridge downplayed the medical independence her nurses displayed as she did not want physicians to view the FNS as competition. Describing her new organization in the *American Journal of Obstetrics and Gynecology* in 1928, she stressed that the mothers her organization served "have no other trained assistance at near hand." Under ideal circumstances all Americans would have access to first-class medical care provided by physicians, but that simply was not the case in many areas.[47]

Breckinridge challenged the women she employed to abandon their ingrained ideas concerning acceptable female behavior. Society dictated that women did not perform heavy labor or supervise male workers, but the FNS's demanding work required staff to ignore traditional prescriptions of what women could be and do. As one of the organization's nurse-midwives proudly pointed out, an individual could not effectively serve in a rugged environment such as Leslie County unless she learned "to be a horsewoman, stable boy, mechanic, carpenter, plumber, acrobat, teacher and bluffer."[48] Couriers, young college coeds who volunteered with the service, especially found themselves stepping outside of their comfort zone. Arriving in "lovely riding boots and the most elegant jodhpurs," these young women soon found themselves rising at dawn, sleeping on cots, and standing in line to brush their teeth. Tasks they would never have imagined performing, such as shoeing horses, cleaning out stalls, or leading livestock between nursing centers, became routine.[49] When female paid staff and volunteers left the FNS, they did so with new skills and a heightened confidence in their abilities.

Breckinridge's confidence and her understanding of women's role likewise expanded throughout her life. As head of the FNS, she won the distinction she craved as a young girl. She wielded a great deal of influence, overseeing a largely male board of directors, managing a sizeable staff that included male physicians, and administering a large budget and a growing endowment. The organization's executive committee voted unanimously in 1925 to give Breckinridge "such executive authority as is customarily given to field directors."[50] Both Breckinridge and the executive committee interpreted her authority broadly, allowing her complete control over the organization, including long-term planning and fiscal matters.

Yet while she exerted full authority over a nationally prominent organization, the director still managed to appear maternal and submissive, an image she carefully cultivated. Observers frequently hinted at the balancing act she performed. An FNS trustee commenting after her death noted, "She was one of the most remarkable women I've ever known. She had the mind of a man and heart of a mother."[51] The FNS's accountant similarly described her as "an intrepid adventurer and pioneer, wearing a girdle of courage, a mantle of faith and hope, a banner of mercy, and a shield of duty; a spirit imbued with an overwhelming and intense love for little children."[52] Breckinridge recognized that the very public role she had adopted could be perceived as threatening her status as a traditional southern woman, and she crafted an image that downplayed the incongruity of her position. Her secretary described her as a "chameleon," equipped with an amazing capacity to adjust to any circumstance in which she found herself.[53] Breckinridge often made light of her accomplishments, claiming she was simply a mother helping other mothers. Few, however, failed to notice that she was the matriarch of her organization.

For Breckinridge, directing the FNS was not just a job; the organization became her life mission, her second family, as well as her path to fame. Breckinridge garnered many awards during her lifetime. She received honorary doctoral degrees from the University of Louisville (1937), the University of Rochester (1940), the University of Kentucky (1942), and Keuka College (1955). Several times she was honored as "Woman of the Week" on radio shows, including Bob Hope's program, which broadcast her accomplishments to listeners across America. The Kentucky Press Association named her Kentuckian of the Year in 1952, the first woman ever to receive the honor. Nine years later, nearing the end of her career, she received the Adelaide Nutting Award for outstanding leadership and achievement in nursing.

Breckinridge's work with the Frontier Nursing Service and her earlier reform efforts were clearly rooted in maternalist ideology.[54] By claiming that she was just a mother serving other mothers and their children, she protected herself from charges that she was stepping beyond her proper sphere. She shielded herself from scrutiny by creating a women's organization that was staffed by women and worked primarily on behalf of women. She took advantage of the exalted status assigned to mothers, celebrating their contributions in her fundraising materials. By spotlighting the valuable and often dangerous service to the nation that Appalachian women provided, and by emphasizing the brave and self-sacrificing work of her nurses, Breckinridge built an extensive financial support base for her organization and won widespread recognition for herself.

When she began work in 1925, Mary Breckinridge had an ambitious goal of providing what amounted to, in today's terms, universal health care. She saw rural women and children as something of an entering wedge—a group that all Americans would agree deserved assistance. From there, she hoped to expand her organization's reach to serve all members of society in all corners of the country. Breckinridge argued that good health was just as essential to the nation's future as universal public education. The whole country would benefit as the health of its citizenry improved; therefore, she insisted, taxpayers should foot the bill.[55]

But taxpayers did not underwrite the costs of the FNS's work. Because the service was almost entirely funded through private donations, Breckinridge had to be constantly alert to her messages and how they resonated with her supporters. During the years of the Great Depression Breckinridge struggled mightily to keep the organization solvent, forcing her to halt expansion into new areas. The financial health of her organization, not to mention her own legacy, depended on remaining relevant to those who paid the bills. The desire to maintain contributors' loyalty made Breckinridge reluctant to change with the times as she grew older; ultimately her desire to protect her base of authority undermined her goal of using government as an equalizing force. Relying on private rather than public funding allowed her to keep a tight rein on her organization, but doing so significantly limited her plan's ultimate reach. While she did tremendous good in Leslie County, Kentucky, her work did not have the far-reaching impact she originally intended.

Her voice, which urged the government to take responsibility for health care in the 1920s, fell silent just as viable opportunities to develop such a system emerged. When Harry S. Truman proposed a national health insurance program in 1945, she did not rally behind this expansion of government as one might expect. She did not publicly criticize the plan, but those close to her knew her position. Breckinridge upheld the states' rights position for which her family had long been known, arguing that a growing welfare state would undermine private initiative. But her concern went beyond this. While at one time she had argued for government-funded health care, she now recognized that such a plan would eliminate the need for her organization. Other mountain reformers had found themselves "municipalized" as government began to attack the problems they had first identified, and Breckinridge feared a similar fate.[56] Writing to U.S. congresswoman Frances Payne Bolton in 1949, she insisted that "the trail the FNS blazed," rather than government aid, provided the best way to meet the health needs of rural areas.[57]

Postwar changes necessitated that the Frontier Nursing Service operate in a very new political, social, and economic context. Increasingly, the federal government assumed responsibility for many of the services private charities had traditionally offered, especially in Appalachia. Even before Lyndon Johnson launched the War on Poverty in 1964, state and federal governments had made economic development in the mountains a priority. During the 1930s and 1940s, new roads appeared to better connect eastern Kentucky to national markets as many argued that isolation was to blame for its poverty. New roads did not provide the magic bullet some predicted, but they did allow for improvements in education.[58] They also allowed for large-scale extraction of Leslie County coal. In 1947 Leslie County produced only 1.1 percent of the coal that came from the eastern Kentucky fields; by 1960 mining employed nearly 50 percent of Leslie County workers.[59] Small farms had once been the mainstay of the area's economy, but by 1960 only twenty full-time farms remained, employing less than 1 percent of the population.[60]

Breckinridge viewed these changes with dismay. She had always styled herself an innovator, offering an alternative to the existing medical establishment, but as she aged she grew less willing to embrace new ideas. She feared that the changes she witnessed in Leslie County and across the country would undermine the need for her organization. FNS nurses had won fame for traveling miles on horseback over dangerous terrain to deliver babies in dark, cold cabins. Although increasingly inaccurate, this was the image the director hoped to preserve. She hesitated to see the area become too modern. If Appalachia no longer appeared different from the rest of the nation, how could she convince contributors, employees, and even patients that hers was a cause still worth supporting?

The desire to protect the service's romantic reputation led Breckinridge to question and in some cases veto improvements that would have made both her employees' and her patients' lives easier. In perhaps the most extreme case, Breckinridge opposed the construction of a highway bridge near one of the FNS outpost centers because, according to one of her colleagues, she feared it would make the area "too sophisticated."[61] Breckinridge recognized that the value of her demonstration hinged on maintaining nursing centers in remote areas.

Similarly, the director hesitated to replace horses with jeeps even as paved roads began to appear in FNS territory after World War II. While Breckinridge recognized that jeeps would "streamlin[e] the stork," she feared the transition would alienate wealthy patrons who found it more exciting to pay for hay and saddles than spark plugs.[62] In the late 1940s a jeep cost nearly $1,500 and lasted only an average of four years in their harsh terrain, whereas horses provided on average ten to fourteen years of service. Hay also cost less than gasoline. As the person responsible for funding the FNS's budget, Breckinridge paid close attention to the price tags of modern conveniences. But with coal trucks rumbling over the county roads, it became too dangerous for FNS nurses to rely on horses for transportation. In spite of her misgivings, Breckinridge gradually replaced the FNS's stables with garages and its horses with jeeps.[63]

Breckinridge hesitated to take other steps to modernize the organization. FNS salaries, which had at one time been competitive nationally, began to lag considerably behind. The executive committee urged her to pay her nurses more, but she resisted, always concerned about the organization's solvency. She admitted that as "an old-fashioned woman," she had "a deep dread of debt."[64] That fear of debt also made her hesitant to hire a much-needed assistant medical director and caused her to defer needed improvements to the FNS's physical plant. By the late 1950s Hyden Hospital was nearly thirty years old and in desperate need of expansion, but again Breckinridge refused to take action until the service was in a better financial position.[65] The FNS eventually would adapt to the postwar environment in which it functioned, accepting Medicare and Medicaid funds and building a new modern hospital, but these changes would not occur until after its founder's death.[66]

Mary Breckinridge was an extremely talented, dedicated professional who came of age in an era when blind ambition, applauded in men, was viewed as unnatural and inappropriate in women. When Breckinridge established the FNS, she purposely created a female organization, directed by a woman, staffed by women, and devoted to improving conditions mothers faced. This combined with the rural setting in which they practiced allowed her and her nurses to assume public positions that carried with them a great deal of autonomy and responsibility without appearing to violate gender norms.

Breckinridge would have adamantly denied that her work with the FNS was fueled in any way by her own ambition, but she clearly relished the power being its director afforded her. Although she wanted what was best for the people of Appalachia, by the end of her career, she saw that new topics of concern were replacing the issues on which she had based her position of authority, and she feared that these shifting winds would make her and her organization irrelevant. Breckinridge walked a careful line during the forty years she directed the FNS, and while her patients praised her devoted service to the area, her need to protect her legacy and her power base ultimately limited the scope of her mission.

Breckinridge remained director of the Frontier Nursing Service until she died on May 16, 1965, at age eighty-four. Though she never created satellite organizations across the United States as she had hoped to do, her ideas have been replicated around the globe by students and observers. The FNS established one of the first nurse-midwifery training programs in the United States in 1939 and continues to be a pioneer in nursing education. Breckinridge poured her heart and soul into the FNS, providing it the financial basis on which to operate long after she was gone. She left the Frontier Nursing Service with an endowment of more than $2 million. All told, she raised almost $10 million for the organization over the course of her lifetime. This money allowed the service to care for nearly 58,000 patients, provide 248,000 inoculations, and deliver more than 14,500 babies in its first forty years.[67] Numbers, however, can never fully gauge the impact Breckinridge's work had on individual lives. Though not eloquent, the following FNS patient perhaps summed up best the contributions the service and its director made to the region: "I think they was a awful lot of children that's growed up healthy that wouldn't have been done if they hadn't been here."[68]

NOTES

1. Mary Breckinridge (hereafter MB), *Wide Neighborhoods: A Story of the Frontier Nursing Service*, 2nd ed. (Lexington: University Press of Kentucky, 1981), 46.

2. "In Memoriam," *Frontier Nursing Service Quarterly Bulletin* (hereafter *FNSQB*) 7 (Autumn 1931).

3. For a fuller discussion of Mary Breckinridge's work with the *FNS*, see Melanie Beals Goan, *Mary Breckinridge: The Frontier Nursing Service and Rural Health in Appalachia* (Chapel Hill: University of North Carolina Press, 2008).

4. I explore the competing messages Breckinridge women received in Melanie Beals Goan, "Establishing Their Place in the Dynasty: Sophonisba and Mary Breckinridge's Paths to Public Service," *Register of the Kentucky Historical Society* 101 (2003): 45–73. See also James C. Klotter, *The Breckinridges of Kentucky, 1760–1981* (Lexington: University Press of Kentucky, 1986).

5. MB, *Wide Neighborhoods*, 21.

6. Ibid., 29–33; Katherine Carson Breckinridge to MB, September 12, 1897, Prewitt Collection, Mary Breckinridge Series, uncatalogued, University of Kentucky Special Collections (UKSC), Lexington, Kentucky. For more information on late nineteenth-century educational options for women, see Barbara Miller Solomon, *In the Company of Educated Women: A History of Women and Higher Education in America* (New Haven, Conn.: Yale University Press, 1985).

7. MB, *Wide Neighborhoods*, 46.

8. Ibid., 51.

9. Susan M. Reverby, *Ordered to Care: The Dilemma of American Nursing, 1850–1945* (Cambridge: Cambridge University Press, 1987), 77.

10. In 1916 a daughter named Mary ("Polly") was born prematurely and lived only six hours. MB, *Wide Neighborhoods*, 66.

11. For records of her activities in this period, see Frontier Nursing Service Collection (hereafter FNSC), UKSC, boxes 336 and 357.

12. Paula Baker, "The Domestication of Politics: Women and American Political Society, 1780–1920," *American Historical Review* 89 (1984): 620–47.

13. Mary Breckinridge Thompson (hereafter MBT), "Motherhood—A Career," serialized in *Southern Woman's Magazine*, November 1916.

14. Child care, once a natural process, had now become measured and regulated. See Julia Grant, *Raising Baby by the Book: The Education of American Mothers* (New Haven, Conn.: Yale University Press, 1998). For Breckinridge's application of these methods and a discussion of Breckie's death, see MBT, *Breckie: His First Four Years* (New York: privately published, 1918).

15. MB to "Chela" [Margaret Gage], January 10, 1952, FNSC, box 352, folder 1.

16. *Mary B. Thompson v. R. R. Thompson*, divorce suit filed in Sebastian County, Arkansas, May 14, 1920, Prewitt Collection, Mary Breckinridge Series, uncatalogued, UKSC.

17. MB, *Wide Neighborhoods*, 66.

18. MBT to Sophonisba Breckinridge, May 23, 1918, FNSC, box 336, folder 4.

19. MB, *Wide Neighborhoods*, 75–110.

20. MB, "Maternity in the Mountains," *North American Review* 226, no. 6 (1928): 765.

21. MB, *Wide Neighborhoods*, 122–56.

22. MB, "Outline for a Demonstration of a Children's Public Health Service in Owsley County, Kentucky," [1923], 1; MB, "Memorandum Concerning a Suggested Demonstration for the Reduction if [*sic*] Infant and Maternal Death Rate in a Rural Area of the South," [February 1923], 2. Both reports can be found in FNSC, box 348, folder 3.

23. MB to Anne Dike, March 28, 1925, FNSC, box 337, folder 6.

24. "A Statement of Facts for Those Who Love Children and for Those Who Wish the Survival of Our Old American Stock," *FNSQB* 1 (October 1925).

25. Executive Group minutes, September 14, 1926, FNSC, box 2, folder 16.

26. "The First Meeting," *FNSQB* 1 (June 1925): 4; organizational meeting minutes, May 28, 1925, FNSC, box 2, folder 2.

27. "Third Annual Report," *FNSQB* 4 (June 1928).

28. Mary B. Willeford and Marion S. Ross, "How the Frontier Nurse Spends Her Time," *FNSQB* 12 (Spring 1937): 5.

29. MB, "Outline for a Demonstration," 4; MB, "Memorandum Concerning a Suggested Demonstration," 3–4.

30. MB to Kitty [Jessie Carson], November 24, 1926, FNSC, box 328, folder 1.

31. MB to Anne Dike, July 20, 1926, FNSC, box 337, folder 8.

32. MB, *Wide Neighborhoods*, 284–85.

33. Statement of Donations and Subscriptions Paid, May 1, 1926, to April 30, 1927, FNSC, box 233, folder 2.

34. "Fifth Annual Report," *FNSQB* 6 (Summer 1930): 4, 69–73.

35. Anna L. Altizer, "The Establishment of the Frontier Nursing Service" (MA thesis, University of Kentucky, 1990), 16.

36. Albert B. Chandler to MB, November 20, 1959, FNSC, box 364, folder 28.

37. "Nurse on Horseback Rides the Lonely Kentucky Trails," *New York Times*, January 18, 1931.

38. "American Appeal," May 1942, FNSC, box 29, folder 14.

39. "An Irish Heroine," *Lexington Herald*, July 24, 1931. Reprinted in *FNSQB* 7 (Autumn 1931): 5–6.

40. Ernest Poole, "The Nurse on Horseback," *Good Housekeeping*, June 1932, 38.

41. Blanche Randolph to Miss MacKinnon, August 1, 1931, FNSC, box 338, folder 6.

42. J. A. Stucky, unpublished article, 1914, J. A. Stucky Papers, box 1, folder 11, Hutchins Library, Berea College, Berea, Kentucky.

43. For "chivalry," see MB, "The Rural Family and Its Mother," reprinted from *The Mother* (April 1944), FNSC, box 356, folder 15. For "heart of the household," see MB, "Where the Frontier Lingers," *Rotarian* 47 (September 1935): 10.

44. "To Lend a Hand," *Johns Hopkins Magazine*, November 1965, 10.

45. MB, *Wide Neighborhoods*, 308.

46. This document provided nurses "standing orders" that covered any emergency that might arise. See Medical Routine, 2nd rev. ed., September 23, 1930, FNSC, box 27, folder 2.

47. MB, "A Frontier Nursing Service," *American Journal of Obstetrics and Gynecology* 15 (June 1928): 8, reprint located in FNSC, box 356, folder 6.

48. Gladys Peacock, "We Built the First Outpost Nursing Center," *FNSQB* 25 (Summer 1949): 39.

49. Caroline Gardner, "Frontier Nurse Chieftain," *Arkansas Gazette* 11 (October 27, 1935): 2.

50. Executive Group Minutes, October 14, 1925, FNSC, box 2, folder 9.

51. Margaret Gage, interview by Marion and W. B. Rogers Beasley, October 16, 1978, 79OH28FNS29, transcript, Frontier Nursing Service Oral History Collection (FNSOHC), UKSC.

52. W. Hifner Jr. to C. N. Manning, May 24, 1935, reprinted in *FNSQB* 11 (Summer 1935): 11.

53. Lucille Knechtly, *Where Else but Here?* (Pippa Passes, Ky.: Pippa Valley Printing, 1989), 73–74.

54. Seth Koven and Sonya Michel, eds., *Mothers of a New World: Maternalist Politics and the Origins of Welfare States* (New York: Routledge, 1993).

55. MB, "Outline for a Demonstration," 2.

56. David E. Whisnant, *All That Is Native and Fine: The Politics of Change in an American Region* (Chapel Hill: University of North Carolina Press, 1983), 166.

57. MB to Frances Payne Bolton, May 4, 1949, FNSC, box 69, folder 7.

58. Mary Jean Bowman and W. Warren Haynes, *Resources and People in East Kentucky: Problems and Potentials of a Lagging Economy* (Baltimore: Johns Hopkins University Press, 1963), 50–51, 212.

59. Ibid., 78–79, 311, 314. For 1960 statistics see Klotter, *Breckinridges of Kentucky*, 269.

60. Ronald D. Eller, *Uneven Ground: Appalachia since 1945* (Lexington: University Press of Kentucky, 2008), 29; Willis A. Sutton Jr. and Jerry Russell, *The Social Dimensions of Kentucky Counties: Data and Rankings of the State's 120 Counties on Each of 81 Characteristics* (Lexington: University of Kentucky College of Arts and Sciences, 1964), 44.

61. Helen E. Browne, interview by Carol Crowe-Carraco, March 26, 1979, 79OH173FNS74, FNSOHC.

62. "Stork Uses a Jeep in Rural Kentucky," *New York Times*, March 30, 1946.

63. T. S. Hyland, "The Fruitful Mountaineers," *Life*, December 1949; MB to Margaret Boncompagni, May 16, 1963, FNSC, box 128, folder 5.

64. EC meeting minutes, June 8, 1965, FNSC, box 8, folder 13; "Editor's Own Page," *FNSQB* 39 (Spring 1964): 22.

65. Peggy Elmore, "Field Notes," *FNSQB* 41 (Spring 1966): 46; Memorandum from MB to Marvin Patterson, January 9, 1961, FNSC, box 125, folder 1.

66. On July 30, 1965, President Lyndon B. Johnson signed Social Security Amendments that created the Medicare and Medicaid programs, just months after Breckinridge's death. The FNS began raising funds for the new Mary Breckinridge Hospital in 1966. It opened in 1975.

67. "Fortieth Annual Report," *FNSQB* 41 (Summer 1965): 4, 6, 15; Forty Year Total, FNSC, box 156, folder 11.

68. Ed Morgan, interview by Dale Deaton, July 7, 1978, 78OH143FNS03, FNSOHC.

Harriette Simpson Arnow
(1908–1986)

A Writer's Life

MARTHA BILLIPS

Harriette Simpson Arnow is known today primarily for her 1954 masterpiece, *The Dollmaker*, a powerful novel of dislocation that charts the downward spiral of the Nevels family once they relocate from the Kentucky hills to industrial Detroit during the waning years of World War II. The common perception of Arnow as a "one-novel author" proves inaccurate, however, as she published four additional works of long fiction during her lifetime: *Mountain Path* (1936), *Hunter's Horn* (1949), *The Weedkiller's Daughter* (1970), and *The Kentucky Trace* (1974). A sixth novel, *Between the Flowers*, which Arnow wrote in the 1930s, appeared posthumously in 1999. In addition to this corpus of work, Arnow also wrote two innovative social histories of the Cumberland region of Kentucky and Tennessee, *Seedtime on the Cumberland* (1960) and *Flowering of the Cumberland* (1963), as well as the autobiographical volume *Old Burnside* (1977). In a career that spanned more than fifty years, she also produced numerous short stories, book reviews, and critical articles. When she died at age seventy-seven in March 1986, she left the substantial but incomplete manuscript of yet another novel, tentatively titled *Belle* and set in Kentucky during the early years of the Civil War.

Based on this range of achievement, Arnow arguably stands as Kentucky's most accomplished woman writer. She undoubtedly ranks as the great chronicler of the lives of the rural residents of the state's southeastern region at a particularly turbulent time in American history—roughly the late 1920s through the 1940s. In her first four novels (including the posthumously published *Between the Flowers*), Arnow depicts an isolated, independent, and agriculturally based mountain culture that she clearly admires; at the same time, she consistently refuses to ignore either the hardships and privations imposed by subsistence farming in a remote area of Kentucky—particularly on women—or the social and economic changes that, in the first half of the twentieth century, drove an increasing number of rural people from the land. Her ambivalence about Kentucky mountain life as she knew and depicted it and her keen awareness of historical change create a major paradox in Arnow's career: her work chronicles and mourns the demise of a much-valued agrarian Kentucky culture, but after acknowledging the diaspora of the people and near destruction of the culture in *The Dollmaker*, Arnow can never again find a subject that inspires her to write novels of the caliber of *Mountain Path*, *Between the Flowers*, *Hunter's Horn*, and, certainly, *The Dollmaker*. After 1954 she turned increasingly to history and historical fiction in an effort, at least in part, to recover the basis of the lost mountain culture. When the subject matter of her work—especially her fiction—changes, its power and its quality decline.

Arnow appears to have experienced in her own life much of the tension and ambivalence toward the region and way of life that permeate her best fiction. She drew inspiration and subject matter from life in rural southeastern Kentucky, but she found she had to leave the area, often for a city, in order to write in any sustained manner. Critic Linda Pannill comments succinctly on this irony, noting that Arnow "always felt a conflict . . . between staying in the mountains and leaving. The people and talk that make up her best work were there, but so was a life that she had found hard on women and inimical to writing."[1] Arnow herself addressed this ambivalence in numerous interviews, including many conducted later in her life. She told Danny Miller in 1982, for instance, "I must still feel I'm a hill person" (despite having lived outside Ann Arbor, Michigan, for more than thirty years), and then added, "If I don't visit my home town [in Kentucky] once a year . . . I feel imcomplete [*sic*]." Earlier in the same interview, however, Arnow insisted, "I did my best and most writing when I lived in the city."[2] Similar statements of ambivalence and frustration run throughout the documentary film, *Harriette Simpson Arnow: 1908–1986*, released by Appalshop two years after the author's death.[3] In her life as in her writing, Arnow seems never to have fully resolved this tension between city and country, between "home" and "away." Like six-year-old Cassie Nevels of *The Dollmaker*, she continued to assert "My country is Kentucky" long after she had relocated to Michigan.[4]

Fortunately, the Arnow Collection at the University of Kentucky contains a trove of meticulously catalogued original documents that provide new insights into the life and work of this fascinating author.[5] Reading the archival material alongside Arnow's published fiction and nonfiction helps shed light on her

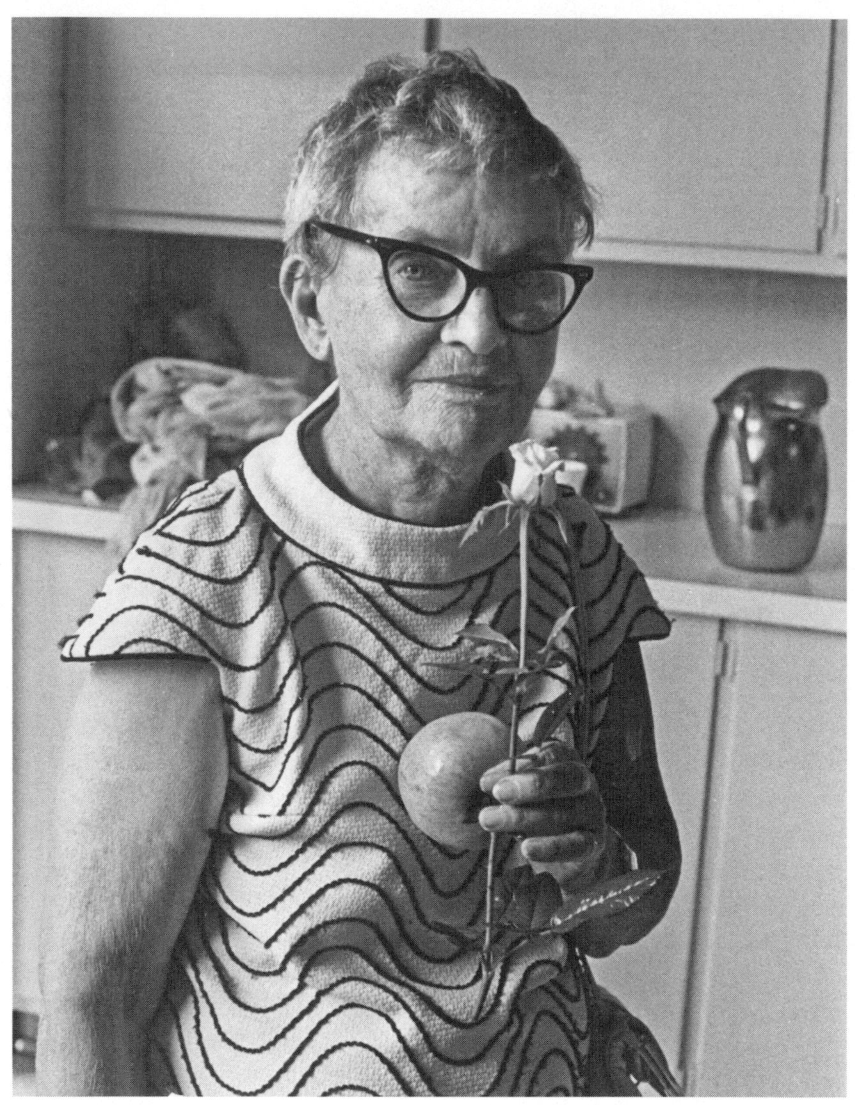

HARRIETTE SIMPSON ARNOW

Photo by Joyce Hancock, *Appalachian Journal* 8, no. 3 (Spring 1981). Copyright *Appalachian Journal* and Appalachian State University. Used with permission.

complex attitude toward her native region and, more generally, the conditions she found necessary for writing. For Arnow, these conditions remained intricately tied to place of residence and, later, to negotiating the demands posed by marriage and motherhood. Despite occasional inconsistencies and even contradictions, all these materials underscore a central reality: Harriette Simpson Arnow always remained motivated by one driving impulse. Her life was "the story of a child, student, teacher, wife and mother who felt compelled to write," whatever the obstacles, contends critic and biographer Sandra Ballard.[6]

Arnow's compulsion proves hardly surprising, for she descended from and grew up in a family of storytellers. Born at home in Wayne County, Kentucky, on July 7, 1908, Harriette Louisa Simpson was the second child and second daughter of Elias Thomas Simpson and Mollie Jane Denney Simpson, both former schoolteachers. (The Simpson family would eventually grow to include five daughters and one son.) Arnow's adult accounts of her early childhood often emphasize the central role of storytelling in the household, and she seems to have retained particularly strong memories of her father's stories. Late in her life, Arnow described her father as "a great story-teller" and associated his stories with her own budding desire to write. Arnow's maternal grandmother, Harriette Le Grand Foster Denney, and her stories also exerted a formidable influence on her young namesake. Arnow recalled that her grandmother "told handed-down stories of the days before our people had come to Kentucky, terrible tales of the French and Indian war." She described many of the stories as "sad as well as bloodcurdling."[7] These family stories Harriette Simpson heard growing up in Kentucky had a strong influence on the young girl; they not only steeped her in the history and oral traditions of her region and her people but also helped spark her own creative imagination.

Along with the stories Arnow heard as a child, the place in which she grew up left a deep impression on the adult author. The Simpson family—now with three children—moved from the small Pulaski County community of Bronston to Burnside in March 1913, a few months before Harriette's fifth birthday. Economics and education motivated the family's move: Elias Simpson had a job "feeding the hog" (or fueling the boiler) at the Chicago Veneer factory in the thriving lumber town; Mollie Simpson wanted her daughters to attend the graded school at Burnside rather than the one-room facility in Bronston.[8] The slim autobiographical volume Arnow published in 1977, *Old Burnside*, provides a vivid account of the author's childhood—and also reveals her subsequent frustration with the changes the Cumberland Dam wrought on the small town of her youth and on the Cumberland River itself.

The Simpson family did not remain in Burnside proper for long. In the mid-autumn of 1913 they moved to a new home on Tyree's Knob just outside (and above) the town itself. Life on Tyree's Knob consisted of chores both inside and outside the house, errands to Burnside, weekly Sunday school and church attendance at the Burnside Christian Church (Disciples of Christ), annual visits by Granma Denney, and, increasingly, talk of the war in Europe. Harriette began first grade at Burnside Graded School in 1914 while living on Tyree's Knob. She loved many things about the school, including making the annual holiday decorations and listening to the stories her teachers read or told; these stories, she recalled, "were the best part of the day for me." Young Harriette also proved quite a good student, earning high grades in "deportment, reading, and numbers" but struggling with penmanship.[9] No matter how hard she worked to form perfect letters or how much she feared her mother's disapproval, any grade higher than a "G" (for good) in penmanship usually eluded her. These early struggles with penmanship prove hardly surprising to those familiar with Arnow's sometimes almost illegible adult handwriting.

Arnow's childhood in and around Burnside anticipates her adult life and career in more significant ways as well. The author's accounts of her early years present young Harriette Simpson not only as a curious, creative, and inquisitive child but also as a strong-willed and independent one who chafed against restrictions, particularly those pertaining to acceptable female behavior. Like the fictional Gertie Nevels of *The Dollmaker*, Harriette hated wearing "appropriate" attire to church services; she decided early on to earn a college degree "but not for teaching school" as her mother insisted; she also wondered "if a girl could be" a geologist.[10] Such questioning of established gender norms and nonconformist aspirations would continue throughout Arnow's adult life.

Arnow's attendance at Burnside Graded School and, in many ways, her childhood came to an abrupt end in 1918. That year Mollie Simpson decided to teach her daughters at home due to the rapid spread of the deadly Spanish influenza; Harriette's beloved grandmother Denney died; her father accepted a more lucrative job as a tool dresser in the oil fields of Wolfe and Lee Counties, Kentucky; and the war escalated. As an adult, Harriette Arnow recalled these events vividly. In a 1973 autobiographical essay she noted: "In one sense childhood ended when I was ten years old; our grandmother died; we did not attend school because of the flu, and our mother taught us at home. Worst of all, our father went away to work . . . in the oil fields."[11] Writing even more dramatically in *Old Burnside*, she admitted, "Grandma dead, Papa gone, the dead and dying in Burnside, the long list of the [war] dead in the daily paper—my world seemed a place forgotten by God or could it be that God had died?" Harriette struggled to put "such a sinful thought" from her mind, but her comments make clear that a combination of personal, familial, communal, and national and international loss and trauma powerfully affected the young girl and that the events of the year 1918 left her profoundly shaken.[12] That year also marked the end of Harriette Simpson's formative early years in Burnside; by then, however, her experiences there had contributed indelibly to the adult writer she would become.

Late in 1918 or early in 1919 Mollie Simpson made the "Great Decision" to join her husband in the oil fields.[13] Although young Harriette Simpson spent a relatively brief period of time in the eastern Kentucky oil fields (the family moved back to Tyree's Knob in the summer of 1921), her experiences there seem to have spurred her lifelong environmental consciousness and provided inspiration for some of her early fiction. In late February or early March 1937 Arnow wrote a long and eloquent letter to her editor at Covici-Friede, Harold Strauss, from her home in Burnside. Strauss had helped Arnow publish her first novel, *Mountain Path*, and the letter largely concerns the manuscript of her second work of long fiction, *Between the Flowers*. Within it, however, Arnow commented on her time in the oil fields, telling Strauss, "When I was ten years old my mother took us and followed my father into the oil fields of Lee and Wolf [*sic*] Counties, a very rough, sparsely inhabited section northeast of here." She then added: "The country there was mostly high sandstone ridges and deep narrow valleys, and in it almost everywhere were signs of the things that had happened to it. Before the coming of the oil men the lumber men had come and gone and left it ugly with rotting limbs of trees and broken underbrush and ruined saplings. They had not only taken but they had destroyed, just as the oil men destroyed everything they touched." Viewing such destruction, the young author "learned to hate something, almost like hating a man who came and ruined and stole and destroyed and then went on to another place to do the same."[14]

This sense of outrage reappears in the comments of Roan Sandusky, a character in *Between the Flowers,* when he discusses the ruined lands in the Kentucky oil fields, and Arnow casts the novel's male protagonist, Marsh Gregory, as a former nitroglycerine hauler who prefers the life of a settled farmer to that of a "roving oil man."[15] Her experience at her father's workplace also seems to have contributed to Arnow's first published work of short fiction, "Marigolds and Mules." This highly realistic story, which appeared in the "little magazine" *Kosmos: Dynamic Stories of Today* in 1935, tells of a nitroglycerine explosion; after the accident, it proves virtually impossible to distinguish the flesh of a human being from that of a mule until a young boy discovers a human hand in the grisly remains. This early story makes clear that Arnow could write scenes of graphic violence from the very beginning of her career; it also indicates that her time in the oil fields continued to assert its influence as she began her life as a published author.

Arnow's first attempt at publication, however, occurred during her junior year at Burnside High School when she surreptitiously used some of her mother's writing paper to type a story, single-spaced, about wildflowers that came to life. She submitted the manuscript to the magazine *Child Life* and eventually received a letter of rejection along with a new copy of the story, double-spaced on standard-sized typing paper. The editors noted that while they could not use the story at the present time, they hoped the young author would continue to submit her fiction to the magazine. Only years later did Arnow realize that the editors had "shown [her] how to prepare a manuscript for submission to an editor and how it should be mailed."[16] In retrospect she recognized this as "a kind thing to do."[17] Mollie Simpson, however, would not have agreed. On discovering the submission, she chastised her daughter for wasting her mother's writing paper and her own time on "scribbling." The adult Arnow later commented wryly, "I continued to want to scribble."[18]

Despite her determination to write, Harriette Simpson entered Berea College in the fall of 1924 to earn a degree in education, as her mother had long insisted she do. In *Old Burnside* she said she chose Berea primarily because "the school required fewer hours of education for an elementary school teaching certificate than did the state's normal schools," which gave her the "opportunity to take botany and geology as electives."[19] In her later life, Arnow did not recall her time at Berea fondly, telling interviewer Danny Miller in 1982, "I put in two years at Berea College, found no one, either teacher or pupil, the least bit interested in writing."[20] Earlier, though, Arnow apparently had more complex and positive feelings about her time at the school. A small pamphlet she wrote in the late 1940s or early 1950s, "What Berea Meant to Me," praises the efforts of a Berea English professor who not only encouraged her to write but also helped her see the advantages of writing about the world she knew.[21] The largely favorable impressions contained in this slim volume serve in many ways to temper Arnow's later comments about the college.[22]

Arnow left Berea, teaching certificate in hand, in 1926, just a few weeks shy of her eighteenth birthday. Although Arnow always remained more interested in writing than in teaching, when faced with the necessity of supporting herself after leaving Berea, she put the teaching certificate to use and "got a job as teacher of a one room school at Hargis . . . on Cave Creek" in a remote corner of Pulaski County.[23] In an introduction she wrote for a 1963 reissue of *Mountain Path*, Arnow explained that in rural Kentucky communities in the 1920s the "average school was a one room frame building, a miscellaneous collection of seats its sole equipment, no toilets of any kind, water from the closest spring, hogs sleeping under the floor, and almost no help from the State of Kentucky."[24] Elsewhere, she recalled that of the nineteen students enrolled, many attended only sporadically, as the older students "often had to stay home to help in some way. They were the sons and daughters of small or subsistence farmers. Young ones couldn't walk the four or five miles to school in bad weather. . . . Mail came twice weekly, as I had come, by mule-back."[25] Despite the privations and challenges that accompanied the position, Arnow stayed the full seven-month term and seldom made the arduous sixteen-mile walk home to Burnside, even on weekends.

This tenure as a teacher in an isolated mountain school, although at first un welcome, proved one of the most important and formative experiences of Harriette Arnow's young adult life. While at Hargis, or "Possom Trot" as the local residents called it, she gained firsthand knowledge of the "world beyond the sound of train whistles," which had captured her imagination since childhood.[26] She boarded with a local family, got to know the parents of all her students, attended local social functions, and "went to church with the people" on Sundays and during revival meetings.[27] In short, she immersed herself in the daily life of the community, its culture, and its traditions. This intense and intimate involvement with the isolated hill community and its residents not only increased Arnow's understanding of and respect for a people and their way of life but also provided the inspiration for her first sustained attempts at writing fiction. Arnow's earliest extant short story dates from the spring of 1927, the period immediately following her departure from Hargis. The untitled piece of thirteen pages centers on Quite Sandusky, a young mountain girl taken from her home in the Kentucky hills by a well-meaning surveyor's wife who hopes to provide her with "the advantages of other children other places."[28] The plan goes awry, however, when Quite chooses to return to the hills after a few months in the city. This apprentice work posits a somewhat simplistic dichotomy between a restrictive "civilized" world and a freer rural one, yet it deserves notice not only because it provides the earliest example of Arnow's fictional treatment of the mountain culture of southeastern Kentucky but also because it anticipates many of the concerns and conflicts of her later, more mature work, including the pressures hill residents feel to devalue their way of life and the condescension of well-meaning outsiders.

Arnow worked in the Pulaski County school system for an additional year, this time as principal "of a large, unruly two room school within boarding distance of home."[29] She variously described the school as "less interesting" than the one at Hargis and a "nightmare."[30] She also complained that her duties as principal left her "neither time nor energy" for writing.[31] At the end of the school term, Arnow decided to return to college to finish her degree at the University of Louisville. Her two years there proved exhilarating for the developing author.

For the first time, she felt herself surrounded by others interested in writing; she joined and participated actively in Chi Delta Phi, a national literary society.[32] Inspired by her reading of Robert Browning, Arnow first attempted to write poetry, specifically dramatic monologues. Although she worked hard on her poems, she ultimately reached the conclusion, "I was not Browning. I was only Harriette Simpson and was no poet."[33] She was, however, a promising writer of fiction, and her friend from Chi Delta Phi, Cora Lucas, recognized Arnow's writing as "more mature, sure and professional than that of the rest of us." Lucas also recalled that in her prose "Harriette wrote of her experiences in her hill-country"—in sharp contrast to her early attempts at writing derivative poetry.[34]

After leaving the University of Louisville, Arnow returned to Pulaski County in part to help support her family; her father had died in July 1929. She quickly obtained a job teaching in a new rural high school. She liked the work very much and received almost a hundred dollars more per month than when she had begun teaching at Hargis.[35] She left the position after three terms, though, to take a job teaching at Louisville Junior High School. She later called herself "an idiot" for accepting the position, letting the idea of proximity to libraries and her friends in Louisville "lure [her] away" from Pulaski County.[36] She taught five groups of students assigned to the lowest-achieving classes in the school based on IQ scores. Exhausted and ill at the end of the semester, Arnow left without attending her final conference with a principal she later described as "Hitlerian."[37]

Perhaps wanting to leave Louisville and teaching behind for a while, once she was well Arnow got a job as waitress in a small resort near Petoskey, Michigan, where she had worked one previous summer. At the close of the resort season, the owner "very kindly" offered Arnow "rent-free, for some weeks, one of her cottages." There, for the first time, the young author had the opportunity to pursue her writing without interruption; she worked hard on the manuscript of a book she conceived of from the outset as "a novel of life in the Kentucky hills."[38] This series of character sketches, then titled *Path*, would eventually grow into her first novel, *Mountain Path*. Inspired by this first period of intensive, uninterrupted writing, Arnow made the momentous decision that she would "rather starve as a writer than a teacher"; instead of seeking another teaching job in Kentucky, as her family expected her to do, she relocated to Cincinnati in the fall of 1934.[39] As Arnow later noted, while the move from Kentucky to Cincinnati was a relatively short one geographically, it proved "a long, long one in [her] life."[40]

Once in Cincinnati, Arnow settled into a furnished room on Garfield Place near the public library and embarked on a rigorous course of reading some of the great European and British novelists, "among them Tolstoy, Dostoyevsky,

Sigrid Undset, Zola, Flaubert, Hardy, and Wladyslaw Reymont."[41] Her reading of these authors not only immersed Arnow in the tenets of what she termed a "grim realism" but also "influenced [her] . . . toward length" in her own novel writing.[42] While in Cincinnati, Arnow read many of the so-called proletariat writers of the time as well, and while she admired some, such as Steinbeck, the work of others, such as Erskine Caldwell's *Tobacco Road*, "sickened" her; she could find little in it consistent with the poor she had known in the hills of Kentucky whom she considered simply as individuals, not as members of an oppressed group. The work of Thomas Wolfe provided Arnow with a rare respite from "proletarianism and grim realism"; she later recalled loving Wolfe's "joyous feeling for life."[43]

Arnow's own writing at the time remained firmly grounded in the hill country she had known in Kentucky. Her first published story, "Marigolds and Mules," which drew on her experiences in the eastern Kentucky oil fields, appeared in *Kosmos* in early 1935. Her second, "A Mess of Pork," which appeared later that year in *New Talent*, tells the story of a Kentucky hill woman who "avenges her husband's murder by sending his killers unsuspecting into a valley of wild hogs." Critic Glenda Hobbs rightly describes "A Mess of Pork" as a "tense, suspenseful vignette" and notes that *New Talent* "received more appreciative letters for this story in a fortnight than it had for any other piece of fiction" it had published.[44] Arnow's next story, "The Washerwoman's Day," was published in the Winter 1936 volume of the prestigious *Southern Review*, then edited by Robert Penn Warren and Cleanth Brooks. Arnow received twenty-five dollars for this story—the first time a journal had paid her for her work—and later said she felt "puffed up with pride" on receiving the check.[45] Her most frequently anthologized story, "The Washerwoman's Day," recounts the funeral of a domestic laborer considered "poor white trash" by the middle-class members of her small Kentucky community, the town members' sanctimonious attempts at charity in paying for the funeral, and the defiance of the title character's daughter in bringing her illegitimate baby to the service.[46]

The author also wrote a number of other stories while in Cincinnati, such as "Fra Lippi and Me" (which shows the continued influence of Browning), which saw publication only later.[47] All these apprentice pieces exhibit the creative energy of a young writer at the start of a promising career, and the three stories published in the 1930s give glimpses of Arnow's mature long fiction. "Marigolds and Mules" and "A Mess of Pork," for instance, include scenes of violence and suspense that anticipate some of her most memorable writing in the later novels, while "The Washerwoman's Day" shows her concern for the working poor and disdain for small-town hypocrisy.

The widely read "A Mess of Pork" had attracted the attention of editor Harold Strauss, whose employer, Covici-Friede, already had the young John Steinbeck under contract.[48] The story so impressed Strauss that he wrote Arnow asking her to send him a novel if she had one in progress. Delighted, Arnow sent Strauss the manuscript of *Path*, which she had begun in Michigan and continued to work on in Cincinnati; this exchange began a long and friendly correspondence between author and editor that led to the publication of *Mountain Path* in August 1936. Although Arnow later claimed that it "was no trouble at all to publish *Mountain Path*," her correspondence at the time indicates that she revised the manuscript extensively, often in response to advice from Strauss.[49]

Set in the mid-1920s, *Mountain Path* tells the story of Louisa (Arnow's middle name) Sheridan, a gifted young university student forced by economic necessity to teach for a year in a one-room school in isolated "Cal Valley," Kentucky. The novel clearly draws from Arnow's earlier experience teaching at Hargis, but she remained impatient throughout her lifetime with those who saw her protagonist as herself and read her novel as a thinly veiled recounting of her own experience. While Arnow "was eager to get into the community [at Hargis] and see what it was like," for instance, Louisa intends to stay aloof from the people of Cal Valley and "to go back to school to chemistry and mathematics and people of her own kind" as quickly as possible.[50] During her seven-month stay in the mountains, however, Arnow's fictional schoolteacher finds that she has much to learn from her pupils and their parents. The outsider's initial condescension changes to respect as she comes to recognize the resourcefulness and adaptability of the mountain people and to see in their lives an emotional immediacy and connection to others missing from her own rather sterile existence. Through Louisa's growing recognition of the values and complexities of mountain life and culture, Arnow dispels many of the stereotypes of the backward or debased Appalachian mountaineer and replaces them with a balanced and realistic portrait of a people materially poor but competent, self-sufficient, and more complex than generally acknowledged in the "outside" world.

Despite Arnow's often positive depiction of the self-sufficient mountain community in her first novel, the author here as elsewhere refuses to ignore the particular toll hill existence takes on women. Hill women of childbearing age, the novel suggests, must deal with hard work, frequent pregnancy, difficult childbirth, the loss of their children to illness or accident, premature aging, and early death. These experiences place physical and psychological burdens on Arnow's women that their husbands, no matter how sympathetic or responsible, simply do not share. Moreover, the novel suggests that these conditions will persist into the future. Observing Rie Calhoun, a young girl in her eighth-grade class and a member of the family with whom she boards, Louisa predicts that in a few years "Rie's waist would twist yet more when she carried her own children instead of her mother's, and the bend of her shoulders grow as she grew with her children, so that at twenty-five she would be an old woman never having been a young one." Like many of Arnow's later young female characters, intelligent and inquisitive Rie Calhoun seems destined to follow the "biological pattern cut out for all things that were female and defenseless against ignorance (and poverty) and pain."[51] Even Arnow's inclusion of a typically male feud plot in the novel subtly shifts the focus from male violence to female experience, for her treatment of the feud calls attention away from the men who perpetuate the fighting and places it squarely on the mountain women who bear its consequences and conspire to end it. As in her later Kentucky novels, Arnow creates in *Mountain Path* a female-centered "domestic plot" that runs counter to, comments on, and ultimately takes precedence over the largely male-centered "action" plot.[52]

Late in her life, Arnow offered interesting glimpses into the composition of her first novel. Speaking of the genesis of *Mountain Path* to her friend John Flynn in 1985, Arnow recalled that her editor, Harold Strauss, "wrote to ask if I had anything longer than the short stories I had been publishing. It was funny. After I got out of the hills, things there seemed more interesting. I had lots of characters written, although nothing in book form. I sent him those." She added that she immediately quit her job, "laid in stocks of coffee, canned milk, oatmeal, bread and vegetables," and worked "like a horse" on the novel while living "in the top of an old building" in Cincinnati.[53] This pattern established the paradigm for Arnow's career; she drew inspiration and characters from her experiences in the Kentucky hills but actually wrote her mountain fiction while living in or near an urban area.

Mountain Path seems to have attracted a fair amount of attention in the city of its composition after the local newspaper, the *Enquirer*, ran an article under the headline "Cincinnati Waitress Revealed as Novelist by Publishers of Kentucky Hills Story."[54] Arnow later recalled the headline simply as "Waitress Writes Book," which she apparently found both condescending and potentially exploitative; she refused an invitation from the newspaper "to pose in her waitress's uniform for a picture accompanying" the article.[55] *Mountain Path* likewise attracted national attention, garnering surprisingly good reviews for a first novel, but it severely displeased at least one reader—Arnow's mother. Mollie Simpson told her daughter, "Everyone will think you fell in love with a moonshiner down there [while teaching at Hargis]."[56] She went further by asking, "Why don't you write about nice people?"[57] These criticisms had little impact, however, for the young author had found her subject matter.

Arnow had to hold firm against forces in addition to her mother in order to remain true to her chosen subject in her second novel, *Between the Flowers*. Strauss cautioned Arnow not to follow up on the success of *Mountain Path* by writing another "hillbilly novel," as some had labeled the earlier work.[58] Arnow remained resolute, however, and *Between the Flowers*, set in the 1930s in and around Arnow's native Burnside (Burdine in the novel), tells the story of Marsh and Delphine Costello Gregory, a young married couple whose conflicting desires create a growing gulf between them. Marsh, the child of itinerant farm workers and a former hauler of nitroglycerin, longs to settle on the land, to establish for himself and his family an enduring home and a way of life that will sustain it. Delph, a native hill woman who has never traveled beyond the county seat town, dreams of a life far from the farm and the small hill community; she desires an education, the wider opportunities available in the larger world, and the possibility of shaping the course of her own life. Arnow treats the dreams of both husband and wife with respect, recognizing that the agrarian life in a small community that nurtures Marsh could all but suffocate a person like his wife. She made this sentiment explicit in a letter to Strauss in which she explained that she did not intend "to glorify farming or any certain way of life at the expense of any other way, but simply to write of two who wanted different things."[59] Arnow achieves this goal in *Between the Flowers*. She writes convincingly of two individuals who want different things in life and whose marriage to one another interferes with the full attainment of their dreams. In the course of the novel, however, the marital conflict between the Gregorys also comes to represent the tension between an insular, self-sufficient, and largely agricultural world and the enticing external world that increasingly draws from it. This tension remains largely unresolved throughout the course of the novel.

Arnow worked on the manuscript of *Between the Flowers* from the middle of 1936 through the fall of 1938 while continuing to live in Cincinnati. Like all her best fiction, the novel contains strong action, convincing characters, and effective evocations of the natural world, but despite its many strengths the manuscript did not find its way into print during Arnow's lifetime. Correspondence between Arnow and Strauss tells the frustrating story of the pair's efforts to see the novel through to publication. These letters indicate that the author faced ongoing opposition to her subject matter and to her depiction of farm life, but *Between the Flowers* probably remained so long unpublished due to the time of its composition. When she began, Covici-Friede was still in business, but the publishing firm folded and was taken over by its printers in August 1938. As Strauss wrote Arnow on September 15, 1939, times "were not very good . . . for novels by little known authors. The war, etc." had made publishers particularly cautious about the market value of the books they chose to put before the public.[60] Fortunately, Michigan State University Press made the novel available to a wider audience when it published Arnow's six-decade-old manuscript in November 1999.

In many ways the "strenuous decade" of the 1930s ended for Harriette Simpson when she married Harold Arnow in March 1939.[61] The two met while working for the WPA Federal Writers' Project in Cincinnati in the late 1930s. They could hardly have had more dissimilar backgrounds. Born in Chicago in 1908 to Louis Arnowitz and Ida Abelowitz, "immigrant European Jews," Harold had worked as a salmon fisherman and fur trader in Alaska "before returning to Chicago as a crime reporter for the *City News Bureau*."[62] Blacklisted in Chicago for his work as a union organizer for the Newspaper Guild, Harold Arnow arrived in Cincinnati around 1936. Harriette later noted that, despite their vastly different backgrounds, she and her future husband "had much in common, particularly writing and a wish to 'get away from it all.'" Acting on that desire, the newlyweds purchased a "worn-out, cut-over boundary of 160 acres of land on Little Indian Creek on the Big South Fork of the Cumberland in a remote corner of Pulaski County" near the small community of Keno, Kentucky.[63] The Arnows intended to practice subsistence farming and devote themselves to writing at Keno. They lived there, in a house they nicknamed "Submarginal Manor," for nearly five years, from 1939 to 1944. Harriette later called their experiment with subsistence farming in a remote mountain area "a silly idea."[64] She insisted that she soon "realized there would never be in that place any time for writing . . . or anything except work."[65] A remarkable journal Harriette Arnow kept of their first year on the farm, "Early Days at Keno," however, paints a much more complex portrait of the experience with subsistence farming than her later comments would suggest. While "Early Days at Keno" details the Arnows' often laborious round of chores and activities, it also includes lyrical passages commenting on the beauty of the surroundings and elegiac ones noting the increasing exodus of people from the land, especially in the lead-up to World War II.[66] The journal contains little of the sense of frustration, despair, and even bitterness evident in so many of the author's later remarks about this period of her early married life.

"Early Days at Keno" does contain, however, glimpses of the tragedy that struck the Arnows during their first months on the farm. Pregnant on their arrival at Keno in August 1939, Harriette mentions in an entry dated November 22 that "there seems to be little I can do except sit by the fire and wait for this procrastinating child to arrive." On November 28 she observes, "It will surely only be a few more days until my confinement," yet the next, undated entry refers to "the weeks of my illness."[67] During this interval in December 1939 the Arnows' first child, a son they named Denny Abel Arnow, arrived stillborn. The Arnows had a healthy child, a daughter, Marcella, in September 1941, but a second daughter died a few hours after birth in 1942 or 1943. The early loss of these two children continued to haunt Harriette throughout her life. Her son Thomas (born December 1946) recalled visiting the "two little markers" in the cemetery near the old house at Keno on childhood trips to Kentucky, and as late as 1985 Harriette mentioned the two babies to her friend John Flynn, telling him, "I was just no good at child bearing."[68] The living conditions in the Kentucky hills, though, probably contributed significantly to the loss of the infants. Prenatal care hardly existed, and women usually delivered their babies at home, often but not always with the assistance of a midwife. These conditions, and the general lack of medical care in the remote mountain area, had serious consequences, especially for women and children. Arnow would later depict these conditions in *Hunter's Horn,* which not only includes a harrowing scene of a woman's death in childbirth but also calculates the emotional cost of the high rate of infant mortality in the mountains. Milly Ballew, the wife of the novel's protagonist, Nunn, has borne seven children and lost two; she continues to think of her dead children as she cares for and worries about her living ones.

The Arnows left the farm in Kentucky for wartime housing in Detroit in 1944—although they never sold their land near Keno. Harold left first and quickly secured a job as a newspaper reporter with the *Detroit Times*; Harriette and Marcella followed him north almost a year later. Although Arnow later claimed to have done almost no writing during the years at Keno, she had published two stories while living on the farm in Kentucky. The first, "Two Hunters," appeared in *Esquire* in July 1942 under the name "H. L. Simpson," as *Esquire* did not then accept submissions from women; when the magazine wanted a picture to accompany the story, Arnow sent them a photograph of one of her brothers-in-law. She later told an interviewer, probably with false contrition, it "was wrong to lie like that. But in the old days many women wrote under pseudonyms."[69] She placed a second story, "The Hunter," in the *Atlantic Monthly* in November of the same year under the name H. Arnow, crediting her husband as coauthor of the piece. Both stories are fragments of the novel Arnow later said "was in [her] head" at Keno—*Hunter's Horn*, published in 1949.[70]

The author may have felt in later years that the period at Keno hindered her efforts to write, but without it she could not have produced the very fine novel she did in 1949, for her experiences subsistence farming in an isolated hill community provided the creative impetus for *Hunter's Horn* as surely as her earlier sojourn as teacher in a one-room school had provided that of *Mountain*

Path. Arnow's stay among the hill people, and her growing maturity as an artist, gave her the confidence to tell the story of her third novel in the voices of the people themselves. After the stay at Keno, she no longer relied on the narrative perspective of the outsider, as in *Mountain Path*, or of the more familiar town farmers, as in *Between the Flowers*. And while *Hunter's Horn* acknowledges the hardships of mountain life and the increasing intrusions on it by an outside culture, it also presents the particular joys and benefits of a self-sufficient life lived close to the land.

Set largely in the back hill farming country of "Little Smokey Creek," Kentucky, *Hunter's Horn* tells the story of Nunnely Ballew, his wife, Milly, and their five children. Nunn farms land that belonged to his grandparents and hunts a great red fox, King Devil. Obsessed with his prey, Nunn feels "tied together [to the fox] with a bond stronger than any made by God or man, be it the link between a man and his child or his wife or his land."[71] When his old hound dog, Zing, dies, Nunn spends money his family desperately needs to buy a pair of pedigreed pups and thus continue the chase. With its focus on Nunn's pursuit of King Devil, *Hunter's Horn* on the surface resembles the hunting tales of Melville or Hemingway. A closer reading of the novel, however, reveals it as what critic Kathleen Walsh appropriately calls "a highly subversive entry" into the genre of the hunting tale, for Arnow remains less interested in Nunn's obsession than in the obligations he neglects in favor of it: the father's obligation to his children, the husband's to his wife, and the farmer's to his land.[72] As she did in *Mountain Path*, Arnow again creates a female-centered "domestic plot" that runs counter to and comments on the male-centered action plot; this "domestic plot" calculates the costs to his family of the hunter's absence.

Nunn's oldest daughter, Suse Ballew, suffers most from her father's neglect. Twelve and hopeful at the novel's beginning, Suse longs to attend high school and, through education and determination, escape the conditions that shape her mother's life. She ends the novel fifteen and pregnant after a single sexual encounter with a nineteen-year-old neighbor, Mark Cramer. Forced by her father and the traditional morality of the hills to marry the father of her child—a man she hardly knows and does not love—Suse ends the novel a victim not only of biology but also of her father's increasing neglect of family and farm. She cannot attend high school simply because Nunn has spent too much money on the hunt to afford her bus fare of fifty cents a week and her school clothes.[73] The novel strongly suggests that had Suse continued her education and received more attention from her parents, she would not have succumbed to the temptation of a clandestine romance.

While *Hunter's Horn* continues to focus on the experiences of mountain women, it also treats many of the other themes and conflicts present in Arnow's earlier fiction as well, primarily the conflict between cultures. *Hunter's Horn* takes place from the late summer of 1939 to March 1942. During this turbulent period in the United States, the cash-based and consumer-oriented economy of the outside world increasingly intruded on and took from the agrarian culture of the Kentucky hills. Many young men left for the war; others (including Mark Cramer) went to northern factories, and few resisted the pull of the "big money" promised by wage labor. Internal problems, such as past environmental damage to the land, posed additional threats to the continuation of a traditional, agriculturally based way of living. Arnow chronicles this process of cultural assault and decline throughout *Hunter's Horn*. Her sense of sorrow at the possible loss of an agrarian mountain existence permeates the novel, and at its end she offers less hope for the survival of a self-sufficient, farm-based way of life in the Kentucky mountains than she did at the conclusion of *Between the Flowers*.

Although Arnow's experiences in the Kentucky hills provided the inspiration, setting, and characters for *Hunter's Horn*, a familiar pattern emerges in its composition: once again, she actually wrote her novel in a city—this time, under demanding circumstances as a wife and mother of two in Detroit. After the Arnows' son Thomas was born in December 1946, the family of four lived in a cramped unit in a crowded development quickly constructed to house the thousands who migrated to the city to support the war effort. As her biographer Wilton Eckley correctly notes, writing and caring for a family "did not make an easy combination, and Harriette was hardpressed to find time for her writing" during these years.[74] Arnow herself more fully described the conditions under which she wrote *Hunter's Horn*, which she referred to as "The Colic Novel," in an unpublished journal. According to Arnow, she would rise "around 4 A.M. or so" to soothe her infant son who suffered from a severe case of colic. "Once up and with the baby quiet," she continued, "it was easier to stay up than go back to bed only to be sleepier than ever at the next awakening." The journal also contains disturbing glimpses of the tensions the author/mother felt between writing and marriage and motherhood. In a particularly anguished passage, she comments: "I knew that now with two children I ought to quit [writing]. Still, I wrote; I had to; I had begun scribbling in childhood, and before marriage had published a novel and a few short stories; now, my head seethed with novels that had to be poured out."[75] Continuing to write, it seems clear, came at a considerable physical and emotional cost to the author.

Fortunately, Arnow managed to complete her novel despite trying circumstances, and *Hunter's Horn* rewarded her efforts by achieving substantial critical and popular success. It reached the *New York Times* best-seller list and was named by the newspaper as one of the ten best novels of the year, while the *Saturday Review of Literature* selected it as Book of the Year—over Orwell's *1984*.[76]

Arnow followed up on this success with the creation of her greatest and most enduring work of fiction, *The Dollmaker*, which appeared five years later in 1954. This novel centers on the Nevels family, sharecroppers in the same Little Smokey Creek area of Kentucky that formed the setting of *Hunter's Horn*. The novel opens in the early years of World War II, and in fact the war pervades the entire work—it ends after the dropping of two atomic bombs on Japan in 1945. In the novel's memorable opening chapter, the novel's mule-riding protagonist, Gertie Nevels, commandeers a car carrying an army officer and his driver along a remote mountain road and forces them to take her and her gravely ill son to the nearest doctor's office; just before performing a crude tracheotomy on the child, she tells him, "I cain't let th war git you too."[77] Readers later learn that Gertie's brother, Henley, has died in action overseas. The war eventually does take the entire Nevels family, however, as Gertie and the five children follow husband and father Clovis to wartime housing in Detroit after he takes a job in a Flint, Michigan, factory to support the war effort. This novel of migration and dislocation powerfully renders the physical and psychic displacement of a self-reliant hill woman who finds herself painfully ill prepared to cope with the dangers and complexities of an urban existence. That Gertie cannot maintain her power and protect and provide for her family in the industrial world forms the heart of *The Dollmaker*'s tragedy.

Despite the seemingly familiar subject matter, *The Dollmaker* differs in several significant ways from Arnow's earlier Kentucky fiction. For instance, when viewed alongside Arnow's other female characters, Gertie Nevels emerges as a rather atypical Arnow mountain woman. Neither long-suffering and fatalistic, like Milly Ballew, nor unhappy with life on a hill farm, like Delph Costello Gregory and Suse Ballew, she works with the land to provide for her family. By the time Arnow writes *The Dollmaker*, she seems determined to create a heroine physically and spiritually strong enough to defy the conditions that oppress other women—and men—in her fiction. Even the powerful Gertie, though, cannot obtain her own land in the hills, thwarted in part in her efforts to buy a nearby farm by her mother's objections and her own inability to resist them.

The Dollmaker differs even more significantly from Arnow's earlier work, however, in that only its first nine chapters take place in the Kentucky hills. The majority of the long novel centers on the Nevels family in the teeming wartime housing project as they struggle to "adjust." Clovis and three of the children do so all too easily, quickly learning to buy consumer goods "on time" and to get along in the competitive worlds of the local alley, the overcrowded school, and the factory floor. Gertie and the other two children do not. The oldest son, Reuben, runs away and returns to Kentucky; the youngest daughter, imaginative six-year-old Cassie, dies in a horrific accident in a train yard. Gertie nearly sinks into madness after these losses, but she recovers in order to care for her husband and remaining children. At the end of the novel, she has a prize piece of cherry wood she has carved for years, hoping to bring out the face of Christ—or Judas—chopped into pieces so that she can make cheap dolls and crucifixes to sell to help support her family. Critics differ as to whether this final action marks Gertie's triumph or defeat, but it seems clear that in having Gertie destroy the piece of wood she brought from Kentucky, Harriette Arnow metaphorically marks the destruction of the self-sufficient agrarian culture of the hills.[78]

In writing *The Dollmaker*, Arnow drew inspiration from both her experiences in the Kentucky hills and her months in wartime housing in Detroit, although she wrote the novel while living on a small, forty-acre farm outside Ann Arbor, Michigan, where the family had moved in 1950. In a 1983 interview, Arnow recalled that witnessing firsthand the heavy migrations of rural people from the "southern part of the Appalachians" to Detroit led her to wonder how mountain "women, who had never used a telephone or seen or used any appliance run by electricity," would fare in an urban environment. She went on to acknowledge that one such woman, Gertie Nevels, did not "learn" to live easily in the urban world, "partly because she didn't really want to."[79] Arnow's heroine did, though, form bonds with many of her women neighbors—Irish, Polish, Catholic, and Protestant. These bonds provide some consolation for all her losses and also mark a way in which *The Dollmaker* remains consistent with Arnow's earlier fiction, despite all its clear differences: once again, female experience proves central. Even in Detroit, amidst all the chaos caused by global events, women depend on one another as they care for and fulfill their responsibilities to their children. A novel both of war and industrialization, *The Dollmaker* focuses firmly on the domestic sphere. It may remain generally overlooked as a World War II text largely because it takes place on the home front rather than the battlefield.

The Dollmaker garnered even more critical and popular success than did *Hunter's Horn*. It sold well and came in second to William Faulkner's *A Fable* for the National Book Award in 1955.[80] In retrospect, *The Dollmaker* actually seems a better book than *A Fable*, despite Faulkner's great achievements throughout his career. Unlike Arnow's other work, *The Dollmaker* has also remained consistently in print since its initial publication, which may have helped contribute in later years to the misperception of Arnow as a "one-novel" author. This frustrated her a great deal, and as her friend John Flynn noted: "More than the additional fame that never came her way for having written two recognized classics, [Arnow] was aggrieved that young people who asked her questions about Gertie Nevels, who was from Ballew, Kentucky, had not been introduced to Nunn Ballew, from *Hunter's Horn*."[81] These feelings of frustration increased when Arnow felt "she was 'being drug into fame on Jane Fonda's coattails'" after Fonda released an Emmy-winning television adaptation of *The Dollmaker* in 1984.[82] Despite this frustration, though, Arnow appreciated Fonda's deep understanding of the novel and admired many aspects of the film.

Harriette Arnow continued to write after *The Dollmaker*, publishing her well-regarded social histories, *Seedtime on the Cumberland* (1960) and *Flowering of the Cumberland* (1963). In these meticulously researched volumes, Arnow represents the early settlement of the region by concentrating on and recreating the daily lives of ordinary people in the late eighteenth century. The works present a markedly egalitarian view of pioneer life in the Cumberland, a view Arnow came to hold after almost two decades of research. Despite the completion and relative success of these long-planned works, the 1960s on the whole proved a very difficult decade for Arnow. She continued to struggle to find time to write while living on the farm, noting her ongoing attempts to give up writing altogether: "I have tried," she writes, "but instead of quitting entirely, have switched from fiction to nonfiction. Research and arrangement of facts take a great deal of time, but the many interruptions do not rupture my day as with fiction."[83]

During much of the decade, Arnow also suffered from a long undiagnosed pituitary tumor. In a manuscript titled "Tumor Tale" and apparently intended for publication, Arnow describes frequent symptoms of "fatigue, thirst, inability to keep warm or cool," and a gradual loss of vision. These physical symptoms contributed to a deep slide into depression; elsewhere in "Tumor Tale" the author acknowledges that "worse, almost than the miseries of my body were those of my mind."[84] She felt alone in the empty house with her children grown and gone; she found it hard to work on the manuscript of *The Weedkiller's Daughter*; she bemoaned the changes to the immediate neighborhood caused by increased construction and suburban sprawl; and she despaired of the escalation of the conflict in Vietnam. A staunch liberal, Arnow frequently told friends that although she happened to live on Nixon Road in Ann Arbor, she "was utterly opposed to the policies" of Richard Nixon.[85]

Arnow had surgery in early 1967 to remove the tumor and her health almost immediately improved, but the tumor returned in just six months. Fortunately, a second surgery eradicated it completely. Restored to health, Arnow completed *The Weedkiller's Daughter* and published it in 1970. Arnow's only novel with a non-Kentucky setting, *The Weedkiller's Daughter* takes place in the area around

Ann Arbor and focuses on a suburban family, the Schnitzers, and the rebellion of their adolescent daughter, Susie, in the face of her parents' paranoia, racism, and determination to "tame" the natural world. Although it includes a memorable appearance by Gertie Nevels, now called "The Primitive" by the neighborhood teenagers, *The Weedkiller's Daughter* as a whole lacks the vibrancy and immediacy of Arnow's earlier fiction, and it received generally negative reviews. Her 1974 novel, *The Kentucky Trace: A Novel of the American Revolution*, fared better with the few critics who reviewed it, but it received little notice overall and did not sell well. Arnow herself judged her final published volume harshly, calling *Old Burnside* "one of those horrible 'I,' 'I,' 'I,' books."[86] Despite the author's harsh assessment, this autobiographical work provides a wealth of insight into both the young Harriette Simpson and the small Kentucky community that helped shape her.

In the final years of her life, Arnow increasingly looked back at her published *oeuvre*, and her remarks in interviews from the 1980s give evidence of many of the same tensions and conflicts she felt throughout her career, especially after her marriage and the birth of her children. When asked by Danny Miller in 1982 if she felt "that women writers have had it harder than men writers," she answered, "Sometimes I feel that way. If you just stay at home and write when you can, then you're really a housewife."[87] In May of the next year, she told Nancy Carol Joyner, "Considering my age and that my first novel was published when I was twenty-eight, I have accomplished very little, but we do have two fine children long since through graduate work and gone," appearing still to counterpose writing and motherhood even many years after her children had reached adulthood.[88] Similar self-deprecating comments appear in other interviews and public lectures as well, and in her unpublished writing she often referred to speaking at conferences and attending writing workshops somewhat derisively as her "literary ladying."[89] At one such conference, a meeting of the Appalachian Writers' Association held at Morehead, Kentucky, in June 1985, she met Sandra Ballard, then a doctoral candidate at the University of Tennessee and now the editor of *Appalachian Journal*. On learning that Ballard planned to write a book about her work, Arnow told her, "If you must write about an author, don't write about me."[90] Arnow may have spoken ironically, but late in life she did seem to undervalue her own considerable achievement as an artist.

Harold Arnow had died suddenly of a stroke in February 1985, a few months before Harriette Arnow met Ballard at the conference in Morehead. His death, not surprisingly, left his widow deeply shaken, for the two had shared a close, mutually respectful, mutually supportive, and deeply affectionate marriage for more than forty-five years. In fact, Harold typed many of Harriette's handwritten manuscripts and saw to other details of publication for her. Somewhat to the family's surprise, Harold had left "a paper in his effects requesting to be buried in the old cemetery" at Keno. Despite the difficulty of reaching the isolated location in February, the family honored his request, borrowing a "six-wheel drive Army truck called a 'Goat'" to reach the destination.[91] Harriette returned to the farm in Ann Arbor after the funeral and continued to live there until her own death on March 22, 1986, one day shy of her wedding anniversary. Two months later her children buried her ashes at Keno "next to Harold and their two still born babies."[92] When Thomas Arnow returned to the gravesite in 2003, he discovered that a "beautiful crushed gravel road" now provided easy access to the old homestead, but with access had come "development" and destruction. The scenes "of destroyed lands" all around his parents' old house, he said, took him "back to high school Latin class, where we learned a verb, *vastare*, translated as, 'lay waste to'"—a description he deemed fitting for what he saw at Keno. "The destruction of the Kentucky land," the son observed, "would have horrified my parents."[93] No doubt, it would have.

NOTES

1. Linda Pannill, "Retrospective," *Belle Lettres* 3, no. 3 (1988): 3.

2. Danny Miller, "A *MELUS* Interview: Harriette Arnow," *MELUS* 9 (Summer 1982): 90, 85.

3. *Harriette Simpson Arnow, 1908–1986*, directed by Herb E. Smith (1988; Whitesburg, Ky.: Appalshop, 2010), DVD.

4. Harriette Simpson Arnow (hereafter HSA), *The Dollmaker* (1954; New York: Avon, 1999), 329.

5. HSA Papers, 1907–2004 (Collection 81M2), Special Collections and Archives, University of Kentucky Libraries, Lexington (hereafter cited as Arnow Papers, UK). This collection consists of 148 boxes measuring a total of 54.71 cubic feet. I would like to thank Kate Black, special collections librarian at the University of Kentucky, for invaluable assistance and insight in helping me conduct the archival research necessary for this essay.

6. Sandra L. Ballard, "Harriette Simpson Arnow's Life as a Writer," in *Harriette Simpson Arnow: Critical Essays on Her Work*, ed. Haeja K. Chung (East Lansing: Michigan State University Press, 1995), 16. This collection of interviews with, lectures by, and critical articles about Harriette Arnow remains the single best source available for those wishing to learn more about her life and work (hereafter cited as *Arnow: Critical Essays*).

7. Miller, "A *MELUS* Interview," 88.

8. HSA, *Old Burnside* (Lexington: University Press of Kentucky, 1977), 31–32.

9. Ibid., 85, 89.

10. Ibid., 101, 74.

11. HSA, "Recollections and Literary History," *Appalachian Heritage* 1 (Fall 1973): 12.

12. HSA, *Old Burnside*, 118.

13. Ibid., 119.

14. Harriette Simpson to Harold Strauss, c. 1937, Arnow Papers, UK.

15. HSA, *Between the Flowers* (East Lansing: Michigan State University Press, 1999), 191.

16. HSA, "Help and Hindrance in Writing: A Lecture," transcribed by Sandra L. Ballard, in *Arrow: Critical Essays*, 285. Arnow delivered the address before the Appalachian Writers Association meeting at Morehead State University in Morehead, Kentucky, in June 1985.

17. Miller, "A *MELUS* Interview," 88.

18. HSA, "Help and Hindrance in Writing," 285.

19. HSA, *Old Burnside*, 125.

20. Miller, "A *MELUS* Interview," 88.

21. Ballard, "Arnow's Life as a Writer," 19.

22. HSA, "What Berea Meant to Me," pamphlet, HSA Papers, 1936–1986, Hutchins Library, Berea College, Berea, Kentucky.

23. Harriette Simpson, handwritten note, Arnow Papers, UK.

24. HSA, introduction to HSA, *Mountain Path* (Berea, Ky.: Council of the Southern Mountains, 1963; Lexington: University Press of Kentucky, 1985), vi.

25. HSA, "Help and Hindrance in Writing," 286.

26. "Possom Trot" in Miller, "A *MELUS* Interview," 89; HSA, introduction to *Mountain Path*, v.

27. Miller, "A *MELUS* Interview," 89.

28. HSA, untitled manuscript about Quite Sandusky, c. 1927, Arnow Papers, UK.

29. HSA, "Recollections and Literary History," 13.

30. HSA, "Help and Hindrance in Writing," 286; "Recollections and Literary History," 13.

31. HSA, "Recollections and Literary History," 13.

32. Cora Lucas, "'A Dream . . . That's What I Came out For': A Recollection and Appreciation of Harriette Arnow," *Adena: A Journal of the History and Culture of the Ohio Valley* 1 (Spring 1976): 128.

33. HSA, "Help and Hindrance in Writing," 287.

34. Lucas, "A Dream," 128.

35. HSA, "Help and Hindrance in Writing," 288.

36. Ibid.; "Recollections and Literary History," 13.

37. HSA, "Recollections and Literary History," 13.

38. HSA, "The Clarence M. Burton Memorial Lecture," in *Arnow: Critical Essays*, 252.

39. Nancy Carol Joyner, "Harriette Simpson Arnow," *Appalachian Journal* 14 (Fall 1986): 53.

40. HSA, "Help and Hindrance in Writing," 288.

41. Danny Miller, "Harriette Simpson and Harold Arnow in Cincinnati: 1934–1939," *Queen City Heritage* 47, no. 2 (1989): 43.

42. HSA, "Help and Hindrance in Writing," 289 ("grim realism"); Miller, "A *MELUS* Interview," 95.

43. HSA, "Help and Hindrance in Writing," 289.

44. Glenda Hobbs, "Starting Out in the Thirties: Harriette Arnow's Literary Genesis," in *Literature at the Barricades: The American Writer in the 1930s*, ed. Ralph S. Bogardus and Fred Hobson (University: University of Alabama Press, 1982), 146.

45. John Flynn, "A Journey with Harriette Simpson Arnow," *Michigan Quarterly Review* 29 (Spring 1990): 246.

46. HSA, "The Washerwoman's Day," in *The Collected Short Stories of Harriette Simpson Arnow*, ed. Sandra L. Ballard and Haeja K. Chung (East Lansing: Michigan State University Press, 2005), 61.

47. HSA, "Fra Lippi and Me," *Georgia Review* 33 (Winter 1979): 867–75. Sandra L. Ballard and Haeja K. Chung also brought out a complete collection of Arnow's previously published and unpublished short fiction in 2005 (see n. 46).

48. Arnow later noted that when the New York publishing house Covici-Friede went out of busi-

ness in the late 1930s, "John Steinbeck and myself both had to find other publishers" ("Help and Hindrance in Writing," 289).

49. Flynn, "Journey with Harriette Simpson Arnow," 246. For correspondence, see Arnow Papers, UK.

50. Miller, "A *MELUS* Interview," 91 (Arnow quotation); HSA, *Mountain Path* (1936; Lexington: University Press of Kentucky, 1985), 12.

51. HSA, *Mountain Path*, 364, 286.

52. For a further discussion of the feud plot in *Mountain Path*, see Martha Billips, "Harriette Simpson Arnow's First Novel: A New Look at *Mountain Path*," *Appalachian Heritage* 40 (Spring 2012): 77–86.

53. Flynn, "Journey with Harriette Simpson Arnow," 246, 247.

54. Miller, "Harriette Simpson and Harold Arnow," 45.

55. Hobbs, "Starting Out in the Thirties," 154–55.

56. Miller, "A *MELUS* Interview," 91.

57. Flynn, "Journey with Harriette Simpson Arnow," 247.

58. Hobbs, "Starting Out in the Thirties," 157.

59. Harriette Simpson to Harold Strauss, c. 1937, Arnow Papers, UK.

60. Harold Strauss to Harriette Simpson, September 15, 1939, Arnow Papers, UK.

61. Hobbs, "Starting Out in the Thirties," 160.

62. Miller, "Harriette Simpson and Harold Arnow," 146.

63. HSA, "Recollections and Literary History," 14.

64. Miller, "A *MELUS* Interview," 93.

65. HSA, "Recollections and Literary History," 14.

66. HSA, "Early Days at Keno," 179-page unpublished manuscript, 1939–40, Arnow Papers, UK.

67. Ibid., 44, 48.

68. Thomas Arnow, "On Being Harriette Arnow's Son," *Appalachian Journal* 14 (Summer 2005): 466; Flynn, "Journey with Harriette Simpson Arnow," 243.

69. Joyner, "Harriette Simpson Arnow," 54.

70. HSA, "Recollections and Literary History," 14.

71. HSA, *Hunter's Horn* (1949; New York: Avon, 1976), 328.

72. Kathleen Walsh, "*Hunter's Horn:* Harriette Arnow's Subversive Hunting Tale," *Southern Literary Journal* 17 (Fall 1984): 55.

73. HSA, *Hunter's Horn*, 335.

74. Wilton Eckley, *Harriette Arnow*, TUSAS United States Authors Series (New York: Twayne, 1974), 42.

75. HSA, "Biography of a Body," unpublished manuscript, c. 1966–70, Arnow Papers, UK.

76. Sandra L. Ballard, "The Central Importance of *Hunter's Horn*," in *Arnow: Critical Essays*, 141.

77. HSA, *The Dollmaker*, 17–18.

78. For positive readings of the novel's ending, see Lee Edwards, *Psyche as Hero: Female Heroism and Fictional Form* (Middletown, Conn.: Wesleyan University Press, 1984), 234–35; Elizabeth Harrison, *Female Pastoral: Women Writers Re-Visioning the American South* (Knoxville: University of Tennessee Press, 1991), 97. Joyce Carol Oates, by contrast, calls *The Dollmaker* "a legitimate tragedy, our most unpretentious American masterpiece." She finds the novel's "beauty" in "its author's absolute commitment to a vision of life as a cyclical tragedy—as constant struggle." See Joyce Carol Oates, afterword to *The Dollmaker*, by Harriette Simpson Arnow (New York: Avon, 1999), 601, 602.

79. Haeja K. Chung, "Fictional Characters Come to Life: An Interview," in Chung, *Arnow: Critical Essays*, 266, 267.

80. Eckley, *Harriette Arnow*, 44.

81. Flynn, "Journey with Harriette Simpson Arnow," 255.

82. Joyner, "Harriette Simpson Arnow," 52.

83. HSA, "Biography of a Body."

84. HSA, "Tumor Tale," unpublished manuscript, c. 1966–70, Arnow Papers, UK. A letter to a Dr. Kahn, dated November 18, 1969, precedes the manuscript; the letter indicates that Arnow planned to publish the text in order to help others suffering from similar symptoms. Given this apparent intent to publish "Tumor Tale," some of its revelations appear surprisingly candid.

85. George Brosi, "Harriette Simpson Arnow: A Remembrance," *Appalachian Heritage* 40 (Spring 2012): 87.

86. Miller, "A *MELUS* Interview," 91.

87. Ibid., 96.

88. Joyner, "Harriette Simpson Arnow," 55.

89. HSA, "Biography of a Body."

90. Flynn, "Journey with Harriette Simpson Arnow," 260.

91. Thomas Arnow, "On Being Harriette Arnow's Son," 466.

92. Flynn, "Journey with Harriette Simpson Arnow," 260.

93. Thomas Arnow, "On Being Harriette Arnow's Son," 467.

Georgia Montgomery Davis Powers

(1923–)

Purpose in Politics

CAROLYN R. DUPONT

By her own telling, Georgia Montgomery Davis Powers stood patting her hair in the mirror when she heard the shots that felled Dr. Martin Luther King Jr. After running into the courtyard of the Lorraine Motel in Memphis that April afternoon in 1968, she looked up to see King's body on the second floor, one knee stuck straight up and one foot dangled over the ledge. As medics loaded him into an ambulance moments later, she climbed in as well, but a discreet Andrew Young pulled her back. "No, Senator," he cautioned. "I don't think you want to do that."[1]

Like the man she mourned that day, Montgomery worked at the core of the social revolutions that dramatically altered America in the mid-twentieth century. She secured a prominent place in gender, civil rights, and Kentucky history by becoming the first woman as well as the first African American ever elected to the Kentucky Senate. Her legacy and influence, however, extend far deeper than "firsts" in the record books. As a Kentucky state senator for twenty-one years, Montgomery used her position to champion the needs of the dispossessed and underprivileged. She won perhaps her most significant legislative battle after only a few months in office, when she introduced and secured the passage of an open housing law. The first such provision in any southern state, the bill struck at one of the most insidious, intractable, and far-reaching sources of discrimination faced by black Kentuckians.

Montgomery's path to these achievements differs significantly from the trajectories of other noted female civil rights leaders. Women such as Diane Nash, Rosa Parks, Victoria Gray, Septima Clark, and Fannie Lou Hamer each set out

GEORGIA MONTGOMERY DAVIS POWERS (THIRD FROM RIGHT)

At the 1964 march on Frankfort, Georgia Montgomery Davis walked just behind Martin Luther King Jr. Here she is seen over his left shoulder (in a coat with a light collar). Jackie Robinson (on left) signs a program. Public Information Photo Collection, Public Records Division, Kentucky Department for Libraries and Archives.

in local, grassroots work for racial equality that later catapulted them into larger political battles. Montgomery, however, found her true calling and came alive in politics itself, and she entered civil rights activism through this door. Her involvement in direct-action initiatives lasted but a short time, while in her long Senate career she furthered equality and opportunity for black, female, elderly, laboring, poor, and disabled Kentuckians.

Yet sex—that most private and intimate of matters—intrudes significantly into this story about a very public life. For in addition to her well-earned recognition for breaking gender and racial barriers and her celebrated legislative achievements, Montgomery claims fame and fascination as the self-confessed lover of Martin Luther King Jr. Indeed, the great leader expended his valedictory sexual energies with Georgia Montgomery only hours before she stood over his mortally wounded body in Memphis. Issues of sexuality have shaped the legacy of many other civil rights heroines, for their long struggle for equality has included a quest to conduct their intimate lives free from patriarchal domination and racial intimidation. Slave women contended with masters' unchallenged access to their bodies, and spokeswomen such as Ida B. Wells decried the racial and sexual double standards that underlay the horrors of lynching. Though black women often adopted rigorous standards of chastity, the opponents of racial equality blasted civil rights activists for sexual improprieties of all sorts. Importantly, Rosa Parks, rather than Claudette Colvin, became a civil rights icon because the fifteen-year-old Colvin's illegitimate pregnancy, it was believed, rendered her an unsuitable figure around which to rally support for a bus boycott. Women, far more than men, have consistently suffered vetting of their private lives when they entered the public arena, but for black women, race raised the bar of gender to nearly insurmountable heights.[2]

Yet the same illicit sex that once disqualified Claudette Colvin for civil rights activism only bolstered the notoriety of Georgia Montgomery. Thus, in the conduct of her sexual life, as well as in her path to civil rights achievements, Montgomery departed from important norms that constrained and defined the behavior of other black female activists. Even as she carved out a long and fruitful political career in the Kentucky Senate—an arena previously occupied exclusively by white men—Montgomery also pursued a private sexual life once only available with impunity to white men. If she gained a place in history by crashing through conventional barriers to achieve her goals, in her teenaged sexual experimentation, marital infidelity, and sensational celebrity affair, she ignored the gender and racial standards that had long dictated the fitness of black women for entry into any public role.

Born on October 19, 1923, in the black settlement of Jimtown, just east of

Springfield, Kentucky, Georgia Lee Montgomery grew up in a segregated and racially oppressive world, and she came of age under strict assumptions about her destiny as a woman. Her family claimed deep roots in rural Kentucky and in a racially mixed reality only thinly veiled by segregation. Mystery shrouded the exact paternity of her father Ben, whose straight, ash-blond hair and light complexion obviously came from a white man rather than his mother's husband, Joseph Montgomery. Though the Montgomerys and most of their relatives lived on the edge of poverty, a great-aunt Celia owned five hundred acres and a large house filled with fine furniture. Born a slave, Celia had remained with her white owners after emancipation, and the patriarch bequeathed her the property in gratitude for decades of service.[3]

When a tornado destroyed their two-room shack in 1925, the family forsook Washington County to join the tide then sweeping rural black Kentuckians into Louisville. Ben Montgomery's white appearance landed him well-paying work in a foundry, and he moved his wife and children into a Grand Avenue enclave in transition from white to black. The family quickly put down roots; with the exception of just a few years in early adulthood, Georgia Montgomery would call Louisville home for the rest of her life. Along with her eight brothers, she attended the city's all-black schools—Virginia Avenue Elementary, Madison Junior High, and Central High. The children lived in the nurturing environment of a loving and well-respected family, and with little consciousness of deprivation, Montgomery grew up vivacious, capable, and confident.

In addition to a stable and happy home life, Montgomery benefited from the stimulation of a vibrant community. Concentrated in Louisville in greater proportions than anywhere else in the state, blacks settled in patterns that reflected class as well as race. The poorest among them lived hard lives in shacks on unpaved streets in "Little Africa," but Montgomery's family moved among the city's middle-class blacks. These businessmen and women built banking, retail merchandise, and real-estate enterprises; they launched voices of advocacy such as the *Louisville Defender* and organized chapters of the NAACP and the Urban League. Unlike their Deep South counterparts, Louisville blacks retained the right to vote. They used this power to send their own to city government and, after 1935, to the Kentucky House of Representatives. The Montgomerys' neighbors included black lawyers, doctors, educators, politicians, and athletes who rose to national prominence, and Montgomery later credited such role models with shaping her aspirations.[4]

Religion also played an important role for Montgomery and many other black Louisvillians, offering moral guidance, hope in times of trouble, and a vigorous social life. Montgomery's parents read the Bible and prayed in the home, and the family attended Triumph the Church and Kingdom of God in Christ, a black holiness church that assembled in an old "shotgun" house. On Friday evenings and all day Sundays, members gathered for lively worship that included singing, shouting, and clapping accompanied by drums and tambourines. In church Montgomery found significant models of female activism and inspiration, and throughout her life she claimed "strong belief in God and the values expressed in the Bible" as important foundations.[5]

Yet in spite of the family's relatively comfortable material circumstances and the support of faith and community, the racial caste system shaped all aspects of their lives. Most theaters, restaurants, and parks in the city segregated blacks or denied them entry altogether, and Montgomery understood at an early age why her family avoided those places. As she grew older and ventured farther from her protective cocoons, Montgomery encountered these racial barriers in more humiliating ways. A white driver once forced her to the back of the bus on an out-of-state trip. Her manager at a lunch-counter job permitted her to serve black customers who wanted to carry their meals out but would not allow them to eat on the premises. Louisville employers pursued racial discrimination with ferocity, and Montgomery once took a job in a factory that segregated the restrooms and even the stairs. Racial lines also manifested cruelly in the attitudes and practices of Louisville law enforcement. In one particularly troubling incident, police burst into the Montgomery home without warning or warrant; they grabbed Montgomery's brother Robert as a suspect in a tire-slashing incident and placed him in the Jefferson County Children's Center.[6]

Though a loving family and close community sheltered Montgomery from the severest abuses of racial oppression, that same family and community reinforced the gender limitations that frustrated her energy and ambition. As the only girl among nine children, she shouldered a wide range of domestic responsibilities and watched with longing as her brothers enjoyed more leisure time. While still a teenager, she worked cleaning white homes, like many other young black women. Everyone in her world—her parents perhaps especially—took for granted that domestic duties would dominate her future, but such assumptions infuriated her. Confident and restless, Montgomery yearned for more, though she could not articulate exactly what she hoped to do with her life. In her own words, she "wanted to get on with it; but what that 'it' was or how and where to search remained a mystery." Indeed, she chafed at the constraints of gender more than race, and when a neighbor raped her at the age of fifteen, female uniqueness seemed an especially harsh burden. At the time, she told no one about the experience.[7]

As Montgomery entered adulthood, her hopes of "something more" grew even more chimerical, but her concrete realities quickly assumed shapes predictable for black women at the time. She could not accumulate the funds to finish her degree at Louisville's all-black Municipal College, though she performed well academically and won a partial scholarship. She hastily agreed to marry a man she did not love, on the promise that he would pay her tuition. When he reneged, the marriage lost its purpose and disintegrated. Then World War II swept her into its arc; she met a serviceman from New York, Norman F. "Nicky" Davis. They married just before he deployed for the European theater in 1943, and Montgomery worked several jobs in defense-related industries while waiting for his return. After the war, the couple settled in Louisville; she found work as a power-machine operator for the Enro Shirt Company and then as a secretary for a black-owned real-estate firm. She and Nicky looked briefly for a better life in California, but a longing to live near family brought them permanently back to her hometown in 1957. Nicky took a job at the DuPont Chemical facility, and Montgomery worked for a time at the Louisville Medical Depot before moving to the Census Bureau.[8]

Well into her adulthood, nothing augured the path Montgomery would later take. By the age of forty-one, she had worked at some nineteen different jobs. Though she performed well and rapidly gained promotions, she displayed little direction or sense of purpose. She and Nicky lived comfortably, but mutual disinterest plagued their marriage. Following quiet if unsatisfying routines, they raised an adopted biracial son, went to work, renovated their house, and participated in church activities.[9]

The city around them, however, buzzed with civil rights activity. In the 1950s a coalition of African Americans and progressive whites waged important struggles that won only uneven and limited victories. In 1952 a huge petition drive and a mass march on the state capitol ended discrimination in state-licensed hospitals, but, in spite of herculean struggles to effect school integration after the *Brown v. Board of Education* decision in 1954, racial mixing in Louisville's public schools registered little above token status. Activists pressed for workplace equality as well, but the city's board of aldermen rejected a fair-employment ordinance, and individual employers refused to alter discriminatory practices. Long and tortured struggles to open public facilities won few gains, housing segregation continued as a major problem, and most restaurants, hotels, and theaters remained segregated or completely closed to blacks.[10]

Frustrated by this slow and spotty progress, black Louisvillians enthusiastically joined the sit-in movement as it washed through the South in the late winter and spring of 1960. Louisville youths led the way, but adults joined the sit-ins, pickets, and boycotts that set the city in an uproar. By April 27, 1961, the city had jailed 685 activists, more than in any other American municipality to that point.[11] Though Georgia Montgomery certainly sympathized with movement aims, she did not participate in this activity proliferating in her city. Louisville's civil rights movement hardly appears in her autobiography before 1964, though by that year the struggle had already profoundly affected the lives of her family and friends.

Indeed, many black political leaders of the 1960s and 1970s entered the door of public service through the path of civil rights work, but Georgia Montgomery followed exactly the reverse course. She found her way to the movement through politics, with a trailhead in the most mundane of circumstances. Referred by a friend for a job with the U.S. Senate campaign of former Louisville mayor Wilson Wyatt, Montgomery held few deep convictions about the candidate and his bid for office. She took the position because it offered better pay and fewer hours than her work with the Census Bureau. The campaign apparently reciprocated her indifference; as the "token black" on the staff, Montgomery suffered subtle workplace discrimination until she gently insisted on equal treatment. As Wyatt lost on election night 1962, Montgomery sported "the only dry eyes in the suite." Yet her experience in the Wyatt campaign office profoundly changed the course of her life. In politics she had tasted the passion she craved.[12]

After Wyatt's defeat, Montgomery plunged into another campaign, this time a successful drive in 1963 that put Edward T. "Ned" Breathitt in the governor's chair. Now Montgomery possessed experience in two high-profile political campaigns, and these credentials made her the ideal office manager for the newly formed Allied Organization for Civil Rights (AOCR). Formed in early 1964 expressly to garner support for a civil rights law pending in the Kentucky General Assembly, the AOCR planned a march on the state capitol in Frankfort. The Frankfort march came at a pregnant moment in Kentucky's and the nation's civil rights travails. The city of Louisville had recently passed a controversial open-accommodations ordinance, and, nationally, the dramatic public theater of the Birmingham struggles and the March on Washington had helped spur support for the measure that would become the Civil Rights Act of 1964. The AOCR hoped to capitalize on this momentum and boost the chances that Kentucky's legislation would pass. In a scant two months, Montgomery and her coworkers pulled together Kentucky's highest-profile civil rights event.[13]

A host of ten thousand from across the state and beyond flocked to Frankfort on March 5, 1964, despite the cold and wet weather. Led by Martin Luther King Jr., Jackie Robinson, and prominent Louisville civil rights leaders, Georgia Montgomery walked in the second row as the throng moved up the city's central artery, spilled across the state capitol's massive steps, and overflowed onto the lawn. On a high platform, the folk group Peter, Paul, and Mary sang, and local and national figures gave soaring speeches. Yet in spite of the inspiring turnout, newly installed Governor Breathitt remained in his office, refusing even to acknowledge the gathering. When a delegation of eight leaders that included King, Robinson, and Montgomery visited him afterward, Breathitt evaded their questions and made no promise to support the civil rights bill. In terms of securing its immediate goals, the march on Frankfort failed. The hoped-for legislation died in committee, and the AOCR closed its office.[14]

However, the march on Frankfort succeeded splendidly in galvanizing Montgomery's political and civil rights sensibilities. Working now with intensity of purpose, she sought and won a seat on the Jefferson County Democratic Executive Committee in 1966, the first black and the first woman to do so. Then a prominent Democratic legislator helped her secure a post in the "bill room" of the Kentucky House of Representatives, a position that involved only routine work but gave her an "up close" look at how government worked. The bird's-eye view, along with the sense that few state lawmakers understood the needs of blacks or of women, fueled her growing sense that her true calling lay in politics. Fortuitously, a vacancy for the state senate from Louisville's thirty-third district appeared in late 1966. Montgomery recognized the opportunity as one for which she had waited and moved to seize it.[15]

Montgomery faced her most serious obstacles in the primary. The local Democratic Party backed her opponent, a white Catholic in a district where this constituency made up about 60 percent of the voters. Furthermore, several factions within the black community, beholden to party operatives, also worked against her. Nonetheless, she secured important endorsements from the Greater Louisville Labor Council, the local AFL-CIO Executive Committee, the Kentucky Education Association, and prominent black professionals. She squeaked to a primary victory by only 160 votes. With the party nomination secured, she fairly sailed through the general election that fall, riding the crest of a wave that swept two other new black legislators, Mae Street Kidd and Hughes McGill, into the Kentucky House of Representatives.[16]

Simultaneously with her new passion for politics, Montgomery plunged into civil rights activism. She helped organize the contingent of Kentuckians who flew to Alabama for the Selma march in 1965. Even while campaigning for the Kentucky Senate, she immersed herself with other black Louisvillians in a drive for open housing, perhaps their most difficult struggle to date. Now Montgomery marched, sat with other activists in front of snarling downtown traffic at five o'clock in the afternoon, and joined demonstrations that elicited some of the city's most violent backlash. Vastly outnumbering the demonstrators, crowds of hecklers threw rotten eggs, tomatoes, and even stones and bricks. In 1968 Montgomery helped organize marchers on the Poor People's Campaign and flew to Washington, D.C., to visit their Resurrection City. Later that year, she joined striking sanitation workers in Saint Petersburg, Florida, where she and other women knelt to pray in the path of trucks driven by strikebreakers. The trucks skidded to a halt just a few feet in front of the women, and police lifted them out of the road one by one.[17]

Much had changed in America's racial landscape by January 1968, when Georgia Montgomery took her seat in the Kentucky Senate, but Frankfort remained beholden to many norms of racial segregation. No hotel would rent her a room, so she found lodging in a private home. Though a few blacks had served in the Kentucky House since 1935, state government seemed ill prepared to deal with the increased diversity brought by the 1967 election. The assembly doorkeeper refused admission to her young friend Raoul Cunningham, who arrived that year as the House's first black reading clerk. Neither was the public used to women in office. A *Louisville Times* feature on the city's three new female assembly members focused on them as "well-organized homemakers," with plans to manage domestic duties by cooking in advance and stocking their freezers with quick-to-prepare meals.[18] Not surprisingly, as both the first black and the first woman in the Kentucky Senate, Montgomery proceeded cautiously in her relationships with colleagues.

These obstacles notwithstanding, Montgomery, with characteristic energy and confidence, introduced a major initiative on open housing in her first session. Residential segregation had long vexed black Kentuckians, and extraordinary turmoil had erupted over housing in her home city the previous year. Though the Supreme Court had outlawed racially restrictive covenants early in the twentieth century, unwritten codes persisted.[19] The limited residences available to African Americans often lay in the worst areas, where poor city services, cheap construction, overcrowding, and high prices dictated choices even for middle-class purchasers. The lending industry bolstered this discrimination, setting higher credit standards and lower loan-to-value ratios for black customers. Because school segregation and other racially charged issues remained tied to housing, even moderate whites fiercely resisted residential integration, as the highly publicized ordeal of Andrew and Charlotte Wade demonstrated. In 1954 the Wades purchased a home in a white Louisville neighborhood from Carl and Anne Braden, who had bought the home with the intent of selling it to the Wades. Their new neighbors, however, would have none of it. The black family suffered violent reprisals intended to drive them from the area, while a grand jury indicted the Bradens for sedition. Though Louisville's racialized housing patterns affected all of Montgomery's friends and relations, the Wade incident had hit especially close to home, since Charlotte Wade was related to Montgomery by marriage.[20]

Just a bit more than a month after taking her seat, Montgomery introduced Senate Bill 264, legislation that would render racial discrimination illegal in the sale or rental of housing. The bill further prohibited lending institutions from discrimination, and it empowered the Kentucky Commission on Human Rights to investigate alleged violations and to pursue legal action. Montgomery presented her bill with an impassioned speech that appealed to her colleagues' pride in Kentucky's reputation as a state with race relations superior to other southern states, to their obligations to black Kentuckians who had served in the armed forces, and to the Christianity that the majority of them professed in common. Yet many of her thirty-seven white male colleagues vividly displayed their indifference by slipping out of the chamber while she spoke, and the rump that remained offered only tepid applause. With little enthusiasm for it, the bill seemed doomed to die in committee like its 1964 predecessor.[21]

Ever the pragmatist, Montgomery quickly honed her political sensibilities as she sought a path for resuscitating her bill and getting it passed. She found five senators willing to cosponsor the bill, and she traded her vote on daylight savings time—another controversial measure that seemed doomed to failure—to legislators who promised to vote for her open-housing initiative. When the vote finally came up in the Senate, the bill that originated with little hope of passage won handsomely, twenty-seven to three. Tellingly, eight senators abstained, no doubt fearful of repercussions in their home districts. The measure also passed decisively in the House. Though Republican governor Louie B. Nunn did not sign the bill, neither did he add it to the growing heap of measures that suffered his veto. The biggest legislative surprise of the session, the Georgia M. Davis, Hughes McGill, Mae Street Kidd Civil Rights Act of 1968 took its place as the first such provision in the South.[22]

Montgomery's historic accession to the Kentucky Senate, her early and dramatic legislative success, and her new civil rights activism catapulted her overnight to a position of considerable stature among civil rights notables and black leaders in Kentucky and the national Democratic Party. Standing ovations greeted her when she went to speak. *Ebony* magazine profiled her alongside congresswomen Barbara Jordan and Shirley Chisholm as part of a rising tide of black women in politics. She flew with A. D. King, brother of Martin Luther King Jr., on a chartered plane to attend the funeral of Robert F. Kennedy in June 1968, and she addressed the Democratic National Convention as it met in Chicago later that summer.[23]

Though none of her subsequent legislative victories acquired landmark status on par with the 1968 Civil Rights Act, Montgomery remained a tireless advocate in the Kentucky Senate for the concerns of African Americans, women, the poor, and labor. Always an outsider because of her race and gender, Montgomery's pragmatically "liberal" positions on economic and social issues furthered her status as a political minority in conservative Kentucky. Her difficulty in finding allies in the Senate eased a bit when, in her second legislative session, she gained appointment as chair of the Health and Welfare Committee. From this position, which she held for the next four sessions, she leveraged support for her own bills. Among her proudest achievements, she introduced amendments to a civil rights bill from 1966, extending its protections against employment discrimination to women and persons over age forty-five, and she secured important amendments that nullified exceptions to her own 1968 Fair Housing Act. In 1974 she introduced legislation that made Kentucky only the second state to establish a holiday in honor of Martin Luther King Jr. A staunch advocate for women's concerns, she won passage of a "displaced homemaker's bill," which benefited older women trying to reenter the workforce. With strong roots among working people and deep ties to the labor community, she acceded to the chairmanship of the powerful Labor and Industry Committee in 1978. From this position she consistently blocked right-to-work legislation and lobbied for prevailing-wage laws and minimum-wage increases.[24]

Montgomery advocated most vigorously for black Kentuckians, both individually and institutionally, at every opportunity. She called government officials to task when they failed to hire black staffers or appoint African Americans to influential commissions. She supported a directive to the Kentucky Historical Society, along with an appropriation of funds, to further research about black Kentuckians. In 1978 she secured the passage of legislation that required recipients of state contracts to employ blacks in proportion to their percentages in the population where the contract would be performed. When reorganization of the state's postsecondary educational system threatened to close Kentucky State University in Frankfort in 1981, she fought successfully to keep it open. She enthusiastically sought to deliver Kentucky's Democrats to Jesse Jackson when he sought his party's nomination for the presidency in 1984, and she lent him her support again four years later.[25]

Montgomery's successes, however, do not describe a linear or complete path to racial or gender equality in Kentucky. Importantly, significant legislative defeats demonstrate the persistence of white patriarchy during the two decades of her Senate career. In the mid-1970s the Ku Klux Klan revived with vigor in response to the court-ordered desegregation of Louisville schools. When Montgomery introduced an antimask bill designed to target this group, she and her family members received personal threats, and the House version of the bill died in committee. She fought the General Assembly's effort to rescind its support for the Equal Rights Amendment, but the male-dominated body followed the lead of other states and withdrew its ratification in 1978. Her efforts to defeat House Bill 125, which limited the use of public funds for abortion, availed little as the measure coasted to a resounding victory. By a decisive majority, Montgomery also lost a valiant struggle against an antibusing provision that undermined school integration.[26]

After her retirement in 1988, Montgomery's seemingly boundless energies craved outlets, and she continued to pursue projects related to race, gender, and social justice. With the help of grant monies, she reactivated a service organization that encouraged church members to build relationships with nursing home residents. When implementation of the 1990 Kentucky Education Reform Act threatened to undo school integration, she sprang into action, writing letters, organizing a rally, and forming an organization to monitor developments related to diversity in public schools.[27] Always interested in history and writing, she wrote and published a novel based on the life of her great-aunt Celia, the former slave whose erstwhile master bequeathed her a large home on a substantial acreage.[28]

In 1995 the then seventy-one-year-old Montgomery published an autobiography, *I Shared the Dream: The Pride, Passion, and Politics of the First Black Woman Senator from Kentucky*. Though the piece richly detailed her life and accomplishments, it also focused extensively on her intimate relationship with Martin Luther King Jr. Indeed, the preface introduced her life story almost entirely in terms of this affair, while the epilogue offered a reflection on it—bookends that suggest its centrality in her own presentation of her legacy. Recent accounts had betrayed her long-held secret; most significantly, the 1989 autobiography of longtime King associate Ralph David Abernathy had directly referenced the leader's liaison with the Kentucky senator. Since the exposure she long feared had finally materialized, Montgomery wanted to dispel rumors and forestall judgment by offering her own authoritative account. She believed that telling the story in her own words—portraying its intimacy without subjecting the reader to sordid details—would mitigate criticism.[29]

Montgomery's autobiography documented several encounters with King, beginning with their first liaison in March 1967 through his death in April 1968. The two rendezvoused whenever King came to Louisville, where at least once he spent the night in her home, and she met him in Chicago when he joined civil rights initiatives there. Though the affair unfolded during her bid for the

Kentucky Senate, she left her busy schedule to "come whenever he called." Her account copiously detailed her conversations with King when they were alone, but it featured no elaboration on their sexual interactions. Offering little more than innuendo—"We drew close to each other. 'Senator . . . ,' he murmured as I moved into his embrace"—Montgomery avoided the salacious while leaving the reader's imagination to fill in the obvious next steps.[30]

Montgomery's account also confirmed Abernathy's claim that she had joined King at the Lorraine Motel in Memphis the night before he died. A few weeks previously, after finishing her exhausting first session in the Kentucky Senate and spending herself on behalf of the Civil Rights Act, Montgomery had accompanied a friend to Florida to recoup and relax on the beach. While there, the two heard news of the sanitation workers' strike in Memphis and the turmoil that attended it. In Montgomery's telling, King called and asked her to come to Memphis, saying, "I need you." After driving all day and arriving at the Lorraine Motel late on April 3, Montgomery spent the night with King. As in descriptions of their other encounters, her memoir offered few details about their final tryst. It explained only that he followed her to her room. Once inside, they spoke both of his extraordinary exhaustion and his satisfaction with the outcome of that night's rally. Then "he sat down on the edge of the bed. 'Senator, our time together is so short,' he said, opening his arms." The next day, as she prepared herself for dinner, she heard the shots that felled him and was among the first who rushed to his side.

Like many well-known figures who aim to shape public perceptions of their infidelities, Montgomery hoped to elevate this affair above the tawdry and to ennoble it as a human bond with genuine emotional depth. Focusing on their verbal interactions rather than the mechanics of their lovemaking, she portrayed a relationship in which "attachment grew stronger until it passed beyond camaraderie into intimacy." In her telling, the two civil rights leaders initiated "a close friendship between two people sharing the same dream, working for the same goals [but] crossed the line into intimacy."[31] Yet assertions that the relationship grew gradually from shared experiences notwithstanding, her account actually described a different development. In fact, King and Montgomery seemed hardly to know one another when he first asked her—using his brother the Reverend A. D. King as the emissary—to meet at a local hotel after a large rally. Montgomery had first met King in 1964, when he came to Kentucky for a single day as a participant in the march on Frankfort. They met again but spent no significant time together when she traveled to Selma for the 1965 march. She recorded no other meetings until King's overt proposition in early 1967.

Like others who write tell-all books in the wake of affairs with high-profile leaders, Montgomery struggled to reckon with questions of her own moral responsibility, guilt toward the betrayed spouse, and the meaning of King's infidelities for his heroic legacy. Not naturally given to deep reflection, Montgomery displayed little sense of moral failure, justifying the relationship as one that offered mutual solace to two beleaguered souls: "When we were together, the rest of the world, whose problems we knew and shared, was far away. Our time together was a safe haven for both of us. There we could laugh and speak of things others might not understand." At one point she described the affair as an opportunity she could scarcely have passed up: "Martin Luther King, the leader of the civil rights movement . . . wanted to be with me. How could I *not* have seized the moment, no matter what my fears, no matter what the obstacles?"[32] Indeed, she maintained, "I have never regretted being there with him."

Of Coretta Scott King, Montgomery wrote only that she offered personal condolences to his grieving spouse: "As I took Coretta's hand, I said, 'I'm sorry.' Sorry for what? I was sorry she had lost her husband; I was sorry the world had lost a savior, and on some level, I think I was also apologizing for my relationship with her husband." She concluded her account of King's death by admitting that she did "regret any hurt inflicted on others because of my actions." Coretta Scott King and all four of the King children remained alive at the publication of Montgomery's memoir, and none commented publicly on it. As to the propriety of writing about the affair, Montgomery maintained in her epilogue that those who believed she should have kept quiet "wish to perpetuate a myth to protect the reputation of a man whose greatness is not diminished by the truth."[33]

On the issue of how infidelity might affect King's legacy as well as her own, Montgomery insisted that their civil rights accomplishments far outweigh their personal shortcomings. Though the autobiography alluded to "those who would cast stones," public criticism of her revelations seemed sparse and muted.[34] Indeed, much had changed between the mid-1960s when the affair took place and 1995 when she revealed it. Not only had the civil rights and women's movements exposed the sexual double standard, an army of writers and thinkers had expended serious intellectual energy deconstructing the ways sex shaped constructions of race and gender. Thus, even as Montgomery pursued a political life that placed gender and racial equality at the fore, her own legacy benefited from the gains of the civil rights and women's movements. Most biographical sketches take the affair for granted, and Montgomery speaks openly and quite casually about her relationship with King in public interviews.[35]

Montgomery's memoir offered glimpses into other intimate aspects of her life in addition to the King affair. With a subtlety even greater than she employed in discussing her encounters with King, she revealed the sexual activity of her teenaged years. Had such activity resulted in out-of-wedlock pregnancy, the course of her life would have been profoundly altered, her political career likely doomed decades before it began. Montgomery also revealed that, from early in her 1943 marriage to Nicky Davis, she had entertained an on-again-off-again relationship with a married father of three, "Big Jim" Powers of Louisville. Montgomery and Davis eventually separated during her bid for the Kentucky Senate and they later divorced, a move she attributed to persistent lack of emotional and sexual intimacy and his disinterest in her political career. After Powers's wife returned to Jamaica to live, Montgomery and Powers began to appear openly as a couple in Louisville. When Powers's wife died suddenly in 1972, he moved in with Montgomery and they married soon afterward.

Though Montgomery's affair with King competes for public interest with her notable civil rights accomplishments, these other aspects of her intimate life offer rich material for illuminating the role of sex in a public life dedicated to breaking race and gender barriers. Indeed, from early on Montgomery ignored the rules of chastity and purity that middle-class standing and religious upbringing might have required. Her lack of reflection on her sexual conduct suggests that she gave little credence to prevailing gendered and racialized notions of sex. In other words, Montgomery pursued sexual independence with an impunity often afforded men but not women, and traditionally available to whites but not African Americans. Ironically, revelation of any of this extramarital sexual activity—teenage sexual experimentation, persistent and longstanding infidelity—would have utterly disqualified her as a candidate for office and, ultimately, as a civil rights leader.

Yet the King affair reeks not of empowerment but of patriarchy. As substantial scholarship has documented, and Montgomery's own testimony underscores, King led an extraordinarily male-dominated arm of the civil rights movement. Women exercised little influence or leadership in the Southern Christian Leadership Conference, and dedicated female activists such as Ella Baker left the organization for more democratic environments. Montgomery presented the King liaison as an outgrowth of a working partnership, but, in fact, when she joined him in Chicago and Memphis, she did not participate in the direct-action initiatives seizing those cities. Rather, she waited at the hotel for him to finish the day's work. The only two women with the King entourage at the Lorraine Motel, Montgomery and her friend Luckey Ward, the consort of A. D. King, had come to Memphis to provide sexual companionship, not to participate in the city's civil rights travails. The entire affair put Montgomery in a weak, undignified, and vulnerable position, as do all transactions that barter sex for vicarious power. She could lay no legitimate claim to King's time, emotions, or assets; neither could she fulfill her own needs to give the same. Indeed, though she tried to accompany the wounded King to the hospital, Andrew Young pulled her out of the ambulance to spare them all the shame of public exposure. Shuttled away and out of public view in a time of grief, Montgomery appeared little more than a starstruck groupie who belonged only in King's bed.

Developments since Montgomery's historic accession to the Kentucky Senate render her a historical anomaly rather than a trailblazer whom others have followed. She remains the *only* black woman *ever* to occupy a seat in the Kentucky Senate. During a portion of her tenure, 1971–77, three black women served in the General Assembly simultaneously, but since her retirement in 1989, Kentucky voters have sent only one black woman to the state house of representatives. Neither does Montgomery's career appear to have opened floodgates for other African Americans to pour into Kentucky politics. Only one African American, Gerald Neal, has served in the Senate since Montgomery. Indeed, in the thirty-two years between 1935 and 1967, thirteen blacks, including Montgomery and her cohort, won seats in the General Assembly, yet even fewer—only twelve—gained seats in the post–civil rights period of the same length, 1971–2003. Montgomery's achievement thus appears more a brief moment of hope and opportunities lost than the ushering in of a new day.[36]

If the composition of Kentucky's General Assembly serves as a historical snapshot of the status of minorities and women, African Americans—especially black women—can claim little progress since the civil rights years. White women, however, have benefited substantially from the revolutions of the 1960s. Nineteen women won General Assembly seats prior to Montgomery, but forty-five followed between 1968 and 2004. As this book is preparing for publication, women make up approximately 20 percent of the delegates in the Kentucky House of Representatives.[37] Though these figures hardly document equality, they do bespeak clear gains for white women that black Kentuckians have not adequately shared.

While such statistics fail to tell the complete story of racial and gender progress, they raise important questions about the most significant paths to social change. As leading scholars have argued in recent years, heroic leaders, dramatic public theater, and legislative victories dominate civil rights narratives, but these compelling stories often distort the actual reality concerning the agents, sites, and means of change. Leaders such as Martin Luther King Jr. and Georgia Montgomery did not make the movement so much as the movement made them, and their achievements represent the labor of thousands of ordinary people who walked rather than rode buses, filled jail cells, conducted freedom schools, and registered to vote against great obstacles. Spectacles such as the marches on Washington and Frankfort offered fleeting images of unity and purpose, though of themselves, they produced little lasting change. Measures such as the Civil Rights Act of 1964 and the Georgia M. Davis, Hughes McGill, Mae Street Kidd Civil Rights Act of 1968 required the vigilance and follow-up of black Americans at the local level and in their daily lives. As many scholars have demonstrated, such legislation often represented the beginning of movement activity rather than the fulfillment of it.

A plethora of organizations and institutions have honored Georgia Montgomery Davis Powers for her work to advance the status of minorities and women. Several of Kentucky's public universities, including the University of Louisville and the University of Kentucky, have conferred honorary doctorates on her. The Kentucky legislature named June 26, 2010, as Georgia Davis Powers Day, simultaneously designating an important portion of Interstate 264 that runs through Louisville the Georgia Davis Powers Expressway. At a special ceremony revealing the new highway sign, Kentucky governor Steven L. Beshear praised Montgomery: "[She] spent her entire career building roads—and bridges—of a different kind. She built connectors for this community and, indeed, for the entire Commonwealth."[38] As of this writing, Montgomery continues to live in Louisville.

NOTES

1. This description is based on her own telling in Georgia Davis Powers, *I Shared the Dream: The Pride, Passion, and Politics of the First Woman Senator from Kentucky* (Far Hills, N.J.: New Horizon Press, 1995), 1–2. Though she is usually known as Georgia Davis Powers and conducted much of her public life under this name, several problems have beset the choice of appropriate moniker for use in this essay. She did not assume Powers as a last name until she was forty-nine years old. During many of the events described in this essay, including her first run for the Kentucky Senate, her civil rights activism, and her involvement with Martin Luther King Jr., she was known as Georgia Davis. Because the name changes might be confusing, I have decided to identify her by her maiden name, Montgomery, throughout this essay.

2. An immense literature documents the role of sex in constructions of race and gender. A few essential treatments are Rennie Simson, "The Afro-American Female: The Historical Context of the Constructions of Sexual Identity," and Jacquelyn Dowd Hall, "'The Mind That Burns in Each Body': Women, Rape, and Racial Violence," in *Powers of Desire: The Politics of Sexuality*, ed. Ann Snitow, Christine Stansell, and Sharon Thompson (New York: Monthly Review Press, 1983), 229–35, 328–49; Paula Giddings, *When and Where I Enter: The Impact of Black Women on Race and Sex in America* (New York: HarperCollins, 1984); Jane Dailey, "Sex, Segregation, and the Sacred after *Brown*," *Journal of American History* 91 (2004): 119–45; Danielle McGuire, *At the Dark End of the Street: Black Women, Rape, and Resistance—A New History of the Civil Rights Movement from Rosa Parks to the Rise of Black Power* (New York: Vintage, 2011).

3. Powers, *I Shared the Dream*, 10–12.

4. Charles W. Anderson Jr., the first African American in the Kentucky legislature, was elected in 1935. Powers, *I Shared the Dream*, 29–30. For descriptions of "Little Africa," see ibid., 74, and Houston A. Baker, *Betrayal: How Black Intellectuals Have Abandoned the Ideals of the Civil Rights Era* (New York: Columbia University Press, 2010), 1–10. This portrait of Louisville's middle-class black community is drawn in part from material in Tracy E. K'Meyer, *Civil Rights in the Gateway to the South: Louisville, Kentucky, 1945–1980* (Lexington: University Press of Kentucky, 2009).

5. Powers, *I Shared the Dream*, 18–21.

6. Ibid., 16 (understanding of segregation); 50–51 (bus incident); 38–39 (lunch counter incident); 57–58 (segregation at factory job); 30–31 (brother's arrest and detention).

7. Ibid., 28, 33 (quotation); 35–36 (account of rape).

8. Ibid., 46–80.

9. Ibid., 63–65.

10. K'Meyer, *Gateway to the South*, 17–76.

11. Ibid., 82–91. This wave of demonstrations in 1960 and 1961 played an important role in securing an open-accommodations ordinance in Louisville in 1963, highly touted as the first such city ordinance in the South. Yet, as K'Meyer has shown, the ordinance was not completely enforced initially and suffered challenges to its constitutionality. Thus, this local ordinance was not enforced until after February 1965, after similar laws had been adopted in other localities and the federal Civil Rights Act of 1964 had been passed, chronologies that undermine the Louisville ordinance's claim as "first in the South."

12. Powers, *I Shared the Dream*, 83–89.

13. *Louisville Defender*, n.d. (February 1964), in Georgia Davis Powers Papers (unprocessed collection), Special Collections and Archives, University of Kentucky Libraries, Lexington (hereafter GDPPUK), box 1, binder 1972–86. The proposed state civil rights bill would have ended discrimination in both accommodations and employment.

14. Powers, *I Shared the Dream*, 91–105; K'Meyer, *Gateway to the South*, 107–8. A fifty-year retrospective on the march appeared in the *Lexington Herald-Leader*, February 2, 2014.

15. *Louisville Times*, December 16, 1964, clipping in box 1, binder 1962–76, GDPPUK.

16. Unidentified newspaper clippings, October 12 and November 8, 1967, in box 1, binder 1972–86, GDPPUK,

17. On Louisville's 1967 open-housing demonstrations, see K'Meyer, *Gateway to the South*, 111–44. Montgomery describes her own experience in this campaign in Powers, *I Shared the Dream*, 141–43. On the Poor People's Campaign, see *Louisville Times*, May 8, and *Cincinnati Enquirer*, May 11, 1968, in box 1, binder 1962–76, GDPPUK, and Powers, *I Shared the Dream*, 242–43. On the Saint Petersburg sanitation workers' strike and Montgomery's role in it, see clippings from *Saint Petersburg Times* in box 1, binder 1962–76, GDPPUK, and Powers, *I Shared the Dream*, 246–52.

18. *Louisville Times*, January 2, 1968, clipping in Georgia Davis Powers Papers (unprocessed collection), Center of Excellence for the Study of Kentucky African Americans, Kentucky State University, Frankfort (hereafter GDPPKSU), box 16, unidentified folder.

19. The Supreme Court decision of *Buchanan v. Warley* of 1917 had actually arisen from a case in Louisville.

20. On the obstacles thrown before Louisville blacks in the realm of housing, see K'Meyer, *Gateway to the South*, 45–76. Both K'Meyer and Thomas Sugrue, *Sweet Land of Liberty: The Forgotten Struggle for Civil Rights in the North* (New York: Random House, 2008), argue that residential segregation formed an essential foundation for other forms of racial subordination, especially school

segregation. The Wade-Braden case is ably recounted in Catherine Fosl, *Subversive Southerner: Anne Braden and the Struggle for Racial Justice in the Cold War South* (New York: Palgrave Macmillan, 2002).

21. Powers, *I Shared the Dream*, 207–9.

22. *Louisville Courier-Journal*, March 13, 14, 16, 1968; *Frankfort State Journal*, March 14, 1968; *Louisville Defender*, March 15, 1968; *Louisville Times*, March 15, 1968; clippings in box 1, binder 1962–76, GDPPUK; Powers, *I Shared the Dream*, 209–16.

23. *Ebony*, 48–52, n.d. [1970], clipping in box 16, unidentified folder, GDPPUK; *Louisville Courier-Journal*, n.d. [August 1968], in box 1, binder 1962–76, GDPPUK.

24. *Louisville Times*, September 7, 1978, box 16, unidentified folder, GDPPKSU (Displaced Homemakers Bill); *Louisville Times*, March 18, 1978, box 1, binder 1972–82, GDPPUK (prevailing wage law).

25. See, for example, Georgia M. Powers to the Honorable Wallace G. Wilkinson, January 5, 1989, in box 7, unidentified folder; Senator Georgia M. Powers to Governor (telegram), September 14, 1979, and Georgia M. Davis to Lt. Governor Wendell Ford (letter), October 10, 1971, box 16, unidentified folder, GDPPKSU (calling government officials to task); *Louisville Courier-Journal*, May 17, 1979, in box 1, binder 1972–82, GDPPUK (legislation to further research about black Kentuckians); material in box 7, unidentified folder, GDPPKSU (advocacy for Kentucky State University); *Louisville Times*, July 18, 1984, in box 7, unidentified folder; and Richard Alatorre, Chair Credentials Committee, to Mrs. Powers, June 25, 1984, box 16, unidentified folder, GDPPKSU (advocacy for Jesse Jackson).

26. *Louisville Courier-Journal*, February 28, 1978, box 1, binder 1972–82, GDPPUK (Klan Bill); *Lexington Leader*, March 15, 1978, box 1, binder 1972–82, GDPPUK (ERA repeal); *Louisville Courier-Journal*, March 13, 1980, box 1, binder 1972–82, GDPPUK (abortion bill). The vote was 65–2 in the House and 25–5 in the Senate. Press release, box 16, unidentified folder, GDPPKSU (antibusing provision).

27. See organizational letter from Georgia M. Powers to Dear Friend, September 26, 1991, box 7, unidentified folder, GDPPKSU.

28. Georgia Davis Powers, *Celia's Land: A Historical Novel* (Louisville, Ky.: Goose Creek, 2004).

29. Ralph David Abernathy, *And the Walls Came Tumbling Down* (New York: Harper & Row, 1989).

30. Powers, *I Shared the Dream*, 161–62.

31. Ibid., 235.

32. Ibid., 234. Montgomery was six years older than King.

33. Ibid., 323.

34. See, for example, Isabelle Wilkerson's critique of Montgomery's autobiography, *New York Times*, June 25, 1995.

35. See, for example, Rachel Platt's interview with Montgomery on Louisville's TV station WHAS, June 16, 2010, http://www.whas11.com/video?id=96514559&sec=553357 (accessed December 4, 2012).

36. Kentucky General Assembly Membership, 1900–2004, prepared by the Legislative Research Commission, November 2004, 377–83, http://www.e-archives.ky.gov/Pubs/LRC/infobull/IB175b.pdf (accessed December 5, 2012).

37. Ibid., 383. For current members of the General Assembly, see http://www.lrc.ky.gov/Legislators.htm (accessed December 5, 2012).

38. http://kysenatedems.com/2010/07/30/highway-sign-honors-former-senator-georgia-davis-powers/ (accessed December 5, 2012).

Martha Layne Collins

(1936–)

Textbooks, Toyota, and Tenacity

JOHN PAUL HILL

Political commentators frequently refer to 1992 as the "Year of the Woman" because four women captured U.S. Senate seats to triple their gender's representation in that body, but in one southern state another year is equally deserving of that title.[1] In 1983 Kentucky lieutenant governor Martha Layne Collins beat back multiple challengers in the Democratic primary and Republican nominee Jim Bunning in the fall to become the commonwealth's first and, to date, only woman governor. From 1979 to 1983 Collins had served ably as lieutenant governor and, before that, had held the clerkship for the court of appeals. Collins's gubernatorial administration (1983–87) was marked by some early setbacks—notably, the state legislature refused to enact her first budget—but she persevered and began to succeed, if not flourish, in the rough-and-tumble world of male-dominated Kentucky politics. Her crowning achievement came in 1985 when she lured the Toyota Motor Corporation to build an $800 million manufacturing plant near Georgetown in Scott County. Now, nearly three decades later, the plant continues to be an economic boon to the region; a University of Michigan study, for example, estimated that the plant generates ten jobs in central Kentucky for every one of the facility's seven thousand on-site positions.[2]

Despite being constitutionally restricted from seeking a second consecutive term, Collins seemed to have a bright political future when she left the governor's mansion in December 1987. Rumors swirled that she would run for the U.S. Senate or possibly receive a cabinet post in a Democratic administration, but her political fortunes waned when her husband, Dr. Bill Collins, a dentist, was found guilty of extortion and sentenced to prison in 1993.[3] Although tainted by her husband's misdeeds, Collins has continued to serve the state in various capacities. For example, she was president of Saint Catharine College in Washington County from 1990 to 1996, helping that institution boost enrollment and increase its endowment.[4] Understanding Collins's political ascendancy and ongoing service to the commonwealth not only helps us appreciate one woman's remarkable story of personal and political triumph but also illuminates the difficulties that women in general, and women in the conservative South in particular, faced in their attempts to gain personal freedom and political power during the late twentieth century.

Born in Shelby County, Kentucky, on December 7, 1936, to Everett and Mary Taylor Hall, Collins displayed early on some of the characteristics that would propel her to political prominence. Growing up, she helped the family set the tobacco crop and learned to drive a tractor before she drove a car. Her parents encouraged their daughter to establish lofty goals, pursue an education, and vie for civic honors and elected school positions. Their support nourished a competitive streak in Collins.[5] Her experience watching her father balance multiple positions, including owning and operating an ambulance service and a funeral home, furthered her ambitions. "There were calls 24 hours a day . . . at two o'clock in the morning," she recalled. "It was a 24-7 job. I carried that [way of life] into running for office and for serving [the state]."[6] Collins did not win every school office or award she sought, but her mother refused to allow setbacks to discourage her. "Now you've got this job," she would say. "It may not be as big as [class] president, but you do a good job here and maybe next time you'll be elected president." Collins heeded her mother's advice and poured her energies into such "small jobs" as serving in church groups, working at the local swimming pool, and helping start a youth center at the public library.[7] Another "small job" gave Collins her first taste of politics. When her parents occasionally worked at the county level for Democratic candidates, she helped them by stuffing envelopes and leaving political pamphlets on doorsteps.[8] Her hard work and perseverance were rewarded when she was named Shelby County Burley Tobacco Queen in 1954 and Kentucky Derby Festival Queen a few years later.[9]

On graduating from Shelbyville High School in 1955, she enrolled at Lindenwood College near Saint Louis. She later transferred to the University of Kentucky (UK) and majored in home economics, hoping to become a teacher. While at UK she maintained a frenetic pace. She was elected president of her dormitory, joined Chi Omega sorority, served on the Baptist Student Union Council, and in 1958 bested students from three other Kentucky colleges in an essay contest to capture the title of Miss Future Home Economist.[10] This last accomplishment, significant in its day, netted Collins "offers of positions from some of the larger

GOVERNOR MARTHA LAYNE COLLINS

Courtesy of the Filson Historical Society, Louisville.

companies of the United States."[11] During the summer between her sophomore and junior years, she met Bill Collins of Hazard at the Cedarmore Baptist Summer Camp in Shelby County, where both of them were working. They quickly fell in love, and in the summer of 1959, only a few weeks after Martha Layne's graduation from UK, they were married. They soon moved to Louisville, where Bill pursued a dental degree at the University of Louisville and she taught at Fairdale High School and later at Seneca High. The couple had their two children during this period: Stephen, born in 1960, and Marla, born in 1963.[12]

In 1966 Martha Layne Collins and her husband moved to Versailles, Kentucky, where he established a dental practice and she taught at the local junior high.[13] While in Versailles she got her first taste of politics since childhood when her and her husband's membership in local organizations, such as the Jaycees and Jayceettes, drew them to area politics. In her spare time, Collins worked in Democratic campaign headquarters during election season. Her efforts caught the attention of party leaders, who sought to help the national party attain its goal of greater political participation by women. In 1971 state senator and majority floor leader Walter D. "Dee" Huddleston approached Collins and asked her to serve as the Sixth Congressional District chair of Lieutenant Governor Wendell Ford's campaign for governor.[14] At first hesitant to increase her commitment to politics due to work and familial responsibilities, she accepted the position at the insistence of her husband. "I was teaching school and had two small children and felt like I just had everything I could do and my husband said, 'Sure, you're going to do it,'" she recalled.[15] She attended to her political duties each day after teaching, sometimes taking her children along to political rallies in the district. "On the way they did their homework. We would be headed for a bean supper or a fish fry. . . . We would eat the supper provided, and after the speeches they'd get back in the car with their pillows and sleep on the way home."[16] Collins excelled at this position, which opened additional opportunities for her. Huddleston soon invited her to serve as campaign coordinator for women's activities in his 1972 run for the U.S. Senate, and state party chair J. R. Miller asked her to come to Frankfort as the full-time coordinator for women's activities at Democratic headquarters.[17] Although she accepted both positions, she was initially unsure whether she wanted to leave teaching behind permanently for politics. She took a year's leave of absence from the classroom to decide her future, but before it had ended, politics had become her new calling.[18]

Collins helped Huddleston win his 1972 Senate campaign, while in her new full-time post in Frankfort she gained a growing reputation for hard work, determination, and political know-how. She expanded her political contacts by attending as many party functions as possible and serving on the Democratic

National Committee. With her name recognition increasing, candidates began approaching her for advice. "In 1975 there were 11 people running for lieutenant governor, and a lot of them were coming to see me," she observed. "So I'd go home and talk it over with my family. Finally my husband said, 'I think you've spent enough time and put in enough miles for everyone else. I think it's time you either run or come home.'"[19] She chose to run for clerk of the Kentucky Court of Appeals. Collins's years of organizing for the party paid off; she bested four male challengers in the Democratic primary and went on to defeat her Republican opponent easily in the fall campaign. Voters that same year elected to create a state supreme court to supersede the appeals court. Collins's clerkship transferred to the Supreme Court once that court was formally established.[20]

Collins served ably during this time of extensive reorganization in the state's judicial system. She maintained a busy speaking schedule on evenings and weekends, fueling speculation that she might be looking ahead to a run for lieutenant governor in 1979.[21] Thelma Stovall had become the first woman elected to that position in the commonwealth's history in 1975, a precedent that seemed to add momentum to the rumors.[22] In an October 1976 interview Collins refused to confirm or deny her intentions of seeking the office. "There are a lot of people encouraging me to do so," she said. "But I'm keeping my options open; I believe if you do your job well, the future will take care of itself."[23]

The reports proved correct. Collins threw her hat into the ring alongside a crowded field of six male challengers in the 1979 Democratic primary for lieutenant governor. Although many people had indeed supported her entry into the race, some political observers believed that she was not prepared for such a high-ranking position, accusing her of "leapfrog[ging]" opportunities to run for lower-level positions that would give her the necessary political seasoning for the post she was then seeking.[24] Moreover, many political prognosticators initially gave her little chance of winning because five of her opponents had greater name recognition and more extensive political experience. Former state representative and former transportation secretary William "Bill" Cox of Madisonville had Governor Julian Carroll's endorsement, Louisville attorney Todd Hollenbach had served two terms as Jefferson County judge and had run unsuccessfully in the 1975 Democratic gubernatorial primary, state senator Joe Prather had served as state senate president since 1975, Richard Hayes Lewis had served as state representative from 1970 to 1975, and Jim Vernon was the current commissioner of public information.[25] On Election Day Collins edged Cox by approximately 3,300 votes, a victory that surprised many. Those familiar with Collins's furious pace and wide-ranging political contacts, however, were hardly taken aback by the election's outcome. As the *Lexington Herald-*

Leader observed, "Many of her opponents were better known, and most had more experience running for office. But Mrs. Collins' organization, nurtured through years of personal contacts at countless fish fries and bean suppers, was hers alone."[26] Enjoying the extra benefit of running on a strong Democratic ticket headed by millionaire businessman John Y. Brown Jr., she defeated future U.S. congressman Harold "Hal" Rogers with 63 percent of the vote in the general election.[27]

The lieutenant governor of Kentucky has few official duties other than presiding over the state senate every other year and serving as acting governor when the governor leaves the state. But Collins worked eighteen-hour days attending public events, trying to help needy Kentuckians who called on her office, and generally serving as the "ombudsman for all of state government." Her extraordinary work ethic was one reason she put in these long hours, but early in her term she admitted that there was another explanation for her hard work: women, she said, were not taken seriously in politics. "I always remind myself that everything you do you have to work twice as hard and do it as well just because you're a woman," she observed.[28] She devoted particular attention to mastering senate parliamentary procedure. These efforts proving successful, Collins won praise from senators as an impartial and knowledgeable parliamentarian. "She does her homework," senate president pro tem Joe Prather remarked. "She anticipates what's coming up and prepares herself for any parliamentary move."[29] Republican state senator Walter Baker of Glasgow maintained that "Collins was well-liked on both sides of the aisle."[30]

Collins was not without her critics, however. Early in her tenure as lieutenant governor, an unidentified state senator, while agreeing that Collins worked "like hell," complained that she was still an unknown commodity. "She's going to have to show some ability outside the purely political in the next couple of years [if she wants to run for governor]." As lieutenant governor Collins never entirely quieted her critics. In May 1983, just a few months before her term was to expire in December, some senators were still insisting that she had never really defined herself or taken any politically meaningful positions. Republican Walter Baker, for one, made this charge, but even some of Collins's fellow Democrats shared this view. A Democrat identified only as "outspoken" and "well known" insisted that she "had just gumshoed it. She's been nice and pleasant and tiptoed through the tulips and not made any enemies." A Democratic state senator, likewise unnamed, was equally blunt in his assessment of Collins: "She never solicited my vote. She's a very nice person, but I never saw any leadership. Most of us were faced with hard decisions. You find out quickly that you can't vote maybe."[31]

While implicitly admitting that she had indeed taken few positions publicly,

Collins countered that these critics had failed to appreciate her behind-the-scenes work on legislation. "I spent a lot of time working with the budget," she insisted. "I worked on various pieces of legislation that never would have gotten out of committee without my help."[32] Collins had, in fact, taken two political stands while presiding over the Senate, one of which put her in direct opposition to Governor Brown. The first was in March 1980, when the Senate deadlocked nineteen to nineteen on a Brown-backed bill that would have made collective bargaining mandatory for public school teachers. Collins, who said that as a former teacher she could never support mandatory collective bargaining, voted no and killed the bill.[33] Again voting no, she later broke another tie on a bill that would have allowed branch banking across county lines.[34]

Despite the mixed reviews, Collins's ready accessibility to constituents—a point she had prided herself on since at least her days as Supreme Court clerk—and her seeming omnipresence at state social and political gatherings left little doubt that she was preparing to run for governor in 1983.[35] In fact, by the spring of 1982 she had already picked a campaign chairman (senate president pro tem and Collins's former primary opponent Joe Prather), raised $200,000, and received the endorsement of western Kentucky congressman Carroll Hubbard.[36] She formally declared her candidacy that November. Joining her early on in the Democratic primary were Harvey Sloane, the mayor of Louisville, and former state human resources secretary Grady Stumbo; rumors also circulated that former state transportation secretary Frank Metts might enter the race. Early polls predicted a close contest between Sloane and Collins. A November poll by the University of Kentucky Survey Research Center, for instance, showed Collins preferred by 41.9 percent of registered Democrats, while Sloane was the choice of 39.8 percent; both Stumbo and Metts (who ultimately opted out of the race to pursue opportunities in the private sector) trailed far behind with less than 10 percent of the vote each.[37]

In the campaign that followed, Collins focused mostly on her platform while rarely mentioning her gender. Education and economic development were her chief planks. She called for competency testing for students and beginning teachers, more computers in the classrooms, and additional funding for education. Her list of ideas for developing the economy was equally comprehensive: tax credits for companies that created new jobs, relief from inheritance taxes for family farms, and increased emphasis on tourism.[38] She also regularly pledged to avoid a tax increase if at all possible.[39] On one of the few occasions she turned her focus to her gender, she used humor to try to persuade Democrats who might be thinking of voting against her because she was a woman to reconsider. "There are those who may say that Martha Layne Collins has the experience, I like what she says, but, well, you know . . . she's a woman. It's true. I'm not going to deny it. I'm also a wife and a mother. I'm a Baptist. I'm right-handed and wear contact lenses."[40]

Although neither Sloane nor Stumbo made Collins's gender an issue, the two candidates hit Collins hard on other fronts. Stumbo focused on what he perceived to be Collins's dearth of concrete political accomplishments. Speaking to reporters, he wondered aloud what she had achieved as lieutenant governor and as acting governor for 480 days of the Brown administration, paused twenty-five seconds, and then, in dramatic fashion, pulled out a red ribbon and cut it with scissors.[41] In a similar vein, he alleged that Collins had failed, during her more than ten years in politics, to make any discernible difference in the lives of average Kentuckians.[42] Making what turned out to be a successful pitch for the labor vote, Stumbo furthermore reminded audiences of Collins's vote against collective bargaining for teachers, especially as he campaigned in the coal-rich counties of western and eastern Kentucky.[43] Finally, in an attack that simultaneously impugned Collins's integrity and charged her with impropriety, Stumbo alleged that her campaign had failed to report all of its campaign contributions.[44] For his part, Sloane joined Stumbo in belittling Collins's political accomplishments. He maintained that he was the only candidate who had actually governed and added that Collins had never exercised any real leadership during her many weeks as acting governor, claiming that she had dawdled away her time in that role issuing routine proclamations.[45] On the issues, Sloane lambasted Collins for not taking a stand on the state's rising utility rates. "Kentucky's taxpayers deserve a governor who will say no to more utility rate ripoffs. I will be that governor," he exclaimed.[46]

Although normally a measured campaigner who preferred to stay above the political fray, Collins responded aggressively to these attacks and even launched some of her own. In a retort reminiscent of her response to those state senators who had charged that she had rarely led as lieutenant governor, she insisted that Stumbo and Sloane failed to give her credit for her hard work out of public view. "The leadership that I have been able to deliver has not always made headlines, but it's been there," she declared.[47] Collins also tried to make Stumbo's labor support an issue by hinting that most of that support came from out-of-state labor leaders rather than rank-and-file Kentuckians. These "labor leaders," she charged, were using Kentucky "as a battle ground" for national issues. Her sharpest reprimand of Stumbo came after he questioned her campaign fund-raising. According to Collins, Stumbo, who usually polled a distant third among the candidates until the final weeks of the campaign, had made the accusation out of desperation. "His motivation had to be to gain publicity for a failing campaign," she proclaimed, "and I am not going to let him do that at the expense of insulting me and my supporters."[48] Collins dismissed Sloane's criticism of her refusal to take a position on rising utility rates as a "political football."[49] Appealing to voters' sense of loyalty to the commonwealth, she also made subtle attacks against Sloane for his birth outside the state (New York), mentioning frequently that she was born and reared in Kentucky.[50] Collins's television advertisements against Sloane castigated him for raising taxes and increasing the city of Louisville's payroll even while the city was losing population and jobs. Finally, in a somewhat surprising move given the fund-raising allegations Collins had endured, she charged that Sloane had accepted thousands of dollars from a Frankfort contractor in return for political favors.[51]

In the waning days of the campaign, Collins saw what had been a tight two-person race between her and Sloane become a close three-way contest after Governor Brown endorsed Stumbo on May 16, eight days before the election. Brown, never particularly close to Collins, said in announcing his decision that he believed the eastern Kentucky physician was more knowledgeable and experienced than his opponents. He added that he had made numerous offers to Collins over the last three and a half years to take a more active role in his administration but that she had always refused.[52]

On the day of the primary Collins eked out a close victory over her two rivals, polling 223,692 votes to Sloane's 219,160 and Stumbo's 199,785. In the aftermath of the race, some political observers wondered whether Brown had inadvertently given the election to Collins by endorsing Stumbo, implying that Stumbo's jump in the polls had come at the expense of Sloane's support rather than Collins's. But this argument failed to recognize that Collins may very well have won the race on her own merits. She had the best organization of the three candidates, which, in Stumbo's mind, had cost him and Sloane victories in many small counties throughout the state and possibly victory statewide. "While you might say an 800 vote margin (in one county) isn't much, when it happens 25 to 30 times it amounts to a lot," Stumbo observed.[53] In a testament to her organizational abilities, Collins also outraised her opponents; as of mid-May she had raised $2.24 million, Sloane $1.878 million, and Stumbo $688,841.[54]

It is difficult to assess what role, if any, Collins's gender played in the election's outcome. At the time Collins seemed to think that some people questioned her suitability for the governor's mansion on account of her gender. "Because I am a woman, I have to do everything better in this campaign [than Sloane and Stumbo]."[55] Some men were openly hostile to Collins's candidacy. One Paris, Kentucky, man told Sloane that "women shouldn't be in a position of authority," while another warned, "You'd better watch that woman. She's pretty but could slip in there and we don't want that."[56] But whatever support she lost among men due to her gender, she more than offset with her support among women. According to one newspaper, "polls seem to indicate that a majority of women—possibly two thirds of them—support Collins."[57] The same newspaper suggested that Collins's support from women was strongest among conservative ones, noting that "feminists appear cool to her," a fact that probably was due to her opposition to abortion except in cases of rape or incest or where the mother's life was endangered.[58] Given her strength among women, it is conceivable that Collins did in fact win the primary because Stumbo and Sloane split the male vote. Regardless of the reasons for it, her victory was a historic achievement that propelled her into a fall showdown with Republican nominee Jim Bunning.

A state senator and former major-league pitcher, Bunning had won his primary easily against minor opposition and entered the campaign against Collins with the state Republican Party hopeful of capturing the governor's mansion for the first time since 1967.[59] GOP hopes of winning proved ephemeral, however. With the help of her husband, Collins outraised Bunning, amassing more than $2 million total, which she used to blitz the airwaves with campaign commercials.[60] Bunning, meanwhile, largely due to a series of campaign gaffes, failed to make appreciable inroads among Kentucky Democrats, who outnumbered Republicans in terms of registration by a margin of 1.2 million to 500,000.[61] Early in the campaign, for instance, Bunning stubbornly and vocally defended right-to-work laws, costing him any chance that he might have had of exploiting Collins's weakness among union households.[62] Bunning also blundered badly in the campaign's only televised debate on October 12, 1983. According to Collins, Bunning's misstep, along with her forceful rejoinder to it, may have helped ease men's concerns about voting for her. She recalled: "We're standing there and . . . he's big and he's tall and we're in the debate and you know you've got a lot riding on that, and I know as a female I have to be careful about mistakes. But some question was asked . . . and I paused, and [before I could answer] he said something. I looked at him, and said: 'You answer your questions, and I'll answer mine.'"[63] Collins's memorable rebuke overshadowed Bunning's debate performance and ended any chance he had of reversing the campaign's momentum.

On Election Day, Tuesday, November 8, Collins rolled to an easy victory over Bunning, receiving 561,674 votes to his 454,650. She was sworn in on December 13 in Frankfort before an estimated 150,000 people. Collins's election was significant in several respects. Not only did she become the commonwealth's first woman chief executive; she was, at the time, the only woman governor in the nation. Moreover, she was only the sixth woman ever to serve as governor of a U.S. state; only the third to win the office without succeeding a husband; and the first southern woman to do so.[64]

Collins opened her administration by pushing an ambitious education agenda. In her January 26, 1984, budget address, the former teacher outlined her plan for the commonwealth's schools. Among other things, she called for more funding for remediation programs, a new writing program for grades seven through twelve, pay increases for teachers in general and extra compensation for excellent teachers in particular, an internship year for first-year teachers, $2.5 million in funds to purchase more classroom computers and train computer programming teachers, and additional money for school repair and construction. Demonstrating her deeply felt commitment to education, Collins called improving Kentucky's schools the most "pressing" need of the commonwealth. "Without quality schools, our state simply cannot provide the opportunities Kentuckians deserve," she maintained.[65]

Collins's education proposals came on the heels of news that her revenue cabinet had revised downward, by $300 million, its estimates of the amount of income available for budgeted programs. This revelation forced Collins—in the same address in which she had announced her education agenda—to propose additional taxes much sooner than her campaign tax pledge had ever anticipated. She realized that requesting a tax increase so soon was politically risky, but she "chose to go ahead and address the issue, education, and ask for the money and approach it that way." Many members of the General Assembly took umbrage at Collins's tax announcement, however, and generally considered it a mistake. Some believed she had been too quick to ask for a tax increase, insisting she had failed to make the case for one with individual legislators before bringing her request before the assembly. "The groundwork had not been laid for a tax increase," declared Michael R. Maloney, chair of the Senate Appropriations and Revenue Committee and fellow Democrat. According to the *Lexington Herald-Leader*, other legislators worried that supporting the tax increase was politically inexpedient in an election year. Although the General Assembly did deliver on some minor education proposals, Collins sensed the lack of enthusiasm for the education reform and revenue package and withdrew it, opting instead for a continuation budget.[66]

The demise of her budget was not the only setback Collins suffered early in her term. On assuming office, she had placed many friends and political supporters in her cabinet and on the board of regents at Morehead State University. The qualifications of the new Morehead board members seemed incredibly thin to some political observers, prompting them to deem the board the weakest ever appointed to a state university in Kentucky. Three of her cabinet appointments—Floyd Poore, Melvin Watson, and Lester Thompson—raised concerns because they had been big campaign fund-raisers for Collins and each had close ties to her husband. Poore, for example, who served Collins as state secretary of transportation until May 1985, had roomed with Bill Collins in college and had invested in a bank that Collins had started in Versailles. Bill Collins's association with these individuals fueled speculation that he might be exerting an undue influence over his wife's administration.[67]

Governor Collins began a political comeback in early 1985 thanks to her prominent role in two nationally important political events. In January 1984 Collins was named chair of the Democratic National Convention, to be held in San Francisco in July.[68] Leading up to the convention, the Kentucky governor was recognized in another way: she was one of seven candidates whom presumptive Democratic presidential nominee Walter Mondale interviewed for the number-two spot on the ticket.[69] Collins was not a finalist for the position, presumably because feminist organizations, which were pressuring Mondale to name a woman to the ticket, deemed her too conservative; however, it was still a distinct honor for a first-year governor to be considered for the ticket at all.[70] At the convention itself, Collins performed adeptly as the presiding officer and gained national television exposure, elevating her status within Democratic Party ranks. Her experience at the convention also reinvigorated Collins politically. According to Mike Ruehling, a friend and political consultant to the governor, the event "was a turning point in her administration. When she went out there and did well, she gained so much confidence."[71]

The energized Collins made education her top priority once more. Signaling her return to the issue, Collins in January 1985 appointed herself secretary of the Education and Humanities Cabinet. The move surprised many Frankfort politicians but generally won positive reviews from them. For example, Harry Snyder, the executive director of the Council on Higher Education, asserted, "I think it was a brilliant stroke. She is clearly the most important person in Kentucky to education," while David Keller, the executive director of the Kentucky School Boards Association, declared that "the governor's action is clear evidence of her dedication to providing the strong leadership needed to improve education." At the same time she assumed the secretariat, for which she refused a salary, she began to cultivate support for education reform. Collins had concluded from the setback of her first education and tax reform package that she had failed to nurture the proper public and legislative support before seeking its approval. To this end, she personally approached several legislators individually and solicited their support and help on the issue. Collins, who could be an uninspiring public speaker, proved persuasive in these one-on-one meetings. One legislator,

House speaker Donald Blandford, vividly recalled Collins's request for his assistance: "I'll never forget her words, 'How can I get you to help me with my education package?' I had never been for education reform. She wanted to get me involved, and she did." Collins asked sympathetic legislators to join her as she canvassed the state seeking public support for education reform. Beginning her tour of the commonwealth in Casey County in January, she eventually took her education message to more than half of the state's counties. During her meetings with legislators and while traveling around Kentucky, Collins—as far as was possible—avoided discussing the new taxes that might be necessary to fund any education program for fear that education reform and higher taxes might become inextricably linked. "Why would you take a tax program [to the people] hand-in-hand with an education program? Are you going to say we haven't improved education if, in fact, we don't pass a tax package? You can't say that," she asserted.[72] As she toured the state, Collins brought the public into the reform process by asking for citizens' input on the condition of Kentucky's schools, a crucial step for not only gathering ideas and gaining inspiration but also building public support for her eventual education package.[73]

In June Collins revealed the details of her plan. It called for $287.7 million in education spending for 1986–87 in five core areas: teacher compensation and professional development, facilities and operations, power equalization (helping poor school districts achieve program parity with wealthy ones), instructional programs such as reducing class sizes in grades one through six, and school effectiveness projects. To fund her plan, Collins proposed a series of corporate taxes that her administration estimated would generate $249.3 million over the next three years. The remaining funding for education would come from anticipated economic growth. These tax proposals caused some grumblings in the business community, but Collins made the taxes more palatable by simultaneously proposing the repeal of an unpopular business inventory tax. Legislators generally seemed amenable to the education bill and impressed by the "thoroughness" of her tax plan. Emboldened by the support she sensed for the plan, Collins called the General Assembly into session in July to consider her proposals.[74] After making some minor adjustments to each, the House and Senate passed the education bill by votes of 79–15 and 28–9 and the tax package by margins of 60–36 and 23–13.[75] A triumphant Collins proclaimed, "We have truly done ourselves proud in Kentucky."[76]

In 1986 Collins requested additional educational measures, with modest success. The legislature approved funding for her proposals for "centers of excellence" at selected universities, whereby students and professors would work together in "a rigorous academic environment," and for increased salaries for professors.[77] The legislature also passed a constitutional amendment at her behest to make the state superintendent of public instruction an appointive rather than an elected post.[78] Collins maintained that authorizing the State Board of Education to name the superintendent would enhance the likelihood that the position would be staffed by a professional educator rather than a politician.[79] The indefatigable Collins personally campaigned for the amendment, sometimes door to door, but voters defeated the measure in November, perhaps because some of them mistakenly believed the amendment would empower the governor to handpick the superintendent.[80]

Concurrent with her pursuit of her educational objectives, Collins sought the fulfillment of her other core campaign pledge: developing the state's economy. This goal assumed greater importance in the summer of 1985, when General Motors announced that Tennessee would be the location for its new Saturn auto assembly plant. Although Collins had tried to woo General Motors to the commonwealth, some Kentuckians accused her of not having done enough. Hurt by this criticism, she resolved that the state would not be outdone in the bidding war that had already erupted among the states in pursuit of a Toyota Motor Corporation assembly plant that the corporation had announced would be built in the United States.[81]

Even before Toyota had revealed its intention to build the facility, Collins had cultivated a relationship with Japanese corporations, in particular Toyota. In March 1985 she and an economic team, led by Secretary of Commerce Carroll Knicely, met Toyota officials in Toyota City, Japan, to introduce themselves, assess the automaker's interest in foreign investment, and suggest Kentucky as a possible investment site. According to Collins, she treated the Japanese as customers whom she sought to please. She also familiarized herself with Japan's history and culture before making her initial visit, a decision she credited to her Baptist upbringing. "In the Baptist church, you study a lot about missionaries that go to these foreign countries, you learn about the geography and terrain of a country, you learn about their food and clothes, and what happens in their homes."[82] In addition, Collins recalled that her gender gave her an advantage over other state governors who were trying to lure Japanese investments. "I would go to Japan and be the only female governor over there. So they never got me mixed up with the other [governors.] That was to my advantage," she recalled.

Initially, about twenty states vied for the Toyota plant. During this period Collins asked her economic team to provide the corporation with as much information as possible, including data on Kentucky's highways and railroads and even information on the state's sewers, waterways, and utility costs. After Toyota named Kentucky one of ten finalists for the plant, it asked the Collins administration for additional data on possible sites. This time, Collins decided that hand-delivering the report, rather than mailing it, would distinguish Kentucky from its competitors. To this end, she dispatched Ted Sauer, the executive director of the Commerce Cabinet's Office of International Marketing, to Asia. She instructed Sauer to stay in Japan as long as was necessary to answer any questions that Toyota officials might have about the report. According to Collins, he spent "four or five days" there.[83]

In October Collins and her economic team again visited Japan.[84] A month later, a Toyota official confirmed that Kentucky was one of five front-runners—Indiana, Kansas, Missouri, and Tennessee were the others—for the automobile factory. Later in November Toyota narrowed the list to Kentucky and Tennessee and proposed to make a final visit to each state. Collins worried that Tennessee might win out if she did not make the Toyota officials' trip to Kentucky stand out. Instead of sending an official to the airport to greet state guests, which was customary, Collins met them herself. She was equally determined to make a positive impression at dinner that evening at the governor's mansion in Frankfort. Convinced from her studies that the Japanese liked fireworks, she asked for the lights to be dimmed in the dining room while baked Alaskas, bedecked with sparklers, were served for dessert. She also knew that the Japanese appreciated the works of Stephen Collins Foster and therefore invited performers from the popular *Stephen Foster Story* in Bardstown to sing some of his songs after dinner. Collins recalled, "It was way past 9 o'clock, and we were singing. They knew all the words, and they were clapping their hands, tapping their feet and having a good time." Collins capped the night with a fireworks display, also well received by the Japanese. "The idea was just to let them know we were friends and appreciated their relationship and that we knew some of the things they liked," Collins stated.[85]

On December 11, 1985, in a downtown Lexington news conference attended by journalists from several national newspapers and magazines, Toyota made the announcement that Collins had fought so long and hard for: the company had chosen to build its plant near Georgetown in Scott County. Most Kentuckians greeted the news enthusiastically, and Collins received praise for her pivotal role in bringing Toyota to Kentucky. Yet some of the initial enthusiasm cooled when the Collins administration revealed the details of the incentives package that it had put together to lure Toyota. The package totaled $125 million, including $10 million to buy the land (which would then be given to Toyota), up to $25 million for site preparation, $33 million for initial employee training, $10 million for a "high-tech Toyota skills development center" for plant workers, and $47 million in highway improvements. "We calculated these incentives just as a business would, that is, based on the return we could expect from each dollar invested," Collins explained. In return for these incentives, the state estimated that the plant would pay $80 million in salaries annually and generate an additional $488.9 million in revenue for the state over its first twenty years of existence. The latter figure included income taxes from the plant's employees and state property and license taxes from Toyota. Commerce secretary Knicely estimated that Kentucky would recover the cost of its investment in five years.[86]

The size of the incentives package dismayed some Kentuckians, a sentiment compounded when a study in the *Lexington Herald-Leader* found that the cost of winning the Georgetown plant might actually be closer to $354 million if interest payments on the bonds purchased to finance the incentives package were factored in.[87] Opponents of the deal did not shy away from criticizing the governor. A group calling itself the Concerned Citizens and Businessmen of Central Kentucky threatened to sue over the incentives package and circulated "Japs Go Home" bumper stickers.[88] Republican state representative Pat Freibert wondered whether the package had been needlessly excessive. "Could we have gotten the Toyota plant for less?" she asked. "I think we could have. You don't necessarily get a better deal when the other side knows that the sky is the limit."[89] Future governor Wallace Wilkinson would claim that the incentives package had made Kentucky the "laughingstock" of the nation.[90] Despite such sentiments, the General Assembly approved the $125 million package during the 1986 legislative session, and the state supreme court, in a test suit launched by the Collins administration itself, declared the incentives constitutional.[91] These actions helped blunt criticism of the Toyota deal, as did the promise of jobs. As one scholar has pointed out, thousands of Kentuckians flooded "state offices with resumes and phone calls asking how to get a job at Toyota."[92]

The Toyota deal was the pinnacle of Collins's success as governor, but she enjoyed one last notable victory before leaving office. Alarmed by the growing deficit in the state's workers' compensation program, business and labor leaders urged the governor to call a special legislative session in 1987 to address the issue. Collins agreed to convene the session on the condition that the legislature first come to her with a consensus solution. The legislature complied, and Collins called the special session in October. The legislation passed, despite strong opposition from coal companies, which balked at the provision that raised assessments on them more than other industries because the majority of workers' compensation claims were for black lung disease. Ron Cyrus, the head of the Kentucky AFL-CIO, praised Collins for calling the session, noting that she could just have easily passed the workers' compensation issue on to her successor. "But she showed leadership and went ahead with it," he declared.[93]

When Collins's term ended in December 1987, speculation naturally turned to what she would do next. Supporters urged her to run for the U.S. Senate or for governor again four years later, while others hinted that she might receive an appointive position in Washington if a Democrat won the 1988 presidential election. Collins herself was vague when asked about her intentions. "I worked hard and gave an awful lot in four years. That was a phase of my life I feel good about. I'm looking at what the next phase might be," she stated in one interview. In 1988 she started Martha Layne Collins and Associates, a small consulting firm that still operates in Lexington, and accepted the position of "executive in residence" at the University of Louisville's business school, allowing her to return to the classroom as a guest lecturer. In 1989 she was one of six fellows at the Harvard Institute of Politics during the spring term. In this position Collins taught a noncredit course on political leadership and decision making and audited courses on international economics and ethics.[94]

In June 1990 Collins accepted the presidency of Saint Catharine College in Washington County, probably her most significant postgubernatorial position. Her decision to take the post surprised some. The two-year college's enrollment was low, its finances were shaky, and it enjoyed little name recognition outside its immediate area—a far cry from the prestige of the governor's mansion—but Collins viewed the job as an opportunity to contribute to the state. As president she concluded that the college had to diversify its curriculum to attract more students. To this end, the school created a successful nursing program and added courses in real estate, banking, environmental science, and arts management, although it remained a liberal arts institution at its core. These efforts raised enrollment, from 257 students when Collins took over to 372 five years later. To enhance the school's profile, she began inviting dignitaries to campus to speak, including former Speaker of the U.S. House Thomas "Tip" O'Neill, and she used her name recognition and political contacts to attract an increasing number of private donations. The college raised $181,340 in private gifts in 1990, for example, but as of June 1995 it had already received $534,100 on the year. After six fruitful years Collins resigned the presidency in June 1996.[95]

Her tenure at Saint Catharine—and ultimately her political legacy—were tarnished in 1993 when a federal court found her husband, Dr. Bill Collins, guilty of influence peddling and sentenced him to five years in prison. Dr. Collins's financial dealings first came under suspicion in 1986, when newspapers revealed that nearly half of his business investors had contracts or appointments with the state. In the 1993 trial prosecutors alleged that during his wife's gubernatorial campaign and also during her administration, Dr. Collins had exchanged state contracts totaling nearly $1.7 million to two out-of-state bond-underwriting firms for political donations and investments in Collins Investments, a horse and real-estate partnership. They also charged him with disguising the kickbacks as legal contributions on tax returns. During testimony Governor Collins, who was not charged with wrongdoing, maintained her husband's innocence and denied firsthand knowledge of his business transactions. "He was doing his business, and I was running the government," Collins asserted. She also claimed to have been unaware that her family's net worth had climbed significantly during her administration, from $274,000 in 1984 to $1.3 million in 1987. Despite insisting that her husband's business dealings were ethical, Collins struggled in defining conflicts of interests while on the stand, even when given specific examples to consider, perhaps a telling moment for someone who had long prided herself on hard work and attention to detail.[96] Whatever her knowledge of her husband's financial affairs, the verdict against him tainted Governor Collins politically, effectively ending her hopes of running for another political office.

After leaving Saint Catharine College, Collins became director of the International Business and Management Center at the University of Kentucky. In this position she helped start a number of new programs, including a sports marketing academy.[97] She left the post in 1998 to join Georgetown College as "executive scholar in residence," a part-time advisory position that she held until 2012.[98] Also in 1998, at the behest of Governor Paul Patton, she headed the state's successful effort to keep United Parcel Service's sorting hub in Louisville.[99]

Collins has received numerous awards and honors since the end of her term as governor. In 1999, for instance, Japan named her an honorary consul in recognition of her role in promoting Japanese investments in Kentucky.[100] In 2003 the commonwealth renamed the Bluegrass Parkway, a seventy-one-mile stretch of road between Versailles and Elizabethtown, the Martha Layne Collins Bluegrass Parkway. This much-welcomed honor was viewed by some politicians as long overdue. Former Versailles city attorney Jim Gay, for example, commented: "I think Martha Layne did an outstanding job in getting Toyota and some other things for our state. I just don't think she's been paid the tribute that's due her." Democratic state representative Joe Barrows of Versailles, meanwhile, declared that Collins "needs to be honored in some fashion, and if this is the way they've chosen to do it, I'm all right with it."[101] In 2009 Collins received the Order of the Rising Sun, Gold and Silver Star, from Consul-General Hiroshi Sato of the Japanese consulate in Nashville at a ceremony in the governor's mansion. Japan awarded the medal to Collins in recognition of her achievements in fostering Japanese-American relations in Kentucky. That same year Collins's native Shelby County announced that a new high school would be named in her honor.[102]

As significant as these rewards and honors might have been, perhaps the greatest recognition Collins has received has been her steadily improving legacy. Although she failed to win passage of her first education reform bill, largely because of political inexperience, she learned from the setback, cultivated the proper political relationships, and secured passage of a sweeping education reform bill in 1985. Other Kentucky governors had attempted, with varying success, to improve the commonwealth's schools, but few, if any, of them match Collins's zeal and resolve for fundamental education reform. Nor could many of them bring to the table Collins's experience as a schoolteacher, which gave her a unique insight into the problems facing Kentucky's classrooms. Unfortunately for Collins, one cannot measure the effectiveness of her education reforms, for in 1989 the Kentucky Supreme Court declared the state's public school system unconstitutional due to funding inequities between poor and wealthy school districts. These inequities had led to lower pay for teachers, inferior classroom facilities, and fewer learning materials, among other things, in poorer school districts. Collins had, in fact, tried to bring greater parity to school districts, and she cannot be held responsible for inequities that had begun long before her term. Nevertheless, the court's ruling effectively struck down her reforms. However, Collins's efforts helped renew the state's focus on education. As Bob Bell, chairman of Kentucky Advocates for Higher Education, put it, "Martha Layne Collins made it both popular and fashionable to support education reform and quality education."[103] In 1990 the General Assembly enacted the sweeping Kentucky Education Reform Act.

The continuing success of the Toyota plant also enhances Collins's reputation. Although the incentives package to lure the plant to the Bluegrass was maligned by some at the time, the economic benefits of Toyota quickly became apparent and silenced the critics. By 1999 the plant had already expanded twice and increased employment from three thousand to more than seven. Moreover, the success of the plant and Collins's systematic efforts to persuade the Japanese to invest in Kentucky had, by that same year, helped lure more than one hundred additional Japanese-owned companies to the commonwealth. A University of Kentucky study estimated that these facilities employed about 35,000 persons. In spring 2006 Toyota celebrated twenty years in Georgetown with a large party in Rupp Arena attended by the plant's employees, their families, and Collins. At that point in the plant's history, Toyota officially estimated its return on Kentucky's investment at 35 percent.[104] Time had proved the naysayers wrong.

The final part of Collins's legacy is purely political—but no less important. Kentucky has not had a woman governor, or a serious contender for that position, since she left office in December 1987. However, her election—and the elections of the five women who had served as governor of a state before her—helped pave the way for even greater electoral success by women. In 1992 the political landscape witnessed the "Year of the Woman" in Congress. In the 1990s and early 2000s an increasing number of women were elected to gubernatorial, House, and Senate positions, including Kentucky's Anne Northup, who served in the U.S. House of Representatives from 1997 to 2007 out of the state's third congressional district.[105] When the 113th Congress opened in January 2013, twenty women took their position in the U.S. Senate and eighty-one in the House, a record in each case.[106] Although there are political gender barriers yet to fall—chief among them the vice presidency and presidency—Collins's hard work, perseverance, and, ultimately, her political success helped shatter the illusion that politics was a man's world and thereby served as an inspiring example for other women thinking about entering the battles of the political arena.

NOTES

1. For more on the "Year of the Woman," see "From Anita Hill to Capitol Hill: A Flurry of Fresh Female Faces Vindicates the Year of the Woman," *Time*, November 16, 1992, 21; Michael X. Delli Carpini and Bruce A. Williams, "The Year of the Woman? Candidates, Votes and the 1992 Elections," *Political Science Quarterly* 108 (1993): 29–36; Kathleen Dolan, "Voting for Women in the 'Year of the Woman,'" *American Journal of Political Science* 42 (1998): 272–93. The four women newly elected to the U.S. Senate in 1992 were Democrats Barbara Boxer and Dianne Feinstein of California, Democrat Carol Mosely Braun of Illinois, and Democrat Patty Murray of Washington. They joined incumbent Republican Nancy Kassebaum of Kansas and Democrat Barbara Mikulski of Maryland in that body in January 1993. See "Women in the Senate" at http://www.senate.gov/artandhistory/history/common/briefing/women_senators.htm (accessed November 25, 2013).

2. *Frankfort State Journal*, March 21, 2006.

3. Ed Ryan and Elizabeth Duffy Fraas, "Martha Layne Collins," in *Kentucky's Governors*, updated edition, ed. Lowell H. Harrison (Lexington: University Press of Kentucky, 2004), 235.

4. *Lexington Herald-Leader* (hereafter *LHL*), June 2, 1990, June 5, 1995.

5. Elizabeth Duffy Fraas, "Career and Administration of Governor Martha Layne Collins," in *The Public Papers of Governor Martha Layne Collins, 1983–1987*, ed. Elizabeth Duffy Fraas, The Public Papers of the Governors of Kentucky Series, ed. Nelson L. Dawson (Lexington: University Press of Kentucky, 2006), 2.

6. *The Guardian* (London), April 8, 1987, quoted in ibid.

7. Mary Taylor Hall, as quoted by Martha Layne Collins in Frances Smith, "Martha Layne Collins," in *The New History of Shelby County, Kentucky*, ed. John E. Kleber (Prospect, Ky.: Harmony House, 2003), 562.

8. *LHL*, May 8, 1983.

9. Anne Cassidy, "The Lady and Her Legacy: Kentuckian Martha Layne Collins Knows That Some Governors' Work Is Never Done," *Southern Magazine*, October 1987, 26.

10. Fraas, "Career and Administration of Martha Layne Collins," 2; *Shelby Sentinel*, July 29, 1998 (reprint of article from July 24, 1958).

11. *Shelby Sentinel*, July 29, 1998. The article shows a beaming Collins posing with U.S. senator Thruston Morton on receiving her crown.

12. Fraas, "Career and Administration of Martha Layne Collins," 2.

13. *LHL*, May 8, 1983.

14. Elizabeth Duffy Fraas, "'All Issues Are Women's Issues': An Interview with Governor Martha Layne Collins on Women in Politics," *Register of the Kentucky Historical Society* 99 (2001): 226.

15. *LHL*, March 23, 1980.

16. F. W. Woolsey, "Martha Layne Collins: What Keeps a Lieutenant Governor on the Go?" *Louisville Courier-Journal Magazine*, February 21, 1982.

17. "Governor Martha Layne Collins Biographical Information," typescript document in Martha Layne Collins Vertical File, Thomas D. Clark Research Library, Kentucky Historical Society, Frankfort; *LHL*, March 23, 1980.

18. Fraas, "Interview with Martha Layne Collins," 227; *LHL*, May 8, 1983.

19. *LHL*, March 23, 1980.

20. Fraas, "Interview with Martha Layne Collins," 217.

21. *Woodford Sun*, October 21, 1976.

22. A political trendsetter, Stovall also served Kentucky twice as state treasurer and three times as secretary of state. See *Louisville Courier-Journal* (hereafter *LCJ*), February 5, 1994.

23. *Woodford Sun*, October 21, 1976.

24. Woolsey, "Martha Layne Collins," *Louisville Courier-Journal Magazine*, February 21, 1982.

25. Fraas, "Career and Administration of Martha Layne Collins," 19.

26. *LHL*, May 8, 1983, March 23, 1980.

27. Fraas, "Interview with Martha Layne Collins," 219.

28. *LHL*, May 8, 1983.

29. *LCJ*, March 15, 1980.

30. *LHL*, May 8, 1983.

31. Ibid., March 23, 1980, May 8, 1983.

32. Ibid.

33. *LCJ*, March 15, 1980; *Park City Daily News* (Bowling Green; hereafter *PCDN)*, August 9, 1979.

34. *LHL*, May 8, 1983.

35. *Middlesboro Daily News*, March 13, 1979.

36. *PCDN*, May 12, 1982.

37. For the poll, see *Kentucky New Era (Hopkinsville*; hereafter *KNE*), November 17, 1982. For Metts's decision to forgo the race, see ibid., January 10, 1983.

38. *LHL*, May 8, 1983.

39. *KNE*, May 2, 1983.

40. *Harlan Daily Enterprise*, May 10, 1983.

41. *KNE*, December 18, 1982. The number of days that Collins presided as acting governor is given in ibid., May 26, 1983.

42. Ibid., May 2, 1983.

43. *Harlan Daily Enterprise*, May 21, 1983.

44. *PCDN*, April 1, 1983.

45. *KNE*, May 2, 1983.

46. Ibid., May 14, 1983.

47. Ibid., May 2, 1983.

48. *PCDN*, April 1, 1983.

49. *Harlan Daily Enterprise*, May 10, 1983.

50. *KNE*, May 26, 1983.

51. *LHL*, May 8, 1983.
52. *Harlan Daily Enterprise*, May 17, 1983.
53. *LHL*, May 26, 1983.
54. *Harlan Daily Enterprise*, May 17, 1983.
55. *KNE*, May 20, 1983.
56. *LHL*, May 17, 1983. Sloane ignored the obvious gender bias of the comments, disregarding the first comment while responding to the second with a line he had used before: "It'll be a tough race against her but we'll do it."
57. *Harlan Daily Enterprise*, May 10, 1983.
58. Ibid. (quotation); *LHL*, May 8, 1983 (Collins's stance on abortion).
59. For Bunning's victory, see *LCJ*, May 26, 1983.
60. *Williamson (W. Va.) Daily News*, November 5, 1983; *Harlan Daily Enterprise*, November 5, 1983.
61. *KNE*, May 20, 1983.
62. *Madison (Ind.) Courier*, November 10, 1983.
63. Fraas, "Interview with Martha Layne Collins," 234–35.
64. *Frankfort State Journal*, December 12, 14, 1983. The five women to precede Collins as governor of a U.S. state were Nellie Tayloe Ross (1925–27) of Wyoming, Miriam A. "Ma" Ferguson (1925–27, 1933–35) of Texas, Lurleen Wallace (1967–68) of Alabama, Ella T. Grasso (1975–80) of Connecticut, and Dixy Lee Ray (1977–81) of Washington. Of these, only Grasso and Ray had not had a husband who had been governor. See ibid.
65. Budget Address, Frankfort, January 26, 1984, in Fraas, *Public Papers of Martha Layne Collins*, 49–52 (quotation on 48).
66. *LHL*, December 6, 1987; Fraas, "Career and Administration of Martha Layne Collins," 5; Withdrawal of Tax Measure: Press Statement, Frankfort, March 21, 1984, in Fraas, *Public Papers of Martha Layne Collins*, 71–73.
67. *LHL*, December 6, 1987; Fraas, "Career and Administration of Martha Layne Collins," 12.
68. *LHL*, January 19, 1984.
69. The other candidates interviewed were Congresswoman Geraldine Ferraro of New York, who received the vice presidential nod from Mondale, becoming the first woman ever so named; Senator Lloyd Bentsen of Texas; Los Angeles mayor Tom Bradley; San Antonio mayor Henry Cisneros; San Francisco mayor Dianne Feinstein; and Philadelphia mayor Wilson Goode. Ibid., July 15, 1984.
70. *Philadelphia Inquirer*, July 15, 1984; *Miami News*, June 30, 1984.
71. *LHL*, December 6, 1987.
72. Ibid., January 12, 20, 1985, December 6, 1987.
73. Education Summit, Louisville, June 28, 1985, in Fraas, *Public Papers of Martha Layne Collins*, 95.
74. *LHL*, June 13, July 6, 1985.
75. *KNE*, July 20, 1985.
76. *Madison (Ind.) Courier*, July 22, 1985.
77. *LHL*, April 6, 1986 (first quotation); Budget Address, Frankfort, January 21, 1986, in Fraas, *Public Papers of Martha Layne Collins*, 119 (second quotation).
78. *LHL*, April 6, 1986.
79. *Harlan Daily Enterprise*, October 29, 1986.
80. *LHL*, November 6, 1986.
81. Ibid., July 30, 1985, December 6, 1987.
82. Fraas, "Interview with Martha Layne Collins," 240–42.

83. Ibid., 240; *LHL*, May 2, 2011.

84. Fraas, "Interview with Martha Layne Collins," 242.

85. *LHL*, November 6, 1985, May 2, 2011. The fireworks display, which had not been announced and took place sometime between 10:30 and 11:00 p.m., frightened some Frankfort residents. Collins later apologized for the late hour of the display. Ibid., November 16, 1985.

86. Ibid., December 12, 18, 1985; Anne Cassidy, "The Lady and Her Legacy," *Southern Magazine*, October 1987, 28.

87. *LHL*, September 28, 1986.

88. Fraas, "Career and Administration of Martha Layne Collins," 21.

89. Cassidy, "The Lady and Her Legacy," 28.

90. Fraas, "Career and Administration of Martha Layne Collins," 8.

91. *LHL*, January 25, May 8, 1986, and June 12, 1987.

92. Fraas, "Career and Administration of Martha Layne Collins," 9.

93. *LHL*, October 23, December 6, 1987.

94. Cassidy, "The Lady and Her Legacy," 30; *LHL*, February 16, 1988, April 2, 1989.

95. *LHL*, June 5, 1995, June 8, 1996.

96. Ibid., October 15, December 23, 1993; *LCJ*, August 20, October 15, 1993.

97. *LHL*, June 8, 1996, August 23, 1998.

98. Ibid., August 23, 1998. See also "An Emotional Day at GC: Hello to Barlow Park, So Long, Thanks to Former Gov. Martha Layne Collins!" at http://www.georgetowncollege.edu/news/2012/08/an-emotional-day-at-gc-hello-to-barlow-park-and-so-long-thanks-to-former-gov-martha-layne-collins/ (accessed June 25, 2013).

99. *LCJ*, January 17, 1998; *LHL*, August 23, 1998.

100. *LHL*, September 15, 1999.

101. Ibid., September 16, 2003.

102. *Shelbyville Sentinel-News*, December 18, 2009, April 2, 2009.

103. *LHL*, December 6, 1987.

104. *LCJ*, December 31, 1999; *LHL*, May 21, 2006; *Frankfort State Journal*, May 21, 2006.

105. For more on women in U.S. politics in the 1990s and early 2000s, see Susan J. Carroll, *Women as Candidates in American Politics* (Bloomington: Indiana University Press, 1994), chap. 9; *Women and Congress: Running, Winning, and Ruling*, ed. Karen O'Connor (New York: Haworth, 2001); Susan J. Carroll and Richard L. Fox, eds., *Gender and Elections: Shaping the Future of American Politics* (Cambridge: Cambridge University Press, 2010), esp. introduction. For more on Congresswoman Anne Northup, see *LCJ*, November 2, 2006; *LHL*, January 21, 2007.

106. *New York Times*, January 3, 2013.

Nancy Newsom Mahaffey

(1955–)

Preserving Heritage Foods in the "Ham Heartland"

MELISSA A. MCEUEN

Twenty-first-century businesswoman and food artisan Nancy Newsom Mahaffey has earned international acclaim and the title "The Ham Lady" by maintaining the highest standards in her craft: the production of country ham. Mahaffey cures a small "crop" of Newsom's Aged Kentucky Country Hams every year, following with precision the recipe that she learned from her father, just as he had learned from his father.[1] That she continues to cure pork as many rural southerners did for generations speaks to Mahaffey's appreciation for tradition and a preservation process that has nearly disappeared in the South. She could generate more profit if she abandoned the time-consuming all-natural curing operation, a decision that most U.S. ham producers made decades ago. But she is committed to helping contemporary southerners and others understand and appreciate what their ancestors knew and ate, known today as "heritage foods."[2]

Mahaffey's unwavering devotion to place and the past characterizes her outlook as an artisan and entrepreneur. After an especially busy year in 2007, she said, "It's not supposed to be easy. And it's not, but it's rewarding. I'm not looking to be a corporate giant. I want to do it our way as long as possible. We have a tradition—we have a traditional product, and I plan to keep it that way." In addition to curing hams, she also owns and runs Newsom's Old Mill Store on Main Street in Princeton, the western Kentucky town where she grew up and, with the exception of two years as a newlywed in Illinois, has always lived. By expanding her retail operation in a historic mill in the 1980s, Mahaffey did

NANCY NEWSOM MAHAFFEY

Photo by Anita Baker. Courtesy of the *Times Leader*.

her part to help revitalize a small-town economy damaged by the "Wal-Mart effect."[3] She understands what historian Anthony Stanonis has identified in *Dixie Emporium* as the "tightly interwoven—indeed, oftentimes inseparable" phenomena of "tourism, foodways, consumerism, and memory." For nearly thirty years she has promoted the role of culinary heritage to foster local pride and regional tourism, taking pleasure in work that she deems "true, traditional, [and] historic."[4]

With purpose, Mahaffey develops meaningful connections with nearly everyone she meets. Described as "an incredibly interesting character and bubbly conversationalist," she enjoys talking with customers, serving them at the store's meat counter or chatting with them on the telephone. Central Kentucky restaurateur and chef Ouita Michel smiles at the mention of Mahaffey's name, exclaiming, "When you call the store, *she* answers the phone. She will actually talk to you. I love that! It's so rare these days." Identifying herself as a "public servant," as her late father Colonel Bill Newsom did, Mahaffey summarizes her principal philosophy as an entrepreneur simply: "'If you have a good product and give good service, people appreciate it.'" Her influence has radiated outward to the Slow Food movement, an international nonprofit organization dedicated to food systems that celebrate regional food traditions and pleasures of the table in sustainable ways. Yet her work illustrates the complications that heritage-food producers in the rural South, especially pork specialists, face as they attempt to provide distinctive products in an industrialized agricultural landscape.[5] The tensions between tradition and modernity in the late twentieth century come into view when we examine Mahaffey's world as a food artisan. Her success in both the retail grocery business and the ham-curing business can be attributed to her ability to sell tradition as she identifies and meets the needs of a new generation of cooks, gardeners, foodies, and tourists.

Mahaffey's family history mirrors that of many other land grant recipients who moved into the trans-Appalachian West in the early nineteenth century. Having started their New World life in Virginia decades earlier, the Newsoms made their way to North Carolina then on to Kentucky in the 1820s to establish themselves in farming. For nearly one hundred years their livelihood depended on agriculture in Caldwell County.[6] Situated in the Pennyroyal region in the western end of the state, Caldwell County soil yielded tobacco, corn, and other grains, and it helped sustain healthy livestock.[7] The county seat, Princeton, served as a "staging area for the settlement of the Jackson Purchase" to the west and could boast both a state land office branch and a Commonwealth Bank of Kentucky branch in the 1820s. At a crossroads of north-south and east-west arteries, Princeton thrived commercially at midcentury; it also was an educational center in the region, earning the title "Athens of the Western Pennyrile."[8] By 1870 the town was home to several industries, including two steam-powered flour mills and a woolen mill. As in other Kentucky towns, railroads "became an obsession" in Princeton, generating economic growth and employment. Large maintenance crews tended locomotives at the town's extensive railroad yard.[9] By the turn of the twentieth century, Princeton's railway depot was "a beehive of activity." In addition to transporting passengers, cars hauled the region's dark-fired tobacco to and from Princeton's tobacco factory and warehouse district.[10] In 1914 the Illinois Central Railroad (ICRR) constructed a new roundhouse and, four years later, gained an imposing industrial neighbor when the Princeton Hosiery Mills began operations down the street. In this thriving and diverse economy, H. C. Newsom, Nancy Mahaffey's grandfather, opened a general mercantile and grocery store on Main Street, on a promontory just north of Big Spring, where water "gushed out from underneath a limestone bluff."[11]

H. C. Newsom Store provided customers a wide array of goods, including "barrels and bags of flour, sugar and meal; nails and building supplies, wagon wheels, tombstones, notions," and household necessities. Newsom also sold hams he had cured at home.[12] In 1933, in the midst of the Great Depression, H. C. Newsom died, leaving his eldest son, William, to assume management of the store and the welfare of three siblings, his mother, and two other relatives. Nancy Mahaffey is the younger of two children of William "Colonel Bill" Newsom (1914–99) and Jane Williams Newsom (1917–2011), a native Mississippian whose family settled in Princeton in the 1920s. Jane's father worked for the ICRR, and her family was accustomed to train travel. Making regular trips to visit an elderly aunt in Chicago, she took one of the fourteen daily passenger trains that rolled through Princeton in the mid-1930s. An inspired seamstress and musician, young Jane Williams met Bill Newsom in a Princeton music studio, where he took voice lessons and she studied piano. They married in September 1940 but were separated in 1942 when Bill left to serve in the European theater of operations in World War II. One of more than 1,400 Caldwell Countians in the wartime military, U.S. Army Staff Sergeant Newsom carried a small leather folder with Jane's portrait inside.[13] Soon after his return to Princeton in 1946, Bill and Jane Newsom started a family. Their son James William (Jim) was born in 1947 and their daughter Nancy Jane on June 11, 1955.

Bill and Jane Newsom were "older parents" compared to those of Nancy's friends. Seeing them exhausted by running a downtown grocery store and maintaining their retail market for country hams, Nancy claims to have "detested the family business as a child" because her parents' customers "took precedence over [her] needs."[14] Yet her childhood was idyllic, as she spent "whole days" playing in the woods behind her family's house.[15] School posed challenges, though, as Nancy had an eye problem that affected her ability to read. She "overcompensated for a learning disability" by studying long hours to earn good grades. Her greatest passions were for music and art. She sang in church choirs beginning at age five and in school choruses at every level. At her mother's insistence, Nancy took a voice lesson at eight o'clock every Saturday morning with Caldwell County High School choral director Bobbie Allo; while her teenage friends enjoyed lazy weekend mornings, Nancy was warming her vocal cords and singing scales. She also took art lessons from a local painter, Frankie Belle Granstaff. She recalls feeling uncomfortable with high school clique culture, recoiling when girls teased each other. To avoid seeing "girls get hurt," she chose to walk away rather than participate in denigrating conversations. She attributes her responses to her parents' lessons about treating people well, which she believes stemmed from their forebears' religious traditions as Quakers and Mennonites.[16]

After graduating from Caldwell County High School in 1973, Nancy spent a couple of summers working in the family grocery—"meeting customers with a smile, answering the phone, stocking the shelves, and running the cash register."[17] She also took classes at Hopkinsville Community College, initially enrolling in a human services program but switching to secretarial preparation at her parents' urging. Her brother Jim had left Princeton in 1965, when Nancy was ten years old, to attend the University of Kentucky in Lexington; he would pursue a career with the Environmental Protection Agency (EPA) and settle in New Jersey. Having worked hard in the family business as a boy, he preferred not to return to it, his sister recalled.[18]

In March 1975, at age nineteen, Nancy married Larry Mahaffey after "a whirlwind romance."[19] The marriage and move from Princeton to her husband's home in Illinois allowed Nancy to withdraw from Hopkinsville Community College's secretarial science program, where the typewriting and shorthand "drills" had bored her. She enjoyed domestic life—cooking, sewing, gardening, canning vegetables, and "paying household bills"—and was thrilled when her husband wanted to move back to Princeton just before their first child was born.[20] Within five years, Nancy had two children, Alisa Jane (b. 1977) and John Carl (b. 1980). Early on she began making her own "healthful baby food from fresh fruits, vegetables and meats." And she helped take care of others' children as well, coordinating nursery care for the First Baptist Church's worship services and serving on the church's daycare center board. In the same five-year span she suffered the loss of her father-in-law, moved his ailing widow to Princeton to care for her, and immediately following Mrs. Mahaffey's death "collapsed mentally and physically."[21] Although it had exacted a toll, caretaking had become a hallmark of Mahaffey's identity as a young woman. She found employment that would allow her to remain home full time with her children, including a stint with Mary Kay Cosmetics, whose philosophy of putting faith and family before one's career she embraced.[22] In a college assignment she completed after both children were grown and had left home, she wrote of motherhood, "Of all the roles in life, I felt this one the most important of all."[23] Before she established herself as a customer-oriented entrepreneur, Mahaffey earned credentials as a woman devoted to family and the traditionally gendered work of caring for others.

Her desire to have time with her five-year-old daughter and two-year-old son as well as "the need for additional income" led Mahaffey back to her parents' business in 1982. She became the overseer of their "prized mail order files," boxes of 3 × 5 index cards containing contact information for all of their customers. Mahaffey began to draft marketing materials and letters to ham buyers.[24] The more physically demanding work at Newsom's Store alongside her father put her at close range to observe his health. In time he would develop both a heart condition and Parkinson's disease, intensifying Mahaffey's wish to learn more about the family business. She was afraid she would end up with "a house full of hams" if her father suffered a fatal heart attack.[25] So Mahaffey learned how to cure hams by studying him at work in the 1980s, quietly "looking over his shoulder" because he did not consider the ham business an appropriate vocational interest for a woman.[26] Her father had learned the steps the same way, "by watching his father do it when he was a boy."[27]

Mahaffey had entered not one but two predominantly male worlds in the rural South—those of independent grocery owners and country ham producers. As she assumed more responsibility in both Newsom businesses in the mid-1980s, she faced challenges similar to those of many women who attempted to capitalize on the gains made by the Second Wave feminist movement. In spite of "legal, institutional, and social reforms" advancing women's positions and opportunities, historian Virginia Drachman contends that "conventional attitudes toward a woman's 'proper place' persist when women entrepreneurs try to venture beyond the service and retail trade industries of fashion, food, and cosmetics."[28] While Mahaffey was in "retail trade" as a grocer, her food-production business was not the kind typically expected of a woman, such as baking, cooking, catering, or serving meals in a restaurant. With the produce suppliers Mahaffey faced a good deal of chauvinism in addition to dishonesty. Thinking Mahaffey would not recognize that she was being cheated, one supplier tried to give her second-class goods after she had paid him first-class prices for his produce. She learned to be cautious and not turn her back at the wholesale produce market. To prove she could handle the work and endure the slights, she demonstrated her physical strength by loading her truck "top to bottom" without assistance. She thought it was the best way to win the respect of men who would play an ongoing role in a business that was becoming more and more her own.[29]

At home in Princeton she followed the same plan. To engage in "heavy labor" alongside her associates in country ham production was how she hoped to achieve "a balance of leadership as a woman with all male employees," she said. The physical work was democratized. By all accounts her formula worked. Ed Thompson, Colonel Newsom's longtime assistant in both the grocery and ham business, stayed on after Mahaffey took the helm and remained committed until his death in 2002; two other longtime associates, Jessie Gray and Lonnie Robinson, have several decades of combined experience with Newsom's enterprises. Mahaffey described their workplace relationships as mutually supportive, built and sustained in an atmosphere of trust and community. With this small coterie of seasoned coworkers, all of them African American men, Mahaffey cultivates an environment built on relationships, saying, "I don't want to come to work and look at a factory."[30] Like women entrepreneurs who characteristically "place a high value on relationships and advice from others," Mahaffey fosters a spirit of teamwork in the two Newsom businesses, both of them historically considered the purview of men and understood to be masculine endeavors.[31]

As a culinary tradition, "country ham is as old as the South itself."[32] Mahaffey's "old-fashioned" method brings together salt, brown sugar, and smoke from green hickory sawdust.[33] Her father altered the process only slightly over the six decades that he cured country hams, making "the final product less salty and hard" to accommodate more modern palates.[34] Mahaffey has addressed contemporary markets in different ways, by curing a few hundred "free-range" country hams each year in addition to a product she calls Newsom's Gourmet Aged Prosciutto Ham Crudo. Mahaffey uses a recipe that dates back to the late 1700s, discovered in a Newsom family will. The Old World–style dry-cured and unsmoked hams are the predecessors and companions of these, yet Mahaffey's version differs slightly in that she gives them just "a slight hint" of hickory smoke and hangs them higher in the ham house, where they are exposed to the greatest heat.[35] Her products reiterate the long-standing place of hogs in southern foodways, bearing out gourmand James Villas's observation that pork is "the only meat in the world that can absorb such flavors as pepper, sugar, and smoke without losing its identity."[36] Time and a hot Kentucky summer intensify the identity of country ham.

While weather has shaped many aspects of southern culture, as historian U. B. Phillips pointed out nearly a century ago, its role in heritage ham production cannot be underestimated.[37] The Upper South's reputation as the "ham heartland" depends largely on its climate.[38] Cold winters and hot summers provide the combination of extremes needed for a traditional ham-curing process, and Mahaffey must watch the weather closely in order to initiate each step at the most opportune moment. Although Mahaffey does not raise her own hogs but buys trimmed pork ready to be aged, she is attuned to the cycles of traditional farm life, following the seasonal tides as the Newsom family and many other Kentuckians did decades ago. Historian Thomas D. Clark wrote of the "first freezing days of early winter" and stated that for Kentuckians there was "perhaps no warmer memory of rural life than that of the moment when fresh meat reached the table after hog killings." One rural woman recalled the marked change "in the air" soon "after Thanksgiving," an indication that her family's annual hog slaughter could proceed safely.[39] Such sentiments reside almost solely in memory today, as little of Mahaffey's pork is Kentucky-raised. Instead she buys meat from several midwestern farms, some of it "free range" and some of it "factory-raised."[40]

The relationship between midwestern hog farmers and southern pork curers developed in the nineteenth century, historian Charles Reagan Wilson points out, because southern pork production "spiraled downward after the Civil War." A few decades later, "southern state legislatures passed laws requiring fenced lands for livestock, bringing a final end to free-range grazing of hogs by small proprietors."[41] In the 1920s trends in modernization and efficiency as well as the prevalence of "industrial production systems" and big business models took hold in the U.S. agricultural sector, followed by increasing bureaucratization of the American food system during the Great Depression and World War II. Industrial farming continued to expand in the postwar era but has felt its greatest boost since the 1980s, as U.S. farm policies "facilitated a transformation of livestock production into factory farming," creating what are known today as concentrated animal feeding operations (CAFOs). Expansive federal subsidies to corporate grain growers allow them to produce cheap animal feed to sustain CAFOs.[42] So while Mahaffey's all-natural country ham-curing process mirrors that of her early Kentucky ancestors, the nature of the meat has changed dramatically in recent decades. As a result Mahaffey and other small independent ham producers have recognized and cultivated a growing market for "free range" hogs and heritage breeds.[43] She could not, however, depend solely on premium-priced pork or she would have to close her doors—particularly to local customers who live at various rungs on the socioeconomic ladder.[44]

The U.S. government not only determines how most pigs are raised in the twenty-first century, but federal regulations also dictate how and where producers must handle pork. Meat must be shipped directly to Mahaffey's ham house, a facility located just a few minutes' drive from her general store in downtown Princeton. After the hams arrive in January, they ride by wheelbarrow into the prep area of the ham house.[45] Mahaffey calculates the total weight and then begins, during the "coldest" weeks of the year, the first of eighteen steps in the curing process—hand-rubbing each ham with salt and brown sugar. The hams are then stacked or "laced" on shelves where they will rest "a certain number of days" according to weather variations. They undergo this process again while they are "in salt." As spring approaches, Mahaffey and her employees hand wash and net each one, after which they are taken a few yards away to the "hanging house" to dry. Mahaffey is proud of the fact that when it is time to smoke the hams, she builds the fire in the iron kettle on her own.[46] She notes, "We smoke for weeks off and on depending on the weather. We are the last to still do an ambient weather curing process of circulating outdoor weather in and around our hams for the full duration of time from the time they are out of salt as the spring is warming, going through the hot, dog days of summer, and into the fall when they are finally ready for sale."[47] Following the "procedure" is vital, Mahaffey contends. A slight alteration or a missed step would affect the cure and therefore the taste. Over time, Mahaffey warns, such negligence could affect historical knowledge. She claims to be "as particular as" her father was about the process, concluding, "I guess it became my obsession like it was his."[48] Mahaffey's all-natural process yields between 2,500 and 3,000 hams each year. Higher numbers would mean loss of quality, she insists, and she keeps a close count by numbering each ham.[49]

As the air circulates, mold develops on each ham's exterior, a "natural and normal indication of proper aging for Kentucky country ham," Newsom's customers learned in the 1970s and have been told ever since.[50] The fact that mold must be explained to consumers used to judging their food's edibility by its appearance indicates a break from a rural past and its collective knowledge. Mahaffey's father once told a journalist who mentioned the hams' appearance, "I don't cure for looks, but for taste."[51] In 2005 Southern Foodways Alliance interviewer Amy Evans visited Mahaffey's ham house, exclaiming on first glimpse of the hams, "Beautiful." Mahaffey dryly replied, "I don't know that they're beautiful. They're aging."[52] Age, mold, and flavor are inextricably bound in country ham production. Mahaffey's father explained to food writer Peter Kaminsky that "the July sweats" promote the expansion of ham flesh "into the outer covering of mold." Months later, as cold weather sets in and the meat contracts, it absorbs "taste-enhancing enzymes" with it.[53] Mold that forms on the hams' exterior is of particular interest to Mahaffey, who enjoys discussing its importance in the curing process. In early 2013, she had a second ham house constructed just a few minutes' drive from the "original" facility built by her father in 1963 to meet U.S. government requirements for meat preparation. The new house's proximity to Big Spring, which opens into Princeton's cave system, has Mahaffey curious about the "kinds of molds" the house will generate. She discusses the microclimate and its possibilities with the passion of a scientist beginning a new experiment.[54]

While "the hotter the summer, the better the ham," the length of time in the ham house matters more. As food writer James Villas learned in the early 1970s from farmers all over the Upper South, the most vital element in "old-fashioned" country ham production is "the length of time it's left to age." One year or longer is ideal, and Newsom's finished hams range from ten to twenty-two months in age. Mahaffey points out that hams cured in January without nitrates will not necessarily be "ready for the Kentucky State Fair in August." Naturally aged hams will not have reached full maturity in terms of taste. Both variables—weather and time—put Mahaffey in the company of farmers and other heritage-food artisans who must allow nature to take its course.[55]

Appreciating her father's legacy of instructing those curious about country ham production, Mahaffey follows in his footsteps as a patient teacher. She identifies Newsom's Aged Kentucky Country Hams as having "an old-fashioned sugar cure." "But the sugar is not your curing agent," she hastens to clarify. "Your salt is the curing agent with smoking a relative preservative in the ham."[56] According to the founder of the Slow Food movement, Carlo Petrini, those committed to the movement embrace "the necessity to keep learning, to respect traditional knowledge and heed its teachings," so that they become what Petrini calls "co-producers." A co-producer "shares ideas and knowledge, shares in the quest for quality and in the quest for happiness, for a new dignity for the countryside and the people who produce food."[57] Mahaffey shares her craft, which she calls a "lost art," with myriad audiences. She has educated chefs, individual buyers, the general public, and other ham purveyors, including Europeans who have been curing pork for centuries. She has discussed her work at the Kentucky State Fair in Louisville, the Southern Foodways Conference in Oxford, Mississippi, the International Food and Wine Expo at Disney World, and the Fancy Food Show in New York.[58] The warnings Peter Kaminsky offered in 2005 about the value of Mahaffey's knowledge still hold true. At the time he challenged lovers of traditional gastronomic arts and "the old ways" to support and cultivate them, urging: "If the Nancy Newsoms of the world go under, in five or ten years, some true ham believer who has just graduated from culinary school is going to set up his or her own business, painstakingly regathering the knowledge that the Newsoms have had for generations." He likened the task to "students of a dead language [who] have to reacquire their knowledge all over again."[59]

Her devotion to the all-natural pork-curing process has made Mahaffey a recognized Kentucky voice in the contemporary Slow Food movement. Louisville restaurateur Kathy Cary, a longtime leader in the state's farm-to-table initiatives, praises Mahaffey for carrying out her work in "the old, 'slow food' way—the way it should be done." Cary has served Newsom's hams at her award-winning restaurant, Lilly's, since 1994.[60] With a focus on the role of place and tradition in foodways, Mahaffey has spoken at events throughout the United States about supporting and eating locally produced heritage foods. In explaining their appeal in 2010, she said: "I think one reason more and more people are liking the kinds of food that take a long time to produce—the 'slow food' kind of food—is that the world is moving ninety miles an hour. . . . All across America there's a growing feeling that it's good to be able to know where your food came from—and know the person that made it."[61] In an interview in late 2012 Mahaffey identified her country hams as part of traditional foodways by linking their production to another facet of the Slow Food movement: the absence of chemicals, dyes, and preservatives. She observed: "We are the smallest national ham-curing business left and the only one using the old-fashioned methods. . . . Our process was born before nitrates were even discovered."[62]

Slow Food advocates and others who support local producers, growers, and artisans have highlighted Mahaffey's work. In November 2005 *Country Home* magazine featured her ham in its Thanksgiving issue, encouraging readers to serve "a meal to remember with heritage foods rich in meaning and flavor."[63] In 2007 Mahaffey shared the stage and the tables with chefs Alice Waters, Mark Williams, and Kathy Cary at the Slow Food Bluegrass Kentucky Harvest Festival outside Louisville.[64] The following year one of her hams was included in Slow Food Nation's "Taste Hall of Fame," and in 2011 Newsom's Free Range Aged Ham won the prize for best charcuterie in the American South at the Seedling Project's Good Food Awards celebration in San Francisco. The awards recognized artisans committed to their "communities and cultural traditions," noted project spokesperson Sarah Weiner.[65] Mahaffey's work is now so widely known that *New York Times* food editor Sam Sifton could expect readers to recognize a passing reference to "Newsom's" in a feature story on southern cooking.[66] The awards Mahaffey has earned focus on local and regional products that lift up and celebrate a sense of place.

Accolades for Newsom's hams began to appear outside the Upper South soon after Mahaffey graduated from high school. Her father's product was discovered and heralded in 1975 by James Beard, the twentieth century's most influential voice in American foodways. Deemed the "dean of American cookery" by the *New York Times* in 1954, Beard traveled all over the United States studying regional cuisines and highlighting local products in his writing and his cooking classes, thereby encouraging Americans' awareness of a national culinary heritage.[67] In addition to writing about Newsom's hams, he also "made sure that many of his friends had a taste and the word was out."[68] Following the James Beard endorsement, Newsom's hams were featured in *Bon Appétit* and *Food and Wine* in the 1970s, along with several other national publications in the next decade. But to Colonel Newsom the fact that Beard "ordered a ham every year" after his first trip to Princeton seemed more important than the extended press coverage. Newsom claimed to be just "a farmer who cures hams," which is why he chose not to enter his pork delicacies in Kentucky State Fair competitions in August each year. He believed that farmers did not stand a chance against the state's bigger ham producers.[69] To recognize and capitalize on her link to the Newsom family's rural roots, Mahaffey designed a business card that heralds the "Real Old Time Farm Flavor" of Newsom's hams, underscoring historical tradition and authenticity.[70]

Mahaffey could not simply inherit a name and a recipe and expect continued success without the ability to identify shifting markets and adapt where necessary. Her hands-on approach, her connection to the work, and her keen interest in what customers need allow the Newsom's ham business to flourish year after year. And perhaps, Mahaffey admits, "the Newsom-Williams independence . . . or stubbornness" contributes as well.[71] Caldwell Countians have benefited from her knowledge just as they did from her father's and his willingness to share it. Family ties were fortified by visits to Newsom's Store. Mahaffey remembers scenes from her childhood where Caldwell County homemakers arrived at the grocery's door with their roasting pans and dutch ovens so that Colonel Newsom could cut each ham to fit each cook's unique kettle. Mahaffey noted that these "women who were raising big families" in the 1950s, 1960s, and 1970s relied on her father to assist them with food preparation, especially during the holidays. One local homemaker said, "I never left the store without having learned something from Mr. Newsom . . . about flowers, fruits, vegetables, or meat."[72] Customers also received instruction sheets regarding the appearance and taste of a Newsom's ham. Mahaffey has continued this tradition by including recipes and reproducing the same visual image, chart, and directions for carving that her father included with each ham he sold.[73] To reassure contemporary ham buyers, Mahaffey emphasized in a recent holiday marketing initiative that the expansion into a new facility was "being done in a limited fashion to maintain the quality and integrity of this heritage ham and its historic flavor."[74]

Most people who know Mahaffey, especially Princetonians who see her on a regular basis, comment on her work ethic. Ardell Jarratt, the former curator of Princeton's Adsmore Museum and a collaborator with Mahaffey on local tourism efforts, stated, "Nancy works herself to the bone," then suggested that such diligence is required for small-town business success.[75]

When challenges have arisen, Mahaffey's combined optimism and creativity have intensified. During one financial low point, she told her dispirited crew, "Anybody with a sad face, just stay out of my way." In another season, when hams began to deteriorate during the curing stages, Mahaffey realized that entire hams did not have to be sacrificed; only the affected parts had to be cut off. Calling the moment a "revelation," she decided that she could sell "half a ham" or a choice section she labeled "Nancy's little filet." By convincing customers that whole hams were not their only option, Mahaffey created markets that had not existed for the Newsom's enterprise. In recent years she has cooked many more hams and sold them ready to serve because, she points out, people "just don't cook much anymore." To get maximum benefit from her small production facility, the "ham house," she began curing a few more expensive "free range, rare breed" hams and prosciutto types that would increase her "high-end market," made up largely of restaurants in New York, San Francisco, and other urban centers.[76]

But Mahaffey knows she must strike a balance between affordable hams for the bulk of her market and more expensive products for the rest. While she has to "do volume" to make ends meet, she rejects a wholesale operation because she prefers "a broad base" of customers. She revels in yearly orders from local families who will put Newsom's hams on their holiday dinner tables. Maintaining her relationships with these customers and other loyal buyers, whom she calls her "national customers," takes the business beyond numbers, projections, and profit margins.[77] Mahaffey has said, "I don't want an order for so many hams that I can't fill it, because that's not my niche. It could be, but I don't want it to be." She enjoys the freedom that comes with keeping her business a manageable size, believing that constant expansion does not ensure success.[78] She also cherishes the role of her store and her country hams for Princeton natives who have moved away but return to visit, often making Mahaffey's store their first or last stop—to take away a slice or a pound or a whole ham, otherwise considered the "taste of home," the ultimate comfort food. It remains a touchstone for Princetonians of various ages and backgrounds.[79] Mahaffey has said, "It's a place where people come; then when they pass their kids come and their kids pass and their kids come."[80] Cultivating emotional ties to home and place through heritage food is one of Mahaffey's longest-lasting accomplishments. It situates her in the company of other heritage-food producers who have helped illuminate the distinctiveness of a region based on its foodways.[81]

In 2009 Mahaffey became the first American and, in fact, the first non-European to receive an invitation to participate in the biennial World Congress of Dry-Cured Hams, in Aracena, Spain, home of the revered Jamón de Huelva or *jamón ibérico de bellota*.[82] The invitation denoted the respect that Mahaffey commands internationally—and in a male-dominated business, no less. Men at the conference initially challenged her but soon realized by the questions she asked them that Mahaffey understood fully the intricate details of her craft.[83] As a result, one of Newsom's hams now hangs in the Jamón Museum in Aracena. In 2005 Peter Kaminsky claimed that Mahaffey's hams "set the bar for America," adding that they would constitute "a million-dollar business" if she lived in Spain.[84] The prized Ibérico hams that Mahaffey saw in Aracena sold for approximately $1,200 each. In contrast, her whole ham prices that year ranged from $74.85 to $99.80, calculated at about five dollars per pound. The free-range hams were higher at $7.49 per pound and her prosciutto hams at $16.99, but all remained significantly below the Spanish ham prices.[85] Mahaffey's visit to the Andalusian town of Aracena led her to consider its similarities to Princeton—a small-town culture with fewer than ten thousand inhabitants in a largely rural area with weather conditions perfect for curing pork. Both towns sit atop complex cave systems and, as Mahaffey emphasizes, are situated at the "same latitude."[86]

Mahaffey's skills and fame as an artisanal ham producer and Slow Food movement spokesperson are only part of her story; her willingness to maintain her family legacy in the face of global economic challenges casts her in the mold of earlier generations of Kentucky women who found ways to adapt to change.[87] According to fellow Kentuckian Wendell Berry's lexicon, borrowed from his teacher Wallace Stegner, Mahaffey would be considered a "sticker" instead of a "boomer." "Stickers" commit. They "settle, and love the life they have made and the place they have made it in," while "boomers" are "those who pillage and run," leaving a trail of careless destruction motivated by their insatiable desires for material wealth and lives of ease.[88] As with her artisanal work challenging conformity in food production, consumption, and taste, Mahaffey has helped counter the influence of retail giant Walmart, which in the late 1970s built a store two and a half miles outside Princeton's town center near a Western Kentucky Parkway exit.[89] Its establishment led to the successive shuttering of numerous family-owned businesses on Main Street, including furniture stores, clothing stores, shoe stores, pharmacies, and other decades-old retail operations.[90] Princeton native and business owner Michael Cherry, a former Kentucky state legislator, said that the "small town, downtown died" as other retailers moved to the town's outskirts where real estate was cheaper and large tracts could be paved over for near-limitless parking. As a result, Cherry claimed, "[Princeton] changed in character."[91] Civic activist and former Main Street Renaissance director Ann Kimmel attributes some of the downtown desertion to construction and resettlement of the public schools in a rural area on the outskirts of Princeton. The commercial boost to Main Street businesses that student foot (and auto) traffic had historically provided slowly disappeared, with each downtown school moving to the new "campus."[92] As family businesses closed their doors one by one in the 1980s, Newsom's Store suffered differently.

Just before dawn on October 7, 1987, the Newsom family's seventy-year-old store burned, destroying everything but the mail-order files and H. C. Newsom's chopping block. Mahaffey saw the building "engulfed in flames" and had to break the news to her father, calling it "one of the hardest things [she] had ever done."[93] Fortunately, country hams were off-site still in the curing stages, but they were all that Mahaffey and her father had left. At age seventy-three, Colonel Newsom saw the fire as a sign that his daughter should devote herself solely to country ham production. The morning after the fire, Mahaffey took a couple of potted mums over to the Newsom's Store doorstep to mark the "grave." "I felt it was the end of an era . . . that the day of the chain store was on," she recalled. But after someone asked to purchase the flowers, she and employee Ed Thompson sold them and brought more to fill the space. Yet another request for a sale prompted Mahaffey to interpret it as a sign that she should reopen the family store, in spite of her father's arguments against it.[94] Determined to "gain back" her most familiar customers, she observed, "the local people were what made me want to continue. . . . We had been on Main Street since 1917 and I couldn't stand for our store not to be there."[95] Mahaffey refused to let the family legacy in retail die.

Just weeks after Mahaffey set mums outside the doors of the burned-out grocery store, she opened her new enterprise next door in a space that had once housed the town's flour and woolen mills. Taking up residence in what Mahaffey called a "relic of the Industrial Revolution," she christened the new business Newsom's Old Mill Store.[96] Heartened by local customers' support, Mahaffey interpreted their devotion to "blessings inspired by the past," namely, her family's commitment "as public servants to the community."[97] But the past figured as well into the entrepreneur's reenvisioning of a business where she was now in charge. Because she knew that "the business was viewed as a cornerstone of history and stability by the local clientele," she continued to carry flowers in late spring and bulk garden seed from Bunton's Seed Company, a Louisville business that had supplied Newsom's store since its founding in 1917.[98] She wanted to maintain the store's "heirloom varieties" that had "a history all their own."[99]

The changes in family life, domestic responsibilities, and even meal preparation by the mid-1980s led Mahaffey to realize that Newsom's Old Mill Store would have to provide more prepared foods and fewer grocery staples than her father had offered. She decided to add pottery and "private-labeled products" to her inventory, moving forward in spite of one banker's quip that she was "beating a dead horse."[100] The remark emphasizes the "skepticism among the financial community about women's experience and long-term commitment to entrepreneurship" in the late twentieth century. In spite of the 1974 Equal Credit Opportunity Act, many women found that access to capital remained their biggest challenge in the 1980s and 1990s.[101] Facing her doubters directly, Mahaffey created a niche with her general store by stocking glass jars of "country" foods that had come to be considered novelties, since fewer individuals took time to preserve their own fruits and vegetables. Jams, jellies, relishes, and various kinds of pickled vegetables lined the shelves in Mahaffey's new iteration of a country store. She explained: "Anything that takes time to make anymore is a gourmet food. Any food that's a natural food that takes time to make is slow food."[102] In the 1990s Mahaffey staked her future on both—gourmet foods in her country store and slow food with her country ham business.[103] She appealed to memory and imagination, transforming Newsom's Old Mill Store into a tourist destination.

Praising Mahaffey as "a good ambassador" for Princeton and her store as "a wonderful place to send tourists," museum curator Ardell Jarratt noted their attractiveness to visitors seeking a cultural experience. More than anything else, tourists want food, she said; Newsom's could provide it, but perhaps more importantly, she emphasized, tourists could "get an authentic experience in an old-time store."[104] Jarratt's observation reflects Dean MacCannell's theory of modern tourism and the tourist's quest for "authenticity."[105] The experience itself matters more than store purchases, because visitors to historic places usually seek "non-economic" or "intangible" gratification. In *Destination Dixie*, historian Karen L. Cox explains: "Perhaps that intangible is the opportunity to encounter history or local traditions or to see how life was lived—what MacCannell calls 'staged authenticity.' The desire to have an authentic experience, MacCannell argues, is what gives social, historical, and cultural importance to tourist travel." Cox emphasizes that "tourism has long played an important role in the development of the South's cultural identity. It has helped both outsiders and native southerners to define the region's qualities and the character traits of its people."[106] If Mahaffey's enterprises are set against tourism theory, then several questions arise:

What elements best provide tourists with what they believe is an authentic experience? A stroll through Newsom's Old Mill Store? A taste of Kentucky country ham? A conversation with Mahaffey or her employees behind the counter?

For nonsoutherners, tourists, or Princeton natives who have moved away and return home seeking "tradition" or the advertised "real" and "genuine" taste provided by a Newsom's ham, many are journeying away from their regular dietary habits into an "exotic" place. Cultural theorist Lucy Long has argued that culinary tourism inside larger tourist endeavors helps travelers shape their identities. Eating heritage foods such as Newsom's ham may help them connect to a rural past or its traditions, even if they or their ancestors never experienced the realities of rural life and work. The presentation of traditional food within the historic environment of Newsom's Old Mill Store offers a combination of experiences to help visitors confront a fast-paced, technologically driven modern society. Some may even find meaning in "repeat journeys" to a place offering what they believe to be authentic. Historian Tom Selwyn suggests that "tourist destinations tend to have their own 'spirit of place,' and local people, especially in rural settings, act as representatives of an 'imagined world' that is both premodern and preindustrial."[107] Promoting the "historic and down home atmosphere" of her store, Mahaffey realizes the vital role that nostalgia plays in her enterprises. She has said that heritage-ham purveyors must recognize that customers are seeking what she calls a "Kentucky nostalgic thing." Mahaffey's identification of country ham with Kentucky specifically brings this Upper South locale into sharp relief, illuminating its distinctiveness and therefore its capacity to serve as a site of wistful longing inside the larger American South.[108]

In the 1990s Mahaffey identified herself as "a tourism advocate," expressing a belief that tourism was "the most friendly of the alternatives for small cities needing additional flow of income." Seeing her business as a general "information center" for "inquisitive visitors" to Princeton, Mahaffey enthusiastically embraced her role with the town's tourism commission and her position on Kentucky's Western Waterlands Tourism Board. She pointed to the strong relationship between Newsom's Old Mill Store and Adsmore Museum, which worked "hand in hand" to provide tourists "a memorable experience while visiting Princeton."[109] In many ways the two downtown tourist attractions had grown up together. In November 1986 Adsmore, a Greek Revival mansion just steps from the courthouse square and a five-minute walk from Newsom's, opened as a historic house museum. Listed on the National Register of Historic Places, Adsmore and all its contents had been given to the city by the home's last resident, Katherine Garrett, for the "enjoyment of the general public."[110] The Garrett fortune had renovated and would sustain the property, under the direction of

Caldwell County's public library board. Adsmore's distinction, compared with other historic house museums in the South, was the vintage condition of *all* of its varied and valuable contents. Fragile family possessions, account ledgers, and exquisite clothing, including a turn-of-the-century wedding gown, had been packed in tobacco leaves, a natural deterrent to pests and other damaging elements in attics and cellars. In terms of tourism, "Adsmore was a *destination*," reported Ardell Jarratt, the site's former curator. A "huge draw," especially for bus tours in the late 1980s and early 1990s, Adsmore hosted up to twelve thousand visitors annually. The relationship between Adsmore and Newsom's was mutually beneficial. Tourists who visited one site often visited the other, because Mahaffey and Adsmore "promoted each other," Jarratt observed.[111]

As early as 1961 historian Thomas D. Clark pointed out that "tourism's economic impact had eclipsed agriculture in several southern states." He projected it might prove even more promising economically than land cultivation. Fellow historian Richard Starnes argues that tourism is "one of the most powerful economic forces in the modern South" and that while "destination tourism can rely on the land and climate" it "most often is based on attractions created by man."[112] Newsom's Old Mill Store, created by a woman, has remained the steadiest tourist destination in Princeton since its opening in 1987.[113] Although Mahaffey admits that the "chain stores, Wal-Mart stores and whatnot" cut into her "rose bush business" and her "bulb business," she stuck by her decision to develop and market private-label gourmet foods and other items that her father derided as "junk." She was able to test her marketing skills with her combined businesses—the general store and her country hams. After publishing magnate Steve Forbes ordered a ham for his father Malcolm Forbes, Mahaffey seized the opportunity to write an advertisement for the Princeton newspaper that read: "For the man who has everything, except . . . Colonel Newsom's Aged Ham."[114] Because women business owners often wish to "gain more independence" as well as experience a "sense of fulfillment" through their vocation, they generate more "energy, inventiveness, and will to succeed" through running their own operations. In a small town, these combine to strengthen the community as well. Mahaffey's innovations and adaptability, marks of female entrepreneurs in the industrialized world, contributed to local economic growth and stability.[115]

After Newsom's Old Mill Store found firm footing as a tourist destination in the early 1990s, Mahaffey decided to return to college with motivation from a number of forces. Her children had entered middle school and were busy with their own activities. She wanted to restore "self-confidence and esteem" after her troubled marriage led to continued "personal sadness." She thought having a college degree would help her find work should Newsom's Old Mill Store ever have to close its doors. The curriculum in human services at Hopkinsville Community College gave her the opportunity to use her fully developed caretaking skills. She thrived on fieldwork that required advising low-income families and new mothers about state programs to assist them; her studies also inspired her to set up a clothing room for them. After earning an associate's degree, Mahaffey enrolled in Murray State University's Bachelor of Integrated Studies program for "non-traditional" students. In her forties she found herself "as scared as a child" to be at a four-year university for the first time.[116] Mahaffey enjoyed the discussions, themes, and assignments in all of her college courses but one, which she dropped immediately. "On the first day, I knew that I didn't like the class. . . . That's just not me or anything I'm interested in," she said about Corporate Finance.[117]

In 1999 Mahaffey's father died, her twenty-four-year marriage ended in divorce, her last child left home after graduating from high school, and she was faced with living alone for the first time in her life. "Those four things together," she said, presented daunting emotional challenges. But she "[took] that pain and put it in a certain place," returning to music for solace and pouring herself even more into Newsom's Old Mill Store and Newsom's ham production. Her two goals were to make sure that her family legacy would endure and that she could support herself financially. She looked in a new direction in order to identify untapped markets; the Internet awaited. In 2000 Princeton journalist Anita Baker helped Mahaffey establish an online presence for both businesses. Newsom's would go into the twenty-first century as a "dot com."[118]

Mahaffey remains critical of the web as a primary means of communication, however, suggesting that the Internet's most significant impact on her enterprises has been its function as an archive. The myriad feature stories and magazine articles that have appeared in print and are available online have been more important to the business's success than Newsom's website, in Mahaffey's opinion. She has used their online presence to make personal contacts, saying, "I like to take mail-order people and Internet people and make regular customers out of them." And she steadfastly believes that "word of mouth is *still* the key" to her success. An entrepreneur may use the Internet to "*get* business, but keeping it" is a different matter, she insists. If novices rely naively on a single year's Internet sales for future projections, they are likely to become too optimistic and take inadvisable financial risks, Mahaffey warns. Another disadvantage of the web, she believes, is that "you've got to be there for it." Mahaffey is not interested in sitting in front of a computer monitor or maintaining various social media accounts; she would much rather answer the store telephone and give directions to the person on the other end who asks, "Where's the ham store?"[119] The actual human connection reinforces the historic, traditional nature of her business, Mahaffey insists.

In a postmodern technological society, cyberspace provides everyone "access" to Newsom's Old Mill Store. But what does the web offer a visitor who experiences the store virtually rather than in person? What kind of authenticity or community will the Internet tourist discover at www.newsomscountryham.com? Mahaffey has said, "You want people to feel comfortable when they come into your store," and more than anything else on the cyber front, she hopes to create the "ambiance of the store" on Newsom's website.[120] In 2013 Princeton mayor Gale Cherry attributed Mahaffey's success to the entrepreneur's ability to attract and keep national customers "through the quality of her products *and* advertising locally and on the Internet."[121] She encouraged other Princeton business owners to follow suit. Although internationally recognized with a global customer base, Mahaffey likes to emphasize the modest and manageable scale of her enterprise, proudly stating her mantra: "We're small but mighty."[122] This approach undergirds the anticorporate atmosphere designed to appeal to a wide range of customers, whether they are foodies, chefs, tourists, or locals looking for a ham sandwich or garden seeds.

In the twenty-first century Mahaffey's devotion to Princeton's Main Street culture has been matched by downtown revitalization efforts. Renaissance on Main grants from the Commonwealth of Kentucky helped fund streetscape improvements and historic property façade renovations.[123] As Mahaffey said of the new downtown lighting, "street lamps say 'interesting, unique, historic.'"[124] Activists Samuel Koltinsky and Phyllis Robertson spearheaded a "Let's Paint the Town!" initiative that served to embellish storefront architecture. The project attracted statewide attention and inspired other grassroots activists to enhance their own historic town centers.[125] Kentucky Heritage Council officials visited Princeton to herald the town's Main Street program efforts and, while there, toured Mahaffey's store in order to study the structure as well as the remains of a mid-nineteenth-century flour mill on the building's top floor.[126] In 2012 Princeton served as the site of the biennial Kentucky Preservation Conference, the first such conference held outside one of the state's larger metropolitan areas. Mayor Cherry speaks with pride about state and national awards that the community has received for its preservation efforts and notes Mahaffey's influence and impact, stating: "Nancy has been a huge asset to the town." Mahaffey's willingness to assist young entrepreneurs in launching their own businesses was particularly helpful in enhancing the town's commercial growth, reports Patsy Oliver, manager of the City of Princeton Main Street Program.[127]

Today Newsom's Old Mill Store is itself an archive, a repository of the store's history—and much of the town's. Newspaper articles, photographs, and other mementos line the walls, as do Mahaffey's many prizes. Her poems, privately printed and illustrated on cream-colored 5½ × 8½ card stock, stand in a rack and are free to anyone who visits. "Dead Soldiers" (2008) is a lamentation for lost trees due to widespread deforestation. In "Gnarled Trees are Best" (2011) Mahaffey hails deep roots over the external and fleeting beauty of youth. Both political and idyllic in tone, her verses resonate with similar themes: reverence for the land and family ties, individual resilience, and appreciation for wisdom that accompanies age. After food journalist Christine Muhlke visited Newsom's in 2010, she described it as a "through-the-looking-glass country store selling some of the country's best ham." What she found inside "was a blast from many pasts, from the penny-candy sticks to the bulk seeds for farming. But Nancy Newsom Mahaffey and her Kentucky hams are clearly the draw."[128] In her brief synopsis Muhlke brought together history, nostalgia, regional tastes, and a slight hint of an unfamiliar wonderland, all together an escape into a pastoral ideal. Mahaffey's wide influence as a keeper of local history and therefore a shaper of Princeton's historical narrative bears out historian Fitzhugh Brundage's argument that "tourism entrepreneurs, not government officials," have often been "the most significant architects of regional and historical identity."[129] Forging the links between tradition, innovation, and community, Mahaffey has created a comfortable place for tourists to discover and regular customers to return to week after week and year after year. Her central use of an iconic food product of the region—country ham—and other food products connected to a bygone rural past have bolstered the town's economic health and shaped its reputation as a heritage-food destination.[130]

In 2013 Louisville chef Laurent Geroli paired a variety of Newsom's cured hams with Kentucky bourbons in a five-course dinner at the Brown Hotel's English Grill. Diners heard Mahaffey describe the all-natural process she has used for nearly three decades. Mahaffey viewed Geroli's event as "a wonderful tribute" to her work as a keeper of traditions—"not just how we craft our hams, but service to the public as well, that have meant so much to each of us—my father and my grandfather before him."[131] She hopes her son John will carry out the family legacy. "He knows what to do with the hams," she says with measured assurance.[132]

Mahaffey's outlook and her heritage-food mission appear closely aligned with the values of a fellow Kentuckian, the writer Wendell Berry. In his 2012 Jefferson Lecture in the Humanities, delivered at the Kennedy Center in Washington, D.C., Berry articulated the links between human imagination and community strength. He believes that imagination

> thrives on contact, on tangible connection. For humans to have a responsible relationship to the world, they must imagine their places in it. To have a place, to live and belong in a place, to live from a place without destroying it, we must imagine it. By imagination we see it illuminated by its own unique character and by our love for it. By imagination we recognize with sympathy the fellow members, human and nonhuman, with whom we share our place. By that local experience we see the need to grant a sort of preemptive sympathy to all the fellow members, the neighbors, with whom we share the world. As imagination enables sympathy, sympathy enables affection. And it is in affection that we find the possibility of a neighborly, kind, and conserving economy.[133]

Nancy Newsom Mahaffey has nurtured the kind of imagination that Berry describes. Appointing herself the caretaker of a historic Main Street store that could have easily disappeared in the 1980s, Mahaffey preserved a bit of the past for her customers and cultivated an environment for those seeking an "authentic" rural southern experience. Her spirit of caretaking and public service reveals itself in the generous amount of time she spends with curious journalists, ham buyers, and local residents who visit regularly. That she expresses genuine interest in all of them illuminates the depth of her affection and the force of her imagination. But these are strengthened by her investment in one of the Upper South's most significant contributions to southern foodways: naturally air-cured, smoked pork. Sustaining this regional culinary tradition as one of its last practitioners, Mahaffey contributes to the notion of southern distinctiveness. Educating new generations about heritage foods in general, and country ham in particular, she has shined a light on her small corner of Kentucky, bringing into sharper focus the links tying contemporary Americans to the South's past, some of it real and some imagined.

NOTES

1. Nancy Newsom Mahaffey (hereafter cited as NNM), conversation with author, Princeton, Kentucky, March 18, 2011; Jeff Bradford, "Pennyrile Country Hams Are among the Best," *Kentucky New Era* (Hopkinsville), April 1, 1982. Newsom's Aged Kentucky Country Hams are hereafter referred to as Newsom's hams.

2. Logan Ward, "The New Frontier of Country Ham," *Garden and Gun*, December 2010/January 2011, http://gardenandgun.com/article/new-frontier-country-ham (accessed December 30, 2013); Jan Greenberg, "Heritage Breeds," *Gastronomica* 4 (Fall 2004): 2–5; "The Heirloom Market," *Coun-*

try Home, November 2005, 162; "Ham Lady News," www.newsomscountryham.com/hamladynews.html (accessed December 30, 2013).

3. NNM quoted in Anita Baker, "Newsom's Marks Milestones in Commerce," *Times Leader* (Princeton, Ky.; hereafter cited as *TL*), November 28, 2007. The "Wal-Mart effect," a phrase coined by economists and now common in American parlance, actually refers to many effects, only one of which is the demise of small, independent, local businesses in small-town America. Charles Fishman, *The Wal-Mart Effect: How the World's Most Powerful Company Really Works—and How It's Transforming the American Economy* (New York: Penguin, 2006).

4. Anthony J. Stanonis, ed., *Dixie Emporium: Tourism, Foodways, and Consumer Culture in the American South* (Athens: University of Georgia Press, 2008), 3; NNM, interview by Amy Evans, Princeton, Kentucky, August 24, 2005, transcript, Southern Foodways Alliance, Center for the Study of Southern Culture, University of Mississippi (hereafter cited as NNM, SFA interview), 11.

5. Steve Coomes, "Made You Look," *Insider Louisville*, January 7, 2013, http://insiderlouisville.com/news/2013/01/07/brown-hotel-chefs-travel-to-newsoms-ahead-of-friday-artisan-ham-dinner/ (accessed December 30, 2013); Ouita Michel, conversation with author, Lexington, Kentucky, September 22, 2012; NNM quoted in Baker, "Newsom's Marks Milestones"; Carlo Petrini, *Slow Food Nation: Why Our Food Should Be Good, Clean, and Fair*, trans. Clara Furlan and Jonathan Hunt (New York: Rizzoli, 2007). Historians have given much wider attention to the preparation and consumption of pork barbeque than to country ham, but questions about the limits of culinary authenticity in the face of industrial hog farming are similar. See, in particular, Michael Pollan, *Cooked: A Natural History of Transformation* (New York: Penguin, 2013), 27–30, 48–52, 66–80; Margot Roosevelt, "Eat Them or Lose Them," *Time*, June 13, 2005, 45–47.

6. Samuel W. Steger, *Caldwell County, Kentucky History* (Paducah, Ky.: Turner, 1987), 244, 259. On immigration and agriculture in early Kentucky, see Thomas D. Clark, *A History of Kentucky* (New York: Prentice-Hall, 1937), 107–8, 223–31.

7. Clark discusses the fertile soils of the "western coalfield" region as comparable to those in the Bluegrass region in *A History of Kentucky*, 7. While Caldwell is located in the Pennyroyal (or Pennyrile), with predominantly limestone shale, the contiguous counties on Caldwell's northern, eastern, and southern boundaries are in the western coalfield. The Newsom family settled in the southeastern end of Caldwell County. See Steger, *Caldwell County, Kentucky History*, 177, 244, 257.

8. Samuel Steger, "Caldwell County," in *Kentucky Encyclopedia*, ed. John Kleber (Lexington: University Press of Kentucky, 1992), 150; Samuel Steger, "Historical Notebook," *TL*, December 24, 1996, on stagecoach routes and Princeton's Globe Tavern. For Princeton's educational history, see Steger, *Caldwell County, Kentucky History*, 51–52. Mary Grace Pettit discusses the classical education offered to mid-nineteenth-century students in Samuel Koltinsky, "My Kentucky Home: Caldwell County," Producer's Cut (Princeton, Ky.: Blue Springs Productions, 2007), DVD.

9. On the history of the town's mills, see Steger, "Historical Notebook," and Clauscine R. Baker, *First History of Caldwell County, Kentucky* (Madisonville, Ky.: Commercial Publishers, 1936), 41. For railroad growth, see *Kentucky: A Guide to the Bluegrass State*, comp. and written by the Federal Writers' Project of the Work Projects Administration for the State of Kentucky (New York: Harcourt, Brace, 1939), 58.

10. Quotation in Clifford J. Downey, *Images of Rail: Kentucky and the Illinois Central Railroad* (Charleston, S.C.: Arcadia, 2010), 77; Bill Cunningham, *On Bended Knees: The Night Rider Story* (Nashville: McClanahan, 1983), 73–76.

11. Downey, *Images of Rail*, 78–79. ICRR historian George Martin discusses the economic impact of railways on Princeton in Koltinsky, "My Kentucky Home." Big Spring described in Baker,

First History of Caldwell County, 46. See also Steger, "Historical Notebook." The spring was a site where Native Americans sought refuge in the 1830s on the forced removal trek known as the Trail of Tears.

12. Baker, "Newsom's Marks Milestones." See also Steger, *Caldwell County, Kentucky History*, 177, 244.

13. NNM, interview by author, Princeton, Kentucky, January 21, 2013; NNM, interview by author, Princeton, Kentucky, May 9, 2013. On trains, see Baker, *First History of Caldwell County*, 49. On Caldwell County during World War II, see Koltinsky, "My Kentucky Home." After William Newsom was commissioned a "Kentucky Colonel" by the governor of the Commonwealth of Kentucky, he thereafter was known as "Colonel Newsom."

14. NNM, "The Journey Forward," undated manuscript, c. 1998, photocopy in author's possession. Mahaffey wrote "The Journey Forward" for a university course assignment in self-reflection and autobiography. See also NNM, SFA interview, 10.

15. NNM, email correspondence with author, May 28, 2013.

16. NNM, interview by author, May 9, 2013; NNM, "The Journey Forward," 1.

17. NNM, "The Journey Forward," 1.

18. NNM, interview by author, May 9, 2013, in which she said, "Daddy worked him hard and he did it even if he didn't want to."

19. Ibid. The two had met at a party in Princeton three months earlier.

20. NNM, "The Journey Forward," 1–2.

21. NNM, interview by author, May 9, 2013. Quotation in "The Journey Forward," 3.

22. NNM, SFA interview, 22. On Mary Kay Ash's principles for her company, see http://www.marykay.com/en-US/About-Mary-Kay/CompanyFounder/Pages/About-Mary-Kay-Ash.aspx (accessed December 30, 2013).

23. NNM, "The Journey Forward," 2.

24. Ibid., 4.

25. NNM, interview by author, May 9, 2013.

26. NNM, conversation with author, March 18, 2011; NNM, interview by author, May 9, 2013.

27. Bradford, "Pennyrile Country Hams," 29.

28. Virginia G. Drachman, *Enterprising Women: 250 Years of American Business* (Chapel Hill: University of North Carolina Press, 2002), 157. On the backlash against women's progress, see Ruth Rosen, *The World Split Open: How the Modern Women's Movement Changed America*, rev. ed. (New York: Penguin, 2006), 295–340; Sara M. Evans, *Born for Liberty: A History of Women in America* (New York: Free Press, 1997), 309–18.

29. NNM, email correspondence with author, May 28, 2013; NNM, interview by author, May 9, 2013.

30. NNM, email correspondence with author, May 28, 2013; NNM, interview by author, May 9, 2013. The atmosphere of the store is captured well in Thomas Hart Shelby's photographs in Sally Van Winkle Campbell, *Saving Kentucky: Greening the Bluegrass* (Louisville: Limestone Lane, 2010), 176–87.

31. Drachman, *Enterprising Women*, 159; Ouita Michel, conversation with author, Lexington, Kentucky, July 10, 2013. For a sense of the gendered work of curing hams, see Bradford, "Pennyrile Country Hams," 29. Recent histories reveal the world of smoked pork to be dominated by men; see, in particular, Pollan, "Fire," in *Cooked*, 25–121, and Wes Berry, *The Kentucky Barbeque Book* (Lexington: University Press of Kentucky, 2013).

32. John Egerton and Frances Abbott, "Country Ham," in *The New Encyclopedia of Southern*

Culture, ed. Charles Reagan Wilson, vol. 7, *Foodways*, ed. John T. Edge (Chapel Hill: University of North Carolina Press, 2006), 157 (hereafter cited as *Foodways*).

33. Carolyn Jung, "High on the Ham," April 21, 2011, http://www.foodgal.com/2011/04/high-on-the-ham/ (accessed December 30, 2013).

34. Bradford, "Pennyrile Country Hams," 29.

35. NNM, interview by author and author's visit to the ham house, May 9, 2013; on Newsom's artisanal prosciutto, see http://www.newsomscountryham.com/prhamnefiarc.html (accessed December 30, 2013).

36. James Villas, *American Taste: A Celebration of Gastronomy Coast-to-Coast* (1982; reprint, New York: Lyons & Burford, 1997), 56.

37. Historian U. B. Phillips opened his classic study of the region, *Life and Labor in the Old South* (Boston: Little, Brown, 1929), with a discussion of the weather. Reiterated and highlighted by sociologist John Shelton Reed, Phillips's focus on the weather ended in his claim that it was "the chief agency in making the South distinctive." Phillips quoted in John Shelton Reed, *My Tears Spoiled My Aim and Other Reflections on Southern Culture* (Columbia: University of Missouri Press, 1993), 7.

38. John and Dale Reed quoted in Charles Reagan Wilson, "Pork," in *Foodways*, 90.

39. Thomas D. Clark, *Agrarian Kentucky* (Lexington: University Press of Kentucky, 1977), 46–47; John Van Willigen and Anne Van Willigen, *Food and Everyday Life on Kentucky Family Farms, 1920–1950* (Lexington: University Press of Kentucky, 2006), 222.

40. NNM, interview by author, May 9, 2013.

41. Wilson, "Pork," 90; Kentucky Statutes, Chapter 20 (1950), http://www.lrc.ky.gov/krs/259-00/210.pdf (accessed June 11, 2013). "Stray cattle" included "any animal of the bovine, ovine, porcine, or caprine species."

42. Deborah Fitzgerald situates the origins of factory farming in the 1920s, when notions of modernization and efficiency, as well as the prevalence of "industrial production systems," took hold in the U.S. agricultural sector. See Fitzgerald, *Every Farm a Factory: The Industrial Ideal in American Agriculture* (New Haven, Conn.: Yale University Press, 2003), 3–9. Amy Bentley discusses the U.S. government's wartime and immediate postwar support of industrial agriculture and production (at the expense of American consumers) in *Eating for Victory: Food Rationing and the Politics of Domesticity* (Urbana: University of Illinois Press, 1998), 144–55. See also Angela Knipple and Paul Knipple, "Barbeque as Slow Food," in *The Slaw and the Slow Cooked: Culture and Barbeque in the Mid-South*, ed. James R. Veteto and Edward M. Maclin (Nashville, Tenn.: Vanderbilt University Press, 2011), 151–66; Pollan, *Cooked*, 28. Quotation in Food and Water Watch, *Factory Farm Nation: How America Turned Its Livestock Farms into Factories* (Washington, D.C.: Food and Water Watch, 2010), 3.

43. Ward, "New Frontier of Country Ham."

44. NNM, interview by author, May 9, 2013.

45. Ibid.; see also Campbell, *Saving Kentucky*, 184.

46. For the fullest description of the curing process, see NNM, SFA interview, 14–17.

47. Jung, "High on the Ham."

48. On "procedure," NNM, conversation with author, Princeton, Kentucky, March 9, 2013; on "obsession," see Coomes, "Made You Look."

49. In 2009 the business shipped "close to three thousand hams" (Campbell, *Saving Kentucky*, 182). In 2013 Mahaffey cured 2,800 hams (NNM, interview by author, May 9, 2013).

50. "The Colonel Says . . . Read the Facts About Colonel Bill's Kentucky Country Hams," undated flyer, c. 1970; various letters and brochures, 1970–2013, in author's possession.

51. Bradford, "Pennyrile Country Hams," 29.

52. NNM, SFA interview, 37. My first reaction on entering the ham house on a warm May day was not the sight but the aroma, an olfactory sensation that stimulated a mélange of memories including home, Christmas Eve, and extended family gatherings, among them mourning rituals.

53. Peter Kaminsky, *Pig Perfect: Encounters with Some Remarkable Swine and Great Ways to Cook Them* (New York: Hyperion, 2005), 21.

54. NNM, conversation with author, March 9, 2013; Coomes, "Made You Look."

55. NNM quoted in Dana McMahan, "120 Eats: A Quest to Taste Kentucky's Best," *Kentucky Monthly*, October 2012, 19; Villas, *American Taste*, 290. On ideal aging time, see Egerton and Abbott, "Country Ham," 156, and "The Heirloom Market," *Country Home*, November 2005, 162. On Newsom's hams, see Campbell, *Saving Kentucky*, 187. Quotation (Kentucky State Fair) in NNM, SFA interview, 16.

56. NNM, SFA interview, 8.

57. Petrini, *Slow Food Nation*, 2.

58. Baker, "Newsom's Marks Milestones"; Campbell, *Saving Kentucky*, 187; Coomes, "Made You Look."

59. Kaminsky, *Pig Perfect*, 22.

60. Cary quoted in Josh Moss, "Pride of Princeton," *Louisville Magazine*, April 2009. Newsom's is number one on Cary's "short list" of "must-visit" food destinations in Kentucky. *Garden and Gun*, October/November 2011, 123.

61. NNM quoted in Campbell, *Saving Kentucky*, 178.

62. McMahan, "120 Eats."

63. Dana Bowen, "Thanksgiving: Back to Our Roots," *Country Home*, November 2005, 138.

64. Baker, "Newsom's Marks Milestones."

65. Sarah Weiner quoted in "Food Is My Art: Newsom's Ham Named Good Food Awards Charcuterie Winner," *TL*, February 2, 2011.

66. Sam Sifton, "A Southern Chef Doesn't Stray Far," *New York Times*, February 9, 2011.

67. Beard's "discovery" of Newsom's hams appears in most stories about Mahaffey, the most descriptive in Kaminsky, *Pig Perfect*, 19.

68. Baker, "Newsom's Marks Milestones."

69. Newsom quoted in Bradford, "Pennyrile Country Hams," 29.

70. "Col. Bill Newsom's Hams" business card, 2013.

71. NNM, interview by author, May 9, 2013.

72. Peggy Brown McEuen, conversation with author, Princeton, Kentucky, September 30, 2012.

73. Various letters and brochures, 1970–2013, in author's possession.

74. NNM, "More Hams This Year," company brochure, November 2013.

75. Charly Anna Morgan, conversation with author, Princeton, Kentucky, March 17, 2013; Ann Kimmel, conversation with author, Princeton, Kentucky, March 19, 2013; Sean Mestan, conversation with author, Princeton, Kentucky, July 6, 2013; Ardell Jarratt, interview by author, Princeton, Kentucky, May 9, 2013.

76. NNM, interview by author, May 9, 2013; Heritage Foods USA, http://www.heritagefoodsusa.com/heritage/index.html (accessed December 30, 2013).

77. NNM, interview by author, May 9, 2013.

78. Campbell, *Saving Kentucky*, 187.

79. NNM, conversation with author, March 18, 2011; Danny Beavers, conversation with author, January 21, 2013; Sean Mestan, conversation with author, July 6, 2013.

80. NNM, SFA interview, 23.

81. I am grateful to enthusiastic audience members at the 2013 International Federation for Research in Women's History/Women's History Network Conference in Sheffield, United Kingdom, who prompted me to consider the emotional force of certain traditional foods as well as their links to socioeconomic class status. On regional distinctiveness, see Joe Gray Taylor and John T. Edge, "Southern Foodways," in *Foodways*, 1–14.

82. Edward Stanton describes "the deep-red, finely-marbled, air-cured hams, made from Iberian pigs fed on acorns, a diet that gives their flesh a delicate, nutty taste that is unmatched by any other meat in the world," in Stanton, *Culture and Customs of Spain* (Westport, Conn.: Greenwood, 2002), 82.

83. NNM, conversation with author, March 9, 2013. The Fifth World Congress of Dry-Cured Hams took place May 6–8, 2009.

84. Kaminsky, *Pig Perfect*, 22. John Egerton and Frances Abbott maintain that "the prime products of western Kentucky and other places in the region are unsurpassed by the best that France, Italy, and other nations have to offer" (Egerton and Abbott, "Country Ham," 155).

85. All prices listed in Newsom's Old Mill Store brochure, December 2009. Mahaffey noted the Iberico ham price in her year-end message to customers. In 1990 Newsom's ham prices started at $2.69 per pound.

86. NNM, interview by author, May 9, 2013. Aracena's population in 2009, when Mahaffey visited, was 7,612; Princeton's population according to the 2010 census was 6,329. Aracena's latitude is 37.8833, whereas Princeton's latitude is 37.1092. The altitudes vary, however, by about 1,700 feet.

87. Helen D. Irvin, *Women in Kentucky* (Lexington: University Press of Kentucky, 1979); Eugenia K. Potter, *Kentucky Women: Two Centuries of Indomitable Spirit and Vision* (Louisville: Big Tree Press, 1997).

88. Wendell Berry, "It All Turns on Affection," Jefferson Lecture in the Humanities, Kennedy Center, Washington, D.C., April 23, 2012. Published in Berry, *It All Turns on Affection: The Jefferson Lecture and Other Essays* (Berkeley, Calif.: Counterpoint, 2012).

89. The Walmart outlet in Princeton, store #204, opened in 1978. It was the third store to appear in Kentucky, behind earlier sites in Fulton (#106) and Benton (#143), small towns located west of Princeton.

90. Baker, "Newsom's Marks Milestones." Princeton resident Marty Presler names several downtown businesses in Koltinsky, "My Kentucky Home."

91. Cherry quoted in Koltinsky, "My Kentucky Home." Cherry and his wife, Gale, also a Princeton native, returned to Princeton in 1993 and became interested in restoring the town's historic buildings, including the 1939 Capitol Theatre.

92. Ann Kimmel, conversation with author, Princeton, Kentucky, March 19, 2013.

93. NNM, "The Journey Forward," 4. Mahaffey describes how the mail-order files survived on Newsom's website, http://www.newsomscountryham.com/allabhamandt.html (accessed December 30, 2013).

94. Mahaffey told Sally Van Winkle Campbell, "I don't believe in coincidence. It was a sign" (Campbell, *Saving Kentucky*, 179).

95. NNM, SFA interview, 19.

96. Steger, "Historical Notebook"; NNM, SFA interview, 5.

97. NNM, "The Journey Forward," 4.

98. Ibid., 5; NNM, SFA interview, 25, in which she also notes, "I deal with one flower company that we've dealt with since 1917, and I deal with one other flower company that we've been dealing with 70 years . . . people that you know have quality things that we've stayed with for a long time."

99. NNM, "The Journey Forward," 4.

100. Ibid., 5; NNM, interview by author, May 9, 2013.

101. Drachman, *Enterprising Women*, 156–57.

102. NNM, SFA interview, 25.

103. NNM, "The Journey Home," 5.

104. Jarratt, interview by author, May 9, 2013. In 1988 the Princeton Downtown Commercial District gained official listing on the National Register of Historic Places.

105. MacCannell's work is the starting point for all cultural studies of tourism. See, for example, "Staged Authenticity: Arrangements of Social Space in Tourist Settings," *American Journal of Sociology* 79 (1973): 589–603, and "The Ego Factor in Tourism," *Journal of Consumer Research* 20 (June 2002): 146–51.

106. Karen L. Cox, ed., *Destination Dixie: Tourism and Southern History* (Gainesville: University Press of Florida, 2012), 4, 2. In her introduction to this collection of essays, Cox nicely outlines tourism theory in relation to heritage tourism in the South. Other recent southern histories, cultural studies, and anthologies that grapple with tourism theory include John D. Cox, *Traveling South: Travel Narratives and the Construction of American Identity* (Athens: University of Georgia Press, 2005); Kevin Fox Gotham, *Authentic New Orleans: Tourism, Culture, and Race in the Big Easy* (New York: New York University Press, 2007); Tara McPherson, *Reconstructing Dixie: Race, Gender and Nostalgia* (Durham, N.C.: Duke University Press, 2003); Stanonis, *Dixie Emporium*; Richard D. Starnes, ed., *Southern Journeys: Tourism, History, and Culture in the Modern South* (Tuscaloosa: University of Alabama Press, 2003). Other helpful essay collections include Jan Nordby Gretlund, *The Southern State of Mind* (Columbia: University of South Carolina Press, 1999); John Shelton Reed, *Minding the South* (Columbia: University of Missouri Press, 2003).

107. Lucy M. Long, ed., *Culinary Tourism* (Lexington: University Press of Kentucky, 2004); on "repeat journeys," see Ellen Strain, *Public Places, Private Journeys: Ethnography, Entertainment, and the Tourist Gaze* (New Brunswick, N.J.: Rutgers University Press, 2003), 3–4, 9–10; Selwyn quoted in Cox, *Destination Dixie*, 3.

108. Newsom's Old Mill Store brochure, December 2013; NNM, SFA interview, 27, in which she acknowledged that Americans may eventually turn away from country ham due to concerns about blood pressure, salt, and fat. Tara McPherson examines the use of nostalgia in southern tourism, arguing that as contemporary globalization "blurs the boundaries of the nation," a region may become "a site of authenticity." Although McPherson applies her theory specifically to the reemergence of a new "Old South" in the late twentieth century, it may be seen where rural pasts are idolized as well. McPherson, *Reconstructing Dixie*, 3, 2, 18.

109. NNM, "The Journey Forward," 8. Mahaffey held memberships in several local historical societies and organizations, working with Caldwell County historian Sam Steger to encourage other local businesses to focus on their historic elements in order to foster tourism. She and Steger surveyed Main Street business owners to gauge prospective participation, and Mahaffey was disappointed after "at least half" of those surveyed claimed they did not have "enough that was interesting" to tourists so did not want to pursue it. In spite of her colleagues' disinterest, Mahaffey continued with her own historic project in Newsom's Old Mill Store, cultivating tourism "long before" other entrepreneurs in town sought to attract visitors. NNM, interview by author, January 21, 2013.

110. Garrett's last will and testament quoted in Steger, *Caldwell County, Kentucky History*, 182.

111. Jarratt, interview by author, May 9, 2013.

112. Clark's argument described in Starnes, *Southern Journeys*, 7; other quotations on 1, 3.

113. Jarratt, interview by author, May 9, 2013; Gale Cherry, interview by author, Princeton, Kentucky, May 8, 2013.

114. NNM, "The Journey Forward," 5, 7.

115. Quotations in Jeanne Halladay Coughlin with Andrew R. Thomas, *The Rise of Women Entrepreneurs: People, Processes, and Global Trends* (Westport, Conn.: Quorum, 2002), 5, 13. On the role of local food in boosting rural economies, see Rebecca Sims, "Food, Place and Authenticity: Local Food and the Sustainable Tourism Experience," *Journal of Sustainable Tourism* 17 (2009): 321–36. See also Gale Cherry, "From the Mayor's Desk," *TL*, May 8, 2013.

116. NNM, "The Journey Forward," 6.

117. NNM, interview by author, January 21, 2013. Mahaffey needs only a couple of courses to complete a bachelor's degree, having earned more than 150 college credits since 1973.

118. NNM, interview by author, May 9, 2013; Baker, "Newsom's Marks Milestones."

119. NNM, interview by author, May 9, 2013.

120. Ibid.

121. Gale Cherry, "From the Mayor's Desk." Emphasis added.

122. NNM, interview by author, May 9, 2013.

123. "Princeton Awarded Renaissance on Main Grant," *TL*, November 4, 2007. Princeton would share $959,855 with seven other cities. Also see "Renaissance on Main Numbers Show Success," *TL*, March 20, 2006.

124. NNM, interview by author, January 21, 2013.

125. "Downtown Business Successes Shared with Cadiz Main Street," *TL*, December 5, 2009. Marvo Entertainment Group LLC has documented several "Let's Paint the Town!" efforts. Kentucky Educational Television aired these programs in February 2012. "Let's Paint the Town!" projects described in *TL*, February 22, 2012.

126. "New Vision: Main Street Group Eyes Local Future," *TL*, July 6, 2011.

127. Kentucky Heritage Council/State Historic Preservation Office, Press release, January 20, 2012, www.preservationkentucky.org/tiny_mce/images/2012_Conference_News_release_1.pdf (accessed December 30, 2013); Cherry, interview by author, May 8, 2013; Patsy Oliver, interview by author, Princeton, Kentucky, May 8, 2013.

128. Christine Muhlke, "My Old Kentucky Ham," *New York Times*, May 21, 2010. Muhlke became executive editor of *Bon Appétit* in January 2011.

129. W. Fitzhugh Brundage, "Identity Market," in Stanonis, *Dixie Emporium*, 89.

130. Sims, "Food, Place, and Authenticity," 322–23. Heritage Foods USA website, http://www.heritagefoodsusa.com/chefs/index.html#9 (accessed December 30, 2013).

131. Brown Hotel News Release, "The English Grill Partners with Col. Bill Newsom's Aged Kentucky Country Ham for Dining Event," December 13, 2012; "Ham Is Hot at the Brown," *TL*, January 30, 2013.

132. NNM, interview by author, May 9, 2013.

133. Berry, Jefferson Lecture.

Selected Bibliography

Apple, Lindsey. *The Family Legacy of Henry Clay: In the Shadow of a Kentucky Patriarch.* Lexington: University Press of Kentucky, 2011.

Aron, Stephen. *How the West Was Lost: The Transformation of Kentucky from Daniel Boone to Henry Clay.* Baltimore: Johns Hopkins University Press, 1996.

Baird, Nancy Disher. "Enid Yandell: Kentucky Sculptor." *Filson Club History Quarterly* 62 (1988): 5–31.

———, ed. *Josie Underwood's Civil War Diary.* Lexington: University Press of Kentucky, 2009.

Baker, Jean H. *Mary Todd Lincoln: A Biography.* New York: Norton, 1987.

Ballard, Sandra L., and Haeja K. Chung, eds. *The Collected Stories of Harriette Simpson Arnow.* East Lansing: Michigan State University Press, 2005.

Berry, Stephen. *House of Abraham: Lincoln and the Todds, a Family Divided by War.* Boston: Houghton Mifflin, 2007.

Billips, Martha. "Harriette Simpson Arnow's First Novel: A New Look at *Mountain Path.*" *Appalachian Heritage* 40 (Spring 2012): 77–86.

Breckinridge, Mary. *Wide Neighborhoods: A Story of the Frontier Nursing Service.* 2nd ed. Lexington: University Press of Kentucky, 1981.

Breckinridge, Sophonisba. *Madeline McDowell Breckinridge: A Leader in the New South.* Chicago: University of Chicago Press, 1921.

Chung, Haeja K., ed. *Harriette Simpson Arnow: Critical Essays on Her Work.* East Lansing: Michigan State University Press, 1995.

Clark, Thomas D. *A History of Kentucky.* New York: Prentice-Hall, 1937.

Clinton, Catherine. *Mrs. Lincoln: A Life.* New York: HarperCollins, 2009.

Cornett, Judy Gail. "Angel for the Blind: The Public Triumphs and Private Tragedy of Linda Neville." PhD dissertation, University of Kentucky, 1993.

Cox, Karen L. *Dixie's Daughters: The United Daughters of the Confederacy and the Preservation of Confederate Culture.* Gainesville: University Press of Florida, 2003.

Ellis, William E. *A History of Education in Kentucky.* Lexington: University Press of Kentucky, 2011.

Ellison, Betty Boles. *A Man Seen but Once: Cassius Marcellus Clay.* Bloomington, Ind.: Author House, 2005.

Faragher, John Mack. *Daniel Boone: The Life and Legend of an American Pioneer.* New York: Henry Holt, 1992.

Forderhase, Nancy K. "'The Clear Call of Thoroughbred Women': The Kentucky Federation of Women's Clubs and the Crusade for Educational Reform, 1903–1909." *Register of the Kentucky Historical Society* 83 (1985): 19–35.

———. "Eve Returns to the Garden: Women Reformers in Appalachian Kentucky in the Early Twentieth Century." *Register of the Kentucky Historical Society* 85 (1987): 237–61.

Fosl, Catherine. *Subversive Southerner: Anne Braden and the Struggle for Racial Justice in the Cold War South*. New York: Palgrave Macmillan, 2002.

Fraas, Elizabeth Duffy. "'All Issues Are Women's Issues': An Interview with Governor Martha Layne Collins on Women in Politics." *Register of the Kentucky Historical Society* 99 (2001): 213–48.

———, ed. *The Public Papers of Martha Layne Collins, 1983–1987*. Lexington: University Press of Kentucky, 2006.

Friend, Craig Thompson. *Along the Maysville Road: The Early American Republic in the Trans-Appalachian West*. Knoxville: University of Tennessee Press, 2005.

———. *Kentucke's Frontiers*. Bloomington: Indiana University Press, 2010.

Fuller, Paul E. *Laura Clay and the Woman's Rights Movement*. Lexington: University Press of Kentucky, 1975.

Goan, Melanie Beals. "Establishing Their Place in the Dynasty: Sophonisba and Mary Breckinridge's Paths to Public Service." *Register of the Kentucky Historical Society* 101 (2003): 45–73.

———. *Mary Breckinridge: The Frontier Nursing Service and Rural Health in Appalachia*. Chapel Hill: University of North Carolina Press, 2008.

Harrison, Lowell H. *The Civil War in Kentucky*. Lexington: University Press of Kentucky, 1975.

———, ed. *Kentucky's Governors*. Revised edition. Lexington: University Press of Kentucky, 2004.

Harrison, Lowell H., and James C. Klotter. *A New History of Kentucky*. Lexington: University Press of Kentucky, 1997.

Hay, Melba Porter. *Madeline McDowell Breckinridge and the Battle for a New South*. Lexington: University Press of Kentucky, 2009.

Helm, Katherine. *The True Story of Mary, Wife of Lincoln*. New York: Harper & Brothers, 1928.

Hollingsworth, Randolph. "'Mrs. Boone, I Presume?' In Search of the Idea of Womanhood in Kentucky's Early Years." In *Bluegrass Renaissance: The History and Culture of Central Kentucky, 1792–1852*, edited by James C. Klotter and Daniel Rowland, 93–130. Lexington: University Press of Kentucky, 2012.

Irvin, Helen Deiss. *Women in Kentucky*. Lexington: University Press of Kentucky, 1979.

Jabour, Anya. "Relationship and Leadership: Sophonisba Breckinridge and Women in Social Work." *Affilia* 27 (2012): 22–37.

Kleber, John E., ed. *Kentucky Encyclopedia*. Lexington: University Press of Kentucky, 1992.

Klotter, James C. "The Black South and White Appalachia." *Journal of American History* 66 (1980): 832–49.

———. *The Breckinridges of Kentucky*. Lexington: University Press of Kentucky, 1986.

Klotter, James C., and Daniel Rowland, eds. *Bluegrass Renaissance: The History and Culture of Central Kentucky, 1792–1852*. Lexington: University Press of Kentucky, 2012.

K'Meyer, Tracy E. *Civil Rights in the Gateway to the South: Louisville, Kentucky, 1945–1980*. Lexington: University Press of Kentucky, 2009.

Marshall, Anne E. *Creating a Confederate Kentucky: The Lost Cause and Civil War Memory in a Border State*. Chapel Hill: University of North Carolina Press, 2013.

Lucas, Marion B. *A History of Blacks in Kentucky*. Vol. 1: *From Slavery to Segregation, 1760–1891*. Frankfort: Kentucky Historical Society, 1992.

Perkins, Elizabeth A. *Border Life: Experience and Memory in the Revolutionary Ohio Valley*. Chapel Hill: University of North Carolina Press, 1998.

Potter, Eugenia K. *Kentucky Women: Two Centuries of Indomitable Spirit and Vision*. N.p.: Big Tree Press, 1997.

Powers, Georgia Davis. *I Shared the Dream: The Pride, Passion, and Politics of the First Woman Senator from Kentucky*. Far Hills, N.J.: New Horizon Press, 1995.

Ramage, James A. *Rebel Raider: The Life of General John Hunt Morgan*. Lexington: University Press of Kentucky, 1986.

Ramage, James A., and Andrea S. Watkins. *Kentucky Rising: Democracy, Slavery, and Culture from the Early Republic to the Civil War*. Lexington: University Press of Kentucky, 2011.

Richardson, H. Edward. *Cassius Marcellus Clay: Firebrand of Freedom*. Lexington: University Press of Kentucky, 1976.

Smiley, David L. *Lion of White Hall: The Life of Cassius Marcellus Clay*. Madison: University of Wisconsin Press, 1962.

Smith, D. Anthony, and Arthur H. Keeney. "Linda Neville (1873–1961): Kentucky Pioneer against Blindness." *Filson Club History Quarterly* 64 (1990): 360–76.

Smith, John David, and William Cooper Jr., eds. *A Union Woman in Civil War Kentucky: The Diary of Frances Peter*. Lexington: University Press of Kentucky, 2000.

Sorrell, Evelyn Ashley. "'Obtuse Women': Venereal Disease Control Policies and Maintaining a 'Fit' Nation, 1920–1945." Master's thesis, University of Kentucky, 2011.

Stanonis, Anthony J., ed. *Dixie Emporium: Tourism, Foodways, and Consumer Culture in the American South*. Athens: University of Georgia Press, 2008.

Steger, Samuel W. *Caldwell County, Kentucky History*. Paducah, Ky.: Turner, 1987.

Stoddart, Jess, ed. *The Quare Women's Journals: May Stone and Katherine Pettit's Summers in the Kentucky Mountains and the Founding of the Hindman Settlement School*. Ashland, Ky.: Jesse Stuart Foundation, 1997.

Turner, Justin, and Linda Turner. *Mary Todd Lincoln: Her Life and Letters*. New York: Knopf, 1972.

Van Willigen, John, and Anne van Willigen. *Food and Everyday Life on Kentucky Family Farms, 1920–1950*. Lexington: University Press of Kentucky, 2006.

Whisnant, David E. *All That Is Native and Fine: The Politics of Culture in an American Region*. Chapel Hill: University of North Carolina Press, 1983.

Wolfe, Margaret Ripley. *Daughters of Canaan: A Saga of Southern Women*. Lexington: University Press of Kentucky, 1995.

———. "Fallen Leaves and Missing Pages: Women in Kentucky History." *Register of the Kentucky Historical Society* 90 (1992): 64–89.

Wright, George C. *A History of Blacks in Kentucky*. Vol. 2: *In Pursuit of Equality, 1890–1980*. Frankfort: Kentucky Historical Society, 1992.

———. *Life behind a Veil: Blacks in Louisville, Kentucky, 1865–1930*. Baton Rouge: Louisiana State University Press, 1985.

———. *Racial Violence in Kentucky, 1865–1940: Lynchings, Mob Rule, and "Legal Lynchings."* Baton Rouge: Louisiana State University Press, 1990.

Contributors

LINDSEY APPLE is professor emeritus of history at Georgetown College in Georgetown, Kentucky. He is the author of *Cautious Rebel: A Biography of Susan Clay Sawitzky* (1997) and *The Family Legacy of Henry Clay: In the Shadow of a Kentucky Patriarch* (2011). He has written numerous articles on local and regional history.

THOMAS H. APPLETON JR. formerly served as editor-in-chief of publications for the Kentucky Historical Society. Since 2000 he has been professor of history at Eastern Kentucky University. He has coedited five books, including *Negotiating Boundaries of Southern Womanhood: Dealing with the Powers That Be* (2000) and *Searching for Their Places: Women in the South across Four Centuries* (2003).

MARTHA BILLIPS is professor of English and associate dean of the college at Transylvania University in Lexington, Kentucky. She is assistant editor of the *Journal of Appalachian Studies*. She has published articles in several journals including *Feminist Formations* and *Appalachian Heritage*. Her research focuses on women's literature, Appalachian literature, and literature of the American South.

JAMES DUANE BOLIN is a professor of history at Murray State University in Murray, Kentucky. He is the author of *Bossism and Reform in a Southern City: Lexington, Kentucky, 1880–1940* (2000). He is writing a biography of legendary University of Kentucky basketball coach Adolph Rupp.

SARAH CASE is managing editor of *The Public Historian* and lecturer in the Department of History at the University of California, Santa Barbara. She is the author of *Educating "Leaders of Their Own Race": Secondary Education for Women in the New South*, under contract with the University of Illinois Press.

JUILEE DECKER is associate professor of museum studies and visual culture at Rochester Institute of Technology. Since 2008 she has served as editor of *Collections: A Journal for Museum and Archives Professionals*. Her research interests include public sculpture as well as new museum theory and reception theory. She is writing a full-length biography of Enid Yandell.

CAROLYN R. DUPONT is assistant professor of history at Eastern Kentucky University. She is the author of *Mississippi Praying: White Evangelicals and the Quest for Black Equality, 1945–1975* (2013).

ANGELA ESCO ELDER is a PhD candidate at the University of Georgia, where she is completing a dissertation on Confederate widowhood. She is a contributing editor at *The Civil War Monitor.*

CATHERINE FOSL is associate professor of women's and gender studies at the University of Louisville, where she also directs the Anne Braden Institute for Social Justice Research. She is the author of the award-winning *Subversive Southerner: Anne Braden and the Struggle for Racial Justice in the Cold War South* (2006) and coauthor, with Tracy E. K'Meyer, of *Freedom on the Border: An Oral History of the Civil Rights Movement in Kentucky* (2009).

CRAIG THOMPSON FRIEND is professor of history and director of public history at North Carolina State University. He is the author of *Kentucke's Frontiers* (2010) and *Along the Maysville Road: The Early Republic in the Trans-Appalachian West* (2005). He edited *The Buzzel about Kentuck: Settling the Promised Land* (1999) and coedited, with Anya Jabour, *Family Values in the Old South* (2010).

MELANIE BEALS GOAN is assistant professor of history at the University of Kentucky. She is the author of *Mary Breckinridge: The Frontier Nursing Service and Rural Health in Appalachia* (2008).

JOHN PAUL HILL is associate professor of history at Warner University in Lake Wales, Florida. He has published entries in the *Encyclopedia of American Political Parties and Elections* (2006) and articles and reviews in the *Filson History Quarterly, Nine: A Journal of Baseball History and Culture*, and *Register of the Kentucky Historical Society.*

ANYA JABOUR is professor of history at the University of Montana. She is the author of *Marriage in the Early Republic: Elizabeth and William Wirt and the Companionate Ideal* (1988), *Scarlett's Sisters: Young Women in the Old South* (2007), and *Topsy-Turvy: How the Civil War Turned the World Upside Down for Southern Children* (2010). She edited *Major Problems in the History of American Families and Children* (2005) and coedited, with Craig Thompson Friend, *Family Values in the Old South* (2010). She is currently working on a biography of Sophonisba Breckinridge.

WILLIAM KUBY is assistant professor of history at the University of Tennessee at Chattanooga. His research explores controversial and legally ambiguous marital practices in the early twentieth century United States. His most recent article appeared in the *Journal of the History of Sexuality.*

KAREN COTTON MCDANIEL is professor emerita at Kentucky State University, where she was the director of libraries. She also has taught at Eastern Kentucky University in the African American Studies and Women's Studies programs. She is general coeditor of the *Kentucky African American Encyclopedia* (forthcoming). She has written essays for *African American National Biography*, *Black Heroes*, *Notable Black American Women*, *Encyclopedia of the Harlem Renaissance*, and *The Encyclopedia of Louisville*, among other publications. Her research focuses on African American women and Progressive Era reform.

MELISSA A. MCEUEN is professor of history and a Bingham Fellow at Transylvania University. She is the author of the award-winning *Seeing America: Women Photographers between the Wars* (2000) and *Making War, Making Women: Femininity and Duty on the American Home Front, 1941–1945* (2011).

MARY JANE SMITH is associate professor of history at St. Lawrence University in Canton, New York. Her most recent publication appeared in the *Georgia Historical Quarterly*. Her research focuses on white southern women activists in the Progressive Era.

ANDREA S. WATKINS is associate professor of history at Northern Kentucky University. She is the coauthor, with James A. Ramage, of *Kentucky Rising: Democracy, Slavery, and Culture from the Early Republic to the Civil War* (2011).

Index

Italicized numbers represent those pages on which illustrations appear.